MONTANA

CARTER G. WALKER

Contents

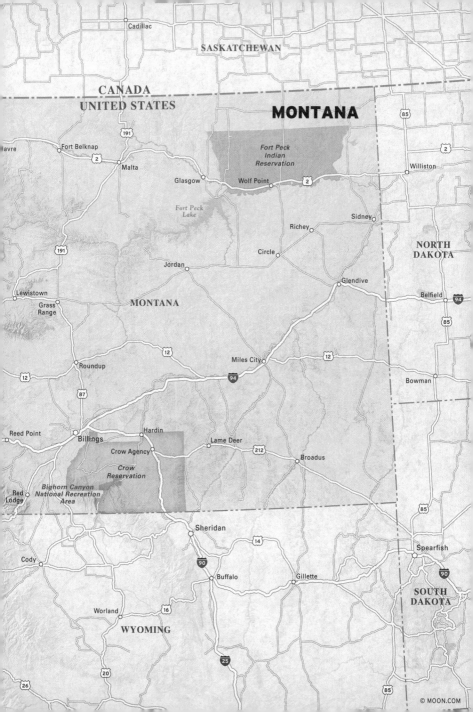

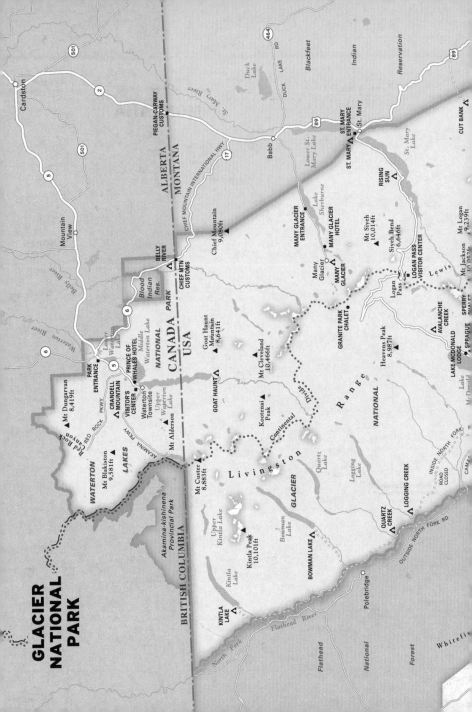

© MOON.COM

DISCOVER

Montana

Montana is as vast as the big sky that blankets it, rich with natural resources—fertile soil, rivers, gold, forests, wind—and overflowing with beauty. The dramatic landscape has been carved over eons by water, wind, fire, and ice. Blue-ribbon trout streams, tumbling and falling, etch themselves ever deeper into green valleys. From Glacier National Park to the Little Bighorn, its sites are enchanting… and sometimes haunting.

The populations are perpetually shifting too, bringing new ideas, new conflicts, and an evolving culture. Pioneer traditions have been embraced by new generations of transplants in cities like Bozeman, where ski bums and artists mingle with fifth-generation farmers. Then there are tiny towns like Loma, at the confluence of the Milk and Marias Rivers, where the headline is still that Lewis and Clark camped just south of town in 1805.

Montana today is defined by the continuing growth in the American West, but it's those little dots on the map that remind us of its almost magical timelessness. Ultimately, it's the forces of nature that make this state so captivating.

Clockwise from top left: relics of Montana's agricultural heritage; tipis at St. Labre Mission; Roosevelt Arch in Yellowstone National Park; fresh flowers at a farmers market; a cowboy; Grinnell Lake in Glacier National Park.

8 TOP
EXPERIENCES

1 **Hike in Glacier National Park:** Glacier is a hiker's paradise. Head to the west side of the park to explore its beloved trails (page 133).

2 **Visit a Dude Ranch:** From rustic to luxe, there are dude ranches across the West where guests can saddle up and ride for their supper—or just ride to their heart's content (page 236).

3 **Go Skiing:** Skiing in Montana is a win-win: phenomenal terrain without the lines of big-name places. Hit up a ski resort like **Whitefish Mountain Resort** (page 208) or **Maverick Mountain** (page 248).

>>>

4 **Soak in the Hot Springs:** From resort-style pools and thermally heated rivers to entire towns built on hot springs, this region offers infinite ways to get wet (page 24).

5 **Learn about Indigenous Cultures:** With seven reservations scattered across the state, you can go to powwows, visit museums, and witness cultural traditions (page 20).

^
^
^

6 **Drive Going-to-the-Sun Road:** The journey is the main event (page 133).

7 **See the Glaciers—While You Still Can:** Head to Glacier National Park's sublime **Many Glacier** (page 147) and **Grinnell Glacier** (pictured; page 148) before they're gone.

>>>

8 **Spot Wildlife:** Take advantage of multiple wildlife refuges to see animals in their prime habitats (page 23).

Planning Your Trip

Where to Go

Billings and the Big Open

Beyond **Billings,** the state's largest and most industrial city, much of eastern Montana is made up of small but tightly knit communities separated by vast swaths of **wide-open country.** It's also where four of the state's seven **Indian reservations** can be found. The landscapes are varied and dramatic—from the rimrocks in Billings and the rolling hills around the **Little Bighorn Battlefield** to the badlands of **Makoshika State Park** outside Glendive.

Great Falls and the Rocky Mountain Front

The **vast plains** erupt into **soaring peaks** along the **Rocky Mountain Front.** The **Bob Marshall Wilderness Complex** is one of the most spectacular and isolated mountainous areas in the Lower 48. Tiny towns like **Choteau** and **Fort Benton** offer a charming sense of community, along with fascinating sites like dinosaur mecca **Egg Mountain** and lovely **historic hotels.** Straddling the division between mountains and plains, **Great Falls** boasts two of the state's best museums: the **C. M. Russell Museum** and **Lewis and Clark National Historic Trail Interpretive Center.**

Glacier National Park

Known as the "Crown of the Continent," **Glacier National Park** embodies the Montana you've always imagined: **rugged mountains** piercing the sky, **crystalline lakes** and **plunging waterfalls, abundant wildlife,** gravity-defying

view from the Hidden Lake Overlook Trail in Glacier National Park

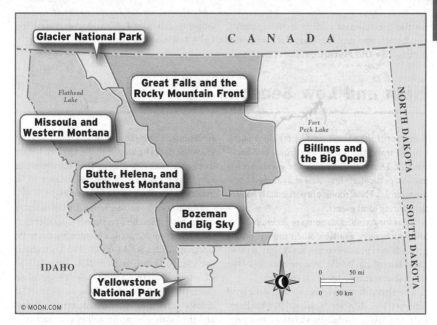

Glacier National Park

CANADA

Great Falls and the Rocky Mountain Front

Flathead Lake

Missoula and Western Montana

Fort Peck Lake

Billings and the Big Open

NORTH DAKOTA

Butte, Helena, and Southwest Montana

Bozeman and Big Sky

SOUTH DAKOTA

IDAHO

Yellowstone National Park

0   50 mi
0   50 km

© MOON.COM

roads, and miles upon miles of trails. For now, the park still lays claim to **25 glaciers.**

Missoula and Western Montana

Western Montana shows off with **lush green mountain ranges** and **towering forests.** In the far north, **Whitefish** is the ultimate mountain town, a **skier's paradise.** Just south, glittering **Flathead Lake** is Montana's Riviera, with sprawling mansions and luxurious lodges at water's edge. The tiny hamlet of **Bigfork** serves up a surprisingly fine selection of both culture and cuisine, not to mention recreation. The scenic **National Bison Range** in Moiese can be visited en route to **Missoula,** a cultural hub and home of the **University of Montana,** with great restaurants and better bars. In the southwest corner of the state, the **Bitterroot Valley** combines a rich history with **world-class fly-fishing.**

Butte, Helena, and Southwest Montana

This corner of the state wears its history like a badge of honor in mining towns like **Bannack,**

Virginia City, and **Nevada City.** Some of the other towns that survived the unforgiving boom-and-bust cycles include charming Victorian **Philipsburg** and **Butte,** and **Helena,** the venerable state capital. Then there is the sweeping **Big Hole Valley,** with **picturesque ranches** and **rivers to fish,** and the **Big Hole National Battlefield,** one of the most haunting battle sites in the state.

Bozeman and Big Sky

The communities surrounding Yellowstone offer a diverse range of experiences. From **skiing, fishing,** and an abundance of outdoor adventures in the booming college town of **Bozeman** to the **art and culinary scenes** just over the pass in **Livingston,** the area's culture is as rich as its landscape. **Big Sky** and **Red Lodge** offer year-round resorts with ample skiable terrain and some terrific places to stay.

Yellowstone National Park

Just over the border in Wyoming, this magnificent park is constantly in motion; nothing here is static. See abundant wildlife, including **bison, elk, bears, and wolves;** marvel at geothermal features like **Old Faithful;** and stay in historic lodges like the **Old Faithful Inn** and rambling **Lake Yellowstone Hotel.**

High and Low Seasons

Summer is the easiest, and by far the busiest, time to travel the roads, both front- and backcountry. Thoughtful planning and advance reservations, particularly for hotels and campgrounds, are essential. Hotel rooms are particularly hard to find during local events.

Rates for accommodations are generally lower and rooms more available when snow is on the ground, except around ski areas, but **winter road travel** can be challenging because of the inevitable storms and possible closures.

The **shoulder seasons** can be a delightful time to travel. **Glacier National Park** is heavenly and less crowded in **autumn,** but keep in mind that winter comes very early at high elevations. There are also little-known ways to enjoy the parks by bicycle in the **spring,** before it opens to cars. Opening and closing times can vary by year (weather and federal budget too), so make sure to check ahead of traveling.

Don't try to see too much in too short a time; this cannot be overstated. Consider that the drive from Montana's eastern border to its western border is 550 miles (890 km), about the same distance as from New York City to Charlotte, North Carolina. Don't spend so much time on the road that you miss the small details—idyllic hikes, roadside burger joints, and the locals who give small towns their true character.

springtime in Yellowstone National Park

Seven-Day Glacier Road Trip

Start your tour of Montana's magnificent northwest corner in Missoula, the hometown of *A River Runs Through It* author Norman Maclean and dozens of the state's literary heroes. Although the city is surrounded by wilderness, the University of Montana community gives the town something of an urban vibe. Those who want to spend less time on the road could start and finish the journey in Kalispell. Because of the mountain terrain, the driving time is often much longer than the mileage suggests.

At Ravalli, choose your direction—northwest toward the **National Bison Range** at Moiese or northeast to the historic **St. Ignatius Mission.** The forks come together again just south of Ronan, where you'll continue north along the east shore of **Flathead Lake** to the waterfront village of Bigfork. Stop along the way to gorge yourself on seasonal **Flathead cherries** or just to stretch your legs and dip your toes in the lake. Just south of Bigfork, settle in at the **Mountain Lake Lodge** for two restful nights.

Day 1
Missoula to Bigfork
100 MILES (161 KM), 2 HOURS
Arrive in Missoula; check out the shops on **Higgins Avenue** and the hip **Missoula Art Museum,** grab a ham and cheese croissant at **Le Petit Outre** or sandwich from **Bernice's Bakery,** and walk along the lovely **riverfront trails.** Next, head north toward Glacier country.

Day 2
Bigfork
Try **white-water rafting** on the Flathead River or **kayaking** on the lake with the **Flathead Raft Company,** or rent your own craft at **Bigfork Outdoor Rentals.** Take an incredible hike—maybe to **Black Lake** or **Twin Lakes**—in the nearby **Jewel Basin.** Leave some time for browsing the cute shops around town, and reward

Lake McDonald

Indigenous Heritage

The culture and history of Indigenous people have powerfully defined Montana's identity. There are tremendous opportunities for those interested in learning about and experiencing Native American history, traditions, and contemporary culture.

LITTLE BIGHORN BATTLEFIELD NATIONAL MONUMENT

This is where thousands of Cheyenne, Sioux, and Arapaho warriors fought under such legendary figures as Sitting Bull and Crazy Horse. Lieutenant Colonel George Armstrong Custer and more than 200 men from his 7th Cavalry died in the brief battle. A wonderful way to explore the monument is by hiring a Native American guide through **Apsalooke Tours.**

CROW FAIR

Held the third week in August since 1904, Crow Fair is considered the largest outdoor powwow in the world. More than 45,000 people come to watch, and many camp out in more than 1,000 tipis erected on the banks of the Little Bighorn River.

BLACKFEET TOURS

Guided trips on and around the Blackfeet Reservation take guests hiking or on horseback into the sacred Badger Two Medicine area near Glacier. Tours can include a visit to the **Museum of the Plains Indian.**

performer at a Crow powwow

BIG HOLE NATIONAL BATTLEFIELD

This moving historic site bears witness to the 1877 battle between Chief Joseph's band of Nez Perce and the U.S. Army.

---

yourself with a gourmet northern Italian meal at **Stone Hill Kitchen + Bar.**

Day 3
Bigfork to Whitefish
34 MILES (55 KM), 0.75 HOUR

Start your day at the **Echo Lake Café** before heading north toward **Kalispell,** where you can check out the contemporary art scene at the **Hockaday Museum of Art.** Consider a hike or bike ride at **Whitefish Mountain Resort,** perhaps hiking the **Danny On Trail,** just 3.8 miles (6.1 km) to the summit, and then taking a

gondola ride down. For dinner, try **Latitude 48 Bistro and Red Room Lounge,** then wander the **art galleries and boutiques.** Settle in for the night, lakeside, at the **Lodge at Whitefish Lake.**

Day 4
Whitefish to Many Glacier
112 MILES (180 KM), 3 HOURS

Get a hearty breakfast and a great piece of pie at **Loula's Café** before heading into **Glacier National Park.** Stop at **Lake McDonald** to soak in the majestic beauty and prepare

It's hard to drive through Montana without running into rodeo action somewhere. Stop. Buy a ticket. The bleachers are fine. These small-town rodeos offer a unique window into life here: Locals wear their Sunday best, and no one seems to mind the dust. Sitting on a sunbaked wooden bench, cold beer in one hand and a bag of popcorn in the other, is the best first date in small towns, where they show off their best without hiding what's real.

MILES CITY BUCKING HORSE SALE (THIRD FULL WEEKEND IN MAY)

Since 1914, the country's best bucking stock—and the most ambitious cowboys—have been showcased at this world-famous event in **Miles City.** The party atmosphere follows the crowds from the rodeo into town and every bar throughout the long weekend for concerts, street dances, and a good old small-town parade. Don't be surprised if you see cowboys, carrying their saddles, hitching a ride to this event: For horses, bulls, and riders, this is *the* place to get noticed.

GARDINER RODEO (MID-JUNE)

Just outside Yellowstone's north entrance, in the shadow of Electric Peak, the annual rodeo in tiny **Gardiner** includes all the standards—bull riding, saddle bronc riding, bareback bronc riding, steer wrestling, barrel racing, and breakaway roping—with a timeless small-town charm.

AUGUSTA AMERICAN LEGION RODEO AND PARADE (LAST SUNDAY IN JUNE)

Held in the hamlet of **Augusta,** at the edge of the spectacular Rocky Mountain Front, this is the largest and oldest one-day rodeo in the state. The town throws its biggest party of the year with rodeo action, a barbecue, a street dance, and even an art show.

LIVINGSTON ROUNDUP RODEO (JULY 2-4)

Offering small-town charm and a big-city purse over the Fourth of July holiday, this festive event puts **Livingston** on the map with big-name rodeo action, a popular parade, nightly fireworks, and more than 10,000 spectators that flood this riverfront community.

WOLF POINT WILD HORSE STAMPEDE (SECOND WEEKEND IN JULY)

Montana's oldest rodeo, the Wild Horse Stampede in **Wolf Point,** on the Fort Peck Indian Reservation, is a three-day event that includes professional rodeo, daily parades and a carnival, the famous wild horse race, street dances, and a kids' stick-horse rodeo.

---

yourself for the vistas still ahead on the **Going-to-the-Sun Road** (where you will need an advance reservation from www.recreation.gov between 6am and 4pm from late May to mid-September). Stop for a hike; the **Hidden Lake Overlook** from Logan Pass is a stunner. Continue east out of the park through **St. Mary** and **Babb,** where you can treat yourself to dinner at **Two Sisters Café** before heading back into the phenomenal Many Glacier Valley to camp or stay at the historic **Many Glacier Hotel.**

Day 5
Many Glacier

Plan to spend the day adventuring around Many Glacier. Possible activities include an endless number of **hiking trails** and **canoeing, kayaking,** or **cruising** on **Swiftcurrent Lake.** One option is to combine a scenic cruise with a hike to **Grinnell Glacier.** Other options include **ranger-led hikes** and **Red Bus Tours.** For dinner, try the bison tenderloin or the wild mushroom stroganoff in the **Ptarmigan Dining Room** at the Many Glacier Hotel.

Day 6
Many Glacier to East Glacier
63 MILES (101 KM), 1.75 HOURS

After a morning hike, head south toward East Glacier. Stop for recreation in **St. Mary** or continue farther south into the isolated **Two Medicine Valley.** Consider combining a 45-minute **cruise** on Two Medicine Lake, cutting 6 miles (9.7 km) off the hike to **Twin Falls.** Another option is to cruise and then hike to **No Name Lake.** Finish the day in East Glacier with a hearty Mexican meal at **Serrano's Mexican Restaurant** and a room at the historic **Glacier Park Lodge.**

Day 7
East Glacier to Missoula
222 MILES (355 KM), 4 HOURS

This is the longest day by far in the car, but there is some magnificent scenery and plenty of places to stop along the way. From East Glacier, drive southwest on US 2 over **Marias Pass,** then north along the west side of Glacier National Park. As you enter Columbia Falls, turn south onto Highway 206 and continue on Highway 35 toward Creston. Take Highway 83, the Swan Highway, south through the scenic **Seeley-Swan Valley.** You'll pass **Swan and Seeley Lakes,** among others. Time it right and you can stop for an incredible lunch and hike at **Holland Lake Lodge.** At Highway 200, continue west back to Missoula, where you can recall the highlights of your trip over an outstanding brick oven pizza at **Biga Pizza.**

Swiftcurrent Lake and Many Glacier Hotel

Yellowstone Getaway

Just over the border in Wyoming, breathtaking Yellowstone National Park proves an irresistible getaway for many Montana visitors. Here's a plan for a quick visit, departing from Bozeman.

Day 1
Bozeman

Bozeman is equal parts college town and mountain town. Fit in a trip to the **Museum of the Rockies** to see where dinosaur guru Jack Horner did much of his work. Throw in a hike up to the large M in the hills above the city (for Montana State University) or on **the Drinking Horse Mountain Trail,** just northeast of town, and end with a shopping stroll on historic **Main Street.** Enjoy a game of pool, a local brew, and an excellent meal at the popular **Montana Ale Works.** After a pre-bed ice-cream cone from the **Genuine Ice Cream** truck, bed down for the night at **The Lark,** a hip, artistically driven hotel.

Days 2-3
Big Sky

It's roughly 44 miles (71 km, 1 hour) to Big Sky. When you arrive, head over to the **Freeheel & Wheel** to rent a bike and then hit the famous **Rendezvous Ski Trails,** where Olympic Nordic skiers have trained. After lunch, drive through

---

TOP EXPERIENCE

Where the Wild Things Are

Appreciating wildlife is as much a part of the culture as mountains are part of the landscape. The most obvious choice for prime wildlife-viewing is over the border in Wyoming's Yellowstone National Park, but Montana has 19 wildlife refuges that offer prime habitat to any number of species. Here are some of the best to visit.

- **Medicine Lake National Wildlife Refuge** is in fact two wildlife refuges and a wetland management district that host more birds than you could ever imagine.

- About 30 miles (48 km) south of Missoula in **Stevensville,** the **Lee Metcalf National Wildlife Refuge** provides habitat for migratory birds including ospreys, eagles, and hawks as well as larger animals including wolves, coyotes, black bears, and badgers.

- Located in **Moiese** between the Flathead and Missoula, the **National Bison Range** is home to around 400 bison, along with white-tailed and mule deer, bighorn sheep, pronghorn antelope, and elk.

- Near **Lima,** the **Red Rock Lakes National Wildlife Refuge** hosts more than 230 species of birds—including the once-endangered

National Bison Range is home to bighorn sheep.

trumpeter swan—and other wildlife including bears, wolves, and moose.

Get Yourself in Hot Water

In the middle of winter, when the cold works its way into your bones, there's nothing quite like soaking in a natural hot spring to restore your energy and well-being. Thanks to the geothermal and hydrothermal activity, most of which can be enjoyed year-round. Options range from middle-of-nowhere holes in the ground to well-known natural features and developed pools in resort-like settings. A good site for a diverse range of hot springs is Montana Hot Springs (http://montanahotsprings.net). Montana's official tourism site (www.visitmt.com) regularly updates their page on hot springs around the state (navigate to Things to Do, then Hot Springs).

Set in the middle of nowhere about halfway between Helena and Butte, **Boulder Hot Springs** (page 267) has both indoor and outdoor pools of varying temperatures and mineral content. There are also separate men's and women's plunge pools and steam baths. The on-site hotel offers simple rooms and great food.

Just up the road from Yellowstone in Montana's Paradise Valley, **Chico Hot Springs Resort** (page 307) is a classic. Founded in the late 1800s and known then for offering miners a bath, a clean bed, and fresh strawberries at every meal, Chico today is known for its wonderful outdoor pools, cozy accommodations, fabulous dining room, and lively tavern.

The **Boiling River** (page 335)—which is not, in fact, boiling—is a magical place and an experience you will not soon forget. Located just inside Yellowstone's north entrance at Gardiner, Montana, the Boiling River is actually a small stretch of the Gardner River where thermally heated water from nearby Mammoth Hot Springs flows into the icy waters of the Gardner, mixing to make a perfect swimming temperature any time of year. The snow-capped peaks and great plumes of steam coming off the water make winter an especially unforgettable time to swim here.

the scenic **Gallatin Canyon** toward Big Sky Resort. There are countless hiking trails and fishing spots along the way. Plan on spending the night at **The Wilson Hotel.** Head to dinner at **Olive B's Big Sky Bistro.**

The next day, plan on a short hike to scenic **Ousel Falls** and then jump in a Montana Whitewater raft to white-knuckle it down the Gallatin River canyon.

Days 4-5
Yellowstone

It's 51 miles (82 km, 1 hour) from Big Sky to **West Yellowstone,** where you can check out the **Grizzly and Wolf Discovery Center** and the adjacent **Yellowstone Giant Screen Theatre.** Don't miss the opportunity to swim in the thermally heated waters of the **Firehole River.** Grab some brisket or pork ribs at **Firehole Bar-B-Que Company** or a gourmet meal at **Bar N Ranch** before calling it a night in a cozy safari tent at **Under Canvas Yellowstone.**

The next day, continue into **Yellowstone National Park.** There are great trails along the way, including an easy jaunt to **Lone Star Geyser.** End your day with dinner and a bed at the at the **Old Faithful Inn.** Old Faithful eruptions in the moonlight are pretty unforgettable. With more time, you can explore deeper into the park. Soak at **Mammoth Hot Springs Terraces,** spot wildlife in the **Lamar Valley,** hike to inspiring views along the rim of the **Grand Canyon of the Yellowstone,** and fish in **Yellowstone Lake.**

1: Lone Star Geyser 2: Grand Canyon of the Yellowstone

The best way to see this place and to know it is to get out and hike. Explore the wilderness. Climb the mountains. Run your fingertips along the bark of trees. Feel the whisper of high grasses on your legs. Earn the best view you've ever seen. Here are 11 of the top hikes, some popular and some lesser known.

BILLINGS AND THE BIG OPEN

High in the Beartooth Mountains, not far from Roscoe, **East Rosebud Trail #15 to Elk Lake** is a 6.7-mile (10.8-km) trail with diverse terrain—forest, canyon, alpine cirque—and a rushing creek nearly the whole way. Wildlife is abundant, views are sublime, and a dip in Elk Lake makes every step worthwhile.

GLACIER NATIONAL PARK

Highline Trail is popular for good reason. Best in midsummer when the wildflowers explode with color, the shorter version of this strenuous hike climbs a total of 1,950 feet (594 m) over 11.8 miles (19 km) and offers outstanding scenery, including a stretch along the Garden Wall, a ledge that will delight thrill seekers.

A short and easy hike through alpine meadows known as the Hanging Gardens, the **Hidden Lake Overlook Trail,** also known as the Hidden Lake Nature Trail, offers extraordinary views of Clements Mountain, the Garden Wall, and Mount Oberlin. The 2.7-mile (4.3-km) round-trip hike crosses the Continental Divide and is often snow-covered, even in midsummer.

BUTTE, HELENA, AND SOUTHWEST MONTANA

A lesser-known but stunning spot for hiking is the **Humbug Spires Wilderness Trail,** south of Butte. There are quartz monzonite towers, a primeval Douglas fir forest, and a gurgling stream. The 3.5-mile (5.6-km) hike travels through dense, lush greenery, even late in summer.

along the Highline Trail

BOZEMAN AND BIG SKY COUNTRY

Sacajawea Peak towers above Fairy Lake and affords hikers spectacular views and a good shot at seeing mountain goats. The trail is just 4 miles (6.4 km) round-trip—but steep, gaining 2,000 feet (610 m) in elevation. For more, continue on the winding **Bridger Mountains National Recreation Trail.** Those who want less can amble around **Fairy Lake,** a flat 1.2-mile (1.9-km) loop.

YELLOWSTONE NATIONAL PARK

Starting with a steep descent to a suspension bridge over the rushing Yellowstone River, the backcountry **Hellroaring Trail** is beautiful but strenuous. Enjoy a 6.2-mile (10-km) stretch through scenic sagebrush plateau to the confluence of Hellroaring Creek and the Yellowstone River.

Billings and the Big Open

Eastern Montana is a vibrant amalgam of history, landscapes, and cultures. It's home to the Little Bighorn Battlefield and four of the state's seven Indian reservations, as well as the city of Billings and starkly beautiful Missouri River Breaks terrain.

Sometimes referred to as Montana east of the mountains, rather than eastern Montana (in truth, the region occupies more than a third of the state's land mass), this region may not have the mountainous grandeur most people expect when they visit Montana, but it has a sense of authenticity, a grittiness that sets it apart from the rest of the state. Plenty of towns in eastern Montana were founded by accident, when someone's wagon broke down and options were limited. A day's drive in this region gives visitors a true sense of the hardscrabble life

Highlights

Look for ★ to find recommended sights, activities, dining, and lodging.

★ **Yellowstone Art Museum:** Housed in an old jail, this art museum is renowned for its permanent collection of Montana artists, both historical and cutting-edge (page 34).

★ **Pictograph Cave State Park:** The caves in this state park contain evidence of human habitation dating back more than 4,500 years, including pictographs of people, animals, and even weapons (page 36).

★ **Little Bighorn Battlefield National Monument:** This historic site is a moving tribute to one of the last armed battles in which Native Americans fought to preserve their land and way of life. An annual reenactment brings to life the terror and tragic meaning of the event (page 47).

★ **Crow Fair:** This five-day celebration on the Crow Indian Reservation features an all-Native American rodeo, daily parades, and horse racing (page 52).

★ **WaterWorks Art Museum:** This gem is housed in a century-old waterworks building (page 57).

★ **Miles City Bucking Horse Sale:** Held the third full weekend in May, this rodeo is packed with cowboy swagger (page 58).

★ **Makoshika State Park:** The colorful rock layers at Montana's largest state park are a fascinating lesson in geological time travel (page 62).

★ **Medicine Lake National Wildlife Refuge:** Walk or drive through this stunning blend of glacial-drift prairie and shallow wetland to see hundreds of migrating birds (page 64).

★ **Pioneer Town in Scobey:** More than 35 buildings from Scobey's past have been restored to their early-20th-century glory (page 70).

★ **Fort Peck Dam:** The dam's interpretive center and museum chronicles not only the remarkable structure itself but the staggering number of fossils unearthed during its construction, local dinosaur finds, and Sioux and Assiniboine culture (page 73).

in these parts, the unavoidable isolation and the enormous value placed on community. And there is beauty here that should not be overlooked. The often crumbling architecture of agriculture—leaning barns, lonely grain elevators, and rusted equipment—is as much a part of the landscape here as mountains are farther west. The tones of golden light are subtle but too plentiful to count. The clouds change their moods often and play tricks with shadows.

Though few and far between, the northern communities in this region—Malta, Scobey, Plentywood, and Wolf Point, to name a few—are strong and tightly knit. They have to be in the face of the Bakken Oil Field— and its ageless boom-and-bust cycle—just over the border in North Dakota. In the northeast corner of the state, the Fort Peck Indian Reservation is home to various bands of both Sioux and Assiniboine people. In this part of Montana, the hunting ethos is as deeply rooted as the agricultural way of life. Farther south, bigger towns like Glendive and Miles City boast strong cowboy culture and some surprisingly important art, and the Crow Indian Reservation is a carefully preserved but living piece of Western history. Billings, Montana's largest city and frankly not known for its beauty, is not unpleasant in its size, modernity, and ease of access. Though decidedly industrial, the city is populated by fiercely loyal and proud residents, many of whom have been in the area for generations. Strong art, theater, and sports scenes are part of the city's pulse; with a number of excellent eateries and performing arts venues, Billings is a wonderful place for an evening out. Plus, outdoor pursuits—on the river and rimrocks or in the mountains—are always a good option. With the post-pandemic influx that has overrun touristy towns like Bozeman and Whitefish, eastern Montana is especially appealing for its lack of crowds.

Whether you see this region as the Big Sky, the Big Open, or just an obvious and easy access point, this is a part of the state that will enchant you with historical and geographic context for everything else Montana has to offer. You may have overlooked the region in the past, but don't. Plenty of folks would say this is the real Montana.

PLANNING YOUR TIME

For travelers who are willing to take their time and let the state unfold slowly as opposed to the drama of the one-two mountain-sky knockout punch, eastern Montana is an ideal place to start a Montana road trip. There is subtlety here in the landscape and the light as well as a feeling of timelessness. When you drive on the prairie, it is not such a stretch to imagine the first travelers to this region. In fact, some Lewis and Clark buffs suggest that the only landscape the explorers would recognize today is rural Montana, simply because it hasn't changed much. Even a stroll down almost any small-town Main Street can feel like a step back in time, with still-bustling local hardware stores and, instead of fast-food or chain restaurants, real bakeries, doughnut shops, and cafés. Take your time in eastern Montana: Stop for pie and to chat. Just slow down and enjoy.

Most visitors traveling by car from the east will arrive in Montana via either I-94 at Wibaux or I-90 near Wyola, just south of the **Little Bighorn Battlefield.**

Although "the Magic City" is the largest in Montana, and one of the easiest to get to by air, **Billings** is not an altogether magical place. Still, the city has an authenticity and a vitality that make a visit worthwhile. Its restaurants and art scene alone make Billings worth the trip. It is also an excellent place to launch explorations of eastern and central Montana. Many people opt to access Cody, Wyoming, or Yellowstone National Park by driving over the Beartooth Highway from

Previous: Little Bighorn Battlefield National Monument; pronghorn, also known as "speed goats," the fastest land animal in North America; performers at Crow Fair on the Crow Indian Reservation.

Billings and the Big Open

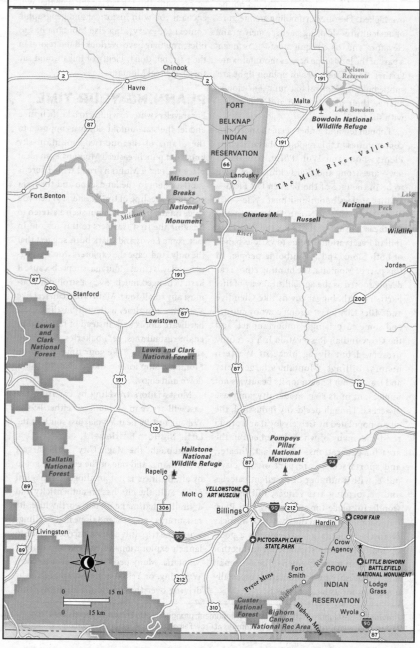

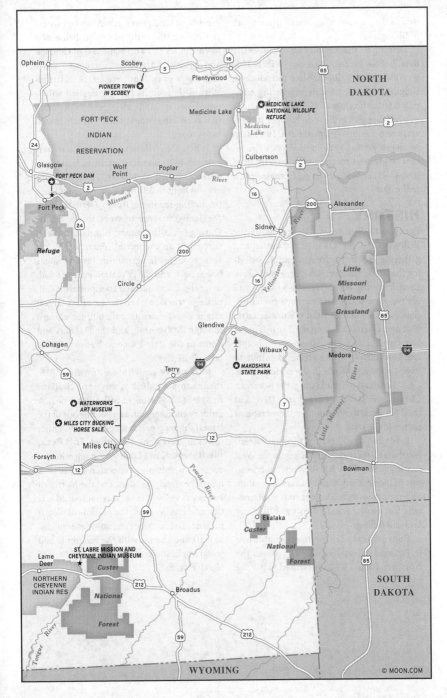

Red Lodge, just over an hour's drive south of Billings.

Driving in this region can eat up entire days, but the journey itself can be incredibly worthwhile. In 2010, the state introduced a tongue-in-cheek, in-state marketing campaign with the slogan "Get Lost," the signs of which are still evident on bumper stickers and the occasional painted barn. In eastern Montana, getting lost—in wide-open spaces, vast wilderness refuges, and friendly little towns—is the best way to get from one place to the next.

HISTORY

For thousands of years, the area along the Yellowstone River was used as hunting and gathering sites by Native Americans, including the Sioux, Blackfeet, Cheyenne, and Crow. Conflicts arose between the U.S. Army and Native Americans, and perhaps no battlefield is better known than the one at Little Bighorn where Custer made his infamous last stand. The Crow, Sioux, Assiniboine, and Northern Cheyenne tribes continue to have a strong presence in the region on the Crow Reservation near Hardin, the Northern Cheyenne Reservation near Lame Deer, and the Fort Peck Reservation in the northeast corner of the state.

Lewis and Clark traveled through eastern Montana on their journey back from the West Coast in 1806. They left the only intentional sign of their entire journey—Clark's signature and the date—on a 200-foot rocky outcropping that Clark named **Pompeys Pillar,** not far from Billings.

Coulson was the first town established in the area by settlers, in 1877. When the Northern Pacific Railway refused to pay the exorbitant land prices asked by the owners in Coulson, the railroad established a new town 2 miles (3.2 km) southeast of Coulson and named it after the Northern Pacific Railway's president, Frederick Billings. Within six months the city bustled with a population of 2,000, giving rise to the city's moniker, "the Magic City," which it still holds today.

When the Yellowstone Valley was irrigated in 1879, hundreds of sugar beet fields were cultivated, and by 1906 a sugar refinery was built in Billings. Soon migrant labor (including Japanese, Russo-Germans, and Mexicans) arrived to work in the fields. During the 20th century, Billings grew and thrived as an industrial center with a diverse economy in agriculture (grains, sugar beets, beef, and dairy cattle), energy (coal, natural gas, and oil), and transportation (air, rail, and trucking). Today, Montana's largest city is a major health care hub for eastern Montana, Wyoming, and the Dakotas and home to the state's second-busiest airport (after Bozeman).

Miles City grew into a town in 1876, thanks to a handful of wayward civilians fired by Col. Nelson A. Miles at his nearby military encampment, and became one of the largest shipping points for bison hides. Other towns in the region—**Glendive, Fort Peck, Plentywood,** and **Scobey,** among others— sprang up with the expansion of railroad lines, the Great Northern and the Northern Pacific, as well as the various homestead acts that lured settlers with the promise of plentiful land. Today, these communities continue to shift and change with the economic and social implications of the massive oil field in North Dakota.

Billings and Vicinity

Though not a tourist attraction per se, Billings (pop. 117,116, elev. 3,124 ft/952 m) is the largest city in the state and the hub for much of eastern Montana. The city is a center for industry, including oil refineries and stockyards, and serves much of eastern and central Montana with two major hospitals, three colleges, and significant shopping options. Billings used to be *the* place to buy a car, see a specialist doctor, or stock up at Costco. That has changed with growth across the state, but Billings still attracts visitors from around the state for both practical and decidedly more entertaining purposes.

The MetraPark is popular as a venue for concerts, trade shows, and rodeos and serves as the fairgrounds each summer. The Alberta Bair Theater for the Performing Arts is the largest of its kind between Minneapolis and Spokane. The Yellowstone Art Museum boasts an impressive collection of contemporary Montana art, in addition to past masters, and is worth a visit. The rimrocks around the city offer wonderful perspectives—you can see five mountain ranges—and there is a great network of hiking and biking trails. At the end of a full day, Billings's lively food and drink culture will sate any appetite.

SIGHTS
Guided Tours

Billings is not as easily navigated on foot as Montana's significantly smaller cities, but tour companies offer opportunities to see its high points. The **Fun Express Bus** (406/254-7180, www.mtfunadventures.com, 11:30am, 2pm, and 7pm Mon.-Fri., 2pm Sat.-Sun. May-Labor Day, 2pm Sat.-Sun. Labor Day-April, $40) offers 90-minute historical tours that feature creepy cemeteries, haunted hotels, and stories of such legends as Calamity Jane, Wild Bill Hickok, and Buffalo Bill Cody. Other tour options—including Lewis & Clark, Wild Mustangs, Battle of the Little Bighorn, Sunset Jeep Tours, and custom tours—can be arranged. The **Billings Trolley and Bus Company** (406/252-1778 or 800/698-1778, www.mttotaltransportation.com) offers

the view from the rimrocks

Billings

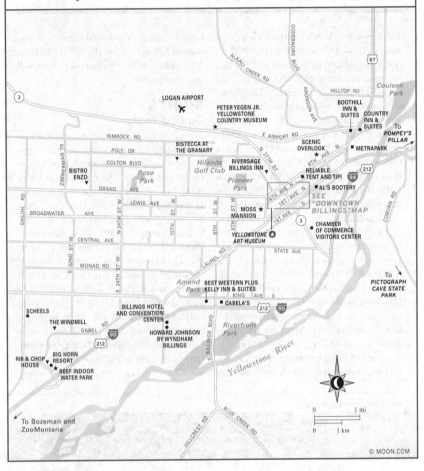

customized and lighthearted tours of the Billings historical district and surrounding areas; the Christmas Light Tour is a winner.

For drinkers, the **Billings Brewery Trail** is a self-guided 1.5-mile (2.4-km) walking tour that includes visits to six breweries, two distilleries, and one cider mill. For more information and to download a map, which may come in handy the farther one gets into the tour, visit www.visitbillings.com/billings-brew-trail.

★ Yellowstone Art Museum

The **Yellowstone Art Museum** (401 N. 27th St., 406/256-6804, www.artmuseum. org, 10am-5pm Tues.-Sun., 10am-8pm Thurs., 10am-8pm first Friday of each month, $15 adults, $6 children 6-18 and students, free for children under 6) is the region's largest contemporary art museum and offers changing exhibitions, education programs, a café, and an art sales gallery. The impressive permanent collection includes works by Russell Chatham, Freeman Butts, John Buck,

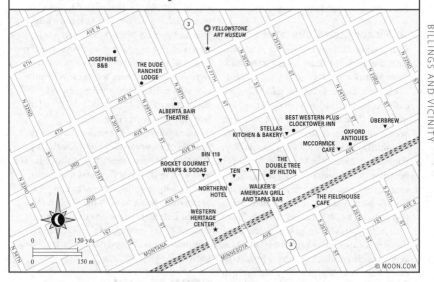

Downtown Billings

AVE N · 6TH ST · JOSEPHINE B&B · THE DUDE RANCHER LODGE · N 32ND ST · N 30TH ST · N 29TH ST · N 28TH ST · 4TH ST · 3RD ST · N 31ST ST · N 33RD ST · N 34TH ST · 2ND ST · 1ST ST · AVE N · AVE N · AVE N · ALBERTA BAIR THEATRE · BIN 119 · ROCKET GOURMET WRAPS & SODAS · TEN ▼ · NORTHERN HOTEL · WESTERN HERITAGE CENTER ★ · N 27TH ST · N 26TH ST · YELLOWSTONE ART MUSEUM ★ · STELLAS KITCHEN & BAKERY ▼ · BEST WESTERN PLUS CLOCKTOWER INN · MCCORMICK CAFÉ ▼ · OXFORD ANTIQUES · THE DOUBLE TREE BY HILTON · WALKER'S AMERICAN GRILL AND TAPAS BAR · N 25TH ST · N 24TH ST · ÜBERBREW ▼ · N 23RD ST · N 22ND ST · THE FIELDHOUSE CAFÉ · S 24TH ST · S 25TH ST · S 26TH ST · AVE S · 1ST ST · MONTANA AVE · MINNESOTA AVE · 3

0   150 yds
0   150 m

© MOON.COM

Deborah Butterfield, and Theodore Waddell. The museum also houses a significant number of works by Will James and early Montana modernist Isabelle Johnson. The Visible Vault gives visitors a glimpse of how and where the museum stores the 3,500 works of art—plus thousands of sketches, photographs, correspondence, and other archival material—in its permanent collection.

Moss Mansion

For 87 years, the family of fabulously successful entrepreneur Preston Boyd Moss lived happily in Billings's **Moss Mansion** (914 Division St., 406/256-5100, www.mossmansion.com, self-paced tours 10am-4pm Wed.-Sat., noon-3pm Sun., guided tours 10am and 1pm Wed.-Sat. June-Aug.; self-paced tours noon-3pm Wed.-Sun. year-round; guided tours 1pm Fri.-Sat. and self-guided tours noon-3pm Thurs.-Mon. Sept.-May; $15 adults guided tours, free for children under 5, $12 adults self-paced tours, $10 seniors and military, $8 students, free for children under 5). The 1903 home, designed by New York architect Henry Janeway Hardenbergh, who also designed

New York City's original Waldorf Astoria and Plaza Hotels, was lovingly maintained by the family and turned into a museum. One-hour guided tours offer a fascinating glimpse into the Moss family's elegant lifestyle. Much of the original furnishings and art decorate the mansion today. Winter holiday tours (guided adults $20, children under 5 free; self-guided $15 adults, $12 seniors, military, and students, children under 5 free) are a special treat starting in mid-November, when the mansion is decorated for Christmas.

Western Heritage Center

Beautifully housed downtown in the former Parmly Billings Memorial Library, the **Western Heritage Center** (2282 Montana Ave., 406/256-6809, www.ywhc.org, 10am-5pm Tues.-Sat., $5 adults, $3 students and seniors, $1 children under 12) is an affiliate of the Smithsonian Institution and has an extensive collection that documents the history of the Yellowstone River Valley, with more than 17,000 objects including historical photos and artifacts, Native American beadwork, architectural drawings, textiles, and Western art.

The museum is one of the few dedicated to recording and collecting oral histories of various regional Native American groups.

★ Pictograph Cave State Park

Southeast of Billings among the sandstone cliffs that form the rimrocks is **Pictograph Cave State Park** (3401 Coburn Rd., 406/254-7342, www.stateparks.mt.gov, park 9am-7pm daily, visitor center 10am-6pm daily third Fri. in May to third Sun. in Sept.; park 9am-5pm Wed.-Sun., visitor centers 10am-4pm Wed.-Sun. third Mon. in Sept. to third Thurs. in May; nonresidents $8/vehicle, $4 walk-in, bicycle, or bus passenger, Montana residents free). The site contains three caves—Pictograph, Middle, and Ghost—with evidence of human habitation that dates back 4,500 years. Pictographs more than 2,000 years old can be seen in one of the caves. Binoculars are helpful since visitors are kept some distance back in order to protect the ancient artwork. After the caves' discovery in 1936, a significant archaeological survey uncovered more than 30,000 artifacts from the site, including barbed harpoon points made from caribou horn. The park was vandalized in the 1950s and 1960s, when much of the artwork was covered with graffiti. Today it has been carefully restored, and in places, tracings from the initial archaeological study have been overlaid on the originals in order to make the vivid images more visible. A nice trail system winds through the 23-acre park, and picnic facilities are available for day use only.

Pompeys Pillar National Monument

Twenty-five miles (40 km) east of Billings is **Pompeys Pillar** (3001 US 212, Worden, 406/875-2400, www.pompeyspillar.org, vehicle access 8am-6pm daily, interpretive center 9am-6pm daily last Sat. in Apr.-Sept., pedestrians permitted dawn-dusk Oct.-Apr. but no services available, $7/vehicle), an age-old landmark that bears the signature of Captain William Clark of the Lewis and Clark expedition. Named by Clark for Sacagawea's son, Jean Baptiste Charbonneau,

nicknamed "Pomp," the sandstone pillar had a storied history both before and after Clark signed it on July 25, 1806: There were Indian pictographs on the 200-foot-tall rock when he first laid eyes on it. In 1873, Custer's troops were camped opposite the pillar along the banks of the Yellowstone River when they were fired on by Sioux warriors. When the gate is locked, October-April, pedestrians can park along the road and walk 1 mile (1.6 km) from the gate to the pillar.

Every year on the last weekend in July, the Friends of Pompeys Pillar host **Clark Days** (406/969-5380), a celebration of the pillar's past with lively history lectures and presentations, nature walks, hot meals, and plenty of activities geared toward the whole family. It is the only night of the year that camping is allowed on the grounds of the pillar, and no admission fee is charged during the two-day festivities.

SPORTS AND RECREATION
Spectator Sports

Under the shadow of the rimrocks, **Dehler Park** (2611 9th Ave. N., 406/657-8371, www.billingsparks.org), built in 2008 to accommodate 6,000 baseball fans in stadium seats, bleachers, and grassy picnic areas, is home to the **Billings Mustangs** (406/252-1241, www.billingsmustangs.com). The stadium's predecessor, Cobb Field, built in 1948, was home to the Pioneer League rookie affiliates for the Brooklyn Dodgers, the Pittsburgh Pirates, and the St. Louis Cardinals. From 1974 to 2020, the Mustangs were affiliated with the Cincinnati Reds, but they became independent in 2021. George Brett is among the most well-known alumni of Cobb Field.

Golf

There are a number of golf courses in Billings, perhaps because the winters are milder

---

1: Moss Mansion 2: Western Heritage Center
3: Pompeys Pillar National Monument

than in much of western Montana and the summers are longer. Twice ranked first in the state by *Golf Digest,* **Briarwood Country Club**'s 18-hole course (3429 Briarwood Blvd., 406/248-2702, www.thebriarwoodgc.com) is open to members and, reciprocally, to members of other private golf facilities in the United States. **Eagle Rock Golf Course** (5624 Larimer Ln., 406/655-4445, www.eaglerockgolfcourse.com) is an 18-hole public course, as are the challenging par-3 **Exchange City Golf Course** (19 S. 19th St. W., 406/652-2553) and the **Lake Hills Golf Club** (1930 Clubhouse Way, 406/252-9244, www.lakehillsgolf.com). Built in 1992, **Yegen Golf Club** (1390 Zimmerman Tr., 406/656-8099, www.yegengolfclub.com) is a beautiful course. Thirteen miles (20.9 km) northeast of Billings is the semiprivate **Pryor Creek Golf Club** (1292 Pryor Creek Rd., Huntley, 406/348-3900, www.pryorcreekgolf.com), one of only two 36-hole facilities in the state. The Elmer Link course is open to members and their guests, while the Johnny Walker course is open to the public.

Disc Golf

Also known as Diamond X Disc Golf Course, **Phipps Park** (Molt Rd., 4 mi/6.4 km west of Billings, www.billingsparks.org) is ranked among the top five disc golf courses in Montana. The 350-acre city park offers 27 holes for disc golfers, panoramic views, and a network of rugged, challenging trails for both runners and mountain bikers. Right in town, the 32-acre **Pioneer Park** (301 Parkhill Dr.) offers disc golf, a wading pool, tennis courts, multi-use trails, barbecue areas, horseshoe pits, and lots of green open space.

Hiking

Hikers can find plenty of trails winding around the rimrocks, including the 2.8-mile (4.5-km) trail at the **Four Dances Natural Area** (2 mi/3.2 km east of downtown Billings, 1100 Coburn Rd., 406/896-5013, www.blm.gov/visit/four-dances), which offers up a wonderful view of the Yellowstone River and

valley beyond from the top of the cliffs. It was named for the vision a Crow Indian had here in the 1830s while on a vision quest. Between April and August there are often peregrine falcons nesting, so hikers are asked to stay away from cliff's edge. The trail drops down to the river as well. From Billings, head east on Highway 90 to exit 452, turn right on Highway 87, then take the first right on Coburn Road for 1.4 miles (2.3 km) to reach the entrance to Four Dances.

For more extreme terrain, there are some phenomenal mountain trails less than an hour from town. The **Island Lake Trail** (trailhead at Mystic Dam Power Station, end of W. Rosebud Rd.), 40 miles (64 km) southwest of Billings in the **Custer National Forest's Beartooth Ranger District** (406/446-2103, www.fs.fed.us/r1/custer), is a 12-mile (19.3-km) out-and-back round-trip in the West Rosebud Valley. There are numerous trout-laden mountain lakes in the region, but the climb is significant, so allow ample time.

Farther afield, 85 miles (137 km) from Billings, but well worth the drive, the popular and well-traveled **East Rosebud Trail #15 to Elk Lake** (406/446-2103, www.fs.fed.us/r1/custer) winds along a stream, through meadows and beneath jagged peaks to an alpine lake. There are waterfalls and sparse conifer forests along the route, which is frequented by hikers and wildlife alike. It's about 3.4 miles (5.5 km) to Elk Lake. There are established campsites at the lake, or ambitious hikers can go on another 2.5 miles (4 km) to the turquoise waters of Rimrock Lake. The out-and-back hike to Elk Lake is 6.7 miles (10.8 km) round-trip; it's 12 miles (19.3 km) to Rimrock Lake and back. To get there from Billings, head east on I-90 to exit 408 for Columbus. Head south on North 9th Street until it ends in a T at Old Highway 10/East Pike Avenue. Take a right and then the first left onto Highway 78. Continue for about 27 miles (43 km) until the town of Roscoe. Turn right onto East Rosebud Road. Watch signs to stay on East Rosebud Road, as there are a few forks and deceptive turns. After 3.8 miles (6.1

km), just after crossing a bridge, turn right to stay on East Rosebud. Continue 10.6 miles (17 km) to the trailhead at the end of the road.

ENTERTAINMENT AND EVENTS

The Arts

Billings offers a host of urban culture options. Numerous theatrical performances and concerts are held at the **Alberta Bair Theater** (2801 3rd Ave. N., 406/256-6052, www.albertabairtheater.org), including the **Billings Symphony Orchestra and Chorale** (406/252-3610, www.billingssymphony.org, Sept.-June). The **NOVA Center for the Performing Arts** (2317 Montana Ave., 406/591-9535, www.novabillings.org) hosts drama, musical theater, improv comedy, opera, and a youth conservatory all under one roof. The **Billings Studio Theatre** (1500 Rimrock Rd., 406/248-1141, www.billingsstudiotheatre.com) offers excellent theater with tremendous community support.

Festivals and Events

A great resource for finding specific events during your visit to Billings is **www.Billings365.com,** which highlights every sort of daily happening from concerts and food-related events to readings, sports, and recreation.

Few artificial objects enhance a skyline as spectacularly as a flock of hot-air balloons. Billings's annual **Big Sky International Balloon Rendezvous** (Amend Park, 5101 King Ave. E., www.facebook.com/bigskyballoonrally), held on a weekend in late July or early August, lights up the sky with early-morning flights, dusk Balloon Glows, and plenty of camaraderie. Check the Facebook page as dates and locations can vary year to year.

Sponsored by the Yellowstone Art Museum, **Summerfair** (Veterans Park, corner of Poly Dr. and 13th St. W., 406/256-6804, ext. 222, www.artmuseum.org, 4pm-9pm Fri., 9am-5pm Sat., 10am-4pm Sun., $5 adults, free

for children under 6) is the largest arts and crafts festival in the region. Typically held on a weekend late June or early to mid-July, the fair includes more than 100 artist booths, loads of activities for kids, live entertainment, and a food court. The weekend pass ($25) admits two adults and three children over 6 for all three days.

The state's largest annual event, **MontanaFair** (MetraPark, 308 6th Ave. N., 406/256-2400 or 800/366-8538, www.montanafair.com, $9 adults, free for children 5 and under), running for nine days starting the second week of August, is an agricultural fair in the classic tradition. In addition to arts and crafts competitions and displays on everything from pigs and tomato-growing to pickles and crochet, MontanaFair events include major concerts, motorsports, bull riding, rodeo, and a good old-fashioned carnival. Check online or call ahead for special deals and concert tickets.

For beer lovers, **Ales for Trails** (downtown Billings, 406/281-1244, www.billingstrailnet.org) in September offers 40 microbrews, local food vendors, and great local music. Since its founding in 2001, the event has raised more than $1 million for the city's trail system, which boasts upward of 50 miles (80 km) of multiuse trails and 31 miles (50 km) of bike lanes.

Growing like mad since its origins in 2001, the two-day music festival **Magic City Blues** (main gate on the 2500 block of Montana Ave., 406/534-0400, www.magiccityblues.com, general admission from $59) held in early August offers an impressive lineup of big-name artists in a unique outdoor setting. Children under 18 are not permitted.

SHOPPING

While Billings is more often thought of as a place for supplies rather than boutique shopping, there are interesting shops worth visiting. The **Toucan Gallery** (2505 Montana Ave., 406/252-0122, www.toucanarts.com, 10am-5:30pm Tues.-Fri., 10am-4pm Sat.) is part gallery, part gift shop and showcases the work of more than 40 emerging and established contemporary artists, both local and regional. In addition to fine art, there are beautiful artisan crafts ranging from jewelry and cards to hats and home decor. They also offer various art classes and workshops.

AAA Oxford Hotel Antiques (1820 1st Ave. N., 406/245-4827, 10:30am-4:30pm Wed.-Sat.) is Billings's oldest single-owner antiques store. The building is a 1908 Victorian Italianate and suits the inventory perfectly. In addition to two floors of furniture, the store has an endless assortment of Montana-related items and other collectibles, including record albums.

Another Billings classic since 1946 is **Al's Bootery & Repair Shop** (2411 Montana Ave., 406/248-2094, www.alsbootery.com, 9am-6pm Mon.-Fri., 9am-5pm Sat.). Promising old-world craftsmanship and stellar customer service, Al's sells (and repairs!) work boots, cowboy boots, hiking boots, hunting boots, shoes, moccasins, and slippers.

A unique piece of Montana can be ordered at **Reliable Tent & Tipi** (501 N. 23rd St., 406/252-4689 or 800/544-1039, www.reliabletent.com), which has been family-owned since 1945. Its tents are designed for the often rugged hunting conditions in Montana, and its specialty Crow and Sioux tipis are designed by Native Americans according to family and tribal traditions. The company also makes a wonderful Backyard Tipi for kids.

For a nice selection of Montana sweatshirts, T-shirts, baseball caps, beanies, and other accessories, visit **Aspinwall Mountain Wear** (103 N. Broadway, 406/702-1586, www.aspinwallmountainwear.com, 10am-5pm Mon.-Sat.), started by a young Billings couple. Their latest commitment is to support the search for a cure for ALS with the sales of specially designed baseball shirts.

The 80,000-square-foot **Cabela's** (4550 King Ave. E., 406/373-7300, www.cabelas.com, 9am-9pm Mon.-Sat., 9am-7pm Sun.) offers a wealth of educational and entertaining displays—including a 7,000-gallon aquarium, indoor archery range, gun library, and museum-quality animal mounts—in addition to the company's top-notch outdoor gear. There's an express deli inside, as well as dog kennels and horse corrals, in case you plan to spend some time. Not to be outdone, **Scheels** (1121 Shiloh Crossing Blvd., 406/656-9220, www.scheels.com, 9am-9pm Mon.-Sat., 10am-6pm Sun.) is 220,000 square feet of sporting goods paradise housing a collection of entertainment venues in addition to individual sport and game shops, brand-name concept shops, and a full-service shop for bikes, skis, skates, and so on. Amenities include a Ferris wheel, saltwater aquarium, shooting gallery, a deli and fudge shop, plus Starbucks.

FOOD

As Montana's largest city, Billings has a lively dining scene and is a good place to splurge. Right downtown, **Bin 119** (119 N. Broadway, 406/294-9119, www.bin119.net, 11am-8:30pm Mon.-Thurs., 11am-9:30pm Fri.-Sat., $10-29) is an American bistro and wine bar with 180 labels and more than 30 wines sold by the glass. Started by local students, it's stylish but not at all pretentious. The food, primarily inspired by Spanish tapas, is geared toward appetizer-size dishes ($10-16). An expanded menu of entrées includes everything from lobster mac and cheese and braised short ribs to rib eye steaks and salmon fillets, a wide selection of pastas, plus soups, salads, and sandwiches.

★ **Walkers American Grill and Tapas Bar** (2700 1st Ave. N., 406/245-9291, www.walkersgrill.com, dining room 4pm-10pm Mon.-Thurs., 4pm-10:30pm Fri., 5pm-10:30pm Sat., 5pm-10pm Sun., $17-39) is big-city chic with excellent food and award-winning wine. The menu is cosmopolitan (salmon crudo) and entirely Montana (elk pot roast), and the ambience is elegant but

---

1: Pictograph Cave State Park 2: the McCormick Café 3: Billings' comfortable and contemporary Northern Hotel

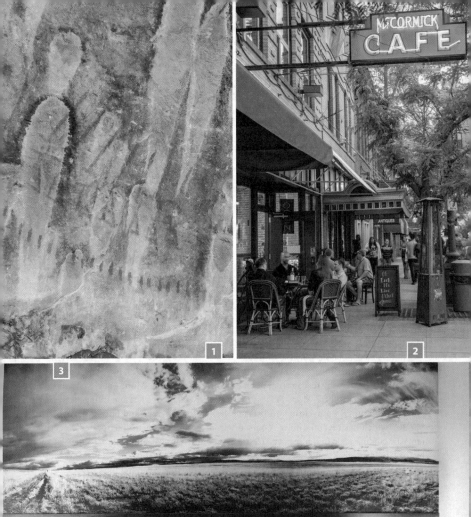

vibrant; Sunday evenings are enhanced by live jazz starting at 7pm.

Bistro Enzo (1502 Rehberg Ln., 406/651-0999, 5pm-9pm Sun.-Thurs., 5pm-9:30pm Fri.-Sat., $14-43) serves up hearty fusion fare—American, Asian, French, Italian—in a comfortable farmhouse. The restaurant imports fresh fish from both coasts daily and cooks many of the entrées on a wood-fired grill; the eclectic menu is a local favorite.

Located in the Northern Hotel, **TEN** (19 N. Broadway, 406/867-6774, www.northernhotel.com/ten, 5pm-10pm daily, lounge opens at 3pm daily, $28-78) offers guests a sophisticated dining experience that emphasizes fresh local produce and meat in decidedly creative ways. From the lamb pierogis and mountain fondue on the small plates menu to bison tenderloin au poivre, Rocky Mountain rack of elk, and a phenomenal range of Angus and Kobe beef steaks, the red-hued restaurant offers an urban and very upscale take on the Montana culinary scene.

Another elegant choice for fine dining is **Bistecca at the Granary** (1500 Poly Dr., 406/259-3488, www.bisteccagranary.com, dining room 5pm-close Mon.-Fri., 4pm-close Sat., lounge 3pm-close Mon.-Fri., $17-30), which has several dining rooms, a fantastic outdoor patio in summer, and classic bistro fare from steaks and seafood to pasta and poultry.

Billings has plenty of casual and entirely family-friendly options as well that are open for both lunch and dinner. **The Windmill** (3429 TransTech Way, 406/252-8100, www.windmillbar51.com, 11:30am-9pm Mon.-Thurs., 11:30am-10pm Fri., 4pm-10pm Sat., lunch $12-32, dinner $15-70) offers an extensive seafood, steak, chicken, and ribs menu as well as a children's menu. The creekside patio can't be beat when the weather is good. Not far away, and right across from the Reef Indoor Water Park, is **Montana's Rib & Chop House** (1849 Majestic Ln., 406/839-9200, 11am-10pm daily, $14-43), an excellent chain with locations across Montana and Wyoming (and now Colorado and Utah too). The menu

is packed (and usually so is the restaurant) with plenty of steaks, seafood, and ribs.

For brewpub aficionados, Billings won't disappoint. A couple of casual favorites are **Überbrew** (2305 Montana Ave., 406/534-6960, www.uberbrew.beer, taproom 11am-9pm daily with last pour at 7:59pm, $10-17), which serves great burgers, sandwiches, elk sausage and the like, and **Montana Brewing Company** (113 N. Broadway, 406/252-9200, www.montana-brewing-company.business.site, 11am-1am daily, $9-13), which has all of your favorite bar fare, including burgers, pasta, and Mexican fare. Both establishments serve a selection of excellent beers brewed on-site.

For breakfast and lunch, **McCormick Café** (2419 Montana Ave., 406/255-9555, www.mccormickcafe.com, 7am-2pm Mon.-Fri., 8am-2pm Sat.-Sun., $7-11) is another local favorite, offering everything from Parisian crepes and wonderful pastries to savory sandwiches, wraps, and healthy salads.

Rocket Gourmet Wraps & Sodas (2809 1st Ave. N., 406/248-5231, www.rocketwraps.com, 10am-3pm Mon.-Fri., $7-9) is an excellent place for a fast and filling meal. The hot and cold wraps and burritos are made from fresh ingredients like roasted chicken, andouille sausage, and albacore tuna. There is an ample selection of salads and kids' meals, and diners can wet their whistles with specialty coffees and Italian sodas.

★ **The Fieldhouse Cafe** (2601 Minnesota Ave., 406/534-2556, www.thefieldhousemt.com, 11am-2pm and 5pm-9pm Wed.-Fri., 9am-2pm and 5pm-9pm Sat., 9am-2pm Sun., dinner $18-29, brunch $12-18) offers weekend brunch and a farm-to-table tapas-style dinner menu that changes weekly based on the freshest local and organic ingredients. From quinoa salad and fish tacos to truffle fries and cashew-parmesan Brussels sprouts, you will want to lick your plate before you surrender it. The happy hour is 4pm-6pm Tuesday through Saturday.

Not exactly healthy—unless your body runs on cinnamon rolls, sour cream coffee cake, sugar cookies, or warm-from-the-oven bread—but completely homemade and utterly delicious, ★ **Stella's Kitchen & Bakery** (2525 1st Ave. N., 406/248-3060, 5:30am-3pm Mon.-Sat., 6:30am-1pm Sun., $3-13) is an excellent choice for warm, doughy comfort food and all-day breakfast. Stella's serves just breakfast items on Sunday.

ACCOMMODATIONS

When it comes to combining luxury and historical grandeur, the only choice is the magnificently restored 1902 ★ **Northern Hotel** (19 N. Broadway, 406/867-6767, www.northernhotel.com, from $209 low season, $249 high season). Reopened in 2013 as part of the Preferred Hotel Group and listed on the National Register of Historic Places, it is indeed a Western boutique hotel, with 160 guest rooms and two excellent restaurants, including the elegant TEN. It is Billings's only four-star hotel, and amenities include 24-hour room service, valet service, triple-sheeted beds, and piles of pillows.

The **DoubleTree by Hilton** (27 N. 27th St., 406/252-7400, www.doubletree3.hilton.com/billings, from $159) in downtown Billings is difficult to miss: It is a towering brick building that dwarfs its neighbors. The hotel is geared to business travelers, and the guest rooms are plenty comfortable. It offers a large assortment of amenities, including complimentary high-speed Internet. The **Montana Sky** restaurant is situated on the 20th floor with terrific views of the city and rimrocks.

On the southwest side of town, the **Billings Hotel and Convention Center** (1223 Mullowney Ln., 406/248-7151, www.billingshotelmt.com, from $174) is another large facility with all the standard amenities. Some rooms are pet-friendly (for a charge), and kids will love the curlicue water slides in the indoor pool.

There are two Best Western options in Billings, both of which offer clean, comfortable, and pet-friendly accommodations. In the heart of downtown,

Best Western Plus Clocktower Inn (2511 1st Ave. N., 406/259-5511 or 800/238-4218, www.bwclocktowerinn.com, from $118 low season, $156 high season) offers guests a "Key to the City," which gives them 10 percent off at many area restaurants and bars within walking distance of the hotel. West of town, near the big-box shopping stores, the pet-friendly **Best Western Plus Kelly Inn & Suites** (4915 Southgate Dr., 406/256-9400 or 800/528-1234, www.bwbillings.com, from $86 low season, $145 high season) offers immaculately clean and spacious rooms, cozy fireplace suites, and an ideal water playland for younger kids.

When it comes to water parks, however, **Big Horn Resort** (1801 Majestic Ln., 406/839-9300 or 877/995-8999, www.thebighornresort.com, from $69 low season, $115 high season) is the real deal and a kid's dream come true. Parents will appreciate the clean, comfortable, quiet rooms and grown-up amenities like free wireless Internet and jetted bathtubs, and kids will delight in the enormous and loud **Reef Indoor Water Park** (406/839-9283, www.thereefindoors.com, $14.95 all-day admission for anyone over 4 ft, $12.95 all-day admission under 4 ft, $12 hotel guest, $12.95/swimmer after 4pm, $5 spectators, free for children under 2). Check the website or call for hours, which are subject to change and closures during COVID-19. The state's largest, this indoor facility includes three-story water slides, a wave pool, interactive playhouse, basketball pool, 25-person hot tub, arcade, and café. There is great dining just across the parking lot at the **Rib & Chop House,** so guests can leave the car parked during a stay here.

Additional hotel offerings worth looking at include the **Country Inn & Suites** (231 Main St., 406/245-9995, www.countryinns.com, from $103 low season, $148 high season) and the **Boothill Inn & Suites** (242 E. Airport Rd., 406/245-2000, www.boothillinn.com, from $125 low season, $145 high season), which has great family suites with a king and queen as well as twin bunks.

Housed in a 1912 historic residence at the edge of downtown, **The Josephine Bed and Breakfast** (514 N. 29th St., 406/248-5898 or 800/552-5898, www.thejosephine.com, $95-170 d) offers a quiet stay in an intimate yet convenient setting. The inn provides airport pickup, free wireless Internet, passes to a 24-hour fitness center, and a gourmet breakfast. At times, the inn only accepts guests for one week or longer, so be sure to call ahead.

A 15-minute drive from downtown Billings in Huntley is **Somewhere in Time Bed & Breakfast** (266 Hogan Rd., Huntley, 406/348-2205, www.ourbedandbreakfast.com, from $100), a lovely 1900 Victorian set in a ranch on Pryor Creek. Although the property is not handicapped-accessible, the rooms are comfortable and, unlike some Victorian establishments, not at all over-cluttered.

The **Dude Rancher Lodge** (415 N. 29th St., 406/545-0121, www.duderancherlodge.com, from $63 low season, $77 high season) is a unique, independently owned frontier hotel built in 1949. It is within walking distance of downtown's shops, restaurants, and nightlife and prides itself on offering Western hospitality. Each guest room is individually furnished, and some come with refrigerators and microwaves.

Other budget-friendly hotels you may want to consider are the pet-friendly **Riversage Billings Inn** (880 N. 29th St., 406/252-6800 or 800/231-7782, from $91 low season, $102 high season, with significant discounts for advance payment) and the **Howard Johnson by Wyndham Billings** (1345 Mullowney Ln., 406/252-2584, from $89-209, with discounts for advance payment).

CAMPING

Native Ways Primitive Campground (4055 High Trail Rd., 406/670-1209, nwpcmt@gmail.com, March 15-Nov. 1, weather dependent, $50-70), 4 (6.4 km) miles southeast of Billings, offers a unique take on camping: four tipis, both Crow and Sioux style, on 25 wooded acres. Each site has its own tipi and

can be fully supplied with sleeping bags ($5) and other necessities if you need them, plus a washbasin, water, a picnic table, a lantern, and a garbage can. For more unique stays, visit www.hipcamp.com.

The **Billings KOA** (547 Garden Ave., 406/252-3104 or 800/562-8546, www.billingskoa.com, Apr.-Oct. 15, limited service the rest of the year, from $40 tents, $58 RVs, from $110 cabins) is considered the world's first KOA and offers 40 tent sites, many of them on the banks of the Yellowstone River, along with 135 RV sites, 11 cabins, and two lodges that accommodate up to six people with bathroom, kitchen, and linens provided. Amenities include a swimming pool and spa for campers, a barbecue, miniature golf, a playground, and broadband Wi-Fi. The campground is conveniently close to town and offers pancake breakfasts and barbecue dinners mid-June to mid-August.

INFORMATION AND SERVICES

The **visitor center** is one floor below the **Billings Chamber of Commerce** (815 S. 27th St., 406/252-4111 or 800/735-2635, www.visitbillings.com, 8:30am-5pm Mon.-Sat., noon-4pm Sun. Memorial Day-Labor Day, 8:30am-5pm Mon.-Fri. Labor Day-Memorial Day).

The **main post office** (841 S. 26th St., 8:30am-5:30pm Mon.-Fri.) is just behind the chamber of commerce. There is also a **downtown post office** (2602 1st Ave. N., 406/657-5748, 8am-5:30pm Mon.-Fri.), and one **branch post office** (724 15th St. W., 406/657-5788) is open on Saturday (10am-2pm).

The **Parmly Billings Library** (510 N. Broadway, 406/657-8258, www.billings.lib.mt.us, 9am-8pm Mon.-Fri., 10am-5pm Sat., 1pm-5pm Sun., closed Sun. Memorial Day-Labor Day) offers free use of computers with Internet access.

You'll find Wi-Fi at a number of **Starbucks** across Billings (910 Grand Ave.,

5am-8pm Mon.-Fri., 6am-8pm Sat.-Sun.; 406 Main St., 5am-8pm Mon.-Sat., 5:30am-8pm Sun.; 1017 N. 27th Ave., 5:30am-3pm daily) and at **Rock Creek Roasters** (124 N. Broadway, 406/896-1600, 6am-4pm Mon.-Fri., 7am-2pm Sat.).

Two conveniently located coin-op laundries are **Speedy Wash** (2505 6th Ave. N., 406/248-4177, 7am-7pm daily) and **Spin Fresh Coin Laundry** (3189 King Ave. W., Ste. 4, 406/652-2993, www.spinfreshlaundry. com, 7am-9pm daily), which has a second self-serve-only location at 410 Lake Elmo Drive (6am-midnight daily).

For emergency medical assistance, **St. Vincent Healthcare** (1233 N. 30th St., 406/237-7000, www.svh-mt.org) and **Billings Clinic Hospital** (2800 10th Ave. N., 406/238-2501 or 800/332-7156, www.billingsclinic. com) both have 24-hour ER service. For minor medical care, the **Billings Clinic** also has walk-in service at three branch locations: Downtown Pediatric Center (2800 10th Ave. N., 406/238-2500, 8am-6pm Mon.-Fri., 9am-1pm Sat.), West (2675 Central Ave., in Lamplighter Square next to Target, 406/238-2900, 8am-5pm Mon.-Fri., 9am-1pm Sat.), and Heights (760 Wicks Ln., across from Walmart, 406/238-2475, 8am-5pm Mon.-Wed. and Fri., 8am-4pm Thurs.).

TRANSPORTATION
Getting There
Billings Logan International Airport (BIL, 1901 Terminal Cir., 406/247-8609 or 406/657-8495, www.flybillings.com) is situated atop the rimrocks off I-90 at the 27th Street exit. Delta, United, Allegiant, Alaska Airlines, American, and Cape Air offer regular flights.

If you arrive early at the airport or have some time to spare before you are picked up, visit the **Peter Yegen Jr. Yellowstone County Museum** (1950 Terminal Cir., 406/256-6811, www.pyjrycm.

org, 10:30am-5:30pm Mon.-Sat., free). Once outside the terminal, follow the road around the west parking lot; the museum is on the right before the airport exit. The museum has artifacts and exhibits highlighting the history of the northern plains from early Native American influence through westward expansion and mining up to the 1950s. There's even a two-headed calf! The museum's deck provides a splendid view of the city below.

The **Greyhound** bus terminal and ticket offices (1830 4th Ave. N., 406/245-5117, www. greyhound.com) are open 24 hours a day year-round.

As the largest city in Montana, Billings is an easy driving destination. It's intersected by I-90, and I-94 begins just outside the town. Billings is 142 miles (229 km) east of Bozeman, 81 miles (130 km) east of Big Timber, 60 miles (97 km) northeast of Red Lodge, and 46 miles (74 km) west of Hardin. In Wyoming, Cody is 106 miles (171) away, and it is 130 miles (209 km) to Sheridan.

Getting Around
At the Billings airport, **Enterprise, Thrifty, Dollar, Hertz, Alamo, Avis, Budget,** and **National** have on-site car-rental counters.

Two taxi services are available: **City Cab** (406/252-8700, www.willsonllc.com) and **Yellow Cab** (406/245-3033). There is no taxi stand at the airport, so call ahead if you want to be picked up.

MET transit (406/657-8218, www.mettransit. com, 5:50am-6:50pm Mon.-Fri., 8:10am-5:45pm Sat., $2 one-way fare adults 19 and up, $1.50 youth 6-18, $1 seniors and disabled citizens, free for children 6 and under, $18 10-ride ticket, $4 day pass) offers bus service throughout Billings, and although there are marked bus stops around the city, you can also flag them down at any corner. Booklets with routes and schedules are available at most banks, convenience stores, grocery stores, the library, and government offices.

Crow and Northern Cheyenne Reservations

Southeastern Montana is a ruggedly beautiful part of the state, with vast prairies, dramatic canyons, and stark badlands. The land is dry and brittle in places, but the people are tenacious, having been ordered to occupy this region in the aftermath of the Fort Laramie Treaty of 1851. The two tribes in this part of the state—the Crow and the Northern Cheyenne—have managed to preserve their cultures with little more than steadfast determination. There is no better place to experience Native American culture—to see and hear their stories, their art, their traditions—than on the reservations.

The Crow Reservation occupies roughly 2.3 million acres of land and is home to some 7,900 Crow, which accounts for 72 percent of the tribe's enrolled members. Nearly 85 percent of those on the reservation speak Crow as their first language. The largest settlement by far and the county seat, Hardin (pop. 3,808, elev. 2,902 ft/885 m) is not on the reservation; communities on the reservation include Crow Agency, Fort Smith, Garryowen, Lodgegrass, Pryor, and Wyola.

Just east of the Crow Reservation is the much smaller Northern Cheyenne Indian Reservation. Today, the reservation is home to roughly 6,012 of the 12,266 enrolled tribal members. Lame Deer is the tribal and government agency headquarters; Busby is the other primary settlement on the reservation.

HISTORY

The story of the Crow Indian Reservation is all too familiar and tragic. The 1851 Fort Laramie Treaty recognized almost all of the Yellowstone Valley as Crow territory. Mining claims and a dramatic increase in the number of settlers traveling through the region led to

conflict and a second treaty in 1868, which, even though unsigned by the vast majority of Crow, significantly reduced the size of their territory. The discovery of gold on Crow land shortly after the second treaty led to a third treaty in 1873, which moved the Crow again to a much smaller reservation in central Montana's Judith Basin. Neither the Crow nor the cattle ranchers settling in the region were pleased with the arrangement, and the Crow Reservation was moved farther east and reduced yet again in size.

The Northern Cheyenne are a division of the Cheyenne tribe who once ranged across the Great Plains from South Dakota to Colorado. The first Cheyenne territory dictated by the U.S. government was in the region around what is now Denver. The Cheyenne were repeatedly attacked by the U.S. government and sustained enormous casualties, all while living according to law in the territory the government had given them. Following the Battle of the Little Bighorn, in which the Cheyenne participated, the army's attempts to capture the Cheyenne increased in intensity. Several Cheyenne chiefs surrendered, expecting to be returned to Colorado, but were instead sent to the reservation for the Southern Cheyenne in Oklahoma.

After disease decimated the tribe and starvation threatened the survivors, fewer than 300 Northern Cheyenne slipped out of the reservation with the intent of going back north. Nearly 10,000 soldiers and 3,000 settlers chased the band for six weeks across Kansas and Nebraska. In the fall of 1878, the remaining Northern Cheyenne split into two groups: those who were willing to surrender with Dull Knife and live at Red Cloud Agency and those under Little Wolf who wanted to continue northward. Dull Knife and his people were captured, brutalized, and ordered back to Oklahoma. Dull Knife refused and again made a daring attempt at escape. In the end, only nine of the people with Dull Knife survived. They were eventually allowed to go to Fort Keogh, near modern-day Miles City, Montana, where Little Wolf and his followers had ended up.

After assisting the army in their pursuit of Chief Joseph and the Nez Perce, the Northern Cheyenne were given a reservation by the U.S. government in 1884. In an atypical move, the government actually expanded the reservation in 1890.

SIGHTS

★ Little Bighorn Battlefield National Monument

The **Little Bighorn Battlefield National Monument** (65 mi/105 km southeast of Billings, 15 mi/24 km southeast of Hardin, 1 mi/1.6 km east of I-90 on US 212, 406/638-2621, www.nps.gov, entrance gate 8am-8pm daily Memorial Day-Labor Day, 8am-6pm daily Labor Day-end of Sept., 8am-4:30pm daily Oct.-Memorial Day, $25/vehicle, $20/motorcycle, $15/pedestrian or bicyclist) is a desolate, somber, and terribly meaningful place, commemorating a tragic battle with no true victors, only bloodshed marking the end of an era. The monument memorializes the battlefield made famous by Lieutenant Colonel George Armstrong Custer, more than 200 men from his 7th Cavalry, and the thousands of Native American warriors who fought under Sitting Bull and Crazy Horse for their way of life against a foreign government that they perceived as dishonest, unreliable, and tyrannical.

In early 1876, thousands of Native Americans from numerous tribes slipped away from their reservations, restless and disgruntled at having been repeatedly lied to and mistreated by the U.S. government. Countless skirmishes throughout the winter and spring reinvigorated the army's pursuit of the Native Americans, and four centuries of conflict between Native Americans and European Americans came to a head in June 1876 at the battle, when Custer and his men attacked an enormous force of Cheyenne, Sioux, and Arapaho and were quickly surrounded. Custer's infamous Last Stand actually lasted less than an hour, and every man under his command on that hill was killed.

The **Little Bighorn Battlefield Visitor Center and Museum** (8am-6pm daily Memorial Day-Oct., 8am-4:30pm daily Nov.-Memorial Day) is a must for those visiting the site. The compact facility powerfully interprets the events leading up to and following the battle. Exhibited artifacts include weapons, photos of the key players, archaeological findings, and, during the off-season, an excellent 25-minute video documentary called *Triumph and Tragedy Along the Little Bighorn*. Rangers give frequent interpretive lectures, and bus tours of the site are available in summer.

Adjacent to the visitor center is the **Custer National Cemetery** for the military, which resembles Arlington National Cemetery on a much smaller scale. The actual monument on Last Stand Hill is on a paved trail within walking distance of the center, and a 4.5-mile (7.2-km) road open to car traffic connects the Custer Battlefield with the Benteen Battlefield.

The granite memorial on **Last Stand Hill** was built in July 1881, and in 1890 marble markers replaced stakes that stood where each soldier had fallen. Starting in 1999, red granite markers were placed to honor the Native Americans who died in the battle, including Cheyenne warriors Lame White Man and Noisy Walking and Lakota warriors Long Road and Dog's Back Bone. Another monument, titled "Peace Through Unity," was dedicated in 2003 to honor the Native American participants who fought and died in the Battle of the Little Bighorn. For those wanting to do a bit of homework before arriving at the site, the organization **Friends of the Little Bighorn Battlefield** (www.friendslittlebighorn.com) maintain an excellent website. If you can time it just right, each

year over a three-day weekend at the end of June the Real Bird family hosts a **Battle of the Little Bighorn Reenactment** (www. littlebighornreenactment.com) with hundreds of Native Americans and U.S. Cavalry on horseback. The remarkable event takes place on the Real Birds' land along the river, where Sitting Bull's camp was located.

A wonderful way to explore the monument, and the starkly beautiful windswept plains that surround it, is by hiring a Native American guide through **Apsalooke Tours** (406/638-3897 or 406/679-0041, daily Memorial Day-Labor Day, $15 adults, $12 seniors 65 and over, $5 children 4-12, free for children under 4), organized through the **Little Big Horn College.** The hour-long tours are generally held on the hour 10am-3pm, and guides can also be hired for group and private tours and as step-on guides.

Big Horn County Historical Museum and Visitor Center

Located in Hardin, 15 miles (24 km) north of the Battle of the Little Bighorn National Monument, the **Big Horn County Historical Museum** (1163 3rd St. E., 406/665-1671, c, 8am-6pm daily Memorial Day-Labor Day, 9am-5pm Mon.-Fri. Labor Day-Memorial Day, historical buildings closed Oct.-Apr., $6 adults, $5 seniors, $3 children 7-18, free for children under 6) contains 24 historical buildings outfitted from the periods in which they originated—a 1922 schoolhouse, a 1917 Evangelical church built by German settlers, a 1906 depot, and buildings from a 1911 working farm. The museum offers excellent hands-on educational programs and a Montana state visitor center.

Chief Plenty Coups State Park

For his bravery and leadership, Plenty Coups was made chief of the Crow Nation when he was only 28 years old. In 1884, he became one

of the first Crow to own and work a farm. Along with his wife, Strikes the Iron, Plenty Coups built a home, worked the land, and operated a general store on his 320-acre plot of land just east of Pryor. Upon his death in 1932, and according to the wishes of the chief and his wife, 195 acres of their land was turned into a public park known as **Chief Plenty Coups State Park** (1 Edgar Rd., 1 mi/1.6 km west of Pryor, 406/252-1289, www.stateparks. mt.gov, 8am-8pm daily mid-May-mid-Sept., 8am-5pm Wed.-Sun. mid-Sept.-mid-May, nonresidents $8/vehicle, $4/bus, bicycle or pedestrian, Montana residents free). The park is home to a **museum and visitor center** (10am-5pm daily mid-May-mid-Sept., 10am-5pm Wed.-Sun. mid-Sept.-mid-May, free) celebrating Crow culture and a gift shop, along with Chief Plenty Coups's log cabin home, his general store, and his grave.

St. Labre Mission and Cheyenne Indian Museum

St. Labre Mission (1000 Tongue River Rd., Ashland, 406/784-4500, www.stlabre.org, 8am-5:30pm Mon.-Fri. Memorial Day-Labor Day, 8am-4:30pm Mon.-Fri. Labor Day-Memorial Day, free) began as the St. Labre Indian School in 1884 under the guidance of the Ursuline Sisters. The school and mission were founded before the Northern Cheyenne Indian Reservation was officially set up by the U.S. government. George Yoakum, a former soldier and Roman Catholic from Miles City, requested that Montana's bishop John Brondel go to help the wandering Cheyenne who were congregating in the Tongue River Valley. Brondel purchased the land, and the St. Labre School was founded in March 1884.

The original three-room cabin, of which there is a replica today, served as the church, the school, and the dormitory for both students and nuns. The school has always blended Cheyenne culture with Roman Catholicism; in 1970 the Cheyenne language was added to the elementary curriculum because many of the children had never learned it. The course was so well received that a night course was added

---

1: Bighorn Canyon National Recreation Area
2: Last Stand Hill 3: angler in the Bighorn River
4: a hiker in the Bighorn Canyon National Recreation Area

Plenty Coups, Visionary Chief of the Crow

Born into the Apsáalooke (or Crow) tribe in 1848, Chief Plenty Coups had a life that spanned two eras. As a young warrior, he rode across the plains hunting, fighting, and conquering. As a middle-aged leader, he embraced life on the reservation as a farmer, trader, and negotiator. He is regarded by many Native Americans and whites alike to be the last of the great Crow war chiefs, and he had a tremendous influence on the tribe's relations with settlers.

Plenty Coups was considered special even as a young child. His grandfather foresaw his role as a chief and named him Alaxchiiaahush, meaning "many accomplishments" or "plenty coups." When he was 11, Plenty Coups went into the mountains on a vision quest. He was gone for three days, and when he returned he shared his dream with the group's elders. He claimed he had seen large herds of buffalo disappearing across the plains and a new strange animal arriving to take their place. He described seeing all the trees in the forest blow over with a great gust of wind until only one remained standing straight and tall. Inside the tree was a single chickadee. The elders declared that his dream was a vision of the future and that it meant the buffalo would disappear and be replaced by settlers' cattle. They believed the forest represented all the Plains Indian tribes, and the settlers, like the wind, would tear through their land and way of life. The fallen trees were interpreted as the tribes that resisted and fought the settlers. The lone standing tree represented the Crow; they would survive because they would work with, rather than against, the settlers. The Crow used this dream as a guide for the next several years, and when it came time to fight, they joined the side of the settlers and fought against other tribes.

Plenty Coups earned several "coups" as a valiant and skilled warrior. He was believed to have had at least 80 feathers on his coup stick, each representing an act of bravery. In addition, he proved to be an eloquent and moving orator. When the Crow people were confined to their reservation, Plenty Coups counseled that they ought to do their best to adapt to this new way of life. He led by example, cultivating his individual allotment of land, opening a general store, and building a log cabin. Plenty Coups was also a great promoter of education, reminding his people that "with education you will be the white man's equal; without it you will be the white man's victim." Plenty Coups negotiated a railroad line through the reservation and made several journeys to Washington DC to represent Native American interests. In turn, Washington recognized him as an important American leader. In 1921 he was invited to speak at the dedication of the Tomb of the Unknown Soldier, which was attended by other important international figures. In reading about Plenty Coups, one can only wonder how much of his story is shaped by the white narrative, the version where the "good Indians" were the ones who learned to live like white men. And by contrast, how much of his story, and his heroism, belongs to the Crow people. As tribes across the continent reclaim their own narratives and establish the authority of their own voices, time will tell.

In 1928, four years before his death, Plenty Coups dedicated a portion of his land as a memorial to the Apsáalooke Nation, stating, "It is given as a token of my friendship for all people, both red and white." Today it is a state park located on the Crow Reservation called Chief Plenty Coups State Park.

for adults. Today, the St. Labre Indian School educates nearly 800 Northern Cheyenne and Crow students from kindergarten through high school on three campuses.

Tragically and unsurprisingly, the St. Labre Indian School was not immune to the epidemic of trauma that so many Indigenous schools across the United States and Canada faced. It's widely reported that the reservations and mission schools were "dumping grounds" for predator priests who'd faced allegations elsewhere. Under both Pope Benedict XVI in 2009 and Pope Francis in 2015, the Catholic Church apologized for the abuse.

A 1971 church on the site was constructed in tipi form, with a cross as the center pole. The Cheyenne Indian Museum (8am-5pm Mon.-Fri. Memorial Day-Labor Day,

8am-4:30pm Mon.-Fri. Labor Day-Memorial Day, free) offers an opportunity to see various Plains Indian artifacts as well as a short documentary film on the St. Labre Indian School. The museum is also open on Saturday on the Memorial Day and Independence Day weekends (9am-3pm), and all weekend over Labor Day (9am-3pm).

SPORTS AND RECREATION

Fishing

The fishing on the **Bighorn River** is legendary, and there is no shortage of fly shops and outfitters available to help visitors find big, beautiful trout. The Bighorn is known for trout that are plentiful in both size and number: browns in this river average 15 inches (38 cm) and rainbows average 16 inches (41 cm). Dry-fly fishing is almost always an option, but nymphing and streamer fishing are useful under certain water conditions as well. Trout fishing on the Bighorn is generally best the 13 river miles (21 km) below the Yellowtail Dam, and estimates put the fish population between 3,000 and 5,000 fish per mile. Although fishing is certainly more popular during the temperate season, the Bighorn is a tailwater fishery—thanks to the Yellowtail Dam—meaning that the river never freezes in winter and stays fishable year-round.

The area's original fly shop and outfitter, **Bighorn Angler** (577 Parkdale Ct., Fort Smith, 406/666-2233, www.bighornangler. com) offers complete outfitting services, with experienced guides, boat rentals, quality tackle, and packages including lodging—ranging from simple but nice motel rooms ($85 single, $115 double) or deluxe lodge rooms ($145 double) to river cabins ($200-250 for up to 4 people) and deluxe lodges ($450 for up to 6 people, $595 for up to 10 people). Stop in for the best advice on where the fish are biting and what they're eating.

Established by Congress in 1966 after the completion of the Yellowtail Dam, the **Bighorn Canyon National Recreation Area** (north entrance via Hwy. 313, Fort Smith, headquarters 406/666-2414, visitor information 307/548-5406, www.nps.gov, $5/vehicle, $30 annual vehicle pass) includes 71 miles (114 km) of Bighorn Lake in a spectacular 55-mile (89-km) canyon. Fishing can be done from shore or in a boat either in the river or on Bighorn Lake—home to brown, rainbow, and lake trout as well as walleye, smallmouth bass, channel catfish, and even ling and shovelnose sturgeon.

Hiking and Boating

Bighorn Canyon National Recreation Area itself straddles the Montana-Wyoming border and also offers excellent boating, bird- and wildlife-watching, swimming, and picnicking. There are 28 miles (45 km) of hiking on 14 separate trails. Hiking guides and other information are available at the **Yellowtail Dam Visitor Center** (off Hwy. 313 near the top of the dam, 406/666-9961, www.nps.gov, 8:30am-5pm daily Memorial Day-Labor Day). Pontoon boats can be rented from the **Ok-A-Beh Marina** (near Fort Smith, 406/666-2349 or 406/629-9041, 10am-7pm Mon.-Fri., 9am-7pm Sat.-Sun. Memorial Day-Labor Day). Numerous free campgrounds are within the boundaries of the recreation area, many of which are open all year.

Horseback Riding

On the Northern Cheyenne Indian Reservation, **Cheyenne Trailriders** (N. Tongue River Rd. and Robinson Ln., Ashland, 406/784-6150) affords visitors an opportunity to explore the reservation on horseback. In order to increase awareness and appreciation of Cheyenne history and culture, the company offers workshops on history, culture, and ethnobotany. Guides are also happy to teach you about gourd dancing, intertribal hand games, round dancing, and Indian sign language around an evening campfire. There are storytellers and flute players to entertain riders, and wagon trips are available for non-riders. Custom overnight trips (from $250 pp), with lodging in a tipi, can be arranged for riders as young as eight years old.

ENTERTAINMENT AND EVENTS
★ Crow Fair

Crow Fair (powwow grounds in Crow Agency, 406/638-3708 or 406/679-2108, www.crow-nsn.gov) is an annual powwow held on the Crow Indian Reservation the third week in August to celebrate the past, present, and future of the Crow people. The event is awash in vibrant color, sound, and taste and is certainly one of the best times to visit the reservation; it's called the "tipi capital of the world" for the more than 1,000 tipis that are erected at the site. Crow Fair is a major event not only for the Crow but also for Native Americans across North America, who come to participate in the competitive dancing and drumming and what is considered to be the largest all-Indian rodeo in the country. There are daily parades and evening grand entries, the ceremonial opening to the evening events, which include flag bearers and dancers in all their finery. There is also horse racing of many varieties and rodeo, in addition to nonstop food and music. Festivities take place mainly at the fairgrounds in Crow Agency, 60 miles (97 km) southeast of Billings off I-90.

Crow Native Days Powwow

A smaller and much newer event than Crow Fair, **Crow Native Days** (powwow grounds in Crow Agency, 406/638-3708, www.crow-nsn.gov) happens over a weekend in late June. The event includes evening grand entries and features the royalty from the upcoming Crow Fair. Like Crow Fair, the event hosts daily parades and dancing competitions for various age groups—from fancy dancing and chicken dancing categories for men to traditional and jingle dancing for women. Unique to Crow Native Days is an Ultimate Warrior competition for both men and women. Each male contestant runs, canoes, and rides three different horses for 6 (9.7 km) miles, wearing a breechcloth and moccasins. Women compete in teams of three, with each member completing one leg of the race.

Little Big Horn Days and Battle of the Little Bighorn Reenactment

Little Big Horn Days (Hardin, 406/665-1672 or 888/450-3577, www.thehardinchamber.com) entails three days of celebrations close to the June 25 anniversary of the famous battle—some festive, others sober—commemorating the region's history and, in particular, its proximity to the Battle of the Little Bighorn. The festivities include a quilt show, a book fair, and a historical dance—the 1876 Grand Ball—as well as arts and crafts sales, a symposium, and a parade, all culminating in the dramatic and well-attended **Battle of the Little Bighorn Reenactment** (E. Frontage Rd. between Crow Agency and Garryowen, www.littlebighornreenactment.com). The reenactment requires more than 200 actors and is performed from the Native American perspective in a script written by historian Joe Medicine Crow. The event takes place on the Real Bird ranch 6 miles (9.7 km) west of Hardin, not far from the actual battlefield, and tickets ($20 adults, $10 children 6-16, free for children under 6) can be purchased at the gate only. Exact change is appreciated.

Powwows on the Northern Cheyenne Indian Reservation

Two powwows are held annually on the Northern Cheyenne Indian Reservation. The largest celebration for the tribe is the **Fourth of July Chief's Powwow and Rodeo** (Kenneth Beartusk Memorial Powwow Grounds, 3 mi/4.8 km south of Lame Deer, 406/477-8222 or 406/477-4847, www.cheyennenation.com, camping permitted), which happens over the course of four days around July 4. There are contests for princesses from all tribes, open dance and drum competitions, parades, grand entries, and daily gourd dancing. Traditional food is available. Guests are welcome, and photography is allowed.

The **Ashland Labor Day Powwow** (at the arbor between St. Labre and Ashland,

The Tipi Capital of the World

Held annually since 1904 during the third week of August, **Crow Fair** is considered the largest outdoor powwow in the world. The five-day celebration was introduced to the Crow people—their traditional name is Apsáalooke, which means "children of the large-beaked bird" but was misinterpreted to mean "crow"—by S. C. Reynolds, an Indian Affairs agent assigned to the reservation around the turn of the 20th century. His goal was to encourage the nomadic Crow to become more settled and agrarian on the reservation, which was neither their traditional homeland nor particularly well suited for farming. He modeled the concept for the fair after the county fairs that were popular around the country at the time. The tribe's initial reaction was purportedly less than enthusiastic. In an effort to increase their willingness to participate, Reynolds relaxed the strict ban on "Indian doings" for the days of the Crow Fair, giving the Crow their only legal opportunity to dance, sing, and speak in their traditional ways. Recognizing it as an opportunity to openly pass on Crow culture to younger generations, the tribe eagerly accepted the opportunity, and the Crow Fair has been held annually ever since, except during the world wars and the Great Depression. Today, close to 85 percent of the tribe speak Crow as their first language, a much higher percentage than among other Native American groups in the state.

The celebration itself is lively and colorful, with some 12,000 people camping out in more than 1,000 tipis erected on the banks of the Little Bighorn River. Native Americans from various tribes in the United States and Canada and visitors from around the world come to participate or just witness the competitive dancing and drumming, the all-Indian Championship Rodeo, the pari-mutuel horse racing, and the family reunion-like camaraderie that pervades this time-honored event. The hot, dusty late-summer air is thick with smells—from Indian fry bread to parade ponies—and sounds, including the bullhorn whine of the camp-crier and the jingling of the tobacco lids that decorate the elaborate costumes of some of the dancers. Crow Fair is a feast for the senses and a wonderful way to appreciate the traditions and culture of some of the people who were here long before the Europeans.

0.5 mi/0.8 km off US 212, 406/477-6824 or 406/477-8844, www.cheyennenation.com) happens every year for four days over Labor Day weekend. Drummers and dancers from tribes across the United States and Canada participate in the festivities. Flag-raising occurs each morning at 9am, and dancing concludes each night at midnight. The powwow welcomes visitors and provides an excellent opportunity to learn about and celebrate Northern Cheyenne culture.

FOOD

In much of Montana, especially in eastern Montana and on the Indian reservations, dining options are few and far between. You have to be willing to look hard and expand your culinary horizons now and again. There are some good places to be found.

Immediately off the highway near the Little Bighorn Battlefield National Monument is the **Custer Battlefield Trading Post and Café** (347 Hwy. 12, at exit 510 off I-90, 406/638-2270, 8am-9pm daily summer, 8am-8pm daily winter, hours vary during COVID-19 so call ahead, $9-27), a tourist shop and restaurant that obviously appeals to locals. There is quite a selection of Crow handicrafts in the shop, and the restaurant offers Indian tacos, buffalo burgers, soups and sandwiches, plus plenty of variations on Montana beef.

In Hardin, you'll find a fantastic little pizza place called **3 Brothers Bistro** (316 N. Center Ave., 406/545-5133, www.3brothersbistro.com, 11am-9pm Mon.-Sat. summer, 11am-8pm Tues.-Fri., 4pm-8pm Sat. winter, pizzas $15-23, entrées $10-18), which offers a menu of pizza, sandwiches, and giant burgers. It also serves fresh salads, homemade pasta, and delicious desserts including Greek-style cheesecake with a glaze made from local sugar beets. Right next to the movie theater (meals can be taken to go), this place is small but cool. Oh, and they have a chef's wine list.

In Ashland, you can try **Maggie's Café** (105 Main St., 406/784-6899, 7:30am-8:30pm daily, $6-12), with an excellent variety of burgers and sandwiches, along with friendly service. In Lame Deer, check out **The Spoon & Fork** (42074 US 212, 406/477-6799, www.thespoonnfork.com, 11am-3pm Mon.-Fri., $7-10), an amazing little farm-to-table restaurant that serves delicious soups, salads, sandwiches, and wraps made with locally sourced meat and produce.

ACCOMMODATIONS

Lodging in this part of the state can be sparse, so day trips from Billings are not a bad idea unless you are an angler and need to be on the river from dusk until dawn. The closest town to the Little Bighorn Battlefield National Monument and easiest place to find accommodations in the area is Hardin. Safe bets include the **Super 8 by Wyndham Hardin** (1324 N. Crawford, 406/665-1870 or 800/800-8000, www.wyndhamhotels.com/super-8-hardin-little-bighorn-battlefield, $80-99) and **Homestead Inn & Suites** (201 14th St. W., 406/665-1870, $89-100). Both have clean and comfortable guest rooms. The **Lariat Motel** (709 N. Center Ave., 406/665-2683, $109-149) is convenient and pet-friendly.

A historical and worthwhile place to stay in Hardin is the **Kendrick House Inn** (206 N. Custer Ave., 406/665-3035, from $99), a 1915 Edwardian boardinghouse with five guest rooms and a couple of suites with private baths, all meticulously decorated with period furniture.

Just 3 miles (4.8 km) south of Hardin, the Orvis-endorsed **Eagle Nest Lodge** (879 Sawyer Loop, Hardin, 406/665-3711 or 866/258-3474, www.eaglenestlodge.com, packages from $2,050 for 3 nights) is a beautiful and traditional log lodge ideally suited for fishing and bird hunting. The lodge has seven well-appointed guest rooms, all with private baths, and the meals—breakfast, field lunch, and dinner—are superb. Guides are on-site,

and owners John and Rebecca are exceedingly gracious and always available to point guests in the right direction. The lodge offers packages catering to fishing, hunting, and cast-and-blast. Shorter stays can be arranged.

Among the many (but still never enough) accommodations for anglers in the Fort Smith area is the Orvis-endorsed **Forrester's Bighorn River Resort** (40754 Hwy. 313, 406/333-1449 or 800/655-3799, www.forrestersbighorn.com, 3-night fishing packages from $1,950). When the fishing is good, you'll need to have booked well in advance.

CAMPING

Immediately adjacent to the Little Bighorn Battlefield National Monument and not far from the Crow Agency fairgrounds, **7th Ranch RV Camp** (Reno Creek Rd., Garryowen, 406/638-2438, www.historicwest.com, from $48 RV sites with water and electric only, from $53 full service RV, from $58 super full service RV) offers a great location and plenty of amenities including free Internet, free showers, and horse stalls. Pets are welcome at no charge.

INFORMATION

In some ways, visiting Native American reservations can be a bit like exploring another country. The tribes have worked fiercely to protect their culture and preserve their history. They also live according to their own values rather than any imposed on them. One result is that time can take on a different meaning: Few things happen precisely when it is stated they will. Travelers should adjust accordingly and learn to be more spontaneous. In addition, the technology that many of us rely on is not nearly as critical to some Native Americans; you may not get an answer the first few times you call someone. And there is no voicemail.

The **Crow Tribal Council Headquarters** (406/638-3708, www.crow-nsn.gov) in Crow Agency is a good source of local information. The **Hardin Chamber of Commerce** (10. E. Railway St., 406/665-1672) is another source for visitor information.

The Northern Cheyenne Tribal Office (www.cheyennenation.com) can be reached at 406/477-6284. The Northern Cheyenne Chamber of Commerce (US 212, Lame Deer, 406/477-8844) is another source of information on the reservation.

TRANSPORTATION

The Crow Indian Reservation is easily accessed from I-90, which runs the length of the reservation. The Northern Cheyenne Indian Reservation is accessed by US 212, which runs east-west, or by Highways 39 or 314, both of which run north-south.

Miles City

Miles City (pop. 8,487, elev. 2,369 ft/722 m) has always been a cowboy town. After the 1876 campaign against the Native Americans, including the Battle of the Little Bighorn, the 5th Infantry established camp at the confluence of the Tongue and Yellowstone Rivers under the leadership of Col. Nelson A. Miles. In 1881 the arrival of the Northern Pacific Railway ensured the longevity of the settlement, and in 1884 the Montana Stockgrowers Association was formed, creating an important and long-lasting link to the cattle market. The brick buildings that line Main Street today are much as they were when this town boomed in the late 1800s and early 1900s.

The biggest event in Miles City, and its claim to fame today, is the annual Miles City Bucking Horse Sale, which at least doubles the population of the town each May and reflects its heritage and openness in all its glory. A Montana Mardi Gras with cowboys and chaps, the weekend celebration is probably one of the five best events in the state.

While Miles City has never shed its rough and weathered exterior or its boom-and-bust sensibility, there is much that makes it relevant. On top of its cowboy culture—stop in any diner before 8am to see the town's old guard—there is a youthful exuberance to the city evident in its cutting-edge art museum, the vitality of the Range Riders Museum, and its excellent recreation facilities. Indeed, surrounded by badlands and prairie, Miles City unites the best of Montana past and present.

SIGHTS

Range Riders Museum

The fabulous Range Riders Museum (435 L. P. Anderson Rd., 406/232-6146, 8am-5pm Wed.-Mon. Apr.-Oct., or by appointment, $10 adults, $8 seniors 60 and up, $5 high school and college students, $3 jr. high and elementary) is a gem. Plan to spend some time, and don't be bashful about striking up a conversation with caretaker-curator Bunny Miller or her husband, Gary. Bunny's parents, Bob and Betty Ann Barthelmess, were the heart and soul of the Range Riders from 1976 until they were well in their 80s. Sadly, Bob passed away, but Bunny and Gary have kept his passion and spirit very much alive at the Range Riders.

The museum was founded in 1939 by a group of locals dedicated to preserving their heritage. Today it has 13 buildings and thousands of artifacts that include old saddles and clothing, machinery, dinosaur bones, phenomenal photographs by L. A. Huffman and Christian Barthelmess (Bunny's great-grandfather, an army photographer born in Germany), and 400 antique firearms in the Bert Clark Gun Collection. Bob commandeered a team of volunteers to build four spectacular dioramas of the 1877 Battle of Lame Deer, Fort Keogh, the Milwaukee Railroad Roundhouse, and the famed L. O. Ranch, once southeast Montana's largest ranch. An almost life-size replica of Main Street in Miles City circa 1877 is another can't-miss exhibit. This museum has been a labor of love for so many, and it captures the spirit of this frontier town.

Miles City

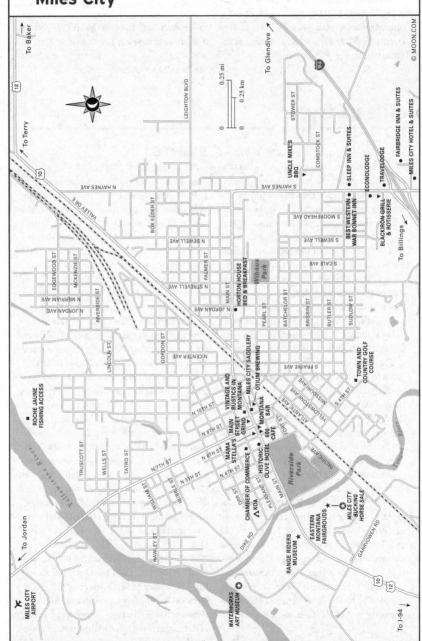

To Baker

To Terry

To Jordan

To Glendive

To Billings

To I-94

© MOON.COM

LEIGHTON BLVD

0.25 mi
0.25 km

MILES CITY
AIRPORT

Yellowstone River

ROCHE JAUNE
FISHING ACCESS

VALLEY DR E

N HAYNES AVE

S HAYNES AVE

STOWER ST

COMSTOCK ST

UNCLE MIKES
BBQ

SLEEP INN & SUITES

ECONOLODGE

TRAVELODGE

FAIRBRIDGE INN & SUITES

MILES CITY HOTEL & SUITES

BOX ELDER ST

N SEWELL AVE

S MOOREHEAD AVE

S SEWELL AVE

BLACKIRON GRILL
& ROTISSERIE

BEST WESTERN
WAR BONNET INN

EDGEWOOD ST

MCKENZIE ST

RIVERSIDE ST

N MERRIAM AVE

N JORDAN AVE

N PALMER ST

N STREVELL AVE

HORTON HOUSE
BED & BREAKFAST

Wibaux
Park

S CALE AVE

MAIN ST

N JORDAN AVE

PEARL ST

BATCHELOR ST

BRISBIN ST

BUTLER ST

SUDLOW ST

LINCOLN ST

GORDON ST

N CENTER ST

S PRAIRIE AVE

TOWN AND
COUNTRY GOLF
COURSE

TRUSCOTT ST

WELLS ST

TATRO ST

N 10TH ST

N 9TH ST

N 7TH ST

N 6TH ST

N 5TH ST

N 4TH ST

VINTAGE AND
RUSTICS IN
MONTANA

MILES CITY SADDLERY

OTTUM BREWING

MAIN
STREET
GRIND

MONTANA
BAR

600
CAFE

MAMA
STELLA'S

HISTORIC
OLIVE HOTEL

ATLANTIC AVE

YELLOWSTONE AVE

MISSOURI AVE

S 4TH ST

WILLIAM ST

HUBBLE ST

ORR ST

PLEASANT ST

MAIN ST

CHAMBER OF COMMERCE

KOA

DIKE RD

Riverside
Park

PACIFIC AVE

Tongue River

HAWLEY ST

RANGE RIDERS
MUSEUM

MILES CITY
BUCKING
HORSE SALE

EASTERN
MONTANA
FAIRGROUNDS

GARRYOWEN RD

WATERWORKS
ART MUSEUM

★ WaterWorks Art Museum

Quite a contrast to the Range Riders Museum but just as compelling is the **WaterWorks Art Museum** (85 Waterplant Rd., 406/234-0635, www.wtrworks.org, 9am-5pm Tues.-Sun. May.-Sept., 1pm-5pm Tues.-Sun. Oct.-Apr., free). Creatively housed in the 10,000-square-foot concrete basins of the 1910 waterworks that provided the city's drinking water for more than 60 years, the award-winning museum specializes in contemporary Montana artists but has regional and national changing shows. Part museum, part gallery, WaterWorks also owns the state's largest public collection of works by photographer L. A. Huffman in addition to photos by Lady Evelyn Cameron, E. S. Curtis, and Christian Barthelmess. Interesting local art, pottery, photos, and books are available in the gift shop. The museum hosts a series of design shows every year or two, focusing on everything from artisanal pieces like handmade fiddles and furniture to industrial design in iconic cars and motorcycles.

Just outside the museum, which is on the Yellowstone River, is a gorgeous park, the ideal spot for a shaded picnic. Century-old cottonwoods tower over a beautifully manicured lawn with picnic benches and a modest playground. If nothing else, this is a perfect spot to stretch your legs.

SPORTS AND RECREATION

For outdoor recreation, one need not travel too far from town. There are **fishing accesses** (and in some cases boat launches) on the Yellowstone River at **Roche Jaune** (Truscott St. and N. 6th St.), **Kinsey Bridge** (10 mi/16 km east of Miles City, on a gravel road intersecting Valley Dr. E.), and **Pirogue Island State Park** (3 mi/4.8 km northeast of Miles City, www.stateparks.mt.gov), where Lewis and Clark camped on their cross-country journey. The 269-acre park is a haven for waterfowl, bald eagles, and white-tailed and mule deer. **Spotted Eagle Recreation Area** (just south of the Eastern Montana Fairgrounds) is a quiet place for walks, picnics, and fishing in the small artificial lake. There are picnic benches as well as accessible fishing. Other fishing access sites can be found through **Montana Fish, Wildlife & Parks** (406/234-0900, www.fwp.mt.gov).

Avid golfers can hit the links in Miles City at the nine-hole **Town & Country Club** (S. 4th St. and Eagle St., 406/234-1600, $22 for 9 holes, $29-34 for 18 holes), which runs along the Tongue River. It has a driving range and holds open tournaments during the season.

ENTERTAINMENT AND EVENTS
Festivals and Events

Montana Shakespeare in the Parks (406/994-3944, www.shakespeareintheparks.org) performs at least one engagement every summer in Miles City at the Pumping Plant Park of the **WaterWorks Art Museum** (406/234-0635, www.waterworksgallery.org). And Miles City's own **Barn Players** (406/951-0560, www.facebook.com/BarnPlayersInc) is the oldest amateur theater group in the state, producing a couple of small performances each year, some of them under the stars at the Pumping Plant Park.

The annual **Eastern Montana Fair** (406/421-5419 or 406/234-2890, www.milescitychamber.com) in late August brings Custer County together with five others for four days of nonstop entertainment, rodeo, concerts, fireworks, exhibits, and a carnival.

The third weekend in September, as the fields turn golden and there is a crispness to the air, the small **Miles City Bluegrass Festival** (406/234-2480 or 406/853-1678, www.milescitybluegrassfestival.com, $25/day adults or $40 weekend pass, free for children under 12) brings people together. The alcohol-free event is held at the Eastern Montana Fairgrounds and features several bands from across the country. The concerts are held indoors, and limited outdoor camping ($15/night) is available. On Tuesday nights throughout summer, the town closes down a few city blocks to car traffic so folks can enjoy live music at the **Cowtown Moosic Festival** (406/234-2480, www.milescitychamber.com).

Each February, the streets of Miles City are filled with yearling bulls for the **Cowtown Beef Breeders Show** (406/234-2480, www. milescitychamber.com). It's a unique sight and brings buyers from far and wide.

★ MILES CITY BUCKING HORSE SALE

Held annually the third full weekend in May, the **Miles City Bucking Horse Sale** (406/874-2825 or 406/234-2890, www. buckinghorsesale.com, $20 general admission, $25 reserved seating, $5 general admission for children 6-12, free for children under 6) is in many ways the granddaddy of all rodeos. Simply stated, it is where the top rodeo contractors come to get their stock, but it has defined Miles City and given it serious swagger since 1951. The image of a headstrong cowboy hitchhiking a lonely highway with nothing in hand but his trusty saddle and the shirt on his back is realized here year after year—they come to ride the best broncs in the business.

In addition to the central bronc sale, the event is rounded out by concerts, bull riding, pari-mutuel horse racing, street dances each night, and a good old-fashioned parade on Saturday morning. The whole affair can be slightly bawdy, and it's true that the town's many bars take out all their furniture to make room for thirsty cowboys. If you arrive Monday morning after the Bucking Horse Sale, you'll see what a hungover town looks like.

SHOPPING

In business since 1909, **Miles City Saddlery** (808 Main St., 406/232-2512, www. milescitysaddlery.com, 9am-5:30pm Mon.-Sat.) is famous for having originated the Coggshall Saddle. The shop is a step back in time with exceptional custom saddles, clothing, boots and belts, hats, tack, and gifts. Across the street, **Vintage and Rustics in Montana** (813 Main St., 406/234-7878,

7:30am-4:30pm Mon.-Thurs., 7:30am-5pm Fri.-Sat.) is a sprawling and eclectic antiques mall with more than 100 vendors, a soda fountain, bakery, and espresso.

FOOD

True to its Cowtown moniker, Miles City is a meat-and-potatoes mecca. The **Black Iron Grill & Rotisserie** (2901 Boutelle St., 406/234-4766, www.milescityrestaurant. com, 11am-10pm daily, $12-40) does not disappoint. From the mouthwatering burgers and chicken-fried steak to applewood-smoked brisket, Black Iron uses local beef and serves it alongside Montana microbrews.

For diners looking for something besides steak, **Mama Stella's Pizza** (607 Main St., 406/234-2922, 10am-10pm daily, $9-24) serves up pizza (including gluten free), wings, sandwiches, and, of course, burgers. And for those who haven't had enough of burgers, there's a bacon cheeseburger pizza. Because the restaurant is attached to the Trails Inn Bar (open till 2am daily), diners can also have a drink with dinner.

A great place for breakfast, lunch, or a cup of joe is **Main Street Grind** (713 Main St., 406/234-9200, 6:30am-3pm Mon.-Fri., $7-12). From the homemade pastries, pies, and granola to the thick, juicy burgers, Main Street Grind is a great find in eastern Montana. They offer free Wi-Fi. New in town in 2021, and already a local favorite, is **Uncle Mike's BBQ & Grill** (3020 Stower St., 406/970-9529, www.facebook.com/UncleMikesBarbeque, 11am-8pm Tues.-Sat. or until they sell out, $10-18). In addition to their barbecue—everything from brisket and pulled pork to ribs and smoked chicken—they host Taco Tuesday and Fish Friday. Every Thursday they offer baby-back ribs prepared a different way. Think sticky Asian ribs or sour cherry with habanero.

The gold standard in Miles City for a community café is **Café 600** (600 Main St., 406/234-3860, 5am-2pm Fri.-Tues., $9-28), which opened in 1946 and still serves up excellent cinnamon rolls, omelets, sandwiches, steak, and more.

For excellent barbecue **Boog's BBQ Food Truck** (406/853-6856, open sporadically, $5-15) is the spot. They keep fans posted on their opening days, times and location through Facebook (www.facebook.com/Boogs-BBQ-101271277905931) Among the favorite offerings are pulled pork, pulled beef, brisket, loaded nachos, and more. Another noteworthy stop is the taproom at **Otium Brewing** (21 S. 9th, 406/234-2337, 4pm-8pm Wed.-Sat.). Started by a young Miles City couple, Otium's four flagship brews include Honey Cream Ale, IPA, Irish Red Ale, and American Stout.

A trip to Miles City would not be complete without a drink at the **Montana Bar** (612 Main St., 406/234-5809, 10am-2am daily). The bar has been serving thirsty patrons since 1902 and has managed to keep its incredible original back bar in beautiful shape all these years. The expansive leather booths, beveled leaded glass, and marble tile floors are all original. The bar stools and the jukebox are just about the only additions in the last century. It is a remarkable place to sip a cold drink and reflect on just how much things haven't changed in little pockets like this across the West. Inside the bar, Tubb's Pub serves standard bar fare. Breakfast is served Saturday and Sunday from 2am to 4am only.

ACCOMMODATIONS

The **Historic Olive Hotel** (501 Main St., 406/234-2450, $69-99) is both a classic and a bargain. The rooms are neither fancy nor grand, but they are clean and accommodating, and the location is unbeatable. There's also a ghost to be reckoned with—but don't worry, she's friendly.

Far more elegant than the Olive, but an equally historic gem in the heart of Miles City, ★ **Horton House Bed & Breakfast** (1918 Main St., 406/234-4422, www.hortonhousebandb.com, $119-139) is a stunning property with rooms dedicated to local historical figures including artist Charlie

Russell, Sitting Bull, and photographer Evelyn Cameron.

Among the chain hotel offerings, the pet-friendly **Fairbridge Inn & Suites** (3111 Steel St., 406/232-3661, www.fairbridgeinns.com, $69-185) has 61 rooms, free Wi-Fi, and a complimentary hot breakfast. More upscale and locally owned, the **Miles City Hotel & Suites** (1720 S. Haynes Ave., 406/234-1000, www.milescityhotelandsuites.com, $109-189) has a presidential suite with a copper ceiling and strict no-pets policy.

You'll find larger chain hotels on the way into Miles City—**Best Western War Bonnet Inn** (1015 S. Haynes Ave., 406/234-4560, $89-115), **EconoLodge** (1209 S. Haynes Ave., 406/234-8880, from $68), **Travelodge by Wyndham** (1314 S. Haynes Ave., 406/232-7040, from $59-186), and **Sleep Inn & Suites** (1006 S. Haynes Ave., 406/232-3000, $95-149).

CAMPING

The **Miles City KOA** (1 Palmer St., 406/232-3991 or 800/562-3909, www.koa.com, from $32 tents, $49-71 RVs, from $68 cabins without bathroom, Apr. 15-Oct. 15) is tucked in the cottonwood trees on the banks of the Tongue River just six blocks from downtown. Free wireless Internet is provided, along with an outdoor swimming pool and bicycle rentals.

Big Sky Camp and RV Park (1294 US 12, 406/234-1511, www.bigskycampandrvpark.com, May-Sept., from $45 full hookup) offers standard amenities, including Wi-Fi, in a beautiful grassy setting alongside impressive rock formations.

INFORMATION AND SERVICES

The **Miles City Area Chamber of Commerce** (511 Pleasant St., 406/234-2890, www.milescitychamber.com, 9am-5pm Mon.-Thurs., 9am-4pm Fri., is a block from Main Street and has maps, brochures for local businesses, restaurant and hotel listings, museum information, and very friendly staff.

1

2

3

RANGE RIDERS MUSEUM

The **main post office** is at 106 North 7th Street (406/232-1224, 8am-5:30pm Mon.-Fri., 9am-noon Sat.).

The historic 1902 **Miles City Library** (1 S. 10th St., 406/234-1496, www.milescitypubliclibrary.org, 9am-5pm Mon.-Fri.) is at Main and 10th Streets; computers with Internet access are available.

The **Express Laundry Center** (1115 S. Haynes Ave., 406/234-9999, www.expresslaundrymc.com, 6am-11pm daily for self-serve, laundry service available 8am-5pm Mon.-Fri., 8am-4pm Sat., 10am-4pm Sun.) offers coin-operated machines and same-day or next-day drop-off service. Plus there's a dog wash and free Wi-Fi.

Holy Rosary Health Care (2600 Wilson St., 406/233-2600, www.holyrosaryhealthcare.org) has a 24-hour emergency room as well as a walk-in clinic (406/233-2500, 7:30am-5:30pm Mon.-Fri., 8am-5pm Sat.-Sun.).

TRANSPORTATION

After a few years of scrambling to keep commercial flights to Denver, and then Billings, Miles City lost all commercial service in May 2013, which means the nearest commercial airport is 140 miles (225 km) away in Billings.

I-94 runs through Miles City, making it an easy destination by car. It is 140 miles (225 km) east of Billings and 78 miles (126 km) southwest of Glendive.

Bus service to Miles City is provided by **Greyhound** (1120 S. Haynes Ave., 800/451-5333, www.greyhound.com) and **Jefferson Lines** (1120 S. Haynes Ave., 858/800-8898, www.jeffersonlines.com), which leave from the McDonald's Restaurant.

Miles City to Medicine Lake

The stretch of road from Miles City to Medicine Lake is sparsely populated and subtly beautiful. This is cattle country and the beginning of the badlands. The Yellowstone River cuts through the rugged country as it flows northeast to the North Dakota border. I-94 parallels the river, echoing the Yellowstone's onetime importance as a means of transportation and shipping. This area was once home to the country's last great bison herd, but the slaughter of these animals in the early 1880s nearly wiped out the species, ending a long and important chapter in North American history.

Though small towns dot the landscape, there is more to the region than human settlements. With intact badlands, grasslands, and wetlands, this part of the state is a birder's paradise. The region is home to national wildlife refuges, wildlife management areas, and tracts of public land, all of which provide marvelous habitat for an enormous number of avian species. Part wetland, part prairie, Medicine Lake National Wildlife Refuge is a spectacular place to see migrating birds at various times of year. Although it is not a common destination, driving through this part of the state is a magnificent way to enjoy the ride on the way from one place to the next.

HISTORY

The small, colorful towns in this part of the state have origins that date back to the Indian Wars and before. **Terry,** named for Gen. Alfred E. Terry, emerged from a dugout that offered food and lodging to soldiers fighting the Sioux. The town later became known for one of its esteemed residents, pioneering photographer Evelyn Cameron, a wealthy Englishwoman who ranched in the area with her husband and captured on film the often gritty life of local homesteaders. A

1: the WaterWorks Art Museum **2:** a photograph at the Evelyn Cameron Gallery in Terry **3:** the Range Riders Museum

museum in town honors her art and legacy. And the town's Kempton Hotel is the oldest continually operating hotel in the state.

The history of **Glendive** dates back even further. Lewis and Clark camped near the present-day town site in 1806 on their way back from Oregon, and they reportedly shot a huge white grizzly bear four times without killing it. An Irish nobleman hunting bison, bears, and ungulates in the region gave the name Glendive to a small tributary of the Yellowstone River. The town itself sprouted up with the arrival of the Northern Pacific Railway in 1880.

Just this side of the North Dakota border, **Wibaux** is named for French cattle king Pierre Wibaux, who left the family textile empire in Roubaix, France, for the wilds of Montana in 1883. Over time, he amassed a herd of 65,000 cattle. In 1884, with money from his father, Wibaux commissioned the construction of St. Peter's Catholic Church by Norman French immigrants, using stunning local fieldstone and lava rock. It is an exquisite piece of noble architecture that still stands today. The tiny town is better known today for its Beaver Creek Brewery.

Farther north, towns such as **Sidney** and **Fairview** survive thanks to a robust sugar beet industry, and across the region, local people's lives are tied to the land through agriculture, ranching, and, more significantly, energy production. The influx of workers eager to make a fortune in North Dakota's Bakken Oil Field brought money and more service jobs to the area, but it was also responsible for sky-high rents, pressure on local infrastructure, and unfortunately, crime. While the population in Sidney grew to its highest levels in 2015, plummeting oil prices and a subsequent downturn have caused the population to slowly decrease at a rate of -0.7 percent annually. It remains to be seen how these towns will fare in the boom-and-bust cycle of the Bakken.

SIGHTS

Prairie County Museum and Evelyn Cameron Gallery

In Terry are the adjacent **Prairie County Museum** (101 Logan Ave., 406/635-4040, 9am-3pm Mon. and Wed.-Fri., 1pm-4pm Sat.-Sun. Memorial Day-Labor Day, free) and **Evelyn Cameron Gallery** (105 Logan Ave., 406/635-4040, www.evelyncameron. org, same hours as the museum, free, donations accepted). The latter pays homage to a fascinating woman who captured the spirit of the often hardscrabble life in eastern Montana with captivating photos and meticulous journals. Thousands of Cameron's negatives were discovered in the late 1970s by Time-Life Books editor Donna Lucey, who published them in her landmark work *Photographing Montana 1894-1928: The Life and Work of Evelyn Cameron*. The gallery is home to many of Cameron's images, both originals and reprints. Her work is a striking testament to the passage of time on the Western frontier and at the same time a reminder of how much remains the same in eastern Montana.

★ Makoshika State Park

Montana's largest state park at more than 11,000 acres, **Makoshika State Park** (1301 Snyder Ave., Glendive, 406/377-6256, www. makoshika.org, 10am-5pm daily Memorial Day-Labor Day, 10am-5pm Wed.-Sun. Labor Day-Memorial Day, $8/vehicle or $4/pedestrian for nonresidents, day use free for Montana residents, $4-34 for rustic and backcountry campsites) is literally at the perimeter of Glendive. The park is an intriguing if not altogether beautiful place, made up of colorful exposed rock layers that look like petrified anthills.

Makoshika (muh-KO-shi-kuh) was established in 1953 and named for the Lakota word for badlands, which literally translates as "pitiful earth." An impressive **interpretive center** gives an excellent overview of the park's geological significance and helps visitors easily navigate the rock layers according to color, distinguishing the Age of Reptiles (dinosaurs!) from the Age of Mammals. Millions of years old, these badlands expose older rock layers than those in North Dakota and have produced some important dinosaur fossils, including a triceratops skull. Hikers have been known to find fossilized shark teeth and alligator teeth, but all rocks and fossils must stay in the park.

The park is well-suited for exploration in a number of different ways. There are 4 miles (6.4 km) of paved roads and 12 miles (19.3 km) of unpaved roads (which can be impassable at certain times of year). Three developed trails offer good hiking opportunities: the **Diane Gabriel Trail,** the **Cap Rock Nature Trail,** and the **Kinney Coulee Hiking Trail.** Trail guide pamphlets and free advice are available at the interpretive center. The park also has picnic benches, shelters, and an 18-basket **disc golf course.** Although there are pines and junipers throughout the park, there is little shade in this compelling play of light and color, so bring water and a hat. The park ties the record for hottest temperature in Montana at 117°F (47.2°C).

Baisch's Dinosaur Digs

An outstanding place to schedule a dig for ages six and over is **Baisch's Dinosaur Digs** (323 Rd. 300, 406/365-4133, http://dailydinosaurdigs.com, $120 pp, $80 half day, free for children under 12 with paying adult). The Baisch family—headed by matriarch Marge, whose father was on the last cattle drive from Wyoming to Montana—offers daily paleontological digs on their land in view of Makoshika State Park. They've uncovered remarkable specimens of *Tyrannosaurus rex,* edmontosaurus, and triceratops. A guide will take you out and show you the best places to dig (and the places to watch for rattlers!). When you've had your fill, head back to the ranch headquarters, a makeshift museum where Marge often goes through each of your finds and tells you exactly what she thinks it is. For visitors who want to take home their own fossil finds—including bone fragments, teeth, and petrified wood—this is the only legal way to do it. And the Baisch family makes the whole experience an absolute pleasure.

Frontier Gateway Museum

Tucked downtown in Glendive is the **Frontier Gateway Museum** (201 State St., 406/377-8168, www.frontiergatewaymuseum.org, 9am-5pm Mon.-Sat., 1pm-5pm Sun. Memorial

Makoshika State Park's rocks can look like elephant skin.

Day-Labor Day, free). The classic small-town museum is home to a full-size stegosaurus replica, plus fossils from triceratops, hadrosaurs, and thescelosaurus.

Glendive Dinosaur & Fossil Museum

Visitors in search of dinosaur bones and fossil exhibits presented from a biblical perspective will find creationist exhibits at the **Glendive Dinosaur & Fossil Museum** (139 State St., 406/377-3228, www.creationtruth.org, 10am-5pm Tues.-Sat. mid-May-early Sept., 10am-5pm Fri.-Sat. Apr.-mid-May and Labor Day-late Oct., $8 adults, $7 seniors 60 and over and students 13 and over, $6 children 3-12). In addition to 20,000 square feet of excellent dinosaur casts, nice fossil displays, and painstaking dioramas with much emphasis on the great flood as told in the Bible, the museum offers daylong and half-day dinosaur digs. It's worth mentioning that this museum was sold to the Foundation Advancing Creation Truth, at which point the exhibits were re-contextualized to promote their ideas about biblical creation. On their website, the museum states that they do not believe in evolution and that all people are descendants of Adam and Eve. Among their 12 stated beliefs is that "the creation of all things occurred in six natural days and was originally 'very good.'" Curiously, for a dinosaur museum, they also state their belief that "marriage is ordained by God and is only between one man and one woman." If it's science you're after, Montana's Dinosaur Trail has plenty of excellent options.

★ Medicine Lake National Wildlife Refuge

The Medicine Lake National Wildlife Refuge is a wetland oasis in a sea of prairie. It is a startlingly beautiful place on a breezy afternoon when the grasses sway in watery waves or on a stormy night when lightning flashes across the sky, illuminating clouds that are 15 shades of blue, pink, and purple—or any time, really; it's just that beautiful. And

like so much of eastern Montana, it is not what you might expect to see in a state known for its mountains.

The **Medicine Lake National Wildlife Refuge** (223 North Shore Rd., 406/789-2305, www.fws.gov) comprises two wildlife refuges and a wetland management district. Established in 1935, the area provides a much-used breeding and stopover habitat for an enormous range of migratory birds, including ducks, geese, swans, cranes, white pelicans, and grebes. As such, the refuge is as much an oasis for landlocked ocean lovers and wildlife photographers as it is for migrating birds. The sounds and smells and even some of the sights can immediately conjure feelings of a favorite coastal haunt.

Opportunities for bird-watching abound, and what you see will depend on the time of year you visit. There are roads to cruise along and trails to explore. Hunting and fishing are permitted on the refuge as well; get up-to-date information about seasons and regulations, licensing, and necessary permits from the **U.S. Fish and Wildlife Service** (223 North Shore Rd., 406/789-2305, www.fws.gov). Camping is not permitted in the refuge, but sites are available in nearby Medicine Lake or Plentywood.

The refuge is on Highway 16, just south of the tiny town of Medicine Lake, which has very limited accommodations (www.medicinelakemt.com), most of which are modest rentals. The nearest towns with significant hotel and motel accommodations and services—Plentywood and Culbertson—are more than 20 miles (32 km) away to the north and south, respectively, so bring what you need for the time you plan to spend exploring the refuge.

SPORTS AND RECREATION
Fishing

Since I-94 parallels the Yellowstone River from Billings to Glendive, **fishing opportunities** are available at just about any exit. The Yellowstone is filled with trout and, oddly enough, paddlefish: These prehistoric

Before Montana had cowboys, Indians, ranchers, and homesteaders, even before the Missouri and Yellowstone Rivers were formed, this was dinosaur territory. The world's first *Tyrannosaurus rex* was discovered in Montana, as were the world's first baby dinosaur bones. Sites across the state are dedicated to celebrating this unique and rich history, and the **Montana Dinosaur Trail** (www.mtdinotrail.org), created in 2005, consists of 14 different facilities in 12 communities. The stops along the trail include museums, parks, educational centers, and field stations, all of which are committed to finding and preserving dinosaur specimens. These sites have numerous well-preserved fossils, complete dinosaur skeletons, perfectly honed replicas, and even some active dig sites that are open to the public.

little dinosaur diggers in Eastern Montana

Malta's **Great Plains Dinosaur Museum and Field Station** (405 N. 1st St. E., Malta, 406/654-5300, www.greatplainsdinosaur.org, 10am-5pm Tues.-Sat. May, 10am-5pm Mon.-Sat. and 12:30pm-5pm Sun. June-Aug., $5 adults 13 and over, $3 children 6-12, free for children under 6) displays rare fossils, including a "mummy" dinosaur considered the world's best-preserved dinosaur. Also in Malta, the **Phillips County Museum** (431 US 2 E., Malta, 406/654-1037, www.phillipscountymuseum.org, 10am-5pm Mon.-Sat. Apr.-Dec., $5 adults, $3 children, free for children under 3) boasts a 700-pound apatosaurus femur, a complete *Tyrannosaurus rex* skull, and "Elvis," a 33-foot-long brachylophosaurus.

In Jordan, the site of the first *T. rex* discovery in 1902, the **Garfield County Museum** (952 Jordan Ave., Montana Hwy. 200, Jordan, 406/557-2308, 1pm-5pm daily June-Labor Day) showcases Cretaceous fossils from the Hell Creek Formation, including a full-size triceratops.

The **Fort Peck Interpretive Center and Museum** (adjacent to the powerhouses on Lower Yellowstone Rd., Fort Peck, 406/526-3493, 9am-5pm daily May-Sept., open by appointment 9am-4pm Mon.-Fri. Nov.-Apr., free) owns one of the most complete *T. rex* skeletons ever found. You are greeted with a life-size model of the ferocious carnivore when you enter the museum.

Glendive is home to the **Frontier Gateway Museum** (201 State St., Glendive, 406/377-8168, www.frontiergatewaymuseum.org, 9am-5pm Mon.-Sat., 1pm-5pm Sun. Memorial Day-Labor Day, free) and **Makoshika State Park** (1301 Snyder Ave., Glendive, 406/377-6256, www.makoshika.org, 10am-5pm daily Memorial Day-Labor Day, 10am-5pm Wed.-Sun. Labor Day-Memorial Day, nonresidents $8/vehicle or $4/pedestrian, day use free for Montana residents), where at least 10 different dinosaur species have been found; the museum displays an impressive collection of dinosaur fossils from around the world.

The farthest eastern stop on the Dinosaur Trail is in Ekalaka, the **Carter County Museum** (306 N. Main St., Ekalaka, 406/775-6886, www.cartercountymuseum.org, 9am-5pm Mon.-Fri. and 1pm-5pm Sat.-Sun. Apr.-Nov., 9am-5pm Tues.-Fri. and 1pm-5pm Sat.-Sun. Dec.-Mar., free). This is Montana's first county museum and displays complete dinosaur skeletons found in the nearby Hell Creek Formation.

monstrosities in the sturgeon family can live up to 60 years and weigh more than 100 pounds (45 kg). They are caught only by snagging and then fighting them, sometimes for hours. The paddlefishing season on the Yellowstone runs from early to mid-May to mid- to late June, assuming the target goal of fish (usually varying between 500 and 1,000) is not met in that time. When the harvest target is met, anglers will be allowed to catch and

release only. As if to reinforce what remarkable adversaries these fish are, there is an archery season for paddlefish below Fort Peck Dam in early July. Paddlefish roe is considered a delicacy among caviar connoisseurs, but it can only be purchased outside Montana.

The Missouri River also flows through the region and offers plenty of trout, salmon, pike, and the occasional paddlefish.

Golf

Despite the abundance of gentle terrain, there are only a few golf courses in the area, most of them nine-holers. The **Cottonwood Country Club** (508 Country Club Dr., 406/377-8797, www.cottonwoodcc.com) in Glendive is a lovely course with long holes, wide fairways, and mature cottonwood trees.

FOOD

This is bar-food country and an excellent place for hamburger and chicken-fried steak lovers. Some of the fun is finding the best piece of pie, the juiciest burger, or the strongest coffee. Don't expect gourmet fare, but you can expect big portions and good, simple food.

In Glendive, the **Yellowstone River Inn** (1903 N. Merrill Ave., 406/377-4433, www.yellowstoneriverinn.net, 6am-close daily, $11-33) is inside a hotel and has a pretty complete menu for breakfast, lunch, and dinner, including wraps, burgers, salads, and steak. For a healthy and light menu with great salads, toasted and grilled sandwiches, breakfast burritos, and more, try **Bloom Coffeehouse & Eatery** (209 Gibson St., Glendive, 406/365-2586, 7am-2pm Mon.-Wed. and Sat., 7am-2pm and 5pm-8pm Thurs.-Fri., $6.50-11).

Since 1965, The **Gust Hauf** (300 W. Bell St., Glendive, 406/365-4451, 11am-9pm Sun.-Thurs., 11am-10pm Fri.-Sat., $7-12.50) has been serving up pizza and bar-type appetizers in a sports bar setting. And it's open on Monday, which a lot of restaurants in this part of the state don't seem to be.

For delicious, authentic Mexican food, try **Los Amigos** (205 N. Merrill Ave., 406/377-5074, 11am-8:30pm Tues.-Thurs., 11am-9pm Fri.-Sat., $9-28). The enormous menu (which includes a kids' menu and American dishes like rib eye, T-bone steaks, and bacon cheeseburgers) has seafood, vegetarian options, combo plates, and a whole page of house specialties, including Carne Mexicana and Chile Colorado. You will not leave hungry.

A great family restaurant just across the street from the Holiday Inn Express is **CC's Family Café** (1902 N. Merrill Ave., Glendive, 406/377-8926, 6am-10pm daily summer, 6am-9pm daily winter, $7-26). The restaurant is decorated with photographs of Montana's beauty pageant winners, which is odd but kind of fun. It's the full menu, though, and the friendly service that make CC's a great stop. It features home cooking, daily specials, breakfast all day, and, yep, really good pie.

ACCOMMODATIONS AND CAMPING

Wherever you find communities in Montana, most often you'll find at least a couple of roadside motels; options in eastern Montana, however, can be somewhat limited. In Terry, the 1902 **Kempton Hotel** (204 Spring St., 406/635-5543, $65-125) has hosted such notable figures as Teddy Roosevelt and Calamity Jane. Stories of ghosts abound. The hotel is showing its age, and long-range plans are in place to restore it to its original glory; for now, this is a choice you make for the experience rather than the comfort. Pets are welcome for a $20 fee.

Glendive is a safe bet for a comfortable, clean room. There are **chain motels** (including La Quinta Inn & Suites, Comfort Inn, Days Inn, Holiday Inn Express Hotel & Suites, and Super 8) thanks to traffic to and from the Bakken Oil Field, but the cream of the crop is the 89-room, pet-friendly **Astoria Hotel & Suites** (201 California St., 406/377-6000, www.glendive.stayastoria.com, $93-109), which offers a business center, indoor swimming pool and fitness center, free Wi-Fi, free breakfast, and on-site dining. All of

---

1: the wetlands near Medicine Lake **2:** a sandstone spire

the nicely appointed and oversize rooms have microwaves, refrigerators, and coffeemakers. This is indeed evidence of the New West.

Perhaps because of the oil and gas traffic, campgrounds in Glendive have been changing hands and going out of business. The most reliable and interesting place to camp is **Makoshika State Park** (1301 Snyder Ave., Glendive, 406/377-6256, www.makoshika.org and www.reserveamerica.com, $12-72 for rustic campsites, campsites, tipi, and large yurt, day use free for Montana residents). Peak season at Montana's state parks is from the third Thursday in May to the third Monday in September, and this campground is open May-October.

INFORMATION AND SERVICES

The **Glendive Chamber of Commerce** (808 N. Merrill Ave., 406/377-5601, www. glendivechamber.com, 9am-5pm Mon.-Fri.) is an excellent resource for everything from guided excursions to daily fishing reports. One of the things that makes this chamber unique is that it offers to clean the paddlefish of any angler willing to donate the fish roe, which the chamber then processes into world-class caviar.

The 25-bed **Glendive Medical Center** (202 Prospect Dr., 406/345-3306 or 800/226-7623) offers 24-hour emergency care and a walk-in clinic in the lower level of the Gabert Clinic (107 Dilworth St., 406/345-3311, 10am-6pm Mon.-Fri., 10am-2pm Sat.).

TRANSPORTATION

Glendive is off I-94 and at the southernmost point of Highway 16, west of the North Dakota border 35 miles (56 km) from Beach.

Bus service to Glendive is available through **Greyhound** (800/231-2222, www.greyhound.com) and **Jefferson Lines** (800/451-5333, www.jeffersonlines.com), which leave from **Robin's Service Station** (406/365-2600) at 1302 West Towne Street.

Fort Peck and the Hi-Line

In the extreme northeastern corner of the state, the Fort Peck Indian Reservation and the Hi-Line are tight-knit places that wear their histories like a badge of honor.

As the state's second-largest, the Fort Peck Indian Reservation encompasses more than 2 million acres of land and is home to some 6,800 Assiniboine and Sioux tribe members, and 3,200 non-Indians. The land itself is made up of gently rolling hills and fertile agricultural land. Although the reservation was established in the late 1800s, the government negotiated a treaty with the tribes that each tribe member on the reservation would be given 320 acres of land, not unlike the Homestead Act. The "surplus lands" were opened up to outside settlers, and by the 1920s the Indians retained ownership of only about half the original reservation. The integration of white settlers and Native Americans is more pronounced on Fort Peck than any other reservation in the state, and stories like those about the Indian hospital versus the white hospital suggest the inherent injustice and hardship of that integration for the Indians. The reservation is adjacent to the site of the Fort Peck Dam, the largest work-relief project to be undertaken during the Great Depression.

Just north of the reservation, the Hi-Line—a string of towns collectively named for their location along the northernmost railroad line in the region—sprouted up with the arrival of the Great Northern Railway in 1887. In fact, many of these small towns—Westby, Scobey, and Medicine Lake among them—up and moved to situate themselves alongside the tracks and make themselves places where the train could bring farmers in and move crops out. This is still a place where you make your own fate, where nothing comes easy.

US 2 runs parallel to the railroad and is the access point for nearly all the communities of any size in this corner of Montana.

PLENTYWOOD

Like all the towns dotting the Hi-Line, Plentywood (pop. 1,825, elev. 2,024 ft/617 m) is primarily a farming community, known in recent years for pulse crops, including lentils, peas, and beans. Because of its size and proximity to nothing much larger, the town has become something of a trade center, a destination for Canadian bargain shoppers, and a stopping point for many of the oilfield workers. Plentywood also attracts a good number of bird hunters every autumn.

The town is proud of some unique chapters in its history—the famous Outlaw Trail ran right through here, bringing with it more than its fair share of unsavory characters—and in the 1920s and 1930s the Communist Party was one of the most active in local politics. An oil boom in the 1970s and 1980s caused a population spike, and for a time, poker chips from the many bars in the area were accepted as legal tender almost anywhere in the county.

Sights

The **Sheridan County Museum** (4642 Hwy. 16 S., 406/765-2145, 9am-4pm Thurs.-Mon. Memorial Day-Labor Day, free) is a small but pleasant county museum, conveniently located adjacent to a 24-hour rest area. The museum houses Montana's longest indoor mural at 74 feet, and nearby a historical monument commemorates Sitting Bull's surrender after five years living in Canada with his Sioux people.

Food

Just about everything in town is within walking distance of the Sherwood Inn. **Cousins Family Restaurant** (564 W. 1st Ave., 406/765-1690, www.cousinsplentywood.com, 6:30am-8pm daily, $5-20) is known locally for good home cooking and breakfast all day. The pictures on the walls of the owners' family—early Plentywood settlers—are fun to see. The **Blue Moon Supper Club** (4316 Hwy. 16 S., 406/765-2491, 11am-2am daily, $7-46) is known for its prime rib and Montana-style fine dining. It's also one of the few places on the Hi-Line you can expect to find lobster tail on the menu. For delicious specialty pizza and wings, head to **Fergie's Pizza** (114 S. Main St., 406/765-1744, 4pm-9pm Mon.-Thurs., 4pm-10pm Fri.-Sat., 4pm-8pm Sun., $12-21).

Accommodations

Sherwood Inn (515 W. 1st Ave., 406/765-2810, www.sherwoodinnplentywood.com, $90-135), complete with a host of Robin Hood-themed businesses (the Robin Hood Lounge, Fryer Tuck's Restaurant, and Maid Marion's Hair Salon) is a rather large hotel with 120 guest rooms and extended-stay apartments in three separate buildings, the most recent of which opened in 2013. This pet-friendly hotel is a nice place for the night, perfectly situated within walking distance to eateries, and is ideal for hunters. Wireless Internet is available throughout the property.

SCOBEY

Just down the road from Plentywood is Scobey (pop. 1,155, elev. 2,450 ft/747 m), an agricultural town with Scandinavian roots, a wealth of wheat farms—in 1924, Scobey was the largest primary wheat-shipping point in North America—and a population of die-hard sports fans. The downtown area is compact and cute, with nice places to eat and a very welcoming attitude. The town has so many unique features because most of its residents are descendants of those who homesteaded the area around the turn of the 20th century. The 1913 Daniels County Courthouse, for example, was once known as One-Eyed Molly's House of Pleasure. There are a few legendary feuds, of course, but mostly people get along and are always willing to lend a hand. When Scobey residents get married, invitations are unheard of; rather, the event is published in the weekly paper, and the entire town shows up with hot dishes, salads, and everything else to make a party worth attending. It is as quaint as it is genuine. Scobey is a wonderful example of small-town Montana. The town achieved some minor fame thanks to an award-winning 2008 PBS documentary, *Class C,* which tells the story of vanishing small towns through the lens of five girls' basketball teams.

★ Pioneer Town

Just west of town is Scobey's beloved **Pioneer Town** (720 2nd Ave., 406/487-5965, 12:30pm-4:30pm daily Memorial Day-Labor Day, by appointment only Labor Day-Memorial Day, $10 adults, $6 children under 12, free for preschool children, includes tour), an extension of the Daniels County Museum and a significant labor of love. It is a collection of more than 40 buildings from Scobey and the surrounding area that were saved from destruction and, to a lesser extent, the ravages of time. Some 35 of the buildings on-site—including a schoolhouse, a barbershop, two churches, and a saloon—have been restored and furnished with period pieces. Pioneer Town comes alive at the end of June each year with **Pioneer Days,** the town's biggest and arguably best event. The weekend includes the *Dirty Shame Show,* a musical variety show in the vaudeville tradition and still a rite of passage for many of Scobey's young women. There is a parade and plenty of food and celebration, and appropriately dressed pioneer guides will walk you through some of the town buildings.

Food

On the west side of town, **Burger Hut** (Hwy. 13 between 1st Ave. and Railroad Ave., 406/487-5030, 11am-8pm Mon.-Sat., 11am-4pm Sun., $5-12) is a summer-only establishment with classic curb service and a menu that puts full-size restaurants to shame. Don't miss the famous and enormous "Ugly Burgers" or the excellent ice cream. Another local favorite is **Ponderosa Bar and Pizza** (102 Main St., 406/487-5954, 11am-8pm Mon.-Wed. and Fri.-Sat., 11am-3pm Thurs., $6-12) which serves salads, burgers, sandwiches, and bar food in addition to pizza.

Accommodations

Just south of town, the **Smoke Creek Inn** (Hwy. 13 S., 406/487-5332 or 800/562-2775, www.smokecreekinn.com, $80-90) offers 30 clean, basic rooms, free Wi-Fi, free continental breakfast, and free guest laundry. Pets are welcome with a $20 fee, and outside kennels are available too. Outside electrical outlets are available to plug in your engine block during winter so that the car starts in the morning. No one said the winters were mild this far north.

WOLF POINT

Nestled on the banks of the Missouri River on the Fort Peck Reservation, Wolf Point (pop. 2,774, elev. 1,997 ft/609 m) has been many things over the course of Montana history: a fur trading post, a cow town, a refueling stop for wood-burning steamships, an Indian trading post, and, more recently, a community hub for the Fort Peck Reservation and an important storage site for much of the region's grain.

The community is made up of roughly equal numbers of tribe members and nonmembers, just as it was in the early 1900s when the U.S. government opened the reservation to homesteaders. The Native American population includes primarily Sioux and Assiniboine people.

Entertainment and Events

Among the most celebrated events in eastern Montana is the **Wolf Point Wild Horse Stampede** (Marvin Brookman Stadium, 0.25 mi/0.4 km east of Main St., 406/653-1770 or 406/653-2102, www.wolfpointchamber.com), Montana's oldest pro rodeo. Held annually the second weekend in July, this event has its origins in Native American celebration and is still an opportunity for participants to show

1: Scobey's Pioneer Town 2: two people waiting for the show

off their equestrian skills. In addition to three nights of spine-tingling rodeo, there are daily parades, a carnival, the famous wild-horse race, and street dances.

The other major event for Wolf Point is the **Wadopana Celebration** (406/650-7104 or 406/650-8724, www.wolfpointchamber.com), the oldest traditional powwow in the state, held annually the first weekend in August. The event includes a special day of activities for young people, naming ceremonies, and an annual community feed on Thursday evening.

Food
Old Town Grill (400 US 2, 406/653-1031, 7am-8pm Mon.-Sat., 7am-2pm Sun., $7-16) is a clean, well-lit place with a curious but tasty assortment of Mexican, Asian, and American food. Breakfast is served all day.

For more classic Montana fare and a slice of local life, try the newly remodeled restaurant at the **Sherman Inn** (200 E. Main St., 800/653-1100, 7am-9pm daily, $8-14), where weekly specials include Wednesday prime rib and Saturday ribs, plus pizza and burgers all the time. Or visit the **Elk's Club Dining Room** (304 Main St., 406/653-1920, 5pm-9pm Thurs.-Sat., noon-10pm Sun. summer, 5pm-9pm Thurs.-Sat. fall-spring, $10-29), where the steak and the karaoke are the main draws.

For those inclined toward liquid nourishment, **Missouri Breaks Brewing, Doc'Z Pub** (326 Main St., 406/653-1467, www.missouribreaksbrewing.com, 4pm-8pm Tues.-Sat.) serves up nine microbrew varieties, all made on-site, as well as homemade root beer and other fancy soda drinks for the under-21 crowd. Check their Facebook page for special events, including live music and trivia nights. Food can be ordered and brought in from the nearby **Wolf Point Café** (217 Main St., 406/653-1388, 11am-8pm Mon.-Fri., $4-14), whose menu includes burgers, sandwiches, wraps, salads, steak, and all-day breakfast. Call ahead; listed hours can fluctuate based on customers and local happenings. For a break from burgers and sandwiches, try the wings, calzones, and yummy pizzas at **The Pizza Joint** (200 1st Ave. S., 406/653-2020, 3pm-9pm Mon.-Sat., $9-28).

Accommodations
The Homestead Inn (101 US 2 E., 406/653-1300, www.homesteadinnmotel.com, from $86) is clean, comfortable, and affordable and offers free coffee and doughnuts every morning.

Right downtown, the **Sherman Inn** (200 E. Main St., 406/653-1100, www.shermaninn.com, from $90) offers 44 rooms, all with single or double queen-size beds.

GLASGOW AND FORT PECK
Glasgow (pop. 3,344, elev. 2,090 ft/637 m) is another northeastern Montana town that has seen its share of heart-stopping boom and heartbreaking bust. Founded around 1887 with the arrival of the Northern Pacific Railway, the town was a supply center for the region's homesteaders before it exploded in 1933 with the construction of the Fort Peck Dam, the largest of President Roosevelt's Public Works Administration projects, which employed more than 10,000 workers at any given time. When the dam was complete, the population and the city dwindled until the mid-1960s, when the Glasgow Air Force Base was commissioned. The population doubled, and the city built an entirely new infrastructure to meet the needs of the new residents. When the air force pulled out suddenly in 1968, 16,000 people left Glasgow, and the city was left to manage the fallout. Today the mostly abandoned and deteriorated base operates intermittently as a testing facility for Boeing and is occupied by a couple hundred retirees.

Both the expansive **Fort Peck Lake,** with as many miles of shoreline as California has coastline, and the Charles M. Russell National Wildlife Refuge are nearby and offer residents and visitors alike a wealth of outdoor opportunities. And as the largest city in this part of the state, Glasgow has plenty of services for those looking for recreation at Fort Peck Lake.

The town of Fort Peck (pop. 246, elev. 2,100 ft/640 m) was an Indian trading post starting in 1867, and even though the settlement was bypassed by the railroad, it was a hub of activity during construction of the dam. Today the town has a few residents and a significant number of lake visitors. The historic Fort Peck Theatre is a magical place to watch a show during the summer season.

★ Fort Peck Dam

The **Fort Peck Interpretive Center and Museum** (adjacent to the powerhouses on Lower Yellowstone Rd., 406/526-3493, www. fws.gov, 9am-5pm daily May-Sept., by appointment Oct.-Apr., free) is a unique combination of exhibits created in a partnership among Fort Peck Paleontology Inc., the U.S. Fish and Wildlife Service, and the U.S. Army Corps of Engineers. The museum features the state's largest aquariums, with examples of the species native to Fort Peck Lake, a life-size model of the *T. rex* uncovered some 20 miles (32 km) southeast of Fort Peck, and the construction history of the Fort Peck Dam. The museum also offers excellent interpretive programs throughout the summer with weekend nature walks on a nice 3-mile (4.8-km) paved trail and experiential programs for kids. Visitors can also sign up for tours of the **Fort Peck Power Plants** (9am, 11am, 1pm, and 3pm Mon.-Fri. and on the hour weekends and holidays Memorial Day-Labor Day, 11am and 1pm daily Labor Day-Sept., by appointment Oct.-Memorial Day), next to the interpretive center. A great day-use area is adjacent to the museum, complete with picnic shelters, playground equipment, and horseshoe pits. There is also a Class A campground.

The **Fort Peck Theatre** (201 Missouri Ave., 406/526-9943 or 406/228-9216, www. fortpecktheatre.org) was built as a temporary movie house in 1934 to entertain the huge number of workers building the dam. Over the years, the structure, designed and built by the Army Corps of Engineers in the style of a Swiss chalet, has become one of Montana's gems. The incredible craftsmanship, right down to the light fixtures, can be appreciated each summer during live performances produced by the Fort Peck Fine Arts Council.

In Glasgow, the **Valley County Pioneer Museum** (54109 Hwy. 2, 406/228-8692, www. valleycountymuseum.com, 9am-5pm Mon.-Sat. summer, 1pm-5pm Tues.-Fri. fall-spring, closed Jan., $3 adults, $2 students, free for children 6 and under) houses everything from dinosaur fossils found nearby and Fort Peck Dam construction information to the country's largest Assiniboine collection and genealogical archives.

Sports and Recreation

With 50 different kinds of fish in **Fort Peck Lake Reservoir,** nearly 1,600 miles (2,575 km) of shoreline, and more than 1 million acres of public land in the surrounding Charles M. Russell (CMR) National Wildlife Refuge, the area is a nature lover's paradise. **Hi-Line Charter Fishing** (6820 US 2 E., Havre, 406/262-2195 or 406/390-6892, www. hilinecharterfishing.com, half day $400 for 3 people, full day $650-700 for 2-3 people) can provide fully equipped boats and guides for fishing expeditions. Depending on the season, fishers can angle for walleye, smallmouth bass, northern pike, sauger, lake trout, and king salmon, among others. To rent a boat, contact the **Hell Creek Marina** (1 Hell Creek Rd., 406/557-2345, www.hellcreekmarina. net), 26 miles (42 km) north of Jordan, or the **Rock Creek Marina** (652 S. Rock Creek Rd., 406/485-2560, www.rockcreekmarina.com), on the southeast end of the reservoir, which also offers stocked cabins (from $100), RV campsites (from $35), and an on-site restaurant and tavern.

Golfers can hit the links in nearby Glasgow at the fairly level nine-hole **Sunnyside Golf Club** (95 Skylark Rd., 406/228-9519, $17 for 9 holes, $30 for 18 holes, carts $12-18).

Food

An upscale burger and steak restaurant,

Durum Restaurant & Bar (1015 US 2, 406/228-2236, dining room 5pm-9pm Tues.-Sat., bar 2pm-2am Tues.-Sat., $11-30) is a nice surprise in this part of the state. The menu is diverse, and the preparations are creative—lamb chops with rosemary plum glaze—meaning the restaurant is often packed. And the bar stays open late if you're in that kind of mood. On Wednesdays, the prime rib can't be beat.

For a good, thin and crispy pizza with loads of create-your-own options, try **Eugene's Pizza** (193 Klein Ave., 406/228-8552, www.eugenespizza.com, 4pm-10pm Sun.-Thurs., 4pm-11pm Fri.-Sat., $8-22.50), which also serves up chicken dinners, burgers, steaks, and fried chicken by the bucket.

The best spot for a cup of coffee or tea in town is **The Loaded Toad** (527 2nd Ave. S., 406/228-4610, 7am-4pm Mon.-Fri., 7am-2pm Sat.), which has delicious pastries and wonderful ambience.

Accommodations

Right in Fort Peck is the rambling **Fort Peck Hotel** (175 S. Missouri St., 406/526-3266 or 800/560-4931, www.thefortpeckhotel.com, May-Nov., $79-168), built at the same time and in similar fashion to the Fort Peck Theatre. The wooden hotel certainly recalls a time gone by, and though the amenities are simple (double and single beds, bathrooms down the hall for the more basic rooms), they are perfectly suitable and quite charming. The hotel serves three wonderful meals daily in the quaint dining room, and guests tend to lounge in oversize Depression-era rockers on the expansive porch. Pets are allowed for a $30 charge for one dog per room.

The pet-friendly **Cottonwood Inn & Suites** (54250 US 2, 406/228-8213 or 800/321-8213, www.cottonwoodinn.net, rooms from $112, RV sites $44-49) in Glasgow is the town's most modern hotel. There are 168 guest rooms, many of them suites that can accommodate up to eight people, an indoor heated pool with two hot tubs, free Wi-Fi, a dining room, lounge and casino, and an adjacent RV park that gives guests full access to hotel amenities.

INFORMATION AND SERVICES

The **Glasgow Area Chamber of Commerce** (54147 US 2, 406/228-2222, www.glasgowchamber.net, 9am-5pm Mon.-Fri. Memorial Day-Labor Day, 8:30am-4pm Mon.-Fri. Labor Day-Memorial Day) is happy to provide visitors with information for the surrounding area, including Fort Peck.

The **Daniels County Chamber of Commerce** (120 Main St., Scobey, 406/487-2061, www.scobeymt.com, 10am-2pm Mon.-Fri. May 15-Sept. 15) is in downtown Scobey.

The **Sheridan County Chamber of Commerce** (108 N. Main St., 406/765-1733, www.sheridancountychamber.org, office hours vary so call ahead) is in Plentywood. There is also a **visitors information** rack filled with brochures and pamphlets at the **Sherwood Inn** (515 W. 1st Ave., Plentywood).

The **Wolf Point Chamber of Commerce and Agriculture** (218 3rd Ave. S., Ste. B, 406/653-2012, www.wolfpointchamber.com, 9am-5pm Wed., and 9am-5pm first Tuesday of the month) also has information about the Fort Peck Reservation.

TRANSPORTATION

Glasgow sits on US 2, 270 miles (435 km) northeast of Great Falls and 50 miles (80 km) west of Wolf Point. Fort Peck is off Highway 24, 47 miles (76 km) southwest of Wolf Point and 18 miles (29 km) southeast of Glasgow.

1: Fort Peck Theatre 2: Fort Peck Lake

The Milk River Valley

The Milk River flows from high in the Montana Rockies, north into Alberta, then east and south, through Havre and across prairie and riparian areas teeming with wildlife, through Fort Belknap, Malta, and Glasgow, eventually joining the Missouri River. The water is indeed milky colored, even late in summer, and it was named by Lewis and Clark, who thought the water looked like "a cup of tea with the admixture of a table-spoonful of milk."

Life along the river seems to follow an equally relaxed pace in nice little towns like Saco, Malta, and Fort Belknap. This is the country of Wallace Stegner, the beloved Western author who spent much of his childhood along Frenchman Creek, a tributary of the Milk River. He didn't always love the austere beauty of the place, but he always captured it in his spare, lovely prose.

This is also prime hunting territory for large game and birds, and there are a number of places to enjoy the water by boat or with a fishing rod. Many people simply come to drink it all in, visiting the scenic wildlife refuges, driving through the open country, stopping in friendly towns along the way, or relaxing at eastern Montana's only hot springs resort.

MALTA

A notable stop on the Montana Dinosaur Trail and something of a mecca for bird hunters, Malta (pop. 2,090, elev. 2,254 ft/687 m) is a hub for the myriad ranches in the area and a nice place to start day trips into the Bowdoin National Wildlife Refuge or organize an exciting fossil dig. Known among Native Americans in the region as "The Big Bend," for the curve of the Milk River here, the town eventually got its name when a blindfolded railroad employee in Minneapolis was told to point his finger at a spot on the globe—and landed on the Mediterranean island. Nearby Saco was named in the same way, when the man pointed to Saco, Maine.

Just west of town is the site of a great train robbery in 1901 by Kid Curry and his gang of outlaws, many of whom were known to frequent the area. The other most famous

weathered agricultural buildings

residents of Malta were of the scaly variety: a 77-million-year-old mummified brachylophosaurus, a rare and precious find, was unearthed north of town in 2000 and has become something of a local hero, along with fellow duck-bills Elvis, Roberta, and Peanut, all of whom are on display in town.

The **Phillips County Museum** (431 US 2 E., 406/654-1037, www.phillipscountymuseum.org, 10am-5pm Mon.-Sat. Apr.-Dec., $5 adults 13 and older, $3 children, free for children under 6) is a stop on the Montana Dinosaur Trail and includes exhibits on mining, Native Americans, outlaws, and, most notably, dinosaurs. The collection includes Elvis, a brachylophosaurus found in 1994, in addition to a complete *Tyrannosaurus rex* skull and an upright full-size albertosaurus, a relative of the *T. rex* and the primary prey of the brachylophosaurus. A beautifully restored 1903 home, built by New York transplant H. G. Robinson, is adjacent to the museum and available for tours.

Another stop on the Montana Dinosaur Trail is the **Great Plains Dinosaur Museum and Field Station** (405 N. 1st St. E., 406/654-5300, www.greatplainsdinosaur.org, 10am-5pm Tues.-Sat. May, 10am-5pm Mon.-Sat. and 12:30pm-5pm Sun. June-Aug., open by appointment only Oct.-Apr., $5 adults 13 and over, $3 children 6-12, free for children under 6). The museum includes rare dinosaur exhibits that show fossilized skin, tendon, and even stomach contents. It also offers excellent field programs as well as experiences in the paleo lab.

The nearby **Bowdoin National Wildlife Refuge** (194 Bowdoin Auto Tour Rd., 7 mi/11.3 km east of Malta off Old US 2, 406/654-2863, www.fws.gov) is a landscape scoured by a runaway continental ice sheet more than 15,000 years ago. The area was established as a migratory bird refuge in 1936. Both saline and freshwater wetlands offer ideal habitat for the thousands of birds—from waterfowl and shorebirds to birds of prey and grassland songbirds—that soar along this flyway. More than 230 species have been identified in the refuge, including one of the largest colonies of inland American white pelicans, as well as double-crested cormorants, great blue herons, ring-necked pheasants, sandpipers, sharp-tailed grouse, and the occasional bald eagle. A 15-mile (24-km) self-guided auto tour route brings visitors face-to-face with much of the region's wildlife. Fishing and hunting in the refuge are strictly regulated and should be coordinated through the refuge office during business hours.

Two other impressive swaths of wildlife-rich land include the vast Charles M. Russell National Wildlife Refuge and the much newer American Prairie Reserve, which may eventually top 3 million acres.

Twenty miles (32 km) northeast of Malta, near the tiny town of Saco, **Sleeping Buffalo Hot Springs** (669 Buffalo Trail, 406/527-3320, www.sbhotsprings.com, 9am-8pm Sun.-Thurs., 9am-9pm Fri.-Sat. year-round, $13 adults ages 12 and up, $12 seniors 60 and up and children 5-11, $8 children 4 and under) is a wonderfully restored slice of Montana history and a great place to soak in warm, medicinal waters. The only hot springs in eastern Montana, Sleeping Buffalo was discovered by a wildcat oil rigger in 1922 and became known as the local "Saturday night bathtub" for the region's cowboys before it was developed by a rancher whose son suffered from polio. The 108°F (42.2°C) mineral water, flowing from 3,200 feet down, worked wonders on the boy, and it wasn't long before other swimmers started coming. The springs fell into grave disrepair and were closed before a massive 2015 renovation. Today, with a new well in 2021, there are three pools, hot enough and cleaned often enough that no chemicals are necessary. A snack bar is on-site, and towels and toys are available for rent. Five deluxe cabins ($149-229), including two with two bedrooms each, are available, as are RV sites ($37-48) and tent sites ($24).

FORT BELKNAP INDIAN RESERVATION

Set between the Little Rockies and the Milk River, the **Fort Belknap Indian Reservation,** established in 1889, put together the Gros Ventre and the Assiniboine who refused to relocate to the Fort Peck Indian Reservation. The two tribes had long been enemies and only formed an alliance to fight the nearby Blackfeet. Today the reservation is a peaceful place encompassing 650,000 acres of grasslands and gently rolling hills. There is an **1877 mission** in Hays as well as some significant recreation sites and festive celebrations. The nearby Charles M. Russell National Wildlife Refuge is a marvelous place for recreation and to appreciate the diverse and abundant wildlife.

CHARLES M. RUSSELL NATIONAL WILDLIFE REFUGE

The **Charles M. Russell (CMR) National Wildlife Refuge** (406/538-8706, ext. 221, or 406/526-3464, www.fws.gov) was established in 1936, and at 1.1 million acres, it is the second-largest U.S. wildlife refuge outside Alaska. In this place of uncommon beauty—from badlands to breaks, coulees to canyons—live thriving populations of mountain lions, coyotes, prairie dogs, pronghorn, and enormous numbers of birds. Twenty-five percent bigger than Rhode Island, the refuge has only two paved roads providing minimal access. The 20-mile (32-km) paved auto tour begins and ends on US 191 and offers two hours of scenery and, most often, abundant wildlife. All other travel is on dirt and gravel roads, on foot, on horseback, or by boat. The region was a frequent hiding place for a number of famous outlaws. The refuge encompasses Fort Peck Lake, a long stretch of the Missouri River, and the rugged Missouri Breaks, extending more than 100 miles (161 km) west to US 191.

AMERICAN PRAIRIE RESERVE

The lofty mission for the **American Prairie Reserve** (406/585-4600 or 877/273-1123, www.americanprairie.org) is to create the largest wildlife reserve in the continental United States by piecing together more than 3.5 million acres of public and private land to be a functioning mixed-grass prairie ecosystem. Wild inhabitants of the area include bison, elk, deer, pronghorn, and even bighorn sheep. Smaller critters include badgers, prairie dogs, swift fox, and a multitude of birds. The reserve, very much a work in progress, is open to hiking, biking, horseback riding, wildlife-watching, and hunting. Guided trips and volunteer opportunities can be arranged and are well worth looking into for anyone seeking real solace in this ocean of grassland. With advance reservations, visitors can stay in huts or camp in their own tents and RVs at designated sites, or camp in the backcountry.

ENTERTAINMENT AND EVENTS

Milk River Indian Days (406/353-2281, www.ftbelknap.org) is a traditional powwow with colorfully clad dancers, Native American drummers, and music. The celebration is typically held in late July at the Fort Belknap Powwow Grounds in Harlem. The **Hays Pow Wow** (406/353-2205) is another excellent celebration of Native American history and culture, staged annually 5 miles (8 km) south of Hays in Mission Canyon. The event features a weekend of Native dancing and singing, along with multiple contests for every age group. Both events are free and open to the public.

FOOD

As this is ranch country, diners often have the choice between steaks and burgers, and you can't really go wrong with either. The **Great Northern Steak House** (2 S. 1st St. E., Malta, 406/654-2100, 6am-8pm Mon.-Thurs., 6am-9pm Fri.-Sat., 6am-noon Sun., breakfast $5-14, lunch $6-25, dinner $14-42) serves the best surf and turf on the Hi-Line, including Saturday night prime rib. As the restaurant is in a hotel, it's open for breakfast and lunch as well, with an extensive menu for both, including Mexican specialties. A coffee shop in the hotel serves specialty coffees plus breakfast and lunch. And the Great Northern Lounge is a nice spot for a drink.

The Tin Cup Bar and Grill (1652 US 191 S., Malta, 406/654-5527, 10am-3pm and 5pm-10pm daily summer, limited hours fall-spring, $9-32) is an elegant full-service restaurant overlooking the Marian Hills Golf Course and the pastoral Milk River Valley. The Hitchin Post (745 N. 1st Ave. E., Malta, 406/654-1882, 6am-3pm Mon.-Fri., 7am-2pm Sat., 8am-2pm Sun., $6-15) is a favorite for homemade soups, pies, rolls, muffins, and daily lunch specials. Breakfast is served all day. Another good choice for breakfast, lunch, or a healthy snack for the road is Lettuce Eat (902 Central Ave., Malta, 406/654-2217, 7am-4pm Mon.-Fri., $7-12), which serves great soups, salads, and sandwiches with friendly service.

ACCOMMODATIONS

A number of small motels are found in Malta, the nicest being the pet-friendly Great Northern Hotel (2 S. 1st St. E., Malta, 406/654-2100, $85-91). It's not charming in a historical sense (the 1904 hotel was rebuilt after a catastrophic fire in 1971), but the rooms are quite comfortable and impeccably clean. There is a nice steakhouse and a coffee shop on the premises. The pet-friendly Riverside Motel & RV Park (8 Central Ave. N., Malta, 406/654-2310 or 800/854-2310, www.riversidemotel-rvpark.com, $62-95) is a good choice for more budget-conscious travelers. The modern rooms are clean and spacious and offer free Wi-Fi plus refrigerators and microwaves.

CAMPING

In Malta, basic motel rooms ($83-85) and RV sites ($42.50-46.50) are available at the Edgewater Inn & RV Park (47176 US 2,

406/654-1302 or 800/821-7475). Amenities include an indoor pool, hot tub, and health club.

You'll find multiple primitive campgrounds in the vicinity of Malta: Fourchette Bay Campground is 60 miles (97 km) south of Malta, Montana Gulch Campground is 1 mile (1.6 km) south of Landusky, and Nelson Reservoir is 17 miles (27 km) east of Malta. But roads and access can be problematic in wet weather, and most sites advise campers to bring three days' worth of food in case they get stranded.

A newer and exciting option for camping in the region, with six tent sites and nine RV sites, is Buffalo Camp at American Prairie Reserve (44704 Regina Rd., 406/658-2252 or 877/273-1123, www.americanprairie.org, $10 without electricity, $15 with electricity), 50 miles (80 km) south of Malta and in the midst of excellent hiking and biking terrain. Tent sites include low-impact platforms with tie-down cleats. The campsite is primitive but does have non-potable water, vault toilets, and an amphitheater. There is no cell phone coverage on the reserve. The Antelope Creek Campground at Mars Vista (61080 US 191, S. Zortman, 406/673-3859, www.americanprairie.org) is 7 miles (11 km) north of the Missouri River along US 191. There are 12 RV sites ($32) with power, eight tent sites ($15), three of which are reserved for walk-ins, and four rental cabins ($61).

INFORMATION

The Malta Chamber of Commerce (2 S. 1st St. E., 406/654-1776, www.maltachamber. com, by appointment) can provide brochures and information. The Tourist Information Center is open mid-May to mid-September in the Phillips County Museum (431 US 2 E., 406/654-1037, 10am-5pm Mon.-Sat.).

TRANSPORTATION

The Milk River Valley can be accessed from US 2, running east from Havre or west from Glasgow, or from US 191 running north from Lewistown or south from Canada.

Great Falls and the Rocky Mountain Front

North-central Montana encompasses much of the geographical diversity that defines the state, with vast plains along the Hi-Line, rolling agricultural fields in Montana's breadbasket, and the dramatic Rocky Mountain Front.

Although this stretch of Montana isn't often among the state's primary tourist destinations, there are many reasons why it should be (chief among them that the area is *not* a tourist destination). The region is rich with natural beauty, culturally significant landmarks, and history. Fort Benton, just east of Great Falls, is considered the birthplace of Montana due to its origins as an important inland port, the westernmost stopping point for steamers loaded with materials and pioneers traveling up the Missouri River. There are two major

Highlights

Look for ★ to find recommended sights, activities, dining, and lodging.

★ **C. M. Russell Museum:** The most beloved and impressive art museum in the state is an extraordinary tribute to the life and work of the consummate Western artist (page 84).

★ **Lewis and Clark National Historic Trail Interpretive Center:** This compelling museum enables visitors to learn about the extraordinary challenges faced by Lewis and Clark and to appreciate how what they found parallels what exists today (page 88).

★ **Fishing on the Missouri River:** America's longest river attracts anglers from all over the world. The tailwater stretch between Holter Dam and Cascade serves up thousands of trout per mile (page 90).

★ **Bob Marshall Wilderness Complex:** More than 1 million acres of pristine wilderness straddle the Continental Divide here. The topography is dramatic, the wildlife is plentiful, and the opportunities to explore are endless (page 101).

★ **Fort Benton:** Touted locally as the birthplace of Montana, this town was an important early trading post. A charming hotel, gourmet food, and a riverside setting make it an ideal destination (page 104).

★ **Havre Beneath the Streets:** Practically an entire city exists underneath the streets of downtown Havre. Guides show you around the 27-bed brothel, saloon, and opium den and the more genteel dentist's office, cigar shop, and bakery (page 108).

★ **Charlie Russell Chew Choo:** This three-hour narrated train ride travels from Lewistown through some of the most starkly beautiful terrain anywhere. The staged holdup might be hokey, but the prime rib and splendid scenery are the real deal (page 114).

★ **Charles M. Bair Family Museum:** In the tiny agricultural town of Martinsdale, this remarkable home and museum tells the story of a Montana family and the way their history and art collection shaped the fabric of the West (page 117).

★ **Red Ants Pants Music Festival:** Started as a celebration of rural Montana, this family-friendly weekend-long festival in late July offers pastoral beauty, fantastic music, and a real sense of community (page 119).

Great Falls and the Rocky Mountain Front

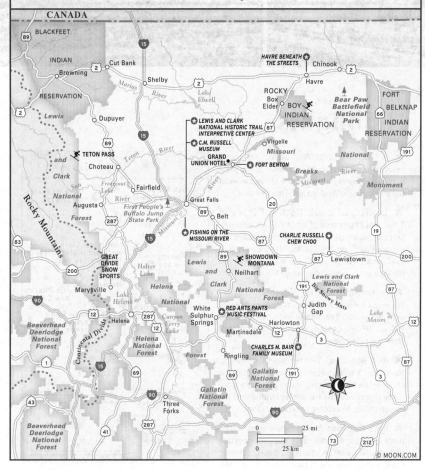

buffalo jumps (butte-like geographical features that Native Americans used to hunt bison) worth seeing, Egg Mountain with its significant dinosaur discoveries, the vast Bob Marshall Wilderness, the placid Smith River, and outcroppings all along the Missouri River that hold the lore of the fur-trapping era. Great Falls, the largest city in the region, is home to the C. M. Russell Museum and some intriguing contemporary art as well as the Lewis and Clark National Historic Trail Interpretive Center. Smaller towns, including Choteau, Lewistown, and White Sulphur Springs, have preserved their culture and history as they have fought to maintain their populations in boom-and-bust economies, and each offers a meaningful glimpse into Montana's

Previous: the Rocky Mountain Front; the Missouri River; farmland near Fort Benton.

agricultural life past and present. The Rocky Boy's and Fort Belknap Indian Reservations offer some wonderful ways to immerse yourself in Native American culture.

PLANNING YOUR TIME

As with most of Montana, there is as much to do in Great Falls as your time will allow. Visitors should plan at least a day in the city to see some of the excellent museums and nearby natural attractions, including First Peoples Buffalo Jump State Park. Known for its consistent wind, this city is ideally located on the Missouri River between the Rocky Mountains and Montana's Big Open. Any number of outdoor adventures can be dreamed up and launched from Great Falls.

Other towns in this region, each with its own unique charm, are often best enjoyed en route from one destination to another. One notable exception is Fort Benton, less than an hour's drive from Great Falls. This picturesque hamlet sits in a canyon along the Missouri and is an ideal spot for visitors, with several museums, a quaint downtown, historic sites, and one of the handsomest old hotels in the state.

The country opens up significantly east of Great Falls. In places it looks as if the only occupants are cattle and oversize windmills. The Upper Missouri River Breaks National Monument, with some of the state's most interesting and isolated terrain, is best explored from the water. Havre is the largest city on the Hi-Line (a stretch of the state that parallels Montana's northernmost or "highest" railroad line) and offers plenty of accommodations and the fascinating Havre Beneath the Streets Tour. Farther south, Lewistown is small but colorful, with plenty of good fishing nearby and a couple of good restaurants.

West of Great Falls, the Rocky Mountains soar skyward, with towns such as Choteau and the reservation town of Browning in their shadows. Dude ranches are available for those who make this region their primary destination, but at the very least this is a magnificent corner to drive through en route to Glacier National Park or southwest toward Missoula. In the fall, this is a bird hunter's paradise. Dinosaur aficionados will want to allow enough time to visit some of the plentiful paleontological sites, including Egg Mountain and the Old Trail Museum in Choteau and The Montana Dinosaur Center in Bynum.

HISTORY

This vast, largely open stretch of Montana was home to numerous Native American groups, including the Blackfeet, Sioux, Assiniboine, Gros Ventre, and Cree, who took up residence and battled for land as early as the late 18th century. The Crow, Nez Perce, and Salish were known to hunt the region.

Settlers were brought by steamboats that navigated along the Missouri all the way to Fort Benton as early as 1859. In 1887, the Great Northern Railway was rapidly constructed. Under the direction of James J. Hill, 643 miles (1,030 km) of track were laid in less than eight months by a crew of 9,000 men and 6,600 horses. In an attempt to populate the area, in 1908, Hill sent agents and exhibition cars to county fairs across the Midwest and on the East Coast to entice farmers. Settlers flocked to the region for their 320 acres of "Poor Man's Paradise," a term made famous by Hill's promotional campaign, which piggybacked on the Homestead Act of 1891, giving every U.S. citizen the chance to claim 320 acres of unoccupied land. Generous rainfall prompted enormous harvests of wheat and kept population growth steady until 1917, when a cyclical drought wreaked havoc on the land and broke the spirits of newcomers. Between 1909 and 1916, some 80,000 people had moved into the region; 60,000 of them were gone by 1922. North-central Montana is still subject to harsh weather and the unpredictable but inevitable boom-and-bust cycle.

When Meriwether Lewis stood atop the rocks beneath the Great Falls of the Missouri River in June 1805, he pronounced the scene as "the grandest sight I ever beheld," a sentiment shared by Fort Benton businessman

Paris Gibson some 75 years later. Gibson committed himself to building a city around the site of the falls. In 1883 he plotted the city, then urged his friend James J. Hill to bring his railroad through. Gibson envisioned a "new Minneapolis" on the banks of the Missouri River. By 1888, with plentiful industry in town and fertile farmland around it, the city of Great Falls, with Gibson as its mayor, boasted more than 2,000 residents. Two years later the population had doubled. But despite Gibson's best efforts and his intelligent and thoughtful city planning, Great Falls floundered when Hill opted not to bring the railroad to town. Though it never fulfilled Gibson's ultimate vision, the city did achieve industrial success with power-producing dams, copper smelting, and eventually a U.S. Air Force base.

Great Falls

At the edge of the mountains and the plains, Great Falls (pop. 58,835, elev. 3,674 ft/1,120 m) has more romantic origins than its modern-day grittiness may suggest. A few days ahead of William Clark, Meriwether Lewis stumbled on the region in June 1805, calling the falls themselves "the grandest sight I ever beheld." Seventy-five years later, Fort Benton merchant Paris Gibson sought the same views that had captivated Lewis and later recollected,

> I had never seen a spot as attractive as this . . . I had looked upon this scene for a few moments only when I said to myself, here I would found a city.

Just three years later, in 1883, the city of Great Falls was named and platted.

With the falls long since dammed to create power—Great Falls is known as the "Electric City" for all its dams and power plants—the city has worked to capitalize on the beauty of the Missouri River with a scenic roadway (River Drive), trails, parks, and picnic areas along the waterway. The Lewis and Clark National Historic Trail Interpretive Center sits atop a bluff and affords visitors an unspoiled view of what the area might have looked like 200 years ago. Another kind of beauty celebrated by this city is art. There are a couple of excellent—and surprising—art museums to visit.

But Great Falls is still a rough-and-tumble Montana town. There is cowboy culture, military culture, and serious wind, all of which give the state's third-largest city a little bit of an edge. Its location between the mountains and plains and amid rivers is ideal for lovers of the outdoors, and Great Falls is an excellent launching point for adventures in any direction.

SIGHTS
Great Falls Trolley

If you only have a few hours and want to see as much of the city as possible, the **Great Falls Trolley** (406/868-2913, www.gotrolleygo.com, June-Sept., late Nov.-Dec. for holiday lights tours, $22/adults, $5/youth ages 5-17, free for children under 5) takes you on a 2-hour tour to the most important natural and human-built places in a cool old streetcar from California. Charters are available too.

★ C. M. Russell Museum

One of the best and most intimate Western art museums in the country, the **C. M. Russell Museum** (400 13th St. N., 406/727-8787, www.cmrussell.org, 10am-5pm Wed.-Mon. May-Oct., 10am-5pm Thurs.-Mon. Nov.-Apr., $14/adults, $11/seniors over 60, $11/scheduled tour groups, $4/students, free for active military and their family members, plus children 5 and under) has amassed the world's largest collection of Charlie Russell art and personal objects, including his illustrated letters. His home has been meticulously maintained on the museum grounds and is open to visitors (11am-4pm Wed.-Mon. May-Oct.). In addition to a significant number of important

Great Falls

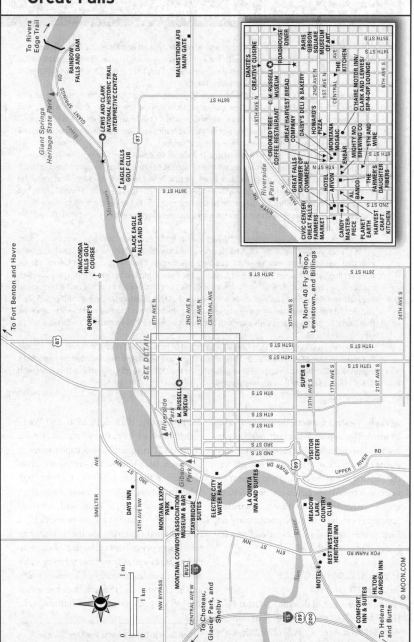

To Rivers Edge Trail

Giant Springs Heritage State Park

Missouri River

GIANT SPRINGS RD

RAINBOW FALLS AND DAM

LEWIS AND CLARK NATIONAL HISTORIC TRAIL INTERPRETIVE CENTER

EAGLE FALLS GOLF CLUB

MALMSTROM AFB MAIN GATE

56TH ST

87

38TH ST S

BLACK EAGLE FALLS AND DAM

ANACONDA HILLS GOLF COURSE

To Fort Benton and Havre

87

BORRIE'S

8TH AVE N
2ND AVE N
1ST AVE N
CENTRAL AVE

26TH ST S

To North 40 Fly Shop, Lewistown, and Billings

SEE DETAIL

Riverside Park

C.M. RUSSELL MUSEUM

15TH ST S
14TH ST S
9TH ST S
6TH ST S
5TH ST S
3RD ST S
2ND ST S

10TH AVE S

SUPER 8

13TH AVE S
17TH AVE S
21ST AVE S
24TH AVE S
26TH ST S
13TH ST S

VISITOR CENTER

89

UPPER RIVER RD
RIVER DR

SMELTER AVE

3RD ST NW

DAYS INN
14TH AVE NW

MONTANA EXPO PARK

Gibson Park

MONTANA COWBOYS ASSOCIATION MUSEUM & BAR

STAYBRIDGE SUITES

ELECTRIC CITY WATER PARK

LA QUINTA INN AND SUITES

MEADOW LARK COUNTRY CLUB

BUS 15

CENTRAL AVE W

6TH ST NW

FOX FARM RD

BEST WESTERN HERITAGE INN

MOTEL 6

Sun River

To Choteau, Glacier Park, and Shelby

NW BYPASS

COMFORT INN & SUITES

HILTON GARDEN INN

15 89 200

To Helena and Butte

To Rivers Edge Trail

1 mi
1 km
0

© MOON.COM

Detail

DANTE'S CREATIVE CUISINE
ROADHOUSE DINER
PARIS GIBSON SQUARE MUSEUM OF ART

16TH ST S
15TH ST S
14TH ST S

8TH AVE N

C.M. RUSSELL MUSEUM

2ND AVE N
1ST AVE N
CENTRAL
THE KITCHEN

5TH AVE S

Riverside Park

PARK DR N

RIVER DR S

CROOKED TREE COFFEE RESTAURANT

GREAT HARVEST BREAD COMPANY

DAISY'S DELI & BAKERY

HOWARD'S PIZZA

MONTANA MOSAIC

O'HAIRE MOTOR INN/ CLARK AND LEWIS SIP-N-DIP LOUNGE

GREAT FALLS CHAMBER OF COMMERCE

HOTEL ARVON

MIGHTY MO BREWING CO

ENBAR

5TH AND WINE

THE FARMER'S DAUGHTER FIBERS

CIVIC CENTER/ GREAT FALLS FARMERS MARKET

CANDY MASTERPIECE

AL BANCO

PLANET EARTH HARVEST CRAFT KITCHEN

1ST AVE S
2ND AVE S

Nancy Russell:
The Force Behind the Artist

Charles M. Russell's name is synonymous with great Western art and Montana. He is not only the pride and joy of Great Falls but a hero to the entire state. Although today Charlie Russell's art is heralded around the world, there is little debate that the world may not have known him had it not been for his savvy and determined wife, Nancy.

Born Nancy Bates Cooper in 1878, she was 14 years younger than Charlie and worked as a housemaid for one of his friends when they met. Their pairing seemed an unlikely match, and when news of the engagement spread, it seemed clear that Charlie was marrying beneath himself. What soon became apparent was that not only could Nancy hold her own in any social circle, she would be the single greatest asset to her husband's career.

Nancy Russell had fended for herself from the age of 16, when her mother had died. She was a strong woman capable of achieving whatever she set her mind to; some would argue that's how she nabbed Charlie. In his book *More Rawhide,* Charlie wrote, "It's the women that make the men in this world," and in his case it was true. There is no doubt that he was a talented artist, but his wife's belief in his work and her drive to see him properly recognized are what made him a success. As his business-minded partner, Nancy ultimately organized the shows that gained him worldwide attention.

Nancy quickly earned the moniker "Nancy the robber" because of the high prices she would ask (and receive) for Charlie's work. Charlie once told a newspaper that the worst fight the couple ever had was when she had asked for $75 for a painting that he thought would sell for $5. Initially setting up a home in the town of Cascade, the couple moved to Great Falls to aid Charlie's burgeoning career. On their arrival, the mayor's wife commissioned a painting, and Nancy asked her husband if she could deliver it. He warned her that the painting was to be sold for $25, and she should not ask for a penny more or the painting would not sell. Nancy met the mayor's wife, delivered the painting, and with a lump in her throat asked for $35. The mayor's wife replied, "I'll get my checkbook."

Ultimately, it was evident that Charlie was proud of his wife and relieved to have her handle the financial part of his business. In 1919, when asked by a reporter if marriage hinders an artist's expression, Charlie replied, "I still love and long for the Old West, and everything that goes with it. But I would sacrifice it all for Mrs. Russell."

works by Western masters, the museum takes an interesting approach to art through its permanent bison exhibit. The iconic western ungulate had significance to Russell himself, and the importance of the animal and its near extinction is traced through more than 1,000 exquisite Native American artifacts. Fascinating temporary exhibits include contemporary art. Don't leave Great Falls without spending a few hours at the C. M. Russell.

Paris Gibson Square
Museum of Art

At the eastern end of downtown Great Falls, the **Paris Gibson Square Museum of Art** (1400 1st Ave. N., 406/727-8255, www.

the-square.org, 10am-5pm Mon. and Wed.-Fri., 10am-9pm Tues., noon-5pm Sat., free) is known as "The Square" and occupies an entire city block. Built in 1896, the impressive structure served the community as Central High School and later as Paris Gibson Junior High until it closed in 1975. Renovated, renamed after the city's founder, and reopened in 1977, this National Historic Landmark houses an impressive permanent collection of contemporary art as well as important traveling exhibitions. In addition to classes, lectures, tours, and performances, the museum has a café and gift shop. Don't miss a stroll through the

1: Roe River in Giant Springs Heritage State Park
2: Great Falls

sculpture garden out on the beautifully landscaped grounds.

★ Lewis and Clark National Historic Trail Interpretive Center

Beautifully built into a bluff overlooking the Missouri River, the **Lewis and Clark National Historic Trail Interpretive Center** (4201 Giant Springs Rd., 406/727-8733, www.fs.usda.gov, 9am-6pm daily Memorial Day-Labor Day, 9am-5pm Tues.-Sat., noon-5pm Sun. Labor Day-Memorial Day, $8 adults 16 and up, free for children under 15 and Federal Pass holders) provides visitors with a hands-on interpretation of the intrepid explorers' cross-country journey. With a two-story diorama of the portage at the Missouri River's five great falls, impressive videos by Ken Burns and others, and ranger-led programs, the center does an excellent job of portraying the importance of Native Americans to the journey along with a comprehensive natural history exhibit. The center offers a wealth of worthwhile special events that include concerts, lectures, and reenactments (check the website for upcoming events). A nice outdoor component to the center includes a network of self-guided trails, one of which leads you to the nearby Giant Springs Heritage State Park.

Giant Springs Heritage State Park

Among the largest freshwater springs in the country, Giant Springs was discovered by Lewis and Clark in 1805. The spring, now in **Giant Springs Heritage State Park** (4600 Giant Springs Rd., 406/454-5840 or 406/727-1212, www.stateparks.mt.gov, sunrise-sunset daily, nonresidents $8/vehicle or $4/pedestrian or biker), produces 156 million gallons of crystal-clear water each day. The water stays at a constant 54°F (12.2°C) all year, making it an ideal spot for fishing. Attractions include a fish hatchery on-site, a **visitor center** (8am-5pm daily), a picnic area, and several trails that wind through

the lush area. There are four Missouri River waterfalls within the park. For trivia buffs, the 201-foot-long **Roe River**, the second shortest in the world, flows from the springs.

First Peoples Buffalo Jump State Park

Considered to be among the largest buffalo jumps in North America, and in use more than 1,000 years before Lewis and Clark explored the area, **First Peoples Buffalo Jump State Park** (342 Ulm-Vaughn Rd., Ulm, 406/866-2217 or 406/454-5840, www.stateparks.mt.gov, park open daily in summer and Wed.-Sun. in winter, visitor center open 8am-6pm daily mid-Apr.-mid-Sept., 10am-4pm Wed.-Sat., noon-4pm Sun. mid-Sept.-Mar., nonresidents $8/vehicle) is exceptional in that it offers an extensive on-site education center that houses buffalo culture exhibits, a storytelling circle, a gallery, and an outdoor powwow area. The site itself is impressive, with a mile-long sandstone cliff from which the bison were chased to their deaths, but more than anything, this is the best place in the state to learn about buffalo jumps. Watch your step on or off the trails for both rattlesnakes and prickly pear cacti. An adjacent prairie dog town is home to protected black-tailed prairie dogs and worth the short detour. The park is 10 miles (16 km) south of Great Falls off I-15 at Ulm; follow signs for the state park 3.5 miles (5.6 km) northwest on a county road. Check the website for upcoming events in the late fall and early winter like the guided **Rock Art Hike** ($4 pp), a strenuous hiking tour that takes visitors to prehistoric petroglyphs and pictographs by Native Americans as well as carvings in stone made by early European settlers.

SPORTS AND RECREATION
River's Edge Trail

The River's Edge Trail is the envy of nearly every town in Montana. With nearly 60 miles (97 km) of trail, some 20 miles (32 km) of which are paved for wheelchair access, the River's Edge Trail accommodates single-track

The History of Buffalo Jumps

Used by Native Americans for more than 5,000 years, buffalo jumps are rocky cliff formations that entire herds of bison were driven over, causing mortal injury to the animals and providing the hunters with ample meat, fur, and bones to make into weapons, tools, and decorative objects. Throughout Montana, the jumps have become significant archaeological sites, with discoveries of bones and tools guiding scientists to a better understanding of the various cultures of the people who hunted in this way.

What is surmised about the process is that the hunters first would spot herds of bison within a reasonable distance of the jump. Using rock cairns, they would carefully construct an ever-narrowing pathway from the base of the jump up the gradual slope to the cliff's edge. Several warriors would dress in animal hides and intersperse themselves undetected among the herd. At a specific moment, the warriors would throw off their hides and stand up to startle the bison into a stampede, hopefully in the direction of the jump. As the bison headed toward the jump, other hunters would line the way, waving a variety of things to frighten the animals and prevent them from leaving the trail. By the time the animals reached the precipice, they were moving so fast that they were unable to stop at the cliff's edge even when they saw it. Hundreds of bison could go over the jump in one event, providing a substantial harvest for the hunters.

All of the animals were processed on-site, a painstaking process since every piece of the animal was used for meat, clothing, shelter, tools, and even toys. Archaeologists have uncovered significant prehistoric camps at the base of many jumps. In some places, bison bones continue to be found more than 15 feet beneath the surface.

Buffalo jumps were used by a great variety of Native American tribes until the 19th century, when the Spanish brought horses to North America and the Indians began hunting on horseback.

and double-track riders on 19 miles (31 km) of dirt, as well as walkers on graveled paths. Started in the 1990s, the trail winds along both sides of the Missouri River, past five waterfalls, including Black Eagle Falls, Rainbow Falls, Crooked Falls, and the renowned Great Falls of the Missouri below Ryan Dam. The trail houses 18 public art pieces and provides access to numerous parks, reservoirs, and other attractions, including the **Lewis and Clark National Historic Trail Interpretive Center** (4201 Giant Springs Rd., 406/727-8733, www.fs.usda.gov). A new addition is the River's Edge Skillz Trail, a 0.5-mile (0.8-km) gently flowing downhill trail where mountain bikers can learn or hone riding skills. There are 11 parking areas for easy access, and a trail map can be downloaded online (www.thetrail.org) or picked up at the **Great Falls Visitor Information Center** (15 Overlook Dr.).

Swimming

Starting in 2000, the city of Great Falls went to great lengths to renovate all of its municipal pools. The **Electric City Water Park** (100 River Dr. S., 406/771-1265, www.greatfallsmt.net, noon-6pm daily, Wed. family nights until 8pm, early June-late Aug., $5-12 adults, $3-10 children 2-17, free for children under 2) is a favorite with kids and includes surfing features, giant slides, a lazy river, and a toddler-friendly water-play structure. The facility boasts the largest heated outdoor swimming pool in the state, **Mitchell Pool,** and concessions are available on-site. Two other outdoor neighborhood pools in Great Falls with small splash parks are **Jaycee Pool** (4th St. and 26th Ave. NE, www.greatfallsmt.net, $3.50 adults, $2.50 children 3-17, free for children under 3) and **Water Tower Pool** (34th St. and 7th Ave. S., www.greatfallsmt.net, $3.50 adults, $2.50 children 3-17, free for children under 3). Both are open daily (1pm-5:45pm late June-mid-Aug.) depending upon weather.

Golf

Golfers not afraid of a stiff breeze can find a few places to play in Great Falls. There are three 18-hole public courses: **Eagle Falls Golf Club** (1025 25th St. N., 406/761-1078, www.playeaglefalls.com, $21 for 9 holes or $34 for 18 holes Mon.-Fri., $21 for 9 holes or $37 for 18 holes Sat.-Sun.), **Anaconda Hills Golf Course** (2315 E. Smelter Ave., Black Eagle, 406/761-8459, www.playanacondahills. com, $19 for 9 holes or $28 for 18 holes Mon.-Fri., $22 for 9 holes or $32 for 18 holes Sat.-Sun.), and **Hickory Swing Golf Course** (1100 American Ave., 406/452-9400, www. hickoryswinggolf.com, $15 for 9 holes or $25 for 18 holes). **Meadow Lark Country Club** (300 Country Club Blvd., 406/453-6531, www. meadowlarkclub.com) is a lovely old private club at the confluence of the Missouri and Sun Rivers that allows reciprocal fees ($90) for members of other private clubs.

★ Fishing on the Missouri River

With no shortage of world-class waters in the region, including the Missouri and Sun Rivers, there are endless opportunities to wet a line in and around Great Falls. Among the fish that can be found in local waters are northern pike, walleye, perch, catfish, large- and smallmouth bass, plus, of course, the venerable trout. For trout fishing on the Missouri, the 30-mile (48-km) stretch of river running from **Holter Dam to Cascade** is the most productive (and the most heavily fished!) for both rainbows and browns. Average size for rainbows is 14-18 inches (36-46 cm), and browns are generally a bit bigger. Blue-winged olive hatches start in late April and often last through June, and then hit again in the fall. The river's biggest hatch, the pale morning dun, can happen anytime from June well into August and gives skilled anglers a thrilling chance to catch very big fish on very small flies. Fish in these parts see a lot of flies and thus are wary of clumsy anglers.

North 40 Outfitters (which used to be Big R) is one of the West's best all-around ranch supply stores, selling everything from baby chicks and barbed wire to snakeskin cowboy boots, and also has a well-respected fly-fishing shop staffed by passionate local anglers. **North 40 Fly Shop** (4400 10th Ave. S., 406/761-7441, www.north40flyshop.com, 7am-7pm Mon.-Sat., 9am-5pm Sun.) is an excellent place to start for advice on local waters and current hatches. For a guided trip on local waters, try **Fin Fetchers Outfitters** (406/240-3715, www.finfetchers.com, from $425 half day, $525 full day for up to 2 people, $625 full-day jet boat for up to 2 people). Owner Brian Neilson was born in Bozeman and raised in Great Falls, and he knows as much as you could ever hope to learn about the sport.

A member of the Blackfeet tribe, Alger Swingley, owner of **Blackfeet Outfitters** (1720 10th Ave. S., 406/450-8420, www. blackfeetoutfitters.com) offers phenomenal guided fishing adventures ($425 half day for 1-2 people, $525 full day for 1-2 people) on the Missouri and on alpine lakes in the Badger Two Medicine area south of Glacier National Park. Each trip is custom planned, and all gear can be provided. Alger also guides visitors on **day hikes** ($275 adults, $137.50 children under 12), three-day/two-night **backcountry pack trips** either hiking ($850 adults, $425 children under 12) or on horseback ($1,250 adults), and **hunting expeditions** ($400-6,000) for everything from upland birds to elk, deer, moose, bighorn sheep, and mountain goats. Certified interpretive guides will teach you the Native names of mountains and valleys, plus flora, fauna, and the relationship between the Blackfeet tribe and the Badger Two Medicine area. Tipis, bedding, fishing gear, and hearty meals are provided. Premium combination trips are available too.

Skiing

Although Great Falls is not often considered a prime alpine skiing destination, with the Rocky Mountains in such close proximity, it is no surprise that there are in fact three developed ski areas within a couple of hours' drive.

High atop the Continental Divide, **Great Divide Ski Area** (7385 Belmont Dr., Marysville, 95 mi/153 km southwest of Great

Falls, 406/449-3746, www.skigd.com, full day $56 adults, $44 students and military, $26 children and seniors over 70, free for preschool children and beginner rope tow; partial-day tickets vary depending on arrival time) touts itself as "Montana's sunniest ski area" and offers an impressive 1,600 acres and 140 trails accessed by six lifts. The hill averages 180 inches (457 cm) of snow annually and offers night skiing.

Showdown Montana Ski Area (2850 US 89, south of Neihart, 1 hour southeast of Great Falls, 406/236-5522 or 800/433-0022, www.showdownmontana.com, $50 full day or $45 half day ages 18-69, $40 seniors, $45 college students with ID and military, $40 children 11-high school, $25 children 6-10 beginner chair only, free for children 5 and under) is one of Montana's oldest ski hills, in operation since 1936. In the middle of the not-so-little Little Belts, Showdown sees an average of 20 feet (240 in/610 cm) of powder annually. There are four lifts and 34 trails on 620 skiable acres at this family-friendly ski hill, with 40 percent of the runs geared to intermediates and 30 percent each aimed at beginners and experts. Mountain biking is also offered when the snow melts, with the primary season running mid-June through October.

Closest to Great Falls, **Teton Pass Ski Resort** (18 mi/29 km west of Choteau, 406/466-2209, www.tetonpassresort.com, $50 adults full day or $45 half day, $45 seniors, military, college students, and youth 7-17, $20 beginner lift, free for kids 6 and under) is a small ski area—three lifts and 36 trails geared largely to experts—with an enormous amount of snow (the area averages 25 ft/7.6 m of snow annually) and some pretty fierce terrain.

ENTERTAINMENT AND EVENTS
Nightlife

An authentic and unforgettable tiki bar in the heart of cowboy country, the **Sip-N-Dip Lounge** (17 17th St. S., 406/454-2141 or 800/332-9819, www.ohairemotorinn.com, 11:30am-midnight Sun.-Mon., 11:30am-2am Tues.-Sat.) is housed in the O'Haire Motor Inn. You can sip exotic cocktails as you gaze at the glass window into the pool behind the bar, watch exhibitionist guests, or, most evenings depending on the season, see mermaid- and (occasionally) merman-costumed performers (check Facebook or Instagram for current schedule). Daryl Hannah, the quintessential mermaid, has even taken a dip here. Sadly, Piano-Pat Spoonheim—who had been singing covers of Elvis, Neil Diamond, and other legendary crooners for nearly 60 years— passed away in 2021. She added to the bar's legendary status. Once voted the best bar on the planet by *GQ* magazine and recognized as one of the world's best bars by *Condé Nast Traveler,* this kitschy, cool watering hole should not be missed.

Another one-in-a-million bar in Great Falls is the **Montana Cowboys Association Museum & Bar** (311 3rd St. NW, 406/453-0651, www.cowboysbarmca.com, 8am-2am daily). Whether this is a bar in a museum or a museum in a bar is open to debate, but either way there is no shortage of cool old stuff to look at while you sip something frosty. An authentic log cabin built in 1941, it boasts two fireplaces and hundreds of artifacts from the Old West, including a sizable gun collection, Charlie Russell's well-worn boots, a rare photo of Jeremiah "Liver-Eating" Johnson, and a handsome collection of saddles. An evening spent bellied up to the bar is bound to be unforgettable. Bring some friends; the bar closes earlier when the number of guests drops below five.

The Arts
GREAT FALLS SYMPHONY

The **Great Falls Symphony** (venues vary, 406/453-4102, www.gfsymphony.org) is a dynamic organization that has been in existence for more than half a century, offering marvelous year-round entertainment in the form of classical symphonic masterpieces and contemporary compositions, chamber music, a youth orchestra, a symphonic choir, and ballet. For an evening of refined culture in the heart of cowboy country, the symphony is a rare treat. Larger performances are held at the **Mansfield Theater** (2 Park Dr. S.) in the lovely 1930s Great Falls Civic Center.

Festivals and Events
WESTERN ART WEEK

With major art-related events held across Great Falls in mid-March, **Western Art Week** puts Great Falls on the map of top destinations for serious Western art collectors. In addition to two major auctions— **Out West Art Show** (1700 Fox Farm Rd., 406/899-2958, www.outwestartshow.com) and **March in Montana** (1411 10th Ave. S., 307/635-0019, www.marchinmontana.com)— the weekend offers an impressive collection of fine art by living and deceased masters, as well as cowboy and Native American collectibles. Considered *the* social event of the year for lovers of Western art, the celebration takes over several hotels, where artists and art dealers set up mini galleries and provide a rare opportunity for collectors to mingle with the artists they collect. Lectures, tours, artist demonstrations, parties, and a quick draw event are scheduled throughout the week. Another major art auction, **The Russell: The Sale to Benefit the C. M. Russell Museum** (400 13th St. N., 406/727-8787, www.cmrussell. org), shifted in 2021 from the March date to late August. The museum plans to continue the event each August.

LEWIS AND CLARK FESTIVAL

Since 1989, Great Falls has been celebrating the Corps of Discovery's 1806 month-long stay in the city. The **Lewis and Clark Festival** (event venues vary, many held at Gibson Park on the River's Edge Trail, 406/452-5661, www. lewisandclarkfoundation.org) takes place each year in June or July. For a full weekend, history comes alive in various locations around the city. Highlighting events from Lewis and Clark's experience in Great Falls, the festival is as much about education as it is about fun. There are children's activities such as a discovery camp and storytelling,

float trips, tours of Lewis and Clark sites, and presentations by Native American groups. Actors help re-create daily life from this period with dramatic readings and plays, and other attractions include a traditional arts and crafts show, concerts, food, nature outings, and exhibits.

MONTANA STATE FAIR

The **Montana State Fair** (Montana ExpoPark, 400 3rd St. NW, 406/727-8900, www.goexpopark.com, general admission $8 adults 18-59, $5 youth 6-17) takes place in Great Falls around the end of July and into August. It is one of Montana's largest parties and a true celebration of the state's unique history and culture. It includes a five-day rodeo (the largest in the state), horse racing, carnival rides, and big-name entertainment at the Montana ExpoPark. There are more than 250 vendor booths selling arts, crafts, clothes, music, and plenty of food as well as local, national, and international exhibits.

GREAT FALLS ORIGINAL FARMERS' MARKET

During summer, wander over to the **Great Falls Original Farmers' Market** (Civic Center Park, 2 Park Dr. S., www. farmersmarketgf.com, 7:45am-noon Sat. June-Sept.), which was started in 1982 by some of the local Hutterite colonists. Claiming to be the largest farmers market in the state, more than 150 vendors gather to sell their goods, and you'll find the best homegrown fruits and vegetables, delicious jams, tasty baked goods, and handmade gifts and crafts. Pony rides are available for the little ones, and musicians wander among the stalls to keep you entertained.

SHOPPING

Unique specialty stores line either side of Central Avenue in downtown Great Falls. You can start at the beginning of Central Avenue at Park Drive and stroll down the avenue. If you have a sweet tooth, don't miss **Candy Masterpiece** (120 Central Ave.,

406/727-5955, www.candymasterpiece.com, 9:30am-5:30pm Tues.-Sat.). Friendly staff are extremely generous with samples, and you'll find a delicious array of sweets, from childhood favorites straight off the candy rack to mouthwatering handmade chocolates. There are 30 different types of fudge: Try the Heavenly Goo (chocolate with marshmallow and caramel) or, for the more adventurous, jalapeño fudge. Leaving Montana without a bag of huckleberry saltwater taffy is a mistake.

Next door to the candy store is the fun and funky **Planet Earth** (116 Central Ave., 406/761-7000, 10am-5pm Tues.-Sat.), a shop full of eclectic gifts. Browse the assortment of cards, accessories, and jewelry. It also has a fragrance bar where you can create your own scent from essential oils and add it to specific bath or skin-care products. **The Farmer's Daughter Fibers** (320 Central Ave., 406/890-8809, www.thefarmersdaughterfibers.com, 10am-5pm Tues., Thurs., and Fri., 10am-8pm Wed., 10am-3pm Sat.) is a gorgeous yarn store that will delight even those who don't know how to knit. Yet! There are classes and workshops, and the owners started a nonprofit in 2020 called Sisters United that aims to empower Indigenous women and girls.

For a selection of just about everything for body and home—including seasonal decor, furniture, women's clothing, jewelry, handbags, candles, wall art, and more—visit **Real Deals on Home Décor & Boutique** (117 Park Dr. S., 406/315-1154, www.realdeals. net, 10am-5pm Mon.-Sat.), where the inventory changes weekly. **Montana Mosaic** (525 Central Ave., 406/761-3226, 10am-5:30pm Mon.-Thurs., 10am-6pm Fri., 9am-5pm Sat.) is an art gallery with a great selection of Montana-made gifts and works in various media by local artists.

FOOD

One of Great Falls' most well-known restaurants is a local pizza joint, **Howard's Pizza** (713 1st Ave. N., 406/453-1212, www. howardspizzamt.com, 4pm-midnight daily, $12-24), started in 1959. Much beloved for its signature thin crust, famous sauce, and homemade ranch dressing, four locations citywide are now available for dining in, takeout, or delivery.

Another iconic restaurant in Great Falls is **Borrie's** (1800 Smelter Ave., 406/761-0300, www.borriesrestaurant.com, 5pm-9:30pm Mon.-Thurs., 4:30pm-10pm Fri., 4pm-10pm Sat., 4pm-9pm Sun., $9.50-44), an old-school supper club with excellent steaks, seafood specials (including Australian lobster), and legendary homemade pasta sauce and ravioli. The atmosphere leaves something to be desired, but this is a classic Montana dining experience with great specials several nights a week.

Though it has changed names and owners many times over the decades, the **Roadhouse Diner** (613 15th St. N., 406/788-8839, www. roadhousegf.com, 11am-8pm Wed.-Sat., last seating at 7:30pm, 9am-2pm Sun., $11-15) is the real deal when it comes to burgers and fries. It has inventive, and strangely delicious, options like the Bacon Mac-N-Cheeseburger and PB&J Burger—which pairs bacon, cheddar, peanut butter, and grape jelly—but the basics are plenty good. Try the breakfast burrito and the hand-cut fries. A true mom-and-pop outfit, the Roadhouse gets as much of its ingredients as possible locally and makes most everything from scratch. It's no wonder they win best burger in just about every contest they enter.

Another Montana success story, **Great Harvest Bread Company** (515 1st Ave. N., 406/452-6941, www.greatharvestgreatfalls. com, 6am-5pm Mon.-Fri., 6am-4pm Sat., $7-10) is a national chain that started in Great Falls in 1976. Its motto starts, "Be loose and have fun," and the food follows suit with inventive offerings that change daily and range from molasses whole wheat to white chocolate cherry bread and the more savory Asiago sun-dried tomato sourdough bread. The menu revolves around freshly baked bread and is filled with delicious hot and cold sandwiches. And the cinnamon rolls, muffins, and "toe-curling brownies" will leave you begging for mercy. For a delicious lunch made from locally grown ingredients, try **Harvest Craft Kitchen** (220 Central Ave., 406/770-0784, 11am-2pm Mon.-Thurs., 11am-3pm Fri., $11-13). The eclectic menu includes Cubanos, Philly Italian pork, *banh mi,* gourmet grilled cheese, salads, and burgers.

Established in 2013, and an excellent addition to downtown Great Falls, is **Mighty Mo Brewing Company** (412 Central Ave., 406/952-0342, www.mightymobrewing.com, 11am-9pm Mon.-Thurs., 11am-10pm Fri.-Sat., lunch $8-10, dinner $10-21). Housed in a beautifully refurbished historical building, this microbrewery serves fine beer with perfectly paired food—wings, pizza, nachos, breadsticks, pretzels, and the like. On Monday nights, 5pm-8pm, Mighty Mo donates $1 from every pint they sell to the featured nonprofit of the night.

For small plates and craft cocktails, **Enbär** (8 5th St. S., 406/952-1520, 4pm-1am daily, brunch 11am-1pm Sat.-Sun., $9-26) is the place. From The Juniper, with Montgomery Distillery gin, fresh blueberries, and house-made mint simple syrup and lime juice, to the Spotted Apple with Spotted Bear tequila, apple cider, lime, and huckleberry, their concoctions are elegant to say the least. They also serve steak, fish tacos, pasta, salmon, and a delicious assortment of tapas. Don't miss the **Enbär fries.**

Dante's Creative Cuisine (1325 8th Ave. N., 406/453-9599, noon-8pm Mon.-Thurs., 11:30am-9pm Fri.-Sat., lunch $13-16, dinner $19-33) is set in a beautiful old brick iron-works building. It's white linens all the way with Italian pasta, seafood, and steak. The Thursday night lobster tail is a local favorite at this decidedly upscale establishment.

Inviting **5th & Wine** (214 5th St., 406/761-9463, www.fifthandwine.com, wine shop and deli 11am-6pm Tues.-Sat., lunch 11am-3pm Tues.-Sat., dinner by reservation only 5:30pm or 7:30pm Wed.-Fri., lunch $13-17, pre-fixe 4-course dinner $65-85 pp) is a find. Part wine shop, part deli, and part restaurant, this place serves delicious meals. The four-course pre-fixe dinners (you choose from three or four choices for every course) are out of this world, with courses like Brussels sprout and bacon salad, lightly spiced candied pork belly bites, roasted peach bruschetta, rib eye, and miso-glazed halibut.

For an excellent cup of coffee and a quick bite, Great Falls has cute coffee shops. Two of the locally owned best are the hip **Al Banco** (202 2nd St., 406/952-0624, www.albanco406.com, 7am-4pm Mon.-Fri., 9am-1pm Sat., breakfast $5-7, lunch $5.50-10), with healthy quinoa bowls, avocado toast, and gourmet salami sandwiches; and the homey and gorgeous **Crooked Tree Coffee and Cakes** (501 1st Ave. N., 406/315-1221, www.crookedtreecoffeeandcakes, 7am-4pm Mon.-Fri., 8am-2pm Sat.-Sun., $2.50-6.50), started by two sisters who love coffee and all that goes with it, including simple breakfast sandwiches and an incredible assortment of treats.

ACCOMMODATIONS

If you are looking for a memorable motel stay in downtown Great Falls, look no further than the ★ **O'Haire Motor Inn** (17 7th St. S., 406/454-2141 or 800/332-9819, $90-160), with 68 pet-friendly guest rooms, an indoor pool, indoor parking, and free Wi-Fi. Its full-service restaurant, **Clark and Lewie's** (7am-9pm Mon.-Thurs., 7am-10pm Fri.-Sat., 7am-8pm Sun., breakfast $7-14, lunch and dinner $12-25), offers up hearty meals—from burgers and barbecue to steak, Mexican, sandwiches, and pasta—and even room service. The biggest draw at the inn is its authentic and unforgettable tiki bar, the Sip-N-Dip Lounge.

The upscale **Hotel Arvon** (118 1st Ave. S., 406/952-1101, www.hotelarvon.com, $114-174) is a 33-room boutique hotel with a coffee shop, wine bar, restaurant, and pub in the city's oldest commercial building. There are standard king and queen rooms, plus suites, gorgeous lofts, and even cooking suites.

Another option just south of downtown is **La Quinta Inn & Suites** (600 River Dr.

S., 406/761-2600 or 800/531-5900, www. laquintagreatfalls.com, $102-243), built in 2000 on the banks of the Missouri River. Ask for a room with a view of the river. The hotel is styled as a Western lodge, with a fireplace in the lobby, as well as an indoor pool and a fitness center. The guest rooms are large and comfortable with amenities such as high-speed Internet, microwaves, and fridges, and continental breakfast is included.

Along the River's Edge Trail, the spacious Staybridge Suites (201 3rd St. NW, 406/761-4903 or 877/238-8889, www.staybridgesuites.com/greatfallsmt, $108-236) is a pet-friendly, all-suite hotel offering fully equipped kitchens, free Wi-Fi, a 24-hour business center, and an indoor pool.

Among the chain hotel offerings in town, the Best Western Heritage Inn (1700 Fox Farm Rd., 406/761-1900, www.bestwestern.com, $86-127) offers 231 rooms plus an indoor swimming pool, fitness center, restaurant, casino, and sports bar. Other comfortable chain hotels in Great Falls include Comfort Inn & Suites (1801 Market Place Dr., 406/455-1000, www.choicehotels.com, from $106), the pet-friendly Days Inn (101 14th Ave. NW, 406/727-6565, www.daysinngreatfalls.com, $69-154), and the Hilton Garden Inn (2520 14th St. SW, 406/452-1000, http://greatfalls.hgi.com, $101-356), which is next to several restaurants, a shopping mall, and a 10-screen movie theater. More budget-friendly options include Motel 6 (2 Treasure State Dr., 406/453-1602, www.motel6.com, $71-91) and Super 8 by Wyndham (1214 13th St. S., 406/564-1976, www.wyndhamhotels.com, $45-78).

INFORMATION AND SERVICES

Most services are conveniently located in a walkable downtown area. The Great Falls Chamber of Commerce (100 1st Ave. N., 406/761-4434, www.greatfallschamber.org, 8am-5pm Mon.-Fri.) and Great Falls Visitor Information Center (15 Overlook Dr., 406/771-0885, www.visitgreatfallsmontana.org, 9am-4pm Mon.-Fri., 10am-2pm Sat.-Sun. Oct.-Apr., 9am-6pm Mon.-Fri., 10am-4pm Sat.-Sun. May-Sept.), under the huge U.S. flag in Overlook Park, both have city brochures, books, Made in Montana goods for sale, and friendly, knowledgeable volunteers.

The main post office (215 1st Ave. N., 406/771-2160, 8:30am-5:30pm Mon.-Fri., 10am-1pm Sat.) is at 1st Avenue and 2nd Street.

The public library (301 2nd Ave. N., 406/453-0349, www.greatfallslibrary.org, 10am-8pm Tues.-Thurs., 10am-6pm Fri.-Sat., noon-6pm Mon.) is just two blocks from the post office and offers computers and free Internet access.

Falls Cleaners & Laundry Center (614 9th St. S., 406/453-9361, 8am-9pm daily) offers same-day laundry service, dry-cleaning service, and coin-op machines to do it yourself.

Benefis Health Systems (1102 26th St. S., 406/455-5000, www.benefis.org) is a first-class hospital with a 24-hour emergency room as well as a walk-in clinic (1401 25th St. S., 406/731-8300, 7am-8pm Mon.-Fri., 9am-6:30pm Sat.-Sun.) for immediate medical care.

TRANSPORTATION
Getting There

The Great Falls International Airport (GTF, 2800 Terminal Dr., 406/727-3404, www.flygtf.com) is southwest of the city. It is served by Alaska Airlines, Allegiant, Delta, and United. The airport's on-site car-rental companies are Alamo, Avis, Enterprise, Hertz, National, and Budget.

Greyhound Bus Lines offers service to other major towns and cities in Montana.

Great Falls is situated directly off I-15, allowing easy access by car. It is 218 miles (355 km) northwest of Billings, 186 miles (300 km) north of Bozeman, 155 miles (250 km) northeast of Butte, and approximately 90 miles (145 km) from Helena (to the south) or Shelby (to the north).

Getting Around

Diamond Cab (406/453-3241) serves the Great Falls area and will pick you up from the airport (look for the direct phone in the terminal) or shuttle you around town.

Blacked Out 406 Limo & 24/7 Taxi Service (406/781-5218) is another option for airport transfers, regular taxi service, or crazy fancy limousine SUVs, buses, and the like.

Rocky Mountain Front

Spanning more than 100 miles (161 km) from Montana into Canada, the Rocky Mountain Front is the startling merger of prairie and mountain—in places the Rockies rise 4,000-5,000 feet (1,200-1,500 m). It is one of the few places in the Lower 48 where grizzly bears still wander onto the plains, much as they did when Lewis and Clark traveled the region. There is a strong cowboy culture in Choteau and a rich Native American culture in Browning. The small agricultural towns have rugged mountain wilderness just a stone's throw away. It is rare to be able to appreciate natural diversity, undistracted by humankind's homogenous development.

The Rocky Mountain Front is also the gateway into the **Bob Marshall Wilderness Complex**, which comprises three wilderness areas totaling more than 1.5 million acres of the remotest wilderness in the Lower 48. The complex runs 60 miles (97 km) north to south along the Continental Divide. The region, named for forester, wilderness preservationist, and Wilderness Society cofounder Bob Marshall, teems with wildlife and stunning topography. The Chinese Wall, for example, a rock escarpment that averages 1,000 feet (305 m) in height, follows the Continental Divide for 22 miles (35 km). For obvious reasons, including its 1,700 miles (2,700 km) of trails, this area is a mecca for outdoors enthusiasts.

BROWNING

Agency headquarters for the Blackfeet Indian Reservation, home to Montana's largest tribe, Browning (pop. 940, elev. 4,377 ft/1,334 m) has retained much of the culture of the Blackfeet people. The setting is spectacular, at the eastern edge of Glacier National Park, but the town doesn't offer anything in the way of striking architecture or high-end hotels. What it does offer, though, is an exceptional opportunity to learn about and experience Blackfeet culture. In addition to the significant Museum of the Plains Indian, there are annual events open to visitors, including North American Indian Days, as well as tours given by well-versed local guides.

Sights

Just west of Browning at the junction of US 2 and US 89 is the **Museum of the Plains Indian** (19 Museum Loop, 406/338-2230, www.doi.gov/iacb/museum-plains-indian, 9am-4:45pm Tues.-Sat. June-Sept., 10am-4:30pm daily Oct.-May, $5 adults, $4 seniors 65 and over, $1 children 6-16 June-Sept., free Oct.-May). The museum exhibits the arts and crafts of the Northern Plains Indians. The permanent collection highlights the diversity of tribal arts and displays artifacts from everyday life, including clothing, weapons, toys, and household implements. Two galleries are dedicated to showcasing contemporary Native American artists. During summer, painted tipis are assembled on the grounds.

Owned by Blackfeet tribe member Alger Swingley, **Blackfeet Tours** (406/450-8420, www.blackfeettours.com) offers authentic all-inclusive Native American culture tours—seeing the country around the reservation, learning the Native names for mountains and valleys, plus flora and fauna—in a variety of ways. You could hike the Badger Two Medicine area with a certified interpretive guide (8 hours, from $275) or do a three-day/

Powwow Etiquette

Attending a powwow on one of the Indian reservations in Montana offers an extraordinary opportunity to learn about and appreciate Native culture and traditions. While most powwows are open to any visitors and spectators, there are some things to know to be properly respectful of the people and events.

- Tipis and wall tents are often used to house powwow participants and are referred to locally as "campgrounds." Calling a powwow a "fair" or the campground "fairgrounds" can be insulting.

- Many powwows have an "intertribal dance" where everyone can mingle and greet one another. The dancers wear regalia or traditional dress, not costumes. These clothes are painstakingly handmade using the finest materials and detail, and are often passed down through the generations. Be sure not to use the word "costume" when referring to these works of art.

- When the honor songs are being performed—such as the flag song during grand entry—men and women should stand and pay their respects to the flag as they would at any event in the United States or Canada, by removing their hats (except for the very elderly) and not talking. Photos should not be taken during honor or prayer songs.

- Dancing contests are meant to be healthy, fun, and inspiring. Visitors should enjoy the celebration; when in doubt, look around to see what other spectators are doing. When you see people standing or removing their hats, follow their lead.

two-night backcountry pack trip either hiking ($850 adults, $425 children under 12) or on horseback ($1,250 adults) into the mountains south of Glacier. Also owned by Swingley, the sister company of Blackfeet Tours, **Blackfeet Outfitters** (1720 10th Ave. S., 406-450-8420, www.blackfeetoutfitters.com) offers **guided fishing adventures** ($425 half day 1-2 people, $525 full day 1-2 people) on the Missouri and on alpine lakes in the Badger Two Medicine area south of Glacier National Park. Hunting expeditions ($400-6,000) for everything from upland birds to elk, deer, moose, bighorn sheep, and mountain goats are also offered.

Entertainment and Events

Held annually the second week in July for four days, the **North American Indian Days** (406-338-7406 ext. 2353, www.blackfeetnation.com) is an excellent powwow and signature celebration in Browning, giving insight into the Blackfeet culture and traditions. Events include contest dancing, games, sporting events, horse relay races, drum contests, and plenty of food.

Set in the shadow of Heart Butte, known among Blackfeet as Moskitsipahpi-istuki, **Heart Butte Indian Days** (406-338-7521 or 406-338-7406 ext. 2353, www.facebook.com/HBNDNDays) is held in one of the oldest traditional communities on the Blackfeet Indian Reservation. It's a four-day celebration, held usually in the middle of August, and features dancing and drumming contests, stickgame tournaments, parades, vendors, and plenty of food.

Shopping

In business since 1946, **Faught's Blackfeet Trading Post** (133 W. Central Ave., 406-338-2275, www.theblackfeettradingpost.com, 9:30am-5:30pm Tues.-Fri., 10am-3pm Sat.) is the real deal, a full-service clothing store, and also the best place to find specialty Native-made crafts and lotions, books, beading supplies, and souvenirs.

Another good bet for local crafts and souvenirs is **Western Curios** (129 Central Ave. E., 406-338-2815, www.westerncurios.com, 9am-7pm daily in summer), which is chock-a-block with every little thing you could think of, from postcards and jewelry to T-shirts and knickknacks.

Food

Right in town, across from the Museum of the Plains Indian, the **Junction Café** (330 W. Central Ave., 406/338-2386, 8am-2pm Mon.-Fri., $3-12.50) is locally owned and serves up hearty breakfasts of corned beef hash, breakfast burritos, and biscuits and gravy, as well as hamburgers and steaks. Try the fry bread! With usually only one server and a local clientele, the restaurant is very friendly. Don't be surprised if a neighboring diner offers to refill your coffee cup.

Another very friendly local restaurant serving everything from burgers to Indian tacos is **Nation's Burger Station** (205 Central Ave., 406/338-2422, www.nationsburgerstation.com, 10:30am-9:30pm Mon.-Fri., 10:30am-10:30pm Sat.-Sun. May-mid-Aug., 11am-8:30pm Mon.-Sat. mid-Aug.-Apr., $7-15). In addition to the aforementioned, Nation's Burger Station serves salads and wraps, plus an impressive menu of frozen treats including root beer floats, slushies, and snow cones. On a hot day, this is the place.

At **Smokin' Blackfeet BBQ** (129 1st Ave. SW, 406/845-2027, noon-6pm Mon.-Fri. or until the meat is gone, $6-13), Virgelle slow smokes everything from brisket to ribs for bone-sucking goodness. It's a tiny little spot, best for takeout or eating outside.

For great coffee and quick bites, try **Glacier Grind Coffee House** (inside Glacier Peaks Hotel & Casino, 22 US 89 N., 406/338-4678, www.glacierpeakscasino.com/glacier-grind, 7am-10pm Mon.-Fri., 8am-10pm Sat.-Sun.). Also inside the Glacier Peaks Hotel & Casino, the **Jackpot Restaurant** (22 US 89 N., 406/338-2274 or 877/238-9946, www.glacierpeakscasino.com, 11am-10pm daily, $8-16) serves three meals a day, including soups and salads, burgers, sandwiches, chicken fried steak, Indian tacos, and more.

Accommodations

By far the largest and newest hotel in Browning is the **Glacier Peaks Hotel & Casino** (22 US 89 N., 406/338-2400, www.glacierpeakscasino.com, $145-350), which has comfortable, well-appointed non-smoking rooms with mini fridges, flat-screen TVs, microwaves, and free high-speed Internet. Amenities include a complimentary hot breakfast buffet, a fitness area, heated indoor pool, and guest laundry area.

Besides the hotel and casino, Browning itself doesn't offer a lot in the way of accommodations; the best bets are toward Glacier National Park. Just 9.5 miles (15.3 km) west of Browning is the comfortable and friendly **Aspenwood Resort** (US 89, 406/338-3009, mid-May-early Oct., suites $196-250), ideally located close to Glacier National Park between Browning and St. Mary. There are two rooms and a two-room suite in the rustic lodge, in addition to RV sites ($50), a campground ($25), and a restaurant that is open from Memorial Day to Labor Day.

Information

The Central Montana Tourism Office (800/527-5348 or 406/761-5036, www.centralmontana.com) is in Great Falls is open year-round but reachable solely online and over the telephone. Their website is excellent.

Transportation

Browning is 123 miles (198 km) northwest of Great Falls on US 89.

CHOTEAU AND AUGUSTA

Established with a post office under the name Old Agency in 1875, Choteau (pop. 1,829, elev. 3,819 ft/1,164 m) is one of the region's oldest active towns. The name was changed in 1882 to honor Pierre Chouteau, president of the American Fur Company and the man responsible for bringing the first steamboat up the Missouri River. This ranching town at the edge of the Rockies is a dinosaur lover's dream, with paleontological museums and sites galore. It also provides unparalleled access to some of the state's most incredible wilderness areas. In addition to its obvious attractions, Choteau is simply a charming Montana town—small, friendly, and ideally situated for visitors.

Just under 30 miles (48 km) southwest of Choteau is the wonderful little town of Augusta (pop. 318, elev. 4,068 ft/1,240 m), another gateway to the Bob Marshall and Scapegoat wilderness areas. The town—with classic Western storefronts and warm hospitality—hosts the state's oldest and biggest one-day rodeo, known as the "Wildest One Day Show on Earth," the last Sunday in June.

Sights

The remains of the most famous inhabitants of Egg Mountain (US 287, between mileposts 57 and 58) were discovered in 1978 by Marion Trexler Brandvold, who started The Rock Shop in Bynum with her first husband, and was still running it with her second husband at 96 years old. Brandvold's findings were studied extensively by dinosaur guru Jack Horner. The discovery has yielded the largest collection of dinosaur eggs, embryos, and baby skeletons in the Western Hemisphere. The findings entirely changed our notion of how dinosaurs raised their young. The baby remains in 14 nests were found alongside an enormous number of adult remains, which scientists determined was a monumental herd of maiasaura (good mother reptile) along with a lesser number of troodons killed in a catastrophic event like a volcanic eruption or a hurricane. Egg Mountain is one of 16 sites in Montana deemed "geological wonders" by a team of historians, geologists, and paleontologists. An interpretive sign on US 287 provides information about the site. There is also a small parking area, and visitors are welcome to wander the site, which is more a hill than a mountain. Naturalist guides occasionally offer narrated tours of the area; for more information contact the Montana Dinosaur Center in Bynum (800/238-6873) or Museum of the Rockies in Bozeman (406/994-2251).

At the north end of Choteau, the Old Trail Museum (823 N. Main St., Choteau, 406/466-5332, www.mtdinotrail.org/old-trail-museum, 9am-5pm daily Memorial Day-Labor Day, $2, children under 3 are free) celebrates both the natural and cultural history of the Rocky Mountain Front. In the Dinosaurs of the Two Medicine paleontology gallery, there are dinosaur bones and fossils aplenty, along with a good maiasaura exhibit. Other interesting local history exhibits include Native American artifacts collected by A. B. Guthrie Jr. and details of Choteau's last hanging.

Almost 14 miles (22 km) north of Choteau in Bynum, The Montana Dinosaur Center (120 2nd Ave. S., Bynum, 800/238-6873 or 406/469-2211, www.tmdinosaur.org, 9am-6pm daily Memorial Day-Labor Day, 10am-5pm daily spring and fall, $5 adults 13-54, $4 seniors over 55, $3 children 4-12, free ages 3 and under), formerly the Two Medicine Dinosaur Center, is a great little museum with paleontology displays on the babies of Egg Mountain and a variety of dinosaur, invertebrate, and plant fossils, as well as cultural artifacts from the region. Perhaps best of all, the museum offers dinosaur digs, from a half day to a two-week paleo training course. The staff are incredibly friendly—if you can visit on the day of their Christmas party, don't miss it—and the little gift shop is wonderful. For paleo fanatics, a visit here should be a priority.

Between Choteau and Fairfield off US 89 is Freezeout Lake (406/467-2646, www.fwp.mt.gov, mid-Mar.-autumn), a birder's paradise and for many Montanans the best place to gauge the imminent arrival of an ever-elusive spring. The scenic lake is a staging area for hundreds of thousands of snow geese and thousands of tundra swans on their way north. The snow geese typically start arriving at Freezeout in mid-March, but peak days can happen almost anytime until mid-April. As with most wildlife, dawn and dusk offer the best viewing opportunities. Other birds passing through the area include raptors and upland game birds in winter, waterfowl in spring and fall, and shorebirds in summer.

The interior roads have ample parking and pullouts, and are open to vehicles mid-March to the beginning of waterfowl season.

Entertainment and Events

Held annually the last Sunday in June, the **Augusta American Legion Rodeo and Parade** (American Legion Rodeo Grounds, Augusta, 406/562-3477, www.augustamontana.com) is the biggest and oldest one-day rodeo in the state. Since 1936, this small town has put on an amazing show with a parade, a Professional Rodeo Cowboys Association-sanctioned rodeo complete with bull riding, and a huge party atmosphere.

Small towns along the Front, or anywhere across the state really, tend to have some wonderful, family-friendly events that will not be like anything you know from home. Make a point of attending some of them to better understand the history and culture of this rare place. In Dupuyer, for example, which is 34 miles (55 km) north of Choteau on US 89, visitors can attend **Doig Day** (late June) in celebration of famed writer and Montana son Ivan Doig. And in early August in Dupuyer, **Grizzly Day** (406/472-3272) celebrates the big bear with a pancake breakfast, an elaborate parade, duck race, human foosball, wagon rides, vendors, chicken bingo, live music, and more.

Shopping

Shopping in small towns is often more about the experience than the items, although visitors will do well with both around Choteau. **Choteau Arts Studio & Gallery** (204 Main Ave. N., Choteau, 406/466-2800, www.choteauarts.org, 10am-5:30pm Wed.-Fri., 10am-12:30pm Sat.) is a beautiful shop that promotes all forms of art and beauty throughout the community with events and workshops. They also have a lovely collection of works in varied media by local and regional artists. Magnificent and affordable surprises can be found at **Full Circle Thrift Shop** (38 Main Ave. N., Choteau, 406/466-2618, 10am-3pm Mon.-Fri.), which sells furniture, clothing, housewares, ski gear, and more. In the spirit of old general stores that had to carry a little bit of almost everything, **Dupuyer Cache** (307 Montana St., Dupuyer, 406/472-3272, 11am-5pm Tues.-Sat.) is a unique place filled with groceries, locally grown merino wool and woolen goods, specialty books, local art and crafts, and more.

One of the best gift shops in the state is **Latigo and Lace** (122 Main St., Augusta, 406/562-3665, 10am-5pm Wed.-Sun. Mar., 10am-6pm Tues.-Sun. Apr., 10am-6:30pm daily May-Dec.), which has books, clothing, an espresso bar, and fantastic local art including ceramics, photography, paintings, jewelry, rugs, baskets, and beadwork. Just up the street, **Allen's Manix Store** (10 Main St., Augusta, 406/562-3333, 7:30am-7:30pm daily Jan.-May and Sept.-Dec., 7am-8pm daily June-Aug.) is a classic country store with everything from groceries and meats to hunting and fishing licenses, sporting goods, and gifts. The staff are friendly and helpful, and just listening to the chatter as you wait in line to check out makes you feel like you know this place a little bit.

Who doesn't love a good rock shop? **Trex Agate Shop** (5500 US 89, Bynum, 406/469-2314, www.trexagateshop.com, 9am-5pm Sun.-Fri. May-Dec. 21, by appointment Dec. 22-April) is the real deal, a rock and gift shop specializing in unique rocks, crystals, fossils, turquoise, and jewelry. The shop was established in 1937 by Cliff and Marion Trexler. Marion, who married John Brandvold in 1965, discovered the first baby dinosaur fossils in North America, at Egg Mountain, in 1978.

Food

Choteau has some good options for regional cuisine. The **Log Cabin Cafe** (102 Main Ave. N., Choteau, 406/466-2888, 11am-9pm Wed.-Sat., 7am-9pm Sun., $6-15) is precisely what you would expect from its name: a cozy spot with hearty servings of good old-fashioned comfort food. The burgers are great, but so are the salads, soups, and breakfast dishes. Don't miss the desserts!

For a quick, fresh lunch or snack, **Outpost Deli** (824 Main Ave. N., Choteau, 406/466-5330, 11am-5pm Thurs.-Sun. summer, 7am-2pm Sun. and 6am-3pm Mon., Tues., Thurs., Fri. winter, $4-8) offers soups, sandwiches, lettuce wraps, smoothies, and a mouthwatering assortment of freshly baked goodies. From the maple sticks and blueberry scones to the ham-and-cheese breakfast rolls and deli sandwiches, **Bylers Bakery** (425 Main Ave. S., Choteau, 406/466-9900, 6am-2pm Wed.-Fri., 6am-noon Sat., $2-8) is a great little coffee shop and café open for breakfast and lunch. For folks who like hot dogs (or bad wiener jokes), look for **The Dirty Wiener** food truck (www.facebook.com/thedirtywiener), which shows up at events around town serving their excellent loaded hot dogs.

In Augusta, the **Buckhorn Bar** (120 Main St., Augusta, 406/562-3344, 7am-2am daily, $9-23) is a great place for a burger and a microbrew and to soak in the scene, particularly during hunting season.

Accommodations

Sadly, most of the small, mom-and-pop motels in Choteau have gone the way of the dinosaur. The best hotel in town today is the relatively new **Stage Stop Inn** (1005 Main Ave. N., Choteau, 406/446-5900, www.stagestopinn.com, $82-150), which is spacious, comfortable, and clean but without any of the charm of days gone by.

The beloved Bunkhouse in Augusta burned down, leaving a big hole in the community. There is a charming old guest ranch 28 miles (45 km) west of Choteau. The **Deep Canyon Guest Ranch** (2055 Teton Canyon Rd., 406/466-2044, www.deepcanyonguestranch.com, from $2,477 weekly pp double occupancy, $1,595 children under 12) is located in the heart of Teton Canyon with easy access to the Bob Marshall Wilderness Complex. Some of the buildings date back to the 1920s, but others were constructed in the 1980s.

Available daily activities include horseback riding, fishing, and hiking.

Another favorite family-friendly guest ranch west of Augusta is the **Triple J Wilderness Ranch** (80 Mortimer Rd., 406/562-3653, www.triplejranch.com, $2,350 weekly pp double occupancy all-inclusive, $2,200 kids 13-17, $2,100 children 6-12), tucked in the magnificent Sun River Canyon above Gibson Lake. In addition to all-inclusive vacations catering to riders, hikers, and fishers, the Triple J offers fantastic kids' programs and awesome pack trips in the Bob Marshall Wilderness Complex. Early June-late September, the ranch offers six-day stays with discounts for children and teens. Shorter stays may be available in June and September.

Information

The **Choteau Chamber of Commerce** (815 Main Ave. N., 406/466-5316 or 800/823-3866, www.choteauchamber.com, 10am-4pm Mon.-Fri. Memorial Day-Labor Day) has office hours in summer. The **Augusta Chamber of Commerce** (www.augustamontana.com) has a great website with information on the area, but no physical presence.

Transportation

Choteau is 52 miles (84 km) northwest of Great Falls along US 89. Augusta is 26 miles (42 km) southwest of Choteau on US 287.

★ BOB MARSHALL WILDERNESS COMPLEX

With more than 1.5 million acres, the Bob Marshall Wilderness Complex is one of the largest and remotest wilderness areas in the Lower 48. The mountains soar above 9,000 feet (2,700 m), and the Continental Divide splits the region into several headwater drainage areas. Numerous lakes and pristine trout-laden rivers are here along with copious animals, including elk, white-tailed and mule deer, gray wolves, Canada lynx, bobcats, bighorn sheep, mountain goats, wolverines, and cougars. The area was named for its

first and perhaps most vociferous champion, Bob Marshall, a forester, author, explorer, and leader in the protection of wildlands. The area was first set aside in 1940, shortly after Marshall's death, and was designated as wilderness by the federal government in conjunction with the 1964 Wilderness Act. If you want wild Montana without the people, and are prepared and respectful, this is an extraordinary place to be. With privilege comes responsibility. In this era of industrial recreation, the Bob is still wild, but it's up to us to keep it that way.

Visiting the Bob

Encompassing three designated roadless wilderness areas, "the Bob," as it is known locally, is a magnificent place to explore. The most famous geological landmark is a dramatic 22-mile-long (35-km-long) escarpment known as the **Chinese Wall.** Technically referred to as the Lewis Overthrust, the incredible rock wall—it is 1,000 feet (305 m) high in places—is the result of a massive geologic upheaval in which the state split from Glacier National Park all the way down to Yellowstone. The Chinese Wall is where the eastern plate slid under the western plate.

Other popular areas for hikers and backpackers include the **South Fork of the Flathead River** valley, where most of the major trails leading into or out of the Bob can be picked up. **Big Salmon Lake** in the South Fork is among the more popular destinations. On the western edge of the wilderness complex, **Holland Lake** in the Swan Valley offers good access for backpackers and outfitters.

The **Sun River Game Preserve,** which lies at the eastern edge of the Bob, is the only portion of the complex where hunting is restricted. The area was established in the late 1920s as a refuge for elk, deer, and grizzlies, among other animals, and remains an important winter range for numerous species.

Access

Though the wilderness complex is roadless by definition, more than 1,000 miles (1,600 km) of trails crisscross the region and provide access for private visitors and commercial outfitters. Ten-day trips into the region to take advantage of hunting, fishing, or just unparalleled wild scenery are popular and can be arranged through licensed outfitters. **Bob Marshall Wilderness Outfitters** (41088 Roberts Rd., Charlo, 406/644-7889 or 406/240-2722, www.bobmarshallwildernessoutfitters.com) offers a range of guided pack trips into the Bob that cater to hunters, fishers, and nature lovers. Eight-day/seven-night trips start at $3,600 per person. **Seven Lazy P Outfitters** (891 Teton Canyon Rd., Choteau, 406/466-2245, www.sevenlazyp.com, four-day trips from $1,950 pp, six-day trips from $2,950 pp) also offers guided trips into the wilderness area. Other outfitters can be found through the **Montana Outfitters & Guides Association** (406/449-3578, www.montanaoutfitters.org).

Information

Road access to the perimeter of the wilderness complex is on US 2 to the north, US 89 and US 287 to the east, and Highways 200 and 83 to the south and west. The complex is managed by four national forests, including the **Flathead National Forest** (406/758-5208, www.fs.usda.gov) in Swan Lake, and five ranger districts.

Transportation

The Bob Marshall Wilderness Complex is roughly 80 miles (129 km) west of Great Falls and can be accessed from numerous communities along the Rocky Mountain Front, including Choteau, Augusta, and Browning.

1: the Chinese Wall and wildflowers in the Bob Marshall Wilderness Complex **2:** typical Montana highway

Fort Benton and the Hi-Line

The farther east you travel from Great Falls, the more the landscape opens up. From the edge of the Rockies the land is pulled tight into the Upper Missouri River valley and the rugged breaks that fracture the vast agricultural land and prairie. It is quiet in these parts but stunning, and there is a remarkable quality of light in which the weather can change the landscape in a moment.

Fort Benton, considered the oldest town in Montana, is a picturesque hamlet on the banks of the Missouri. Farther north, on the Milk River, is Havre, a rough-and-tumble railroad town with a colorful history. Tight-knit communities like Cut Bank, Shelby, and Chinook span the Hi-Line and reflect its boom-and-bust cycle.

★ FORT BENTON

Established in 1846 as an American Fur Company trading post, Fort Benton (pop. 1,410, elev. 2,644 ft/806 m) became one of the most important trading centers in the Northwest as a critical inland port. Starting in 1860, each year in spring and early summer some 50 steamboats would arrive, loaded with trappers, traders, gold seekers, and mountains of supplies destined for places across the West. When the Great Northern Railway arrived in Helena in 1887, the river traffic to Fort Benton all but dried up. The last steamboat to unload in Fort Benton left in 1922.

The infrastructure created in Fort Benton's heyday—including a glamorous hotel—still lures visitors today. In fact, the entire town is recognized as a National Historic Landmark, and the people of Fort Benton have done much to preserve and promote their storied past. The old steamboat levee, along what was once known as the "bloodiest block in the West," has been transformed into a tranquil walking path. The original fort has been partially rebuilt in the center of town, and there are two wonderful museums and one of the best historic hotels in the state.

Sights

Fort Benton has an inordinate number of museums for its population, all of which are worth seeing. A **two-day museum pass** ($15 adults, $12 seniors, $7.50 military, $5 children 12-17, $1 children 6-11) can be purchased at any of the museums and enables you to visit both the Museum of the Upper Missouri and the Museum of the Northern Great Plain.

Dedicated to the region's 19th-century history, the **Museum of the Upper Missouri** (Old Fort Park, 406/622-5316, www.fortbenton.com, 10am-5pm Mon.-Sat., noon-4pm Sun. late May-late Sept., winter hours by appointment) has exhibits that hark back to Fort Benton's glory days as the Northwest's most important inland port. Twice-daily guided tours take visitors on a walk around the fascinating Old Fort.

The **Museum of the Northern Great Plain** (1205 20th St., 406/622-5316, www.fortbenton.com, 10:30am-4:30pm Mon.-Sat., noon-4pm Sun. late May-late Sept., winter hours by appointment) pays tribute to the agricultural heritage and homestead era.

The **Upper Missouri River Breaks Interpretive Center** (701 7th St., 406/622-4000 or 877/256-3252, www.mt.blm.gov, 8am-4:30pm daily Memorial Day-late Sept., 8am-4:30pm Mon.-Fri. winter, $5) is an impressive facility celebrating the natural and cultural history of the river and its surrounding environment. A must-see for boaters on the Missouri, the center offers technical information as well as historical and interactive exhibits. Among the treasures here is Chief Joseph's surrender rifle. Winter hours can change depending on budget, so call ahead if you plan to visit.

The **Upper Missouri River Breaks National Monument** (406/538-1900 or

The Legend of Shep

The story of a dog named Shep is a tear-jerking one, and Shep has become something of an icon for the town of Fort Benton. Some sort of border collie mix, Shep was born in Montana in the late 1920s. He was a sheepdog and, by all accounts, a very faithful companion. When his sheepherding master fell ill during the Great Depression and had to be taken by buckboard to the hospital in Fort Benton, Shep followed along and waited for days outside the hospital for his owner. A nurse at the hospital, Sister Genevieve, noticed the dog and began to leave scraps of food and drinking water for him. When his master was loaded onto an eastbound train at the Fort Benton depot in a casket, Shep began a nearly six-year vigil, meeting every train, waiting for his master to disembark. Each time a train pulled out of the station, Shep would vanish into the hills, only to return to greet the next arrival.

After several months, Shep stayed closer to the station, carving a little nook for himself under the platform. The son of one of the railroad workers made a point of bringing Shep regular meals, and the depot agent eventually coaxed the wary animal into the station with a warm bed. Another railroad worker recognized Shep as having belonged to a sheepherder whose lifeless body was shipped to his family back East. He explained to Shep's new caretakers that the dog had been waiting at the station since then. Over the span of a few years, the legend of Shep began to grow, along with the number of his admirers.

Shep was written up in newspapers around the world, and the Great Northern Railway had to hire a secretary just to handle the mail—which included everything from money to dog bones—addressed to Shep from people worldwide.

By 1942, Shep was quite old and deaf. Despite his celebrity, he still greeted every train in search of his master. On an icy January morning, Shep wandered out to the tracks and was tragically hit and killed by an inbound train. The whole town mourned his loss, and hundreds came to pay their respects at his funeral. His concrete gravestone still stands sentry high atop a hill next to where the depot once stood.

In 1994, the city fathers presented a beautiful bronze statue of Shep to the people of Fort Benton. His sweet story was immortalized in a wonderful children's book, *Shep: Our Most Loyal Dog*, by Sneed B. Collard III and Joanna Yardley.

877/256-3252, www.mt.blm.gov) comprises 378,000 acres centered on a 149-mile (240-km) stretch of the Missouri, designated a National Wild and Scenic River. The remoteness of the region adds to its ecological and cultural significance. Boaters have the rare opportunity to travel in an area virtually untouched since Lewis and Clark's era, and the white cliffs and sandy beaches have as much appeal today as they did 200 years ago. The water is wide and reasonably flat, so whitewater equipment and expertise are not necessary. However, because of its remoteness, great care should be taken, and careful planning is necessary. Day trips, shuttles, and full-service camping trips through the white cliffs and badlands sections can be arranged through outfitters, including **Upper Missouri River Guides** (2206 Main St., 406/616-2001 or 406/261-3297, www.uppermissouri.com), which offers three-day/two-night trips from $845 per person and plenty of other options up to the full 148 miles (238 km) in seven days and six nights for $1,675 per person. **Missouri River Outfitters** (406/622-3295 or 866/282-3295, www.mroutfitters.com, 3-day trip from $825, 4-day trip from $1,000, 6-day trip in June and July from $1,400, 7-day trip in August and September $1,550) offers guided trips and shuttle service as well as canoe, kayak, and camping equipment rentals. Boaters interested in planning their own trips should contact the **Fort Benton River Management Station** (701 7th St., 877/256-3252, www.blm.gov).

For an altogether different experience,

check out the tiny town of **Virgelle,** in the heart of the national monument and accessible by road or **river ferry** (406/378-3110). This former ghost town has been restored without being overly modernized, and bed-and-breakfast-type accommodations in small cabins and even sheepherder wagons are available. The tiny town and its do-everything mercantile store truly offer a step back in time.

Food

Inside the Grand Union Hotel, ★ **The Union Grill** (1 Grand Union Sq., 406/622-1882 or 888/838-1882, www.grandunionhotel.com, 5pm-9pm Wed.-Mon. summer, 5pm-9pm Wed.-Sun. winter, $15-39) is exquisite and offers some of the most innovative cuisine in this part of the state. In the summer you can sit on the riverside patio and indulge in everything from green curry mussels and harissa roasted carrots to wild mushroom carbonara and filet of beef tenderloin. The menu is ever-changing and incorporates as much fresh local meat and produce as possible. The wine list and the desserts are equally exceptional, and even the bar menu is inspired.

For something decidedly more casual, **The Freeze** (722 Front St., 406/622-3739, 11am-8pm Tues.-Sat., 11am-7pm Sun. Apr.-Oct., open weekends in October "until the snow gets deep") has great burgers, pork chop sandwiches, onion rings, and phenomenal soft-serve ice-cream flavors like Blue Goo, which tastes like cotton candy. There's even a cone for dogs. ★ **Wake Cup Coffee House & Restaurant** (1500 Front St., 406/622-5400, www.wakecupcoffeehouse.com, 7am-4pm Tues., 7am-8pm Wed.-Fri., 8am-8pm Sat., breakfast $7-16.50, lunch $8-16.50, dinner Thurs.-Sat. only $11-28) is a full-service restaurant with outstanding food and a welcoming ambience. From huevos rancheros to Texas style brisket, Montana pork shoulder, and even pizza, it's impossible to leave here unsatisfied. Oh, and the coffee. It's out of this world.

Housed in a beautiful, 1880 mercantile

building, **Golden Triangle Brew Co.** (1220 Front St., 406/622-3307, 3pm-9pm Thurs.-Mon., www.goldentrianglebrews.com, $2.50-10) is known for creating field to glass beers with custom malts and ingredients from family farms just minutes from the brewery. In addition to their inspired beverages—consider the Ryedn' Dirty hazy IPA, the Sir Stubbs Habanero Honey Hefeweisen, and the Fresh Sesh hop pale lager—they serve plenty of snacks, from chicken nuggets and Bavarian pretzels to pulled pork sliders and cheddar brats. Taco Mondays and Trivia Thursdays are popular with locals.

Accommodations

If you could only stay in one place in Montana, the ★ **Grand Union Hotel** (1 Grand Union Sq., 406/622-1882 or 888/838-1882, www.grandunionhotel.com, $120-215) might be it. The hotel was built in 1882 at the height of Fort Benton's steamboat era and a full seven years before Montana became a state. After more than 100 years of operation, the hotel closed its doors in the mid-1980s and continued to decay. Montanans Jim and Cheryl Gagnon purchased the once-glorious hotel in 1997 and undertook a massive, award-winning renovation. Today the 26-room hotel lives up to its original splendor with gorgeous mahogany woodwork, lofty ceilings, and elegant furnishings throughout. It's interesting to note that the 3rd floor was originally designed for cowboys, workers, and their occasional female companions. It's accessed by a back staircase, rather than the grand central staircase to the 2nd floor, which was occupied by VIPs. The entire hotel is lovely and worth the splurge.

Accommodations in Virgelle, in the heart of the Upper Missouri River Breaks National Monument, are available in rustic but comfy homestead-era cabins (from $70 pp) with a shared bathhouse or in charming B&B rooms ($140-250 including breakfast) above the **Virgelle Mercantile** (7485 Virgelle Ferry Rd. N., 406/378-3110, www.virgellemontana. com). Pets are not permitted.

Information

The **Fort Benton Chamber of Commerce** (1421 Front St., 406/622-3864, www.fortbentonchamber.org, 10am-4pm daily May-Sept.) is part of the Information Center inside the old fire station next to the walking bridge.

Transportation

Fort Benton is 40 miles (64 km) east of Great Falls on US 87.

CUT BANK

At the edge of the Blackfeet Reservation between Browning and Shelby, Cut Bank (pop. 3,058, elev. 3,733 ft/1,138 m) is famous for being the site of Lewis and Clark's only armed encounter with Native Americans. On July 26, 1806, Meriwether Lewis, joined by George Drouillard, Joseph Fields, and Reuben Fields, met with eight Blackfeet. When Lewis revealed that the U.S. government intended to outfit all the Plains Indians with hunting rifles, the Blackfeet became angry because they had controlled the firearms trade among Native Americans through their relationship with the Hudson's Bay Company. The Blackfeet took off with the men's horses, a fight ensued, and two Blackfeet were killed.

In addition to the town's proximity to the reservation and its cultural influence, five Hutterite colonies in the area also welcome visitors. The **Glacier County Historical Museum** (107 Old Kevin Hwy., 406/873-4904, www.glaciermuseum.org, 10am-5pm Tues.-Sat. Memorial Day-Labor Day, by appointment Labor Day-Memorial Day, $5 12 and up) presents exhibits on Lewis and Clark, homesteading, artist John Clark, and the town's oil boom. On summer weekends, costumed guides reenact homestead life circa 1915.

The **Glacier Gateway Plaza** (1130 E. Main St., 406/873-2566 or 800/851-5541, www.glaciergateway.com, $50-89) has large, clean rooms. This place is nothing fancy, but they offer amenities like an indoor pool and high-speed Internet. There's also a **Super 8 by Wyndham** (609 W. Main St., 406/873-8325, www.wyndhamhotels.com, from $71) in town.

Cut Bank is 30 miles (48 km) south of the Canadian border on Highway 213, 106 miles (171 km) northwest of Great Falls via I-15 and US 2, and 35 miles (56 km) east of Browning on US 2.

SHELBY

The humble story of Shelby's origins involves a discarded boxcar around which a town eventually developed. The town saw enormous growth thanks to the railroad, the Homestead Act, and a 1921 oil discovery. Shelby even hosted the 1923 World Heavyweight Championship fight between Jack Dempsey and Tommy Gibbons. Today, Shelby (pop. 3,078, elev. 3,086 ft/941 m) is a small trade center that attracts plenty of Canadians through the state's busiest port of entry. The nearby Sweet Grass Hills are a beautiful place for a hike, and Lake Sheloole offers plenty of recreation opportunities. Most recently, the town came together to restore a 1936 carousel with 900 lights and hand-painted animals. It can be visited at the **Carousel Rest Area** (441 11th Ave. N., 406/424-8444, carousel 10am-8pm Mon.-Sat. summer, noon-8pm Sat. in winter) in Shelby and is well worth the stop.

The **Marias Museum of History and Art** (1129 1st St. N., 406/424-2551, www.toolecountymt.gov, 1pm-7pm Mon.-Fri., 1pm-4pm Sat. June-Aug., 1pm-4pm Tues. Sept.-May, free) is a classic county history museum with plenty of interesting displays of Native American artifacts, dinosaur bones, homestead-era relics, and re-created historical interiors.

Anyone looking to do a little shopping or find a good cup of coffee in Shelby will want to visit the **Prairie Peddler** (319 Main St., 406/434-5446, www.prairie-peddler.com, 9am-5:30pm Mon.-Fri., 9:30am-3pm Sat.), a delightful coffee and gift shop that is clearly a special place in this community. The shop is loaded with jewelry, clothing, housewares, books, and more. For a serious Montana steak dinner in the best supper club tradition, **Frontier Bar & Supper Club** (28904 US 20, 10 minutes east of Shelby in Dunkirk, 406/432-3600, 5pm-midnight Wed.-Sun., $8-38) is the place. They serve drinks in giant pickles for starters, and all their entrées—including hand-cut steaks, pan-seared fish, and made-from-scratch pasta—are sure to satisfy. For a good old-fashioned drive-in restaurant with corn dogs, burgers sandwiches, pitas, and of course ice cream, visit the **Dash In** (702 W. Roosevelt Hwy., 406/434-5888, 11am-8pm daily Apr.-mid-Sept., $4.25-10.50), which is only open in spring and summer.

Overnight accommodations are available at **Comfort Inn & Suites** (455 McKinley, 406/434-2212, www.choicehotels.com, $76-204) and the three-star **Best Western Shelby Inn & Suites** (1948 Roosevelt Hwy., 406/424-4560, www.bestwestern.com, $110-250).

The **Shelby Chamber of Commerce** (100 Montana Ave., 406/434-7184, www.shelbymtchamber.org, 9am-noon Mon.-Fri.) and the **Shelby Visitors Information Center** (406/434-9151, 11am-6pm Mon.-Fri., 1pm-6pm Sat. mid-May-Sept., 9am-noon Mon.-Fri. Oct.-mid-May) are located in the historic Shelby Town Hall (100 Montana Ave.) at the eastern edge of town and can fill you in on local events and guided tours. There is free Wi-Fi on the premises.

Shelby is 84 miles (135 km) north of Great Falls along I-15.

HAVRE

Named for the birthplace of the French homesteaders on whose land the town was sited, Havre (HAV-er, pop. 9,362, elev. 2,494 ft/760 m) is a railroad town anchoring the Hi-Line, with an economy that is increasingly diversifying even as the population slowly decreases. As with so many towns along the Hi-Line, the existence of the settlement can unquestionably be attributed to railroad titan James J.

Hill, who sent his construction crew to the area in 1887.

The city itself is defined by various natural features: the Bears Paw Mountains to the south, the wide-open plains in every direction, and the Milk River, which borders Havre. With the exception of the Havre Beneath the Streets Tour, which is remarkably well done, Havre has not done well in preserving and promoting its historical attractions, many of which, in Havre's defense, were not actually discovered until the 1960s and 1970s. This is an agricultural and college town—Montana State University-Northern—as well as the trade center for many of the smaller towns in the region.

★ Havre Beneath the Streets
When the city of Havre nearly burned to the ground in 1904, business owners moved underground in an effort to stay afloat while the city was rebuilt. The **Havre Beneath the Streets Tour** (120 3rd Ave., 406/265-8888, 1-hour tours 9:30am-3:30pm daily Memorial Day-mid-Sept., 10am-4pm Mon.-Sat. mid-Sept.-late May, call for specific tour times and reservations, $17 adults, $9 children 6-12, free for children under 6) takes visitors into this phenomenal maze of turn-of-the-20th-century establishments that include a faithfully re-created saloon, brothel, bakery, sausage factory, opium den, and more. The guides are passionate and have juicy stories of Havre's wild days and wilder characters. The underground passages were only discovered in 1976 when the city undertook a street-widening project, but the care with which the businesses have been restored is remarkable, making it one of the best historical tours in the state. Each year in early June, actors in period garb bring the underground city to life with a **Living History Weekend.**

1: Fort Benton **2:** Grand Union Hotel in Fort Benton **3:** Main Street in Lewistown **4:** old steamer on display in Havre

Other Sights

If you don't get your fill of Havre history on the underground tour, visit the **H. Earl Clack Memorial Museum** (Holiday Village Mall, 1753 US 2, 406/265-4000, www.hearlclackmuseum.org, 11am-5pm Mon.-Sat., noon-5pm Sun. May-mid-Sept., 1pm-5pm Tues.-Sat. mid-Sept.-Apr., free), oddly located in a shopping mall, for illustrative dioramas on the development of Havre, an assortment of 75-million-year-old dinosaur eggs and embryos, and, most interestingly, artifacts from the adjacent **Wahkpa Chu'gn Archeological Site** (406/265-4000, 9am-4pm daily, weather permitting, June-Labor Day, $15 adults, $11 seniors, $9 students 13-17, $5 students 6-12, free for children under 6), a 2,000-year-old buffalo jump that was discovered in the early 1960s. Unfortunately the site is located immediately behind the mall and surrounded by a chain-link fence that detracts from the perceived significance of the place, but it is one of the best-preserved buffalo jump sites in the state. A fascinating hour-long guided tour—the only way visitors are permitted into the site—takes visitors through bison kill areas and campsite deposits, some of which are 20 feet deep. At the end of the tour, visitors have the opportunity to throw the atlatl, the weapon favored by the Besant people who utilized the site 2,000 years ago.

Sports and Recreation

Winter visitors to Havre, hardy souls indeed, should do whatever they can to ski at **Bear Paw Ski Bowl** (66 Saddle Butte Dr., Rocky Boy's Reservation, 29 mi/47 km south of Havre, 406/395-4040, 10:30am-4pm Sat.-Sun. Jan.-Mar., $25 adults, $20 children 9-17, free for children under 9 with paying adult, free for Chippewa Cree Tribal members with ID). Known as the "Last Best Ski Hill," Bear Paw is an old-fashioned ski area with two lifts, excellent advanced terrain, and an entirely volunteer staff. Rentals are available Friday evenings and Saturday and Sunday mornings at **Bear Paw Winter Sports** (417 1st St., Havre, 406/390-4788). The hill is open only on weekends, but it's a day of skiing with a side of nostalgia that you will never forget.

Entertainment and Events

The biggest event of the year by far in the Havre area is the **Rocky Boy Pow Wow and Rodeo** in Box Elder, usually held around the first weekend in August. The four-day event includes a rodeo, a dance, and costume and drumming competitions for more than $100,000 in prize money. There are cultural demonstrations, grand entries twice daily, and plenty of food vendors. The venues are decided each year and can be located through the **Rocky Boy Agency** (406/395-5705 or 406/395-5439), which also has a regular presence on Facebook.

Food

Murphy's Pub & Casino (1465 US 2 NW, 406/265-4700, www.murphyspubmontana.com, 11am-10pm Tues.-Sat., $9-24) has a surprisingly international menu that ranges from the rather Irish fish-and-chips, corned beef or hot pastrami on rye, and black and tan onion rings to Asian chicken salad, a gyro platter, quesadillas, and even a South Texas burger. The food is good, and the beer and liquor selection is excellent.

Equally inexplicable but just as delicious is **Nalivka's Original Pizza Kitchen** (1032 1st St., 406/265-4050, noon-9pm Tues.-Sun., large pizza $19-27, sandwiches $5.50-11), owned and operated by a Russian American family since 1957. Nalivka's serves outstanding pizza—the crust is rich and flaky like a quiche—along with sandwiches, soups, and salads. The service is takeout or delivery only. They do not accept credit cards, so have cash or a personal check ready.

For great sandwiches and homemade soup in the less-than-scenic ambience of the Atrium Mall, **Grateful Bread** (220 3rd Ave. S., 406/265-2370, 7am-2pm Mon.-Fri., $5-13) is an excellent choice. Another great place for baked goods in Havre is **Infinity Bake Shop** (309 3rd Ave., Suite B, 406/879-8100, 8am-5:30pm Tues.-Fri., 8am-3pm Sat.,

$3-12), which serves homemade donuts and pastries, savory breakfast rolls, quiche, soup, and sandwiches. Traveling pooches will be especially grateful for the dog bones. For a meal on the go, try a sandwich or loaded potato at **Spud's Grub Hut** (1903 5th Ave., 406/262-7992, 11am-4pm Mon. and Sat., 11am-7pm Tues.-Fri., $5-8).

If you haven't had your fill of big, juicy burgers and hand-cut fries or old-fashioned milk shakes by this point, **Wolfer's Diner** (126 3rd Ave., 406/265-2111, 11am-8pm Mon.-Sat., $6.50-9.25) won't disappoint.

Accommodations

Havre has a plentiful assortment of hotels and motels, and surprisingly they are often fully booked with business travelers, so advance reservations are a good idea. On the west end of town, the **AmericInn** (2520 US 2 W., 406/395-5000 or 877/634-3444, www.wyndhamhotels.com, $89-220) is one of the largest, with an indoor pool, oversize rooms, Wi-Fi, and hearty breakfasts. Other options include **Best Western Plus** (1345 1st St., 406/265-4200 or 877/237-8791, www.bestwestern.com, $114-187), **Havre Super 8 by Wyndham** (1901 US 2 W., 406/265-1411 or 800/800-8000, $55-119), and **Quality Inn of Havre** (601 W. 1st St., 406/564-1145, www.choicehotels.com, $68-125).

For campers, just 20 miles (32 km) south of town is **Beaver Creek Park** (17863 Beaver Creek Rd., 406/395-4565, http://bcpark.org, permits $10/night), which has a special site on the north face of the Bears Paw Mountains. At 10,000 acres, it is the largest county park in the United States and offers nature trails, two lakes for fishing, and a private campground. The Bear Paw Nature Trail, leaving from the Lions campground, has paneled signs over 2 miles (3.2 km) to interpret wildlife, archaeology, and history of the park.

A phenomenal option for luxury-loving bird hunters in the region is **Sage Safaris** (406/219-4025, www.sagesafaris.com, Sept.-Nov., from $6,950 pp for three-night trips), which offers all-inclusive guided wing-shooting safaris in luxurious wall tents with three gourmet meals daily.

Information

One block south of 1st Avenue at the corner of 5th Avenue is the **Havre Area Chamber of Commerce** (130 5th Ave., 406/265-4383, www.havrechamber.com, 9am-4pm Mon.-Fri.), which has a good selection of visitor and recreation information.

Transportation

The **Havre City-County Airport** (HVR, 5404 9th St. W., 406/265-4671) is 3 miles (4.8 km) west of the town. **Cape Air** (800/227-3247, www.capeair.com) offers two flights daily to Billings from Havre.

Havre is 114 miles (184 km) northeast of Great Falls along US 87.

The **Empire Builder** is the most popular **Amtrak** (800/872-7245, www.amtrak.com) long-distance train in the United States, traveling between Chicago and either Portland or Seattle. One train passes in each direction daily, and much of the route through Montana, known as the Hi-Line, runs in the north along US 2. The first stop for westbound trains in Montana is Wolf Point, and the last is Libby. The route goes over the Continental Divide and along the southern border of Glacier National Park, a portion of the trip that is unforgettable, and trains are supposedly timed so that passengers are able to enjoy a view of the majestic Rockies regardless of which direction they are traveling. The busiest stops for the train are Whitefish, Shelby, and Havre. If you have plans to travel west and can spare the time, consider taking the train.

CHINOOK

With such an auspicious name—*chinook* is a Native American word meaning "warm wind"—it's no wonder that Chinook (pop. 1,230, elev. 2,428 ft/740 m) is a cattle town with more cows than people. Here the grasses are grazeable even in January and February. Set on the rolling plains alongside the Milk River and just north of the Bears

Paw Mountains, Chinook is a lovely and solemn place most closely associated with the heartbreaking battle and subsequent surrender of Chief Joseph.

Bear Paw Battlefield

Sixteen miles (26 km) south of Chinook and just 40 miles (64 km) south of the Canadian border on Highway 240 is the haunting **Bear Paw Battlefield** (sunrise-sunset daily year-round), one of three historic Nez Perce sites in the state and the site of a five-day battle between the U.S. Army and Chief Joseph's band of 700 Nez Perce, who had already traveled more than 1,000 miles (1,600 km) in an effort to escape the army and were only 40 miles (64 km) from freedom in Canada. There is a self-guided 1.25-mile (2-km) trail, and ranger-guided tours can be arranged in summer by contacting the **National Park Service** office in Chinook (301 Ohio St., 406/357-3130, www.nps.gov).

For a comprehensive introduction to the site, visit Chinook's **Blaine County Museum** (501 Indiana St., 406/357-2590, 9am-5pm Mon.-Sat., 1pm-5pm Sun. Memorial Day-Labor Day, 8am-noon and 1pm-5pm Mon.-Fri. Sept. and May, 1pm-5pm Mon.-Fri. Oct.-Apr., $5 adults, $4 students) before you head to the battlefield. The museum offers a gripping multimedia presentation, *Forty Miles from Freedom*, as well as maps of the battlefield. The museum is also on the Montana Dinosaur Trail and houses a dozen exhibits from the area's once massive inland ocean.

Other Sights

Wildlife lovers will very much appreciate the artistic taxidermy of the **Blaine County Wildlife Museum** (417 Indiana St., 406/357-3102, www.bcwildlifemuseum.com, 9am-5pm Mon.-Sat., 1pm-5pm Sun. June-Aug., $6 adults, $4 students, children 5 and under free, tours available by appointment), which includes an ever-growing number of exhibits covering everything from a buffalo jump and wetlands to peaks, plains, nocturnal woods, and a moose-grizzly encounter.

Entertainment and Events

Unlike the vast majority of Montana towns that pack the calendar with events during summer, Chinook offers worthwhile entertainment in the fall. The **Bear Paw Battle Commemoration** (406/357-3130, www.nps.gov) pays tribute to the 1877 battle with a traditional pipe ceremony. It is normally scheduled for 10am the first Saturday in October. Photos and filming of the pipe ceremony are not permitted.

Worth seeing during summer is the **Blaine County Fair & Bear Paw Roundup** (300 Cleveland Rd. W., 406/357-2988 or 406/357-3742), a small-town fair with a great rodeo, a carnival, country music, agricultural exhibits, and even lawn mower races.

Food

Rad's Pizza & Deli (315 Indiana St., 406/357-3606, 11am-9pm Mon.-Sat., $9-23) is a quaint little place with excellent soups and sandwiches as well as pizza, salads, wraps, nachos, and homemade cookies.

If you don't get too full at Rad's, just a couple of blocks away is **The Creamery** (415 US 2 W., 406/357-4260, noon-9pm daily Apr.-Sept.), a perfect spot for any soft-serve ice-cream concoction imaginable when the weather is warm. Try the shiver, a combination of ice cream and slushie.

Accommodations

The **Bear Paw Motel** (145 Cleveland Rd., 406/357-2221, lawanna.harvey@hotmail.com, $85-120) has guest rooms with queen beds and free Wi-Fi. Pets are allowed for a fee. The nearby pet-friendly **Chinook Motor Inn** (100 Indiana St., 406/357-2248, www.chinookmotorinn.com, $84-100) is bigger and slightly more modern, also with Wi-Fi. There's also a restaurant on-site, the Chinook Grille, serving both Chinese food and the ubiquitous Montana burger.

The Battle of Bear Paw

Sixteen miles (26 km) south of Chinook is the historic Bear Paw Battlefield, an area that looks much as it did in 1877 when the Nez Perce fought the last in a series of battles known as the Nez Perce War. Originally from the Wallowa Valley in northeastern Oregon, the Nez Perce, under the leadership of Chief Joseph, had refused to relocate to a reservation in Idaho. General Oliver O. Howard planned an attack to force Joseph's band onto the reservation. Before arriving at this site in Montana, the band of 700 Indians, 200 of whom were warriors, undertook a journey that has come to be known as one of the most spectacular military retreats in U.S. history. They spent three months covering more than 1,000 miles (1,600 km), crossed four states, and engaged in numerous skirmishes with the U.S. Army as they fled capture and sought refuge in Canada.

Bear Paw Battlefield in Nez Perce National Historical Park

On September 29, 1877, the Nez Perce chose to rest at Snake Creek, just north of the Bears Paw Mountains and 40 miles (64 km) from the Canadian border. General Howard had pursued them relentlessly, but believing that they had a good lead on his troops, the Nez Perce chose to set up camp. Unbeknownst to the Nez Perce, Col. Nelson A. Miles and his 7th Cavalry were quickly approaching from the southeast. With the help of Cheyenne and Lakota scouts, they spotted the Nez Perce camp. Although almost 300 troops attacked the Nez Perce, the skilled warriors were able to stand their ground and rapidly fortify the encampment.

The Nez Perce earned great praise not only for their fighting but also for their humane treatment of others. During this battle, as wounded army soldiers lay on the battlefield, the Nez Perce moved among them looking for ammunition and weapons but did no further harm to the injured men. There is even a legend that an injured soldier kept crying out to his comrades for water. A warrior approached him, removed the soldier's ammunition belt, and left a container of water.

After five days of fighting, Joseph had seen enough. There may have been an opportunity to escape, but he refused to leave the wounded, sick, and elderly behind. On October 5, 1877, Joseph, Howard, and Miles spoke though translators. Joseph made a poignant speech, finishing with the famous words: "From where the sun now stands, I will fight no more forever." Although it was a conditional surrender and both Miles and Howard assured Joseph that he and his people would be returned to their home in the Northwest, that was not the case. The U.S. government moved the Nez Perce first to a reservation in Kansas and later to Indian Territory in present-day Oklahoma. Not until 1885 were they moved to Washington State, still not their original homeland. Joseph died there in 1904, the cause of death diagnosed by his doctor as "a broken heart."

The Bear Paw Battlefield is one of several sites located within the **Nez Perce National Historical Park** (406/357-3130 or 208/843-7009, www.nps.gov, year-round). A ranger is on-site beginning at noon each day late June-September.

Information

The **Chinook Chamber of Commerce** (313 Indiana St., 406/357-3115, www.chinookmontana.com) has an informative website. Information is also available at the **Blaine County Museum** (501 Indiana St., 406/357-2590) and *Blaine County Journal* (217 Indiana St., 406/357-3573).

Transportation

Chinook is 135 miles (217 km) northeast of Great Falls via US 87 and US 2.

Lewistown and the Central Plains

In many ways, the heartland of Montana doesn't look all that different from the heartland of the United States. Small towns with strong identities and long, hard histories lie amid vast swaths of agricultural land, rolling fields, and—here is where things are different—humble mountains on the horizon. Though Lewistown is holding on to its population and the culture that accompanies it, other towns, like Judith Gap, Harlowton, and White Sulphur Springs, have struggled to hang on to their residents, most of whom earn a living on the land. There is great charm in the fact that some places don't change much, and visiting them can be like stepping back in time.

LEWISTOWN

Long the heart of this region both geographically and for trade, Lewistown (pop. 5,952, elev. 3,950 ft/1,204 m) was built by a diverse group of immigrants, something that is reflected in the town's beautiful architecture. The stonework, using local sandstone, was done largely by Croatians, and the interiors were crafted by Norwegians. The town itself was incorporated in 1899, and the area was settled by landless Métis, gold seekers, farmers, and ranchers. It is splendidly set amid open fields, rolling prairie, and three mountain ranges. Although there are three ghost towns in the area—access to which is limited because they are almost entirely on private land—Lewistown itself is thriving and has become something of a model for renaissance in Montana. The combination of beautiful scenery, old-fashioned hospitality, good fishing, and great food has served Lewistown well.

Lewistown Art Center

Across from the historic courthouse, the **Lewistown Art Center** (323 W. Main St., 406/535-8278, www.lewistownartcenter.org, 10am-5pm Tues.-Sat., free) is the artistic hub of this artsy community. Monthly gallery shows feature primarily Montana artists, and the center is the site of numerous arts-related events throughout the year, including music and theater performances. The center's gift shop sells regional pottery, jewelry, fused glass, hitched horsehair, and fine art.

★ Charlie Russell Chew Choo

One of the best ways to see and appreciate the area is aboard the fabulous and kitschy **Charlie Russell Chew Choo** (406/535-5436 or 866/912-3980, www.montanadinnertrain.com, selection of Sat. evenings June-Sept., special events in the fall and Dec. holidays, $100 adults, $50 children 12 and under, VIP packages $135 adults and $70 children), a 56-mile (90-km), three-hour ride that takes visitors on a narrated tour through the mountains and prairies of the region aboard an elegant 1950s passenger train. A full-course dinner featuring prime rib and all the fixings is served. There is also entertainment in the form of musicians, cowboy poets, and the occasional good-natured train robber. The boarding station is a 40-minute drive from Lewistown. At Christmastime, the train runs as the **North Pole Adventure Train** (www.montananorthpoleadventure.com, 5pm and

7:30pm weekly late Nov.-Dec., $30 pp) on a 90-minute adventure that includes hot cocoa, cookies, a story, songs, games, and a visit from Santa and Mrs. Claus.

Ghost Towns

Three primary ghost towns are located outside Lewistown, all of which were gold-mining towns around the turn of the 20th century. **Maiden** (off US 191, northeast of Lewistown, 406/535-5436) was home to some 6,000 people in 1881 and produced more than $18 million worth of gold in its heyday. By 1896 the population had dwindled to 200, and after a fire destroyed every building in 1905, Maiden was never rebuilt. Today, the town's abandoned structures are entirely on private property, so you can only view them from the road.

The town of **Kendall** (on US 87, north of Lewistown, at the base of the North Moccasin Mountains, 406/535-5436) took off in 1901 with the advent of the Kendall Gold Mining Company. It was among the first mines to use the cyanide process for separating gold and mined an average of $800 worth of gold daily in its prime. At its height, Kendall had a 23-room hotel complete with hot running water, hot-air heating, and electricity. There was also an opera house, several saloons, two churches, four stagecoach lines, and other businesses. By 1920 the town had died, the mines were closed, and many of the buildings collapsed into the mine shafts. Today, only three stone buildings are left standing, and interpretive signs guide visitors at the ruins.

Built in 1893, **Gilt Edge** (off US 191, 20 mi/32 km northeast of Lewistown, 406/535-5436) was considered to be among the premier towns in the country at its heyday in 1900. Calamity Jane was a frequent visitor, and not unlike Jane herself, who grew quite familiar with the town's jail, Gilt Edge's residents experienced a host of legal problems. The mine manager, Colonel Ammon, was eventually tried and convicted for stealing $25,000 worth of bullion intended as wages for the miners. He ultimately served time in New York's Sing Sing prison for stock swindling. Today, the jail and brothel are two of three buildings left standing. But beware: An open well behind one of the buildings poses a real danger for hikers.

Before you seek out any of the ghost towns, call the **Lewistown Chamber of Commerce** (408 E. Main St., 406/535-5436) for precise directions and information about private land. For more history and detailed driving directions, visit www.montanahikes.com.

Sports and Recreation

The land, mountains, and rivers around Lewistown make this area an ideal destination for anglers, hunters, and nature lovers. It's one of the few cities in Montana that offer outstanding fishing within the city limits, at **Big Spring Creek,** the area's premier water source, supplying water for the city and a significant trout hatchery. There are also numerous public and privately stocked ponds and springs. For a guided fishing trip on Big Spring Creek, contact **Brad Hanzel of S&W Outfitters** (406/640-1673, www.sandwoutfitters.com, $550 full-day walk/wade for 1-2 anglers, includes lunch, $325 half-day walk/wade for 1-2 people) or stop by **Sport Center** (120 2nd Ave. S., 406/535-9308, 9am-6pm Mon.-Sat., 10am-4pm Sun.) for some flies and advice.

Entertainment and Events

Held in late July, the **Central Montana Horse Show, Fair and Rodeo** (1000 US 191 N., 406/535-8841, www.centralmontanafair.com, $15 adults 13 and over, $10 youth 7-12, free for children 6 and under) is a great small-town fair with an equestrian bent. In addition, there is live country music entertainment, a PRCA rodeo, AMX auto racing, and a demolition derby. Winter visitors will delight in the offerings at the eight-day **Montana Winter Fair** (406/538-2200, www.montanawinterfair.com), which happens in late January, the coldest part of winter, before lambing and calving commence. Events celebrating Montana's agricultural history and the Western way of life happen all over town.

The second-oldest such event after the National Cowboy Poetry Gathering in Elko, Nevada, the **Montana Cowboy Poetry Gathering & Western Music Rendezvous** (406/538-4575, www.montanacowboypoetrygathering.com) is held each year over four days in mid-August. The event—which features readings and musical performances across town—aims to preserve and celebrate the history, heritage, and values of the American cowboy in the upper Rocky Mountain West.

The annual **Chokecherry Festival** (Main St., 406/535-5436, www.lewistownchokecherry.com) is held the first Saturday after Labor Day. Nearly 5,000 people attend the breakfast (pancakes with chokecherry syrup, of course) and other festivities, which include a fun run and walk, chokecherry culinary contests, kids' activities, chokecherry pit-spitting contests, and arts and crafts booths.

An awesome festival in central Montana is the **Montana Bale Trail,** held each year on the Sunday after Labor Day. Sponsored by the Friends of the Hobson Library, the event sees inventive and artistic farmers in the area—between Windham, Hobson, and Utica—build magnificent sculptures using hay bales along a 21-mile (34-km) loop south of US 87 on Highways 239 and 541. The voting day takes place in conjunction with the **Hobson-Utica Day Fair.** Oftentimes the more than 50 sculptures stay up long after the voting, making this route the ideal choice for a Sunday drive.

Food

Set in the breadbasket of Montana, Lewistown has established a reputation for fine dining, and among its gems is **The Mint Bar & Grill** (113 4th Ave. S., 406/535-9925, 5pm-8:30pm Wed.-Sat., $14-32), housed in a 1940s car dealership. The chefs specialize in savory sauces to accompany succulent steaks, ribs,

seafood, and pasta. Like the best Montana restaurants, it uses fresh local ingredients and pairs hearty meals with an impressive wine list.

Worth a visit is **Big Spring Brewing** (220 E. Main, Suite 1, 406/535-2337, www.bigspringbrewingmt.com, 11:30am-9pm daily), which brews five mainstay beers and roughly 10 rotating seasonal drafts. **Central Feed Grilling Co.** (220 E. Main, 406/535-2337, www.centralfeedgrillingco.com, 11:30am-9pm daily, $8-40) is destined to become a classic. Set in the historic Mercantile Building, this restaurant is part steakhouse, part wine bar, and a mecca for craft beer lovers. The food and drinks are excellent, and the ambience is warm and inviting.

Open since 1952, the **Dash Inn** (207 NE Main St., 406/535-3892, 10am-10pm daily, $3-11) is a classic drive-through-only burger joint with everything you'd expect from a drive-in diner: ice-cream drinks, buckets of crispy chicken, and its famous wagon-wheel sandwich. Another local favorite is the casual **Harry's Place** (631 NE Main St., 406/538-9510, 11am-9pm Mon.-Sat., $7-26), which serves sandwiches, salads, soups, wraps, burgers, chicken sandwiches, steak, and prime rib.

For a quick bite, a fancy coffee, and a good read, check out **Rising Trout Café & Book Store** (217 W. Main St., 406/535-4999, 7am-5:30pm Mon.-Sat., 8:30am-1pm Sun., lunch $7.50-8.50), which serves soup in bread bowls, salads, sandwiches, and lots of delicious baked goodies.

Accommodations

For in-town convenience, the pet-friendly **Yogo Inn of Montana** (211 E. Main St., 406/535-8721 or 800/860-9646, www.yogoinn.com, $95-175) has 123 well-appointed guest rooms and suites catering to business travelers. The indoor pool is a hit with kids.

Originally built as a girls' dormitory in 1912, **The Calvert Hotel** (216 7th Ave. S., 406/535-5411 or 877/371-5411, www.thecalverthotel.com, $139-219) is a beautifully refurbished 28-room historic property with all the perks of a boutique hotel.

There is also a **Super 8 by Wyndham** (102 Wendell Ave., Hwy. 87 W., 406/538-2581, www.super8.com, $88-115) in town.

For more privacy on a ranch setting 10 miles (16 km) from town, **Cottonwood Log Cabins** (4197 Lower Cottonwood Creek Rd., 406/538-8411, www.cottonwoodlogcabins. com, $150 for 2 people, $40 each additional person over 5 years old) has four cute log cabins with full kitchens, bathrooms, grills, and picnic benches. All the cabins are pet-friendly for a $20 per night/per pet fee, and two have hot tubs. The cabins are surrounded by open country, big views, and nearly 5 miles (8 km) of walking trails.

Information

The **Lewistown Area Chamber of Commerce** (408 E. Main St., 406/535-5436, www.lewistownchamber.com, 8am-5pm Mon.-Fri.) is housed in the Central Montana Museum building in Symmes Park, on the east side of town.

Transportation

Lewistown is 106 miles (171 km) southeast of Great Falls on Highway 3 and 125 miles (201 km) northwest of Billings via US 87.

WHITE SULPHUR SPRINGS

Named for the white deposits found around the hot sulfur springs here, White Sulphur Springs (pop. 935, elev. 5,043 ft/1,537 m) was a gathering spot for various Native Americans tribes for years before James Brewer stumbled on the area in 1886 and developed the hot springs into a resort. The town boomed, first as the "Saratoga of the West," then with lead and silver mines, and then as a cattle town and commercial region for this vast agricultural area. There is nothing booming about White Sulphur Springs these days, but it does have its own charm. In the midst of the prairies, it is close to excellent floating on the Smith River and skiing at Showdown Ski Area, and

there are wonderful relics from its glory days: A castle sits atop the hill in town, and the hot springs still gurgle with purportedly healing waters. There's a two-hour drive called the Arts & Cultural Trail that loops through White Sulphur Springs, Martinsdale, and Ringling, with points of interest marked by barn quilt signs. And every summer the Red Ants Pants Music Festival brings great musicians (country, folk, bluegrass) to a dreamed-up stage in the middle of a cow pasture in the middle of nowhere.

Castle Museum

Built in 1892 by merchant Bryon Roger Sherman, **The Castle** is a remarkable Victorian mansion that now houses the **Meagher County Museum** (310 2nd Ave. NE, 406/547-2324, www.intothelittlebelts. com, 10am-5pm daily May 15-Sept. 15, last guided tour of the day at 4:30pm, $7 adults, $5 seniors and children 5-12, free for children under 5). It was constructed with hand-cut granite blocks hauled by oxen from the Castle Mountains, 12 miles (19 km) away. It is appointed with period furniture and original fixtures—Italian marble sinks as well as crystal and brass light fixtures. Sherman supplied electricity to the entire town, making White Sulphur Springs one of the first towns in the state to have electricity.

★ Charles M. Bair Family Museum

Thirty-five miles (56 km) east of White Sulphur Springs off US 12 in the little town of Martinsdale, the **Charles M. Bair Family Museum** (2751 Hwy. 294, 406/572-3314, www.bairfamilymuseum.com, 10am-5pm daily May 15-Sept. 15, $5 adults, $3 seniors, $2 children under 13) is a phenomenal little museum dedicated to preserving and perpetuating the historic and artistic significance of the Bair family legacy. Charles Bair arrived in Montana in 1883 from Paris, Ohio, intent on making his fortune. He worked as a train conductor and sheep rancher (where he befriended the Crow chief Plenty Coups) before

Floating the Smith River

In the center of Montana and the middle of nowhere runs the Smith River, a blue-ribbon trout stream and one of the most sought-after rivers in the state for float trips. There are no services and no road access along the 59-mile (95-km) stretch of river between Camp Baker and Eden Bridge. The remoteness of the Smith, coupled with limestone canyons and giant swaths of ranch land, makes this river an idyllic destination.

Aside from the splendid scenery, the fish add to the river's appeal. The rainbow and brown trout populations are thriving, as are the native whitefish, which are somewhat unfairly maligned. Perhaps because they are easier to catch (thanks in part to a bigger and more circular "sucker" mouth), or because they don't have the dramatic colors of a trout, or maybe just because they compete for food and space with trout, whitefish are often called "trash fish" by fly-fishers. But anyone who's ever had the good fortune to eat smoked whitefish on crackers with horseradish would never stoop to name-calling.

Because of the river's popularity, it is closely managed by Montana Fish, Wildlife & Parks (FWP), which oversees a lottery system for the roughly 1,000 permits issued annually, compared to more than 15,000 applicants in 2021. There are 27 boat camps and 52 campsites scattered along the river, which can most often be floated in four days. The season varies dramatically depending on snowpack, rainfall, and the timing of irrigation use, but mid-April to early July is considered the prime season, and occasionally floaters can hit the Smith as late as September. To apply for a permit, which is due in mid-February, contact the **Montana FWP Smith River Reservation Line** (406/454-5861, www.fwp.mt.gov). Another option for those unlucky in the lottery is to book a Smith River trip with one of eight permitted outfitters. **Lewis and Clark Expeditions** (Twin Bridges, 406/684-5960 or 406/459-2030, www.hwlodge.com, 4-day/5-night trips from $4,950) offers excellent trips with world-class guides and gourmet grub. In addition to his fantastic commercial trips and Healing Waters Lodge, owner Mike Geary has teamed with Project Healing Waters to sponsor river-fishing trips for disabled veterans.

making it big with a ground-thawing device used in Alaska's gold rush. He used his earnings to buy land around Martinsdale, where he ran 300,000 sheep. Charles, his wife, Mary, and their daughters, Alberta and Marguerite, lived all over the country as he worked in mining, oil, and business, and traveled around the world, but they always came back to the ranch in Martinsdale. Avid art collectors and good friends with artists like Charlie Russell and Joseph Henry Sharp, the family filled their Montana home full to bursting with glorious artworks, antiques, and artifacts from their travels across the globe. After youngest daughter Alberta died in 1993 at the age of 97, the family home was opened to the public as a museum. In 2011, a 7,000-square-foot art museum containing the family's treasures opened. Visitors can tour both the home and the museum in summer and early fall to see family photos and memorabilia, original paintings, and Native American artifacts.

Sports and Recreation

One of Montana's most isolated, the **Smith River** is 59 miles (95 km) of dramatic canyons, open ranch land, and rugged forest between Camp Baker and Eden Bridge. The high season is when the water is high, typically late spring-early summer. On average, floaters take four days to travel through this spectacular roadless area.

Because of its popularity with Montanans, it is the only river in the state that can be used only with a permit. Permits are issued annually by Montana Fish, Wildlife & Parks (FWP) in a lottery that runs early January to mid-February. For more information, contact the **Great Falls FWP office** (406/454-5840). To inquire about remaining launch dates or cancelled permits, call the Smith River

Reservation Line (406/454-5861) beginning in mid-March.

Entertainment and Events
★ RED ANTS PANTS
MUSIC FESTIVAL

Voted the Best Event of the Year for the state of Montana in 2018, **Red Ants Pants Music Festival** (Jackson Ln., 3 mi/4.8 km northeast of White Sulphur Springs, 406/209-8135, www.redantspantsmusicfestival.com, $60 day pass, $155 3-day pass, $30-35 camping pass, free for kids 12 and under) is held in late July. It's a family-friendly, three-day weekend of music, food, and camping for those who don't mind the dust. Past headliners have included Dwight Yoakum, Shooter Jennings, Lucinda Williams, Lyle Lovett, and the Wailing Jennies. There's a kids' tent, a beer garden, hayrides, great food vendors, and room to dance. It can be hot and windy with very little shade (bring your own!), but this is a wholesome place to listen to great music. Tickets go on sale with early bird specials in early April. The festival was founded in 2011 by Sarah Calhoun, the genius behind the Red Ants Pants brand of workwear for women. Along with her staff and army of volunteers, she is transforming the region by bringing youth and vibrancy and music. In town, stop into **Red Ants Pants** (206 E. Main St., 406/547-3781, www.redantspants.com, 10am-5pm Mon.-Sat.), which sells T-shirts, gifts, and awesome work gear, including pants that don't wear out and are made for women's bodies.

Food

White Sulphur Springs sometimes calls itself a small drinking town with a big elk hunting problem. This is rugged country with hardy folk, but White Sulphur Springs has an assortment of great and kind-of-fancy bars. **The Jawbone** (11 E. Main St., 406/544-7643, www.thejawbonemt.com, 5pm-9:30pm Thurs.-Sun., $24-38) calls itself a cocktail lounge and eatery, and is one of the newest additions to town. An elegant spot serving sophisticated drinks (it's a mixologist, not a bartender), the Jawbone serves up delectable dishes like brie *en croûte*, *burrata* caprese, watermelon salad with feta and mint, mahi-mahi, and Montana filet mignon. Another great place for dinner and a glimpse of the local nightlife is the **Stockman Steakhouse and Bar** (117 E. Main St., 406/547-9985, kitchen 3pm-9pm Mon.-Thurs. and 3pm-10pm Fri.-Sun., bar opens 11am daily, $9-41) where you can

The Red Ants Pants Music Festival near White Sulphur Springs is one of the best events of the summer.

order a perfectly cooked steak, a juicy burger, or any of their mouthwatering pastas, salads, and seafood. For another gourmet experience in the New West, try ★ **Bar 47** (24 E. Main St., 406/547-6330, 11am-11pm daily, $10-29), which serves excellent and inspired comfort food, including poutine, sea salt caramel fries, cheese curds, pulled pork sliders, phenomenal burgers, street tacos, and steaks. There's also a kids' menu and awesome desserts. Try the grown-up milk shakes too!

In the parking lot of the Spa Hot Springs Hotel, **Haugen Express** (298 W. Main St., 406/461-0936, 6am-6pm daily, $4-9) is the perfect stop for an espresso drink, a cinnamon roll, a breakfast burrito, or any of their delicious sandwiches. The food is prepped while you wait, so it's not always fast, but it's good. Another outstanding spot for coffee and from-scratch baked goods is **Wild Oats Bakery and Coffee** (15 1st Ave. E., 406/547-2253, www.wildoatsbaking.com, 7am-2pm Wed.-Sun.) in the old county library.

Twenty-two miles (35 km) down US 89 from White Sulphur Springs is the tiny town of Ringling, named for one of the five brothers who launched the circus, and the old **Ringling Bar** (4 Main St., 406/547-2300, noon-2am Thurs.-Sun., $28-57). The building is old, and there is history galore. But the food and the prices are New West all the way. There are only steaks on the menu, and shrimp (no burgers available at dinner), but they are the tenderest steaks you will have eaten all year. They serve prime rib on Saturday night, but reservations are required. This is the Montana from the past, and the one we are becoming.

Accommodations

To enjoy White Sulphur Springs in the way the earliest settlers intended, make a point to visit the pet-friendly **Spa Hot Springs Motel and Tenderfoot Cabins** (202 W. Main St., 406/547-3366, www.spahotsprings. com, $99-149). The guest rooms are basic and clean, though some have been recently updated and have pillow-top mattresses, leather recliners, and flat-screen TVs. Some pet-friendly rooms are available for a $10 fee. Across the street, the Tenderfoot Cabins are basic but clean and they come with a microwave and small fridge, and some have full kitchens. But it's the three hot springs pools that make this place special. Outside, two pools are kept at 98°F (26.7°C) and 103°F (39.4°C). Inside, the pool is 105°F (40.6°C), and all are drained and cleaned nightly so that no chemicals have to be added to the natural hot water. Nonguests can use the pools for a fee ($10 adults, $9 seniors and youth 13-17, $8 children 6-12, $5 children 3-5, $3 children under 3). The springs are open 7am-10pm daily year-round.

For nonswimmers, the nearby **All Seasons Inn & Suites** (808 3rd Ave. SW, 406/547-8888, www.allseasonsinnandsuites.net, $126-218) is a smoke-free modern hotel with a hot tub, free Wi-Fi, and continental breakfast. Dogs are welcome for a $30 fee.

Information

For information about White Sulphur Springs, contact the **Meagher County Chamber of Commerce** (101 Main St., 406/547-2250, www.meagherchamber.org). Hours vary daily and seasonally, so please call before you visit.

Transportation

White Sulphur Springs is 97 miles (156 km) south of Great Falls and 79 miles (127 km) north of Bozeman on US 89 and 75 miles (121 km) east of Helena via US 12 and US 89.

Glacier National Park

Known as the "Crown of the Continent," Glacier

National Park is one of the largest intact ecosystems in the Lower 48, an amalgam of stunning landscapes that, for many visitors, defines the entire state.

The beauty of Glacier is rugged, raw, and dynamic. The mountains thrust skyward, and the gravity-defying roads are ribbons that snake toward the summits. The legendary Going-to-the-Sun Road is one of the West's most impressive engineering feats and one of the best scenic drives in the country. There are still 25 "active" glaciers (at least 25 acres in area) to be found within the park, along with countless waterfalls and hundreds of crystalline lakes. In summer the landscape is heavy with huckleberries and dotted with fuzzy white bear grass.

Highlights

Look for ★ to find recommended sights, activities, dining, and lodging.

★ **Lake McDonald:** The largest lake in the park and arguably one of the most beautiful, glacially carved Lake McDonald is easy to access. Pack a picnic for the rocky beach or cruise the waters on a boat tour (page 132).

★ **Going-to-the-Sun Road:** Stretching just over 50 miles (80 km), this phenomenal feat of engineering gives viewers an extraordinary overview of Glacier (page 133).

★ **Hiking:** Among the best-loved trails in the park is the Highline Trail, the shorter version of which climbs 1,950 feet (594 m) over 11.8 miles (19 km), then drops more than 2,200 feet (671 m) over the last 4 miles (6.4 km) back to Going-to-the-Sun Road. The views are staggering but not for the faint of heart (page 133).

★ **Many Glacier:** Prime hiking, canoeing, and horseback riding country, this stunning area in the northeast section of the park is popular but rarely crowded (page 147).

★ **Grinnell Glacier:** Since scientists anticipate that the glaciers in the park could disappear entirely by 2030, seeing Grinnell Glacier may be a once-in-a-lifetime opportunity. The ranger-led hike is especially worthwhile (page 148).

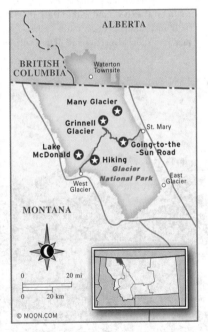

ALBERTA

BRITISH COLUMBIA

Waterton Townsite

Many Glacier

Grinnell Glacier

St. Mary

Lake McDonald

Going-to-the-Sun Road

Hiking

Glacier National Park

West Glacier

East Glacier

MONTANA

0   20 mi
0   20 km

© MOON.COM

While wildlife-viewing from the road can be challenging in this mountainous terrain, the animals—grizzly and black bears, mountain goats, bighorn sheep, wolves, and more—are here in abundance. With 1,583 square miles of alpine majesty, the scenery, if not the altitude, will leave you breathless.

Glacier National Park is a haven for nature lovers, and visitors can enjoy the natural beauty in a number of ways—hiking, bicycling, boating, and cross-country skiing, to name a few. There are 746 miles (1,200 km) of trails throughout the park and a smattering of historic lodges and chalets for cozy accommodations. Yet despite its extensive offerings, Glacier still provides visitors a rare and precious sense of solitude. The crowds are gone as soon as your feet hit the trail, and there are miles of shoreline where the only other picnickers are four-legged. More than just the Crown of the Continent, Glacier is like no place on earth.

PLANNING YOUR TIME

Depending on the amount of time you have to spend in Montana, Glacier National Park could easily absorb all of it, but often it is a spectacular route to get from one side of the Continental Divide to the other, in which case some sights take priority.

The 50-mile (80-km) Going-to-the-Sun Road, which now requires an advance reservation, is one of the most scenic drives you will ever take and the best way to get an overview of the park if your time is limited. The alpine vistas provide a marvelous sense of the geography, and the park's history comes alive for those who stop to notice the architecture of the road itself. The drive will likely take at least two hours, not accounting for construction, traffic, or weather-related delays, but if time permits even just an extra hour, there are plenty of turnouts and hiking opportunities along the way. Hidden Lake

Overlook is a wonderful 2.7-mile (4.3-km) round-trip hike from the Logan Pass Visitor Center that provides opportunities to view seasonal wildflowers and wildlife. Any time in Glacier's backcountry will be time well spent, but visitors should be prepared for changes in the weather (dress in layers and bring water) and wildlife encounters.

With more than a day, visitors can see some of the park's idyllic corners. Many Glacier is a launching spot for day hikes to numerous alpine lakes and glaciers. Lake McDonald, the park's largest, is a favorite place to spend the day. The southern section of the park, accessed from US 2, is especially popular in winter with cross-country skiers who make tracks from the Izaak Walton Inn in Essex.

Planning is critical in Glacier, as accommodations within and immediately surrounding the park fill up as much as a year in advance. The 1,009 campsites throughout the park, on the other hand, are filled primarily on a first-come, first-served basis (with a few notable exceptions: Fish Creek and St. Mary can be reserved in advance, as can half the individual and group sites at Apgar and some of the campsites at Many Glacier). Still, last-minute travelers are not necessarily out of luck (see page 138 for more information). For park brochures, which can be immensely helpful in planning your trip, visit www.nps.gov/glac. For those who are willing to stay outside of the park and launch day trips, the gateway towns of Whitefish and Kalispell have many more choices for accommodations.

INFORMATION AND SERVICES

If you have questions before arriving in Glacier, visit the Plan Your Visit section on the Glacier National Park website (www.nps.gov/glac) or call the Park Headquarters (406/888-7800, 8am-4:30pm daily year-round).

Previous: Hidden Lake; kayaking Lake McDonald; fireweed in summer.

Glacier National Park

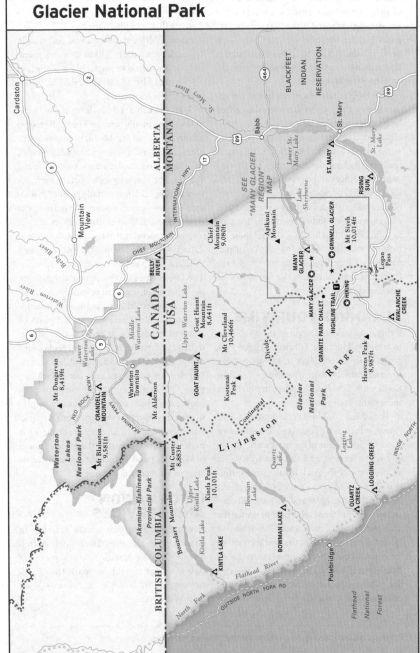

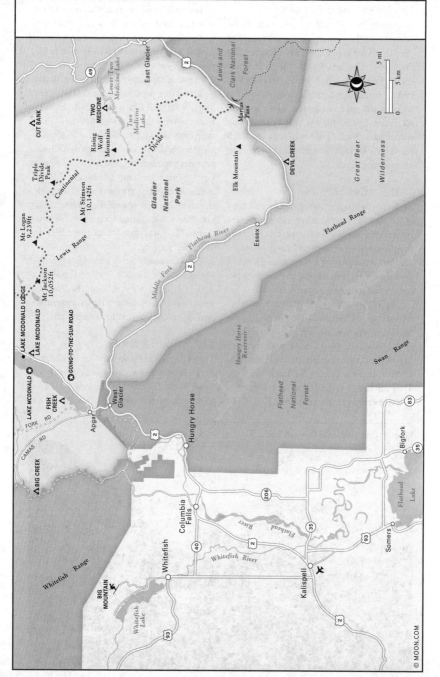

© MOON.COM

Park Fees and Passes

Entrance to **Glacier National Park** (406/888-7800, www.nps.gov/glac) costs $35 per vehicle for seven days May-October, $30 for motorcycles, and $20 for hikers and bikers. An annual park pass for Glacier costs $70, and an annual America the Beautiful Pass is $80 and will gain you entrance into any and all national parks for one year. A seven-day winter pass (Nov.-Apr.) for Glacier costs $25 per vehicle and $20 for an individual on foot, bike, or motorcycle.

Visitor Centers

At the park entrance, visitors are given a copy of *Vacation Planner,* which provides important general information about the park. Once inside the park, visitor centers and ranger stations are the best sources of information. Hours of operation vary, but during the summer the centers and stations are open every day.

The **Visitor Information Headquarters Building** (64 Grinnell Dr., 8am-4:30pm Mon.-Fri. year-round, excluding holidays) is just inside the West Glacier park entrance before the actual entrance station; turn right after passing the Glacier National Park sign. They can issue a variety of passes and permits as well as answer most questions.

The park's visitor centers all have knowledgeable staff, guidebooks and maps, and basic amenities. In West Glacier, visit the **Apgar Visitor Center** (8am-4pm daily May and late Sept.-Oct., 7am-5pm daily June-third Sat. in Sept., only open Sat.-Sun. in winter as staffing permits) in the central part of Apgar Village. It is two doors down from the **Backcountry Permit Center** (406/888-7800, open daily late May-mid-Sept., or by appointment when closed for the season), which also provides trip planning. The **St. Mary Visitor Center** (8am-5pm daily late May-early Oct.), inside the eastern park entrance, is the park's largest visitor center and offers backcountry permit services when staffing allows. Be aware that St. Mary was closed throughout 2021 due to limited staffing.

The **Two Medicine Ranger Station** and **Many Glacier Ranger Station** (both 8am-4:30pm daily late May-mid-Sept., backcountry permits available), close to the campgrounds, provide visitor information and permits.

Entrance Stations

The two main entrances to Glacier National Park are at either end of Going-to-the-Sun Road. **West Glacier,** on the west side of the park, can be accessed from US 2, and **St.**

hikers on the Hidden Lake Overlook Trail

Ranger Programs

Some of the best resources on Glacier National Park are the Park Service rangers—encyclopedias in hiking boots. Their stations are conveniently located at major sites throughout the park, and the rangers host a number of outdoor educational events geared to the whole family. Though COVID-19 severely limited the number of hosted events, the ranger programs in Glacier normally begin in late spring and run throughout the summer, with most activities offered at St. Mary, Apgar, Logan Pass, Many Glacier, Goat Haunt, and Two Medicine. Rangers typically lead several guided hikes each day that allow visitors to learn about the park's geology, history, wildlife, flora, fauna, and more. The St. Mary Visitor Center, Fish Creek Amphitheater, Lake McDonald Lodge, and Many Glacier Hotel host slide lectures as part of the ranger program. Full-day hikes, boat tours, and Junior Ranger programs also are available.

One of the most noteworthy park programs is "Native America Speaks," where members from the Blackfeet, Salish, Kootenai, and Pend d'Oreille tribes provide campfire talks about their life, culture, and influence in Glacier. The speakers range from artists and musicians to historians who intersperse their talks with personal stories and Native American legends. These talks are given at the Apgar, Many Glacier, Two Medicine, and Rising Sun Campgrounds. July-August, the St. Mary Visitor Center also hosts weekly Native American dance troupes. For times, locations, and descriptions of the ranger programs offered, pick up the free "Ranger-led Activity Schedule" available at any of the park's visitor centers.

For information on ranger stations or programs and to download park brochures, contact **Park Service Headquarters** (406/888-7800, www.nps.gov/glac).

Mary, on the park's east side, can be accessed from US 89. Entrance stations on the west side are at **Camas Creek** and the **Polebridge Ranger Station** off Outside North Fork Road, and on the east side at **Two Medicine** off Highway 49, **Many Glacier** off US 89, and at **Waterton Lakes National Park** accessible from Alberta Provincial Highways 5 and 6. Entrance fees must be paid even when entrance stations are closed. There is a self-registration area available at the entrance stations when the stations are not staffed. Alternatively, visitors can buy them online in advance through www.recreation.gov.

Services

Lodging in Glacier is available through separate providers. **Glacier National Park Lodges** (855/733-4522 or 303/265-7010 outside the U.S., www.glaciernationalparklodges. com) Cedar Creek Lodge, Many Glacier Hotel, Swiftcurrent Motor Inn & Cabins, Rising Sun Motor Inn & Cabins, Lake McDonald Lodge, and Village Inn at Apgar. **Glacier Park Collection by Pursuit** (844/868-7474, www.

glacierparkcollection.com) operates Grouse Mountain Lodge, Glacier Park Lodge, St. Mary Village, Belton Chalet, Apgar Village Lodge & Cabins, Motel Lake McDonald, West Glacier RV Park & Cabins, West Glacier Cabin Village, and Prince of Wales Hotel. Granite Park Chalet (www.graniteparkchalet.com) and Sperry Chalet (www.sperrychalet.com) are booked and managed independently.

If you arrive and discover you are missing some important piece of recreational equipment—or more important, bear spray—almost anything you need can be rented from **Glacier Outfitters** (196 Apgar Loop, 406/219-7466, www.goglacieroutfitters.com). From camping gear and backpacks to bicycles, paddleboards, kayaks, canoes, fishing rods, GoPro cameras, and, yep, bear spray, this is the place to make sure you have what you need in the way of toys and gear.

Pets

Although pets are allowed in drive-in campgrounds, picnic areas, and on roads open to car traffic, they are required to be on a leash

Hands-On Learning

Founded in 1983, the Glacier Institute (406/755-1211, www.glacierinstitute.org) is a private nonprofit organization that offers hands-on educational experiences using its official partners, Glacier National Park and Flathead National Forest, as its classrooms. Its mission is "strengthening connections to the natural world through outdoor education." The Glacier Institute fulfills its mission by providing field-based experiences in and around the park for all ages and levels of fitness.

The Glacier Institute offers 3- to 5-day youth camps, starting at $125-450, which have a variety of focuses. Whether it is the first overnight camp experience for children away from their parents, an introduction to the basic concepts of ecology, or a focus on art and nature, the institute offers experienced guides and experts to foster each child's learning. For those too young to spend the night away, there is a day camp ($75 day) for kids offered throughout the summer in Columbia Falls. The institute has outdoor education courses open to young and old. You can enroll for a daylong course ($50-100) with expert instructors on topics such as, for instance, wolves of the North Fork Valley, for a unique learning experience.

To peruse the institute's extensive and fascinating offerings, visit its website; if you see a course that interests you but is not being offered when you plan to be in Glacier, the Glacier Institute creates custom programs and can plan a half-day to several-day course just for your group (1-6 people, $500-700) based on the courses or expert instructors that you select.

no longer than 6 feet (1.8 m) at all times. They are not permitted on any trails within the park, and park officials strongly discourage the presence of pets in Glacier. Because of this policy, it is nearly impossible to find pet-friendly accommodations in the area. Well-socialized pups can enjoy a very ritzy stay with open plan sleeping and tons of outdoor green space at K9 Camp & Boarding Retreat (Hwy. 35, Kalispell, 406/755-7487, www.k9campandboardingretreat.com).

TRANSPORTATION
Getting There
BY AIR

The closest airport to Glacier is 30 miles (48 km) away in Kalispell. The Glacier Park International Airport (FCA, www.iflyglacier.com) is served by Delta, Alaska Airlines, United, Allegiant, and seasonal flights on American, Sun Country, JetBlue, and Frontier. At the airport Avis, Budget, Hertz, and National/Alamo have car-rental counters, and Dollar, Thrifty, and Enterprise have car-rental lots off-site but near the airport. Arrow Shuttle (406/300-2301, www.arrowshuttletaxi.com) and Wild Horse Limousine (406/756-2290 or

800/841-2391, www.wildhorselimo.com) offer taxi and limo services, respectively.

Great Falls International Airport is 130-165 miles (209-265 km) to the southeast of entrances at St. Mary, Two Medicine, and Many Glacier.

Missoula International Airport is roughly 150 miles (242 km) south of the park entrance at West Glacier.

BY CAR

By car, the park is accessible from US 2 and Highway 89. It is about 150 miles (252 km) north of Missoula and 150 miles (252 km) northwest of Great Falls.

BY TRAIN

Amtrak runs the Empire Builder from Chicago to Seattle, with daily stops in both directions in East Glacier (summer only), Essex, and West Glacier.

Getting Around
PRIVATE VEHICLES

Vehicles and vehicle combinations longer than 21 feet (6.4 m), including bumpers, and wider than 8 feet (2.4 m), including mirrors, or taller than 10 feet (3m) are not permitted on

Going-to-the-Sun Road between Avalanche Campground and the Rising Sun Parking Area. Stock trucks and trailers can access Packers Roost on the west side and Siyeh Bend on the east side.

SHUTTLES

Glacier's **free shuttle system** (406/892-2525, 7am-7pm daily July-Labor Day) picks up and drops off at 16 different stops, including Apgar Visitor Center, Avalanche Creek, Logan Pass, St. Mary Visitor Center, and a number of trailheads. West-side shuttles depart every 15-30 minutes and east-side shuttles depart every 40 minutes. Starting in 2021, Glacier implemented a **Ticket-to-Ride** system ($1 per ticket, www.recreation.gov) in an effort to reduce long lines at visitor centers and transfer points. Tickets can be reserved in one-hour increments between 7am and 2pm, and are good for the day. You must validate your ticket in the hour for which it was purchased or have it expire. The shuttle is an excellent option for hiking from the Logan Pass Visitor Center, which regularly has a full parking lot otherwise, or for doing trails that start at one trailhead and end at another. To travel the entire Going-to-the-Sun Road from the Apgar Visitor Center to the St. Mary Visitor Center and back, or vice versa, takes approximately seven hours on the shuttle. The last service to Logan Pass with time to visit and return departs Apgar Visitor Center at 4:15pm and St. Mary Visitor Center at 6:31pm. Check daily schedules for early morning express service from Apgar Visitor Center to Logan Pass. And since the number of stops along the route has decreased, be sure you confirm on the map that you can board and disembark where you planned.

TOURS

Scenic, interpretive **Red Bus Tours** (855/733-4522 or 303/265-7010 from outside the U.S., www.glaciernationalparklodges.com, $70-140 adults, $40-70 children) are another way to see the park. These snazzy vintage buses, known locally as "Jammers," were originally built by the White Motor Company 1936-1939. The vehicles, which have been overhauled for safety purposes, are 25 feet long, seat 17 passengers, and have the added bonus of roll-back canvas tops, ideal for sunny summer days. Numerous tours of varying lengths are available, from 2.5 to 9.5 hours, and informative guides entertain with facts and stories about Glacier. It's an excellent way to leave the driving to someone else.

Slightly less flashy but quite comfortable are the air-conditioned and large-windowed coaches of **Sun Tours** (406/226-9220 or 800/786-9220, www.glaciersuntours.com, June-Sept. 1, $55-100 adults, $35-52 children 5-12, free for children under 5). Tours last four, six, or eight hours, and what makes them unique is that they are guided from a Blackfeet perspective. Plants and roots used for Blackfeet medicine are pointed out, for example, as are the natural features that relate to the Blackfeet Nation. The coaches can accommodate 25 passengers and depart daily from East Glacier, Browning, St. Mary, and West Glacier. Sun Tours also offers a hiker shuttle service and private custom tours.

PLANTS AND ANIMALS
Plants

With more than 1 million acres, Glacier National Park offers a staggering number of microclimates, including forests, alpine meadows, lakes, rocky peaks, and glacial valleys, that are home to an incredible diversity of plant and animal life.

With two climate zones (Pacific maritime and prairie/arctic), three major watersheds (Pacific, Atlantic, and Arctic), and a range of biomes at various elevations, Glacier is home to a broad selection of plantlife. There are 20 different tree species and at least 1,132 species of vascular plants, 858 nonvascular, including 127 nonnative species. There are nearly 900 species of moss and lichen, almost 1,000 species of wildflowers, and more than 100 species of plants that are listed by the state as "sensitive." Amazingly, some of the tiny,

Bear Safety

Glacier has significant concentrations of both grizzly and black bears, both of which can be threatening in any encounter. The keys to safe travel in the backcountry are acting to prevent bear encounters and knowing what to do in the event you do meet a bear. The following are simple guidelines for responsible behavior in bear country:

- **Don't surprise bears.** Make noise, even on well-traveled trails, to allow bears the opportunity to get away from you. Bells can be effective, as can singing, hand-clapping, and loud talking. Never assume that a bear has better senses than you and will see, hear, or smell you coming.

- **Don't approach bears.** Be aware of their feeding opportunities and behavior so that you can avoid potential feeding locations and times of day. Avoid hiking through berry patches, cow parsnip thickets, or fields of glacier lilies. Never approach a carcass, which could be under the surveillance of a bear. Try not to hike at sunrise or at dusk, both active times for bears. Always keep children in close proximity.

- **Minimize the possibility that a bear would be attracted to your belongings or campsite.** Abide by all the park regulations about hanging your food and garbage away from your sleeping area. Don't carry odiferous food, and never bring anything potentially edible, including medicines and toothpaste, into your tent. Take special care with used feminine hygiene products by sealing them in several zip-top bags with baking soda to absorb the odor.

- **Be prepared for an encounter.** Carry pepper spray that is not out of date and know how to use it. Familiarize yourself with the behaviors most likely to ensure your safety in a bear encounter.

If you do surprise a bear, keep your wits about you. While there is no easy or universal answer about how to react—bears are as individual and unpredictable as humans—the following are accepted behaviors outlined on Glacier's website:

- **Talk quietly and calmly.** If you have surprised a bear, don't attempt to threaten it; if possible, try to detour around it.

- **Never run.** Don't turn your back; instead, back away slowly, unless it agitates the bear. Running could trigger its predator instincts.

- **Use peripheral vision.** Bears may perceive direct eye contact as aggressive behavior on your part.

- **Drop something (not food) to distract the bear and keep your pack on for protection.** If you have bear spray, grab it and be prepared to use it in the event of an attack.

- **Protect yourself if the bear attacks.** Protect your chest and abdomen by falling to the ground on your stomach or assuming the fetal position. Cover the back of your neck with your hands, and if the bear tries to roll you over, attempt to stay on your stomach. If the attack is defensive, the bear will leave once it has determined you are not a threat. If the attack is prolonged, fight back!

seemingly delicate alpine plants that are beaten and battered by the harsh climate year after year can live to be more than 100 years old.

Visitors from the northern part of North America will find familiar flora in Glacier. Divided into four floristic provinces,

Glacier's plant species are 49 percent cordilleran (which includes the southern and central Rockies as well as the Cascade Mountains in Washington), 39 percent boreal (which includes much of Canada), 10 percent arctic-alpine, and 1 percent Great Plains. The continent's easternmost hemlock forest thrives in the moist environment around Lake McDonald on the park's west side, offering a stark contrast to the wind-sculpted open forests and grasslands of the east side. There are also significant shifts in plant life from the north to the south as a result of changes in annual precipitation.

Animals

Glacier's diversity of habitats is a critical factor in the spectrum of wildlife that calls the park home. From the minute pygmy shrew, which weighs about as much as a dime, to indicator species like the grizzly bear, gray wolf, and mountain lion, Glacier is home to 71 species of mammals and more than 276 documented species of birds. Missing are bison and woodland caribou, both of which were grossly overhunted in the region prior to the park's designation in 1910.

Today the park is a safe haven for the Canada lynx and the grizzly bear, both of which are threatened, and the once-endangered gray wolf. There are healthy populations of elk, primarily in the grasslands of the park's eastern side, as well as moose, mountain goats, and bighorn sheep. Though rarely seen and few in number, wolverines, cougars, and fishers also live here. Glacier's tailed frog is considered the most primitive frog in North America, and the only one that fertilizes the female's eggs internally. It is most closely related to frogs in New Zealand, which has led scientists to believe that its origins date back 250 million years.

The addition of nonnative species and removal of native species can have far-ranging and catastrophic results. The healthy red-backed vole population on the park's west side eats primarily fungus, and they consequently spread fungal spores as they travel. The rootlets of the spores are almost entirely responsible for the regeneration of conifer trees in the region. Without the voles, there would be no forest. Without the fungus, there would be no voles. The ecosystem is as delicately balanced as it is captivating.

Evidence indicates that this area was inhabited as far back as 10,000 years ago, and the Salish, Kootenai, Flathead, and Blackfeet have all called Glacier home. The Blackfeet came to the region later than the others, entering the region sometime in the early 1700s and extending their territory through the eastern part of the park and onto the plains. The Blackfeet fought quite a few battles for territory with other tribes; the French, British, and Spanish fur trappers who entered the region in the 1800s in search of beaver pelts were wary of the Blackfeet.

When the Blackfeet Indian Reservation was created in 1855, it included the eastern part of the park up to the Continental Divide. In 1895 the Blackfeet sold the land to the U.S. government for $1.5 million with the agreement that they would still have unrestricted access for hunting, ceremonies, and other use. However, the U.S. government reneged on that agreement when they outlawed all hunting in Glacier National Park in 1910. Today the Blackfeet Indian Reservation borders the eastern edge of the park, and the Flathead Indian Reservation—which is home to the Confederated Salish, Pend d'Oreille, and Kootenai tribes—lies to the southwest.

In 1891, the Great Northern Railway completed its route over Marias Pass in the southern part of the park. By the turn of the 20th century it had become a tourist destination; visitors arrived by train and ventured into the park on horseback, on foot, or by boat. In 1910 the railroad started building hotels, lodges, and chalets to further entice visitors. There were few roads at the time, and visitors spent days working their way through the mountains, spending nights in different hotels and chalets. As the Great Northern Railway worked to attract visitors, George Bird Grinnell, a journalist who had first come west to cover the plight of the Blackfeet and who also founded the first Audubon Society, worked arduously to see this magnificent area achieve national park status, and in 1910

President Taft made Glacier the nation's 10th national park.

With the railroad, tourist facilities, and national park status, Glacier did attract a fair number of visitors, and soon there was demand for road access into the park. Going-to-the-Sun Road, a 50-mile (80-km) highway across the Continental Divide that runs from West Glacier to St. Mary, was completed in 1932 after years of treacherous surveying and more than a decade of construction. The road is an impressive engineering feat, now designated a National Historic Landmark, and offers visitors breathtaking (or stomach-churning, depending upon your tolerance for heights) views of the park. With the addition of the road, the number of visitors to the park skyrocketed, and the experience shifted. Now people were able to spend less than a day driving through the park as one of many stops on a cross-country car trip.

In 1932, as a gesture of goodwill between the United States and Canada, the park was joined with Canada's Waterton Lakes National Park to become Waterton-Glacier International Peace Park.

West Glacier Area

A bustling entrance to Glacier, West Glacier (pop. 166, elev. 3,220 ft/982 m) has the feeling of "last chance to get bug spray" and "first non-PB&J in a while." It is clearly not a destination but a portal, and a good place to find lodging, dining, and supplies in immediate proximity to the park.

The town itself grew up around the Belton Chalet, a lodge built by the Great Northern Railway in 1910, the same year Glacier became a national park. The Belton, an arts and crafts-style gem, was the first permanent lodging on the west side of Glacier, and thanks to a painstaking restoration in 2000 and a wonderful restaurant, it remains one of the best accommodations in the area.

SIGHTS
★ Lake McDonald
The largest lake in the park at 9.4 miles (15.1 km) long and 464 feet (141 m) deep, Lake McDonald was gouged out by a glacier that was likely 2,200 feet (671 m) thick. Surrounded by jagged peaks on three sides, it is bordered by the Lewis Range to the east, which creates a rain block and makes the Lake McDonald Valley one of the mildest and lushest environments in the region. Not unlike the Pacific Northwest, the Lake McDonald Valley boasts dense forests of towering western red cedars and hemlocks.

Although the lake and surrounding forests are exquisitely serene, the area is a hub of activity in the summer months for human visitors and the bear population alike. Modeled after a Swiss chalet and opened in 1914, the grand and slightly worse-for-wear **Lake McDonald Lodge** sprawls along the northeast shore and provides expensive lodging with unmatched views. The dining room, lounge, and pizzeria are open to nonguests. Stop in to warm yourself by the massive fireplace, check out the animal mounts that have decorated the place since its origins, or lounge lakeside on the veranda with a beverage.

There are many great hiking trails around the lake, including those to Fish Lake, Mount Brown Lookout, and the mellow Johns Lake Loop. Plenty of fish swim in the lake—17 varieties in all, mainly trout. Boat tours also depart from the lodge, as well as Red Bus Tours and ranger-led activities.

Bowman Lake
Some 32 miles (52 km) north of the west entrance to Glacier in the North Fork area, and only 30 miles (48 km) south of Canada, is Bowman Lake, another crystalline alpine gem ringed with mountains and forest. A long

bumpy ride is required to get here, and as a result it is less likely to be crowded. The density of mosquitoes tends to discourage visitors, too. But the 7-mile-long (11.3-km-long) lake is beautiful, and there is such a thing as bug spray. Boats are permitted, with restrictions on engines. Kayaks and canoes are a wonderful way to explore this photogenic setting. The lake is filled with fish, primarily kokanee and cutthroat trout, and the fishing is legendary, particularly in late spring. There are plenty of worthwhile hikes from the area, including the arduous 13.1-mile (21.1-km) round-trip **Quartz Lakes Loop,** but be warned that this is the heart of grizzly country, and visitors should come prepared with bear spray and a solid understanding of and respect for bear behavior and habitat. Camping is available on a first-come, first-served basis at the primitive **Bowman Lake Campground** (48 sites, late May-mid-Sept., $15), where several of the trailheads can be accessed. Vehicles over 21 feet in length and vehicles with trailers are prohibited at Bowman Lake due to the long, narrow, winding dirt road to the campground and tight parking spaces throughout. Be aware that as of 2022, the park requires an entry ticket ($2, www.recreation.gov) for the North Fork daily from 6am-6pm late May through mid-September.

TOP EXPERIENCE

★ Going-to-the-Sun Road

Completed in 1932, the famed Going-to-the-Sun Road is a marvel of modern engineering. Spanning 50 miles (80 km) from West Glacier to St. Mary, the road snakes up and around mountains that include its namesake, Going-to-the-Sun Mountain, giving viewers some of the most dramatic vistas in the country. The road, which crosses the Continental Divide, required more than two decades of planning and construction. It climbs more than 3,000 feet (900 m) with only a single switchback, known as **The Loop.** Going-to-the-Sun is an architectural accomplishment as well: All of the bridges, retaining walls,

and guardrails are built of native materials, so the road itself blends seamlessly into its majestic alpine setting.

In addition to being an experience all on its own, Going-to-the-Sun is also the primary access road to the park and the only way to get to some of the park's best-known highlights: the visitor center at Logan Pass, the Highline Trail, Lake McDonald, and an array of hiking trails. For visitors who are not keen on driving the road themselves, there are a few excellent options, including free shuttles, vintage tours, and Blackfeet tours, to see the road as a sightseer.

In 2021, with visitor levels hitting an historic high, the park service initiated a **vehicle reservation system** for the Going-to-the-Sun Road, as well as the North Fork area of the park from the Polebridge Entrance Station. As of 2022, entry tickets ($2, www.recreation.gov) are needed late May through mid-September, from 6am-4pm daily for the Going-to-the-Sun Road corridor, and from 6am-6pm daily in the North Fork area. A printed or digital copy of the ticket will be scanned at the park entrance station and is valid for 3 days for the Going-to-the-Sun Road, and for 1 day in the North Fork area.

SPORTS AND RECREATION

TOP EXPERIENCE

★ Hiking

Glacier is a hiker's paradise, and the west side of the park around the Lake McDonald Valley offers a unique opportunity to hike through primeval forests of western red cedars, hemlocks, and other species that thrive in this moist, moderate climate. For a number of reasons—including wildlife, weather conditions, and maintenance—hiking trails can be closed at any time. To check on the status of many of the park's most popular trails, visit www.nps.gov/glac or www.hikinginglacier.com.

Among the most popular and well-traveled trails near Lake McDonald is the **Johns Lake**

Loop, a relatively flat 1.8-mile (2.9-km) round-trip through prime moose habitat with waterfalls and lake views. It can be found just northeast of Lake McDonald Lodge. Also popular is **Trail of the Cedars,** an easy 0.7-mile (1.1-km) loop on a wheelchair-accessible boardwalk through spectacular forest. Leaving from Avalanche Campground, less than 5 miles (8 km) east of Lake McDonald Lodge, the trail crosses an impressive footbridge over Avalanche Gorge. Also leaving from Avalanche Campground, **Avalanche Creek Trail,** 4.5 miles (7.2 km) round-trip with a 730-foot (223-m) elevation gain, takes hikers to the picturesque, mountain-ringed Avalanche Lake. Parking at both trailheads tends to fill early, so the park's shuttles are a good option.

A longer and somewhat more strenuous hike is the trail to **Akokala Lake,** climbing roughly 600 feet (183 m) over 5.7 miles (9 km) one-way (11.4 mi/18 km out-and-back). The trailhead is at the north end of **Bowman Lake Campground** (a bumpy 32 mi/52 km north of West Glacier on Inside North Fork Rd. and Bowman Lake Rd.), and the trail runs over moderate terrain, through burned areas, to the remote Akokala Lake, which is filled with native cutthroat trout. The fishing is great, especially halfway around the west side of the lake, where the water is deep next to the shore. Reuter and Numa Peaks tower over the lake and provide a sublime backdrop. Like many of the trails in Glacier, this one cuts through grizzly country, and hikers should be well prepared with bear spray, humility, and awareness.

Certainly among the best-loved, and most heavily traveled, trails in the park is the **Highline Trail.** Leaving from Logan Pass at the summit of Going-to-the-Sun Road, the high-altitude trail to Granite Park Chalet is 15.2 miles (24.5 km) round-trip, out and back, over moderate terrain with a 500-foot (154-m) elevation gain. A **shorter option,** which

requires a shuttle, is to hike one way from Logan Pass to the Loop Trail, for a total hiking distance of 11.8 miles (19 km). Those who start at The Loop will hike up 2,300 feet (701 m), whereas those who start at Logan Pass will have more downhill than up. The trail can be crowded during summer but is breathtakingly scenic. The first part of the trail cuts into the Garden Wall above Going-to-the-Sun Road and is not for those with a fear of heights; the ledge can be frightening but provides remarkable views. En route to Granite Park Chalet (7.6 mi/12.2 km), the trail passes in the shadow of Haystack Butte, Mount Gould, and Mount Grinnell. Mountain goats and bighorn sheep often share the trail with a good number of hikers. If you're making it a day hike, plan on lunch at the chalet (888/345-2649, www.graniteparkchalet.com) before returning to the trailhead.

An alternative day-hike option is to make a loop using the park's shuttle service, which requires a $1 Ticket-to-Ride (www.recreation.gov). At Granite Park Chalet, the **Granite Park Trail** drops more than 2,200 feet (671 m) over 4 miles (6.4 km) back to Going-to-the-Sun Road at The Loop, where you can catch a shuttle back to Logan Pass.

Another popular and scenic hike from Logan Pass is along **Hidden Lake Overlook Trail,** sometimes referred to as Hidden Lake Nature Trail. It's a 2.7-mile (4.3-km) round-trip hike that starts as paved pathway from the west side of the Logan Pass Visitor Center. The paved trail becomes boardwalk, which allows passage even when there is snow, ice, and meltwater on the trail. The trail offers views of the striking Clements Mountain, the Garden Wall, and Mount Oberlin. After a little more than half a mile, the boardwalk ends and the trail heads toward Bearhat Mountain. At just over 1.2 miles (1.9 km), hikers arrive at the Continental Divide; the Hidden Lake Overlook is at 1.35 miles (2.2 km). On clear days, Sperry Glacier can be seen in the distance. Mountain goats frequent the area and wildlife encounters can happen anytime.

1: Lake McDonald shoreline **2:** Heavens Peak from The Loop **3:** rafting the Middle Fork of the Flathead River **4:** a view from Going-to-the-Sun Road

Be prepared for bighorn sheep, marmots, wolverines, and grizzly bears.

Boating

Before Going-to-the-Sun Road was completed, most of Glacier's adventurous visitors saw the park by boat. Today this nostalgic mode of travel offers benefits all its own. Both Lake McDonald and Bowman Lake offer excellent boating and fishing opportunities in the form of kayaking, canoeing, and even semi-restricted motorboating. Boat rentals are available at Apgar and Lake McDonald Lodge. For hour-long boat tours—think sunset cocktail cruises in a historic wooden boat on Lake McDonald—and rentals, the **Glacier Park Boat Company** (406/257-2426, www. glacierparkboats.com, tours $22.25-33.25 adults, $11-16.75 children 4-12, free for children under 4) is the ultimate resource. Rowboats and double kayaks can be rented for $22 per hour, paddleboards for $15 per hour, and 8 horsepower motorboats for $28 per hour.

Rafting

Although there is no rafting inside the park, white-water outfitting services in West Glacier offer trips on the 87-mile (140-km) Middle Fork of the Flathead River. The North Fork of the Flathead, which forms the western boundary of the park, can be rafted as well. **Glacier Raft Company** (106 Going-to-the-Sun Rd., West Glacier, 406/888-5454 or 800/235-6781, www.glacierraftco.com, half day from $79 adults, $69 children 12 and under, full day from $159 adults, $134 children 12 and under) offers everything from half-day and dinner floats to multiple-day expeditions. The company caters to all floaters, from novices to adrenaline junkies. In addition, the company offers horseback riding excursions, fly-fishing, and kayaking.

Montana Raft Company (11970 US 2, West Glacier, 406/387-5555 or 800/521-7238, www.glacierguides.com, all-inclusive half day from $72 adults, $59 children 12 and under, full day from $127 adults, $99 children) is the sister company of Glacier Guides and has some of the most well-rounded and knowledgeable guides in the area. Group numbers tend to be smaller (9 in a boat as opposed to 14), and the company offers an expansive range of options including rafting and horseback riding, overnight adventures, inflatable kayak trips, family-friendly day trips, raft and dinner trips, and scenic floats. Because of water conditions, in June the minimum age for rafters is eight; from July through the rest of the season, rafting is available to those ages six and up.

Another noteworthy outfitter offering rafting trips in the region is **Wild River Adventures** (11900 US 2 E., West Glacier, 406/387-9453 or 800/700-7056, www.riverwild. com, half day from $62 adults, $52 children). All-day trips, including lunch, are $101 for adults and $81 for children. Minimum age for rafters in May and June is 12, and 6-year-olds and up can raft from July onward. They also offer evening dinner white-water rafting (adults $94, children $76), sport raft wild side tours ($89 adults), inflatable kayak tours ($105 full day adults, $69 half day adults), and custom overnight adventures ($210-230 adults per day, $170-210 children per day) on both the Middle Fork and North Fork.

Bicycling

Biking in Glacier is not for the nonchalant. The climbs are treacherous, the edges precipitous, and the automobile traffic even worse. But the thrill of reaching the summit of Going-to-the-Sun Road, seeing how far you've come, soaking in the scenery, and whooshing back down again is unrivaled.

Still, as with any activity in Glacier, cyclists should be well aware of the conditions, restrictions, and potential hazards. Common sense prevails: Use helmets and reflectors; wear brightly colored and highly visible clothing; and watch for falling rocks, wildlife, and ice on the road. Bicycles are prohibited 11am-4pm daily June 15-Labor Day between Apgar Campground and Sprague Creek Campground. From Logan Creek to Logan

Pass, eastbound (uphill) bicycle traffic is prohibited 11am-4pm daily June 15-Labor Day. It takes roughly 45 minutes to ride from Sprague Creek to Logan Creek, and three hours from Logan Creek to the summit of Logan Pass. Bicycles cannot be ridden on any of the hiking trails, other than on a few marked trails in Waterton Lakes National Park. For more information on restrictions and current road closures, check online at www.nps.gov/glac.

Bicycles can be rented at Apgar Village from **Glacier Outfitters** (196 Apgar Loop, 406/219-7466, www.goglacieroutfitters. com). It rents e-bikes (ages 16 and up, $80 for 4 hours, $125 for the day), hybrid road-mountain bikes ($26 for 2 hours, $39 for 4 hours, $52 for the day), road bikes ($34 for 2 hours, $52 for 4 hours, $67 for 24 hours), kids' bikes ($22 for 2 hours, $33 for 4 hours, $44 for 24 hours), and even bike racks ($15-20) for regular and e-bikes.

Helicopter Tours

If seeing the park from atop Going-to-the-Sun Road is not quite dramatic enough, consider **Glacier Heli Tours** (406/728-9363, www. minutemanaviation.net, rates depend on helicopter availability), which can give adventuresome visitors a bird's-eye view of Iceberg Lake and Gunsight Pass, the Chinese Wall, and more. Operated by Minuteman Aviation out of Missoula, the company's primary role is to use their fleet for firefighting, so tours can only happen when helicopters are not fighting fires.

Golf

Golfers not afraid of a little distraction in the form of stunning mountain scenery can hit the links at the 18-hole **Glacier View Golf Club** (640 Riverbend Dr., 406/888-5471, www.glacierviewgolf.com, $20-45 for 18 holes, $10-30 for 9 holes, $18 for cart per seat for 18 holes) in West Glacier.

Horseback Riding

Another historical form of transportation in Glacier can be enjoyed even today: Guided

horseback rides, from one hour to a full day, are available in good weather late May to mid-September at the corrals at Apgar, Lake McDonald, and Many Glacier from **Swan Mountain Outfitters** (406/387-4405 or 877/888-5557, www.swanmountainglacier. com), the only outfitter that can offer trail rides inside the park. Options include hour-long rides ($55), 2-hour trips ($85), and full-day trips ($225). They also offer options for rides and cookout meals ($85-150). Rates do not include gratuities, which are encouraged. Reservations are required.

Cross-Country Skiing

When the white stuff blankets the park, cross-country skiers and snowshoers find themselves in a winter paradise. Many of the hiking trails double as ski and snowshoe trails, but nothing is groomed, so keen and constant orientation is critical. The **Lower McDonald Creek** trailhead is just south of McDonald Creek Bridge, and the trail is 2-3 miles (3.2-4.8 km) round-trip of gentle, forested terrain that parallels the creek in some spots. Another fairly level but longer option is the **Rocky Point** trail, which is 6 miles (9.7 km) round-trip and rewards skiers with a phenomenal view of Lake McDonald. The trailhead can be found 0.2 mile (0.3 km) north of Fish Creek Campground. Farther north, toward Avalanche Campground, **McDonald Falls** (4 mi/6.4 km round-trip), **Sacred Dancing Cascades** (5.3 mi/8.5 km round-trip), and the **Avalanche Picnic Area** (11.6 mi/18.7 km round-trip) make excellent day trips.

Since many of the roads in the park are unplowed and impassable for cars in winter, they can make excellent ski trails. Going-to-the-Sun Road is one of the best, although because of avalanche danger, it can often be closed east of Avalanche Creek.

Although it's not in the park, one of the region's best-known and beloved areas for cross-country skiing is the **Izaak Walton Inn** (off US 2, Essex, between East Glacier and West Glacier, 406/888-5700, www. izaakwaltoninn.com), which has repeatedly

Planning a Last-Minute Trip to Glacier

Rooms in Glacier's historic lodges and chalets can already be full up to a year ahead, but spontaneous travelers are not necessarily out of luck. Last-minute cancellations and room openings are possible and well worth a couple of phone calls. **Glacier Park Collections by Pursuit** (844/868-7474, www.glacierparkcollection.com) is the booking service for the Grouse Mountain Lodge, Glacier Park Lodge, St. Mary Village, Apgar Village Lodge & Cabins, Motel Lake McDonald, West Glacier Motel & Cabins, and Prince of Wales Hotel. Call and ask specifically for cancellations. You may have better luck if you are open to whatever they have to offer; being flexible with your dates helps.

Glacier National Park Lodges/Xanterra (855/733-4522, www.glaciernationalparklodges.com) is the booking service for Cedar Creek Lodge, Many Glacier Hotel, Swiftcurrent Motor Inn & Cabins, Rising Sun Motor Inn & Cabins, Lake McDonald Lodge, and Village Inn at Apgar. In this case, too, a phone call to ask about cancellations can lead to a windfall.

view from Granite Park Chalet

For visitors willing to hike in to their accommodations, **Granite Park Chalet** (888/345-2649, www.graniteparkchalet.com, from $117 pp, $82 additional person in same room, optional linen and bedding service $25 pp) is a fantastic option and well worth a call to see if they have last-minute openings. The 17 rooms in **Sperry Chalet** (888/345-2649, www.sperrychalet.com, $241 first person, $160 each additional person per room) burned to the ground in a 2017 wildfire, but the historic property was ambitiously rebuilt and opened in 2020. There are also a handful of workshops put on at Sperry Chalet each summer on topics including glaciers, high alpine ecology, and Glacier Park history that include two nights in the chalet. Still rustic—there is no heat, electricity, or running water—and only accessible on foot, Sperry offers beds with bedding and three informal meals with each night's stay.

For true spontaneity, pitch a tent in one of Glacier's 1,000-plus campsites in 13 campgrounds, at least some of which are open May to mid-October. With the exception of St. Mary, Fish Creek, half the campsites at Many Glacier, and half the group sites at Apgar, all campgrounds are available on a first-come, first-served basis, with nightly fees of $10-23. An excellent page on the National Park Service website (www.nps.gov/glac) shows updated availability at campsites across the park, and even gives the time of day each campground was filled the day before. Apgar is the largest campground, with 194 sites, followed by Fish Creek (178 sites), St. Mary (148 sites), and Many Glacier (109 sites). For advance reservations no more than six months ahead of time at Fish Creek or St. Mary, contact the **National Park Reservation System** (877/444-6777, www.recreation.gov).

In the spirit of spontaneity, almost anything you need for your recreational purposes can be rented from **Glacier Outfitters** (196 Apgar Loop, 406/219-7466, www.goglacieroutfitters.com), from bear spray to camping gear.

been named one of the best cross-country ski resorts in the Rockies. With trails groomed for skiers mid-Dec.-late Mar., the resort boasts approximately 20 miles (32 km) of groomed trails, and its proximity to the park invites backcountry travel. Ski rentals are available for classic ($20 day adults, $15 day children size 36 and smaller), skate, and backcountry skis ($30 day). Plus, a night or two at the inn will be something to remember.

FOOD

Even if you are not planning to stay at the Belton Chalet, the hotel offers two distinct and rich dining experiences that are definitely worth a visit in this land of burgers and grilled cheese. The **Belton Dining Room** (12575 US 2 E., 406/888-5000 or 844/868-7474, www.beltonchalet.com, 5pm-9pm daily summer, $17-38) provides an intimate, exquisite dining experience in the historic 1910 chalet. The menu changes seasonally, and chef Earl offers innovative dishes incorporating the freshest ingredients from local Montana growers and the chalet's own Flathead Lake orchard. For dinner you could sample heirloom tomatoes and *burrata* cheese, a farm-to-market pork shank, or Montana meatballs made from beef, pork, and bison. For equally delicious lighter fare and a more moderately priced experience, you can visit the hotel's **Belton Tap Room** (3pm-9pm daily summer, $8-12), where you may choose to accompany a locally brewed Montana beer with pork belly sliders or a lamb burger.

The **Glacier Highland Restaurant** (12555 US 2, 406/888-5427, www.glacierhighland.com, 7:30am-10pm daily July-Aug., off-season days and hours vary, breakfast $8-13, lunch $10-16, dinner $13-21) is an authentic West Glacier diner experience. Located just before the entrance to the park and across from the Amtrak depot, this is an easy stop if you are craving a 5-ounce burger with all the toppings and freshly cut fries. Hearty homemade soups and delicious sweet treats, baked each day in the bakery, are also on offer.

For breakfast and lunch with outdoor seating options in Apgar Village, **Eddie's Café & Mercantile** (236 Apgar Loop Rd., 406/888-5361, www.eddiescafegifts.com, 7am-9pm daily summer, breakfast $9.25-14.25, lunch and dinner $9-17.50) serves up excellent grub including biscuits and gravy, breakfast burritos, bison burgers, and pulled pork.

The closest restaurant to the entrance at West Glacier is the **West Glacier Restaurant** (190 Going-to-the-Sun Rd., 406/868-7474, 7:30am-9pm daily mid-May-Sept., $8-17). Set in a classic Park Service-like building, the restaurant offers casual dining with homemade soups, salads, burgers, and yummy baked goods. The attached full-service **Freda's Bar** serves up delicious cocktails, wine, and beer, not to mention sports on satellite TV for those who are so inclined.

A long ways down a dirt road in Glacier's North Fork Valley is a special off-the-grid spot that is worth every bump and then some. The remote and wonderful **Polebridge Mercantile** (265 Polebridge Loop, 406/888-5105, www.polebridgemercantile.com, 7am-9pm daily Memorial Day-Labor Day, 9am-6pm daily Labor Day-last Sun. in Oct. and late Mar.-Memorial Day, $3.50-9) offers world-class baked goods—don't leave without at least a couple of huckleberry bear claws—and a full deli in addition to groceries and gifts. Lodging and gear rentals are also available.

ACCOMMODATIONS

The West Glacier area has a good selection of places to stay, but once inside the park, or even within view of it, accommodations do not come cheap. If you are on a tight budget, camping is the best option. The hotels listed are only open during the summer season, when Glacier is busiest. However, for avid cross-country skiers who want to take advantage of the park during the winter, the **Izaak Walton Inn** (off US 2, Essex, between East Glacier and West Glacier, 406/888-5700, www.izaakwaltoninn.com, $139-409), a charming old railroad hotel that is on the National Register of Historic Places, is open year-round. In addition to homey rooms in the lodge, guests can select from unique accommodations including family cabins and beautifully restored railcars.

Also in Essex, 20 miles (32 km) from West Glacier and 35 miles (56 km) from East

Glacier, is **Glacier Haven Inn & Healthy Haven Café** (14305 US 2 E., 406/888-5720, www.glacierhaveninn.com, $130-189), which offers clean, comfy accommodations in addition to great home-style cooking.

A reasonably priced motel in the West Glacier area is the **Apgar Village Lodge & Cabins** (Lake View Dr., West Glacier, 406/892-2525 or 844/868-7474, www.glacierparkcollection.com, $169-369), 2 miles (3.2 km) east of West Glacier village at the south end of Lake McDonald. There are 28 cabins with Western decor that sleep up to eight, most with kitchens with stoves and refrigerators, and each with its own picnic table. Ask for a cabin on McDonald Creek; you can literally fish from your front door. There are also 20 modestly furnished, clean motel rooms, some overlooking the creek, with either a queen or two twin beds.

On the shores of Lake McDonald, the **Village Inn at Apgar** (1.3 mi/2.1 km from the entrance at West Glacier, 855/733-4522, www.glaciernationalparklodges.com, $129-309) is a quaint, 1950s motor inn with 36 rooms and a listing on the National Register of Historic Places. As one of the less expensive accommodations in the park, it is typically booked a year in advance.

West Glacier Village Motel & Cabins (200 Going-to-the-Sun Rd., West Glacier, 844/868-7474, www.glacierparkcollection. com, motel rooms from $149) is divided between two properties—half the motel units are about 1 mile (1.6 km) from the park entrance in West Glacier, and the cabins and other motel units are on a secluded bluff that overlooks the Flathead River. It's a great value for the price and location. Pets are not allowed. The cabins on the bluff require a minimum stay of two nights and offer kitchenettes but no air-conditioning or television. There's also an RV park with spaces that start at $105 per night.

Also in West Glacier, just across the street from the Amtrak depot, is the **Glacier Highland Resort** (12555 US 2 E., 406/888-5427, www.glacierhighland.com, May-Oct., from $145), which offers 33 clean, simple rooms.

If you are willing to spend a bit more, two historic lodges are worth a night's stay. **Lake McDonald Lodge** (Going-to-the-Sun Rd., 12 mi/19.3 km from West Glacier, 855/733-4522, www.glaciernationalparklodges.com, $121-531) was built in 1914 by the furrier John Lewis and adheres to the Swiss chalet style of architecture. Though the lodge and cabins are showing their age, they still outshine the 1950s motor inn on-site. The 82-room lodge emanates rustic charm and still has personal touches, such as Lewis's hunting trophies displayed in the lobby. As it was built before there were roads running through Glacier, visitors arrived at the lodge by boat, and the hotel's original entrance faced the lake. Today most guests arrive by car, and the hotel is conveniently located off Going-to-the-Sun Road on the shore of Lake McDonald. Upon entering the lodge, visitors are struck by its warmth and charm. The spacious lobby is surrounded by balconies on three sides. Guests and visitors can enjoy sipping a cocktail on the sprawling veranda, a serene setting that affords a beautiful view of the lake. The guest rooms are rustic yet comfortable, and the location allows easy access to trailheads and boat tours. Fishing lessons and day trips by horseback are available and can be arranged by the hotel.

The most memorable stay in West Glacier is at ★ **Belton Chalet** (12575 US 2 E., 406/888-5000 or 888/235-8665, www. glacierparkcollection.com, rooms $160-250, cottages $270-385) at the west entrance to the park. This was the first hotel built by the Great Northern Railway and dates to 1910. It was fully restored in 2000 and is a National Historic Landmark. Guests can experience a piece of history while enjoying modern amenities. All 25 guest rooms come with a queen bed and private bathroom and are beautifully furnished with antiques. The two cabins on the grounds each have three bedrooms to accommodate up to six people. Although the lodge is mostly closed during the winter season, the cabins are available to rent

Backcountry Camping

That Glacier National Park is a wild place cannot be overstated. Backcountry camping in this wild and potentially dangerous place requires thoughtful planning and meticulous attention to the rules and regulations. A strong dose of common sense can go a long way. Backcountry campers have to be smart about orientation, wildlife encounters, rapidly changing and adverse weather, and stream and snowfield crossings, all of which can be potentially deadly. Here is a list of simple but critical guidelines and etiquette for backcountry travel.

- **Make a plan and chart your route.** Carefully examine elevation gain and loss. Carrying a heavy pack more than 10 miles (16 km) in a day with a 2,500-foot (762-m) elevation change is an extremely ambitious and perhaps overly rigorous endeavor. Topographical maps and hiking guides are available at park visitor centers and ranger stations as well as online through the **Glacier National Park Conservancy** (www.glacier.org). Make sure you are aware of trail and campsite closures, fire restrictions, weather forecasts, local bear activity, and so on. Glacier offers an excellent online trip planner at www.nps.gov/glac.

- **Secure all your permits.** All backcountry campers must camp in established campsites and have a backcountry-use permit ($7 pp per night) for the duration of the trip. Campsites can be reserved in advance when you apply for the permit, or within 24 hours of the trip. Application forms can be downloaded (www.nps.gov/glac) but are accepted starting March 15 online only, and the application fee is $40, not including the $7 per person per night camping fee, which must be paid in person when you pick up the permit. Permits must be picked up at one of five permit-issuing stations (St. Mary Visitor Center, Many Glacier Ranger Station, Two Medicine Ranger Station, Polebridge Ranger Station, and Waterton Lakes National Park Visitor Reception Centre) no sooner than one day before the trip and no later than 4:30pm on the day of departure.

- **Pack intelligently.** All campers should be prepared for a dramatic range of weather conditions by packing appropriate footwear and layered clothing, rain jacket and pants, and footwear for crossing streams. Other items to remember when packing include an appropriate amount of low-odor food, a tent and sleeping bag with pad, a compass and topographical maps, a first-aid kit, weatherproof food and garbage bags, 25 feet (7.6 m) of rope to hang bags, a water container and purifying system, a camp stove and fuel, an emergency signaling device, and a trowel. Bear spray is an absolute necessity.

- **Obey all rules and practice the seven principles of Leave No Trace.** Plan ahead and prepare, travel and camp on durable surfaces, leave what you find, properly dispose of waste, minimize campfire impacts, respect wildlife, and be considerate of other visitors. The goal anytime you are in the backcountry is to use your skills and be motivated by an ethic of responsibility for the natural resource, taking care of it conscientiously.

For visitors seeking the backcountry experience without all the preparatory work, guided trips can be arranged through **Glacier Guides** (406/387-5555 or 800/521-7238, www.glacierguides.com), and equipment can be rented from **Glacier Outfitters** (196 Apgar Loop, 406/219-7466, www.goglacieroutfitters.com).

GLACIER NATIONAL PARK
WEST GLACIER AREA

throughout the year. The hotel does not provide TVs, phones, or air-conditioning, as they can detract from the natural setting, but Wi-Fi is available at no charge. The lodge is immediately adjacent to both the highway and the train tracks, so silence is not possible. A fabulous restaurant on-site offers innovative and satisfying meals, and a fully stocked taproom specializes in Montana brews. You can enjoy a good book in the lobby's reading area or curl up by the large stone fireplace. The incredibly friendly staff even offer wake-up calls for northern lights and bear sightings. Visitors looking for a bit of luxury, or relief for sore hiking muscles, will find a spa offering massages on-site.

CAMPING

Glacier has 13 front-country campgrounds with more than 1,000 sites, at least some of which are open May to mid-October. With the exception of St. Mary and Fish Creek, half the individual and group sites at Apgar, and half the campsites at Many Glacier, all campgrounds are available on a first-come, first-served basis, with nightly fees ranging $10-23. You'll increase your chances of finding a site by showing up earlier in the day and scheduling your trip midweek rather than on the weekend. An excellent page on the National Park Service website (www.nps.gov/glac) shows updated availability at campsites across the park. **Apgar** ($20) is the largest campground, with 194 sites, followed by **Fish Creek** ($23), with 178 sites; **St. Mary** ($23), with 148 sites; and **Many Glacier** ($23), with 109 sites. For advance reservations at Fish Creek or St. Mary, contact the **National Park Reservation System** (877/444-6777, www.recreation.gov).

If your decision to camp is last-minute and you find yourself without such critical items as a tent or sleeping bag, **Glacier Outfitters** (196 Apgar Loop, 406/219-7466, www.goglacieroutfitters.com) can help with its stock of rentable items.

East Glacier Area

Located on the Blackfeet Indian Reservation at the southeast corner of the park, East Glacier (pop. 388, elev. 4,799 ft/1,463 m) has long been a primary entrance into Glacier National Park. Early visitors from the east often arrived by rail at East Glacier and spent the night in the grand Glacier Park Lodge before heading into the wilds of the park.

Today the town of East Glacier bustles year-round and is a hub of activity during the summer months as visitors stream in and out of the park. There are numerous accommodations, including the still-majestic Adirondack-style Glacier Park Lodge, several good restaurants, local outfitters, and a smattering of shops. There is also a tremendous amount of wilderness to be explored both inside the park and in immediate proximity to East Glacier. The stunning Two Medicine Valley is just a few miles away, and hiking, skiing, and even snowmobiling trails are within steps of the main drag.

SIGHTS
Two Medicine Valley

Geographically, Two Medicine Valley is not at the heart of Glacier, but this remote southeastern corner is staggeringly beautiful and seemingly less known among the mass of summer visitors. The rocky peaks and glacially carved valleys meet in clear alpine lakes, and the area offers plenty of activity. There are boat tours that intersect with hiking trails, numerous waterfalls to ogle, fishing, and a lovely campground.

SPORTS AND RECREATION
Hiking

More of a stroll than a hike, the trail to **Running Eagle Falls** is 0.6 mile (1 km) round-trip, kid-friendly, and wheelchair-accessible. The waterfall is interesting, as it changes from a double fall in spring and early summer to a single one by late summer; it appears to emerge from within the rock wall. The trailhead for this easy but scenic hike is on the park road roughly 1 mile (1.6 km) west of the Two Medicine entrance.

Visitors who want to explore the region with an expert local guide can contact Alger Swingley of **Blackfeet Tours** (406/450-8420, www.blackfeettours.com) to plan a hike in the Badger Two Medicine area with a certified interpretive guide (8 hours, from $275) or do a three-day/two-night backcountry pack trip either hiking ($850 adults, $425 children under

12) or on horseback ($1,250 adults), into the mountains south of Glacier.

One particularly exquisite, and perhaps nostalgic, way to explore Glacier is by combining a boat ride with a hike. An excellent place to do so is in the Two Medicine Valley. The **Glacier Park Boat Company** (406/257-2426, www.glacierparkboats.com, $16.75 adults, $8.25 children 4-12, free for children under 4) offers 45-minute cruises, with optional guided hikes, from the Two Medicine Lake boat dock to the far end of the lake, cutting 6 miles (9.7 km) off the hike to **Twin Falls** and **Upper Two Medicine Lake.** It's backcountry hiking without the blisters. From the upper (unloading) dock, the hike to Twin Falls is just 0.9 mile (1.4 km), and an additional 2.2 miles (3.5 km) to the gorgeous upper lake. **No Name Lake,** at the base of the sheer Pumpelly Pillar, is another spectacular hike made easier with a boat shuttle. Instead of 5 miles (8 km) one-way, with the boat it is 2.2 miles (3.5 km) with an 800-foot (244-m) elevation gain. For those looking to put more miles on their feet, there are trails on either side of Two Medicine Lake, making a variety of loops possible. Farther north of Two Medicine, the **Cut Bank Trailhead** offers fantastic hiking with even fewer visitors—perfect for solitude seekers. As is true throughout Glacier, hikers should carry bear spray and be prepared for wildlife encounters.

Bicycling

There aren't many places in the country where you can hop on a bike, head to the nearest highway, and pedal through spectacular scenery in every direction. Although the inclines can be steep and the declines precipitous around East Glacier, the air is fresh and the mountain vistas unrivaled. The traffic—human and animal—needs to be minded.

For avid cyclists, it's possible to do a 137-mile (221-km) loop in and around the park: Head southwest from East Glacier on US 2 to West Glacier, then over Going-to-the-Sun Road to St. Mary, then south on US 89 and Highway 49 back to East Glacier. Remember that eastbound Going-to-the-Sun Road is closed to cyclists from Logan Creek to Logan Pass, 11am-4pm daily June 15-Labor Day, so plan accordingly. In the vicinity of East Glacier, biking to the Two Medicine Valley, 12 miles (19.3 km) northwest of town, is also a popular route.

The closest place from which to rent bicycles is on the west side of the park, at Apgar Village, from **Glacier Outfitters** (196 Apgar Loop, 406/219-7466, www.goglacieroutfitters.com).

Golf

Somewhat surprisingly, the **Glacier Park Lodge** (US 2 and Hwy. 49, 406/226-5642 or 406/892-2525, www.glacierparkcollection.com, late-May-Sept. as weather permits, $40 for 9 holes with cart) has a unique nine-hole golf course. Built in 1928 by Great Northern Railway tycoon James J. Hill, the course is the oldest grass course in Montana and permits soft spikes only. The course was originally named Oom-coo-ska-pes-che (Big Green Blanket) by Chief Earl Old Person. It was designed by a New York architect, but because the course was built within the boundaries of the Blackfeet Indian Reservation, each of the holes is named after a former chief of the Blackfeet Nation. Clubs, carts, and pull carts can be rented from the pro shop. A pitch-and-putt course is on-site as well.

Horseback Riding

For horseback riding outside the park on the Blackfeet Indian Reservation, **Glacier Gateway Trailrides** (Hwy. 49, across from the Glacier Park Lodge, 406/226-4408, off-season 406/338-5560, from $80 for 2 hours) offers excellent guided rides through magnificent country June-September. Trips range from two hours to full-day excursions; children must be at least seven years old. The guides are Native Americans, who offer a unique cultural perspective on places like Looking Glass and Two Medicine River Gorge.

Boating

As on the west side of the park, the **Glacier Park Boat Company** (406/257-2426, www.glacierparkboats.com, tours $16.75 adults, $8.25 children 4-12, free for children under 4) is the ultimate resource. Rowboats and double kayaks can be rented for $22 per hour, paddleboards for $15 per hour, and 8 horsepower motorboats for $28 per hour. Excellent 45-minute cruises on Two Medicine Lake take place at least four times daily mid-June to early September. The 2.5-hour guided hike to Twin Falls can be added at no extra cost.

FOOD

For a town with just over 300 year-round residents, East Glacier has a number of good restaurants that cater to Glacier-bound visitors. Often the best way to select a spot to eat is to walk around and see where the wait is shortest. **Serrano's Mexican Restaurant** (29 Dawson Ave., 406/226-9392, www.serranosmexican.com, 5pm-9pm daily May-Memorial Day and Labor Day-early Oct., 5pm-10pm daily Memorial Day-Labor Day, $8.50-29.50) is inside the oldest house in East Glacier. Nothing is old-fashioned, however, about the menu: There are classic and delicious Mexican favorites alongside local offerings that include Indian tacos and huckleberry carrot cake. American plates include chicken, steaks, and burgers. The food is good, and the atmosphere is quite festive. The fact that it's been in business for more than 25 years means something in this part of the world.

Two Medicine Grill (314 US 2 E., 406/226-9227, www.seeglacier.com/two-medicine-grill, 6:30am-9pm daily summer, 6:30am-8pm daily winter, breakfast $5-10, lunch and dinner $7.50-14.25) is a great spot for budget travelers. The menu has pretty standard fare for the region—bison burgers, homemade chili, chicken-fried steak—but the quality is excellent, and the staff are friendly and generous with advice and insights on the area. The

1: Two Medicine Lake **2:** hikers in Two Medicine Valley

huckleberry shakes are the stuff of legend, as is the double-crusted huckleberry pie. For a quick morning bite, **Rock 'n Roll Bakery** (34 Dawson Ave., 406/226-5553, 7:30am-3pm daily in summer, $2.50-5.75) has wonderful pastries, both sweet and savory braided breads, and pie. You can buy just a slice or, better yet, the whole shebang ($28 fruit, $39 huckleberry). You won't be sorry.

Getting rave reviews from locals and tourists alike is **Summit Mountain Lodge Steakhouse** (16900 US 2, 406/226-9319, www.summitmtnlodge.com, 5pm-9pm Tues.-Sun., $19-38), housed in an old train station with a beautiful outside dining area. The food is marvelous and locally sourced whenever possible. There is a good wine list, and pairing suggestions are offered. Entrées include saltimbocca, grilled beef tenderloin, wild prawns piccata, and a variety of salads and pasta. You could eat dirt on a summer night, with a view like this, and be happy. But luckily, you don't have to.

ACCOMMODATIONS

East Glacier has several small, kitschy motels that are ideal for a night or two before heading into the park, but they are not well suited for a week's stay. The standout alternative is the stately ★ **Glacier Park Lodge** (US 2 and Hwy. 49, 844/868-7474, www.glacierparkcollection.com, late May-late Sept., $149-399), which opened to guests in 1913. An Adirondack-style hotel commissioned by the Great Northern Railway, it was constructed of massive fir and cedar timbers, each weighing at least 15 tons. The local Blackfeet who watched the structure go up called it *omahkoyis,* or "big-tree lodge." The grounds are beautifully manicured—there's even a historic and very playable 9-hole golf course in addition to a pitch-and-putt. The 161-room hotel offers fine and casual dining, a cocktail lounge, a gift shop, an outdoor swimming pool, and a day spa. The rooms are modest but comfortable. Travelers with children will appreciate the family rooms with multiple beds. Although the setting at the edge of East

Glacier village is not quite as captivating, the Glacier Park Lodge is certainly in the same class as the Lake McDonald Lodge and even the Old Faithful Lodge in Yellowstone National Park.

Slightly off the main drag is the tidy and comfortable **Mountain Pine Motel** (909 Hwy. 49, 1 mi/1.6 km north of US 2, 406/226-4403, www.mtnpine.com, May-Sept., $100-300), with 25 units plus the Bear's Den cottage that sleeps up to 8.

The **Whistling Swan Motel** (512 US 2, 406/226-4412, www.seeglacier.com, $99-189 motel rooms, $169-249 cabins) is a long, skinny building that feels a bit like train cars—somewhat appropriate given that the Amtrak station is just across the street. The guest rooms are spotlessly clean and quite comfortable. Hosts Mark and Colleen are exceptionally hospitable and go out of their way to make every guest feel welcome and accommodated. This motel is also within easy walking distance of the local eateries and shops.

The **East Glacier Motel & Cabins** (1107 Hwy. 49, 406/226-5593, June-July 1 $130-200, July 2-Aug. 15 $150-250) offers six motel units and 11 cabins at an excellent value.

On the east side of town, offering cute, park-style cabins complete with kitchenettes, gas fireplaces, and covered front porches, **Traveler's Rest Lodge** (20987 US 2, 406/226-9143 summer or 406/378-2414 winter, www.travelersrestlodge.net, Apr. 15-Oct. 1, $149-189) is a great choice. There are discounts for staying more than one night.

Two miles (3.2 km) west of town on what used to be a dude ranch is **Bison Creek Ranch** (20722 US 2, 406/226-4482, www.bisoncreekranch.com, $89-140), a lodge offering simple sleeping cabins and larger A-frames. The same family has been pouring heart and soul into the ranch for more than 60 years, and it shows in every detail from the artwork to the housekeeping. Pets are permitted for a $15 fee.

A few miles from town is **Summit Mountain Lodge** (16900 US 2, 406/226-9319, www.summitmtnlodge.com, from $169), which offers eight cabins with modern amenities. Single cabins have one queen bed and a full kitchenette. Double units have two queen beds and a living area. Family cabins (from $295) sleep six. The setting and the views are world-class. And the on-site steakhouse, housed in an old train station, is a special place for a memorable meal.

If you are willing to hike to your accommodations, **Granite Park Chalet** (888/345-2649, www.graniteparkchalet.com, from $117 pp, $82 each additional person, optional linen and bedding service $25 pp) is a fantastic option. The last of the railroad chalets to be built, Granite Park Chalet is a hiker's hostel geared toward do-it-yourselfers. The rooms are private; hikers prepare their own meals and, although linens can be ordered ahead of time, generally sleep in their own sleeping bags. The most popular trail in to Granite Park is the 7.6-mile (12.2-km) **Highline Trail**, accessed from Logan Pass. A shorter 4-mile (6.4-km) trail through burned country and with a steep 2,300-foot (701-m) climb can be accessed from Going-to-the-Sun Road switchback known as The Loop, which is in fact not a loop. The 17 rooms in **Sperry Chalet** (888/345-2649, www.sperrychalet.com, $241 first person, $160 each additional person per room) burned to the ground in a 2017 wildfire, but the historic property was ambitiously rebuilt and opened in 2020. There are also a handful of workshops put on at Sperry Chalet each summer on topics including glaciers, high alpine ecology, and Glacier Park history that include two nights in the chalet. Still rustic—there is no heat, electricity, or running water—and only accessible on foot, Sperry offers beds with bedding and three informal meals with each night's stay.

CAMPING

Less than 20 miles (32 km) from East Glacier are a couple of scenic and shady campgrounds. Set on the lake, **Two Medicine Campground** (mid-May-late Sept., $20), with 100 sites and 10 RV sites, is 13 miles (20.9 km) outside town in some of Glacier's most breathtaking wilderness. It is well developed with potable water and flush toilets, an amphitheater for nightly ranger presentations, and one of the original Great Northern Chalets, which has been converted into a camp store and gift shop. Outside the regular season, primitive camping ($10) is possible late September-late October. Shuttle service, boat tours, and Red Bus Tours are all available from the campground. Sites are available on a first-come, first-served basis, and hiking in the area is as limitless as it is sublime.

Farther north is a smaller (14 sites) and more secluded spot, **Cut Bank Campground** (June-Aug. 23, $10), accessed 5 miles (8 km) down a dirt road from US 89. The campground has no water, so campers have to bring their own. Sites are available on a first-come, first-served basis, and day hikes in the area are top-notch. RVs are not recommended due to the nature of the road and the campground layout. Shuttles are only available from the highway.

St. Mary to Many Glacier

This place feels like it's at the edge of two worlds: mountains to the west, vast plains to the east. St. Mary is a small village nestled between St. Mary Lake and Lower St. Mary Lake that marks another entrance to the park and the start of Going-to-the-Sun Road. With all the splendor of the jagged peaks and the wide-open vistas created by sparse stands of aspen and sweeping prairie, the recreational opportunities are abundant and the scenery spectacular.

Farther north, Many Glacier is the ideal base camp for avid and active outdoors lovers, with extensive opportunities for hiking, canoeing, and horseback riding. The popular boat tours and Red Bus Tours are also accessible from Many Glacier. Grinnell Glacier is a dwindling but still phenomenal work of nature, and daily ranger-led hikes take visitors up to its toe. The Many Glacier Hotel is a historic 1915 Great Northern Railway Swiss chalet-style lodge that welcomes guests with a rambling veranda and cozy guest rooms.

SIGHTS

St. Mary Lake

One of the most photographed lakes in the park for its absurdly beautiful mountain backdrop, St. Mary Lake is among the best places in Glacier to watch the sun rise. The lake and its many hiking trails are accessible from Going-to-the-Sun Road. The **Sun Point Nature Trail** is 1.4 miles (2.3 km) round-trip, and the trailhead is 9.5 miles (15.3 km) west of the St. Mary Visitor Center. It is worth the short walk for views of Baring Falls and the lake itself. An even quicker stop is **Sunrift Gorge**, 0.6 mile (1 km) west of Sun Point, an incredible cascade slicing between two rock walls; it is just 200 feet (61 m) from the parking area. **Baring Falls** is another 0.3-mile (0.5-km) walk down the trail.

TOP EXPERIENCE

★ Many Glacier

The Many Glacier region is a palpable reminder of why Glacier has long been known as the Switzerland of America. Marked by grand accommodations and a landscape that was visibly scoured and carved by glaciers, from the U-shaped valleys and milky-blue glacial lakes to the rocky moraines and the last remaining glaciers themselves, this region is among the most dramatic and startlingly beautiful in the park.

This is not a place to be enjoyed from inside a car, although those on a tight schedule would still benefit from making the journey just to walk around the hotel to drink in the stunning surroundings. Many Glacier is best suited for active travelers: The hiking and

Many Glacier Region

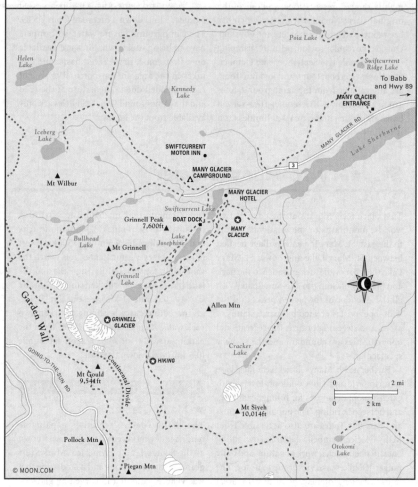

© MOON.COM

boating are exceptional, and it is one of the rare places in the Lower 48 where a day hike can lead you to an actual glacier. Come to Many Glacier to see the splendid scenery, but if possible, stay a few days to truly enjoy it.

TOP EXPERIENCE

★ Grinnell Glacier

Named for conservationist and explorer George Bird Grinnell, Grinnell Glacier lies in the heart of Many Glacier and is a symbol both of the park's wilderness and of the dramatic climatic changes that are occurring. Because the glacier is accessible within a day's hike, its startling shrinkage—from 710 acres in 1850 to 220 acres in 1993 and 152 acres in 2005—has been captured on film. Still, as long as it exists, this glacier is well worth visiting.

The options for seeing the glacier up close and personal are to hoof it from the **Many Glacier Hotel** (5.5 mi/8.9 km one-way with a 1,600-ft/488-m elevation gain) or to take a boat across Lake Josephine with **Glacier Park Boat Company** (406/257-2426, www.glacierparkboats.com, $33.25 adults, $16.75 children 4-12, free for children under 4) and hike the remainder of the trail from the head of Lake Josephine (3.8 mi/6.1 km one-way with a 1,600-ft/488-m elevation gain). There is also an excellent ranger-guided hike to the glacier that makes use of the boat, leaving the Many Glacier dock daily at 8:30am starting in mid-July (weather and conditions permitting). The 8.5-mile (13.7-km) round-trip outing lasts almost nine hours. The trail twists and climbs above impossibly blue alpine lakes and within sight of the aptly named Salamander Glacier. In the early season, hikers will get wet with runoff from the overhanging waterfalls along the trail. Come prepared! Though the trail is one of the oldest and most popular hikes in the park, and thus heavily trafficked, wildlife is plentiful in the area too, and grizzly bears are commonly spotted on or near the trail. The trail often does not open until late July and is seldom clear of snow until well into August.

Upper Waterton Lake and Goat Haunt

You won't necessarily need your passport to see one of the natural highlights of Canada's Waterton Lakes National Park, although the fjord-like valley is reminiscent of Norway, especially when it is shrouded in fog and mist. Upper Waterton Lake runs north-south, straddling the border. Prior to COVID-19 boats ran between the Canadian town of Waterton (headquarters for the park) and **Goat Haunt** at the lake's southern end, accessible only by hiking or by boat. Boats did not run in the area in 2020 or 2021, and a decision had not been made in 2022 as to when to restart service to the area. If you have plans to explore the area, be sure to check the NPS website or call ahead for updates.

On the Canadian side, **Crypt Lake Trail** (10.8 mi/17.4 km round-trip) is an ambitious hike that includes a natural tunnel through a rock wall, stomach-dropping heights, waterfalls galore, and a dazzling hidden cirque. There are several hikes, ranging from mellow to death-defying, from the Goat Haunt ranger station. Check online or call ahead to see if there are ranger-led hikes from the ranger station. A few favorites are **Rainbow Falls** (2 mi/3.2 km round-trip, no elevation gain), **Kootenai Lakes** (5 mi/8 km round-trip, 200-ft/61-m elevation gain), **Lake Janet** (6.6 mi/10.6 km round-trip, 750-ft/229-m elevation gain), and **Lake Francis** (12.4 mi/20 km round-trip, 1,050-ft/320-m elevation gain). For those willing to huff and puff, but only briefly, **Goat Haunt Overlook** (2 mi/3.2 km round-trip, 800-ft/244-m elevation gain) offers a phenomenal view of the valley. The isolation and lack of roads tends to keep visitor numbers down around Upper Waterton Lake, but the mosquitoes are abundant; come prepared.

There is a limited port of entry at Goat Haunt that was open 11am-5pm daily before COVID-19. The crossing was closed 2020-2021. As of 2022, a decision to reopen had not been made. If and when the entry reopens, travel between Waterton Lakes National Park, Canada, and the Goat Haunt Ranger Station on the U.S. side will require an official government-issued photo identification card for U.S. or Canadian citizens or permanent residents; all others must carry a valid passport. Persons seeking to travel beyond the Goat Haunt Ranger Station into the United States must present documents that are WHTI compliant.

SPORTS AND RECREATION
Hiking

One could quite literally spend a lifetime hiking in the St. Mary, Many Glacier, and Upper Waterton Lake region. For a close-up look at a couple of stunning waterfalls in the St. Mary area, head to the **St. Mary Falls** trailhead, just west of Sunrift Gorge. The trail is just 0.8 mile (1.3 km) one-way, with a 260-foot (79-m) elevation drop, to St. Mary Falls, and another 0.7 mile (1.1 km) one-way, with

Waterton Lakes: Glacier's Canadian Sister

Just north of Glacier, across the Canadian border in the southwest corner of Alberta, lies Waterton Lakes National Park. Similar in terrain to Glacier, the park is much smaller (about 203 sq mi compared to Glacier's 1,600 sq mi) and houses a small town, Waterton Park, within its borders. As in its neighbor to the south, the stunning landscape of this park was formed by melting alpine glaciers more than 10,000 years ago and later shaped by floods, fires, wind, and its natural wildlife and flora.

Before European settlement, various nomadic groups of Indigenous people passed through the area, gathering plants and hunting local wildlife. The most prominent in the area were the Kootenai, who eventually clashed with the Blackfeet that had followed the buffalo into Alberta and taken control of the plains. In 1858 the English explorer Thomas Blakiston was looking for a railroad pass through the Rockies. He encountered some members of the local Kootenai tribe, who directed him to a pass in the south. Traversing this path, he eventually came to an opening that looked on a chain of three lakes. He named the lakes after fellow British explorer and naturalist Charles Waterton, known to be quite eccentric. It became a national park in 1895, and the Great Northern Railway established the Prince of Wales Hotel in 1926, helping put the park on the map for tourists traveling from Glacier to Banff and Jasper in Alberta.

The star of Waterton's lakes is **Upper Waterton Lake,** situated on the U.S.-Canada border. It is the deepest lake in the Canadian Rockies and can be explored on a two-hour cruise that leaves from the Waterton marina and dips down into Montana before venturing back. If you have the time, you can disembark from the boat to follow the **Crypt Lake Trail,** considered one of the best hikes in Canada. Numerous trails around the lake lead past waterfalls, through valleys, and on to spectacular vistas.

Arguably one of the most photographed hotels in the world for its sublime setting, the **Prince of Wales Hotel** (Alberta 5, Waterton Park, 844/868-7474, www.glacierparkcollection.com, CA$259-809) is a magnificent Swiss chalet-inspired lodge that overlooks the lake and the town below. Although pricey, it is a great place to stay to have the full Waterton experience. If a night's stay is not in your budget, try to stop in for afternoon tea, which is served daily in the hotel lobby.

During the summer of 2017, two major wildfires roared through Glacier and Waterton Lakes National Parks. The Sprague Fire burned roughly 17,000 acres, primarily in Glacier's backcountry. The Kenow Fire burned more than 47,500 acres in Waterton Lakes, blackening entire valleys and altering the landscape for decades to come. The slopes on both sides of the Akamina Highway were burned and are visible to tourists. It's worth remembering that fire is a critical part of the ecosystem here; many species of trees rely on fire to reseed. So even though the scars are prominent, healthy regrowth is happening already and provides visitors a unique lens into the forces of nature.

Completed in the fall of 2021 after the existing visitor center burned in the wildfire, the gorgeous new **Visitors Reception Centre** (403/859-5133) is at 404 Cameron Falls Drive. It is open year-round (8am-4pm Mon.-Fri., 9am-5pm Sat.-Sun., but hours can change according to season and budget) and can provide you with plenty of information on the region.

a 285-foot (87-m) elevation gain, to the taller **Virginia Falls,** making a relatively easy and lovely 3-mile (4.8-km) round-trip hike.

For bear-savvy hikers with a penchant for floating ice, **Iceberg Lake** is an extraordinary day hike. The trail, 5 miles (8 km) one-way, with a 1,300-foot (396-m) elevation gain, is well traveled by hikers of the two-legged variety, but it also has one of the densest concentrations of grizzly bears in the park thanks to an abundance of huckleberries. Bear encounters are common, and no overnight camping is allowed. The well-marked

1: hiker above Grinnell Lake **2:** touring Swiftcurrent Lake **3:** Wild Goose Island in St. Mary Lake **4:** Iceberg Lake trail trailhead is at the very end of Many Glacier Road, the only road in this section of the park.

The lake itself is a sublime glacial blue with chunks of ice floating in it, often as late as September, but the chunks are bigger and more plentiful in July and August. The elevation is gained slowly, except for a short steep stretch at the beginning, which is enough to turn some hikers around, and passes through meadows bursting with wildflowers. Mountain goats and bighorn sheep are often visible on the last stretch of the hike. Ptarmigan Falls is halfway to the lake—a perfect resting spot. The bridge over Iceberg Creek is erected each summer and taken down each fall to prevent it washing out in spring. Most mornings in July-August, hikers can join a ranger-led hike to the lake, an especially good option for those with more than a healthy concern about bears.

It's always a good idea in Glacier, and this area in particular, to have a backup plan in place for trail closures, which are exceedingly common due to bears, other wildlife, and trail conditions.

Boating

Boats are permitted on St. Mary Lake, but you'll have to bring your own as there are no rentals on-site. There are 90-minute tours available several times daily through the **Glacier Park Boat Company** (406/257-2426, www.glacierparkboats.com, $27.50 adults, $13.75 children 4-12, free for children under 4). The tours depart from the Rising Sun boat dock, 6 miles (9.7 km) inside the east entrance on Going-to-the-Sun Road, and offer views of various waterfalls, Sexton Glacier, and Wild Goose Island. A 15-minute walk to Baring Falls is also an option on the St. Mary Lake cruise. Twice daily, the cruises can be combined with a guided hike to St. Mary Falls (less than 2 mi/3.2 km round-trip, 200-ft/61-m elevation gain) for a 3.5-hour outing.

In the Many Glacier area, rowboats ($18/hour), kayaks ($15/hour), and canoes ($18/hour) are available to rent at **Swiftcurrent Lake,** adjacent to the Many Glacier Hotel.

The **Glacier Park Boat Company** (406/257-2426, www.glacierparkboats.com, $33.25 adults, $16.75 children 4-12, free for children under 4) also provides scenic cruises on Swiftcurrent Lake and Lake Josephine. There are up to seven trips daily during summer, and cruises can be combined with guided hikes or used as a shuttle for hiking trips. A highlight for many is seeing the Grinnell Glacier on a cruise across Lake Josephine.

Fishing

While fishing permits or licenses are not necessary in Glacier National Park, it is imperative that anyone fishing abides by the regulations. A brochure can be picked up at any of the visitor centers or downloaded from the **National Park Service website** (www.nps.gov/glac).

Because of the altitude in Glacier, the water is colder, and some of the lakes in the park are sterile. St. Mary Lake is not especially productive water, but it sure is nice to stand in and soak up the scenery. There are some rainbow trout, brook trout, whitefish, and the rare bull trout in the lake for the patient angler. No bull trout may be kept. Shore fishing is possible, but the chances for catching increase significantly out in the deeper waters. St. Mary Lake can get rough quickly, with 2- to 3-foot swells, so keep a constant eye on the conditions.

In Many Glacier, presumably because of its proximity to the hotel and the road, the trout in crystal clear **Swiftcurrent Lake** see the most action, but they seem to have wised up. Brook trout in the 10-inch (25-cm) range are the most common catches here. **Lake Josephine** and **Grinnell Lake** have brook trout populations that seem more willing to take the bait or go for flies.

Some backcountry lakes are worth hiking into if fishing is the goal. **Red Rock Lake,** located along Swiftcurrent Creek, for example, is accessible by a fairly level 2-mile (3.2-km) hike and holds plenty of brook trout in the 10- to 12-inch (25- to 30-cm) range. Dry-fly anglers will do best in the morning or evening, the same time bears are most active, but will have to go deep in the afternoons.

FOOD

Without a doubt, the fanciest (and priciest!) place to go for a meal in St. Mary is the **Snowgoose Grille** (3 Going-to-the-Sun Rd., 406/732-4431, www.glacierparkcollection. com, 8am-9pm daily late May-late Sept., hours can vary so call ahead, $18-40) in the St. Mary Village. This slightly modern take on the Western steakhouse offers steak frites, bison stroganoff, huckleberry salmon, and wild game gnocchi, as well as plenty of vegetarian options, for both lunch and dinner. There are burgers, soups, and salads too. The adjacent **Curly Bear Café** is primarily a sandwich and ice-cream joint. Outside seating is available and highly desirable when the weather cooperates.

Two Dog Flats Grill (1380 Wisconsin Ave., 855/733-4522, www. glaciernationalparklodges.com, 6:30am-10am and 11am-10pm daily, $8-28) at the Rising Sun Motor Inn & Cabins is operated by Glacier National Park Lodges. It offers standard fare, from burgers and chicken to steak and pasta, and is open for three meals daily during the season. Basic boxed lunches are available with no substitutions.

The nearby ★ **Park Café** (3147 US 89, 406/732-9979, www.parkcafeandgrocery. com, 8am-7pm daily early June-mid-June, 7:30am-9pm June 20-Aug., 8am-7pm daily Sept. 1-mid-Sept., $12-26), in St. Mary, is staffed by people who know and really love Glacier National Park. The pies—nine flavors daily—are mouthwatering and worth every mile on the trail you'll need to work them off. The food is mostly American, from steaks and fish to outrageous baked potatoes, and for the most part as healthy as it is inventive and delicious. There's also a fantastic gift store and grocery on-site. This place should not be missed!

Up the road in Babb is the ★ **Two Sisters Café** (US 89, 4 mi/6.4 km north of St. Mary, 406/732-5535, www.twosistersofmontana.

com, 11am-9pm daily June-Sept., $5-29), a colorful place that is worth the scenic drive along Lower St. Mary Lake. Although the decor is rather outrageous, the food is sublime—a hiker's dream come true. Try the roasted Mexican chicken or their famous Red Burger and a slice of whatever pie they made that morning.

For those not cooking their own supper over a fire pan in Many Glacier, there are only a few options. The **Ptarmigan Dining Room** (Many Glacier Hotel, 855/733-4522, www.glaciernationalparklodges.com, 6:30am-10am, 11:30am-2:30pm, and 5pm-9:30pm daily mid-June-mid-Sept., breakfast $4-11, lunch and dinner $6-26) offers such flavorful entrées as pan-seared duck breast, bison tenderloin, burgers, and more. Lighter fare, including appetizers, burgers, salads, and cocktails, are available in its **Swiss Lounge** (11:30am-10pm daily, drinks until 11pm, $6-21). Many Glacier Hotel also has a snack shop and espresso stand on-site.

In the nearby Swiftcurrent Motor Inn & Cabins is a casual eatery, **'Nell's** (855/733-4522, www.glaciernationalparklodges.com, 6:30am-10am and 11am-10pm daily mid-June-mid-Sept., $10-18). It serves standard fare for three meals daily including pizza, pasta, and chicken, all of which can taste outstanding after a long day on the trail. Boxed lunches are available when ordered a day ahead.

ACCOMMODATIONS

Although options abound in both St. Mary and Many Glacier for hotels, motels, and cabins, there are not many budget-friendly choices. The prices seem to reflect the scenery, which is spectacular, rather than the amenities, which can be quite modest. Campgrounds and RV parks are more common, but small cabins can be found as well. The **Cottages at Glacier** (300 Going-to-the-Sun Rd., St. Mary, 406/309-4231, late May-Oct., $310-945) offer views of St. Mary Lake and comfortable two-bedroom accommodations with a steep price tag. Still, for those who want a full kitchen, Wi-Fi, and satellite TV, these cottages are excellent. In business for more than 70 years, **St. Mary Village** (US 89 and Going-to-the-Sun Rd., 844/868-7474, www.glacierparkcollection. com, mid-June-late Sept., $169-400) is a full resort with all the modern amenities. From tipis to cabins to luxury lodge rooms, this resort has 127 guest rooms among six facilities.

Adjacent to St. Mary Lake is the 1940s-era **Rising Sun Motor Inn & Cabins** (Going-to-the-Sun Rd., 855/733-4522, www. glaciernationalparklodges.com, mid-June-early Sept., $181-197), offering simple, clean, motel-style rooms and on-site dining.

In Many Glacier, the standout is clearly the **Many Glacier Hotel** (855/753-4522, www.glaciernationalparklodges.com, mid-June-mid-Sept., $225-472), a historic Swiss chalet-style lodge built in 1915 by the Great Northern Railway. The hotel is right on the shore of Swiftcurrent Lake, and there is no limit to the natural beauty of the region or the number of ways in which to enjoy it. The hotel is being refurbished, wing by wing, but the rooms are still simple and charming; the steep prices speak more to the hotel's setting in the Many Glacier Valley than its amenities.

There are no televisions in the rooms and the Wi-Fi is extremely limited. There is nightly entertainment and a wealth of activities that include boat cruises, ranger-led hikes, evening programs, Red Bus Tours, and horseback riding from the lodge.

Nearby, the **Swiftcurrent Motor Inn & Cabins** (855/753-4522, www. glaciernationalparklodges.com, mid-June-mid-Sept., $122-183) is decidedly less grandiose and equally less expensive. But this place also has a history; it was established as a tipi camp in 1911 by the Great Northern Railway. Three main lodgings are available: motel rooms, duplex-type cottages, and one-bedroom cabins without private baths. It has its own charm as a longtime stopping point for adventurers and road-trippers, and the location cannot be beat. For the price, it is an excellent place to stay.

CAMPING

Two park campgrounds are available near the village of St. Mary. **St. Mary Campground** (www.recreation.gov, $23) has 148 sites, including 22 sites that can accommodate RVs and truck-trailer combinations up to 35 feet (10.7 m), as well as water and flush toilets. It is the park's largest campground, only 0.5 mile

camping in the Many Glacier region

(0.8 km) from the St. Mary Visitor Center, and has limited shade but superb views. The regular season is late May-mid-September, but primitive camping ($10) is available early April-late May and mid-September through November. Winter camping is also possible December-March. Sites can be reserved up to six months in advance for June through the first Sunday in September online at www. recreation.gov.

The second is **Rising Sun** (www.recreation. gov, mid-June-early Sept., $20), which has 84 sites with 10 sites for RVs, water, flush toilets, and showers. It is halfway along St. Mary Lake in the shadow of Red Eagle Mountain. Some sites are exposed, while others are tucked into the trees. All are available on a first-come, first-served basis.

Not far from the Many Glacier Hotel, the **Many Glacier Campground** ($23) has 109 sites, including 13 sites for RVs up to 35 feet (10.7 m), as well as water, flush toilets, and showers available at the nearby Swiftcurrent Motor Inn & Cabins. The regular season is late May-late September, but primitive camping ($10) is available late September-October. In 2020-2021, camping was by reservation only (www.recreation.gov). The views are phenomenal, and the access to hiking and boating is amazing. Arguably the most popular campground in the park, Many Glacier fills up early, so plan accordingly.

Missoula and Western Montana

From the towering pines and massive cedars to

the mountain of huckleberry ice cream clinging to your cone, just about everything is larger than life in western Montana.

The region is home to three Native American tribes on one major reservation, an assortment of wildlife refuges, and enticing towns such as Missoula and Whitefish. The craggy Mission Mountains beside Flathead Lake and the Bitterroots, just south of Missoula, are but two of the ranges that make up the spine of the Rockies in this lush, green corner of Montana, the only place in the state that boasts some promising wineries. Western Montana is steeped in Western history, from Lewis and Clark to the Nez Perce and the state's earliest missions, and home to one of the state's fastest-growing areas, the Bitterroot

Highlights

Look for ★ to find recommended
sights, activities, dining, and lodging.

★ **Carousel for Missoula and Caras Park:** Built from the dream of one man and the outpouring of the entire community, this extraordinary hand-built carousel is a magical place to spend a beautiful summer day (page 160).

★ **St. Ignatius Mission:** A jewel of a mission founded by Jesuit priest Adrian Hoecken, this massive brick Catholic church is still impressive, but it has a troubling history (page 187).

★ **Cherry Picking:** Timing your visit to Flathead Lake for the annual cherry harvest promises sweet, juicy memories to savor (page 193).

★ **Hiking at Jewel Basin:** With 27 lakes, 35 miles (56 km) of trails, and no motorized vehicles or horses permitted, this is a hiker's paradise (page 193).

★ **Skiing at Whitefish Mountain Resort:** This phenomenal ski area has a view over Whitefish Lake and perhaps the best après-ski scene in the state (page 208).

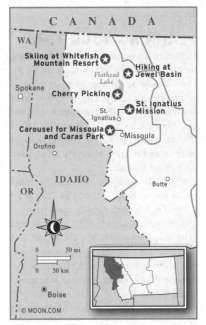

Valley, as well as the National Bison Range. The region feels like the Pacific Northwest in some ways—lush greenery, ancient trees, snowcapped peaks, and, rather unfortunately, the scars of hyper-ambitious logging, which often led to catastrophic wildfires that, as recently as 1910, devoured entire cities in a matter of minutes.

As is true of the state in general, western Montana is a slice of paradise for outdoors enthusiasts. From the sublime Flathead Lake in the north, with its boating, fishing, and unbeatable swimming, and the nearby Jewel Basin, famous for hiking, huckleberries, and grizzly bears, to the Rattlesnake National Recreation Area and Wilderness just outside Missoula and the rugged Bitterroot Mountains in the south, this corner of the state, some 12,000 square miles of diverse and magnificent habitat, is for many the embodiment of the Wild West and the Montana dream brought to life.

PLANNING YOUR TIME

Missoula is a natural stopping point along both east-west I-90 and north-south US 93, and it's easier to get here by air than much of the state, but the city is also a great destination in itself. From boutique shopping and hip eateries near the University of Montana to adventurous athletic pursuits in town and nearby, Missoula is Montana with an urban edge.

Using Missoula as a base, many visitors cruise down the Bitterroot Valley for an active day trip with fishing opportunities, historic missions and mansions, and cool little mountain towns like Hamilton and Stevensville. Another option is to stay at one of the numerous guest ranches in the Bitterroot Valley that have quick and easy access to Missoula.

Almost any part of western Montana can be accessed within a day's drive of Missoula, including the tiny but bustling villages lining the sandy shores of Flathead Lake—don't miss charming Bigfork with its galleries, eateries, and theater—as well as Glacier National Park and its gold-letter gateway town of Whitefish, a marvelous destination with great restaurants and world-class recreation. Whitefish's proximity to Glacier Park and the Flathead National Forest makes it an obvious vacation spot for outdoors enthusiasts. Just south of Whitefish, the larger and slightly less picturesque Kalispell has plenty of lodging options, easy air access, and a couple of interesting, offbeat museums.

HISTORY

Because of harsh winters, unforgiving terrain, and territorial Native Americans, this land was not as quick to be settled by Europeans as other parts of Montana. The earliest inhabitants were the Salish, Kootenai, and Pend d'Oreille people, who fished the lakes and hunted the forests and valleys. Fur trappers and traders—attracted by the abundance of beaver in the lakes—entered the area in the early 1800s. David Thompson, the famous Canadian explorer and fur trapper, set up trading posts in the area 1807-1812, including the first trading post established west of the Rockies.

When the Salish traveled through the Missoula valley in search of bison, the Blackfeet would ambush them as they entered the canyon. French trappers who passed through the canyon in the early 1800s encountered the gruesome remains of various massacres and dubbed the area "Hell Gate." Not far from Hellgate Canyon, Lewis and Clark met the Blackfeet, who introduced them to the main flower of the valley, a staple of the Indian diet, but Lewis found it bitter and inedible, thus giving the bitterroot lily, and eventually the valley, its name.

The Flathead (or Salish) were responsive to conversion by missionaries, and by 1840 St. Mary's Mission had been established; the

---

Previous: Bitterroot Mountains; the Carousel for Missoula; fishing near Kalispell.

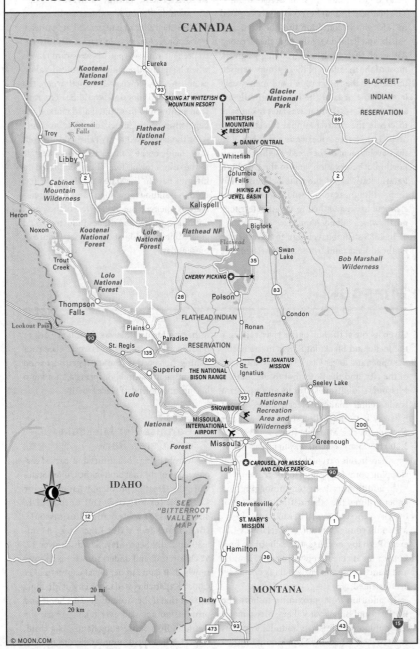

Missoula and Western Montana

CANADA

Kootenai National Forest

Eureka

93

★ SKIING AT WHITEFISH MOUNTAIN RESORT

WHITEFISH MOUNTAIN RESORT

★ DANNY ON TRAIL

Glacier National Park

BLACKFEET INDIAN RESERVATION

89

Troy

Kootenai Falls

Flathead National Forest

Whitefish

2

Libby

2

Columbia Falls

★ HIKING AT JEWEL BASIN

Cabinet Mountain Wilderness

Kalispell

Heron

Noxon

Kootenai National Forest

Lolo National Forest

Flathead NF

Bigfork

Flathead Lake

Swan Lake

Bob Marshall Wilderness

Trout Creek

Lolo National Forest

35

★ CHERRY PICKING

28

83

Thompson Falls

Polson

Condon

Lookout Pass

Plains

90

St. Regis

135

Paradise

FLATHEAD INDIAN

RESERVATION

Ronan

Superior

Lolo

200

★ THE NATIONAL BISON RANGE

St. Ignatius

★ ST. IGNATIUS MISSION

Seeley Lake

National

93

SNOWBOWL

Rattlesnake National Recreation Area and Wilderness

200

Greenough

Forest

MISSOULA INTERNATIONAL AIRPORT

Missoula

90

Lolo

★ CAROUSEL FOR MISSOULA AND CARAS PARK

IDAHO

SEE "BITTERROOT VALLEY" MAP

Stevensville

ST. MARY'S MISSION

12

Hamilton

38

1

MONTANA

0   20 mi

0   20 km

Darby

473   93

43

15

© MOON.COM

St. Ignatius Mission was moved from Lake Pend d'Oreille to Mission Creek in 1854. The Flathead Indian Reservation was created in 1855 on the condition that the Kootenai, Salish, and Pend d'Oreille share the territory. Although their leaders begrudgingly agreed, most of the members of these groups refused to move to the reservation until many years later. Two-thirds of the land originally assigned to the reservation was later taken back to create the many national forests in the area. The Native Americans contributed to the development of the area by selling a small portion of reservation land to the Northern Pacific Railway, at the time believing that their willingness to sell would lead the government to expand their reservation territory north, which did not happen.

In 1885 steamboats began to travel across Flathead Lake, and by the 1890s settlements had appeared on the lake's eastern side. The Northern Pacific Railway laid tracks through the town of Missoula at the same time, and by 1891 the railroad had arrived at Flathead. In response, Charles Conrad, a wealthy entrepreneur who stopped his westward travels when he fell in love with the Flathead Valley, established the town of Kalispell, where the main railroad junction would be. The railroad's entry into this region also marked the beginning of its timber industry: Not only were the trees used to lay railroad lines, but they could now be transported across the state to the rest of the nation. The wood played an integral part in the state's mining industry, used in building mine shafts and fueling numerous smelters. But like the rest of the state's natural resources, the timber industry would create boom-and-bust cycles that endure to present day.

Missoula

Given its site at the hub of five river valleys—the Jocko and Blackfoot Rivers to the north, the upper and lower Clark Fork east and west of the city, and the Bitterroot to the south—Missoula's longtime status as an important trade center makes perfect sense. About halfway between Yellowstone and Glacier National Parks, Missoula (pop. 73,489, elev. 3,200 ft/975 m) is on the way to just about everywhere in this part of the state and a natural stopping point for visitors to the region.

In addition to its history of logging and paper milling, the other defining element of the city—the University of Montana—keeps Missoula young, vibrant, and relatively liberal. Perhaps because the school is best known for its creative writing, art, drama, and dance programs, Missoula is decidedly arts-oriented.

In addition to its proximity to both the Flathead and Bitterroot Valleys, Missoula offers outdoors enthusiasts abundant options right in town—hike the M on Mount Sentinel or hang glide off it, kayak the Clark Fork or bike along its shores. There is world-class river fishing, hot-potting (the art of getting to and swimming in natural hot springs), mountain biking, and no end of places to hike.

SIGHTS

★ Carousel for Missoula and Caras Park

Aside from being a beautiful hand-carved carousel, one of the first built in the United States since the Great Depression, what makes the **Carousel for Missoula** (101 Carousel Dr., 406/549-8382, www.carouselformissoula. com, 11am-7pm daily June-Aug., 11am-5:30pm daily Sept.-May, $2 adults over 12, $1 children 12 and under) so sweet is the way in which it came to be. Local cabinetmaker Chuck Kaparich vowed to the city of Missoula in 1991 that if they would "give it a home and promise no one will ever take it apart," he would build a carousel by hand. As a child, Kaparich had spent summer days in Butte at

Missoula and Vicinity

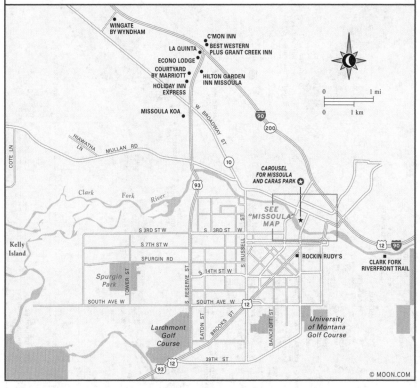

WINGATE BY WYNDHAM

C'MON INN

LA QUINTA

BEST WESTERN PLUS GRANT CREEK INN

ECONO LODGE

COURTYARD BY MARRIOTT

HILTON GARDEN INN MISSOULA

HOLIDAY INN EXPRESS

MISSOULA KOA

W BROADWAY ST

90

200

0   1 mi

0   1 km

HIAWATHA LN

MULLAN RD

COTE LN

10

Clark   Fork   River

93

CAROUSEL FOR MISSOULA AND CARAS PARK

SEE "MISSOULA" MAP

Kelly Island

S 3RD ST W   S. 3RD ST W

S. RUSSELL ST

12   90

S 7TH ST W

SPURGIN RD

ROCKIN RUDY'S

CLARK FORK RIVERFRONT TRAIL

Spurgin Park

TOWER ST

S. RESERVE ST

14TH ST W

SOUTH AVE W   SOUTH AVE W

12

Larchmont Golf Course

EATON ST

BROOKS ST

BANCROFT ST

University of Montana Golf Course

93   12

39TH   ST

© MOON.COM

WESTERN MONTANA
MISSOULA

the Columbia Gardens riding the carousel. For four years, he carved ponies, taught others to carve, and worked to restore and piece together the more than 16,000 pieces of an antique carousel frame he had purchased. The town raised funds and collectively contributed more than 100,000 volunteer hours. In May 1995 the carousel opened with 38 ponies, three replacement ponies, two chariots, 14 gargoyles, and the largest band organ in continuous use in the United States.

The jewel-box building opens to the surrounding green of **Caras Park** in summer and keeps the cold and wind out during the rest of the year. A fantastic adjacent play area, **Dragon Hollow,** was built with the same remarkable volunteerism over a substantially shorter time period. The entire playground

was constructed by volunteers in just nine days in 2001.

Missoula Art Museum

With the tagline "Free Expression Free Admission," the **Missoula Art Museum** (MAM, 335 N. Pattee St., 406/728-0447, www.missoulaartmuseum.org, 10am-5pm Tues.-Sat., free) honors the past and celebrates the future. The building itself represents such a marriage, brilliantly combining a 110-year-old Carnegie library with a contemporary glass, steel, and wood addition. The museum has six exhibition spaces that host 20-25 solo and group exhibitions annually, most of them quite contemporary and provocative. Don't miss the museum's own impressive Contemporary American Indian

Missoula

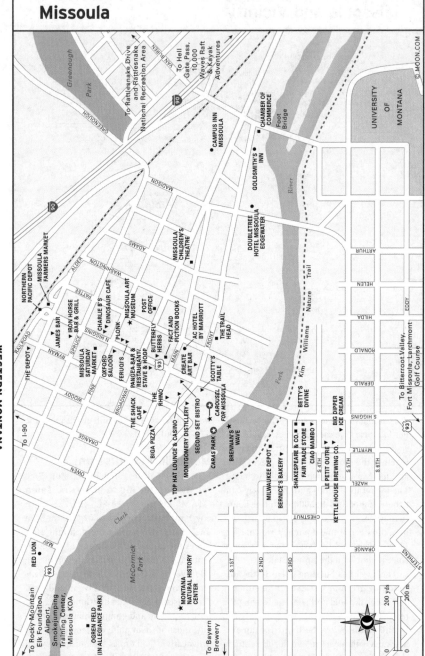

© MOON.COM

Missoula: Montana's Most Liberal Town?

In 1992, when I decided to move to Montana and was vacillating between Missoula and Bozeman, my older brother broke it down according to an age-old and surprisingly right-on generalization when he asked which I liked better: "cowboys or hippies?"

Missoula has long been associated with a hippie lifestyle (the herbs store is one of the busiest shops in town) but its origins as a center for labor movements and civil disobedience go back more than a century. In 1909 a pregnant 19-year-old by the name of Elizabeth Gurley Flynn came to Missoula on behalf of the Industrial Workers of the World to organize the region's lumber and migrant farm workers. She and her husband organized heated rallies around town. Eventually city leaders passed a law making public speaking on Missoula streets a crime. Flynn's plan to start a freedom-of-speech battle across the Northwest worked, and before long people willing to be arrested for the cause arrived by the trainload. City jails quickly filled and overflowed, forcing the city to back down and reinstate the right to speak publicly.

Among the Missoula locals who have contributed to its reputation was Jeannette Rankin, who, in 1916, became the first woman to be elected to the U.S. House of Representatives, two years after Montana granted women the right to vote but four years *before* the 19th Amendment gave women across the country the right to vote. Among the early graduates from the University of Montana in 1902, Rankin was a tried-and-true pacifist, casting one of 50 votes against the resolution to enter World War I in 1917 and the lone vote against entering World War II, a move that sealed her political demise. Rankin famously stated, "You can no more win a war than you can win an earthquake." She was a founding vice president of the American Civil Liberties Union and an outspoken antiwar activist during the Vietnam War era.

The university has also contributed significantly to Missoula's reputation for liberal leanings. When the school was dedicated in 1895, speaker William Fisk Sanders implored, "Hold not up to these pupils hopes of money or office . . . their high service is to save the world from shame and thrall." In 1915, the removal of the University of Montana's popular president, Edwin Craighead, triggered the first of many organized protests on campus, including major incidents around freedom of speech, freedom of the press, civil rights, and the Vietnam War.

Art Collection, among the largest of its kind in the country.

Fort Missoula

Originally established to protect settlers against Indian attacks, **Fort Missoula** (3400 Captain Rawn Way, 406/728-3476, www.fortmissoulamuseum.org, 10am-5pm Mon.-Sat., noon-5pm Sun. Memorial Day-Labor Day, noon-5pm Tues.-Sun. Labor Day-Memorial Day, $4 adults, $2 students, $3 seniors, $10 family, free for children under 6) was never used for its intended purpose. When no attacks occurred, the fort was used to house the African American 25th Infantry in 1888 and as an alien detention center for Italian Americans and Japanese Americans during World War II. The museum houses exhibits about the fort's history

as well as rotating historical exhibits. The fort grounds, for which admission is free, are open year-round. While the museum is housed in the fort's original buildings, other historical buildings, including a one-room schoolhouse, an 1860s church, and a homesteader cabin, have been relocated to the grounds.

Montana Natural History Center

The **Montana Natural History Center** (120 Hickory St., 406/327-0405, www.montananaturalist.org, 11am-4pm Tues.-Sat., $4 adults, $1 children 4-18, free for children under 4, $8 family, $3 seniors and veterans) is one block south of McCormick Park. Originally housed on the University of Montana's campus, the center was created by educators who wanted to work with schools and the public to help nurture an understanding and appreciation of nature. It offers workshops, including children's activities, as well as field trips and evening lectures conducted by local scientists and naturalists. To see what is being offered on specific dates, look under Community Activities on the website.

University of Montana

The **University of Montana** (32 Campus Dr., 406/243-0211, www.umt.edu) was founded in 1895 at the base of Mount Sentinel. To secure Missoula as the site of the state's university, city leaders bribed state legislators with 5 gallons of whiskey, a case of beer, a case of wine, and 350 cigars. Regardless of its shady beginnings, the university has flourished into a flagship liberal arts and research institution with campuses across the state, a broad interest in the performing arts, a well-respected creative writing program, and an ability to produce numerous Fulbright and Rhodes scholars each year. There's both a business and law school at U of M, plus a college of education, a college of forestry and conservation, a college of health, and a college of arts and media. In 2015, Jon Krakauer wrote a damning book that chronicled the stories of five women who reported rapes or attempted rapes at the University of Montana between 2010 and 2012, and the failures of the university, the local police, and the judicial system. The events, and the book, had an impact on the school, and enrollment continues to drop from 15,669 students in 2011 to 10,106 students in 2021.

The university has a beautiful campus to explore. **University Center,** on the east side of the campus almost directly under the M on the hillside, is the hub of campus life. Wander in to grab a bite at the food court or peruse the well-stocked bookstore. To find out what lectures, plays, concerts, or other entertainment is happening on campus, visit the website (http://events.umt.edu).

Rocky Mountain Elk Foundation Visitor Center

Promoting the view that hunters are often the most resolute conservationists, the **Rocky Mountain Elk Foundation Visitor Center** (5705 Grant Creek Rd., 406/523-4500 or 800/225-5355, www.rmef.org, 8am-5pm Mon.-Fri., 10am-5pm Sat. Jan.-Apr., 8am-6pm Mon.-Fri., 9am-6pm Sat.-Sun. May-Dec., free) has protected and enhanced millions of acres of wildlife habitat across North America since its humble origins in 1984. The center

Missoula has one of the state's longest lists of National Register of Historic Places.

does an impressive job of putting the elk in the context of a wide range of wildlife and emphasizing the importance of habitat conservation. A favorite among hunters due to its wealth of trophy mounts, the visitor center is like a natural history museum, and in addition to a pleasant wooded walking trail on the property's 22 acres, there are some great kid-friendly interactive exhibits and wildlife conservation films. Tours can be arranged by emailing in advance, and free youth seminars are held monthly on such subjects as fire, archery, big game, and horns versus antlers. The center was closed for remodeling in 2021 with no stated date for reopening. Check the website or call ahead.

Aerial Fire Depot and Smokejumper Center

Sharing space with the largest smokejumper training base in the country, the **Aerial Fire Depot and Smokejumper Center** (5765 W. Broadway, 0.5 mi/0.8 km west of the Missoula airport, 406/329-4934, www.smokejumpers.com, 8:30am-5pm daily Memorial Day-Labor Day, by appointment Labor Day-Memorial Day, free admission, free tours daily in summer) is a fascinating place for those interested in wildfires and the firefighters who parachute in to battle them. There is a memorial to those killed on duty and a replica of a 1930s fire lookout; visitors on the 45-minute tour have access to the smokejumper loft where the jumpers work when they are not fighting fires.

Brennan's Wave

Although there is no street address, everyone in Missoula knows exactly where Brennan's Wave is. Located on the Clark Fork River, right next to Caras Park, this engineered white-water masterpiece was built in honor of Brennan Guth, a Missoula native and world-class kayaker who perished in 2001 while paddling in Chile. Brennan's Wave hosts big competitions—the 2010 U.S. Freestyle Kayaking Championship brought 200 competitors to town and thousands of spectators—and plenty of everyday paddlers looking for a thrill. The banks are always lined with enthusiastic spectators, and the Wave is a popular gathering spot whenever the river is not covered by ice.

SPORTS AND RECREATION

Rattlesnake National Recreation Area and Wilderness

Less than 5 miles (8 km) north of town, the 60,000-acre **Rattlesnake National Recreation Area and Wilderness** (406/329-3814, www.fs.usda.gov) is fed by some 50 creeks and has 30 lakes, waterfalls, and many miles of trails, some of which lead up to McLeod Peak, the highest spot in the area at 8,620 feet (2,627 m). The area is a dream for hikers, runners, mountain bikers, campers, cross-country skiers, and anglers; it is home to deer, elk, coyotes, mountain goats, bighorn sheep, black bears, and more than 40 species of birds in spring and fall. Dispersed camping is permitted anywhere beyond the 3-mile (4.8-km) radius from the Rattlesnake's main trailhead.

To get to the area from Missoula, take the I-90 Van Buren Street exit at the east end of town and travel 4.5 miles (7.2 km) north on Rattlesnake Drive.

Missoula PaddleHeads Baseball

At Ogren Field in **Allegiance Park** (700 Cregg Ln.), the **Missoula PaddleHeads** (406/543-3300, www.milb.com/missoula, $10 adults), whose mascot is a moose, take on other Pioneer League teams in some great small-town minor league baseball. Missoula is known for its softball, so it's no surprise that the community shows up in force to watch their hometown PaddleHeads, whose name is also a nod to Missoula's active boating scene. Though the PaddleHeads (called the Osprey 1999-2019) had been affiliated with the Arizona Diamondbacks as a Rookie Advanced league, in 2021 the Pioneer League became an independent baseball league and was granted status as an MLB Partner League.

Hiking and Biking

Hugely popular with walkers, runners, and bikers, the flat riverfront trails (www.ci.missoula.mt.us/2209/Riverfront-Trails)—**Ron's River Trail** (2 mi/3.2 km) on the north side of the river and **Milwaukee Trail** (1.8 mi/2.9 km) on the south—are 3.8 miles (6.1 km) long and provide access to **Caras Park, Bess Reed Park,** and **Kiwanis Park** on the river's north bank and **McCormick Park, Clark Fork Natural Park, John Toole Park,** the **University of Montana River Bowl,** and **Jacob's Island Park** on the south bank. The trail, graveled in places and paved in others, connects to other intersecting trails and runs on both the north and south sides of the Clark Fork River. It is easily accessible throughout town, but the most abundant parking can be found at Caras Park near the Carousel for Missoula.

Running for 7 miles (11 km) along both the north and south shores of the Clark Fork River, Missoula's **Riverfront Trail** (www.ci.missoula.mt.us/2209/Riverfront-Trails) feels like an important artery through the city. It connects with myriad hotels, businesses, and parks. It links downtown and the Hip Strip with the university. It's a popular bike path and everyone seems to walk their dog on it. Different sections have different names and nothing is well signed, but it is a wonderful way to get out into the natural world in the center of downtown Missoula, and it is absolutely part of the culture here

The Riverfront Trail connects to the 2.5-mile (4-km) **Kim Williams Nature Trail,** a converted railroad bed near the base of Mount Sentinel (where you can hike the M) that winds through a 134-acre natural area in Hellgate Canyon. The trail is wide and level, and it is open to pedestrians, equestrians, and cyclists. It's also frequented by wildlife, so keep your eyes open. The trail runs through Hellgate Canyon and connects to the Deer Creek-Pattee Canyon Loop. The trail can be accessed easily from Jacob's Island Park near the Van Buren Pedestrian Bridge. Leashed dogs are welcome on all of Missoula's trails.

M TRAIL ON MOUNT SENTINEL

For a bird's-eye view of the city, hike up the **M Trail on Mount Sentinel.** It is a popular trail, so there will be others huffing and puffing up the hill with you. There are 13 switchbacks on the west-facing slope, and the views over Missoula and the Bitterroot Valley at sunset are worth the sweat.

Skiing

Twenty minutes north of Missoula, **Snowbowl** (1700 Snowbowl Rd., 406/549-9777 or 800/728-2695, www.montanasnowbowl.com, $60 adults full day or $55 half day, $57 students and seniors full day or $55 half day, $27 children 6-12 full or half day, $5 beginner tow rope, free for children under 6) is a nice little ski hill with an average of 300 inches (762 cm) of snow annually, 2,600 feet (793 m) of vertical drop, and a run that covers 3 miles (4.8 km). In summer, the mountain is open Friday-Sunday late June to mid-September for mountain biking, disc golf (folf), and diggler, which is a cross between mountain biking and snowboarding (rentals available).

There is no shortage of cross-country ski trails around Missoula. One unique destination is the **Garnet Resource Area** (406/329-3914, www.garnetghosttown.net), with 50 miles (80 km) of trails in a ghost town. In summer, hiking and mountain biking are popular. To get to Garnet, follow Highway 200 east of town and turn south at the Garnet Range Road, between mile markers 22 and 23, about 30 miles (48 km) east of Missoula. Follow the range road approximately 12 miles (19 km) to the parking area. The road

1: Brennan's Wave in downtown Missoula
2: swimming in the Clark Fork River
3: hiking the M Trail on Mount Sentinel

Hang Gliding in Missoula

While it makes some people crazy, for others the combination of wind and mountains in Missoula means only one thing: hang gliding. It's not uncommon to see these colorful oversize-kite contraptions launching off Mount Sentinel and soaring over the city. But what goes up must come down, and when Bill Johnson (widely considered to have been the first hang gliding pilot in the state) landed on top of the university fieldhouse, reports of a plane crash swiftly clogged the emergency services switchboard. When the fire department arrived, Johnson had broken down his glider, packed it neatly in a bag, and even asked the firefighters for help getting down. The firefighters were too busy scanning the scene for a crashed plane to realize that they were aiding Johnson in his getaway.

The sport took hold in the state in the 1970s when gear was cheap and mostly homemade. By October 2006 the number of launches off Mount Sentinel gave pause to Missoula's air traffic controllers, who feared a plane-versus-glider crash, and the area was closed to flight for nearly a year. The state's hang glider pilots joined with people in Missoula who appreciated the life and color that the sport brought to town, and in July 2007 Mount Sentinel opened again to hang gliding. **Glide Missoula** (www.glidemissoula.org) is a good source of information.

Owned by pilot and math teacher Jennifer Bedell, **Blackbird Paragliding** (406/212-3792, www.blackbirdparagliding.com) offers P2 certification training ($1,950), tandem flights ($225), and entry-level lessons or refreshers ($150). **Missoula Paragliding** (406/529-5135) is another flight school in town.

is closed January-April, when access is limited to snowshoers, cross-country skiers, and snowmobilers.

There are also more than 150 miles (242 km) of cross-country ski trails in the **Lolo National Forest** (406/329-3814, www.fs.usda.gov/lolo).

Fishing

While access to the Clark Fork River right in town is easy, the river is still recovering from decades of pollution. Better bets are the Bitterroot River, the Blackfoot River, and Rock Creek. One guiding outfit that does them all is **A Classic Journey Outfitters** (877/327-7878 or 406/880-0541, www.montanaflyfishingguide.com, $595 full-day float, $525 half-day float, multiday trips with lodging available). Owner Joe Cummings grew up fishing on a ranch in nearby Stevensville and left to play professional football. But his heart has always been where the big, wild trout are. He and his guides fish year-round, have a passion for dry flies, and know the area backward and forward.

Another guide who is a phenomenal naturalist in addition to being a world-class fishing instructor is Tom Jenni of **Tom Jenni's Reel Montana** (406/539-6610 or 866/885-6065, www.tomjenni.com, $475 full day for 1 angler, $575 full day for 2 anglers). Jenni grew up in Missoula and has been fishing its rivers for more than 40 years. He also offers multiday trips up to four nights/five days on some of the best waters in the state.

Boating and Water Sports

With five rivers in the vicinity, Missoula is a boater's town. There is even an artificial practice wave, Brennan's Wave, right in town for kayakers to play safely in. Try **10,000 Waves Raft & Kayak Adventures** (131 E. Main St., 406/549-6670 or 800/537-8315, www.10000-waves.com, $69 adults and $59 kids 6-12 half day, $89 adults and $79 kids 6-12 half day) for everything from scenic rafting to whitewater adventures, sit-on-top kayaks, and kayak instruction on numerous sections of the Blackfoot and Clark Fork Rivers. There are also overnight trips ($495 adults, $465 children 5-12) and gourmet dinner trips ($115 adults, $90 children 5-12), plus half-day trips

($69 adults, $59 children 6-12) and full-day trips ($89 adults, $79 children 6-12) on the Clarks Fork and in the Alberton Gorge, as well as on the Blackfoot River.

Another local outfitter that specializes in all things white-water is **Zoo Town Surfers** (1001 S. 4th St. W., Suite 5, Missoula, 406/546-0370, www.zootownsurfers.com). They offer scenic and white-water rafting trips ($60-125), scenic kayak tours ($100-125), river surfing ($125-225), and stand-up paddleboarding (half day $100-125) experiences on local lakes and rivers.

Golf

Although there are a couple of nine-hole courses in town, including the **University of Montana Golf Course** (515 South Ave. E., 406/728-8629, $17 for 9 holes, $30 for 18 with discounts on weekdays) and **Linda Vista Public Golf Course** (4915 Lower Miller Creek Rd., 406/251-3655, $25-27 for 18 holes), the only 18-hole public course in Missoula is the **Larchmont Golf Course** (3200 Old Fort Rd., 406/721-4416, $34 for 18 holes on foot, carts $18-36).

Horseback Riding

Less than 30 minutes south of Missoula in Lolo, amazing trail ride experiences can be had at **Dunrovin Ranch** (5001 Expedition Dr., 406/273-7745, www.dunrovinranchmontana.com), where the emphasis is on community, education, science, and the arts. Animals are at the center of the experience and make every visit remarkable, from the family of smooth-gaited Tennessee Walking Horses to "diva donkeys," beloved dogs, and ospreys and other wild animals that call the ranch home. Though Dunrovin offers lodging and the full guest ranch experience, it also offers riding opportunities for nonguests. Trail rides off the ranch are available to anyone older than eight, starting from 1.5 hours ($120-160 pp). Saturday Spa Days ($25 pp) allow for 2-3 hours of interaction with horses, including bathing, brushing, grooming, braiding, and handwalking. Rides might climb up to

magnificent mountain views or travel along and across the river or through lush forests, and private rides can be arranged as well. Dunrovin Ranch also offers a historical ride perfect for history buffs and mountain men wannabes.

ENTERTAINMENT AND EVENTS
Nightlife

Home to college students and artists, Missoula has no shortage of watering holes, and a brief walk will take you to establishments that are pulsing with activity. Microbrew enthusiasts will enjoy the **Bayern Brewing's Edelweiss Bistro** (1507 Montana St., 406/721-1482, www.bayernbrewery.com, 11am-8pm daily, $6-16), which always has six of its beers available along with its own coffee blends and a sizable and delectable sampling of German food, including sausages, meats, cheeses, salads, stews, schnitzel, and pretzels. The beer garden is a great place to relax in summer, and brewery tours are available by appointment. The **Kettle House Brewing Co.** (313 N. 1st St. W. and 602 Myrtle St., 406/728-1660, www.kettlehouse.com, Myrtle St. taphouse 2pm-10pm Mon.-Tues., noon-10pm Wed.-Sun., Bonner taproom 2pm-8pm Mon.-Thurs., noon-8pm Fri.-Sun.) is home of the famous Cold Smoke and has two locations for visitors to sample excellent local brews.

For more of a late-night scene, try tried-and-true favorites like **The Rhino** (158 Ryman St., 406/721-6061, 11am-2am Mon.-Sat., noon-2am Sun.), with more than 50 beers on tap; **Feruqi's** (318 N. Higgins Ave., 406/728-8799, 4pm-2am Mon.-Sat., 7pm-midnight Sun.), an intimate spot known for its martinis and setting in a historic building; or the **Oxford Saloon & Café** (337 N. Higgins Ave., 406/549-0117, www.the-oxford.com, 24 hours daily), which dates back to the 1880s and still offers live poker nightly at 8pm. Though it no longer serves brains and eggs, the Oxford still makes a pretty tasty Garbage Omelet. **Charlie B's** (428 N. Higgins Ave., 406/549-3589, 8am-2am daily) is a longtime favorite and has a reputation for hard drinking that starts early in the day. The adjacent **Dinosaur Café** (11am-9pm Mon.-Fri., noon-9pm Sat., $3.50-8.25) offers inexpensive and excellent Cajun food to go with your booze. Complete with a Hunter S. Thompson quote etched on the outside of the building, **James Bar** (127 W. Alder St., 406/721-8158, noon-2am Tues.-Fri., 11am-2am Sat.-Sun., $7-15) is a classy joint for cocktails and good, local cuisine—including bison, crab, falafel, and lamb sliders, and the best fries—instead of standard bar fare.

Music lovers will do well at the **Top Hat Lounge & Casino** (134 W. Front St., 406/830-4640, www.logjampresents.com, 11am-10pm Mon.-Thurs., 11am-11pm Fri.-Sat.), which has been bringing live music of every genre to Missoula since 1952. The place can pack in 700 bodies, and the tapas-style menu, including Korean street tacos and chicken and waffles, does not disappoint. A bit mellower and far more upscale is **Plonk** (322 N. Higgins Ave., 406/926-1791, www.plonkwine.com, 3pm-midnight daily, $18-38), which pairs exquisite wine, inspired cocktails, and elegant food with eclectic music. Too pricey for the average college student, Plonk tends to appeal to an older crowd.

The upscale **Create Art Bar** (140 E. Front St., 406/830-3941, www.createartbar.com, 5pm-10pm Tues.-Thurs., 3pm-10pm Fri., noon-10pm Sat., noon-5pm Sun.) is both a bar and the city's only DIY workshop and art studio. They offer a menu of crafting projects—from jewelry and wall art to leather goods—all the tools and materials, plus step-by-step instructions to complete any project on your own. The servers can help if you get stuck.

Montgomery Distillery (129 Front St., 406/926-1725, www.montgomerydistillery. com, noon-7:45pm daily) is a family business that serves their award-winning whiskey, rye, vodka, gin, aquavit, and more. A speakeasy that was built to pay homage to the 1896 building it's in, **Stave & Hoop** (223 N. Higgins, alley entrance, 406/493-0282, www.staveandhoop.com, 4:06pm-12am-ish Tues.-Sat.) serves craft cocktails, beer, wine, and Montana comfort food, from flatbread and bacon-wrapped dates to elk burgers.

The Arts
MISSOULA CHILDREN'S THEATRE
Certainly one of the state's most beloved theater companies, the **Missoula Children's Theatre** (425 E. Broadway, 406/728-7529 or 406/728-1911, www.mctinc.org) mounts several productions annually of such family favorites as *Hansel and Gretel* and *Snow White and the Seven Dwarfs* with children as cast members. Most significantly, MCT has become known for its performances in 16 countries around the world that include local children. The company arrives in town the Monday before a Friday performance, casting and rehearsing local children to light up the stage (or the gym, as is often the case in small-town Montana). At the same time, the company performs pieces that include Broadway musicals and poignant comedies in its home performance space.

Festivals and Events
WEEKLY SUMMER EVENTS
With an active, outdoorsy, and independent population, Missoula hosts weekly events during summer that encourage everything from outdoor dining to art appreciation. **First Friday Gallery Night** (406/532-3240) is held 5pm-8pm on the first Friday of every month. Some 15-20 galleries open their doors, often to display new exhibitions, and they provide complimentary hors d'oeuvres and refreshments to art strollers. **Out to Lunch** (406/543-4238, www.missouladowntown. com, 11am-2pm Wed. June-Aug.) in Caras Park is a riverside performing arts picnic for the whole city, with talented local musicians and more than 20 food trucks. Also in Caras Park and run by the Missoula Downtown Association, **Downtown ToNight** (406/543-4238, www.missouladowntown.

Montana Wineries

Since 1984, when Tom Campbell Jr. and his father first started experimenting with growing grapes along the shores of Flathead Lake, in prime Montana cherry territory, several other wineries have sprouted up across the state, primarily in the western region. Many have disappeared after hard winters and rough economies, but a handful are proving that Montana vintners have what it takes. Though many vintners buy grapes from out of state, there are several growers among them, including a few that opt for unconventional but delicious base fruits like cherries, huckleberries, chokecherries, apples, pears, currants, and rhubarb.

- **Glacier Sun Winery & Tasting Room** (3250 US 2 E., Kalispell, 406/257-8886, www. glaciersunwinery.com, 2pm-8pm daily) grew out of the idea of a small, roadside fruit and veggie stand. Today the winery still sells fruits, veggies, and prepared foods, but also produces 10 varietals made from locally grown fruits and regionally grown grapes. They've added their line of Rough Cut hard cider to the menu and have up to seven brews available on tap.

- **Mission Mountain Winery** (82420 US 93, Dayton, 406/849-5524, www. missionmountainwinery.com, tastings noon-5pm daily May-Sept.) is the state's first bonded winery and produces more than 6,500 cases annually of more than 17 different award-winning varietals. Its vineyards grow the grapes for its highly regarded pinot noir, pinot gris, and small amounts of riesling, chardonnay, and gewürztraminer.

- **Ten Spoon Vineyard and Winery** (4175 Rattlesnake Dr., Missoula, 406//549-8703, www. tenspoon.com, tastings 4pm-9pm Thurs.-Sat. or by appointment) is among the fastest-growing wineries in the state and has a marvelous origin story. Owner Connie Poten bought some pastureland in the Rattlesnake Valley outside Missoula to protect the rapidly disappearing open space. She met Andy Sponseller on a local preservation campaign, and their shared love of wine led to the backbreaking work that built the vineyard and set the stage for their subsequent success with more than 20 varietals, including Moonlight pinot noir, Ranger Rider Red, Flathead cherry dry, Farm Dog Red, and Sweet Talk Riesling.

- **Hidden Legend Winery** (1345 US 93 N., Suite 5, Victor, 406/363-6323, www. hiddenlegendwinery.com, tours and tastings 11am-6pm Tues.-Fri.) in the Bitterroot Valley specializes in honey-based mead with Montana twists like chokecherry and elderberry.

- **Trapper Peak Winery** (75 Cattail Ln., Darby, 406/821-1964, tours and tastings by appointment), also in the Bitterroot Valley, produces an affordable selection of cabernet sauvignon, petite syrah, merlot, cabernet franc, and muscat using California grapes.

- **Tongue River Winery** (99 Morning Star Ln., Miles City, 406/853-1028, www. tongueriverwinery.com, 8am-6pm Mon.-Sat., 2pm-7pm Sun.) is the only winery in southeastern Montana. It offers an expansive list of award-winning wines, and tours of both the vineyard and winery can be arranged.

com, 5:30pm-8:30pm Thurs. June-Aug.) features live music, food vendors, and a beverage garden.

Known as the Garden City, Missoula boasts three fabulous farmers markets, including the **Clark Fork Market** (101 Carousel Dr., next to Dragon Hollow, 406/880-9648, www.clarkforkmarket.com, 8am-1pm Sat. May-Sept., 9am-1pm Oct.), which offers an abundance of local produce, meat, and other products, including hot prepared food. There is live music 10am-12:30pm, and plenty of parking is available. The **Missoula Farmers Market** (Circle Square, north end of Higgins Ave., 406/274-3042, www. missoulafarmersmarket.com, 8am-12:30pm Sat. May-Oct., 5pm-7pm Tues. June 19-Sept.) features more than 100 vendors of fresh local produce, flowers, eggs, honey, and more. The **Missoula People's Market** (inside the Iron Horse Bar & Grill, and outside on E. Pine and N. Higgins Ave., 406/830-3216, www.

missoulapeoplesmarket.org, 9am-1pm Sat. May-Sept.) has prepared food and features art and crafts by local artisans.

INTERNATIONAL WILDLIFE FILM FESTIVAL

Since 1977, the **International Wildlife Film Festival** (718 S. Higgins Ave., 406/728-9380, www.wildlifefilms.org) has been celebrating conservation and film with an eight-day event based at Missoula's famed Roxy Theatre. The event runs annually in late April and features a phenomenal array of wildlife films from around the globe.

INTERNATIONAL CHORAL FESTIVAL

Held every three years (the next one is scheduled for mid-July 2022), the **International Choral Festival** (406/721-7985, www.choralfestival.org) is a true Missoula community event. Nonprofit and noncompetitive, it began in 1987 with the goal of promoting cultural awareness and understanding through music. The four-day event takes place at different venues around the city, and the first day usually includes free preview concerts. Hundreds of international and national choral groups apply each year, but only a handful are selected to participate. In 2016, participants came from Hong Kong, Cuba, Costa Rica, Estonia, and Canada, among others.

SHOPPING

The Fair Trade Store (519 S. Higgins Ave., 406/543-3955, 10:30am-3:30pm Mon., 10:30am-5pm Tues.-Sat.) is operated by the Jeannette Rankin Peace Center and promotes equitable and fair partnerships between producers and distributors of goods. There is a distinctive and colorful selection of merchandise from around the globe, including textiles, pottery, silver, and handmade cards.

In addition to being Missoula's oldest espresso bar, **Butterfly Herbs** (232 N. Higgins Ave., 406/728-8780, www.butterflyherbs.com, 9am-6pm Mon.-Fri., 9am-5:30pm Sat.-Sun.) is a fun and eclectic gift shop. It sells whole herbs, teas, coffee, and spices in bulk as well as soaps, lotions, handmade jewelry, candles, and other decorative goods.

Rockin Rudy's (237 Blaine St., 406/542-0077, www.rockinrudys.com, 9am-9pm Mon.-Sat., 11am-6pm Sun.) uses as a tagline, "A place. Sort of." More than just a place, Rockin Rudy's is *the* place in Missoula for music, posters, cards, gag gifts, jewelry, and on and on. Big and random, this place is part of Missoula culture.

The Trail Head (221 E. Front St., 406/543-6966, www.trailheadmontana.net, 10am-7pm Mon.-Fri., 9am-6pm Sat., 11am-6pm Sun.) is a part of the Missoula community and thrives by knowing the area as well as its activities and specific conditions. Trail Head staff participate regularly in volunteer efforts to preserve and enhance recreational opportunities in the region. The store has fantastic gear for nearly every activity in the area, including skiing, boating, camping, and climbing. Since 1974, great adventures have started here.

It would not be a trip to Missoula without a visit to the thrift shop, and **Betty's Divine** (509 S. Higgins, 406/721-4777, www.bettysdivine.com, 10am-7pm Mon.-Sat., 11am-5pm Sun.) is as good as it gets anywhere. There is an assortment of both vintage and vintage-inspired garb, and though the prices are not cheap, the quality is outstanding, as are the friendly service and the groovy tunes. It's a women-owned, women-run business that prioritizes financial, social, and environmental responsibility. Alongside their clothing, Betty's Divine sells shoes, jewelry, records, and, as of COVID, hip face masks.

Bookstores

In a famously literary town, **Fact and Fiction Books** (220 N. Higgins Ave., 406/721-2881, www.factandfictionbooks.com, 10am-6pm Mon.-Fri., 10am-5pm Sat., noon-4pm Sun.) is a Missoula institution and a good place to learn about local culture and regional authors.

For new books, postcards, cards,

Montana's Literary Treasures

Few states can boast a nearly 1,200-page, 5-pound tome dedicated to the remarkable literature that has come from and defined the state. (The state's "Big Sky" moniker even came courtesy of A. B. Guthrie Jr.'s classic 1947 novel *The Big Sky*.) Montana's literary anthology, *The Last Best Place*, was published in 1988, and the state's literary status only continues to grow. This may partly be attributed to poet and professor Richard Hugo, who directed the University of Montana's renowned creative writing program from 1964 until his death in 1982. The less prosaic might ascribe the inordinate number of well-known authors and poets to things like the light, space, and quality of life here, or the long cold winters and limited distractions. Among the state's best-known writers are Wallace Stegner, Norman Maclean, Bill Kittredge, James Welch, Tom McGuane, Maile Meloy, James Crumley, Deirdre McNamer, Ivan Doig, Mary Clearman Blew, Richard Ford, Sandra Alcosser, David Quammen, Annick Smith, and Rick Bass.

Montana's literary heritage is very much alive in Missoula, where one of the area's softball teams goes by the name "The Montana Review of Books," which once had an outfield lineup with 12 published novels among them. The city boasts some fabulous independent bookstores that promote and often host local writers, including **Fact and Fiction** (220 N. Higgins Ave., 406/721-2881). But perhaps the literary spirit is most alive in any number of watering holes, some more savory than others. **Charlie B's** (428 N. Higgins Ave.), a favorite haunt of the late James Crumley, has no sign, tinted windows, and a big wooden door. Crumley was also a regular at **The Depot** (201 Railroad St. W.). During his tenure at the University of Montana, Bill Kittredge and plenty of creative writing students frequented **Diamond Jim's Eastgate Casino and Lounge** (900 E. Broadway) just over the Van Buren footbridge from campus. **The Rhino** (158 Ryman St.) was identifiable in Jeff Hull's short stories and his 2005 novel. Probably the best known among Missoula's thirsty literary geniuses, Dick Hugo often wrote about bars—**The Dixon Bar** (Hwy. 200, Dixon), which is, for the moment anyway, a bar and grill; **Trixi's Antler Saloon** (Hwy. 200, Ovando); and more famously, the **Milltown Union Bar** (11 Main St., Milltown), which is now the Milltown Moose Lodge, home to the fraternal Moose club, and is virtually unrecognizable.

journals, gifts, and magazines, the independent **Shakespeare & Co.** (103 S. 3rd Ave., 406/549-9010, 11am-6pm Mon.-Sat., 11am-5pm Sun.) is a real find on the Hip Strip.

FOOD

Missoula's dining scene offers more cultural diversity than much of the rest of the state, with plenty of sushi and Thai offerings, but its strong suit is still fresh Rocky Mountain cuisine. Among the best is **Scotty's Table** (131 S. Higgins Ave., downstairs in the Wilma, 406/549-2790, www.scottystable.net, 11:30am-2pm and 5pm-9pm Wed.-Fri., 9:30am-1:30pm and 5pm-9pm Sat.-Sun., brunch/lunch $11-17, dinner $17-42), serving American bistro fare with a global twist. It's an upscale restaurant for the whole family—the gourmet kids' menu was inspired by the chef's own child. Entrées include mouthwatering cioppino and chicken

souvlaki, but the appetizers are enchanting—try the fried Brussels sprouts and cauliflower, roasted beets with black pepper and honey mascarpone, mussels and fries, or the cheese plate; you might not even make it to the main course.

Located in the historic Florence building downtown and combining a love of food and music, **Second Set Bistro** (111 N. Higgins Ave., 406/830-3233, www.secondsetbistro. com, 5pm-9pm Mon.-Sat., $20-55) opened in 2019 to rave reviews. From the rib eye and the bone-in pork chop to steak frites and shrimp scampi, their fresh Montana approach to American classics is delicious. It also might be the only place in the state to get a lobster roll. Don't leave without tasting the sticky toffee pudding.

For a creative take on Italian food, **Ciao Mambo** (541 S. Higgins Ave., 406/543-0377, www.ciaomambo.com, 5pm-9pm Sun.-Thurs., 5pm-10pm Fri.-Sat., $15-28), a Montana-started franchise, serves up everything from Italian nachos and fried mozzarella balls to wood-fired pizza, pasta, and steaks.

For the best local pizza, you can't beat the wood-fired offerings from **Biga Pizza** (241 W. Main St., 406/728-2579, www.bigapizza. com, 11am-9pm Mon.-Sat., pizzas $12-22). From the simple house pie with garlic oil, tomato sauce, fresh basil, and fresh mozzarella to the maple chipotle pizza with sweet potato and bacon, to the prosciutto di Parma with herbed mascarpone fig paste, toasted almonds, and mozzarella, its combinations are nothing short of mouthwatering. Gluten-free crusts are available, as are calzones, salads, sandwiches, and antipasti.

A thriving brewpub in Missoula, the **Iron Horse Bar & Grill** (501 N. Higgins Ave., 406/728-8866, www.ironhorsebrewpub.com, 11am-2am Wed.-Fri., 10am-2am Sat.-Sun., $12-22) is set in the old train depot. The place is always hopping, and terrific outdoor seating is available when the weather permits. The menu is extensive, serving up everything from ahi tuna and nachos to spicy tandoori chicken, salads, burgers, and small plates. Another great spot for drinks and dinner is **Pangea Bar & Restaurant** (223 N. Higgins Ave., 406/493-1190, www.mtpangea.com, 11am-10pm Mon.-Thurs., 11am-11pm Fri., 10am-11pm Sat., 10am-3pm Sun., brunch/lunch $10-15, dinner $14-39), which won a Wine Spectator Award for Excellence. Their curries and fish are outstanding, as is the bison prime rib on Tuesdays. They also have a nice selection of burgers, flatbreads, and salads.

A community favorite since 1949 and serving breakfast and lunch in a classic Pontiac-Oldsmobile dealership setting, **The Shack Café** (222 W. Main St., 406/549-9903, www. theshackcafe.com, 8am-2pm Fri.-Sun., $6.50-16.95) specializes in food grown and raised locally. Don't miss the huckleberry pancakes for breakfast; it may be the best breakfast in town. Lunch includes hefty sandwiches, various house-made soups, and burgers.

For a quick and scrumptious bite with a killer cup of coffee, try **Bernice's Bakery** (190 S. 3rd St. W., 406/728-1358, www. bernicesbakerymt.com, 6am-6pm Mon.-Sat., 8am-4pm Sun., sandwiches $6-10), a real-butter and from-scratch kind of place featuring high-quality organic ingredients, menus that change daily, and sheer artistry in everything it does. The staff support a strong coffeehouse vibe and a commendable commitment to community. If you leave without indulging your sweet tooth, you've made a mistake. **Caffé Dolce** (Southgate Mall, 406/549-4914, www.caffedolce.com, 10am-4pm Mon.-Sat., sandwiches $4.50-8.25) offers fresh, healthy, and utterly delicious fare for breakfast and lunch, plus excellent coffee. For real French pastries and espresso, visit **Le Petit Outre** (129 S. 4th St. W., 406/543-3311, www.lepetitoutre.com, 7am-4pm Mon.-Fri., 8am-4pm Sat., 8am-2pm Sun.), where there is almost always a line because no one wants them to be out of ham and cheese croissants when it's their turn to order. Le Petit makes beautiful bread, too.

If you're just starting your Montana adventure, you'll need to get in shape for all the ice-cream offerings. A good place to start is **Big Dipper Ice Cream** (631 S. Higgins Ave., 406/543-5722, and 2700 Paxson St., suite F, 406/926-1160, www.bigdippericecream. com, noon-10pm daily, $4-8), which has unexpected but out-of-this-world flavors like cardamom, El Salvador coffee, Mexican chocolate, and mango habanero sorbet in addition to the lip-smacking classics. Don't miss daily special flavors like cotton candy, Thai peanut curry (really), and Elvis (peanut butter, banana, chocolate chip, chocolate, and bacon). During summer, the walk-up window is open 11am-11pm daily, and there's almost always a line in the evening. Hours can vary throughout the year, so call ahead or check the website.

ACCOMMODATIONS

As one of Montana's bigger cities, Missoula has plenty of lodging options. The old-school independent motels line much of East and West Broadway, while some of the newer chain hotels can be found on Reserve Street. Among the well-known and well-maintained chains in town are the **C'mon Inn Hotel & Suites** (2775 Expo Parkway, 406/543-4600 or 888/989-5569, www.cmoninn.com, $120-340), **Courtyard by Marriott** (4559 N. Reserve St., 406/549-5260, www.marriott.com, $157-289), the sleek **AC Hotel by Marriott** (175 N. Pattee St., 406/549-0119, www.marriott.com, $161-379), the pet-friendly **Econo Lodge** (4953 N. Reserve St., 406/542-7550, www.choicehotels.com, $63-209), **Hilton Garden Inn Missoula** (3720 N. Reserve St., 406/532-5300 or 877/782-9444, www.hiltongardeninn3.hilton.com, $112-338), **Holiday Inn Express & Suites** (150 Expressway Blvd., 406/830-3100 or 800/315-2605, www.hiexpress.com, $107-290), and **La Quinta** (5059 N. Reserve St., 406/549-9000 or 800/753-3757, www.laquintamissoula.com, $81-260).

In the heart of Missoula on the banks of the Clark Fork River is the pet-friendly **DoubleTree by Hilton Missoula Edgewater** (100 Madison St., 406/728-3100 or 800/222-8733, www.missoulaedgewater.doubletree.com, $131-497), an enormous hotel with all the amenities, including room service. Ask for a room facing the river.

A couple of medium-size hotels offering good value near the university and downtown, respectively, are **Campus Inn Missoula** (744 E. Broadway, 406/549-5134 or 800/232-8013, www.campusinnmissoula.com, $110-227) and **Red Lion** (700 W. Broadway, 406/728-3300 or 800/733-5466, www.redlion.com/missoula, $66-178).

A few miles from downtown is the quiet, comfortable, and pet-friendly **Best Western Plus Grant Creek Inn** (5280 Grant Creek Rd., 406/543-0700 or 800/780-7234, www.bestwestern.com, $109-334). Kids will love the indoor-outdoor heated pool. But for avid swimmers, the only hotel to consider in Missoula is **Wingate by Wyndham** (5252 Airway Blvd., 406/541-8000 or 866/832-8000, www.wingatemissoula.com, $148-309), which boasts clean and comfortable rooms with an indoor water park that will delight little ones with a kiddie pool, froggy slide, and mushroom waterfall. Bigger kids will like the three-story water slides.

As a university town with some beautiful old homes, Missoula used to have an abundance of appealing B&Bs. The combination of the pandemic and the growth of Airbnb, which has some great offerings in town, has created challenges for the traditional bed-and-breakfasts, a few of which have turned their rooms into apartments and studios that are available on the site. Others have been sold or not reopened. Still, if B&Bs are your favorite way to stay, **Blue Mountain Bed & Breakfast** (6980 Deadman Gulch Rd., 406/251-4457 or 877/251-4457, www.bluemountainbb.com, from $190) is nestled on a mountainside outside of town, offering guests a tranquil spot where you can explore nature and even bring your own horse.

Twenty minutes north of Missoula is the **Gelandesprung Lodge at Snowbowl** (1700 Snowbowl Rd., 406/549-9777, www.montanasnowbowl.com, $72-133), a European-style ski-in ski-out lodge on the mountain and open throughout the ski season and on weekends in summer. Some rooms have private baths, others share a hall bath. For the ultimate family or friend reunion, you can rent the whole place for $1,026 night. Rates are announced seasonally, so call ahead or check online.

At the other end of the spectrum is an ultraluxe experience that will thin your wallet considerably. The five-star family-friendly **Resort at Paws Up** (40060 Paws Up Rd., 406/244-5200, www.pawsup.com, luxury tents $1,988-4,818/night for 2 adults and 2 children) in Greenough, about 32 miles (52 km) east of Missoula, is among the most glamorous spots in the state. There are luxury homes and luxury tents that are unimaginably elegant, with heated floors, electricity, king-size feather beds, a dining pavilion with your own personal chef, a camping butler, and nightly bonfires with s'mores. This is camping fit for a high-maintenance king. The food is exquisite, as is the spa, and the activities and adventures are limitless. The company's newest adults-only offering, **the green o** (4069 Backcountry Rd., Greenough, 877/251-2841 or 406/244-4934, www.thegreeno.com, from $2,048 night for 2 adults) offers 12 spectacular architectural homes, one 23 feet high in the trees, and a selection of seasonal experiences from horseback adventures and fly-fishing to mountain biking, shooting, and hot air ballooning. The food is as glorious as you imagine it would be, and of course you can get a massage as part of the spa and fitness program.

CAMPING

There are only a handful of private campgrounds in Missoula, but the **Lolo National Forest** (406/329-3750, www.fs.usda.gov/lolo) has a wide range of campsites in beautiful settings, among them Lolo Creek, Ninemile, and Rock Creek. Camping is also permitted in certain sections of the **Rattlesnake National Recreation Area and Wilderness** (406/329-3814) beyond a 3-mile (4.8-km) radius from the main trailhead.

For in-town convenience with RV-specific sites, try the **Missoula KOA** (3450 Tina Ave., 406/549-0881 or 800/562-5366, www.missoulakoa.com, year-round, $42-52 tents, $43-88 RVs, $62-237 cabins, $212 tipis). The tree-lined property offers 200 RV and tent sites in addition to amenities like a heated pool, two hot tubs, bike rentals, minigolf, free Wi-Fi, nightly ice cream, and a café that serves breakfast daily in summer. Offering 70 nice, shady sites just outside of town is the Good Sam-recognized **Jim and Mary's RV Park** (9800 US 93 N., 406/549-4416, www.jimandmarys.com, RV sites $57-59 plus $3 pp over 12 years old, including water, sewer, electric, cable TV, and Wi-Fi). There are discounts for weekly stays.

INFORMATION AND SERVICES

The **Missoula Chamber of Commerce** (825 E. Front St., 406/543-6623, www.missoulachamber.com, 8am-5pm Mon.-Fri.) and **Destination Missoula** (101 E. Main St., 800/526-3465 for travel consultation, www.destinationmissoula.org, 9am-7pm Mon.-Fri., 9am-5pm Sat., 10am-3pm Sun.) are both great sources of information for visitors.

The **U.S. Forest Service** (26 Fort Missoula Rd., 406/329-3511) and the **Montana Department of Fish, Wildlife and Parks** (3201 Spurgin Rd., 406/542-5500, 8am-5pm Mon.-Fri.) offices offer good information about hiking, camping, and fishing in the national forests.

The **main post office** (8:30am-5:30pm Mon.-Fri., 9am-1pm Sat.) is at 1100 West Kent Avenue; the downtown location is 200 East Broadway. The gorgeous new **Missoula Public Library** (455 E. Main St., 406/721-2665, www.missoulapubliclibrary.org, 8am-8pm Mon.-Wed., 8am-6pm Thurs.-Sat.) is an incredible place to explore on a snowy afternoon.

The main hospitals are **St. Patrick's** (500 W. Broadway, 406/543-7271) and **Community Medical Center** (2827 Fort Missoula Rd., 406/728-4100), both of which have 24-hour emergency rooms. There are several walk-in urgent care facilities in town. The **CostCare Walk-In Clinic** (3031 Russell St., 406/728-5841, www.costcare.com, 8am-6pm Mon.-Fri., 9am-2pm Sat.-Sun.) has several locations and expanded hours, including weekends.

The **Green Hanger** laundry (960 E. Broadway St., 406/728-1919, and 146 Woodford St., 406/728-1948, www.greenhangermissoula.com, 7am-9pm daily) offers two locations with dry cleaning and laundry facilities (including Wi-Fi and free laundry soap), plus drop-off laundry services and a car wash.

TRANSPORTATION
Getting There

Just 4 miles (6.4 km) northwest of the university, **Missoula International Airport** (MSO, 5225 US 10 W., 406/728-4381, www.flymissoula.com) is served by Alaska, Allegiant, American, Delta, Frontier, and United. On the 1st floor of the terminal are **Alamo, Avis, Enterprise, Thrifty**, and **Hertz** car-rental agencies. **Dollar** has shuttles to and from the airport. Most hotels offer free shuttle service to and from the airport; the **Airport Shuttler** (406/880-7433, www.msoshuttle.com) also provides transportation into town.

The **Greyhound** bus station (1660 W. Broadway, 406/549-2339) has several buses in and out of town daily.

I-90 runs directly through Missoula, making it an easy destination by car. Missoula is 115 miles (185 km) west of Helena and the same south of Kalispell, 120 miles (193 km) northwest of Butte, and about 200 miles (320 km) northwest of Bozeman.

Getting Around

The **Mountain Line** (406/721-3333, www.mountainline.com, 6am-8:45pm Mon.-Fri., 9am-6pm Sat., free) is the free city bus service; the city has worked hard to make this a zero-fare public transportation system.

For taxi service, call **Yellow Cab** (406/543-6644, www.yellowcabmissoula.com) or **Green Taxi** (406/728-8294), which only uses hybrid cars.

Hamilton and the Bitterroot Valley

The pastoral and dramatically beautiful valley known as the Bitterroot, named by Meriwether Lewis, has a fascinating history; the region's past has been filled with promise and heartbreak since Lewis and Clark's visit in 1805.

In 1854, John Mullan, who masterminded the Mullan Road overland route to the Pacific, predicted that while much of the region was unpopulated rugged wilderness, the Bitterroot Valley would soon be "one villaged valley, teeming with life, and bustle and business." In the 21st century, his prediction has panned out; the Bitterroot Valley is one of the fastest-growing regions in Montana but still retains a gorgeous swath of green-drenched mountains with sparkling rivers, quaint little towns, and no end of opportunities for outdoor adventures. The drive through towns like Florence, Stevensville, Victor, Corvallis, Hamilton, and Darby is utterly scenic and a splendid way to spend a day or two. The largest of the towns in the Bitterroot Valley, Hamilton was founded by copper king Marcus Daly and named for James Hamilton, one of Daly's employees.

Calamity Jane was among the town's most notorious residents.

The climate here is milder than in other parts of the state, sandwiched as it is between the Bitterroot and Sapphire mountain ranges. Anglers, cyclists, and hikers will not want to leave, and history buffs and antiques hunters will be content as well.

LOLO HOT SPRINGS RESORT

Although not among the state's fanciest, the hot springs at **Lolo Hot Springs Resort** (38500 W. US 12, 877/541-5117, www.lolohotsprings.com, deluxe cabins $243 for up to 6 people, heated camping cabins $103 for 2-3 people) are among those that were known to Indigenous people long before Lewis and Clark arrived in the region. The area was a natural mineral lick for wildlife and an ancient meeting spot for Native Americans. It was also a well-known rendezvous site for trappers and prospectors. As early as 1888, the springs were advertised in Missoula newspapers for board, room, and bath for $11 per

The Bitterroot Valley

10am-9pm Sun.-Thurs., 10am-midnight Fri.-Sat. winter, $7 adults, $6 seniors 55 and over, $5 children 5-12) are sublime at any time of year. Entrance to the pools is included with cabin rentals.

TRAVELERS' REST STATE PARK

Just 0.5 mile (0.8 km) west of the town of Lolo on US 12, **Travelers' Rest State Park** (406/273-4253, www.travelersrest.org, 9am-5pm daily year-round, visitor center 9:30am-4:30pm daily spring-summer, 10am-4pm daily fall-winter, $8/vehicle, free with Montana license plates) is a critical stop for any Lewis and Clark buff. The park is a large grassy area with a tree-lined creek that occupies about 50 acres. Historically it was a resting place for Native Americans, who would set up camp here before crossing the Bitterroot Mountains; it is also where Lewis and Clark's Corps of Discovery camped twice, in September 1805 and June 1806. They named the creek nearby "Travellers Rest." In 2002 an archaeological team discovered physical evidence that confirmed the campsite had been used by the Corps of Discovery—it's the only Lewis and Clark campsite with verified physical evidence, which came in the form of high mercury levels. It was determined from the Corps' journals that the men were given mercury pills, which caused immediate evacuation of their bowels, to cure any number of ailments. The high mercury content of the soil was limited to a pit that served as the latrine. A kitchen was discovered army regulation distance away. It was also at this campsite that Lewis and Clark decided to part ways on their return journey east.

LEE METCALF NATIONAL WILDLIFE REFUGE

The **Lee Metcalf National Wildlife Refuge** (4567 Wildfowl Ln., 406/777-5552, www.fws.gov, dawn-dusk daily year-round) is about 30 miles (48 km) south of Missoula on US 93 in Stevensville, along the Bitterroot River. It was

week. Today the resort offers deluxe cabins, heated camping cabins, tipis, and RV and tent sites. There is a restaurant and bar on-site.

In summer this is a great camping spot, with immediate access to both the Lolo and Bitterroot National Forests as well as many miles of prime river access. In winter the area is popular for snowmobilers, and snowmobile rentals are available daily on-site. The naturally heated mineral pools (8am-10pm Mon.-Thurs., 10am-midnight Fri.-Sun. summer,

established in 1963 by locals in response to the negative effects on wildlife habitat caused by ranches, farms, and the logging industry, and it was named in 1978 after a U.S. senator from Montana who was dedicated to the conservation movement. Its main purpose is as a refuge for migratory birds, including osprey, eagles, and hawks. Larger animals such as white-tailed deer and coyotes can be spotted in the area as well. In the summer, after the nesting season has finished, a 2-mile (3.2-km) hiking trail is opened that loops through the wildlife-viewing area; two shorter trails are available year-round. Wildfowl Lane, a county road, runs through the refuge and provides many viewing opportunities from the car.

STEVENSVILLE

Known primarily for the beautifully preserved mission built by Belgian-born Jesuit priest Pierre-Jean De Smet, **Stevensville** (pop. 2,156, elev. 3,323 ft/1,013 m) is surrounded by the Bitterroot and Sapphire Mountains and the Lee Metcalf National Wildlife Refuge. It provides superb access to hiking, biking, and fishing for outdoors enthusiasts. The town's history comes to life at Fort Owen, St. Mary's Mission, and the Stevensville Museum.

St. Mary's Mission

As the first permanent settlement in the state, many see **St. Mary's Mission** (315 Charlo St., 406/777-5734, www.saintmarysmission.org, Apr. 15-Oct. 15, tours 11am-3pm Tues.-Sat., grounds free, museum $3 adults, $2 students, free for children under 6, tours $8 adults, $7 seniors 60 and over, $6 students, free for children under 6, check the Facebook page for special events) as the birthplace of modern Montana. Its origin dates to the winter of 1823-1824 when two dozen Iroquois were employed as trappers by the Hudson's Bay Company. Twelve of the Iroquois stayed in the Bitterroot Valley that winter, were adopted by the Salish people, and married Salish women. Having been introduced to Christianity 200 years earlier, the Iroquois shared stories of the men they called "blackrobes," who could speak to God. The Salish and neighboring Nez Perce were so riveted by the stories that they wanted to bring the blackrobes to their encampments. Four separate missions were dispatched to make contact with the black-robes in St. Louis; all were futile until 1839, when the Indigenous people met Jesuit priest Pierre-Jean De Smet. In 1841, De Smet arrived in the Bitterroot Valley with two other priests and three laypeople. When they reached what would become Stevensville, De Smet and his men erected a cross and built the church, naming it St. Mary's Mission.

Four years later, the mission was commandeered by an Italian Jesuit priest named Anthony Ravalli. Ravalli was a physician, surgeon, pharmacist, architect, and artist who built the first flour mill and sawmill in the state. He respected the Salish, and although he was loved by his constituents, the mission was temporarily closed in 1850 when many of the Salish rebelled against practices meant to diminish their own traditions and way of life. During its closure the facility was sold to John Owen, and when the Jesuits could not return, as stipulated in the conditions of the sale, the church was burned; in its place Owen built a trading post known as Fort Owen. Ravalli stayed among the Native Americans in western Montana as their physician and spiritual guide.

In 1866, Ravalli built a new chapel and hospital just 1 mile (1.6 km) south of Fort Owen; it was doubled in size in 1879 to include Ravalli's house and pharmacy, a cabin for Salish chief Victor, and a cemetery where Jesuits and Salish were buried side by side. After Ravalli's death in 1884 and the subsequent forced exodus of the Salish from their homeland, the mission was permanently shuttered.

Today the buildings have been painstakingly restored to their original simple beauty. The chapel's colorful interior reflects the Italian Renaissance and re-creates the original colors Ravalli achieved using vermillion clay for the reds, blue from indigo traded among the Native Americans,

and yellow from a sacred cave near the Judith River in central Montana. This place has been so lovingly restored that its sacred spirit is palpable; a visit here is time well spent. Mass is said in this historic chapel twice annually, on opening day and the third Sunday in September, in conjunction with the Salish pilgrimage.

Fort Owen State Park

Established in 1850 on the grounds of the original St. Mary's Mission, **Fort Owen State Park** (100 Stevensville Cutoff Rd. E., 406/273-4253, 9am-6pm daily Mar.-Oct., 9am-5pm daily Nov.-Feb., $8 vehicle, $4 walk-in or bicycle, free for Montana residents) is a great place for a picnic. Considered to be the site of the first permanent white settlement in the state, the site was a trading post established by Major John Owen, and visitors can wander around the restored rooms of the east barracks, which are appointed with period furnishings. Pets are welcome, and facilities include a picnic table and a vault toilet. Donations are appreciated.

Entertainment and Events

The third weekend of June is the time for **Western Heritage Days** (406/777-3928, www.visitbitterrootvalley.com), a celebration of old-time traditions with historic home tours, wagon rides, a parade, cook-off, and more, in downtown Stevensville. During the first week of August, visitors can enjoy the **Stevensville Creamery Picnic** (www.creamerypicnic.com), with its live music, brew fest, kiddie parade, Montana State BBQ Championship, dancing, and more. The Creamery Picnic lays claim to being the oldest ongoing community festival in the state.

HAMILTON

The business and trading center of the Bitterroot Valley, Hamilton (pop. 5,080, elev. 3,572 ft/1,089 m) is a bustling and vibrant

little community with a significant historic house, the Marcus Daly Mansion, as well as a museum set in a beautiful old courthouse, an important national research laboratory that arose from government concern over a spotted fever outbreak around the turn of the 20th century, and an abundance of great restaurants and art galleries. If you want to spend more than a day in the area, Hamilton makes an excellent base.

Marcus Daly Mansion

Among the original copper kings, Marcus Daly was an Irish immigrant who came to Butte and founded the Anaconda Copper Company, which dominated Montana's economy for more than 50 years. Daly became fabulously wealthy and built a dream life for himself in the Bitterroot Valley, with elaborate horse barns complete with hospitals and Turkish baths for his world-class racehorses, 15,000 acres of farmland that included extensive livestock holdings, and a 24,000-square-foot mansion with more than 25 bedrooms. So many hundreds of people staffed the mansion, the racehorse operation, and the ranching and farming outfits that Daly had to build a town—Hamilton—to accommodate them all.

The home itself was purchased by the Daly family in 1886 and remodeled extensively several times until 1910, when it was transformed into its present Georgian revival style. The **Marcus Daly Mansion** (251 Eastside Hwy., 406/363-6004, www.dalymansion.org, tours on the hour 10am-3pm daily mid-May-early Oct., holiday tours Nov. 28-Dec. 20, $15 adults, $14 seniors, $8 children 6-17, free for children under 6) has been impeccably maintained and can be visited only on tours, which include the mansion itself, the laundry house, the greenhouse, the playhouse, the swimming pool, and the tennis courts. Weddings and parties are often held on the magnificently landscaped grounds, known as the **Margaret M. Daly Memorial Arboretum and Botanic Garden** (grounds open during tour season 9am-5pm daily). Check the

1: St. Mary's Mission **2:** the Marcus Daly Mansion in Hamilton website for scheduled events ranging from lawn parties to Shakespearean performances to murder mystery weekends. **Daly Days,** a two-day celebration of the Daly family and the town of Hamilton's heritage held in late July, is an ideal time to visit. But the mansion is a lovely, quiet place to spend any afternoon, imagining the kind of lives that were once lived here.

Ravalli County Museum

The **Ravalli County Museum** (205 Bedford St., 406/363-3338, www.ravallimuseum.org, 10am-4pm Tues., Wed., and Fri., 10am-8pm Thurs., 9am-1pm Sat., $3 adults, $1 seniors and students, $6 families, free for children, free for everyone on Thurs. and Sat.) is housed in the 1900 county courthouse. Operated by the Bitterroot Valley Historical Society, it is dedicated to preserving the cultural heritage of the valley. In addition to their rotating exhibits, the museum's permanent collection focuses on telling the stories of the Salish, Kootenai, and Pend d'Oreille people, as well as early settlers in the area.

Entertainment and Events

The **Hamilton Farmers Market** (205 Bedford St. between 2nd St. and 4th St., 406/961-0004, www.hamiltonfarmersmarket. org, 9am-12:30pm Sat. early May-early Oct.) offers a bounty of local produce, much of it organic, along with local baked goods, arts and crafts, prepared food, and family entertainment. **First Friday Hamilton** (406/360-9124, www.hamiltondowntownassociation. org) happens the first Friday of each month in summer and is an arts-oriented street party with special sales and great food and drinks. Keep an eye open for Hamilton's **Music on Main** (406/360-9124, www. hamiltondowntownassociation.org), which closes down Main Street for a townwide party with live music and street vendors selling food, wine, and beer. It generally happens the second Friday of the month in summer, but visit the website for specific dates and band names.

The first week in June at the Ravalli County Fairgrounds is **Montana Mule Days** (www. montanamuledays.com), featuring riding, driving, Western pleasure, and gymkhana events. The family-friendly **Ravalli County Fair** (100 Old Corvallis Rd., 406/363-3411, www.ravalli.us, $9 adults, $7 students, seniors, and military, free for kids 5 and under, $25 4-day pass adults) is a festive event, held in early September, with a carnival and rodeo, live music, food vendors, and all the good old country fair competitions you can imagine. Held the first Saturday in October at the Ravalli County Museum, the **Annual McIntosh Apple Day** (205 Bedford, 406/363-3338, www.ravallimuseum.org) is hailed as the biggest bake sale under the Big Sky. There are arts and crafts, food and produce vendors, and the signature bake sale.

DARBY

Once the terminus of the Northern Pacific Railway, Darby (pop. 836, elev. 3,888 ft/1,185 m) is perhaps best known for its place in some of the great logging debates of the 1960s-1980s, along with one of the largest pro-logging organized protests in the country in 1988. Referred to as "the Great Log Haul," some 300 fully loaded logging trucks delivered their loads to the Darby Lumber Company on May 13, 1988, to call attention to the plight of the loggers and mill workers who were affected by the big timber companies' flooding of the market, which led to plummeting prices and the subsequent closure of public land to prevent further logging. Much of western Montana, and the Bitterroot Valley in particular, had relied on logging for nearly a century; layoffs and mill closings had an enormous impact.

Entertainment and Events

Marking the end of an era, Darby cancelled its famed Darby Logger Days celebration in 2019. The event had celebrated the region's logging history and the skill and bravery of those men and women who worked the timber. Still, there are plenty of offerings in town.

On the third Saturday of July, the Darby Fire Department hosts **Strawberry Days,** an annual fundraiser and celebration featuring strawberry shortcake, music, and entertainment. Also in late July, the **Hard Times Bluegrass Festival** (424 Forest Hill Rd., 406/821-3777, www.hardtimesbluegrass.com, weekend pass $30 adults, $15 kids 6-12, single day $20 adults, $10 kids 6-12, Sunday only $15 adults, $7 kids 6-12, dry camping $25 for the weekend) brings folks together to see performances all weekend long by 11 bands. As you can imagine, there is plenty of jamming.

SPORTS AND RECREATION
Fishing

Without a doubt, this valley offers some of the best fishing in the West. The Bitterroot River runs north from Connor, where the East Fork and West Fork (both of which offer great fishable waters) join to form the Bitterroot, up the valley to Missoula, where it flows into the Clark Fork River. In addition to its breathtaking beauty and relatively easy access via its proximity to the road, the Bitterroot River offers diverse waters, with everything from riffles and pools to flats and gravel bars. Rainbow trout are the most plentiful fish, but browns and cutthroats can be found in the upper portion of the river, upstream from Hamilton. The best-known insect hatch is probably the spring skwala hatch, which usually starts in March, one of the earliest in the state, and lasts well into April. All fishing during the skwala hatch is strictly catch-and-release. In late June-early July, after the river has cleared of spring runoff, the big hatches are the green drake and brown drake hatches, which can last for several weeks. In the fall, September-October, the tiny trico hatch offers some of the best (and toughest) fishing on the river. In general, the farther you get from Missoula, the fewer the anglers and the better the fishing. Still, there is wonderful wading and floating all along the river.

With so much productive water, it's no surprise that there are plenty of guides in the region. **Freestone Fly Shop** (701 S. 1st St., Hamilton, 406/363-9099, www.freestoneflyshop.com, 9am-5pm Mon.-Sat., 9am-2pm Sun., $550/day 1-2 anglers, $450/half day 1-2 anglers) is a good place to start, both for guided fishing and for equipment and flies. The shop provides lodging and fishing packages as well. Missoula native Tom Jenni of **Tom Jenni's Reel Montana** (406/539-6610, www.tomjenni.com) guides in the area and is an exceptional all-around guide offering both day trips ($475/day 1 angler, $575/day 2 anglers) and multiday trips ($1,100 pp 2 days/1 night up to $2,750 pp 5 day/4 nights).

Hiking and Biking

With two mountain ranges on either side of the valley, the hiking and biking opportunities in the Bitterroot are endless. The **Stevensville Ranger Station** (88 Main St., Stevensville, 406/777-5461, www.fs.usda.gov) and the **Bitterroot National Forest Office** (1801 N. 1st St., Hamilton, 406/363-7100, www.fs.usda.gov) are great places to get maps and ideas.

It's possible in this valley to hike portions of both the **Lewis and Clark Trail** through the Bitterroot Mountains and the **Nee-Me-Poo Trail** (www.fs.usda.gov), the route of the Nez Perce on their fateful 1877 flight from the U.S. Army. The Nee-Me-Poo Trail is at the southern end of the valley near Sula, and the Lewis and Clark Trail is farther north near Lolo Pass.

Among the most popular areas to hike because of its supremely rugged beauty is **Blodgett Canyon,** 5 miles (8 km) northwest of Hamilton in the Bitterroot Mountains. The out-and-back hike is spectacular from the get-go with a nice stream and canyon walls. There are several waterfalls along the way, including a beautiful one at 3.6 miles (5.8 km), and the most dedicated can hike a full 12.5 miles (20.1 km) to Blodgett Lake, making it a 25-mile (40-km) round-trip. The trail is never too steep, and there is plenty of wildlife—including moose, deer, and elk—farther into the canyon. To find the trailhead, turn west off US 93 2 miles (3.2 km) north of Hamilton onto Bowman Road, and follow it for 0.6 mile (1 km). Turn left onto Richetts Road, follow it for 2 miles (3.2 km), and then turn west onto Forest Road 736 for 2.4 miles (3.9 km) to the intersection of Blodgett Canyon Road. Turn right and drive 1.5 miles (2.4 km) to the trailhead.

Another wonderful quick hike that offers an excellent overlook of Blodgett Canyon and signs of the great fires of 2000 is the **Blodgett Canyon Overlook.** It is a short 3-mile (4.8-km) round-trip trail, but it is steep, with 1,100 feet (335 m) of elevation gain on a switchbacking trail to a heart-stopping overlook. There are benches along the way and an interpretive exhibit on forest fire ecology. To find the trailhead, follow the directions to the Blodgett Canyon Trailhead above, but at Blodgett Canyon Road, turn left (west) and drive 3 miles (4.8 km) to the trailhead.

The U.S. Forest Service maintains three mountain bike trails in the valley: the 10-mile (16-km) **Bass Creek Recreation Area Day Use Trail** (Bass Creek Rd., 5 mi/8 km northwest of Stevensville), the 17-mile (27-km) **Hart Bench Mountain Bike Loop** (off Forest Rd. 5711) near Darby, and the 19-mile (31-km) **Railroad Creek Mountain Bike Loop** (Skalkaho-Rye Rd., 16 mi/26 km southeast of Hamilton). Road cyclists will be grateful for the paved path between Lolo and Florence that eliminates the need to ride on the highway. Rentals, service, and repairs are available at **Valley Bicycles and Ski** (219 S. 1st St., Hamilton, 406/363-4428, 10am-6pm Mon.-Fri., 10am-3pm Sat.). The best resource in the area for race-worthy mountain bikes is **Red Barn Bicycles** (399 McCarthy Loop, Hamilton, 406/363-2662, www. redbarnbicycles.com, 10am-6pm Tues.-Fri., 10am-4pm Sat.).

Horseback Riding

In addition to numerous guest ranches in the area (listed at www.montanadra.com), guided trail rides are available in Lolo,

about 30 minutes' drive north of Hamilton, at **Dunrovin Ranch** (5001 Expedition Dr., 406/273-7745, www.dunrovinranchmontana. com), where the emphasis is on community, education, science, and the arts. Trail rides off the ranch are available to anyone older than eight, starting from 1.5 hours ($120-160 pp). Saturday Spa Days ($25 pp) allow for 2-3 hours of interaction with horses, including bathing, brushing, grooming, braiding, and handwalking. Rides might climb up to magnificent mountain views or travel along and across the river or through lush forests, and private rides can be arranged. Dunrovin Ranch also offers a historical ride perfect for history buffs and mountain men wannabes.

Golf

The 18-hole **Hamilton Golf Club** (1004 Golf Course Rd., 406/363-4251, www. golfhamiltonmt.com, Mar.-Oct., $35 for 18 holes, $21 for 9 holes, $20 cart for 18 holes, $10 cart for 9 holes), 3 miles (4.8 km) east of Hamilton, was established in 1924 and is still considered among the best public courses in the Northwest. The mild weather in the valley g=ives this course more playable days than almost any other in the state. A snack bar serves everything from breakfast sandwiches to burgers.

Winter Recreation

For downhill skiing, head down the valley to **Lost Trail Ski Area** (Conner, 406/821-3211, www.losttrail.com, 9:30am-4pm Thurs.-Sun. Dec.-Apr., extended hours around holidays and in spring, $53 adults full day or $48 half day starting at 12:45pm, $45 full day and $40 half day ages 60-69, $24 full day or $21 half day seniors 70 and up, $43 children 6-12 full day or $39 half day, free for children 5 and under), which sits high atop the Continental Divide and straddles the Idaho-Montana border. It is a great small-town Montana family-friendly mountain with fantastic terrain and more than 300 inches (762 cm) of snow annually. There are one-ride passes and discounted rates for the bunny hill only. They rent both alpine and cross-country ski gear at the hill.

Cross-country skiers will be in heaven in the Bitterroot with places like **Chief Joseph Cross-Country Ski Trail** (Hwy. 43, 40 mi/64 km south of Hamilton), which offers 19 miles (31 km) of groomed trails for every level of ability. Groomed by the Bitterroot Cross-Country Ski Club, the trails and warming hut are open December to mid-April or as the snow permits.

At the end of a long winter's day, why not soak in the warm waters at **Lost Trail Hot Springs** (283 Lost Trail Hot Springs Rd., Sula, 406/821-3574, www.losttrailhotsprings. com, $9.25 ages 14-59, $7.25 seniors 60 and over, $7.25 children 3-13, $3.25 children 1-2) in Sula, not far from either ski area. The rustic resort offers a marvelous hot pool in any weather as well as lodging, food, and plenty of history.

FOOD

It is possible to get the impression that Bitterroot Valley residents live on a liquid diet of coffee and beer, as there is plenty of both to be had. But with its comparatively milder climate and abundance of local produce, the valley also boasts some excellent restaurants.

In Hamilton, **Bitter Root Brewing** (101 Marcus St., 406/363-7468, www. bitterrootbrewing.com, 11:30am-8pm daily, $11-21) offers great local beer, brewed on-site, along with some delicious tacos, burgers, both vegan and gluten-free bowls, sandwiches, and standard pub food. For eclectic ethnic food, Hamilton's **Spice of Life** (900 1st St., 406/361-8241, www.thespiceinhamilton. com, 5:30am-9am breakfast and 11am-2pm lunch Mon.-Fri., dinner 5pm-9pm Wed.-Sat., breakfast $2-8.50, lunch $9-18, dinner $18-36) serves a compelling assortment of dishes—from hearty salads to pasta, fish, and steak—with international flair. Don't miss the daily specials, and both kids and their parents will be happy with the children's menu.

For freshly baked goods in Hamilton, you can't go wrong at **Coffee Cup Café** (500 S.

1st St., 406/363-3822, 6am-10pm daily, $4-16), which serves breads, cakes, muffins, soups, sandwiches, and more made from scratch daily. For pie lovers, this is the place. For a unique Montana meal, **Mineshaft Pasty Co.** (111 N. 2nd St., 406/361-8170, 8:30am-4:20pm Mon.-Fri., $6-8) serves traditional Cornish meat pies, called pasties (PASS-tees), long favored for their hearty taste and convenience by Montana miners. You can get yours filled with everything from eggs, cheese, onions, and potatoes to beef tenderloin and mushrooms. Mineshaft also has a full-service coffee bar and plenty of sweet treats. For Montana takeout, nothing beats **Naps Grill** (200 W. Main St., 406/363-0136, www.napsgrill.com, 11am-9pm Mon.-Thurs., 11am-10pm Fri.-Sat., 11am-8pm Sun., $4-36) for its burgers, cheesesteaks, fried chicken, and steaks.

In Florence, **Glen's Café** (157 Long Ave., 406/273-2534, www.glenscafe.com, 9am-3pm daily, $4.50-14) is a wonderful old log cabin that serves up hearty meals, homemade pies, and local art in equally delicious amounts. The breakfast is served all day.

In Corvallis, **The Wild Mare** (283 2nd St., 406/961-8938, www.thewildmare.com, 5pm-9pm Wed.-Sat., $11-35) serves incredible food—from steaks and pasta to lamb, ribs, and seafood—in an elegant but welcoming atmosphere. **Bowers Market** (1000 Main St., 406/961-4830, 6:30am-9pm Mon.-Sat., 7am-9pm Sun.) is a terrific market with delicious prepared foods. Dine-in service and takeout are available.

In the heart of Stevensville, **Mission Bistro** (225 Main St., 406/777-6945, www. missionbistromt.com, 5pm-10pm Wed.-Sat., 9am-3pm Sun., $16-37) serves excellent Northwest cuisine with French flair. There's lots of seafood on the menu, and comfort food, plus a broad selection of wine and local beer. Their Sunday brunch is a favorite with the locals. For Southern-style barbecue in Stevensville, try **Moose Creek Barbecue** (104 Kootenai Creek Rd., 406/363-9152, www.moosecreekbbqmt. com, 11am-8pm Tues.-Sat., $11.95-33.95), which has awesome barbecue sandwiches, Kobe beef burgers, and seafood, in addition to the classics: pork ribs, pulled pork, Texas beef brisket, smoked turkey and chicken, and even housemade pastrami on rye.

In Darby, get your fill of hand-tossed pizza, burgers, and wraps at **The Little Blue Joint** (119 N. Main St., 406/821-0023, www. littlebluejoint.com, 11am-8pm Tues.-Thurs., 11am-8:30pm Fri.-Sat., 8am-7pm Sun., $7-14.50). On weekends, chef Michael changes up the menu to add fine dining options including seafood.

ACCOMMODATIONS

The greatest number of hotels can be found in the valley's largest town, Hamilton, but the Bitterroot overall offers a handsome range of accommodations, from the ultra-luxe, adults-only **Triple Creek Ranch** (5551 West Fork Rd., near Darby, 406/821-4600 or 800/654-2943, www.triplecreekranch. com, $1,200-2,800 per night for 2 people, all-inclusive) to the budget-friendly and pet-friendly **City Center Motel & Annex** (415 W. Main St., Hamilton, 406/363-1651, www. remlcsportmanslodging.com, from $58), which has standard rooms with microwaves and mini-refrigerators or full kitchenettes.

Among the larger properties in Hamilton is the pet-friendly, 65-room **Bitterroot River Inn and Conference Center** (139 Bitterroot Plaza Dr., 406/375-2525 or 877/274-8274, www.bitterrootriverinn.com, $118-247), which has all the standard amenities and comfortable, Western log decor.

A historic property that is long on charm is the **Stevensville Hotel** (107 E. 3rd St., Stevensville, 406/777-3087 or 888/816-2875, www.stevensvillehotel.com, $125-170), housed in the 1910 Thornton Hospital building. In bed-and-breakfast tradition, the rooms are individually decorated with period furnishings, and the continental breakfast is delicious. Dogs are welcome in the Dr. Quinn room. It's free for the first dog and $20 for the second.

A delightful, homey, one-bedroom rental within easy walking distance to downtown shops and restaurants and the River Park Trail System is **Withy Gate** (701 S. 3rd St., Hamilton, 406/360-7019, www.vbro. com/275459, from $120).

For vacation rentals throughout the valley, ranging from cozy, remote cabins to condos and farmhouses, try **Cardinal Properties** (320 S. 2nd St., Hamilton, 406/363-4430, www.cardinalproperties.net) or **Sweet Sage MT** (406/369-0644, www.sweetsagemt.com).

CAMPING

Camping options in the valley are almost unlimited, with dozens of Forest Service campgrounds nearby. A good place to start is to contact the **U.S. Forest Service** (406/363-7100, www.fs.usda.gov) for camping in the Bitterroot National Forest.

A really beautiful campground is the **Lake Como Campgrounds** (County Rd. 82, 4 mi/6.4 km north of Darby, 406/363-7100, early June-early Sept., $25), which has 12 tent sites and 12 RV sites.

The **Bitterroot Valley RV Park and Campground** (1744 US 93 S., 406/363-2430 or 406/531-1390, www.bitterrootvalleyrv.com, year-round, $25 tents, $32 full-hookup RVs) is a pleasant and budget-friendly private campground 8 miles (12.9 km) south of Hamilton.

INFORMATION AND SERVICES

The **Bitterroot Valley Chamber of Commerce** (105 E. Main St., Hamilton, 406/363-2400, 8am-5pm Mon.-Fri.) is in Hamilton.

The nearest 24-hour emergency rooms are in Missoula, 47 miles (76 km) north of Hamilton and about an hour's drive, at **St. Patrick's** (500 W. Broadway, 406/543-7271) and **Community Medical Center** (2827 Fort Missoula Rd., 406/728-4100). **Bitterroot Valley Urgent Care** (1230 N. 1st St., 406/363-4120, 9am-5pm Mon. and Fri., 10am-2pm Sat.-Sun.) is in Hamilton.

TRANSPORTATION
Getting There

The best way to visit the valley is by car. No major bus lines serve the area, and the closest international airport is **Missoula International Airport** (MSO, 5225 US 10 W., 406/728-4381, www.flymissoula.com), served by Alaska, Allegiant, American, Delta, Frontier, and United.

US 93 runs directly through the valley and can often be congested. To get a beautiful view of the Bitterroot Mountains and a sense of this historic part of Montana, take scenic Highway 269 between Stevensville and Hamilton. South from Missoula, Lolo is 9 miles (14.5 km), Hamilton is 50 miles (80 km), and Darby is 64 miles (103 km).

Getting Around

On the 1st floor of the Missoula International Airport terminal are the **Alamo, Avis, Enterprise, Thrifty,** and **Hertz** car-rental agencies. **Dollar** has shuttles to and from the airport.

The Flathead and Mission Valleys

Home to the largest freshwater lake in the western United States, a mountain range that will take your breath away, and the wide-open space of the National Bison Range, this part of Montana truly is God's country. The Flathead Valley, home to such towns as Kalispell, Whitefish, Polson, and Bigfork, is situated just west of the Continental Divide amid the Swan, Mission, Salish, and Whitefish mountain ranges. The Mission Valley is south of Flathead Lake and the Flathead Valley and includes the communities of St. Ignatius, Ronan, and Hot Springs, all three of which are located on the Flathead Indian Reservation. All tiny, with populations ranging from 606 in Hot Springs to 2,174 in Ronan, these are fascinating places with rich histories but not many services. St. Ignatius is home to a remarkable Catholic mission, built in 1854. Ronan was settled in 1883 and provides excellent access into the Mission Mountains Wilderness Area and the Ninepipe and Pablo National Wildlife Refuge complex. Hot Springs was founded in 1910 around the natural mineral springs that still attract visitors today.

Between the wildlife refuges and the 1.3-million-acre Flathead Indian Reservation, the area is of great significance, historically and today. Time spent in these valleys can be quiet and contemplative; there are many opportunities to learn. Flathead Lake has created a vacation culture all its own, with luxe lodges, sprawling lakeside manses, and high-end shops and eateries in and around Bigfork. Endless recreational opportunities are available as well, including hiking, boating, and soaking in hot springs. On the way to Glacier, these valleys and their small but vibrant communities should not be overlooked.

ST. IGNATIUS

The oldest town on the Flathead Reservation, and among the oldest settlements in the state, St. Ignatius (pop. 840, elev. 2,939 ft/896 m) is the site of the St. Ignatius Mission, built in 1854 by Jesuit priest Adrian Hoecken, who moved from Washington State to be closer to the Indigenous people he wanted to reach. The town grew quickly as nearly 1,000 Native Americans resettled near the mission, and in 1864 a group of nuns added schools and a hospital to the community.

The building considered to be the oldest in the state, constructed in 1846, is at Fort Connah, just 6 miles (9.7 km) north of St. Ignatius on US 93. It is all that remains of the last trading post built in the United States by the Hudson's Bay Company. The post was in operation until 1871.

★ St. Ignatius Mission

The beloved redbrick chapel standing today on the **St. Ignatius Mission** (300 Bear Track Ave., 406/745-2768, https://stignatiusmission.org, 9am-7pm daily summer, 9am-5pm daily winter, mass 9am Sun., free, donations accepted) was built in the 1890s, but the mission itself was settled as early as 1854 by Jesuit priest Adrian Hoecken and hundreds of Native Americans who set up camp near him. In 1864, a group of nuns from Montreal, the Sisters of Providence, came to the mission to open a boarding school for girls, a hospital, and eventually, with the help of Ursuline nuns, an orphanage, a kindergarten, and a school for boys. At its peak in the mid-1890s, some 320 children attended school at the mission. The boys' school was burned down by students in 1896, and when the federal government ceased aiding the mission, all schooling was turned over to the Ursuline Sisters. In 1941, they adopted coeducation. The school was shuttered permanently in the 1970s.

When you visit any of the missions and boarding schools attended by Native American children, it's important to recognize the stories that weren't heard for years, for decades. St. Ignatius Mission and its schools were not immune to the child abuse that plagued so many missions and Indian schools across North America. In 2011, 45 former students sued the Ursuline Academy/St. Ignatius Mission School for physical, sexual, and emotional abuse. The suit was resolved with a multimillion-dollar settlement in 2015. In 2018, the Jesuits West Province released a list of 111 members from 10 western states—dating 1880-1982—who abused or might have abused children or vulnerable adults, many of them in Montana and some at Ursuline Academy/St. Ignatius Mission School. A vigil was held at the mission church in the summer of 2021 to honor the Indigenous children who were taken from their families and forced to stay at boarding schools, and to recognize and name the intergenerational trauma that continues to affect Native American families and their communities. It was a solemn event, but one with tinged with hope for healing and reconciliation.

The brick chapel was completed in 1894 with 58 original murals painted by Joseph Carignano, who worked in the kitchen and as a handyman for the mission. Carignano taught himself to paint and managed to complete the frescoes in only 14 months despite working on them only when he wasn't doing his primary job. The paintings tell the life story of St. Ignatius Loyola. In the summer of 2016, significant cracks in the frescoes were being monitored, and the church is trying to raise the money to preserve them.

In addition to the chapel, a small museum and gift shop can be found in the log house that was the original residence of the Sisters of Providence.

National Bison Range

Established in 1908 when the population of bison across North America had dropped from upward of 30 million animals down to just a few hundred, the **National Bison Range** (58355 Bison Range Rd., 406/644-2211, www.fws.gov, gate hours 6:30am-10pm daily summer, shorter hours in spring, fall, and winter depending on sunlight, $10/vehicle May-Oct.) is one of the oldest animal refuges in the country and well worth a visit. Its origins date back to a Qĺispé (or Pend d'Oreille) man named Little Falcon Robe who gained permission from various tribal leaders to bring orphaned bison calves across the Continental Divide to the Flathead Indian Reservation. Those few calves prospered under Native stewardship and number 400 today. Located off Highway 212 in Moiese, the refuge comprises 18,500 acres and is home to the bison, white-tailed and mule deer, bighorn sheep, pronghorn, and elk.

There are two driving routes: The year-round West Loop and Prairie Drive is a short 5-mile (8-km) tour that takes about 30 minutes, and the other is a 17-mile (27-km) one-way loop, Red Sleep Mountain Drive, that climbs about 2,000 feet (610 m) and takes close to two hours. The longer route, open in summer, is incredibly scenic and definitely worth the time. The roads through the refuge are gravel; no bicycles or motorcycles are permitted on them, but parking is available at the **visitor center** (8am-7pm daily in summer with shorter hours depending on daylight in fall, winter, and spring). Several short hiking trails leave from the day-use area as well as from Red Sleep Mountain Drive, which closes earlier in the day and entirely when snow blankets the range.

Before beginning your tour, stop in at the visitor center for informative displays, knowledgeable park rangers, and a large relief map of the refuge marked with small lights indicating where bison can likely be seen that day.

RONAN

Named for the first Indian agent, Major Peter Ronan, who wrote the history of the Flathead people and was respected by them, the town of Ronan (pop. 2,174, elev. 3,048 ft/929 m) was once part of the Flathead Reservation before it was opened to sale and settlement in 1910.

Ronan's history is marked by tragedy and travesty. In 1912, a fire erupted in an automobile garage on a particularly windy afternoon. Within hours, the entire town lay in ruins. In June 1929, a robbery at the Ronan State Bank made a group of seven robbers $3,000 richer. The group of 20-somethings went on a spree of robberies across the state with police always a few steps behind. Eventually all but the ringleader were caught and either killed during the pursuit or sent to prison. A woman who accompanied them, known dramatically as "the woman in white," was eventually found murdered in a Helena brothel.

Today Ronan is known for its proximity to two of the state's most beautiful wildlife refuges: the Ninepipe National Wildlife Refuge and, farther south, the National Bison Range.

Ninepipe National Wildlife Refuge

Five miles (8 km) south of Ronan and just north of the National Bison Range on land of the Confederated Salish and Kootenai Tribes, the **Ninepipe National Wildlife Refuge** (www.fws.gov) is a waterfowl preserve. Established in 1921, these wetlands are at the base of the Mission Mountains and situated around a large reservoir. The marshlands

are difficult to walk through, but good birdwatching is possible from the parking areas surrounding the reservoir. The refuge is situated on a popular migratory path for numerous birds, including mallards, gadwalls, great blue herons, and swans. It has become an important breeding and resting area for the Flathead Valley Canada goose population. The refuge is closed during waterfowl hunting season (fall) and the nesting season (spring). Signed access to the refuge is off US 93. Other roads allowing access to the area from US 93 are Olsen Road and Highway 212.

Ninepipes Museum of Early Montana

The **Ninepipes Museum of Early Montana** (69316 US 93, Charlo, 406/644-3435, www. ninepipesmuseum.org, 10am-5pm Mon.-Fri., 10am-4pm Sat. Mar.-mid-Dec., $7 adults, $6 seniors and veterans, $5 students, $3 children 6-12, group rates available) is halfway between Missoula and Kalispell next to the Ninepipe waterfowl refuge. It documents daily life on the Flathead Reservation over the last 100-plus years and even includes a complete replica of a Native American camp. In addition to Native American life, the history of early trappers, miners, loggers, and ranchers is on display, including photos, artwork, costumes, and artifacts from people in these different walks of life.

HOT SPRINGS

At the western edge of the reservation, in the shadow of Baldy Mountain, Hot Springs (pop. 606, elev. 2,841 ft/866 m) is a town whose main attraction is evident from its name. Known as "the Little Bitterroot," the region is home to numerous natural hot springs and mud pots that for centuries have been thought to possess healing powers. Native Americans camped in the area to make use of the "big medicine." When the area opened to settlers in 1910, the springs became increasingly commercial and were advertised around the West. The local newspaper's slogan, printed beneath the masthead, read, "Limp In?. . . Hop Out!"

Preserving the American Bison

The National Bison Range is a wonderful place to learn about these giant animals.

Before Lewis and Clark set foot in the West, more than 50 million bison roamed the Great Plains and most of North America, from southern Canada into northern Mexico. Early settlers recorded seeing herds so large it took a full day for the animals to pass by. Lewis and Clark came across herds covering entire plains and valleys. By 1900, however, it was believed that less than 100 wild bison existed in the United States.

Indispensable to the Native American way of life, the bison provided Indians with everything—food, clothing, shelter, weapons, and utensils. The eradication of the bison devastated their culture, making it easier to force them onto reservations. Land was also freed up for cattle grazing,

The original bathhouse closed in 1985, but if hot mineral water is your thing, there are modern versions worth soaking in.

The largest and most developed of the local hot springs, **Symes Hot Springs Hotel & Mineral Baths** (209 N. Wall St., 406/741-2361, www.symeshotsprings.com, 7am-8pm Sun.-Thurs., 7am-10pm Fri.-Sat., $10 non-guests, $5.50 children 11 and under, rooms $71-200) was built in 1929 as a grand Mission-style hotel. In addition to the outside mineral pools, two of which have been recently renovated, spa treatments are offered in private pools. The guest rooms are modest and quaint, and there is often live music at the hotel. There are also tent ($35) and RV sites ($35-45) on the grounds.

Developed in the 1930s, **Alameda's Hot Springs Retreat** (308 N. Spring St., 406/741-2283, www.alamedashotsprings.com, $60-155) is part motel and part spa with in-room soaking tubs filled with natural hot spring water. The retreat is popular for health-related gatherings and workshops, and the rooms are simple but clean. Although the retreat does not have an outdoor pool, it can direct guests to other places to soak within walking distance.

POLSON

Polson feels like the kind of town where there is almost always a fair going on or some other reason to celebrate. Historically the economy has been based on lumber, steamboat trade, and ranching. Founded around a trading post at the southern end of Flathead Lake in 1880,

railroads, and pioneers. During the "Great Slaughter" of 1820-1880, bison were hunted for their meat, hides, or just for sport. Their massive carcasses were often left to rot on the open plains.

In the 1870s, when the number of bison had put the species at the edge of extinction, an Qlispé (or Pend d'Oreille) man named Little Falcon Robe got approval from tribal leaders to bring orphaned bison calves across the Divide to the Flathead Indian Reservation. The herd grew under the tribe's stewardship and was eventually sold to local ranchers Michel Pablo and Charles Allard. By the turn of the 20th century, the Pablo-Allard herd was the largest herd of plains bison in the world.

Meanwhile, William T. Hornaday, with the support of fellow conservationist President Theodore Roosevelt, founded the American Bison Society in 1905. In 1908, the National Bison Range was established when the U.S. government forced the Confederated Salish and Kootenai Tribes (CSKT) to sell land at the center of their reservation for $1.56 per acre, something a U.S. Court of Claims determined in 1971 was not fair market value at the time. The conflict continues today as the CSKT work to reclaim the land unfairly taken from them. It was the first time a refuge had been created to preserve a single species in Montana.

Once they had the land, the American Bison Society needed to acquire the bison for it. They solicited donations through letter-writing campaigns, newspaper ads, and neighborhood women's groups—many came from individuals in the amount of $1-5. By year's end, they had the equivalent of almost $250,000 in today's dollars. The majority of the first 40 bison to enter the range came from the private herd of Charles Conrad in Kalispell, 36 of which were direct descendants of the six orphaned bison calves brought to the Mission Valley by Little Falcon Robe 20 years earlier. The first bison arrived on the range in 1909, and 11 calves were born by the spring of 1910. Between 1910 and 1922, white-tailed and mule deer, pronghorn, and elk were also donated to the range in small numbers. The last animals added to the refuge were mountain goats, in 1964.

Today there are 300-500 bison on the range with 50-95 bison removed each year. This protects the genetic integrity of the bison and ensures the land can support all of its inhabitants. The bison that are removed are either sold or donated to other refuges or private herds. The range also donates bison to the Flathead tribal government to support bison restoration on Native American land.

the town was named for David Polson, a local rancher who married a Nez Perce woman and who played the fiddle at dances and powwows across the region. Settlement from 1910 greatly increased the size of the town, and when much of the state was losing population during the Great Depression, Polson actually doubled in size with farmers who came to try their luck with the Flathead Irrigation Project and people seeking work at the Kerr Dam construction project.

Today Polson (pop. 5,152, elev. 2,931 ft/893 m) is a lakeside town, the heart of Montana's cherry-growing district, and the busiest town along Flathead Lake. Its proximity to the magnificent lake, the Flathead River, and the Mission Mountains makes Polson a natural playground.

Miracle of America Museum

An eclectic little museum, to say the least, the Miracle of America Museum (36094 Memory Ln., 406/883-6804, www.miracleofamericamuseum.org, 9am-5pm daily, $10 adults, $5 children 2-12) likes to think of itself as the "Smithsonian of the West." Indeed, the founders were passionate collectors of Western artifacts, and the inspired museum is packed to the rafters with more than 100,000 objects including moonshine stills, antique motorcycles, entire buildings, and military paraphernalia. The museum is kid-friendly, with coin-operated music machines and other paraphernalia children love. Behind the main building is the museum's Pioneer Village, which has 35

buildings spread across 4 acres. There's a helicopter to play in, a replica of Laura Ingalls Wilder's sod-roofed home, and a couple of kiddie trains that still operate.

BIGFORK

Arguably the most beautiful of the lakeside hamlets, year-round resort town Bigfork (pop. 4,668, elev. 2,979 ft/908 m) was named for its location along the fork of the Swan River. At the northeast corner of Flathead Lake, Bigfork has unlimited outdoor recreation opportunities, a handsome offering of live theater, art, fine dining, boutique shopping, and elegant accommodations. The feeling here is of an East Coast beach village 50 years ago—small, quaint, and lovely.

SPORTS AND RECREATION

The thing about the beauty in this part of the state is that it's all very user-friendly. The mountains can be climbed, the rivers fished, the lake swum. And although public land is harder to find, especially along Flathead Lake, there are still plenty of great places to hike.

★ Cherry Picking

Picking fresh, sweet Flathead cherries, or just eating them, is an idyllic way to spend an afternoon. Several orchards dot the east side of the lake between Polson and Bigfork, so don't be shy about stopping at roadside stands to do a little taste-testing; in this valley, you can't go wrong. The primary harvest is late July-mid-August. The average season lasts just 7-10 days. Try **Bowman Orchards** (19944 East Shore Rd./Hwy. 35, 10 mi/16 km south of Bigfork at mile marker 21.5 on the east shore of Flathead, 406/982-3246, 9am-6pm daily), a family-owned business since 1921 that grows a variety of cherries and sells both the fresh fruit and a number of delicious cherry products. **Hockaday Orchards** (25 Hockaday Ln., Lakeside, 406/844-3547, www.hockadayorchards.com, 8am-6pm daily as long as crop lasts) lets cherry lovers climb up the ladders to harvest their own crop. Bring your own bucket or box, as the cherries will get crushed in a bag. At just $1.25 per pound if you pay with cash, you can afford to eat cherries all day long.

★ Hiking at Jewel Basin

One of the best and most distinctive places in the state to hike is **Jewel Basin** (Forest Rd. 5392, 10 mi/16 km northeast of Bigfork, 406/387-3800, www.fs.usda.gov), a wilderness area with high peaks, lush forests, 27 lakes, and 35 miles (56 km) of dedicated hiking trails. Camping is permitted, and the trails can be crowded on weekends. Some of the best day hikes include those into **Black Lake** (8 mi/12.9 km round-trip), the **Jewel Lakes** (9 mi/14.5 km round-trip), or the **Twin Lakes** (5 mi/8 km round-trip). The best map for the area is published by the **Glacier National Park Conservancy** (406/892-3250, www.glacier.org). Note that grizzlies frequent the area, particularly in late summer when the huckleberries are ripe.

Boating

Polson offers rafting opportunities on the warm, clear lower **Flathead River.** The only outfitter on the river, **Flathead Raft Company** (50362 US 93 N., 406/883-5838 or 800/654-4359, www.flatheadraftco.com, full-day scenic raft trips $80 adults, $65 children 6-12, full-day kayak trips $99 adults, $89 children 8-12, paddleboard rentals $15/hour, $40/half day, $60/24 hours) offers great scenic and white-water trips as well as white-water kayak instruction, river boarding, or sea-kayaking trips on **Flathead Lake.**

A couple of outfits rent boats in Polson, including **Absolute Watersports Rentals** (303 US 93, Somers, 406/883-3900) and the **Flathead Boat Company** (50230 US 93 S., Polson, 406/883-0999, www.flatheadboatcompany.com, $240-375 for 4 hours, $350-550 for 8 hours).

1: St. Ignatius Mission **2:** Flathead cherry crop **3:** The Ninepipe National Wildlife Refuge was established in 1921.

In Bigfork, you can rent ski boats, WaveRunners, kayaks, paddleboards, and pontoon boats from **Bigfork Outdoor Rentals** (110 Swan River Rd., 406/837-2498, www.bigforkoutdoorrentals.com) and have them delivered. At **Marina Cay Resort** (180 Vista Ln., Bigfork, 406/837-5861, www.marinacay.com), you can also rent a variety of watercraft, including fishing charters. For more information on Flathead Lake and the work being done to protect it, contact the non-profit **Flathead Lakers** (406/883-1346, www.flatheadlakers.org).

Golf

With so many resorts, golf courses also abound in the area. The **Polson Bay Golf Club** (111 Bayview Dr., Polson, 406/883-8230, www.polsonbaygolf.com, $51-56 for 18 holes, $25-30 for 9 holes, carts $38 for 18 holes, $26 for 9 holes) has two courses with a total of 27 holes. The twilight deal, available daily after 3pm, offers 18 holes with a cart and a drink in the clubhouse afterward for $51-56, depending on season and day of week. In Bigfork, golfers can hit the links at the renowned 27-hole **Eagle Bend Golf Course** (279 Eagle Bend Dr., 406/837-7310, www.eaglebendgolfclub.com, visit the website for current greens fees).

ENTERTAINMENT AND EVENTS

One of the most important events on the Flathead Reservation is the annual **Fourth of July Powwow** (888/835-8766, www.arleepowwow.com) at Arlee. The celebration has played out each year since 1898 (minus 2020 and 2021 for COVID) with camping, competition dancing, drumming and singing, traditional games, and a host of food and arts and crafts vendors. Though the U.S government ban on "Indian doings" in the 19th and 20th centuries forbade such celebrations, Native Americans held the event on the Fourth of July so that the army would see it as a patriotic display. The **People's Center Annual Powwow** (53253 US 93, Pablo, 406/675-0160) is held the third Saturday in August in nearby Pablo.

In Polson, the **Polson Farmers Market** (3rd Ave. W., 406/675-0177, www.polsonfarmersmarket.com, 9am-1pm Fri. May-Oct.) features local produce, crafts, jewelry, photography, handmade soaps, and more. The **Mission Mountain NRA Rodeo** (320 Regatta Rd., 406/883-1100, www.polsonfairgroundsinc.com) is generally held in late June; the professional rodeo action and small-town fun always ensure a big crowd. The biggest event of the year in Polson is probably the **Polson Main Street Flathead Cherry Festival** (Main St., 406/883-3667, www.polsonbusinesscommunity.com). It has a fair-like environment and celebrates everything cherry, including pie-eating contests, seed-spitting contests, exhibitions, and entertainment throughout the weekend. The event is typically held at the end of July, and it is among the best ways to enjoy the phenomenal cherry harvest.

The repertory theater at **Bigfork Summer Playhouse** (526 Electric Ave., 406/837-4886, www.bigforksummerplayhouse.com, performances 8pm Mon.-Sat. plus occasional matinees 2pm Sun., mid-May-Labor Day, $32 adults, $27 seniors 65 and older, $25 military, $19 children under 10) is a standout in the Northwest. For more than 50 years the company has been staging award-winning productions of musical classics like *Fiddler on the Roof, Dirty Rotten Scoundrels, Newsies, The Little Mermaid,* and *Sugar Babies.* The contemporary theater is quite comfortable and roomy with 400 seats and air-conditioning. Also running all summer in Bigfork is the **Riverbend Concert Series** (Everit Slider Park, downtown Bigfork, 406/837-5888, www.riverbendconcertsbigfork.com, 7pm Sun. late June-late Aug., $3 adults, $1 children), held every Sunday. The bring-your-own-seating concerts range from jazz to big band and light opera. Held annually the first weekend

1: swimmers on a dock in Flathead Lake **2:** Jewel Basin viewpoint over the Flathead Valley in August, Bigfork's **Festival of the Arts** (406/837-5888 www.bigforkfestivalofthearts. com, 9am-4:30pm Sat.-Sun.) has been attracting visitors and artists alike since 1978 with more than 150 booths, food, and entertainment.

SHOPPING

The **Four Winds Indian Trading Post** (US 93, 3 mi/4.8 km north of St. Ignatius, 406/745-4336, www.fourwinds indiantradingpost.com, 10am-6pm daily summer, noon-5pm daily winter) is the oldest operating Indian trading post in the state. Opened in 1870, the Four Winds has long supplied local Native Americans with a variety of wares, including beads, face paint, animal hides, and dance bells. The store is authentic and sells traditional Native American crafts alongside history books and made-in-Montana products.

A good place to stop in Polson for some warm Montana bedding is **Three Dog Down** (48841 US 93, 406/883-3696 or 800/364-3696, www.threedogdown.com, 9am-5pm daily), known in the region for custom-made comforters and pillows. Shopping here is a Montana experience—you can buy everything from soap to moccasins to saltwater taffy—and bargain hunters should know that singing the "Star-Spangled Banner" will earn you a discount. A number of art galleries, gift shops, and jewelry stores are also in town.

In tiny Bigfork, art is the thing, so stop in at a few galleries during your visit. You could cover the entire town, easily, in a day. Several artists have their own galleries in Bigfork to represent their work exclusively. Other galleries include the colorful and playful **ArtFusion** (471 Electric Ave., 406/837-3526, www.bigforkartfusion.com, 10am-5:30pm Mon.-Sat., 11am-5pm Sun.), representing more than 60 Montana artists, including ceramicists, painters, jewelers, and photographers.

Persimmon Gallery (537 Electric Ave., 406/837-2288, www.persimmongallery. com, 11am-5pm Mon.-Sat., noon-4pm Sun.

June-Sept., 11am-5pm Tues.-Sat., noon-4pm Sun. Oct.-Dec., 11am-5pm Wed.-Sat., noon-4pm Sun. Feb.-May) has a wonderful collection of more than 70 Montana and Northwest artists working in such media as jewelry, painting, mixed media, ceramics, glass, and fabric. One favorite is Judy Colvin, from St. Ignatius, who uses wool from the sheep raised on her ranch to make felted items that include gorgeous purses, scarves, wraps, hats, and wall hangings.

FOOD

If you cannot survive on cherries alone, there are a number of good restaurants concentrated around Bigfork. Steeped in local history, **Traditions Restaurant at the Bigfork Inn** (604 Electric Ave., 406/837-6680, www. bigforkinn.com, 4:30pm-midnight daily summer, 5pm-9pm Wed.-Sat. off-season, $28-44) is a lovely spot for a hearty meal. Choose from specialties like duck two ways a l'orange, king salmon, rack of lamb, and elk tenderloin.

★ **Stone Hill Kitchen + Bar** (7951 Hwy. 35, 406/837-2720, www.stonehill.kitchen, 5pm-9pm Thurs.-Mon., $26-56) offers an elegant approach to Montana cooking using fresh, local ingredients in dishes including salads, pastas, steak, and fish. The menu can change daily depending on the ingredients available, and such freshness can be savored in everything from the filet mignon to the pan-seared scallops and crispy pork belly carbonara.

Flathead Lake Brewing Company (116 Holt Dr., 406/837-2004, www. flatheadlakebrewing.com, noon-8pm Wed.-Sat., $12-17) serves casual but delicious fare—from seared scallops with beet puree to braised pork shank, rib eye, and house-made pizzas and pastas—in a festive environment. Lovers of craft spirits will enjoy a tasting at **Whistling Andy Distillery** (8541 Hwy. 35, Bigfork, 406/837-2620, noon-8pm daily), where the whiskeys, gins, vodkas, rums, and more are handcrafted using local ingredients—from cherries to grains—for big flavor. In addition to tastings and tours

(2pm and 4pm daily), the tasting room serves outstanding cocktails.

For a casual bite, American small plates, sandwiches, soups, and salad, **Great Northern Gourmet** (425 Grand Dr., 406/837-2715, www.gngmt.com, 11am-3pm Tues.-Wed., 11am-3pm and 5pm-8pm Thurs.-Fri., 5pm-8pm Sat., lunch $11-15, dinner $19-29) offers lots of farm-fresh organic options, from Szechuan pork belly to chicken tikka masala to ruby red trout and beef tenderloin.

For breakfast and lunch, the hands-down favorite in the Flathead Valley is the ★ **Echo Lake Café** (1195 Hwy. 83, Bigfork, 406/837-1000, www.echolakecafe.com, 6:30am-2:30pm daily, $9-15), where everything is homemade and fabulous. Be prepared to wait in line with locals for a table. Right downtown, **Pocketstone Café** (444Electirc Ave. #1, 406/837-7223, www.pocketstonecafe. com, 7am-2:30pm Tues.-Sat., $7-17) has all the breakfast specialties you could want, plus great sandwiches, burgers, salads, and soups for lunch.

In Polson, **Cherries BBQ Pit** (105 2nd St. E., 406/571-2227, 11am-7pm Mon.-Sat., $10-27) serves up tender and flavorful barbecue using—yep—Flathead cherries in a selection of ribs, pulled pork, brisket, chicken, and sandwiches with any of the meats. Kind of nice for a roadside barbecue joint with mostly outside dining or takeaway, Cherries also offers a delicious big salad and a kids' menu. One block over, **Mrs. Wonderful's Café** (103b 3rd Ave. E., 406/319-2080, www. mrswonderfulworld.com, 5pm-8pm Wed., 9am-9pm Fri., 10am-2pm Sat.-Sun., $7-22) serves locally grown and organic breakfast, lunch, and early dinner. There's also a store selling specialty foods and a gorgeous selection of wine, selected by an on-staff sommelier. On Wednesday nights, diners can build their own 10-inch pizzas.

Also in Polson, lovers of all things pink will delight in the pinkaliciousness at **Betty's Diner** (49779 US 93, 406/883-1717, www. bettysdiner.net, 7am-3pm Mon.-Sat., 6am-3pm Sun.). The goodness starts with breakfast ($4-11.25), including specialties for "kids and old farts." Lunch ($8-12) includes such classic diner favorites as burgers, cheesesteaks, patty melts, and other sandwiches. Dinner ($11-17) is everything from New York strip to shrimp baskets and chicken-fried steak.

For authentic Thai food in Polson, try **Hot Spot Thai** (50440 US 93, 406/883-4444, 11:30am-8pm Mon.-Fri., noon-8pm Sat., $10.50-15.50). It has a wonderful Thai chef and is open for lunch, dinner, and takeout. The spot doesn't have a liquor license, but diners can bring their own wine.

Lake City Bakery & Eatery (49493 US 93, Polson, 406/883-5667, 7am-3pm Tues.-Sat., $4-12) is a wonderful spot for breakfast all day or lunch. The great old brick building was a grocery store in 1939. Everything is made from scratch. For a great beer, try **Glacier Brewing Company** (6 10th Ave. E., Polson, 406/883-2595, www.glacierbrewing. com, 11:30am-9pm daily), a German-style ale house serving its own impressive line of beer and homemade soda. Hours change with the seasons and without advance notice but are posted on the Facebook page.

ACCOMMODATIONS

There are a handful of places to stay in the vicinity of St. Ignatius. The **Bear Spirit Lodge B&B** (38712 St. Mary's Lake Rd., 406/745-3089, www.bearspiritlodge.com, $135-150) is a cozy place in a phenomenal setting, and the hosts, Ann and Great Bear, are beyond compare. Take a sauna or a hot tub under the starry skies, and you will never want to leave this welcoming place.

About 12 miles (19 km) up the road in Charlo is **Ninepipes Lodge** (69286 US 93, 406/644-2588, www.ninepipeslodge.com, $119-225), set against the backdrop of the Mission Mountains and adjacent to the Ninepipes Reservoir. It's a full-service resort with a great restaurant, **Allentown Restaurant** (breakfast $7-13, lunch $11-16, dinner $11-27) serving steaks, pasta, seafood, and salads. On warm nights, eat outside on the deck overlooking the kettle pond with unrivaled mountain views.

Plenty of choices for lodging exist in Polson and Bigfork, but a room with a view in these parts can get pretty expensive. Among the best bargains in the area is the rustic **Mission Mountain Resort** (3 minutes from Polson on Hwy. 35, 406/883-1883, www.polsonmtresort.com, holiday cabins from $150 for 2 people, $250 for 4 people, $225 for up to 6 people, $10 each additional person), a collection of cabins and lodge rooms on 75 acres set back from the lake.

The waterfront **Best Western KwaTaqNuk Resort and Casino** (49708 US 93 E., Polson, 406/883-3636 or 800/882-6363, www.kwataqnuk.com, $124-319), which is owned and operated by the Flathead Nation, has 107 guest rooms and an extensive menu of activities that includes lake cruises, boat rentals, fishing tours, and plenty of gaming at the on-site casino. Pets are permitted for a $20 per night fee. For standard pet-friendly accommodations right on the lake, try **America's Best Value Port Polson Inn** (49825 US 93, Polson, 406/883-5385 or 800/654-0682, www.bestvalueinn.com, $89-180).

Luxuriousness and prices rise as you get closer to Bigfork. Depending on the size of your group, a vacation rental can be the most economical choice. In addition to listings on Airbnb, there are a few vacation rental companies in town, including **Bayside Property Management** (406/883-4313, www.rentalsinpolson.com) and **Flathead Lake Vacation Rentals** (406/883-3253, www.flatheadvacationrentals.com), which offers a variety of properties around the lake.

Five miles (8 km) south of Bigfork, the **Mountain Lake Lodge** (14735 Sylvan Dr., Bigfork, 406/837-3800 or 877/823-4923, www.mountainlakelodge.com, $139-299) is elegant and cozy with great vistas of the lake and plenty of amenities, including an outdoor infinity pool, a hot tub, a putting green, and a fire pit along with two restaurants on-site. The 30 rooms include a fireplace. Pets are welcome in some of the rooms for $20 per day per pet.

Also south of town, just a short walk from the pebbled shores of Flathead Lake is **Flathead Lake Resort** (14871 Hwy. 35, Bigfork, 406/837-3333, www.flatheadlakeresort.com, $26-308), which offers a variety of accommodations from queen motel rooms to two-bedroom cabins, dry sleeping cabins, restored campers, plus RV and tent sites, in an idyllic setting.

Just down the road is the funky **Islander Inn** (14729 Shore Acres Drive, Bigfork, 406/837-5472, www.sleepeatdrink.com, $108-297), which boasts colorful and cozy boutique-style bungalows, each designed to reflect Anguilla, Crete, Jamaica, Maui, Wild Horse, Zanzibar, or Bali. A gift shop, bakery, and restaurant is on the property, so you may not want to leave. Right in Bigfork, the **Bridge Street Cottages** (309 Bridge St., 406/837-2785, www.bridgestreetcottages.com, $395-750 June-Sept., $295-650 Oct.-May) offers 13 luxury cottages, both on the river and in the trees. They are all nicely appointed and homey.

Right in town, and on the water, is the **Marina Cay Resort** (180 Vista Ln., 406/837-5861, www.marinacay.com, $109-545). The largest property in the vicinity, and the hub of water sports activities, Marina Cay boasts a number of accommodations, including condos and townhomes, as well as dining. The resort is within easy walking to the lake and the town's shops and restaurants. For a phenomenal guest ranch experience, **Averill's Flathead Lake Lodge** (150 Flathead Lodge Rd., 406/837-4391, www.flatheadlakelodge, weeklong all-inclusive trips from $4,417 adults, $3,444 children 6-17, $2,058 children 3-5, $210 children 2 and under) is a historic family ranch set right on the water. From sailing to horseback riding, fly-fishing to mountain biking, this ranch is exceptional.

CAMPING

If you can get a tent site, camping is one of the best ways to stay as close to Flathead Lake as possible and truly enjoy the region. Among the most popular are **Wayfarers State Park**

(8600 Hwy. 35, 0.5 mi/0.8 km south of Bigfork, 406/837-4196, www.stateparks.mt.gov/wayfarers, mid-Mar.-mid-Nov., $4-34), **Finley Point State Park** (31543 S. Finley Point Rd., 11 mi/17.7 km north of Polson, then 4 mi/6.4 km west on County Rd., 406/887-2715, May-Sept., $4-34), and **Yellow Bay State Park** (23861 Hwy. 35, 15 mi/24 km north of Polson at mile marker 17, 406/982-3034, mid-May-mid-Sept., $4-34). All the parks and camping amenities can be seen online at www.stateparks.mt.gov.

INFORMATION AND SERVICES

The **Polson Chamber of Commerce** (402 1st St. E., 406/883-5969, www.polsonchamber.com, 10am-3pm Mon.-Fri., 10am-2pm Sat. Memorial Day-Labor Day, 10am-2pm Mon.-Fri. Labor Day-Memorial Day) is an excellent resource for the south end of the Flathead Valley, and the **Bigfork Area Chamber of Commerce and Visitor's Center** (Old Town Center, 8155 Hwy. 35, 406/837-5888, www.bigfork.org, 9am-5pm Mon.-Fri., 10am-3pm Sat.-Sun. Memorial Day-Labor Day, 10am-3pm Mon.-Sat. Labor Day-Memorial Day) is open to visitors on the east side of Flathead Lake.

The largest hospital in the area with 24-hour emergency care is **Logan Health Medical Center** (310 Sunnyview Ln., 406/752-5111, www.logan.org), 20 miles (32 km) north of Bigfork, just north of downtown Kalispell. There is a walk-in clinic, **Logan Health Primary Care** (8299 Hwy. 35, Bigfork, 406/837-5541, www.loganhealth.org, 8am-5pm Mon.-Fri.) in Bigfork.

TRANSPORTATION

Nestled between lake and mountains south of Whitefish and north of Missoula, Polson and Bigfork can be accessed from US 93. Polson is 70 miles (113 km) north of Missoula and 67 miles (108 km) south of Whitefish. Bigfork is 33 miles (53 km) north of Polson on Highway 35, known as the East Shore Route.

Seeley-Swan Valley

Much quieter than Flathead and set between the magnificent Mission and Swan mountain ranges, the Seeley-Swan Valley is a remarkable destination. Visitors feel like they are stepping back in time. There are unlikely to be any towns you've ever heard of in this valley, and no chain hotels, fast-food restaurants, or interstate highways. Instead you'll find pristine lakes and seemingly endless forests, wonderful old lodges, and handsome guest ranches. The communities in this valley—Swan Lake (pop. 168), Condon (pop. 247), and Seeley Lake (pop. 1,286)—are old timber camps that now cater to lake-loving summer crowds and outdoors enthusiasts, cross-country skiers, and snowmobilers.

This is a place to spend lazy lakeside days and cozy fireside evenings, and if lazy isn't your style, there are mountains in every direction for hiking as well as rivers and lakes for boating and fishing. For those who want to venture into the **Bob Marshall Wilderness Complex,** this valley is an excellent launching point. If you don't have time to stop and stay awhile, at least plan to drive this route from the Flathead and places north to Missoula, Helena, or Bozeman. In fact, the 91-mile (147-km) stretch of Highway 83 through the Seeley-Swan Valley is the shortest route between Yellowstone and Glacier National Park. The scenery and solitude make the trip worthwhile.

SEELEY LAKE

Seeley Lake (pop. 1,286, elev. 4,028 ft/1,228 m) is clearly a recreation town, and the lake itself is among the chain of lakes through which the Clearwater River flows. A resort town in the most classic sense—think rustic lodges and lakeside retreats with cabins dotting the forest—Seeley Lake is popular but not yet overcrowded. There are plenty of fish in the lake, including bass, kokanee salmon, bull trout, perch, and bluegills, in addition to year-round activities that include boating, hiking, excellent cross-country skiing, and snowmobiling.

Sports and Recreation
BOATING

The **Clearwater Canoe Trail** is a 3.5-mile (5.6-km) stretch of flat water that takes paddlers down the Clearwater River from north of the town of Seeley Lake into the lake itself. Magnificent wildflowers, a variety of birds, and other wildlife are often seen along the way. A canoe trip takes 1-2 hours. A roughly 1-mile (1.6-km) hiking trail alongside the river leads paddlers back to the trailhead parking lot. Canoes ($35/half day, $50/full day, $10/hour) and other sporting equipment, including ski boats, pontoon boats, kayaks, paddleboards, and WaveRunners, can be rented from **Tamarack Resort Rental Shack** (3481 Hwy. 83 N., mile marker 17, 406/677-2433, www.tamaracks.com, 9am-6pm daily Memorial Day-Labor Day). Their Clearwater Canoe Trail package ($55 single, $65 double) includes a half-day rental and portage to the trailhead. Advance reservations for all rental gear is strongly recommended. Canoes, stand-up paddleboards, kayaks, and floating island lounges can be rented ($10/hour, $35/half day, $50/full day, delivery charges apply) from **Heritage Outdoors** (3195 Hwy. 83 N., 406/304-8271, www.heritageoutdoors.com).

HIKING AND BIKING

Among the most popular hiking trails in the region is the **Morrell Lake and Falls Trail,** a 5-mile (8-km) round-trip hike on relatively even terrain to a beautiful mountain lake and a series of towering cascades, the largest of which is 90 feet (27 m) high. From Seeley Lake, drive north less than 0.5 mile (0.8 km) to Morrell Creek Road (also known as Cottonwood Lakes Rd. or Forest Rd. 477). Turn right (east), drive 1.1 miles (1.8 km) to the junction of West Morrell Road, and turn left. Drive 5.6 miles (9 km) to another junction and turn right. Drive 0.7 mile (1.1 km) to the trailhead. The trail is well marked and follows the creek to a pond, Morrell Lake, and then the falls.

Mountain biking is permitted on a variety of Forest Service roads and trails, including a 14-mile (22.5 km) round-trip ride at the

Seeley Lake

Seeley Creek Nordic Ski Trails (www. seeleylakenordic.org). From Highway 83, turn east onto Morrell Creek Road (also known as Cottonwood Lakes Rd. or Forest Rd. 477) and drive 1.1 miles (1.8 km) to the trailhead on the north side of the road. Mountain e-bikes can be rented from **Seeley Adventures** (3181 Hwy. 83, 406/499-2415, www.seeleyadventures.com, 9am-5pm daily, from $69, rental to ages 25-plus, must be 21 to ride). They also offer an array of ATV and side-by-side rentals. The area's most comprehensive rental shop recently closed, so even though other outfits are trying to fill the gaps, you might have to rent bikes in Missoula or Kalispell if biking is your thing.

For more information on Forest Service trails, contact the **Seeley Lake Ranger District** (3583 Hwy. 83, 406/677-2233, www. fs.usda.gov).

WINTER RECREATION

Seeley Lake is a cross-country skier's paradise. Several of the local resorts, including the **Double Arrow Lodge** (301 Lodge Way, 2 mi/3.2 km south of Seeley Lake, 406/677-2777 or 800/468-0777, www.doublearrowresort. com), offer groomed ski trails. The cream of the crop in this region is the **Seeley Creek Nordic Ski Trails** (www.seeleylakenordic. org). This trail system has been under development since 1978, initially created from old logging camps and hilly logging roads, and has a degree of difficulty that resulted in the slogan, "Get good or eat wood." With 20 miles (32 km) of groomed classic and skate trails that can be combined to form some impressive routes, the area offers something for every ability level, and an annual 50-kilometer (31-mi) race is held the last Saturday in January. From Highway 83, turn east onto Morrell Creek Road (also known as Cottonwood Lakes Rd. or Forest Rd. 477) and drive 1.1 miles (1.8 km) to the trailhead on the north side of the road. Nearby are dogsled and snowmobile trails.

For a selection of winter gear—from fat bikes ($20 half day, $30 full day) and snowshoes ($20 half day, $30 full day) to ice skates ($10 half day, $20 full day), cross-country skis ($20 half day, $30 full day), and ice-fishing gear ($20 half day, $30 full day), head to **Tamarack Resort Rental Shack** (3481 Hwy. 83 N., mile marker 17, 406/677-2433, www.tamaracks.com, 9am-5pm daily Memorial Day-Labor Day).

For backcountry skiers who want plenty of adventure with a side of luxury, **Yurtski** (406/721-1779, www.yurtski.com) offers a wide range of services. From extraordinary guided trips for newer skiers to gourmet-catered trips, self-service trips with yurt rental ($250-400 per night for up to 8 people), or just shuttling gear, Carl and his team make use of their awesome backcountry yurts, local knowledge, and mad culinary skills.

Around Seeley Lake are more than 350 miles (565 km) of snowmobile trails. For information on specific trails and snowmobile-specific maps, contact the **Seeley Lake Ranger Station** (3583 Hwy. 83, 406/677-2233, www.fs.usda.gov/lolo) at Lolo National Forest. Snowmobiles and guided tours are available from **Kra-Z's Snowmobile Rentals and Backcountry Guide Service** (125 Beach St, 406/677-0713, www. krazsmontana.com, 9am-5pm daily, $245-295 full day plus $60 insurance), **Tamarack Resort Rental Shack** (3481 Hwy. 83 N., mile marker 17, 406/677-2433, www.tamaracks. com, 9am-5pm daily Labor Day-Memorial Day, $150-250 half day, $250-350 full day), and **Freshies Built Snowmobiles, Guiding, and Rentals** (1036 Spruce Dr., 406/781-9408, 7am-5pm daily, call for options and prices).

CONDON

Just 27 miles (43 km) up Highway 83 from Seeley Lake is tiny Condon (pop. 247, elev. 3,785 ft/1,154 m), another gem in the string of lake towns between the Mission and Swan Ranges. Condon is surrounded by the **Mission Mountains Wilderness Area** to the west and the **Bob Marshall Wilderness**

Complex to the east, making the region a favorite for outdoor recreation. Holland Lake is a gorgeous 400-acre lake with prime opportunities for fishing and boating.

Sports and Recreation

Stunning Holland Lake is the main attraction here and offers plenty of recreational opportunities, including boating, fishing, and swimming. The relatively easy and well-traveled Holland Falls Trail leads hikers on a 3-mile (4.8-km) round-trip hike to a waterfall. From the trailhead on Holland Lake Road just beyond the Holland Lake Campground, the trail skirts the north shore of the lake and climbs roughly 600 feet (183 m) before reaching the 40-foot (12-m) falls. There are natural seating areas for picnickers and waterfall gazers. The trail is often used by outfitters packing into Upper Holland Lake and the Bob Marshall Wilderness Complex.

SWAN LAKE

An hour's drive north of Seeley Lake and 16 miles (26 km) south of Bigfork is the quaint little village of Swan Lake (pop. 168, elev. 3,198 ft/975 m), on Highway 83 at the southern end of the lake of the same name. The area is a natural stopping point for migrating birds, making the Swan River National Wildlife Refuge a wonderful place for avid birders. The lake itself offers excellent fishing for northern pike, kokanee salmon, and rainbow trout. A few services are available in town, including lodging and dining options, but most people come to Swan Lake for recreation. There are 50 miles (80 km) of trails for cross-country skiers and many options for hiking.

Sports and Recreation

From Swan Lake, numerous lengthy trails get hikers and horseback riders into the Bob Marshall Wilderness Complex. The Upper Holland Loop, from the trailhead on the north shore of Holland Lake, is a steep and rugged trail that climbs nearly 4,000 feet (over 1,200 m) over nearly 7 miles (11.3 km) or 13.3 miles (21.4 km) round-trip, which

can be tackled on a well-planned full-day hike. The trail passes the Sapphire Lakes and Upper Holland Lake before descending again down along Holland Creek. For maps and information, contact the Swan Lake Ranger District (200 Ranger Station Rd., off Hwy. 35, Bigfork, 406/837-7500).

The Swan River National Wildlife Refuge (Hwy. 83, 1 mi/1.6 km south of Swan Lake, 406/727-7400, www.fws.gov) is nearly 1,800 acres of glacially carved grassy floodplain that provides habitat for more than 170 species of birds, including waterfowl, bald eagles, various types of hawks, owls, and songbirds. The bald eagles generally arrive in February, and visitors can often see eaglets fledging in mid-May. There are also plenty of other animals—moose, elk, beavers, bobcats, and the occasional grizzly bear—wandering through this quiet and undeveloped place. The refuge is closed for nesting season (Mar. 1-July 15), except for the viewing platforms.

Swan Mountain Outfitters (406/387-4405, www.swanmountainoutfitters.com) offers everything from two-hour trail rides (from $85) in the national forest or Glacier (from $90) to daylong rides into Glacier (from $255) to six-day pack fishing trips (from $2,425/person). They also lead dinner rides, llama treks, and snowmobiling adventures in winter.

FOOD

For a hearty meal, the Hungry Bear Steakhouse (6287 Hwy. 83, between mile markers 38 and 39, Condon, 406/754-2240, 8am-9pm daily in peak season, 11am-9pm Wed.-Sun. in off-season, $9-21) serves burgers, sandwiches, soups, and pizza with a full-service bar and kids' menu. Breakfast ($4.25-12) and lunch ($5-14) are served as well. The Swan Valley Café (6800 Hwy. 83, 406/754-3663, 7am-4pm Sat.-Thurs., 7am-8pm Fri., $6-15) is a great family-style restaurant with a sizable menu that is sure to please.

For a real culinary and visual treat, dine lakeside on gourmet fare at ★ Holland Lake Lodge (1947 Holland Lake Rd., Condon,

406/754-2282, www.hollandlakelodge.com, 8:30am-9:45am, noon-2pm, and 5:45pm-8:45pm daily mid-June-late Oct.). The beautiful inn serves breakfast ($8-12), lunch ($9-15), and a four-course dinner ($32-39) with a menu that changes daily. Sample entrées include gruyère egg bake, green chili burger with cheese and lodge salsa, and wild Alaskan halibut. Reservations are required as hours can change depending on special events and guest occupancy.

The **Laughing Horse Lodge** (71284 Hwy. 83, Swan Lake, 406/886-2080, www.laughinghorselodge.com, 5pm-9pm Wed.-Sun., May-Dec., days and hours can vary with private functions, $19-42) is a wonderful place to eat (and you can stay there as well). The outside patio is heavenly. Chef Kathleen cooks up everything from double-Frenched pork chops to huckleberry peach pie. On the second and fourth Tuesday between late June and September, the lodge hosts a six-course tasting menu spotlighting cuisine and wines from around the globe. Nights are limited to 32 diners and sell out months in advance, so book ahead.

In Seeley Lake, the local favorite is the lakefront **Lindey's Prime Steak House** (Hwy. 83, Seeley Lake, 406/677-9229, 5pm-10pm daily May-Sept., 5pm-9pm Sun.-Thurs. and 5pm-10pm Fri.-Sat. Oct.-May, $29-35), where the steaks are of the same caliber as the great view. There is not much on the menu besides steak (and Alaska king crab legs when they can get them), but meat lovers will be exceedingly happy with this authentic Montana steakhouse. For a quicker, more casual bite, **Bayburgers** is a food truck run by Lindey's; it's just down the hill, at dock's edge, serving hot dogs, hamburgers, chili, steak sandwiches, and ice cream ($6-15, hours vary by season and weather so call ahead or check the website).

Another reliable spot for a meal in Seeley Lake almost any time of day is the **Filling Station Restaurant** (3189 Hwy. 83, 406/677-2080, 11am-10pm Mon.-Fri., 8am-10pm Sat.-Sun., $10-14); the bar offers karaoke on Friday and Saturday nights, and the huckleberry barbecue pork ribs should not be missed. The award-winning menu and wine list in the Double Arrow Resort's **Seasons Restaurant** (301 Lodge Way, 2 mi/3.2 km south of Seeley Lake, 406/677-2777, www.doublearrowresort.com/dining, 7am-9pm daily, breakfast $8-14, lunch $9-16, dinner $24-32) feature classic country cuisine—from rattlesnake and rabbit sausage to baby back ribs and bison tri-tip—in a welcoming and warm log lodge environment. They serve hearty breakfasts and lunch too, and the outdoor patio is a lovely place to be.

ACCOMMODATIONS

For the most part, the accommodations in the Seeley-Swan Valley are lovely and somewhat rustic. The **Double Arrow Resort** (301 Lodge Way, 2 mi/3.2 km south of Seeley Lake, 406/677-2777, www.doublearrowresort.com, cabins $110-860, main lodge rooms $120-175) is a handsome log lodge with history and character in a ranch-like setting. The accommodations are beautiful cabins and lodge rooms, all with private baths. Activities including fishing, golf, sleigh rides, horseback riding, and winter sports can be arranged on-site. Another great old-school family resort in the area is **Tamaracks Resort** (3481 Hwy. 83 N., Seeley Lake, 406/677-2433 or 800/477-7216, www.tamaracks.com, $160-500), which has 17 great old-school cabins, some remodeled in 2021, that can accommodate up to 10 people. Camping ($30-35) and RV ($40-55) sites are also available, as are boat rentals. Both of the roadside motels in Seeley Lake—the Wilderness Gateway Inn and the Seeley Lake Motor Lodge—were purchased in 2021 to be used as employee housing by the not-far-away, ultra-luxe Paws Up Resort in Greenough.

By far the fanciest spot in the region is the **Holland Lake Lodge** (1947 Holland Lake Rd., Condon, 406/754-2282, www.hollandlakelodge.com, cabins $380 double occupancy, lodge rooms $340 double occupancy), where the rates for their six rooms and nine cabins include phenomenal meals.

Activity options at this lakefront idyll include hiking, canoeing, horseback riding, swimming, fishing float trips, and floatplane excursions. The cabins and rooms are modest for the steep price, but the meals, scenery, and solitude more than make up for it. The **Laughing Horse Lodge** (71284 Hwy. 83, Swan Lake, 406/886-2080, www.laughinghorselodge.com, May-Sept., $138-182) is a cozy and fun bed-and-breakfast where pets are welcome and the activity menu is unlimited. Chef Kathleen whips up farm-to-table masterpieces in the kitchen, and the lodge also offers a six-course tasting menu on the second and fourth Tuesday June-September.

CAMPING

With so much public forest and wilderness in the vicinity, the multitude of camping options in the area attracts large numbers of campers on summer weekends. **Placid Lake State Park** (5001 N. Placid Lake Rd., 406/542-5500, $12-42) has 40 sites, flush toilets, and drinking water; it is 3 miles (4.8 km) south of Seeley Lake on Highway 83, then 3 miles (4.8 km) west on a county road. **Salmon Lake State Park** (2329 Hwy. 83, 5 mi/8 km south of Seeley Lake, 406/677-6804, May-Nov., $12-42) is another of the better options.

The **Holland Lake Campground** (Holland Lake Rd., 406/646-1012, www.recreation.gov, Memorial Day-Labor Day, $20) has 40 sites, flush toilets, and an incredible setting right on the lake. Paddleboards, kayaks, and canoes are available for rent. The **Swan Lake Campground** (Hwy. 83, Swan Lake, 877/444-6777, www.recreation.gov, $20-75) is a Forest Service campground 0.5 mile (0.8 km) northwest of Swan Lake on Highway 83.

INFORMATION AND SERVICES

The **Seeley Lake Chamber of Commerce** (2920 Hwy. 83, 406/677-2880, www.seeleylakechamber.com) is in a beautiful old barn on Highway 83 at mile marker 12.5, just south of the town. The **Swan Lake Chamber of Commerce** (22778 Hwy. 83, www.swanlakemontana.org) is in the town of Swan Lake. For more information on the region, you can contact the **Flathead Convention & Visitor Bureau** (800/543-3105, www.fcvb.org), **Glacier Country** (800/338-5072, www.glaciermt.com), or **Travel Montana** (800/847-4868, www.visitmt.com).

TRANSPORTATION

The Seeley-Swan Valley is a 91-mile (147-km) corridor along Highway 83 between the Mission Mountains to the west and the Swan Mountains to the east. From Missoula, Highway 200 leads to Highway 83. The distance from Missoula to Seeley Lake is 55 miles (89 km). From the north, US 93 in Kalispell accesses Highway 82, which then turns into Highway 83. From Kalispell to Swan Lake, the distance is 35 miles (56 km). From Swan Lake to Seeley Lake is 57 miles (92 km).

Kalispell and Whitefish

The northern town of Kalispell (pop. 25,857, elev. 2,956 ft/901 m) exists because of James Hill's Great Northern Railway and survives in spite of it. Freight and mercantile baron Charles Conrad founded the town of Kalispell when he convinced his friend Hill to run the railroad through it in 1891. By 1904, the Great Northern had abandoned its Kalispell route in favor of the more geographically amenable Whitefish line just 15 miles (24 km) to the north. The people of Kalispell were furious, but the town's economy survived due to Conrad's National Bank and the booming timber industry. Today it is still rather

Kalispell

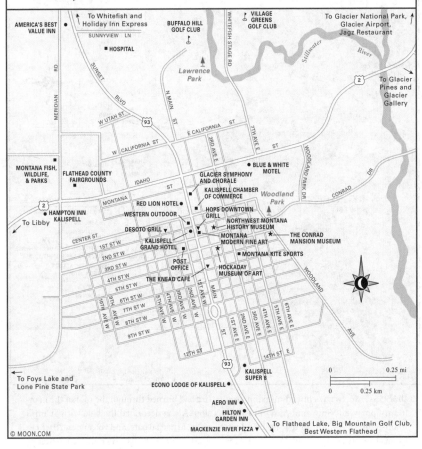

To Whitefish and Holiday Inn Express

SUNNYVIEW LN

AMERICA'S BEST VALUE INN

BUFFALO HILL GOLF CLUB

VILLAGE GREENS GOLF CLUB

To Glacier National Park, Glacier Airport, Jagz Restaurant

HOSPITAL

Lawrence Park

MERIDIAN RD

SUNSET BLVD

N MAIN ST

WHITEFISH STAGE RD

Stillwater

River

To Glacier Pines and Glacier Gallery

W UTAH ST

E CALIFORNIA ST

7TH AVE E

ST

W CALIFORNIA ST

3RD AVE E

WOODLAND PARK DR

CONRAD DR

MONTANA FISH, WILDLIFE, & PARKS

FLATHEAD COUNTY FAIRGROUNDS

IDAHO ST

BLUE & WHITE MOTEL

GLACIER SYMPHONY AND CHORALE

KALISPELL CHAMBER OF COMMERCE

Woodland Park

MONTANA ST

RED LION HOTEL

HOPS DOWNTOWN GRILL

WESTERN OUTDOOR

HAMPTON INN KALISPELL

To Libby

DESOTO GRILL

NORTHWEST MONTANA HISTORY MUSEUM

MONTANA MODERN FINE ART

THE CONRAD MANSION MUSEUM

CENTER ST

KALISPELL GRAND HOTEL

1ST ST W

2ND ST W

POST OFFICE

MONTANA KITE SPORTS

3RD ST W

4TH ST W

THE KNEAD CAFÉ

HOCKADAY MUSEUM OF ART

WOODLAND AVE

5TH ST W

6TH ST W

6TH ST W

7TH ST W

8TH ST W

9TH ST W

10TH AVE W

9TH AVE W

4TH AVE W

5TH AVE W

3RD AVE W

2ND AVE W

1ST AVE W

MAIN ST

1ST AVE E

2ND AVE E

3RD AVE E

5TH AVE E

6TH AVE E

12TH ST

14TH ST E

KALISPELL SUPER 8

To Foys Lake and Lone Pine State Park

ECONO LODGE OF KALISPELL

0   0.25 mi

0   0.25 km

AERO INN

HILTON GARDEN INN

MACKENZIE RIVER PIZZA

To Flathead Lake, Big Mountain Golf Club, Best Western Flathead

© MOON.COM

industrial compared to Whitefish's resort-like atmosphere—a nuts-and-bolts kind of town that serves as a natural supply and shopping center and has some wonderful museums, parks, and an ideal location between Flathead Lake and Glacier National Park.

Given a great boost when the train was rerouted from Kalispell in 1904, Whitefish (pop. 8,915, elev. 3,036 ft/925 m) grew up around Whitefish Mountain (long called Big Mountain) and the sport of skiing, and today is Montana's largest year-round resort community. Although Whitefish is clearly a ski town, it is also an art town, a gateway to Glacier, a summer hot spot, and a great place to find gourmet cuisine.

SIGHTS

The Conrad Mansion National Historic Site

Just a block from Woodland Park in Kalispell sits the palatial historic home of Charles Conrad, the founder of the city. The **Conrad Mansion** (330 Woodland Ave., Kalispell,

Whitefish

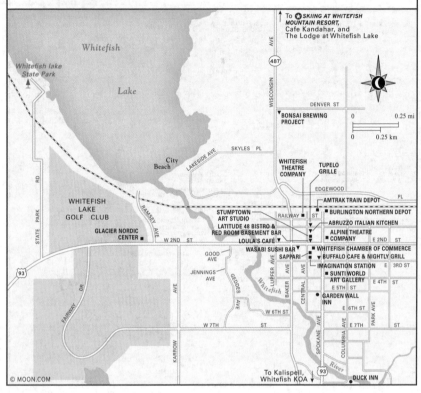

To **SKIING AT WHITEFISH MOUNTAIN RESORT,** Cafe Kandahar, and The Lodge at Whitefish Lake

WISCONSIN AVE

487

DENVER ST

0   0.25 mi

0   0.25 km

Whitefish

Lake

Whitefish lake State Park

City Beach

SKYLES PL

LAKESIDE AVE

BONSAI BREWING PROJECT

WHITEFISH THEATRE COMPANY

TUPELO GRILLE

EDGEWOOD

AMTRAK TRAIN DEPOT

PL

STATE PARK RD

WHITEFISH LAKE GOLF CLUB

GLACIER NORDIC CENTER

RAMSEY AVE

W 2ND ST

STUMPTOWN ART STUDIO

LATITUDE 48 BISTRO & RED ROOM BASEMENT BAR

LOULA'S CAFÉ

RAILWAY

ST

BURLINGTON NORTHERN DEPOT

ABRUZZO ITALIAN KITCHEN

ALPINE THEATRE COMPANY

E 2ND ST

93

FAIRWAY DR

GOOD AVE

JENNINGS AVE

WASABI SUSHI BAR

SAPPARI

GEDDES AVE

Whitefish

LUPFER AVE

BAKER AVE

CENTRAL AVE

WHITEFISH CHAMBER OF COMMERCE

BUFFALO CAFE & NIGHTLY GRILL

IMAGINATION STATION

SUNTI WORLD ART GALLERY

E 3RD ST

E 4TH ST

E 5TH ST

GARDEN WALL INN

E 6TH ST

PARK AVE

KARROW AVE

W 6TH ST

W 7TH ST

River

SPOKANE AVE

COLUMBIA AVE

E 7TH ST

93

To Kalispell, Whitefish KOA

DUCK INN

© MOON.COM

406/755-2166, www.conradmansion.com, 10am-5pm Wed.-Sun. mid-May-mid-June, 10am-5pm Tues.-Sun. mid-June-mid-Oct., 10am-4pm Tues.-Fri. mid-Oct.-mid-May, self-guided tour $15 adults, $10 students 5-17, docent guided tour $20 adults, $10 children 5-17) was completed in 1895 and designed by the renowned Spokane, Washington, architect Kirtland Cutter. The Conrads made sure that the residents of Kalispell felt some connection to the house: On Christmas Day of the year it was finished, the Conrad family invited people from around town who would otherwise have spent the holiday alone to share in their feast. The entire city was invited to a grand New Year's Eve ball a week later. Over the years, Alicia Conrad hosted famous parties, including a Halloween gathering just after a

fire had burned through the roof of the mansion. Alicia decorated the hole with Spanish moss, artificial bats, and volcanoes. After her death in 1923, the family continued to occupy the home until the mid-1960s. Conrad himself had only lived in the house for seven years before his death at age 52. In 1974, his youngest daughter donated the residence to the city of Kalispell. The 26-room, nine-bedroom Norman-style mansion has been beautifully restored and is furnished with the family's original furniture. There is also a large collection of family clothing and three generations of children's toys.

Hockaday Museum of Art

The **Hockaday Museum of Art** (302 2nd Ave. E., Kalispell, 406/755-5268, www.

hockadaymuseum.org, 10am-6pm Tues.-Sat. and noon-4pm Sun. June-Aug., 11am-5pm Tues., 11am-4pm Wed.-Sat. Sept.-May, $5 adults, $4 seniors 60 and over, $2 college students, free for children K-12) was originally begun by local artists in the late 1960s, and today it is a well-established public museum known for showcasing some of the region's most important art and artists. Visitors will find works by T. J. Hileman, John Fery, and Charles M. Russell, among others. It has the largest collection of Glacier Park art in the country and also a large permanent collection dedicated to the Blackfeet Nation. Public tours of the museum are offered for free, with admission, on Thursday and Saturday at 10:30am. Hockaday hosts the **Arts in the Park** program each July, and the gift shop has a broad selection of original works, including jewelry, pottery, and prints by local artists.

Northwest Montana History Museum

The Central School building was opened in 1894 and for more than 100 years housed different educational institutions but was slated for demolition in the early 1990s. The city of Kalispell instead invested more than $2 million renovating the historic building.

Since 1999 it has been used by the Northwest Montana Historical Society, which oversees the **Northwest Montana History Museum** (124 2nd Ave. E., Kalispell, 406/756-8381, www.nwmthistory.org, 10am-5pm Mon.-Fri., 10am-2pm Sat. June-Aug., 10am-5pm Mon.-Fri. Sept.-May, $5 adults, $4 seniors, free for children), formerly known as the Museum at Central School. The museum is dedicated to preserving the unique history of northwestern Montana and especially the history of Kalispell. Permanent exhibits include a historical examination of the Flathead Valley, the growth of the logging industry in Montana, a historical look at recreation in Glacier National Park, and a fascinating look at Demersville, a once-active community in the Flathead and now a stretch of deserted road. On Thursdays 5pm-8pm late June-late August, live music, food vendors, arts and crafts, a farmers market, and a beer and wine garden converge on the grounds of the museum.

Whitefish Mountain Resort

SPORTS AND RECREATION

★ Skiing at Whitefish Mountain Resort

When it comes to skiing in Montana, it doesn't get much better than skiing at the **Whitefish Mountain Resort** (3840 Big Mountain Rd., 406/862-2900, www.skiwhitefish.com, full day $89 adults 19-64, $76 seniors 65-69 and teens 13-18, $45 juniors 7-12, $29 super seniors 70 and over, and free 6 and under, half day $79 adults, $70 seniors and teens, $38 juniors 7-12), which offers 111 marked trails, 11 lifts, 2,353 feet (717 m) of vertical drop, and a 3.3-mile (5.3-km) run. When the snow conditions are just right, the trees all across the top of the mountain look like enormous snow monsters. It's magical—or terrifying, depending upon your point of view. This is a *big* mountain, with serious skiing and family fun at its best. The mountain stays open year-round for hiking, mountain biking, zipline tours, and an alpine slide, among other activities. In addition to offering regular 9am-4pm lift hours, it's also one of the few mountains in Montana that offer lighted night skiing ($27), 4pm-8:30pm.

Cross-Country Skiing

For cross-country skiers, fabulous groomed trails can be found locally at the **Glacier Nordic Center** (1200 US 93 W., Whitefish, 406/862-9498, www.glaciernordicclub.com, $15 adults 18-69, $7 children 8-17, $7 seniors 70 and over and veterans, free children 7 and under) on the Whitefish Lake Golf Course. There are 15 kilometers (9.3 mi) of skate and classic trails on gently rolling terrain, and lighted night skiing on 4 kilometers (2.5 mi) of trails until 11pm. A Nordic shop (406/862-9498) on-site sells passes and rents gear for kids and adults by the half day, full day, or week. Private and group lessons are also available.

Hiking and Biking

In addition to having Glacier National Park as a backyard, both Kalispell and Whitefish have excellent hiking and biking trails. Among the adventures at **Whitefish Mountain Resort** (3840 Big Mountain Rd., Whitefish, 406/862-2900 or 877/754-3474, www.skiwhitefish.com, 8am-6pm daily mid-June-early Sept., Fri.-Sun. only through late Sept.) are serious mountain biking opportunities for the hardcore and not-so-hard-core, who might prefer to limit rides to downhill only. There are more than 30 miles (48 km) of lift-accessed ($49 adult full day, $35 adult 2 hours, $34 junior 7-12 full day, $28 junior 2 hours) single-track and cross-country trails on the mountain. For hikers, the **Danny On Trail** winds 3.8 miles (6.1 km) from the base of the ski hill to the summit. The lift can be taken up or down to make the hike shorter and easier.

Just 4 miles (6.4 km) southwest of Kalispell, **Lone Pine State Park** (300 Lone Pine Rd., Kalispell, 406/755-2706, www.stateparks.mt.gov/lone-pine, $8/vehicle nonresidents) has a nature trail, 7.5 miles (12.1 km) of hiking and biking trails with scenic overlooks, and a year-round visitor center with flush toilets and a picnic shelter. A variety of programs—from yoga to full-moon hikes—are scheduled throughout the summer at the visitor center and picnic shelter. Young kids, ages 4-7, will be excited about the **Junior Ranger Club,** where they can learn about the natural world through activities and games.

Golf

Both Kalispell and Whitefish are big golfing destinations as soon as the snow melts. Public courses in Whitefish include the North and South Courses at the **Whitefish Lake Golf Club** (1200 US 93 N., 406/862-5960, 406/862-4000 for tee times, www.golfwhitefish.com, $49-63 for 18 holes, $26-33 for 9 holes, $40 for 18 holes on the South Course after 2pm). Five public courses are in Kalispell, including the **Northern Pines Golf Club** (3230 US 93 N.,

1: downtown Kalispell **2:** downtown Whitefish

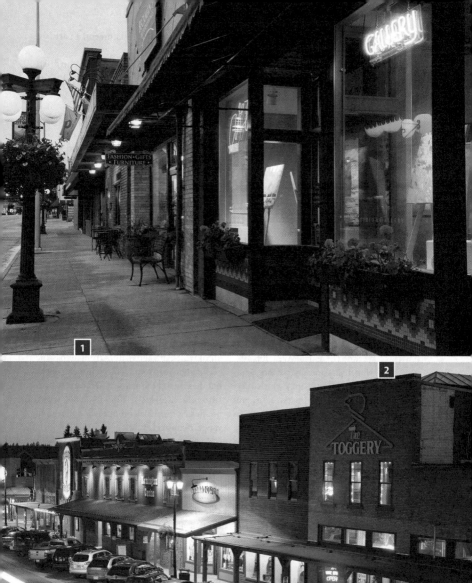

406/751-1950, www.northernpinesgolfclub.com, $30-72 for 18 holes, $20-40 for 9 holes), the 36-hole **Buffalo Hill Golf Club** (1176 N. Main St., 406/756-4530, www.golfbuffalohill.com, $39-70 for 18 holes, $18-27 for 9 holes, discounts for juniors and military), and the **Village Greens Golf Club** (500 Palmer Dr., 406/752-4666, www.montanagolf.com, $32-59 for 18 holes, $22-35 for 9 holes, discounts for seniors over 62 and juniors 7-15).

ENTERTAINMENT AND EVENTS

With so much to do year-round in this part of the state, the calendar is always full with seasonal events. In northwestern Montana, summertime means farmers markets, and a good one is the **Kalispell Farmers Market** (777 Grandview Dr., 406/260-5102, www.kalispellfarmersmarket.org, 9am-12:30pm Sat. early May-mid.-Oct.), held on the campus of Flathead Valley Community College. In Whitefish, summer brings the **Downtown Farmers Market** (1 Central Ave., 406/407-5272, www.whitefishfarmersmarket.org, 5pm-7:30pm Tues. late May-late Sept.), which offers local produce and art, handmade crafts, prepared food, and entertainment, often including live music.

Another market, which focuses on locally made arts and crafts, is the **Artists and Craftsmen of the Flathead Summer Outdoor Show** (920 S. Main St., Kalispell, 406/881-4288, www.artistsandcraftsmen.org), held over a weekend in the first part of July. Among the annual festivals celebrating local art, food, and culture are the **Whitefish Arts Festival** (406/862-5875, www.whitefishartsfestival.org), usually held the first weekend in July in Depot Park; the **Festival Amadeus** (Whitefish, 406/407-7000, www.gscmusic.org), a weeklong classical music festival held in late July or August; and the **Huckleberry Days Art Festival** (Depot Park, Whitefish, 406/862-3501, www.whitefishchamber.org), held over three days in mid-August, which celebrates the juicy purple berry with music, entertainment, an art fair, and lots of family fun.

In mid-May, the annual **Feast Whitefish** (O'Shaughnessy Center, 1 Central Ave., Whitefish, across from the train station, 406/862-3501, www.feastwhitefish.com) is the region's premier food event. It includes a weeklong dinner series with exquisite nightly meals by regional chefs and a one-day distiller's fest that focuses on local vodkas, whiskeys, and other spirits by seven regional distilleries.

Perhaps the most anticipated event of the year is the **Northwest Montana Fair & Rodeo** (fairgrounds, 265 N. Meridian Rd., Kalispell, 406/758-5810, www.nwmtfair.com, fair admission $8 adults 13-65, $5 seniors 65-plus and children 6-12, free for children 5 and under), usually held in mid-August and kicked off with a parade. The nearly weeklong event includes plenty of local agricultural exhibits, a carnival, three nights of professional rodeo, and live entertainment, all of which attract visitors from across the region. For year-round entertainment, check out the **Glacier Symphony Orchestra and Chorale** (Kalispell, 406/407-7000, www.gscmusic.org), which produces an interesting range of musical events.

In winter, the area celebrates the snow with festivities like the **New Year's Eve Rockin' Rail Jam and Torchlight Parade** (Whitefish Mountain Resort, 406/862-2900, www.skiwhitefish.com) and the **Whitefish Winter Carnival** (www.whitefishwintercarnival.com), a silly and fun event meant to help locals survive the gray middle of winter, held annually in early February.

Despite its small size, Whitefish has a remarkably savvy theater crowd, with offerings from both the **Alpine Theatre Project** (600 2nd St. E., 406/862-7469, www.atpwhitefish.org), a highly respected repertory theater company, and **Whitefish Theatre Company** (1 Central Ave., 406/862-5371, www.whitefishtheatreco.org), which offers eight community plays annually plus concerts, professional dance, improv performances, workshops, camps, and films.

SHOPPING

Western Outdoor (48 Main St., Kalispell, 406/756-5818 or 800/636-5818, www.westernod.com, 9am-6pm Mon.-Sat., 10:30am-4:30pm Sun. summer, 10am-6pm Mon.-Sat., 11am-4pm Sun. fall-spring) is one of the most popular shopping attractions. This Western goods store boasts more than 2,500 pairs of boots and close to 1,500 hats in every size, shape, and style imaginable. If you've always wanted real cowboy duds, the salespeople here are very attentive and will do their best to make sure you are outfitted properly.

Think Local (140 Main St., Kalispell, 406/260-4499, 9am-5pm Mon.-Fri., extended summer and holiday hours) showcases amazingly diverse works by 51 local artists, including photographers, painters, rope and barn-wood artists, and copper jewelers, all of them from Montana. A coffee shop in the back makes time spent browsing all the more enjoyable. A perfect winter shop in Kalispell is **Montana Kite Sports** (405 3rd Ave. E., 530/356-2758, 11am-5pm daily), which introduces the sports of "power kiting" and "ice boating" to the willing. Hours can change with the weather, so call ahead. In addition to sales, you can take a lesson! For art lovers, Kalispell's **Montana Modern Fine Art** (127 S. Main St., 406/755-5321, www.montanamodernfineart.com, 11am-6pm Tues.-Sat.) is a rare way to see phenomenal artworks and meet artists like Marshall Noice. He works in oils and pastels and captures the western landscape in brilliant color and luscious form.

The streets of downtown Whitefish are filled with bars, restaurants, spas, and art galleries. Several galleries line Central Avenue, including **Stumptown Art Studio** (145 Central Ave., 406/862-5929, www.stumptownartstudio.org, 10am-6pm Mon.-Sat., noon-5pm Sun.), a marvelous gallery for buying, learning about, and even making art.

Sunti World Art Gallery (345 Spokane Ave., 406/862-1084, www.suntiworldartgallery.com, 9am-5pm Tues.-Sat.) is a gallery that embraces both foreign cultures and old masters. In addition to gorgeous paintings, the gallery also sells American-made raku, antique Turkish rugs, Khmer Cambodian-style wood carvings, and *zardozi* embroidery from India. Both galleries participate in the popular **Whitefish Gallery Nights** (www.whitefishgallerynights.org) the first Thursday evening of each month May-October. Thirteen galleries are involved, each sponsoring a different artist each night of the event. It's a great way to view art, meet the artists, sample good food, and experience the community.

Imagination Station Toys (221 Central Ave., Whitefish, 406/862-5668, and 132 S. Main St., Kalispell, 406/755-5668, 10:30am-5:30pm Mon.-Sat.) began about 20 years ago when the owners realized that they missed the toys of their youth. Their classic toy selection has grown over the years and is a lot of fun for adults and children alike. They also stock their store with the latest wooden toys from Europe, have a good selection of educational toys, and like to keep a lot of puzzles and board games on hand as well. For a well-curated selection of clothing, housewares, jewelry, gifts, and Montana designers, head to **Sappari** (215 Central Ave., Whitefish, 406/862-6848, www.sappariwhitefish.shopsettings.com, 10am-6pm Mon.-Sat., noon-5pm Sun.).

If you have the time, a stop at **Kettle Care Organics** (3575 US 93, Whitefish, 888/556-2316, www.kettlecare.com, 9am-5pm Wed.-Fri.) is well worth the visit. This business is committed to producing fine all-natural body-care products while remaining conscious of its carbon footprint. The ingredients come from its certified organic farm and are created, packaged, and labeled for sale on-site. The store has a small showroom stocked with products; a trip to this store provides visitors an opportunity to see a successful homegrown green business in action.

FOOD

Some fantastic local restaurants are well worth finding. **The Knead Café** (21 5th St. E., Kalispell, 406/755-3883 www.theknead. com, 8am-3pm Tues.-Sat., $10-16) is a great little Mediterranean-inspired breakfast and lunch joint that rightly calls itself a "spirited fusion of food, art, and music." An excellent choice for a gourmet dinner is the family-friendly **Jagz Restaurant** (3796 Hwy. 2 E., Kalispell, 406/755-5303, www.jagzrestaurant. com, 4:30pm-8:30pm Sun.-Thurs., 4:30pm-9pm Fri.-Sat., $10-42), which serves a wide assortment of steaks, seafood, and pasta. **Hops Downtown Grill** (121 S. Main St., 406/755-7687, Kalispell, www.facebook.com/HopsDowntownGrill, 5pm-9pm Sun.-Thurs., 5pm-9:30pm Fri.-Sat., $10-28) is known for a wide selection of craft beer and gourmet burgers. Chicken, lasagna, ribs, and steak round out the menu. Where else can you order bison frites? Calling themselves Rockabilly barbecue, **The DeSoto Grill** (227 1st St. W., Kalispell, 406/314-6095, www.desotogrill. com, 11am-9pm Tues.-Fri., $12-26) is set in a really cool old forge. While you can't go wrong with any of the barbecue, their elk sausage and smokehouse nachos are especially tasty.

In keeping with the number of strip malls in town, Kalispell has an abundance of chain restaurants, many of them quite good, including **Mackenzie River Pizza** (2230 US 93 S., 406/756-0060, and 45 Treeline Rd., 406/756-3030, www.mackenzieriverpizza. com, 11am-9pm Sun.-Thurs. and 11am-10pm Fri.-Sat., $8-22), which serves pies from the traditional to the gourmet and rounds out the menu with a healthy selection of sandwiches, pasta dishes, salads, and foodie appetizers.

Whitefish has a surprising number of excellent restaurants. One of the all-around best places to go for a hearty, delicious meal is the budget-friendly **Buffalo Café & Nightly Grill** (514 3rd St. E., 406/862-2833, www. buffalocafewhitefish.com, 7am-2pm and 5pm-8:30pm Tues.-Sat., 7am-2pm Mon., 8am-2pm Sun., breakfast $5.50-13, lunch $10-14, dinner $12-18). From old-fashioned milk shakes and blueberry granola pancakes to Mexican specialties and baby back ribs, this local favorite has mastered comfort food for more than 30 years. And the service is both friendly and speedy.

When breakfast or pie (or any meal whatsoever) is on the docket, one should not overlook the incredible ★ **Loula's Café** (300 2nd St. E., Whitefish, 406/862-5614, www. whitefishrestaurant.com, 7am-2pm daily, $11-22). Breakfast ($6.50-13) is everything from Yuppie Scrambles to Ski Bum Biscuits and Gravy, eggs Benedict, and breakfast burritos. Save room for pie. Lunch ($8.50-14) is a selection of mouthwatering burgers, sandwiches, soups, and salads. And pie. Don't forget the pie. If you happen to be in Loula's when the pies come out of the oven and you don't jump to buy at least one, you will regret it for the remainder of your trip. I'm not kidding. Eating a huckleberry cherry pie, straight from the box and still a bit warm, on the shores of Lake McDonald is a memory that will stay with you forever.

Although Montana is not known for its sushi, Whitefish residents could not live without **Wasabi Sushi Bar** (419 E. 2nd St., 406/863-9283, www.wasabimt.com, from 5pm daily May-Oct., from 5pm Mon.-Sat. Nov.-Apr., rolls $5-24), with classic nigiri and sashimi, a contemporary twist on sushi and tempura, and plenty of grill items that include steak, duck, scallops, fish tacos, and more.

While a handful of elegant high-end eateries are in Whitefish, **Tupelo Grille** (17 Central Ave., 406/862-6136, www.tupelogrille. com, 5pm-9:30pm Sun.-Thurs., 5pm-10pm Fri.-Sat., $14-56) is a unique choice with a wonderfully Southern-inspired menu and an exceptional wine list. Just down the block is another gem: **Latitude 48 Bistro and Red Room Lounge** (147 Central Ave., 406/863-2323, www.latitude48bistro.com, 5pm-9pm Wed.-Thurs. and Sun., 5pm-10pm Sat.-Sun., $12-42) is an urban oasis with a phenomenal menu that offers small plates like seared beef tips and lamb sirloin, creative wood-fired pizzas, and substantial main courses in a fusion of traditional and contemporary trends.

Open since 2017, **Abruzzo Italian Kitchen** (115 Central Ave., Whitefish, 406/730-8767, www.abruzzoitaliankitchen.com, 4pm-9pm Sun.-Tues. and Thurs., 4pm-10pm Fri.-Sat., $15-36) puts their focus on the quality of the ingredients and the simplicity of preparation. Everything is from scratch. There are Italian cocktails and wine, wood-fired pizzas, salads, and entrées like wild boar ragu, spaghetti carbonara, chicken cacciatore, and, of course in Montana, steak. Beer lovers will want to stop by **Bonsai Brewing Project** (549 Wisconsin Ave., Whitefish, 406/730-1717, www.bonsaibrew.com, noon-8pm daily), where the current tap list usually has more than 10 offerings, from blond ales, pale ales, and IPAs to brown ales, barleywine, and aged sour pale ales. Plus they have plenty of other selections in bottles. They serve snacks, salads, soul bowls, and tacos ($6-13) for those who don't want to leave their seat.

For foodies looking for another unforgettable meal, **Café Kandahar** (3824 Big Mountain Rd., Whitefish Mountain Resort, 406/862-6247, www.cafekandahar.com, seatings at 6pm and 7:30pm Wed.-Sun. mid-Dec.-late Mar. and mid-June-late Sept., 3-course menu from $65, 3-course meal with paired wines from $105, 4-course meal from $75, 4-course meal with paired wines from $125) on the ski hill cannot be over-touted. The menus change nightly, but in addition to the à la carte masterpieces, the chef always offers 3- and 4-course tasting menus. Sample dishes include pork belly confit, halibut lox, and bison or elk tenderloin. But it is the way that chef Andy Blanton masterfully combines delicate flavors and exquisite ingredients that captivates diners. Make no mistake, this will be a pricey meal—but a phenomenal one.

ACCOMMODATIONS

Kalispell is definitely the best place to find an assortment of more budget-friendly chain hotels and motels, but prices can rise when the town is packed with travelers en route to or from Glacier or Flathead. Next to the airport, the **Aero Inn** (1830 US 93 S., 406/755-3798 or 800/843-6114, www.aeroinn.com, $55-160) has 61 no-frills guest rooms and is reasonably priced. Another good value can be found at the 106-room pet-friendly **Blue & White Motel** (640 E. Idaho St., 406/755-4311 or 800/382-3577, www.blueandwhitemotel.com, $43-95), which, in addition to cool neon signage, has decent rooms, standard amenities, and a 24-hour restaurant next door (making it a favorite with truckers). Among the larger chain hotels and motels in Kalispell are **America's Best Value** (1550 US 93 N., 406/756-3222, www.abvkalispell.com, $56-179), **Best Western Plus Flathead Lake Inn and Suites** (4824 US 93 S., 406/857-2400 or 888/226-1003, www.bestwestern.com, $87-409), **Econo Lodge of Kalispell** (1680 US 93 S., 406/752-3467 or 800/843-7301, www.choicehotels.com, $48-212), **Hampton Inn Kalispell** (1140 Hwy. 2 W., 406/755-7900 or 800/426-7866, www.hamptoninn3.hilton.com, $98-341), the fairly glamorous for these parts **Hilton Garden Inn** (1840 US 93 S., 406/756-4500, www.hiltongardeninn3.hilton.com, $99-529), **Holiday Inn Express & Suites** (275 Treeline Rd., 406/755-7405, www.ihg.com, $109-300), and **Kalispell Super 8 by Wyndham** (1341 1st Ave. E., 406/203-1905, www.wyndhamhotels.com, $49-195).

For a more historic experience, try the pet-friendly **Kalispell Grand Hotel** (100 Main St., 406/755-8100 or 800/858-7422, www.kalispellgrand.com, $139-350) downtown. This stately brick property is the last of eight hotels that once lined downtown. Less historic but reliable and pet-friendly, the **Red Lion Hotel** (20 N. Main St., 406/751-5050 or 800/733-5466, www.redlion.com, $62-444) is conveniently located next to the Kalispell Center Mall in the heart of downtown.

Given its proximity to Whitefish Mountain, Whitefish Lake, and Glacier National Park, it's no surprise that Whitefish has an abundance of accommodations—but true to its resort-town vibe, beds don't come cheap. The largest and most diverse, without a doubt, is the **Whitefish Mountain Resort** (3840 Big Mountain Rd., 406/862-2900, www. skiwhitefish.com, $159-1,500), the resort community around Whitefish Mountain with eight different lodging options, 90 percent of which are condominiums that range from modest and economical guest rooms in the **Hibernation House** to palatial five-bedroom townhouses. Rates are generally higher in winter, and particularly around holidays. Navigating the reservation system can be a feat, so practice patience and be clear about what you want and what your budget is.

Another sizable full-service resort, on the shores of Whitefish Lake and just over 1 mile (1.6 km) from downtown, is the ultra-appealing **Lodge at Whitefish Lake** (1380 Wisconsin Ave., 406/863-4000 or 877/887-4026, www.lodgeatwhitefishlake.com, $149-761). The lodge is pretty spectacular, and the rooms are all luxurious. The attached condos are sizable and great for larger groups, but somewhat less romantic. The immediate lake access is a disincentive to ever leave, and the on-site restaurants will keep you well fed and happy.

Smaller options for lodging in the town of Whitefish include the riverfront 15-room **Duck Inn** (1305 Columbia Ave., 406/862-3825 or 800/344-2377, www.duckinn.com, $156-245) and the charming five-bedroom **Garden Wall Inn** (504 Spokane Ave., 406/862-3440 or 888/530-1700, www.gardenwallinn.com, $225-395).

CAMPING

There are quite a few camping options, both public and private, around Kalispell, but nothing for tent campers in town. Among the best RV resorts is the 50-acre **Montana Basecamp RV Park** (1000 Basecamp Dr., Kalispell, 406/756-9999, from $79), which is wide open and grassy and includes free Wi-Fi and access to laundry. Instead of sites, each

RV has a yard with pavement, fire pit, picnic table, and mountain views. A good primitive option for tent campers is **Ashley Lake Campgrounds** (North Shore Rd., off Ashley Lake Rd., 17 mi/27 km west of Kalispell, 406/758-5204, www.fs.usda.gov, Memorial Day-Labor Day, no fees for day use or overnight camping, 5-day stay limit), which offers 11 lakefront sites with no services other than a vault toilet.

By far the most economical accommodations in Whitefish are the campgrounds. There are beautiful national forest campgrounds as well as two private campgrounds, including the **Whitefish KOA** (5121 US 93 S., 2 mi/3.2 km south of Whitefish, 406/862-4242 or 800/562-8734, www.glacierparkkoa.com, mid-May-mid-Sept., $58-125 RV and tent sites, $123-246 cabins), which has every imaginable amenity. **Tally Lake** (913 Tally Lake Rd., 17 mi/27 km west of Whitefish, 406/646-1012, www. recreation.gov, late May-late Sept., $20-100) is a gorgeous and popular spot with a nice campground. Closer to town, **Whitefish Lake State Park** (1615 E. Lakeshore Dr., 406/862-3991 or 406/751-4590, www. stateparks.mt.gov, year-round, water and showers available May-Sept., $12-44) offers 25 waterfront tent and RV sites that go quickly at this beautiful, convenient spot.

INFORMATION AND SERVICES

The **Kalispell Chamber of Commerce** (406/758-2800, www.kalispellchamber. com, 8am-5pm Mon.-Fri.) and **Flathead Convention and Visitor Bureau** (406/756-9091, www.fcvb.org, 8:30am-4pm Mon.-Fri.) are housed in the historic Great Northern Depot building (15 Depot Park, Kalispell). The **Whitefish Chamber of Commerce** (505 E. 2nd St., Whitefish, 406/862-3501, www.whitefishchamber.org, 9am-5pm Mon.-Fri.) is open year-round.

The **Flathead National Forest Headquarters** (650 Wolf Pack Way,

Kalispell, 406/758-5208, www.fs.usda.gov/flathead, 8am-4:30pm Mon.-Fri.) has helpful information for campers and hikers.

Kalispell has the **Flathead County Library** (247 1st Ave. E., 406/758-5820, www.imagineiflibraries.org, 10am-8pm Mon.-Wed., 10am-6pm Thurs.-Fri., 10am-5pm Sat.), and the **main post office** (248 1st Ave. W., 800/275-8777, 9am-4pm Mon.-Fri.) is at the corner of 3rd Street.

The **Logan Health Medical Center** (310 Sunnyview Ln., 406/752-5111, www.logan.org) has a 24-hour emergency room and is just north of downtown Kalispell. There are also several urgent care facilities in town, including **MedNorth Urgent Care** (2316 US 93, 406/755-5661, www.solvhealth.com, 9am-5pm Mon.-Fri., 9am-2pm Sat.-Sun.) and **Logan Health Primary Care** (1287 Burns Way, 406/752-8120, www.logan.org, 8am-5pm Mon.-Fri., 9am-5pm Sat.-Sun.). In Whitefish, **Logan Health Whitefish** (1600 Hospital Way at the intersection of US 93 and Hwy. 40, 406/863-3500, www.logan.org) is a private critical access hospital with a 24-hour emergency room and 25 patient rooms.

TRANSPORTATION
Getting There
Just 14 miles (22 km) south of Whitefish, Kalispell is the larger of the two cities and has commercial flights and bus service, while Whitefish has daily train service. Both cities have taxi services.

The **Glacier Park International Airport** (FCA, 4170 US 2 E., Kalispell, www.iflyglacier.com) is served daily by Delta, Alaska, American and United. Seasonal and twice- or three-times-weekly flights can be found on Sun Country, Jet Blue, Frontier, and Allegiant. There are on-site car-rental counters for **Avis, Budget, Hertz,** and **National/Alamo; Dollar** (406/892-0009, www.dollar.com), **Enterprise** (406/755-4848, www.enterprise.com), and **Thrifty** (406/257-7333, www.thrifty.com) are off-site but near the airport.

Shuttle service is available from **Airport Shuttle Express** (403/509-4799, www.airportshuttleexpress.com), **Arrow Shuttle** (406/300-2301, www.arrowshuttletaxi.com), and **Mountain Shuttle** (406/493-2345, www.mountainshuttlemt.com).

Greyhound (2075 Hwy. 2 E., Kalispell, 406/755-7447) offers daily bus service in and out of Kalispell.

Amtrak (500 Depot St., Whitefish) runs the **Empire Builder** from Chicago to Seattle with daily stops in Whitefish in each direction.

Kalispell and Whitefish are easily accessible by car: Kalispell is 115 miles (185 km) north of Missoula at the junction of US 2 and US 93; Whitefish is just 14 miles (22 km) farther north on US 93.

Getting Around
Taxi service is available from **Airport Shuttle Express** (403/509-4799, www.airportshuttleexpress.com), **Arrow Shuttle** (406/300-2301, www.arrowshuttletaxi.com), and **Mountain Shuttle** (406/493-2345, www.mountainshuttlemt.com).

Mountain Climber (406/758-5728, http://flathead.mt.gov/eagle, 7am-6pm Mon.-Fri.) is the public transit in town and operates on-demand and commuter rides in Kalispell.

Butte, Helena, and Southwest Montana

From the first major discovery of gold along

Grasshopper Creek in 1862, southwestern Montana attracted prospectors, miners, and those who would build communities around them.

Within a year of that major gold discovery, President Abraham Lincoln signed a bill creating Montana Territory. In many ways, this region gave rise to the state.

Two of the state's best-known mining camps, Helena and Butte, prospered and diversified, becoming a pair of Montana's most interesting and historically significant cities. Others, like Virginia City and Bannack, all but disappeared before rising again as well-maintained tourist attractions. Indeed, history comes to life in southwestern Montana, from the mines in and around Butte to the battlegrounds

Highlights

Look for ★ to find recommended sights, activities, dining, and lodging.

★ **Old Butte Historical Adventures:** Spend some time with one of the passionate and knowledgeable guides here, where you'll see history both above and below the ground (page 222).

★ **World Museum of Mining:** This museum, built atop the Orphan Girl mine yard, is packed with artifacts from more than a century of hard-rock mining (page 225).

★ **Philipsburg:** This fabulous mining town is experiencing a rebirth, with a couple of fantastic restaurants and a cool hotel (page 237).

★ **Big Hole National Battlefield:** A memorial to the Nez Perce and U.S. Army soldiers who died in battle, this site is both beautiful and haunting. The tipi frames stand where they did the fateful morning of the attack (page 245).

★ **Skiing Maverick Mountain:** A well-kept secret, Maverick has tow ropes, Carhartt, and the most family-friendly ski atmosphere you can imagine (page 248).

★ **Fishing the Big Hole:** Flowing 155 miles (250 km), the Big Hole River is one of the classics in the Montana fishing oeuvre, filled with rainbow, brown, and brook trout as well as rare native grayling (page 249).

★ **Virginia City and Nevada City:** These neighboring mining towns boast more than 100 historic buildings, a 1910 steam locomotive, and plenty of locals willing to re-create the rowdy mining era (page 253).

★ **Lewis and Clark Caverns:** Montana's first state park is a fine example of limestone caves (page 255).

★ **Last Chance Gulch and Reeder's Alley:** One of the few pedestrian malls in Montana is both the historic and modern heart of Helena (page 262).

along the Big Hole River, the ghost towns above Philipsburg, and the cobblestone streets of Montana's capital city of Helena.

But there's much more to this corner of the state than museums and mine shafts. Vast open spaces, like the glorious Big Hole, are dotted with cattle and lined with blue-ribbon trout waters. There are plentiful hot springs, old-school family-oriented ski hills, and some of the region's most scenic drives. And although the region is developing—a hip contemporary art scene in Helena, for example, and a Jack Nicklaus golf course built into the Old Works smelting site in Anaconda—there are stretches that look and feel untouched. The ranchers in the Big Hole Valley still use big wooden beaver-slide contraptions during haying season, and the Beaverhead-Deerlodge National Forest is a vast swath of breathtaking scenery that encompasses 3.5 million acres and two pristine wilderness areas. Southwest Montana and its best-known cities offer visitors a unique look into Montana's past and an authentic view of Montana's most appealing present.

PLANNING YOUR TIME

This corner of the state is vast and relatively diverse, both geographically and in terms of its offerings. History buffs will be easily sated just about anywhere, from the big cities of Helena and Butte to the tiny ghost towns that dot the landscape. And while southwestern Montana could easily absorb a week or more, it can also be appreciated in three days or less for visitors trying to see more of the state.

Butte is a fascinating destination, not so much for its present-day incarnation, which can be fairly described as a bit rowdy and somewhat bleak, but for its older glory: the remarkable architecture that still stands, the underground city that is coming to light, and the mines that made Butte the "richest hill on earth" and one of the country's largest cities west of the Mississippi for nearly 50 years. Butte is a marvelous place to spend at least

a day, and more if you are interested in mining or history.

For good reason, nature lovers and outdoors enthusiasts will be itching to get out of Butte. **The Big Hole,** southwest of the city, is a natural wonderland of wide-open spaces, supremely good fishing, a ski hill, an important Native American battle site, and a couple of great hot springs. Indeed, this region could be a vacation on its own, and it requires at least a day to cover the terrain.

Farther west, **Philipsburg,** less than 1 mile (1.6 km) from the ghost town of **Granite** and just 10 miles (16 km) from **Georgetown Lake** and **Discovery Ski Area,** is an ideal spot to enjoy a hearty meal, get a good night's rest, and perhaps even catch a show.

Finally, a host of other places in the region make great add-ons or stand-alone destinations. **Virginia City, Nevada City,** and **Bannack** are meticulously preserved ghost towns. The state's capital, **Helena,** is a bustling city that has successfully transitioned into modernity while still carefully preserving its past. As is true almost anywhere in Montana, the recreational opportunities just outside the city are plentiful, from the **Gates of the Mountains,** named by Lewis and Clark, to **Holter, Hauser,** and **Canyon Ferry Lakes,** which offer boating, fishing, and only-in-Montana activities like ice sailing during winter.

HISTORY

Although this area's past was dominated by mining, southwestern Montana's history predates the first precious-metal find. The region long had great appeal to both mountaineers and fur trappers. On their epic journey west, this is where Lewis and Clark were given vital assistance by the Native Americans who frequented the region. Just 14 miles (22 km) north of present-day Dillon, Sacagawea recognized Beaverhead Rock as the area where she had been kidnapped as a

Previous: Virginia City, one of the most well-preserved and lively ghost towns in the state; the Sweet Palace in Philipsburg; The Big Hole.

Butte, Helena, and Southwest Montana

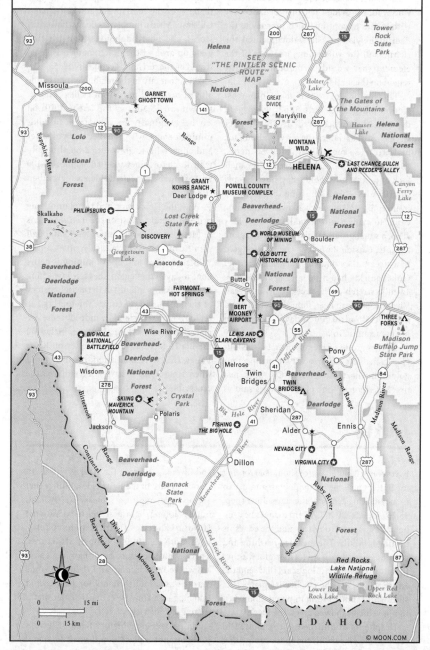

Tower Rock State Park

Helena

SEE "THE PINTLER SCENIC ROUTE" MAP

Helena National Forest

Holter Lake

The Gates of the Mountains

GREAT DIVIDE

Marysville

MONTANA WILD

HELENA

Hauser Lake

Helena National Forest

LAST CHANCE GULCH AND REEDER'S ALLEY

Missoula

GARNET GHOST TOWN

Garnet Range

Lolo National Forest

Sapphire Mtns

Skalkaho Pass

PHILIPSBURG

GRANT KOHRS RANCH
Deer Lodge

POWELL COUNTY MUSEUM COMPLEX

Beaverhead-Deerlodge

Canyon Ferry Lake

Helena National Forest

WORLD MUSEUM OF MINING

OLD BUTTE HISTORICAL ADVENTURES

Boulder

Lost Creek State Park

DISCOVERY

Georgetown Lake

Anaconda

Butte

National Forest

69

Beaverhead-Deerlodge National Forest

FAIRMONT HOT SPRINGS

BERT MOONEY AIRPORT

LEWIS AND CLARK CAVERNS

55

THREE FORKS

Madison Buffalo Jump State Park

BIG HOLE NATIONAL BATTLEFIELD

Wise River

Wisdom

SKIING MAVERICK MOUNTAIN

Jackson

Polaris

Beaverhead-Deerlodge National Forest

Crystal Park

Melrose

Twin Bridges

FISHING THE BIG HOLE

Big Hole River

Sheridan

Jefferson River

Tobacco Root Range

Beaverhead-Dearlodge

Pony

Ennis

Madison River

Madison Range

Alder

NEVADA CITY

VIRGINIA CITY

TWIN BRIDGES

Continental Divide

Bitterroot Range

Dillon

Bannack State Park

Beaverhead-Deerlodge

Beaverhead River

Beaverhead Divide Mountains

Red Rock River

National Forest

Ruby River

Snowcrest Range

National Forest

Red Rocks Lake National Wildlife Refuge

Lower Red Rock Lake

Upper Red Rock Lake

0   15 mi

0   15 km

I D A H O

© MOON.COM

child. With this information, the men set out to encounter her former people, the Shoshone, who would provide the Corps of Discovery with horses to continue their journey to the Pacific. Lewis and Clark documented the richness of the wilderness, unaware of the element that would permanently put the region on the map—gold.

The history of Montana's Gold West Country begins in July 1862, when gold deposits were discovered in Grasshopper Creek. A year later, the city of Bannack had attracted more than 3,000 residents. Although many initially arrived to try their luck at panning for gold, they stayed to ply their trades—blacksmithing, butchery, or innkeeping—all of which allowed the mining camp to evolve into a small town. In May 1863, a small group of men set out to explore the area outside Bannack. They struck gold in a stream they named Alder Creek. Alder Gulch quickly had nine mining camps on a 14-mile stretch of the creek. Within a year, Virginia City had been founded and boasted a population of 10,000 (today its population hovers around 216).

Next, a group of men known as "the four Georgians" left Virginia City to prospect for gold in uncharted territory. "OK, boys, just one last chance," one of the miners said as

he dipped his pan in the Prickly Pear Creek and came up with enough gold to keep them there. The word soon spread, and Last Chance Gulch spawned a jumble of saloons, makeshift stores, and boardinghouses. The city that grew up around the gulch, named Helena, would be the territorial capital by 1875.

The other city in the region defined by the almost maniacal pursuit of riches is Butte, known for decades as the "richest hill on earth." Originally an assortment of gold-mining camps, with the discovery of silver and copper Butte grew into a bustling city with dozens of mines and 10,000 miles (16,100 km) of tunnels beneath its increasingly urban streets.

With the Depression and the plummeting price of metals, most of the mining towns in Montana suffered similar fates, although significantly less dramatically than Butte. While a limited amount of mining is being done today in the region, the state is working to draw visitors interested in the rich history of the area—and, of course, by touting the region's natural splendor. Indeed, there are places in southwestern Montana, including the Big Hole Valley and the Jefferson River Valley, that were unscarred by mining and where time seems to have stood still over the centuries.

Butte

Everyone in Montana is (or should be) rooting for Butte. Once the cosmopolitan and urban moneymaking center of the state, Butte (pop. 35,267, elev. 5,700 ft/1,737 m) today is beat-up but still scrappy; "rough around the edges" is putting it mildly. The most far-reaching and present reminder of its former glory, other than the open-pit mining scars that rend the entire valley, are the car license plates that start with 1, Butte's rank in population when motor vehicles showed up on the scene.

Despite its diminished status, Butte is a remarkable place with the most compelling

and diverse history in the state as well as an infrastructure of fabulous old buildings that are just waiting for a renaissance. In fact, Butte is among the largest registered National Historic Landmark Districts in the country, with more than 4,000 historic structures. There is more culture here than just about anywhere in Montana, and there are some marvelous establishments for dining and imbibing—and one hotel in particular that is staging a comeback.

Unless you are a history fanatic, Butte is probably not a place you'll want to spend

Butte

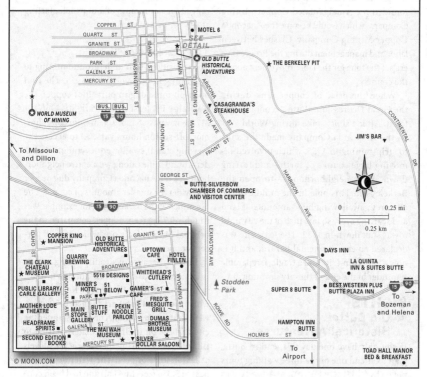

COPPER ST
QUARTZ ST
GRANITE ST
BROADWAY ST
PARK ST
GALENA ST
MERCURY ST
IDAHO ST
WASHINGTON ST
MAIN ST
WYOMING ST
ARIZONA ST
MOTEL 6
SEE DETAIL
★ OLD BUTTE HISTORICAL ADVENTURES
★ THE BERKELEY PIT
▼ CASAGRANDA'S STEAKHOUSE
★ WORLD MUSEUM OF MINING
BUS. 15 BUS. 90
MONTANA ST
MAIN ST
UTAH AVE
FRONT ST
CONTINENTAL DR
JIM'S BAR ▼
To Missoula and Dillon
15 90
GEORGE ST
AVE
■ BUTTE-SILVERBOW CHAMBER OF COMMERCE AND VISITOR CENTER
HARRISON AVE
0   0.25 mi
0   0.25 km
LEXINGTON AVE
DAYS INN ●
LA QUINTA INN & SUITES BUTTE ●
▲ Stodden Park
SUPER 8 BUTTE ●
BEST WESTERN PLUS BUTTE PLAZA INN ●
15 90
To Bozeman and Helena
ROWE RD
HAMPTON INN BUTTE ●
HOLMES ST
To Airport ↓
TOAD HALL MANOR BED & BREAKFAST ●

IDAHO ST
★ COPPER KING MANSION
OLD BUTTE HISTORICAL ADVENTURES
GRANITE ST
★ THE CLARK CHATEAU MUSEUM
QUARRY BREWING
BROADWAY ST
UPTOWN CAFE
HOTEL FINLEN
5518 DESIGNS
WHITEHEAD'S CUTLERY
■ PUBLIC LIBRARY/ CARLE GALLERY
MINER'S HOTEL
51 BELOW
GAMER'S CAFE
PARK ST
MONTANA AVE
MAIN ST
WYOMING ST
■ MOTHER LODE THEATRE
MAIN STOPE GALLERY
BUTTE STUFF
PEKIN NOODLE PARLOR
FRED'S MESQUITE GRILL
HEADFRAME SPIRITS ■
GALENA ST
DUMAS BROTHEL MUSEUM
■ SECOND EDITION BOOKS
THE MAI WAH MUSEUM
MERCURY ST
★ SILVER DOLLAR SALOON
© MOON.COM

an entire week; to see Montana, you need to get out in the fresh air and enjoy the natural beauty. A weekend in Butte gives visitors to the state an incredible opportunity to learn about Montana's past and see firsthand what happens to a place when all of its natural resources are exploited as quickly as possible. Indeed, there is something of *The Lorax* in Butte, and something of *The Giving Tree.* But no copper king or corporation can rob this place of its fascinating past and modern-day spirit. And no one is willing to rule out a renaissance—least of all the citizens of Butte.

HISTORY

Like many of the towns in this part of the state, Butte grew up as a mining camp after a gold strike in 1864. After discovery of both silver and copper ores, many big companies moved into town to extract, process, and distribute the metals, making Butte the state's first industrialized city. Urban and fiercely proud, Butte residents were known to describe their city as "Butte, America," rather than "Butte, Montana," to distinguish themselves from the rural sensibilities of the rest of the state. By the late 1800s, Butte was one of the world's largest silver and copper producers and among the most populated cities in the United States. Throughout the boom, a diverse range of immigrants flooded into the area looking for opportunities. Irish, Italian, Eastern European, and Chinese newcomers all contributed to the culture and history of the city.

By the early 1900s, with the introduction of electricity and the demands of World War I, Butte's copper production was in full swing, and big business wanted the largest piece of the pie. In 1899 the Standard Oil Company founded the Amalgamated Copper Mining Company, which would become the Anaconda Copper Mining Company. Clashes between labor and management during the Progressive era set the tone for the labor movement across the country.

When the price of copper sank during the Great Depression, Butte's economy suffered. After a short spike during World War II, the Anaconda Company made the shift to strip-mining in 1955, which involved removing large chunks of earth—and tearing down entire neighborhoods—to open the Berkeley Pit. This hole in the middle of the city grew, swallowing huge amounts of land and scarring every square inch of the city until it was shut down in 1982. The toxic site was declared an environmental hazard, and it is now a Superfund site and a tragic, irreparable reminder of the end of the city's mining era.

SIGHTS
★ Old Butte
Historical Adventures
If you only have one day to spend in Butte, plan to attend one of the three walking tours put on by **Old Butte Historical Adventures** (117 N. Main St., 406/498-3424, scheduled tours 10am, noon, and 2pm Mon.-Sat., by reservation only Sun. Apr.-Sept., by reservation only Nov.-Mar., Underground City and Dellinger Tours $20 adults, $15 seniors, military, and students with ID, East Walking Tour $25 pp and a minimum of 4 people). It offers a variety of walking tours of Butte's underground city, complete with a speakeasy, a barbershop, and an old city jail. Other tours stay above ground and visit the Myra brothel, Finntown, Tony's Tinshop, and the Cabbage Patch shantytown, or a number of offices inaccessible from 1938-2005. Ghost tours, labor history tours, and ethnic culture walking tours can also be arranged. What makes these tours so compelling, other than the mind-blowing history, is the passion and knowledge of the guides—you may just fall in love with Butte. Reservations are strongly recommended, and custom tours can be arranged for a minimum of four people starting at $25 per person.

The Berkeley Pit
The transition from underground mining to pit mining in Butte began in 1955. The first open-pit mine dug in pursuit of copper, the **Berkeley Pit** (east end of Park St., 406/723-3177, www.pitwatch.org, 9am-5pm daily summer, off-season hours vary, $2 to access the viewing stand) swallowed several of the underground mines along with entire neighborhoods as the Anaconda Company dug deeper and wider for smaller amounts of copper. The ore mined at the Berkeley Pit, for example, was roughly 0.75 percent copper, compared to the original Marcus Daly ore, which was 30 percent copper.

In 1982, because of steadily falling copper prices, the Berkeley Pit was shut down. With it, the pumps from the nearby Kelley Mine, which had kept the pit dry for nearly 30 years, were shut down as well. The mines under the city and the pit itself immediately started to fill with water bearing the same acidity levels as lemon juice or cola. The water depth surpassed 5,356 feet (1,633 m) and had been continuously climbing, with 2.6 million gallons (9.8 million liters) flooding in every day until remediation started in 2019. In 2019, however, as the water started approaching the lowest level of the pit rim, called the protective water level, pumps started pumping out and treating about 3 million gallons (13.6 million liters) per day. The water itself is highly toxic and appears various shades of brown, blue, green, and red, depending on the concentration of chemicals and subsequent chemical reactions.

In 1994, the EPA established a "critical water level" of 5,410 feet (1,649 m), stipulating that when the water in the pit reaches that level, it could seep into Silver Bow Creek or the alluvial groundwater aquifer and contaminate the

1: uptown Butte 2: the Berkeley Pit, the first open-pit copper mine in Butte 3: the World Museum of Mining 4: the historic Hotel Finlen

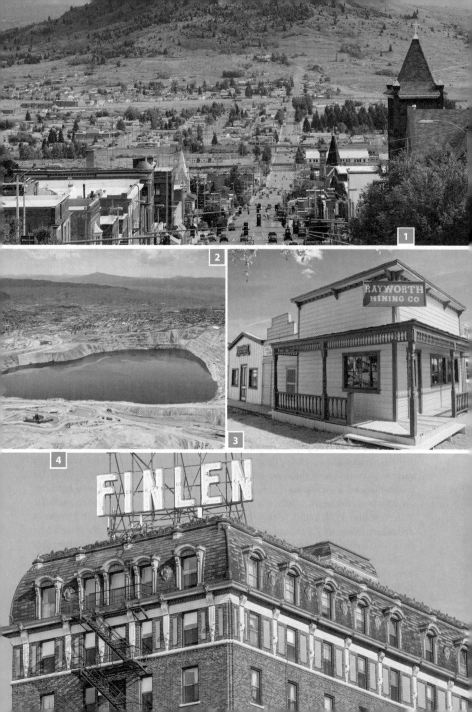

Montana's Superfund Sites

Big Sky Country is most often associated with images of pristine lakes, majestic mountains, and wide-open grasslands. But toxic wastelands? And one of the worst in the country? It seems far-fetched. However, Montana's mining industry wreaked havoc on the natural environment, scarring the landscape and contaminating both water and soil.

The 1980 Superfund program was created to clean up hazardous waste sites posing a threat to public health and the environment. The area surrounding the Upper Clark Fork River, which encompasses Butte, Anaconda, and Missoula, is among the largest Superfund areas in the country.

In the late 1800s, Butte's smelters were adjacent to the mines, and the toxic fumes created massive amounts of thick smoke. In mines without smelters, the copper sulfide ore was spread over large piles of logs and ignited in toxic piles that burned for weeks, contaminating air, soil, and water. The mining and smelting in Butte not only decimated Butte Hill but was carried downstream and downwind as far as Milltown, 120 miles (193 km) northwest.

Butte was famously without vegetation, and its citizens were often sick with burning eyes, bloody noses, gagging, and lung disease. The copper baron William Andrews Clark was quoted as saying, "I must say that the ladies are very fond of this smoky city . . . because there is just enough arsenic there to give them a beautiful complexion." Eventually an antismoke ordinance was passed, but it was never enforced because smelter operators threatened to shut down if the laws were applied. No one questioned who had the power in Butte.

When the copper smelter was erected in Anaconda in 1894 by Marcus Daly, Butte's air improved dramatically. But Deer Lodge ranchers and farmers who lived in the valley between Butte and Missoula suffered devastating crop failures and livestock losses. The Anaconda Company built an enormous smokestack in 1918 (at 585 ft/178 m, it surpasses the Washington Monument) to disperse the smoke, but farmers argued it was just spreading the poison over a wider area. The case went all the way to the Supreme Court, and the company won.

By the 1970s it was apparent that the air and water pollution was still hurting livestock and agricultural soil throughout the Deer Lodge Valley. The EPA rated the area the most polluted in the country, worse than Love Canal in New York, and although the cleanup is underway, it will likely last decades and cost hundreds of millions of dollars.

region's water supply. The government requires the parties responsible for treating the groundwater to pump and treat the water before it reaches that level or incur fines of $25,000 per day. That treatment began in 2019.

In November 1995, a flock of snow geese landed in the Berkeley Pit; fog and snow kept them from flying off, and after several days 342 birds were found dead in the water. Since then, a program has discouraged migrating birds from landing on the pit water. In November 2016, more snow geese landed in the pit in a single day than often do in an entire year. Crews employed a number of ways to encourage the birds to leave after a short rest—fireworks, bird wailers, drones—but several thousand stayed for a few days and, sadly, perished as a result.

One curious creature that managed to live in and around the pit for years was a dog known by miners as "The Auditor." He greeted workers daily for 17 years but never came close enough for anyone to touch. He was a white (OK, gray) dog with dreadlocks that dragged on the ground. The miners built him a shanty and left food and water; they pointed to The Auditor as proof that there were indeed things able to withstand the toxicity of the Superfund site. The pit's unofficial mascot died in 2003, but not before the community raised enough money to commission a bronze statue of the mangy mutt, which is on display at the pit viewing stand.

Our Lady of the Rockies

High atop the crest of the Continental

Divide is **Our Lady of the Rockies** (tours leave from 3100 Harrison Ave., 406/782-1221, www.ourladyoftherockies.net, 10am and 2pm daily weather permitting, gift shop 11am-4pm Mon.-Sat. June-Oct., $25 adults, $20 juniors 12-17 and seniors 63 and up, $10 children 11 and under), a 90-foot statue of the Virgin Mary meant to watch over this predominantly Catholic town. Between 1979 and 1985, the statue was built and erected entirely by volunteers, many of them miners who had lost their jobs when the Berkeley Pit, Butte's last operating mine, closed down. Bob O'Bill, who worked for the Anaconda Mining Company for years, vowed that if his wife recovered from illness, he would hoist a statue of the Virgin Mary on the East Ridge overlooking the city. When the final piece was set in place by helicopter, Butte came to a screeching halt to watch in proud silence. Indeed, the statue is a reflection of this city's indomitable spirit. The roughly 2.5-hour tours leave from the gift shop in the Butte Plaza Mall on Harrison Avenue and include a trip inside the metal sculpture.

★ World Museum of Mining

Off West Park Road, across from the Montana Tech campus, is the **World Museum of Mining** (155 Mining Museum Rd., 406/723-7211, www.miningmuseum.org, 9:30am-5:30pm daily Apr.-Oct., hours subject to change after Labor Day, $9 adults, $8 seniors 65 and over, $5 students 5-17, free for children under 5), which sits on the now-defunct Orphan Girl mine yard. It houses numerous large-scale exhibits, and the mine yard is filled with a variety of equipment covering a century of use, including smelter cars, ore carts, and trucks. When you purchase your entry ticket to the museum, you may also want to buy a ticket for the 1.5-hour **underground mine tours** (from $21). Visitors to the underground mine wear hard hats, cap lamps, and battery belts and descend 65 feet (20 m) into the mine. The tours are led by former mine workers who tell their personal stories. They also explain how equipment was used

and how the ore was mined and removed from the pit. Combined tickets can be purchased for the museum and the underground tour. Children under five are not permitted on the underground tour.

A highlight of the museum is its **Hell Roarin' Gulch**, a full-scale, authentic reproduction of an 1890s mining town. There are 50 buildings on the site, 15 of which are original historic buildings that have been relocated to the museum. Visit a bank, general store, school, and Chinese herbalist whose shelves are stocked with original herbs and medicines. The buildings have been painstakingly re-created using as many antiques and original materials as possible. A rock and mineral room in the museum will delight rockhounds, and there's a remarkable doll and dollhouse collection.

Copper King Mansion

The **Copper King Mansion** (219 W. Granite St., 406/782-7580, www.thecopperkingmansion.com, 10am-4pm daily May-Sept., by appointment Oct.-Apr., tours at 10am, noon, 2pm, and 3:30pm, $20 adults, $10 children 5-12, discounts for seniors and military, free for children under 5) is both a museum and bed-and-breakfast ($125-250). Guided tours show off this 34-room Victorian home built in 1898 for the infamous King of Copper, William Andrews Clark. Considered one of the wealthiest men in the world in his day, Clark could easily afford to import all the material for the house's construction as well as the European artisans needed to do the work. The cost to construct the mansion is estimated at around $500,000, which represents one-half day's wages for Clark at the peak of his career. His personal fortune is thought to have exceeded $50 million by 1900. Each room has a fresco painted on its ceiling by artists personally commissioned by Clark. There is elaborate woodwork throughout the house, including the fireplaces, bookcases, and stairways. Tiffany stained-glass windows and magnificent chandeliers enhance the elegance. It is an exquisite way to truly appreciate the wealth in this city around the turn of the 20th century.

Clark Chateau Museum

W. A. Clark's son, Charles, also commissioned a house in 1898. The **Clark Chateau Museum** (321 W. Broadway, 406/565-5600, www.clarkchateau.org, noon-4pm Thurs.-Sun. May-Aug., noon-4pm Sat.-Sun. Sept.-Apr., 1-hour tours at 1pm, $10 guided tour, $7 general admission) is a replica of a chateau Charles had admired in France. Today the house is a period museum and Butte's community arts center. Up the gorgeous spiral staircase to the 2nd and 3rd floors is the museum's permanent collection, dedicated to showcasing the diverse cultural and ethnic heritage of the city. Two galleries offer current shows, and the exhibits change over the course of the season. Weekday tours can be arranged off-season by emailing clarkchateau@gmail.com.

Dumas Brothel Museum

Butte also happens to be home to "America's longest-running house of prostitution." The Dumas Brothel was the center of Butte's red-light district back in its mining heyday. Opened in 1890, it only closed its doors in 1982. The brothel reopened as the **Dumas Brothel Museum** (45 E. Mercury St., 406/530-7878, call for hours and admission prices), allowing visitors to get a glimpse into the seedier side of the city's history. At its height, the brothel used all 43 rooms and was open 24 hours a day to cater to the miners, who worked around the clock. There were even underground tunnels that led to other downtown buildings, providing secret entry for some of its more distinguished clientele. Since the building was actually constructed to serve as a brothel, it has some unique design elements, including windows lining the hallway. The rooms themselves, known as "cribs," are small enough to hold a bed and not much more. Naturally, the brothel is rife with ghost stories, including the tale of Madame Elenor Knott, who agreed to run away with her married lover in 1955. When he didn't show up for their rendezvous, Elenor took her own life. Her ghost is often reported, and even photographed, in the building. The museum was purchased in 2012 by Travis Eskelsen and Michael Piche, who committed themselves to its preservation and restoration. Tragically, Piche died in 2018. It was sold again in 2019 to Charlee and David Prince, who are working to clean up and restore the brothel. Always call before visiting, since the restoration process often requires closures. During COVID, the museum was open "every other weekend or so." This is a labor of love in every way imaginable, like so much of Butte's restoration. Be patient and flexible—it's worth it.

Mai Wah Museum

The **Mai Wah Museum** (17 W. Mercury St., 406/723-3231 or 406/565-1826 off-season, www.maiwah.org, 10am-4pm Tues.-Sat. June-Sept., $8 adults, $5 kids, students, and seniors, free for children under 5) is dedicated to documenting and preserving Butte's Chinese heritage. By 1910, Butte's Chinatown had more than 2,000 Chinese residents, and the 1914 directory listed 62 Chinese businesses that included gambling parlors, noodle shops, herbalists, and grocery stores. The permanent exhibit tells the story of Chinese immigrants to the city who came in search of lucrative jobs in the mining industry 1860-1940. It houses exhibits containing photos, artifacts, and interpretive materials. The museum is in the Wah Chong Tai and Mai Wah buildings, just off China Alley, the heart of Butte's Chinatown. Originally the buildings were a mercantile store and noodle shop that historically served as meeting places and a major point of social interaction for the Chinese immigrant community.

SPORTS AND RECREATION

United States High Altitude Sports Center

A unique facility with an outdoor speed-skating rink and a training facility for

Olympic athletes from all over the world, the **United States High Altitude Sports Center** (1 Olympic Way, 406/494-7570, free) hosts various competitions and is open to the public.

Stodden Park

During Butte's mining heyday, the only greenery in town could be found at the beloved Columbia Gardens, which sadly burned down. Today there is plenty of green space in town, and **Stodden Park** (Sampson St. and Utah St., 406/494-3686 or 406/494-6200, www.co.silverbow.mt.us) tops the list with a swimming pool, tennis courts, horseshoes, an awesome playground that celebrates the city's mining heritage, a nine-hole golf course ($14 for 9 holes, $23 for 18 holes), and Ridge Waters Waterpark (noon-3pm and 4pm-7pm, $6 adults 18-60, $4 seniors 61 and up, $4 youth 3-17, free for 2 and under), complete with a lazy river and two slides.

Hiking and Bouldering

Hikers and climbers driving into Butte from the east over Homestake Pass might get tingly as they see the hoodoos scattered across the terrain. A wonderful and quite similar place to explore, without the distraction of highway traffic, is the **Humbug Spires Wilderness Trail,** 26 miles (42 km) south of Butte in the Humbug Spires wilderness area. This is primitive Bureau of Land Management territory that has granite outcroppings, for which the area is named, in addition to primeval Douglas fir forest and a small stream chockfull of little cutthroat trout. The relatively flat 7-mile (11.3-km) round-trip trail can be accessed by taking I-15 to exit 99 for Moose Creek and then heading east on Moose Creek Road for 3.4 miles (5.5 km) to the parking lot and trailhead.

ENTERTAINMENT AND EVENTS

Nightlife

Like a puckish teenager, Butte's reputation has always preceded it. This is a scrappy town where no one likes to back down. Even the most elegant older women love to tell of carrying pearl-handled revolvers every time they traveled into or through Butte. It's a fighting town, which means Butte is a drinking town.

Butte has numerous bars, many of them good ones, but the best one—the M&M Cigar Store—burned to the ground in May of 2021. Opened in 1890, the M&M remained unlocked for more than 100 years, bearing witness to Butte's glory days from a front-row seat. There was once a bowling alley in the basement, a dining and drinking room on the 1st floor, and a gambling lounge upstairs. The cigars were added during Prohibition as a polite show of compliance, but the liquor was never locked up. In a 1970 *Esquire* article, Jack Kerouac wrote a poignant description of a late night spent at the M&M, summing it up: "It was the end of my quest for an ideal bar." But this is Butte. And no one gives up here. A letter from the owner on the M&M website (www.mandmbarandcafe.com) promises "This is not the end." The only thing they managed to save was the wonderful neon sign out front. Keep an eye out. This is Butte. Anything can happen.

The **Silver Dollar Saloon** (133 S. Main St., 406/782-7367, 4pm-2am daily) is another legendary Butte watering hole, established on the border between Chinatown and the redlight district. The adjacent building was both a brothel and a boardinghouse for Chinese laborers. One of the hubs of the St. Patrick's Day festivities, the Silver Dollar is known for its live music offerings.

For a more family-friendly place with outstanding beer, try **Quarry Brewing Company** (124 W. Broadway St., 406/723-0245, www.wedig.beer, 3pm-8pm daily) in the old Grand Hotel. Its five different German-style beers are brewed on-site, and kids will appreciate the play area, free popcorn, and homemade root beer and orange cream soda.

Jim's Bar (2720 Elm St., 406/782-3431, 3pm-2am daily) is kind of a biker bar, with plenty of fun and rowdy events such as biker rodeos and beach volleyball. Closing time is dependent on the number of customers.

The newest bar on the scene in Butte, and a really interesting one in how it pays homage to Butte's history, is **Fifty One Below Speakeasy** (53 W. Park St., 406/723-8928, www.theminershotel.com, 4pm-9pm Mon.-Wed., 4pm-10pm Thurs., 2pm-11pm Fri., 10am-11pm Sat.), located in the boutique Miner's Hotel, a building with fantastic, gritty history. The bar is intimate, as you would expect in a speakeasy, and they serve a huge selection of whiskey cocktails, plus signature cocktails with every other spirit under the sun. There are nine different varieties of Moscow Mule, for example.

The Arts

For a selection of contemporary gems, try **Main Stope Gallery** (14 S. Dakota St., 406/723-9195, www.mainstopegallery.com, 11am-5pm Wed.-Fri., 9am-2pm Sat.), which sells pottery, paintings, photography, and other fine art by contemporary Montana artists. Located on the 3rd floor of the Butte public library, the **Carle Gallery** (226 W. Broadway, 406/723-3361, www.buttepubliclibrary.info, 10am-5pm Mon. and Fri.-Sat., 9am-7pm Tues.-Thurs.) pays tribute to Butte artist John Carle, known for his paintings of the city's buildings and people, and hosts monthly shows. The gallery also hosts rotating exhibits from the World Museum of Mining and Mai Wah Museum.

MOTHER LODE THEATRE

Seeing an event at the **Mother Lode Theatre** (316 W. Park St., 406/723-3602, http://buttearts.org) is an event in itself. Built entirely with private funds by the Masons in 1923 as the 1,200-seat Temple Theatre, the glorious building was converted into a movie house during the Depression. As the mines were abandoned, so was the theater. In the 1980s, the only other theater in town was condemned and razed. True to form in Butte, people made it a priority to restore the building. The only more pressing project at the time

was a complete overhaul of the city's water system. The Butte Center for the Performing Arts formed as a nonprofit organization to raise the funds necessary and oversee the construction work. The Masons donated the building to the city, and $3 million was raised for the overhaul, completed in 1996. A 106-seat children's theater known as the Orphan Girl Theatre (named for a mine in Butte) was added in 1997 thanks to another big donation.

Today, the Mother Lode provides performance space for the Butte Symphony, Montana Repertory Theatre, Missoula Children's Theatre, traveling Broadway productions, concerts, and numerous other events and organizations.

SILVER BOW DRIVE IN

Since 1977, the **Silver Bow Twin Drive In** (116054 S. Buxton Rd., 406/782-8095, www.silverbowdrivein.com, spring-early-Sept., $6 ages 4 and up) has been an absolute classic. There really isn't a better way to see a movie under the Big Sky. Two screens allow for a capacity of nearly 500 cars. Don't bring food with you—a concession stand (that until 1973 was at a drive-in theater in Deer Lodge) serves great popcorn and other goodies including Tombstone pizza and ice cream. The audio can be found on your FM dial, or a few portable radios are available to rent for those without a working car radio or who want to sit outside. This is old-timey goodness under the Big Sky.

Festivals and Events

CHINESE NEW YEAR

A reflection of Butte's diverse population and cosmopolitan history, each **Chinese New Year** the community gathers to celebrate with a parade from the courthouse to the **Mai Wah Museum** (17 W. Mercury St., 406/723-3231, www.maiwah.org). For the year of the dragon, the Mai Wah pulls out its 60-foot paper dragon—a gift from the people of Taiwan—to dance through the streets of uptown Butte. The event is punctuated by 10,000 fireworks and has been described as

The Irish in Butte

Sometimes referred to as Ireland's fifth province, Butte has long had a significant Irish influence. Of the city's 47,635 residents in 1900, some 12,000—nearly one-quarter of the population—were Irish. For many years, despite its wildly disparate climate and geography, Butte maintained the largest concentration of Irish immigrants in the United States. Copper king Marcus Daly, himself an immigrant from Ireland, was known to preferentially hire Irish workers in his mines and smelters whenever possible. Other well-known Irish figures in Butte included Cornelius "Con" Kelly, a lawyer who ran both the Anaconda Company and later the Montana Power Company; William McDowell, Montana's lieutenant governor and eventually U.S. ambassador to Ireland; and Jeremiah J. Lynch, a local judge who was an important leader of the Irish community in Butte. At times, being Irish was practically a prerequisite for success. Consider a rug merchant named Mohammed Akara, who in the early 1900s changed his last name to Murphy "for business reasons."

The majority of the Irish in Butte came from western Ireland—Cork, Mayo, and Donegal. Of the 1,700 people who emigrated between 1870 and 1915 from County Cork to the United States, 1,138 landed in Butte. A collection of Irish neighborhoods developed around the mines, Corktown and Dublin Gulch among them. Irish pubs sprang up on just about every corner, many of which still stand today. The Irish Times Pub, a modern-day addition, has booths made out of church pews that originally stood in a Dublin church. A stone at the front door, imported from County Clare, allows patrons to touch Irish rock as they enter. Other bars with Irish influence include Maloney's and the Silver Dollar Saloon.

But Irish culture in Butte extends beyond drinking establishments, thankfully. Each summer the community gathers to celebrate their Irish heritage at the **An Rí Rá Montana Irish Festival,** an outdoor celebration of Celtic music and dance complete with footraces, concerts, and dance performances. Another Butte program, **Project Children,** brings Irish children and young adults of different faiths to Butte to work on projects like Habitat for Humanity to show them that religious differences need not prevent cooperation and communication.

Undoubtedly the best-known Irish event in Butte is the annual **St. Patrick's Day** celebration. Some 30,000 people descend on the city, creating bedlam that some see as a fabulous party. The day kicks off with a parade in uptown Butte led by the Ancient Order of Hibernians. There's a piper luncheon, concerts, and dances, and the city's plentiful bars host massive crowds for green beer and Irish festivities. This Montana version of New Year's Eve in Times Square is more than a little rough-and-tumble: One gets a real sense of what life as a Butte miner must have been like around the turn of the 20th century.

the "shortest, loudest, and (sometimes) coldest parade in Montana." Alongside St. Patrick's Day, this is one of the city's most fascinating and defining events.

ST. PATRICK'S DAY

In a town largely composed of Sullivans, Shannons, Harringtons, O'Neills, Sheas, Driscolls, and O'Briens, is it any wonder that the annual **St. Patrick's Day** celebration is probably the biggest party of the year? Some 30,000 people descend on the city in March to celebrate the strong Irish community with a parade in uptown Butte led by the Ancient Order of Hibernians. Events are held all over the city, including a piper luncheon, concerts, dances, and, of course, no shortage of places to fill up on frosty green beer.

MONTANA FOLK FESTIVAL

One of the largest free outdoor music festivals in the Northwest, the **Montana Folk Festival** (www.montanafolkfestival.com, free) is held annually early to mid-July and features performances by more than 200 musicians, dancers, and craftspeople. There are six stages including a family stage and a dancing pavilion for participatory dancing, as well as marketplaces and a food court. Music styles run the gamut from Ethiopian funk to

Western swing, Latin dance, gospel, blues, and, of course, bluegrass. For history buffs (who will love the setting) and music lovers, this is a fantastic event.

AN RÍ RÁ

Held annually the second week of August, **An Rí Rá Montana Irish Festival** (Park St. between N. Main St. and N. Montana St., www.mtgaelic.org, free) is the less bawdy cousin to St. Patrick's Day. The event focuses less on drinking (there are no alcohol sponsors and no alcohol sold at the festival itself) and more on Irish culture and traditions, with music and dancing, drama, and historical lectures along with lots of events geared to families with children. The event is sponsored by the Montana Gaelic Cultural Society and includes fun runs, live music and other entertainment, speakers, and food vendors. The Montana Gaelic Cultural Society sponsors education and entertainment opportunities throughout the year as fundraisers for the festival.

CHRISTMAS STROLL AND ICE CARVING CONTEST

Typically the **Christmas Stroll** and **Ice Carving Contest** are held on successive weekends in early December and celebrate the past, present, and future of uptown Butte. Held most often on the first Friday of December, the Christmas Stroll offers activities for the whole family. It is a community-centered event with food vendors, music, dancing, a parade, a visit from Santa, and a tree-lighting ceremony. Many businesses get involved by offering treats and special events to strollers. There are also plenty of places along the parade route to stop in for a toddy.

Resulting in dozens of marvelous ice sculptures placed around town, the annual Ice Carving Contest is another family-oriented event that often kicks off with a breakfast with Santa and culminates in the judging of the sculptures. The event is held the second Saturday of December. Progress on the carving can be monitored throughout the day as you stroll around uptown Butte.

Information on both events is available from **Mainstreet Uptown Butte** (66 W. Park St., Ste. 211, 406/497-6464, www.mainstreetbutte.org).

SHOPPING

Once home to 100,000 people and a number of copper kings, it's no surprise that Butte offers plenty of antiques shopping in the historic uptown. Several antiques stores are located in the area bounded by Main, Montana, Granite, and Galena Streets. **Broadway Antiques** (45 W. Broadway St., 406/723-4270, 10am-5pm Thurs.-Sat.) is packed with trinkets and treasures. Not exactly an antiques store, but more of an antique, **Whitehead's Cutlery** (73 E. Park St., 406/723-9188, www.whiteheadscutlery.com, 11am-5pm Mon.-Sat.) was founded in 1890 and is considered to be the oldest continuously operated family-owned small business in the state. Its founder, Joseph Whitehead, made his living by traveling to mining camps in the region selling and sharpening knives. His first grinder in Butte was powered by a St. Bernard that ran on a treadmill to run the wheel. While his own line of products expanded from knives to include straight razors, barber supplies, and hockey and figure skates, Joseph's son Edward collected knives and swords from around the world. The impressive collection is on display and worth a visit.

Another Butte treasure is **Second Edition Books** (112 S. Montana St., 406/723-5108, www.secondeditionbooks.com, 9am-5:30pm Mon.-Sat.), a second-generation, family-run used bookstore. In addition to a great selection of Butte books, both common and rare, Second Edition Books carries a nice selection of books on Montana, mining, engineering, geology, Yellowstone, and Glacier. There is also a children's section.

For Butte T-shirts (including "Long Live the M&M"), hoodies, hats, stickers, and other Butte souvenirs, try **5518 Designs** (27 N. Main St., 406/299-3471, noon-6pm Mon.-Fri., 11am-5pm Sat., noon-4pm Sun.) or the appropriately named **Butte Stuff** (55 W.

Park St., 406/565-1692, www.buttestuff.com, 10am-4pm Mon.-Tues., 10am-5:30pm Wed.-Fri., 9am-4pm Sat.), which sells Butte- and Montana-related glassware, T-shirts, coffee, cutting boards, dish towels, and more.

If you lack space in your suitcase for antique treasures and have a taste for spirits, stop into **Headframe Spirits** (21 S. Montana St., 406/299-2886, www.headframespirits.com, 10am-8pm daily), founded in 2010 but steeped in Butte history. You can sip and sample the Neversweat Straight Bourbon, Destroying Angel Whiskey, Anselmo Gin, High Ore Vodka, and Orphan Girl Bourbon Cream Liquor. Tours of the distillery are likely to be resumed post-pandemic and offered Thursday at 5pm, Friday at 4pm, Saturday at 2:30pm and 4:30pm, and Sunday (in July only) at 2pm. Or you can skip the tour and relax with a cocktail in the tasting room. It's really quite a fitting way to spend an afternoon in Butte.

FOOD

No other Montana town can match the culinary history and culture of Butte. The Butte pasty, inspired by the Cornish dish, is a flaky pastry filled with meat and potatoes for the ultimate miner's lunch; when in Butte, it is the thing to try. The **Gamer's Café** (15 W. Park St., 406/723-5453, 7am-2pm Mon.-Sat., 8am-2pm Sun., breakfast $4-10, lunch $7-12) is a quaint little spot, founded in 1905, that feels like an old ice-cream parlor. There are no irritating keno machines, despite the name (those are next door in the casino), and the home-cooked food is excellent. Breakfast is served all day, and lunches include homemade soups, burgers, and sandwiches. Still, this is Butte, and you've got to try a pasty: The ones here are made with New York steak from Montana beef and potatoes grown just down the road in Twin Bridges. Don't miss the apple dumpling for dessert, warm with a scoop of ice cream.

Another fun and historic establishment is the **Pekin Noodle Parlor** (117 Main St., 406/782-2217, 5pm-9pm Wed.-Sun., $8-18), Butte's oldest Chinese restaurant, open since 1911. The place is casual and utterly authentic

with private booths hidden behind curtains. Everything is the color of a Creamsicle. Reading the menu is a lesson in history, and an evening in the parlor is time well spent. Hours can vary depending on the number of customers, so call ahead.

The locals love **Fred's Mesquite Grill** (205 S. Arizona St., 406/723-4440, 11am-8pm daily, $10-27), a casual place with ample outdoor seating and the best ribs and kebabs in town. Fred was a salty character with a heart of gold and had a penchant for motorcycles and great food. Though he died in 2007, his legacy is still alive—and delicious.

Long considered the best restaurant in Butte, the ★ **Uptown Café** (47 E. Broadway, 406/723-4735, www.uptowncafe.com, 11am-2pm Mon.-Fri., $12.75-16) is a gourmet restaurant with sophisticated style and plenty of Butte spirit. Sadly, because of pandemic-related staff shortages, they stopped serving dinner, but hopefully will start up again soon. It's worth a call. Still, the lunches are excellent, from beef stroganoff and Cajun chicken pasta to Butte pasties and Wiener schnitzel, and more.

Newer on the scene and serving outstanding cuts of meat, in addition to pasta, chicken, seafood specialties, and sushi, is **Casagranda's Steakhouse and Guido's Bar** (801 S. Utah St., 406/723-4141, www.casagrandassteakhouse.com, 5pm-9pm Sun.-Wed., 5pm-9:30pm Thurs.-Sat., wine bar from 4pm, $13.50-47). Every Thursday night is sushi night, but the hand-cut steaks, sourced locally and regionally, are unbeatable, with various preparations to choose from, including au poivre, demiglace, fungi, Oscar style, and more. Set in a restored 1900 warehouse, the inviting restaurant also has a full-service bar.

ACCOMMODATIONS

Although Butte has quite an assortment of nice chain-type hotels, a couple of places will have significantly more appeal to those caught up in the saga of Butte's past and present. William Andrews Clark's ★ **Copper King**

Mansion (219 W. Granite St., 406/782-7580, www.thecopperkingmansion.com, $125-250) is also a bed-and-breakfast. Guests sleep in accommodations ranging from the butler's room to the Clarks' master bedroom. Because it is a functioning museum, check-in is at 4pm and guests must check out by 9am to accommodate the tour schedule. Guided tours are free for guests, and a full breakfast is served in the formal dining room.

In the heart of uptown Butte is another fantastic old building striving to achieve its former glory. Hotel Finlen (100 E. Broadway, 406/723-5461 or 800/729-5461, www.finlen.com, $105-192) was built in 1924 on the site of the old McDermott Hotel, one of the grandest in the Northwest. Modeled after the Astor Hotel in New York City, the Finlen is a nine-story Second Empire building with a copper-shingled roof. Over the years, Hotel Finlen was visited by Charles Lindberg, Harry Truman, John F. Kennedy, and Richard Nixon. As is true of all of Butte, Hotel Finlen fell into disrepair and neglect as the mining economy dried up. The Taras family purchased the hotel in 1979 and has worked hard to restore the lobby and mezzanine, both of which are more beautiful than ever. The 30 guest rooms are basic, and the 25 guest rooms in the motor inn are dated; still, there is history here, and with some luck, a future.

A brand-new boutique hotel that pays homage to the city's history, the Miner's Hotel (53 W. Park St., 406/763-8928, www.theminershotel.com, $139-209) is listed on the National Registry of Historic Places. Housed in the 1913 Miner's Savings and Trust Co., the building has a lot of history. At one point the hotel was a boarding house and was occupied at the same time by government Prohibition agent Carrol Olson and known bootlegger Henry Alexis. The rooms are comfortable and elegant. The 51 Below Speakeasy offers craft cocktails in the basement of the hotel.

For classic charm on the lush grounds of the Butte Country Club, Toad Hall Manor Bed & Breakfast (1 Green Ln., 406/494-2625, www.toadhallmanor.com, $130-185) is

an excellent choice. From a goblet of sherry or port upon arrival to feather beds, Jacuzzi tubs, and decadent breakfasts, Toad Hall Manor offers classic B&B style.

Butte also has its fair share of reliable chain hotels, but none of them capture the town's amazing history as well as the independent hotels and inns that can be found uptown. Options spread along Harrison Avenue and close to the interstate include the Best Western Plus Butte Plaza Inn (2900 Harrison Ave., 406/494-3500 or 800/780-7234, www.bestwestern.com, from $139), Days Inn Butte (2700 Harrison Ave., 406/272-7525 or 855/224-2016, www.wyndhamhotels.com/days-inn/butte, $87-174), Hampton Inn (3499 Harrison Ave., 406/494-2250, www.hilton.com, $91-188), La Quinta Inn & Suites (1 Holiday Park Dr., 406/494-6999, www.wyndhamhotels.com, $119-314), Motel 6 (220 N. Wyoming St., 406/723-4391, www.motel6.com, $59-89), and Super 8 by Wyndham (2929 Harrison Ave., 406/565-4418, www.wyndhamhotels.com, $68-119).

INFORMATION AND SERVICES

The front of the Butte-Silver Bow Chamber of Commerce and Visitor Information Center (1000 George St., 406/723-3177, www.buttechambersite.org, 8:30am-5pm Mon.-Sat., 9am-4pm Sun. summer, 10am-5pm Mon. and Fri.-Sat. winter) is stocked with brochures, pamphlets, and tour information; in back, you can usually find a helpful chamber employee to answer questions. A terrific Butte online resource is www.butteamerica.com.

The Butte-Silver Bow Public Library (226 W. Broadway, 406/723-3361, www.buttepubliclibrary.info, 10am-5pm Mon. and Fri.-Sat., 10am-7pm Tues.-Thurs.) is at Broadway and Idaho Street. The main post office (406/494-2107, 8:30am-5:30pm Mon.-Fri., 9am-1pm Sat.) is at 701 Dewey Boulevard.

The emergency room at St. James Healthcare (400 S. Clark St., www.sclhealth.org, 406/723-2500) is open 24 hours every day. Butte has walk-in medical facilities, including **St. James Rocky Mountain Clinic** (435 S. Crystal St. #300, 406/496-3600, www.sclhealth.org, 8am-5pm Mon.-Fri.) and **Express Care** (435 S. Crystal St. #200, 406/221-1563, www.sclhealth.org, 8am-5pm Mon.-Fri.).

For laundry, **Front Street Laundromat** (1000 E. Front St., 406/723-3666, www.frontstreetlaundromat.com, 5am-midnight daily, staff available 8am-6pm Mon.-Fri., 9am-6pm Sat.) offers high-capacity washers, self- or full-service, and free Wi-Fi.

TRANSPORTATION
Getting There
The **Bert Mooney Airport** (BTM, 101 Airport Rd., 406/494-3771, www.butteairport.com) in Butte is served by Delta Connection with daily direct flights to and from Salt Lake City. NetJets also serves the airport.

The car-rental agencies at the airport are **Hertz, Avis,** and **Budget. Enterprise** (3825 Harrison Ave., 406/494-1900, www.enterprise.com) has an off-site service center.

Bus service from **Greyhound** and **Rimrock Stages** (406/723-3287) is available at 1324 Harrison Avenue. Butte is 64 miles (103 km) south of Helena, 82 miles (132 km) west of Bozeman, and 120 miles (193 km) southeast of Missoula.

Getting Around
The **Butte-Silver Bow Transit System** (406/497-6515, www.buttebus.org, free) offers bus service 7:15am-5:45pm Monday-Friday, with shorter hours on Saturday. You can pick up a bus schedule at the public library or download a copy online. **Mining City Taxi** (406/723-6511) offers service 24 hours every day.

The Pintler Scenic Route

This stretch of the state is wide open, with sweeping valleys, soaring mountains, and some authentic small communities that were involved in different stages of Montana's boom-and-bust economy.

Set in a grassy valley that was known by Native Americans for its abundance of deer, Deer Lodge was both a mining town and a ranching community during its evolution. It has also long been a county seat, giving Deer Lodge an interesting if somewhat random collection of specialized museums, including the slightly creepy, always cold, and really cool Old Montana Prison Museum.

Historic and charming Philipsburg is another study in Montana's boom, bust, and renewal economy. Today's visitors come for proximity to wild beauty, quaint architecture, and good food.

Named for the Anaconda Copper Mining Company, Anaconda was by all accounts a company town. But it's managed to hang on and is working to redefine itself since

the company pulled out in 1980. Structures like the **Anaconda City Hall, Deer Lodge County Courthouse,** and **Washoe Theatre** hark back to the town's glory days, when it vied for the status of state capital. Its proximity to **Georgetown Lake** and the Jack Nicklaus-designed **Old Works Golf Course** keep Anaconda hopping with visitors in the warmer months, and **Discovery Ski Area** is a marvelous place to spend a winter's day.

DEER LODGE
Nestled between the Flint Creek and Garnet mountain ranges sits the small, and shrinking, town of Deer Lodge (pop. 2,733, elev. 4,521 ft/1,378 m). Although initially a trading and trapping town like the other towns in the area, Deer Lodge grew when gold was discovered just a few miles outside town. With the gold and quartz mining, businesspeople, among them copper king W. A. Clark, flocked in to set up mills.

Today Deer Lodge is best known for being

The Pintler Scenic Route

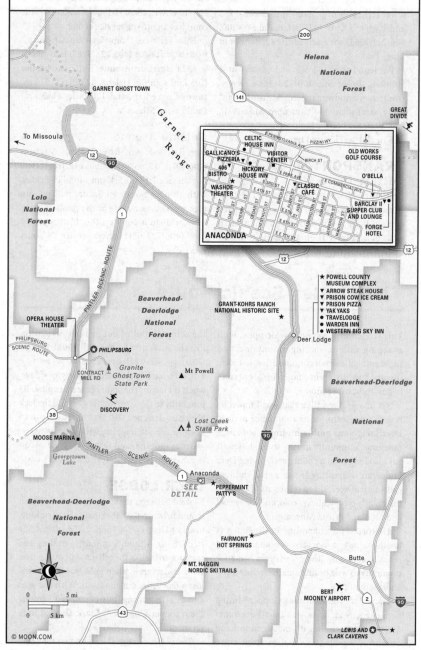

GARNET GHOST TOWN

Garnet Range

To Missoula

GREAT DIVIDE

Helena National Forest

Lolo National Forest

PINTLER SCENIC ROUTE

ANACONDA (detail)

CELTIC HOUSE INN
GALLICANO'S PIZZERIA
406 BISTRO
WASHOE THEATER
VISITOR CENTER
HICKORY HOUSE INN
CLASSIC CAFÉ
OLD WORKS GOLF COURSE
O'BELLA
BARCLAY II SUPPER CLUB AND LOUNGE
FORGE HOTEL

E. PENNSYLVANIA AVE
PIZZINI WY
BIRCH ST
E PARK AVE
E COMMERCIAL AVE
E 3RD ST
E 4TH ST
E 5TH ST
E 6TH ST
E 7TH ST
E E 7TH ST
E 8TH ST
MAIN ST
OAK ST
CHERRY ST
CEDAR ST
CHESTNUT ST
BIRCH ST
ALDER ST
ASH ST
WASHINGTON ST
ADAMS ST
JEFFERSON ST
MADISON ST

Beaverhead-Deerlodge National Forest

OPERA HOUSE THEATER

PHILIPSBURG SCENIC ROUTE

PHILIPSBURG

CONTRACT MILL RD

Granite Ghost Town State Park

GRANT-KOHRS RANCH NATIONAL HISTORIC SITE

★ POWELL COUNTY MUSEUM COMPLEX
▼ ARROW STEAK HOUSE
▼ PRISON COW ICE CREAM
▼ PRISON PIZZA
▼ YAK YAKS
● TRAVELODGE
● WARDEN INN
● WESTERN BIG SKY INN

Deer Lodge

Mt Powell

DISCOVERY

Lost Creek State Park

Beaverhead-Deerlodge National Forest

MOOSE MARINA

Georgetown Lake

PINTLER SCENIC ROUTE

Anaconda
SEE DETAIL
★ PEPPERMINT PATTY'S

Beaverhead-Deerlodge National Forest

FAIRMONT HOT SPRINGS

Butte

MT. HAGGIN NORDIC SKI TRAILS

BERT MOONEY AIRPORT

LEWIS AND CLARK CAVERNS

0   5 mi
0   5 km

© MOON.COM

home to the state penitentiary. But that fact aside, it also proclaims itself the museum capital of Montana, and it does have more museums per capita than any other city in the state. Old West aficionados and collectors will definitely find Deer Lodge worth a stop.

Sights
GRANT KOHRS RANCH
The **Grant Kohrs Ranch** (266 Warren Ln., 406/846-2070, ext. 250, www.nps.gov, 9am-5:30pm daily Memorial Day-Labor Day, 9am-4:30pm daily Labor Day-Memorial Day, free) is a National Historic Site and a wonderful piece of Montana history. Originally, cattle were grazed in these lush grasslands on the open range. Canadian Richard Grant and his sons Johnny and James were able to build up their herd trading with pioneers moving west along the Oregon Trail. They offered travelers a nicely fattened cow for two travel-worn brutes.

In 1862 Johnny established a base ranch on the grounds, and as fortune would have it, the area soon flooded with hungry beef-eating gold prospectors. In 1866, Grant sold the ranch to Conrad Kohrs, who went on to become the King of Cattle, making the ranch the headquarters of a 10-million-acre cattle empire that stretched over three states. Although it was reduced in size over time, the ranch stayed in the Kohrs family until 1972, when it was bought by the National Park Service to preserve its historical significance.

Today it is a 1,600-acre small-scale working cattle ranch with 80 historic buildings, walking trails, guided tours, and ranger-led talks. You can take a tour of the 23-room main house, built in 1862 and later expanded by Kohrs. Sign up for the tours at the visitor center; tour size is limited to 12 people, and they do fill up quickly in the summer. Ranger talks are also available in the summer and cover topics such as the life of cowboys on the open range, the importance of the chuck wagon to cowboys on the trail, and the role of the blacksmith. **Wagon tours** (1pm, 1:30pm, 2pm, 2:30pm, 3pm, 3:30pm Wed. late June-Aug.) are a fun way to see a good portion of the park with a ranger as your guide.

POWELL COUNTY MUSEUM COMPLEX
The real highlight of a trip to Deer Lodge is the **Old Montana Prison Museum** (1106 Main St., 406/846-3111, www.pcmaf.org, 8am-6pm daily summer, 10am-4pm Wed.-Sun. fall-spring), which is part of the larger **Powell County Museum Complex** (www.pcmaf.org, $18 adults, $10 children 10-15, free for children under 10, $14.50 for AARP, AAA, Sam's Club, seniors, and veterans, guided tours at 11am and 2pm in summer). Tickets are a two-day pass that grants visitors admission to all the museums.

Deer Lodge was home to the first prison in Montana Territory, built in 1871. The impressive redbrick, iron-gated prison you see today was built in the 1890s using inmate labor. Prisoners also made the 1.2 million bricks used to build the cell block and other buildings. Visitors can take self-guided tours through the rows of vacant cell blocks, the maximum-security area, and the "galloping gallows," and learn about the rules and daily regimen for both prisoners and guards. There are a few macabre histories of some of the more interesting characters who occupied these cells. Prisoners who were seen as potential escapees, for example, were forced to wear work shoes with concrete soles, each weighing about 20 pounds, to inhibit their flight. The building itself is impressive and somewhat beautiful (but bleak and very cold), resembling a castle with turreted stone towers at each corner. For visitors who love to be scared, the prison offers **ghost tours** (406/846-3111, 9:30pm-2:30am, reservations required, $50 pp). Also housed in this building is the **Montana Law Enforcement Museum,** which pays tribute to officers who have lost their lives in the line of duty.

The **Montana Auto Museum** was recognized by *USA Today* as one of the best auto museums in the country. It houses more than 150 cars, many of them beautifully restored,

Dude Ranch Vacations

Southwest Montana is a natural destination for ranch vacations, with an age-old ranching history, wide-open spaces, and spectacular mountain scenery. Indeed, the challenge is choosing among the dozens of wonderful and welcoming ranches in the region. One of the best resources, aside from a good friend who will steer you to a personal favorite, is the **Montana Dude Ranchers' Association** (406/260-6596, www.montanadra.com). In addition to a number of ways to choose a ranch (by location, type of experience, and so on), the website offers some helpful advice in finding the best fit for you.

- **Location:** Imagine yourself on horseback, and then think about the type of landscape you want to explore. Do you want to lope through open meadows or wind up mountain trails? Do you want to be out in the middle of sublime nowhere, or would you like to be just a quick ride from town? Determine where you want to be, and then look for ranches in the immediate vicinity. Consider distance from the nearest airport, too.

- **Type of riding:** What is your main objective, and your comfort level, for your time in the saddle? Would you like to be on a working ranch, helping with daily chores like rounding up cattle? Or are you more interested in working on your riding skills in clinics? There are ranches that can accommodate both. There are also places where you can just ride as the means to take in the incredible scenery. Your choice will come down to working ranches, dude ranches, and ranch resorts.

- **Size and season:** Think about size. Do you want to be among just a handful of guests, or would you like to be among a much larger group of people? And when would you most like to go—summer, spring, or fall?

- **Activities:** Are you exclusively interested in horseback riding, or do you want other options as well—fishing, golf, activities for kids? Sightseeing and day trips away from the ranch?

- **Accommodations:** You'll need to decide whether you want to immerse yourself in ranch life and cowboy style (a working ranch or some dude ranches), whether you just want to casually play cowboy or cowgirl for a week (a dude ranch), or whether you want some serious luxury with a little bit of Western flavor tossed in for good measure (a ranch resort). Accommodations can range from lodge rooms to individual cabins, and amenities vary dramatically, from no cell service or TV to full-on Wi-Fi, massage, and luxury accommodations.

hard-to-find vintage models, including a 1911 Ford Model T.

The other museums are open during summer but closed during winter. **Frontier Montana** covers the history of the Old West and displays a vast and impressive gun collection. **Desert John's Saloon Museum** has a large amount of whiskey memorabilia and brings the saloons of the Old West to life. The **Powell County Museum** covers local history, which includes mining history, of course; exhibits include antique furniture, historical photos, and a weapons collection from both world wars. **Yesterday's Playthings** is a toy and doll museum with a fun collection of antique dolls, mohair teddy bears, baby carriages, horse-drawn carriages, and tea sets that date back to the mid-1800s. The newest attraction in the museum complex is **Cottonwood City,** a completely reconstructed historic mining town with a school, a mortuary, and a blacksmith's shop where blacksmithing demonstrations take place daily in season.

GARNET GHOST TOWN

About 40 miles (64 km) outside Deer Lodge, off I-90 at the head of First Chance Creek, you can explore the tucked-away mining ghost town of **Garnet** (www.garnetghosttown.org,

9:30am-4:30pm daily year-round). Named after the semiprecious stone mined in the area, Garnet is an unspoiled, well-restored, authentic Montana ghost town. Founded in 1895, about 30 buildings are on-site along with a visitor center to welcome guests. It is open all year, but the road is closed to wheeled vehicles January-April, making it a popular cross-country ski trip. In its heyday around 1898, the town had a population of 1,000, with a school, hotels, saloons, and even a Chinese laundry. By 1950 the town was virtually abandoned. In the summer, visitors can take guided tours, walk in and out of the buildings, and rent cabins to stay overnight. If you are interested in ghost sightings, Kelly's Saloon reportedly has spectral sounds of laughter, music, and voices even in the dead of winter.

Food

The Broken Arrow Steak House (317 Main St., 406/846-3400, 10:30am-midnight daily, $9-30) serves a variety of steak platters for lunch and dinner. Yak Yaks (200 Main St., 406/846-1750, 7am-2pm Mon.-Fri., 8am-2pm Sat., $5-9) offers deli sandwiches with fresh veggies, gyros, tacos, wraps, and a plethora of different lattes, Italian sodas, and milk shakes. Nowhere but Deer Lodge is it recommended to eat in a place called Prison Pizza (818 Main St., 406/846-4800, 11am-11pm Mon.-Thurs., 11am-midnight Fri.-Sat., 4:30pm-11pm Sun., $7-15). But it's good. The pizza is made from scratch and to order. And they have wonderful homemade soups daily, plus pastas, salad, milk shakes, Italian sodas, and more. And since you're on a roll, why not stop for a cone at Prison Cow Ice Cream (1106 Main St., 406/846-3111, noon-8pm daily in summer), which serves delicious Montana-made ice cream. They even offer pup cups for your furry friend.

Accommodations

All the accommodations in Deer Lodge fall in the budget-motel category. The most centrally located (across from the Old Montana Prison Museum) is the very comfortable and clean Warden Inn (809 Main St., 406/987-2234, www.wardeninn.com, $109-139). Rooms come with free Wi-Fi, smart TV, mini-fridge, and microwave. The pet-friendly Western Big Sky Inn (210 N. Main St., 406/846-2590, www.westernbigskyinn.com, $69-83) is at the other end of town, nicely located for a trip out to the Grant Kohrs Ranch. It also offers free breakfast muffins, fruit, yogurt, granola bars, and the like. Plus they have free Wi-Fi, cable TV, and pillow-top mattresses in all king rooms. The only chain hotel in town is the Travelodge (1150 N. Main St., 406/545-2858, www.wyndhamhotels.com, $70-94).

Information

A good source of visitor information is the Powell County Chamber of Commerce (1109 Main St., 406/846-2094, www.powellcountymontana.com, 8am-4pm Mon.-Fri.). The Old Montana Prison Museum also has a visitor center (1106 Main St., 406/846-3111, 9am-6pm daily summer, 10am-4pm Wed.-Sun. fall-spring).

Transportation

Deer Lodge is immediately off I-90. It is 37 miles (60 km) northwest of Butte and 83 miles (134 km) southeast of Missoula.

★ PHILIPSBURG

The little town of Philipsburg (pop. 929, elev. 5,280 ft/1,609 m) is something of a hidden gem. Off the main drag but right on the Pintler Scenic Route, also known as Highway 1, P-burg, as it is known locally, is an 1890s silver-mining town ideally located just minutes from recreational hot spots like Georgetown Lake, Discovery Ski Area, and the Old Works Golf Course. Still, P-burg can stand on its own merits. Surrounded by mountains—the Pintler Range to the south, the Sapphire Mountains to the west, and the Flint Range to the east—Philipsburg is populated by a beautiful collection of brightly painted Victorian brick buildings that have been brought back from the dead—the state's oldest operating school, jail, and theater are all here—by an exceedingly proud and active local population, many of whom are transplants from faraway places. Highlights include a wonderfully restored hotel, some good restaurants, a fantastic brewery, a candy store straight out of your childhood dreams, and many other reasons to come to Philipsburg and stay awhile. Like all mining towns in these parts, P-burg has seen its own rise and fall. The ups and down are immortalized in a poignant poem by Richard Hugo titled "Degrees of Gray in Philipsburg." Before you go, look it up.

Sights

The **Opera House Theatre** (140 S. Sansome St., 406/859-0013, www.philipsburgtheatre.com) was built in 1896, complete with a sod basement, elaborate dressing rooms, and indoor plumbing. Countless performers played the stage here for throngs of culture-hungry miners. In 1919 the elegant boxes were removed to make way for sound equipment, and the theater continued to attract a wide range of entertainers. It is still undergoing restoration that started in the late 1990s. but you can call ahead and arrange a tour. This is the oldest continually operating theater in the state, with one of the youngest theater companies, the **Opera House Theatre Company** ($20 adults, $10 children 15 and under), performing live theater and vaudeville shows to much fanfare every summer. Inside, look for five original backdrops painted by Charlie Russell contemporary Edgar S. Paxson.

Just northeast of town, off Highway 1 near mile marker 36, is a marked but rough dirt road that leads 4 miles (6.4 km) up the mountain to **Granite Ghost Town State Park** (347 Granite Rd., 406/287-3541, www.stateparks.mt.gov, dawn-dusk May-Sept., $8/vehicle nonresidents), once the site of one of the world's richest silver-mining districts. Today it's a fascinating and entirely abandoned ghost town.

Granite's first silver strike came in 1865 at the hands of Hector Horton. In the fall of 1872, the Granite mine was established, then relocated in 1875. But when the mine failed to produce anything of substance, a telegram was sent from mine owners on the East Coast that it should be shut down; the telegram was fatefully delayed. As foreman Charles D. McClure prepared to give his workers the bad news, the miners struck silver ore that would produce 1,700 ounces of silver to the ton, yielding $40 million. Because of the great demand for silver by the U.S. government for coinage, the population of Granite swelled to more than 3,000 almost overnight with miners in pursuit of the $4-per-shift wages. The town grew on the steep mountainside with a two-level main street and many buildings on stilts. Local establishments included not only the usual abundance of saloons, brothels, and churches but also a sophisticated reading room, a bathhouse, and a toboggan run that zoomed 2,000 vertical feet down the mountain to Philipsburg.

Two mines ran full-bore, making Montana the country's largest silver producer until 1893, when Congress voted to end silver purchases, leading to a rapid mass exodus from Granite. The barely staffed mines eventually merged and produced a modest supply of silver for another decade or so until they flooded in 1915. A 1958 fire demolished what was left of the buildings. Today the town is like a graveyard, filled with brick foundations, rusting equipment, and the faded memories of Montana's biggest silver boom.

By far the most scenic—if somewhat hair-raising—way to get from Philipsburg's Flint Creek Valley to the Bitterroot Valley south of Missoula is by way of **Skalkaho Pass,** a largely graveled 50-mile (80-km) high-mountain road. Highway 38 heads up through the thickly forested Sapphire Mountains 6 miles (9.7 km) south of P-burg and brings adventurous drivers down 3 miles (4.8 km) south of Hamilton. The road is primitive, not for trailers or the faint of heart (particularly driving east, which puts cars along some pretty precipitous cliffs), seasonal, and well worthwhile.

Skalkaho Pass was long used as a trail by Native Americans traveling between the valleys. A more permanent road was built in 1924 to connect the mining areas around Philipsburg with the agricultural resources in the Bitterroot. There are two campgrounds along the road as well as the spectacular **Skalkaho Falls.** The summit is at 7,260 feet (2,213 m), and the region is home to an abundance of wildlife, including moose, elk, deer, black bears, and mountain goats. Though not well traveled due to its altitude and spotty road conditions, the area does offer incredible recreation opportunities, including hiking, mountain biking, cross-country skiing, and snowmobiling on the plentiful trails.

Sports and Recreation

With all the rivers and lakes in this region—Rock Creek, the Clark Fork, Blackfoot, and Bitterroot Rivers, Georgetown Lake, and more—there are plenty of good places to wet a line. You can get geared up in Philipsburg at **Flint Creek Outdoors** (116 W. Broadway, 406/859-9500, www.blackfootriver.com, 9am-6pm daily summer, 7:30am-5pm Fri.-Sun. fall-spring), a fishing aficionado's version of the Sweet Palace across the street. The owners of Flint Creek also offer guided fishing trips as **Blackfoot River Outfitters** (from $500 for half-day floats, from $550 for all-day walk/wade trips). Once you're geared up, head out to **Rock Creek,** a gorgeous 29-mile (47-km) stream known for its late May-early June salmonfly hatch, 15 miles (24 km) west of town. The creek, which looks and fishes more like a river, is chock-a-block with rainbow, cutthroat, and brown trout. You'll likely be wade fishing here, and although the Rock Creek Road is bumpy and winding, and the fish tend to be a bit smaller than they are closer to the confluence with the Clark Fork River, the access is broad and the anglers are fewer than on other stretches.

Food

Visitors to Philipsburg are advised to arrive in town with an empty belly; the town has a couple of great places to eat. The first stop should always be at ★ **The Sweet Palace** (109 E. Broadway, 406/859-3353 or 888/793-3896, www.sweetpalace.com, 10am-6pm Sun.-Fri. June-Aug., 9am-5pm Sun.-Fri. Sept.-May), itself a Victorian confection. Though they don't serve food, this old-fashioned store is all nostalgia and sugar, and it is certainly among the best candy shops in the state.

The **Doe Brothers Restaurant and Old Fashioned Soda Fountain** (120 E. Broadway, 406/859-6676, 11am-6pm daily summer, 11am-5pm Wed.-Sun. winter, call ahead to confirm hours, $11-16) is a malt shop in its most classic form, housed in a faithfully restored 1887 drugstore. The counter is lined with sweetheart chairs, and the tables come with boards for chess and checkers. The owners, transplants from North Carolina, have lovingly intertwined some of their own family history with that of Philipsburg. The service is beyond compare, and the food is terrific. The homemade bread is dusted with sugar, the ice cream is all Montana-made, and the entrées—ranging from mouthwatering buffalo or Wagyu beef burgers to elk stew, Butte-style pasties, crab cakes, and bison or elk meatloaf—are large and savory. Don't miss the onion rings, which are served hanging on little stands, or the beer-battered fried pickles. And whatever you do, don't forgo dessert.

Brick's Pub (102 W. Broadway, 406/240-1616, 11:30am-8pm Mon., 4pm-10pm Thurs. and Sun., 11:30am-10pm Fri.-Sat., $10-17) is a casual eatery and full-service bar offering build-your-own burgers, fish tacos, Philly cheesesteaks, mac and cheese, and more. **Kiko's Mexican Restaurant** (127 E. Broadway, 11am-8pm Fri.-Tues., $10-17) is a festive place serving standard Mexican fare. For breakfast, the place to go in town is **Sunshine Station** (3830 Hwy. 1, 406/859-3450, 7am-9pm daily but hours change unpredictably so call ahead, $6-13), where you can get anything from a simple breakfast sandwich to a chicken-fried steak and egg sandwich to biscuits and gravy. And because there is always room for ice cream,

be sure to visit **Philipsburg Creamery** (119 W. Broadway St., 406/596-0843, www.philipsburgcreamery.com, 11:30am-2pm Wed., 11:30am-5pm Thurs.-Sun., extended hours in summer) for some real made-in-Montana goodness. Summer strawberry and Hungry Horse huckleberry are but two of the delicious flavors.

If you're looking for a delicious, easy-on-the-palate craft beer, head over to **Philipsburg Brewing Company** (101 W. Broadway, 406/859-2739, 10am-8pm daily) for a pint or a growler. Opened in 2012 in a stunning Victorian building, the bar even boasts a copper plate, cooled with glycol lines, so that mugs set on the bar never get warm. Not unlike the dance floors on springs that Philipsburg was once known for, this is P-burg technology at its best.

Accommodations

For such a tiny town, P-burg has no shortage of wonderful and unique accommodations, with nary a chain hotel to be found.

The frontrunner in town is ★ **The Broadway Hotel** (103 W. Broadway, 406/859-8000, www.broadwaymontana.com, $145-225), a cozy hotel with individually themed guest rooms in a beautifully restored 1890 building. There are only nine guest rooms and a couple of cabins, so book early. Guests enjoy amenities that include a continental breakfast, a coffee bar, ample common areas, wireless Internet, and a local library. Ski packages for nearby Discovery Ski Area can be arranged for a good deal.

The newest hotel in town is also the oldest: **The Kaiser House Lodging** (203 E. Broadway, 406/859-2004, www.kaiserhouselodging.com, $104-195). Completed in 1881, the building was a fine restaurant and hotel. The basement was a game room, where high-stakes billiards and cards were played. The place has been beautifully restored, and each of the five rooms has historic charm and modern

amenities including telephone, satellite TV, free Wi-Fi, and air-conditioning. The morning breakfasts are a treat.

Nestled creekside along the Skalkaho Pass Road is the ultra-swanky **Ranch at Rock Creek** (79 Carriage House Ln., off Hwy. 38, 877/786-1545, www.theranchatrockcreek.com, $2,000-14,400 night for 2-8 people, all-inclusive), which offers an unmatched setting, exquisite service and amenities, and extraordinary accommodations including riverfront cabins, glamorous wall tents, rooms in a converted hayloft, and a five-bedroom riverfront home. Luxury is infused in every detail.

Information

A good source of information on the local area is the **Philipsburg Chamber of Commerce** (109 E. Broadway, 406/859-3388, www.philipsburgmt.com, 9am-5pm Sun.-Fri.), which happens to be in the Sweet Palace.

Transportation

Philipsburg is 78 miles (126 km) southeast of Missoula and 55 miles (89 km) northwest of Butte. From either city, I-90 leads to Highway 1, which can be accessed at Drummond. From Drummond, Philipsburg is 27 miles (43 km) south.

ANACONDA

The much smaller sibling of Butte, Anaconda (pop. 9,162, elev. 4,756 ft/1,450 m) boomed with the mines and suffered when the company hurriedly pulled out of the region. But this fierce little town has not given up. Far from it. The population is rising slowly, after a downturn of more than 6 percent between 2000 and 2010. The townspeople are working to restore some of their most glorious buildings, including the 1888 Montana Hotel, and they've transformed slag heaps and mining refuse into recreational opportunities including the **Old Works Golf Club,** one of the finest in the state. There's a new hotel and several new restaurants. Anaconda is working to make the most of their location, too, just minutes from **Georgetown Lake**

1: Philipsburg 2: Granite Ghost Town State Park

and **Discovery Ski Area.** In winter, the scene in the town's central park, **Kennedy Commons**—ice skaters, the community Christmas tree—looks like a tableau in the *Saturday Evening Post*. Not an obvious destination for anything other than golf, Anaconda is a proud and tight-knit community that is not ready to be ruled out.

Sights

A fantastically pink art deco building, the **Washoe Theatre** (305 Main St., 406/563-6161, movies and frequent live performances daily year-round, check Facebook for schedule) was built in 1936 with massive murals as well as silver, copper, and gold leaf to be a movie palace in the truest sense. It is one of the few art deco theaters standing today and was ranked fifth in the nation for its architectural value by the Smithsonian Institution.

Sports and Recreation
GOLF

The only Jack Nicklaus signature course in the state, the publicly owned **Old Works Golf Club** (1205 Pizzini Way, 406/563-5989, www.playoldworks.com, $41-125 for 18 holes, discounts for booking online 5 or more days in advance) is a fabulous and challenging course built entirely on a Superfund site. The design makes impressive use of the black slag for all its bunkers, along with many relics from the original smelter, including the remains of flues and ovens. The course offers generous fairways and beautifully maintained greens, and the fishable Warm Springs Creek offers water challenges on several holes. And there's a restaurant in the clubhouse, **Jack's Grille** ($9-14), serving burgers, sandwiches, salads, and appetizers. If you only play one course in Montana, this is the one.

GEORGETOWN LAKE

A vast artificial lake that dates back to the mining era and has been a longtime respite for residents of Butte, Georgetown Lake is a popular recreation area for boating, fishing, camping, and windsurfing. The elevation

tops 6,000 feet (1,829 m)—the local ski area is visible from the lake—so the wind can pick up and the weather can change quickly. In addition to rainbow trout, the lake has a healthy population of kokanee salmon. There are four public boat ramps and a number of campgrounds, and in the winter ice fishing and snowmobiling are among the most popular activities. Services are limited, but that is part of Georgetown's charm. The lake feels like something out of the 1950s, when people went to their cabins or brought their campers and simply enjoyed the great outdoors. Surrounded by Beaverhead-Deerlodge National Forest, Georgetown Lake is 90 miles (145 km) southeast of Missoula and 18 miles (29km) west of Anaconda off MT Highway 1.

Boats can be rented, and flies or worms acquired, at the tiny **Moose Marina** (24443 Hwy. 1 W., 406/563-3277, 8am-8pm Mon.-Sat., 8am-6pm Sun. May-Sept.), the only marina on the lake. In addition to docks, a boat launch, and boat rentals that range from canoes to small motorized fishing boats, Moose Marina offers gasoline, fishing licenses, hand-tied flies, and a small assortment of food and sundries.

SKIING AND WINTER RECREATION

Just across from Georgetown Lake is **Discovery Ski Area** (180 Discovery Basin Rd., 406/563-2184, www.skidiscovery.com, $68 adults 13-64 full day, $56 adults half day, $54 seniors 65 and over with ID, $35 children 6-12, free for children 5 and under), a diverse mountain with varied terrain for all ability levels. There are seven lifts and 67 runs, with a vertical drop of 2,388 feet (728 m). This is a very family-friendly ski hill, with the longest run being 1.5 miles (2.4 km) and an annual average snowfall of 215 inches (546 cm). It also has a terrain park and 3 miles (4.8 km) of groomed cross-country ski trails. On summer weekends, the mountain and lifts are open for mountain bikers (11am-5pm Sat.-Sun.).

For Nordic skiing enthusiasts, **Mt. Haggin Nordic Ski Area** (Mill Creek Rd./Hwy.

274, 11 mi/18 km south of Hwy. 1, 406/498-9615, www.milehighnordic.org, donations appreciated) offers more than 17 miles (27 km) of groomed trails in what used to be a series of logging camps. This is not an ideal place for new skiers, but hard-core enthusiasts and racers will be delighted. Fantastic loops are available on varied terrain. The trails also provide access to backcountry skiing along the Continental Divide. Naturally, the wildlife-rich area is ideal for hiking when the snow melts. Maintained by volunteers, usually on Saturday morning, the trails are not patrolled. Though Mt. Haggin isn't dog-friendly, Fido is welcome on the groomed trails at **Moulton Reservoir** (Moulton Reservoir Rd., 406/498-9615, www.milehighnordic.org) above Butte. The trails aren't groomed to the same standards as Mt. Haggin, but the skiing is excellent.

Food

After a big move into the stylish Forge Hotel, **Barclay II Supper Club and Lounge** (1300 E. Commercial Ave., 406/563-5541, 5pm-9pm daily summer, closed Mon. off-season, $12-40) is the most popular fine-dining restaurant in town, and has been for some 40 years. In the classic tradition of seven-course meals, Barclay II's offers friendly service, hearty food, and good old-fashioned relish trays. Entrées include steak, seafood, chicken, veal, and pasta.

Inside the gorgeous 1888 Montana Hotel, **406 Bistro** (200 Main St., Suite 2, 406/298-0605, 7am-2pm Wed.-Sat., $7-10) dishes up breakfast burritos and breakfast sandwiches, in addition to a larger menu of salads, sandwiches, and wraps. They also serve espresso drinks and freshly baked goodies. For classic Italian cuisine, **O'Bella** (1515 E. Commercial Dr., www.obellarestaurant.com, 11am-9pm daily, $11-32) serves hand-tossed pizza, pastas, and specialties like Delmonico steak and chicken piccata. They also have a beer and wine menu. Another Italian option in town is **Gallicano's Pizzeria** (118 E. Park St.,

406/563-7776, www.gallicanospizzeria.com, 11am-8pm Tues.-Fri., 3pm-8pm Sat., lunch-only slices start at $2.50, entrées to large pizzas $7-30), which has a sizable menu of pizzas with every topping you could want. They also serve sandwiches and pasta. They don't take credit cards, so bring some cash.

For big burgers, made-from-scratch pizza, sandwiches, salads, and an extremely family-friendly atmosphere (you can eat in a Volkswagen Bug or on a table made from an engine block), **Classic Café** (627 E. Park Ave., 406/563-5558, 11am-9pm Tues.-Thurs., 11am-10pm Fri., 8am-10pm Sat., 8am-9pm Sun., $7.50-18) is an excellent choice for friendly service and a diverse menu; the food is consistently good. Almost as much a tradition as the pasty in Butte is the pork chop sandwich in Anaconda. For an excellent version with gravy fries, the place to go is **Peppermint Patty's** (1212 E. Park Ave., 406/563-7428, 11am-8pm daily, $4-13).

Accommodations

For a long time there was little more than run-down roadside motels in Anaconda. But that's changing thanks to the indomitable spirit of this community and the visitors who keep showing up. Opened in 2021, the $10 million **Forge Hotel** (100 Union Ave., 406/797-4100, www.bestwestern.com, $112-247) offers sleek, comfortable rooms, full breakfasts, in-room microwave and refrigerator, and a great on-site restaurant.

Another notable exception to the run-of-the-mill roadside motels in these parts is the **Hickory House Inn** (218 E. Park St., 406/563-5481, www.hickoryhouseinnanaconda.com, $100-138), a bed-and-breakfast that has been beautifully maintained. The house was originally the rectory of St. Paul's Church and offers five lovely guest rooms. Another historic option is the **Celtic House Inn** (23 Main St., 406/563-2372, $60-80), a brick building that was a bordello at the turn of the 20th century. The hotel has 10 basic guest rooms, some with kitchenettes; because it is located over the Harp Pub, light sleepers should request one of the quieter guest rooms or, better yet, find another place.

Outside town is a great option for a family-friendly, full-service resort. ★ **Fairmont Hot Springs** (I-90 exit 211 and follow the signs, 800/332-3272, www.fairmontmontana. com, rooms from $195, suites from $225 plus resort fee) is a sizable property built around the hot springs. Guest rooms are nothing fancy, but it's the water that makes this place special. An enormous, warm (88-94°F/31-34°C) indoor pool, with one end shallow enough for toddlers to walk around, is complemented by a smaller indoor hot pool (100-104°F/38-40°C) and two outdoor pools, one warm, one hot. Fairmont's enclosed three-story, 350-foot water slide ($2/run or $11.50 full-session pass, $9.50 half-session pass) is a blast, particularly when cold weather causes so much steam that you can't see what's right in front of your face. The pools are open 24 hours daily for hotel guests, for whom entrance is included at no additional charge. During the pandemic, the pool was open to hotel guests and members only. Call ahead for ongoing operations, hours, and prices during COVID. The hotel has two restaurants, a snack bar, and a small game room. Other attractions include an RV park, golf course, spa, tennis courts, an outdoor playground, and a small petting zoo.

At Georgetown Lake, the way to go is **vacation rentals,** where you can provide your own meals. Websites for perusing vacation rentals in the area include www. airbnb.com and www.vrbo.com.

Camping

Two miles (3.2 km) east of Anaconda is a surprisingly lush and beautiful campground at **Lost Creek State Park** (5750 Lost Creek Rd., 406/287-3541, www.stateparks.mt.gov, May-Nov., $12-42), set amid pink and white granite cliffs that soar 1,200 feet (366 m) above the canyon floor. There is a lovely waterfall, and campers can often spot bighorn sheep and mountain goats on the cliffs. There are 25 sites, vault toilets, fire rings, picnic tables, and drinking water.

Numerous campgrounds, both public and private, are at Georgetown Lake. Among the closest to the lake is **Lodgepole Campground** (11 mi/17 km south of Philipsburg on Hwy. 1, 406/210-8199, www. reserveamerica.com, May-Sept., $16), which has 31 sites, fire pits, picnic tables, and vault toilets. The campground is across the highway from the lake. **Fairmont Hot Springs Resort** also offers tent sites (from $35) and RV sites ($54-58) with day use fees for all visitors, and pet fees.

Information

Visitor information is available from the **Anaconda Chamber of Commerce and Visitors Center** (306 E. Park Dr., 406/563-2400, www.anacondamt.org, 9am-4pm Mon., 9am-4:30pm Tues.-Fri., 9:30am-1:30pm Sat.). The visitor center offers a wonderful two-hour antique bus tour of the city (call for times and prices) mid-May through mid-September. A printed guide for walking tours is also available.

Transportation

Anaconda is just a short jog off I-90 on Highway 1, the Pintler Scenic Highway. The town is 108 miles (174 km) southeast of Missoula and 24 miles (39 km) northwest of Butte.

The Big Hole

The Big Hole Valley is high, wide, and handsome, not unlike Montana's larger breadbasket to the east, but the emphasis here is on high. Most of this massive valley is a relatively high mountain plateau, entirely flat terrain at or above 6,000 feet (1,800 m) ringed by mountains that soar more than 10,000 feet (3,000 m) into the sky. It's beautiful in the most sweeping sort of way and relatively untouched by the developments of our modern world; technology runs a distant second to tradition here.

The oldest town in the valley, Wisdom (pop. 91), was settled in 1898. Located on the Big Hole River, Melrose (pop. 125) is an angler's paradise, as is Wise River (pop. 266), which is set at the confluence of the Wise River and the Big Hole. Jackson (pop. 113), known for its hot springs resort and awesome snowmobile terrain, is a winter haven. Polaris (pop. 107) is considered a populated mining ghost town with a wonderful old-school hot springs resort, Elkhorn Hot Springs, and a classic ski hill, Maverick Mountain.

The Big Hole is a unique corner of the state with virtually all the attractions Montana is known for: big skies, vast agricultural lands, towering mountains, historically significant sites, world-class fishing, and rugged but charming small towns.

★ BIG HOLE NATIONAL BATTLEFIELD

Among the most moving historic sites in the state, the Big Hole National Battlefield (16425 Hwy. 43, 10 mi/16 km west of Wisdom, 406/689-3155, www.nps.gov, visitor center 9am-5pm daily summer, 10am-4:30pm fall-spring, battlefield sunrise to sunset daily, free) is an important stop for visitors interested in the state's Native American history and, more specifically, the flight of the Nez Perce. The site bears the ghosts of the battle on August 9, 1877, between Chief Joseph's band of Nez Perce, often referred to as the nontreaty Nez Perce, who were fleeing the U.S. Army from their homeland in the Wallowa Valley in Oregon rather than be sent to a reservation, as the U.S. government insisted. Thinking they were safe once they had crossed the border from Idaho into Montana, the Nez Perce set up camp on the picturesque stream to celebrate their freedom and rest after the rugged journey. Thanks to the invention of the telegraph, the army was able to learn of their movements and catch up to them during the night. The Nez Perce lost nearly 90 people, many of them women and children, in the early morning ambush, and Col. John Gibbon lost 31 of his soldiers. Visitors learn the tragic details as they amble around the well-preserved battlefield.

All visits should start at the visitor center, where rangers are on hand to answer questions in addition to showing an excellent 18-minute video and museum exhibit on the battle, the key players, the events leading up to the Nez Perce War, and the fateful encounter at the Big Hole.

Several excellent self-guided trails (buy the printed guide available in the visitor center or at the trailhead; the details it provides are more than worth the $1-2) lead visitors to various scenes of the battle. On hot summer days or wet spring days when the river bottom is soggy or buggy, take the trail that leads up into the forest for a firsthand look at the location from which the army mounted its surprise attack. You can still see small mounds, called rifle pits, where the soldiers scratched the earth by hand or with their rifles to protect themselves from the Nez Perce's return fire. The Nez Perce sniper areas are pointed out, as well as the location where the Nez Perce managed to take control of an army cannon. When the lower trail along the river bottom is dry, visitors can walk among the tipi frames erected where historians have learned the 89 camps stood. Markers indicate where numerous Nez Perce died.

The battlefield is as serene and beautiful today as it is haunting. The National Park Service has done an extraordinary job of presenting information about the Nez Perce War and this battle in particular. Because so little has changed in this region—from the actual landscape to the overall view—it is easy to imagine the events that gave this spot its bloody legacy.

MELROSE

Once a mining outpost and then a railroad town, today Melrose (pop. 125, elev. 5,184 ft/1,580 m) is a fishing town midway between Butte and Dillon. Easy access to both the Wise River and the Big Hole River ensures a steady stream of anglers in this otherwise tiny village.

The Sportsman Lodge (540 N. Main St., 406/835-2141, www.sportsmanlodgemt. com, motel rooms $89-104, cabins $113-150, call for home rates) offers one-stop shopping: In addition to the pet-friendly motel and cabins, there is an RV park with tent sites (from $38 full hookups, $15 tent sites), plus you can hire a guide and rent a raft on the premises. Hunters are just 10 minutes from

the Beaverhead-Deerlodge National Forest. Owners Ken and Bonnie can point you toward some great adventures, including hikes to the otherworldly **Canyon Creek Charcoal Kilns,** a series of beehive-shaped kilns built in the 1870s to produce charcoal for the silver and lead smelters. A few buildings still stand in what was the mining town of **Farlin** on Birch Creek, including some old mining cabins, a school, a butcher shop, and the old smelter. To tour the area on the back of a horse, contact **Wagoner Training** (406/660-1679, www. wagonertraining.com, $55/hour, $75/1.5 hours) for guided trail rides or riding lessons.

Another terrific option for anglers just steps away from the Big Hole River is **Pioneer Mountain Cabins** (47 Trapper Creek Rd., 406/596-1007 or 406/835-2711, www.pioneermountaincabins.com, $120/ night or $720/week), which are modern, clean, and very comfortable with air-conditioning, satellite TV, microwave, refrigerator, and coffee machine—all the standard amenities that feel like luxuries when you're out in the middle of nowhere.

WISE RIVER

Although it's too small to be an incorporated town, Wise River is another fishing paradise.

tipi frames at Big Hole National Battlefield

The non-town—a collection of modest drinking establishments that are long on character—grew up around the place where the Wise River flows into the Big Hole.

While the area around Wise River offers no end of opportunities for entertainment—fishing, hunting, rockhounding, hiking, snowmobiling—the facilities in Wise River are rather sparse. The notable exception is the **Wise River Club** (65013 Hwy. 43, 406/832-3258, www.wiseriverclub.net, $92.50 rooms with shared bath, $120 cabins with private bath for up to 2 people, $10 per additional person, tent sites with shower $10 night, $45-55 RV sites), which has been a restaurant, bar, hotel, and unofficial community center, all in one, since 1896. The menu in the restaurant (8am-9pm Sun.-Thurs., 8am-1am Fri.-Sat., $9.50-34) lists standard Montana fare, including burgers, steaks, chicken-fried steak, and perhaps the best broasted chicken in the state. The bar is open from noon daily, and there is live music Friday nights 7pm-10pm and Sunday afternoons 2pm-6pm. The countless antlers on the ceiling in the club actually came from a single elk that lived across the street for years. People came from miles around to visit the bull, and each year when he shed his antlers, someone would bring them to hang up in the club.

In the nondrinking hours—meaning during fly-fishing time—the best resource in town is **The Complete Fly Fisher** (66771 Hwy. 43, 406/832-3175 or 435/659-1069), a beautiful facility that caters to discriminating anglers for multiday all-inclusive guided fishing stays (3 nights/2 days $3,300 pp, 4 nights/3 days $4,400 pp, 5 nights/4 days $4,800 pp, 6 nights/5 days $5,400 pp, 7 nights/6 days $6,000 pp). The gourmet meals are exquisite (including streamside lunches where your guide will wow you with linens and a menu), and the accommodations are top-notch. The guides are absolute pros, and everything you could possibly need—from fishing licenses to the latest and greatest fly—is available on-site. As a lodge, it can also arrange other activities such as horseback riding, hiking, and nature tours.

WISDOM

Another great fishing town in a spectacular setting, Wisdom (pop. 91, elev. 6,050 ft/1,844 m) is the name that Lewis and Clark initially gave to the Big Hole River. The Beaverhead and Ruby Rivers were named Philosophy and Philanthropy. Together the three formed the Jefferson River, and the names were meant to honor the three "cardinal virtues" possessed by President Thomas Jefferson.

Wisdom still doesn't have much cell phone coverage, but there is a wonderful restaurant, well worth the drive. **The Crossing Bar & Grill at Fetty's** (327 County Rd., 406/689-3260, 8am-8pm Fri.-Tues., closed Wed. mornings and Thursday, but call ahead because hours can change without warning, $11-40) was established in 1932 as Fetty's and reopened in 2011 by the Havig family, whose own restaurant and art gallery across the street burned down in 2010. The Havigs spruced the place up and expanded the menu with more gourmet options, but the restaurant was sold again in 2021 so there could be change. The hope is that the new owners will stay true to Fetty's promise of "authentic cowboy cuisine since 1932." Never mind that the building dates to 1960; the black-and-white photos tell a treasured history of the area. The Crossing is as famous for its burgers as for its Rocky Mountain oysters (don't ask, just try them). From the kitchen you can hear the muffled sound of the local police scanner, and the snickerdoodles are homemade and always available to go. What could be better than such old-school goodness?

JACKSON

From the cool little town of Jackson (pop. 144, elev. 6,407 ft/1,953 m), it's 25 miles (40 km) to Idaho on foot and 45 miles (72 km) by car. More to the point, though, why leave? There is a great hotel, restaurant, and hot springs complex, not to mention spectacular scenery and terrain worth exploring in every direction along with fishing access. This is an outdoors lover's paradise at any time of year.

The best place to launch an adventure—or recover from one—is the ★ **Jackson Hot Springs Lodge** (108 Jardine Ave., 406/834-3151, www.jacksonhotspringslodge.com, Thurs.-Sun., $75-156 rooms and sleeper cabins, $35 RV sites). The rooms are not fancy, by any stretch, and the Wi-Fi is only available in the lodge, but the outdoor pool fed by natural hot springs (nonguests $10 adults, $7 children, veterans, teachers, and seniors) is divine, and the gigantic Western bar (8am-12:30am Thurs.-Sun., 8am-11am Mon.) and dance hall are authentic and welcoming. Live bands often play, and the massive Montana-size dance floor invites fancy footwork. An on-site restaurant serves breakfast (8am-11am Thurs.-Mon., $7.50-17), lunch (11am-5pm Thurs.-Sun., $7.50-16), and dinner (Thurs.-Sun. 5pm-9pm, $7.50-22), plus bar food all day. Pets are allowed in some of the rooms and need to be confirmed when booking.

POLARIS

Essentially a ghost town with a surprising number of people (mostly ranchers) still in residence, Polaris (pop. 107, elev. 6,352 ft/1,936 m) was an important silver-mining center near Grasshopper Creek as early as 1885. The smelter was destroyed in 1922, and by 1955 the only structure left standing was the Polar Bar, a small white cabin on the side of the road that served up frosty beers to weary travelers. It's been closed since the 1990s.

Most people coming through Polaris today are headed for skiing at Maverick Mountain or soaking at Elkhorn Hot Springs, both worthwhile pursuits.

Elkhorn Hot Springs

After a full day of skiing, nothing is better than submerging in naturally heated mineral waters, and Elkhorn Hot Springs (Hwy. 284, 13 mi/21 km north of Hwy. 278, 406/834-3551 or 800/722-8978, www.elkhornhotsprings. com, single-room rustic cabin $90 for 2 people, multiroom rustic cabin $130 for up to 4 people, modern cabin $150 for 2 people, from $35 single and $60 double dorm-style

rooms) is just the place to do so. Set in the forest and very basic (the rustic cabins do not have running water, and heat is provided by a fireplace or wood-burning stove), Elkhorn Hot Springs is a playground for outdoors enthusiasts. The two outdoor pools (8am-10pm Sun.-Thurs., 8am-11pm Fri.-Sat., $10 adults 16 and up, $7 children, free for children 3 and under, admission included with any lodging package) range 92-102°F (33-39°C), and an indoor wet sauna ranges 104-106°F (40-41°C). These are not sparkling clear pools; dark green algae grows on the bottom of them. But the water is natural and right out of the ground. So if you prefer greenery to chemicals, this is the place. The large outdoor pool is cleaned on Tuesdays ($5 admission). A restaurant on the premises serves standard Montana fare for three meals daily in summer (breakfast buffet is included with lodging) and lunch and dinner Friday-Sunday in winter (lunch $8-14, dinner $11-32).

In addition to all the other amenities at this relatively time-worn resort, there is immediate access to more than 200 miles (320 km) of groomed snowmobile trails and 20 miles (32 km) of cross-country ski trails.

SPORTS AND RECREATION

TOP EXPERIENCE

★ Skiing Maverick Mountain

North of the town of Polaris, Maverick Mountain (1600 Maverick Mountain Rd., 406/834-3454, www.skimaverick. com, Thurs.-Sun. and holidays Dec.-late Mar., full day $40 adults, $34 seniors 65 and over, $27 juniors 12 and under) boasts 24 trails, 350 skiable acres, and just over 2,000 feet (610 m) of vertical drop. There are two lifts, one of which is a rope tow, and a nice breakdown of beginner (30 percent), intermediate (40 percent), and expert runs (30 percent). The area receives an average of 250 inches (635 cm) of the white stuff annually.

An antidote to ski areas like Aspen and Sun Valley, the real charm of Maverick is its total lack of pretense: You're likely to ride a chairlift with a rancher in Carhartt coveralls or a Hutterite girl in a dress and braids. Skiing at Maverick is a little bit like skiing somewhere small but fantastic in about 1968, with no lift lines and wide-open skiing. It is as family-friendly as a ski hill gets, and the terrain is excellent.

★ Fishing the Big Hole

If Butte is a city built on mining, the Big Hole is a region defined by fishing and hunting. For generations, the land and rivers here have provided pristine habitat for an abundance of wildlife and terrific access for anglers and hunters.

The 155-mile-long (250-km-long) **Big Hole River** is spectacularly beautiful and offers a diversity of terrain, from its origin high in the Bitterroot Range through the wide flats of the Big Hole Valley. It is known for early-season salmonfly hatches and then a golden stone hatch in late June and early July. It is also considered the last river where an angler can catch all five species of trout.

The access to the river is pretty good, thanks to designated fishing access sites and informal road access sites. Considered the most scenic of the stretches, the upper river from its origin to Squaw Creek is known for huge brook trout and smaller cutthroat and rainbows. There are native grayling too, which can be caught but must be released. Brookies, which can exceed 16 inches (41 cm) on this stretch, are primarily fished higher up on the upper river, while rainbows and cutts, usually 12 inches (31 cm) or less, are more plentiful downstream from Wisdom. Don't forget to pack your mosquito repellent, especially in June and July. The skeeters love all this water and are delighted with the fresh blood of anglers. By August, they are usually not as much of a problem.

The stretch of river from Wise River to the Salmon Fly Fishing Access Site is ideally suited to big browns and can be accessed along Highway 43 or from various fishing access sites.

There are numerous outfitters eager to introduce anglers to the trout in the Big Hole River. Among them are **Sunrise Fly Shop** (472 Main St., Melrose, 406/835-3474, www.sunriseflyshop.com, 8am-4pm daily Apr.-Oct., call for off-season days and hours, $595-615 full-day guided float trip for 1-2 anglers) and **Troutfitters** (62311 Hwy. 43, 2 mi/3.2 km west of Wise River, 406/832-3212, $650-690 full-day guided float trip for 1-2 anglers, $75 rod fee for trophy ponds), both of which can also provide lodging.

Rockhounding

There is a reason this part of the state is known locally as Gold West Country. There are a number of places still open to rockhounding. One of the best places to look for gems is at **Crystal Park** (Pioneer Mountains Scenic Byway/Rd. 73, 406/683-3900, www.fs.usda.gov, May 15-Sept. 30 depending on road conditions, $8/vehicle day use), at 7,800 feet (2,377 m) high in the Pioneer Mountains, where visitors can dig for quartz crystal and amethyst, among other stones. Amenities include picnic benches and grills on-site as well as toilets.

Hiking

The Big Hole is surrounded by the **Beaverhead-Deerlodge National Forest** (406/683-3900, www.fs.usda.gov), the state's largest national forest, which encompasses several mountain ranges and innumerable phenomenal hiking trails. Three of the longest running through the region are the **Continental Divide National Scenic Trail,** the **Nez Perce National Historic Trail,** and the **Lewis and Clark National Historic Trail.**

A great day hike near Elkhorn Hot Springs is the trail to beautiful **Sawtooth Lake,** filled with colorful lake trout. It's a 4-mile (6.4-km) hike to the lake (and 4 mi/6.4 km back), climbing just over 1,500 vertical feet

(455 m). The trailhead is off Willman Creek Road (Forest Rd. 7441). Go east on Willman Creek Road through the Taylor subdivision for 1.8 miles (2.9 km) until it forks; keep right for 0.3 mile (0.5 km) to the trailhead, where you'll see the parking lot and vault toilet. The trail crosses the creek twice, which can be treacherous at high water or anytime the logs are wet.

CAMPING

There are countless campsites in the vast **Beaverhead-Deerlodge National Forest** (406/683-3900, www.fs.usda.gov). You can choose RV campgrounds, tent sites, or even cabin rentals by location on the website.

The **Boulder Creek Campground** (406/689-3243, $8 summer, free in winter) near Wise River has 13 sites in a high-elevation and heavily wooded site; another with only 5 sites but set right on the Big Hole River is the **East Banks Recreation Site** (Hwy. 43, 8 mi/13 km west of Wise River, 406/533-7600, no fees for day use or camping).

INFORMATION

The website of the **Big Hole Tourism Association** (www.bigholevalley.com) offers information on the towns, businesses, attractions, and accommodations in the region. Information is also available through the **Beaverhead Chamber of Commerce** (10 W. Reeder St., Dillon, 406/683-5511, www.beaverheadchamber.org, 9am-5pm Mon.-Fri.).

TRANSPORTATION

The Big Hole Valley can be accessed most directly from Butte via I-15 south to Highway 43 and Highway 278, and from Dillon via I-15 south to Highway 278.

Dillon and the Southwest Corner

This part of the state is where mining meets agriculture, and where history and adventure are intertwined. There are wide-open spaces, snowcapped peaks, and limestone caves that snake deep underground. It is an area that will enchant history buffs with preserved mining settlements like Virginia City, Nevada City, and Bannack, and transfix lovers of sports and nature with incredible wildlife habitat, phenomenal fishing in rivers and lakes, and plenty of wild space just to get lost in for a while.

Dillon, the economic and service hub of the region, was an important stopping point for the Lewis and Clark expedition. Lewis and Clark met the Shoshone in Dillon and were able to cache their canoes and some supplies for the return trip. In the latter part of the 19th century, Dillon was an important shipping point between the goldfields of Montana and Utah. Agriculture has also shaped the area. Cattle were first brought to Dillon in 1865, followed by sheep in 1869. The University of Montana Western, which emphasizes agriculture, thrives in Dillon today and adds youthful energy to the town. Dillon's downtown offers the largest number of shops (including the Patagonia Outlet), hotels, and eateries in the region.

DILLON

The area around Dillon (pop. 4,369, elev. 5,096 ft/1,553 m) was significant on Lewis and Clark's westward journey. One site earned the name Camp Fortunate when Lewis and Clark met the Shoshone people and managed to cache supplies for their return voyage.

After gold strikes in Bannack, Helena, and Butte, the area around what is now Dillon became an important shipping route between the booming mining camps and more-developed Utah, often the source of equipment, supplies, and labor. Eventually the railroads came through the region, but not until a deal was struck between Irish rancher Richard Deacon, the railroad owners, and the merchants who made their living following the railroad construction crews. A staunch opponent of the railroad and a shrewd businessman, Deacon raised the price on his land to a whopping $10,500, which the railroad agreed to pay. The town of Dillon, named for Sidney Dillon, president of the Utah and Northern Railway, grew quickly as the construction crews completed the rail line during the winter of 1880-1881. Its longevity was ensured when the county seat was moved to Dillon from nearby Bannack later that year. The town prospered with the construction of a teachers college in 1892, leading some to predict that Dillon would become "the very Athens of the West."

If not quite Athens, today Dillon is a thriving (and growing!) little community and home to the University of Montana Western. The town has preserved its local history—from Native American influences to agriculture and mining—and achieved a reputation as an excellent launching point for outdoor adventures that include hunting, fishing, hiking, biking, and rockhounding. Mostly, though, it is Dillon's proximity to historic mining centers like Bannack, Virginia City, and Nevada City that makes it an obvious destination.

More reliable than the first frost, outdoorsy Montanans mark the end of summer with the **annual Labor Day weekend sale** at the **Patagonia Outlet** (16 S. Idaho St., 406/683-2580, www.patagonia.com, 10am-6pm Mon.-Sat., 11am-5pm Sun.). Sales on the already reduced selection of ecofriendly and always cutting-edge outdoor gear jump to 40 percent discounts. Just as Montanans buy their ski passes before the first flake falls, so too do they get their gear when the getting's cheap.

BANNACK STATE PARK

Twenty-five miles (40 km) west of Dillon is **Bannack State Park** (4200 Bannack Rd., 406/834-3413, www.bannack.org, visitor center 11am-5pm or by appointment weekends only in May and Oct., 10am-6pm daily late May-Sept., townsite open 8am-5pm daily in spring/fall/winter, 8am-9pm daily Memorial Day-first week of August, 8am-sunset second week of Aug.-Sept., $8/vehicle nonresidents), which comprises the original mining settlement of Bannack. First established in 1862 when John White discovered gold on Grasshopper Creek, the town waxed and waned for years until World War II, when all nonessential mining was prohibited. In 1954, much of the area and its

Bannack State Park

50-plus buildings were donated to the state for preservation.

The townsite is well preserved but not restored or commercialized, which makes it an interesting place to visit. Bannack's history is fascinating, and many of its stories come to life in the buildings and grounds in the state park. Henry Plummer, the sheriff of both Bannack and Virginia City, was famously hanged here by a group of vigilantes in 1864. He is reportedly buried at the site. The gallows and cemetery can be visited, and nearly all the buildings can be entered.

Two types of guided tours are on offer at Bannack when staff are available: **Mill Tours** (about 50 min., noon Sat.-Sun. summer or by appointment, $4 pp) and **Town Tours** (about 60 min., 2pm Mon.-Fri., 10:30am and 2pm Sat.-Sun. summer, free with park admission). Rangers suggest calling ahead to see if tour schedules have changed. The visitor center is open 11am-5pm on weekends only in May and October and 10am-6pm daily late May through September. Held annually the third weekend in July, **Bannack Days** is a celebration of the way life was when Bannack was in its prime. The weekend kicks off with a break-fast (7am Sat.) at **Hotel Meade.** Throughout the day there are pioneer demonstrations, in-cluding quilting, basket making, blacksmith-ing, and shooting a black-powder rifle. Lots of old-time delicacies—think kettle corn, fry bread, and fresh lemonade—are available, along with live music and an abundance of theatrics.

There are two campgrounds: **Vigilante Campground** and **Road Agent Campground** (855/922-6768, $28 summer, discounts available for Montana residents, hike-in/bike-in campers, seniors, and disabled). Restrooms, water, picnic tables, and fire rings are available, and a tipi (mid-May-early Oct., $42 for nonresidents or $30 with park pass) can be reserved at the Vigilante Campground.

RED ROCK LAKES NATIONAL WILDLIFE REFUGE

Known for its alpine and riparian beauty and its phenomenal habitat for birds and other wildlife, including bears, wolves, and moose, the **Red Rocks Lake National Wildlife Refuge** (27650B S. Valley Rd., Lima, 406/276-3536, www.fws.gov, 8am-4:30pm Mon.-Fri. year-round except federal holidays) is a spectacular area for naturally inspired recreation. Some 232 bird species have been recorded at the refuge, including 53 that are rare or considered accidental. The refuge was founded in 1935 to protect the majestic trumpeter swans, which are still happily in residence. In 1932, there were thought to be fewer than 70 in existence worldwide, half of them in this area. Today there are nearly 46,000 trumpeter swans, including roughly 500 that live in Montana, Wyoming, and Idaho. Up to 2,000 tundra and trumpeter swans gather in the refuge in early fall along with 50,000 ducks and geese. Springtime provides opportunities to see (and hear!) nesting sandhill cranes. Hunting and fishing are permitted at specific places and seasons within the refuge, but regulations change frequently and can be found through **Montana Fish, Wildlife & Parks** (406/444-2535 or 406/444-2950 for out-of-state licensing, www.fwp.mt.gov). One of the few marshland wilderness areas in the country, the area is in its original natural state. Physical facilities are kept to a minimum, and formal trails are not maintained or designated. This is a place to get away from the crowds and explore at your own pace with minimal impact. To get to the refuge, turn off I-15 at Monida and drive 28 miles (45 km) east on the gravel and dirt road. There are several cool 1.5- to 3-hour drives to take, including the South Valley Road at the base of the Centennial Mountains, the Refuge Loop, to the Sand Dunes, Hellroaring Creek, and more. Visit the website for descriptions of each drive. Primitive camping ($7 night) is available at the **Upper** and **Lower Red Rocks Lake Campgrounds.**

★ VIRGINIA CITY AND NEVADA CITY

Another 57 miles (92 km) east of Dillon are Virginia City and Nevada City, two thriving ghost towns left over from Montana's glorious gold-mining era. In May 1863, a party of six prospectors left Bannack after a string of bad luck. While they set up camp for the night along Alder Creek, the men discovered what would become one of the richest gold deposits in North America. Nine camps grew up along the creek almost overnight, the largest of which would be named Virginia City.

Within a year, the town had upward of 10,000 residents and became the first territorial capital. It was also the site of the state's first newspaper, the first public school, and the first Masonic Lodge. The town's history is intertwined with the Vigilantes of Montana, the group that hanged Sheriff Henry Plummer, among others, in 1864.

By 1875, much of the mining activity in the region had abated, and Virginia City's population had dwindled to less than 800. Over the years, as new technologies developed, including the mining dredges, the area was mined over and over for traces of what might be left. Still, between 1863 and 1889, some $90 million worth of gold had been extracted from the region. Today, that amount of gold would be worth $40 billion.

In 1961, Virginia City was designated a National Historic Landmark and protected as an important historic site. Since then, many of the buildings have been restored to function as shops, restaurants, and a hotel. The display of artifacts in both Virginia and Nevada City constitutes the largest collection of Old West memorabilia outside the Smithsonian. The growing population of 216 people works hard to re-create the atmosphere of Virginia City at its peak. Throughout the summer, nightly cabaret entertainment at **Brewery Follies at Gilbert Brewery** and nightly 19th-century melodrama courtesy of the **Virginia City Players at the Opera House** entertain visitors. There are **train rides** on a 1910 locomotive between the cities, and living history exhibits are scattered around the sites. Plenty of services—accommodations and restaurants—are available for visitors who plan to stay.

For more than six decades, the illustrious **Virginia City Players** (338 W. Wallace St., Virginia City, 406/843-5314 or 800/829-2969, ext. 2, www.virginiacityplayers.com, 4pm Tues.-Thurs., 7pm Fri.-Sat., 2pm Sat.-Sun., times can vary year to year so check the website or call ahead, $25 adults, $20 college students, seniors, and military, $15 children 17 and under) have been entertaining the crowds at the Virginia City Opera House with turn-of-the-20th-century-style melodrama, vaudeville, and variety acts. They generally offer three shows over the course of the summer season and also play silent movies on one of only two operating photoplays in the world. Reservations are strongly encouraged. Babies, children, and even dogs are welcome in the theater, but the company warns that dogs who might be frightened by (and bark at) occasional gunfire should probably stay at home.

For more outlandish theater and comedy geared strictly to adults, **Brewery Follies** (200 E. Cover St., Virginia City, 800/829-2969, ext. 3, www.breweryfollies.net, 8pm Tues.-Wed., 4pm and 8pm Thurs.-Mon. Memorial Day weekend-Sept., $25 adults, $20 seniors and veterans) at the Old H. S. Gilbert Brewery offers the unique setting of a restored 1864 brewery with bawdy entertainment and excellent microbrews.

Visitor services are available at four staffed areas throughout summer: **Virginia City Depot Visitors Information Center, Virginia City Depot Gift Store, Nevada City Open Air Museum,** and the **Alder Gulch Shortline Railroad.** More information is available from the **Montana Heritage Commission** (406/843-5247, www.montanaheritagecommission.mt.gov).

Cell service can be spotty in both Virginia and Nevada cities.

SHERIDAN AND THE RUBY RIVER VALLEY

Nestled between the Ruby and Tobacco Root mountain ranges, the Ruby River Valley is lush, fertile, and known for its fishing and bird hunting. Among the small but scenic hamlets in this valley are **Silver Star, Twin Bridges, Sheridan,** and **Alder.** Between Sheridan and Alder is **Robber's Roost,** a notorious hangout for thieving road agents in the gold rush era. The landmark hideout cabin is marked by a roadside sign and can be toured in a matter of minutes.

JEFFERSON RIVER VALLEY

The Beaverhead, Big Hole, and Ruby Rivers come together at Twin Bridges to form the Jefferson River, which flows 77 miles (124 km) through dry, scrubby, and relatively untouched country before joining the Missouri alongside the Madison and Gallatin Rivers at Three Forks. Along the way are small towns like **Whitehall, Cardwell, LaHood,** and the tiny but charming **Willow Creek.** Much of the valley looks the same as it did when Lewis and Clark made their way through it more than 200 years ago.

★ Lewis and Clark Caverns

Among the sights Lewis and Clark missed on their travels through the region is the **Lewis and Clark Caverns** (25 Lewis and Clark Caverns Rd., 17 mi/27 km east of Whitehall off Hwy. 2, 406/287-3541, www. stateparks.mt.gov, $8/vehicle nonresidents), a phenomenal limestone cave several hundred yards above the Jefferson River on which the explorers traveled. The caverns are among the largest in the Northwest and were Montana's first state park. They are filled with several rooms and lined with stalactites, stalagmites, columns, and helictites. The temperature in these colorful caverns stays at around 50°F (10°C)

year-round, making them the perfect spot to escape the increasingly common blisteringly hot days in southwest Montana.

The caves can only be accessed on a **two-hour guided tour** (9am-4:30pm daily May-mid-June and mid-Aug.-Sept., 9am-6:30pm daily mid-June-mid-Aug., classic cave tour $15 ages 12 and up, $10 children 5-14) that includes a roughly 2-mile (3.2-km) hike up to and down from the caverns. On hot days, the hike can be grueling, but the cool, dark, moist caverns are the perfect reward. The natural bat nursery inside is daunting to some, but fascinating to others. Wait times can be anywhere from a half hour or less in early and late season and on weekday mornings and evenings during peak season. During midday peak season, wait times can be well over an hour. **Wild Cave Tours** ($40 ages 15 and up), **Paradise Tours** ($15 ages 12 and up, $10 youth 5-14 and seniors, free for children under 5), and **Candlelight Tours** ($25 ages 15 and up, $15 youth 5-14, children under 5 not permitted) can be reserved ahead of time.

A **campground** at the caves has 40 sites ($12-42), restrooms with showers, a dump station, three **cabins** ($54-66), and a **tipi** ($30-42) for rent. Within the 3,000-acre park are 10 miles (16 km) of hiking trails with trailheads at the campground, a fishing access site, two picnic areas, and a gift shop and restaurant.

Rockin' the Rivers Festival

Considered "Montana's homegrown rockfest," the 3-day **Rockin' the Rivers festival** (1865 Highway 2, Cardwell, 406/285-0099, www. rockintherivers.com) has been held annually at the bridge in Cardwell for more than 20 years. People bring their lawn chairs and camp (showers are available for $5) for the weekend to watch acts that have included Journey, Joan Jett, Little Feat, and plenty more over the years. Tickets for all three days start at $170.

1: Lewis and Clark Caverns **2:** cemetery overlooking Virginia City **3:** the ghost town of Nevada City

SPORTS AND RECREATION

With so many fantastic rivers in the region, it's no surprise that southwest Montana is known as a fishing paradise. Anglers can choose from the Beaverhead, Big Hole, Jefferson, Ruby, and Red Rock Rivers, all within this corner of the state. The Beaverhead, which is easily accessed from Dillon, is among the state's most productive and prolific tailwaters, with dense bug populations and upward of 4,000 fish per mile. The Jefferson River does not give up its savvy fish easily, but streamer fishing and terrestrial fishing are fantastic. The Ruby River offers great wading and superb caddis and mayfly hatches. It's a serene river that offers small stream-like settings. The Red Rock River flows out from Lillian Lake into the Centennial Valley. Its upper portion, known for cutthroat, rainbows, and grayling, is narrow and ideally suited for wading. There is also great brown and rainbow trout fishing beneath the Lima Reservoir.

With so many fish, there are numerous outfitters in the region eager to get anglers on the water. Among them is Justin Hartman of **Tight Line Adventures** (406/925-1684, www.tightlinemontana.com, from $2,295 pp 3 nights lodging/2 days fishing), who can guide you to the huge trout and also offers accommodations. Another excellent resource is **Frontier Anglers** (680 N. Montana St., Dillon, 800/228-5263, www.frontieranglers. com, from $625 full-day float/walk/wade for up to 2 anglers including flies and tackle, from $595 for 2 anglers using their own gear and flies), a full-service fly shop offering everything from boat and gear rentals to equipment and supplies, guide services, fly-fishing lessons, and even vacation home rentals.

FOOD

Paula and Bill Kinoshita, owners of ★ **The Old Hotel** (101 E. 5th Ave., Twin Bridges, 406/684-5959, www.theoldhotel.com, closed to in-house dining during COVID, open for takeout 4pm-7pm Fri.-Sat., breakfast and bakery 8am-1pm Sat., call ahead for changing hours and services, $14-24), are phenomenal chefs who have mastered everything from Le Cordon Bleu classics to Pacific Rim flavors and their own brilliant invention, cowboy sushi—a classic nigiri roll filled with thinly sliced vegetables and their own barbecue beef, then dipped in tempura batter and fried, served with red chili aioli. The creative menu changes weekly and is always paired with carefully selected wines from around the world. The restaurant serves anglers, ranchers, and range-roving foodies year-round. And their breakfast pastries and goodies—French almond croissants, caramel and pecan sticky buns, BLTs on croissants—are well worth a long drive. Because the tiny size and remote location of the Old Hotel are entirely disproportionate to the incredible fusion of flavors, reservations are strongly recommended. But do call ahead to see if they are open for dining and what their seasonal hours are.

While the cuisine at the Old Hotel is surely the most surprising and remarkable in the region, this is not plain burger-and-fries country (although the beef in southwestern Montana is notably good). There is fine dining at **Wells Fargo Steakhouse** (314 W. Wallace St., Virginia City, 406/843-5556, 4pm-9pm Wed.-Sun. mid-May-mid-Sept., $16-45), a stately building with tall, tin ceilings and a grand horseshoe bar. In addition to gourmet cuisine like mussels *fra diavolo*, pork scaloppini, pasta, and of course mouthwatering steaks, the Wells Fargo often hosts live music in its ballroom-size dining room.

The ★ **Star Bakery Restaurant** (1576 Hwy. 287, Nevada City, 406/843-5777, www.aldergulchaccommodations.com, 7am-3pm Thurs.-Sun. and 5pm-8pm Fri.-Sat., Memorial Day-Labor Day, $15-30) has been serving delicious and hearty meals since 1863 when it was a hot spot with miners. Today the clientele is more family-oriented, and the menu has plenty to appeal to everyone, including homemade sandwiches, beer-battered shrimp, and sodas from the early-1900s soda fountain. The restaurant is known for its fried pickles, so you might want to indulge. The emporium offers quick sugary goodies like ice cream, fudge, and penny candy, too. The restaurant was closed for dinner during COVID, but check back to see if they are open again.

In Dillon, a good bet for a relatively quick bite (depending on the crowd of hungry college students) is Sparky's Garage (420 E. Poindexter St., Dillon, 406/683-2828, www.sparkysrestaurant.com, 11am-9pm Mon.-Thurs. and Sun., 11am-9:30pm Fri.-Sat., $6-19), a neat little barbecue joint with tender brisket, mouthwatering pulled pork, and delicious sweet-potato fries. They also have burgers, sandwiches, soup, and salad. The locals' favorite—and something of a Dillon institution—is the Fiesta Mexicana Taco Bus (510 N. Montana St., 406/660-0915, 9am-9pm daily, $2-14) which serves amazing tacos, enchiladas, fajitas, burritos, and combo platters. This is the real deal. For a juicy steak, head to Blacktail Station Steak House (26 S. Montana St., 406/683-6611, www.blacktailstation.com, 5pm-9:30pm Sun.-Thurs., 5pm-10pm Fri.-Sat., $10.50-35), a sports bar, grill, and casino that has a nice selection of steaks, plus ribs, seafood, pasta, and burgers.

In the Ruby River Valley, though the beloved Shovel & Spoon closed during the pandemic after eight years, there are a couple of other good spots to wet your whistle or grab a bite. Bread Zepp (107 S. Main St., Sheridan, 406/842-7777, www.breadzepp.com, 2pm-8pm Tues.-Sat., pizzas $16-21) serves delicious and inventive pizza, sandwiches, and salads. Plus they make the most amazing bread and sweets, from brownies and cookies to cinnamon rolls. From inside Bread Zepp, there's a window into the neighboring establishment, Ruby Valley Brewing (111 S. Main St., Sheridan, 406/842-5977, www.rubyvalleybrew.com), serving up handcrafted brews like Cow Puncher Kölsch, Mad Cou Heifer Weizen, Chompin' at the Pit Cherry Porter, and Maverick Mary IPA. They usually have 12 brews on tap, including root beer for the little ones. Make it a pizza and beer night. You won't be sorry.

ACCOMMODATIONS

While Dillon is home to what was once a grand railroad hotel, the Metlen Hotel & Saloon is showing its age. Ripe for a restoration, the Metlen was for sale in 2021, so keep an eye on it. It could be glorious again. Meanwhile, a good local choice is the budget-friendly and pet-friendly Sundowner Motel (500 N. Montana St., 406/683-2375, $58-88), which offers 32 basic rooms with continental breakfast and Wi-Fi included. It is the best rate in town, the staff are super-friendly, and the rooms are consistently clean and comfortable. There's a coin laundry across the street, and the taco bus is just steps away.

Among the chain hotels and motels in Dillon are Best Western Paradise Inn of Dillon (650 N. Montana St., 406/683-4214, www.bestwestern.com, $82-289), Quality Inn (450 N. Interchange, 406/683-6831, www.choicehotels.com, $98-185), and Motel 6 of Dillon (20 Swenson Way, 406/683-5555, www.motel6.com, $96-138).

For a historical lodging experience, the Fairweather Inn (305 W. Wallace St., Virginia City, 406/843-5377 or 800/829-2969, ext. 4, www.aldergulchaccommodations.com, June-mid-Sept., rooms with shared bathrooms from $150, rooms with private baths from $165) is a building from 1863 with plenty of charm. There are 14 guest rooms, six of which have en suite baths; the others share facilities. Don't expect to find a bed larger than a double in this property. The ★ Nevada City Hotel & Cabins (1578 U.S. 287, Nevada City, booking 855/377-6823, or 406/843-5377 or 800/829-2969, ext. 4, mid-May-late Sept., from $165 for 2 people) has a more rustic exterior with slightly more elegant interiors. All the guest rooms have private baths, and two Victorian suites have their own balconies. The cabins are true sod-roofed pioneer cabins that have been updated with comfortable accommodations and modern amenities. Both hotels offer ideal access to all the sights in Virginia City and Nevada City plus some local discounts.

INFORMATION AND SERVICES

The **Beaverhead Chamber of Commerce** (406/683-5511, www.beaverheadchamber. org, 9am-5pm Mon.-Fri.) is at 10 West Reeder Street in Dillon.

The **Virginia City Chamber** (406/843-5555 or 800/829-2969, www.virginiacity.com) does not have a physical address but provides information by phone and on its website. The **Montana Heritage Commission** (300 W. Wallace St., Virginia City, 406/843-5247, www.montanaheritagecommission.mt.gov, summer) is a good source of information because it manages most of the sights in Virginia City and Nevada City.

For information about the towns in the Ruby River Valley, the **Greater Ruby Valley Chamber of Commerce and Agriculture** (www.rubyvalleychamber.com) makes visitor information available at the public library (206 S. Main St.) in Twin Bridges.

TRANSPORTATION

The closest airport to Dillon is the **Bert Mooney Airport** (BTM, 101 Airport Rd., 406/494-3771, www.butteairport. com) in Butte. Car-rental agencies at the airport include **Avis, Budget,** and **Hertz. Enterprise** has an agency off-site.

Greyhound bus service is available to Dillon from various cities in Montana. The station is at 1324 Harrison Avenue (406/723-3287 or 800/454-2487).

Dillon is about 65 miles (105 km) south of Butte and 115 miles (185 km) southwest of Bozeman. Virginia City and Nevada City are both 70 miles (113 km) southeast of Butte or southwest of Bozeman.

Helena

Montana's capital, Helena (pop. 34,256, elev. 4,090 ft/1,247 m) is an elegant city, the demure and pious little sister to Butte. The city has done a particularly good job of preserving its history by maintaining architecture. The Montana State Capitol building, for example, is Greek Renaissance style, and the myriad mansions around town are largely Victorian. With its soaring spires and remarkable stained glass, the **St. Helena Cathedral** would look at home in Europe. Humble miners' cabins and historic businesses line the streets in Last Chance Gulch, the site of the city's origins.

But Helena is not living in the past. The city is growing rapidly, and with that growth comes culture. Helena is becoming recognized as the arts capital of the state, with an edgy, contemporary fine arts scene in addition to extensive performing arts. And the tourism office is not shying away from technology: Look for its self-guided walking tour app that tells the juicy stories behind the city's stately buildings and mansions, or go on a geocaching adventure.

But it's not technology that draws people to Montana. Located as it is in a wide-open valley surrounded by mountains, lakes, and rivers, Helena also offers endless opportunities to get out of the city and into nature.

HISTORY

Founded in 1864 with a gold strike on a site that would become the heart of the city, Helena was initially named Crabtown by the four prospectors who made the discovery. Eventually, as the camp filled with miners, the name was changed to St. Helena after a town in Minnesota. It was a gold-mining town, after all, so the saint was eventually dropped.

As was common at the time, these small towns would boom and bust, and commerce and government would move from one gold strike to the next; by 1875 the territory's capital was in Helena, the city that had grown

Helena

To Lakes and Steve's Café →
■ EATON TURNER JEWELRY

To Delta Hotels Helena Colonial, Townsend, and Butte →

To The Dive Bakery and Café →

★ MONTANA HISTORICAL SOCIETY

★ MONTANA STATE CAPITOL BUILDING

▼ STEVE'S CAFÉ

★ LAST CHANCE SPLASH WATERPARK AND POOL

LAST CHANCE GULCH

★ GREAT NORTHERN CAROUSEL AND EXPLORATION WORKS

GREAT NORTHERN TOWN CENTER

● BEST WESTERN GREAT NORTHERN

■ CARROLL COLLEGE

ST. HELENA CATHEDRAL ✦

THE SANDERS, HELENA'S B&B ●

● ORIGINAL GOVERNOR'S MANSION

MYRNA LOY CENTER FOR THE PERFORMING ARTS

GENERAL MERCANTILE
HOLTER MUSEUM OF ART ★
MONTANA BOOK & TOY CO.
BENNY'S BISTRO ▼

FUNKY TRUNK

HELENA CHAMBER OF COMMERCE

▼ ON BROADWAY
WINDBAG SALOON ●
LASSO THE MOON

THE PARROT CONFECTIONERY
DOUBLETREE BY HILTON ●
PARK AVENUE BAKERY ●
● LAST CHANCE GULCH

GRANDSTREET THEATRE

REEDER'S ALLEY

REEDER'S ALLEY

MANSION DISTRICT

▼ SUNFLOWER BAKERY

To Montana WILD, Broadwater Hot Springs, Spring Meadow State Park, Archie Bray Foundation, and Missoula →

MONROE AVE
HARRISON AVE
GILBERT ST
POWER ST
HOLTER ST
MADISON ST
DEARBORN ST
LAWRENCE ST
PARK AVE
ADAMS ST
HAUSER BLVD
STUART ST
FLOWEREE ST
EUCLID AVE
BENTON AVE
LYNDALE AVE
E 14TH ST
GETCHELL ST
NEILL AVE
HELENA AVE
WARREN ST
EWING ST
RODNEY ST
DAVIS ST
15TH ST
11TH
9TH
8TH
6TH
BROADWAY
MONTANA AVE
PROSPECT AVE
ROBERTS ST
HOBACK ST
CRUSE AVE

.25 mi
.25 km

▲ Mt Helena

© MOON.COM

up around Last Chance Gulch. The city of Helena persisted because just as its gold supply dwindled, other valuable materials were discovered, including quartz, silver, and lead. Helena had also established itself as an important center of trade for the region, and when Montana became a state in 1889, Helena had more millionaires per capita than any other city in the country. Although there had been a fierce battle between Helena and Anaconda, pitting copper kings Marcus Daly and William Andrews Clark against each other, Helena was named the capital of Montana Territory, and 13 years later ground was broken on the state capitol.

SIGHTS

Last Chance Tour Train

One of the best ways to get an overview of the city and some historical perspective is by hopping on one of the Last Chance Tours (tours depart from Montana Historical Society, 225 N. Roberts, corner of E. 6th Ave., 406/442-1023, www.lctours.com, Mon.-Sat. June-Sept. 15, $11 ages 13-59, $10 seniors 60 and over, $9 children 4-12, free for children under 4). The wheeled trains and trolley cruise around town with commentary on places like Reeder's Alley, the Old Fire Tower, Last Chance Gulch, and the city's tree-lined Mansion District. Tours depart at 11am and 3pm June 1-14 and September 1-15; 11am, 1pm, and 3pm June 15-30; 9am, 11am, 1pm, and 3pm July-August. Plan to arrive 15 minutes before departure time for any tour.

Montana State Capitol

Visible for miles around with its weathered copper dome, the Montana State Capitol (1301 E. 6th Ave., 406/444-2694 or 406/444-4789, www.visit-the-capitol.mt.gov, 7am-6pm Mon.-Sat., 11am-5pm Sun.) unites Montana's past and present in a very ornate and interesting way. The building itself is something of a Greek Renaissance masterpiece. Started in 1898, the main portion of the building was completed in 1902, and the wings were unveiled 10 years later. The building is filled with dramatic art by some of Montana's most recognizable legends, among them Charles M. Russell and Edgar Paxson.

Self-guided tours are possible 9am-5pm daily. Guided tours (free) are offered on the hour 10am-2pm Monday-Saturday in summer and on the hour 10am-2pm Saturday only mid-September to mid-May. When the legislature is in session, in odd-numbered years, tours are offered 9am-2pm Monday-Saturday January-April. The capitol is always closed on state holidays and on Sunday when the legislature is in session.

Montana Historical Society

With a phenomenal collection spanning 12,000 years of history, the Montana Historical Society (225 N. Roberts St., 406/444-2964, www.montanahistoricalsociety.org, 8am-5pm Mon.-Sat., $5 adults, $1 children, $12 family) is the best historical resource in the state. Exhibits include an impressive art gallery, photo archives, a Native American collection, and decorative arts—more than 50,000 artifacts in all. A wonderful long-term exhibit explores what Montana must have been like at the time of Lewis and Clark. There are several special exhibits and traveling exhibits. The institution was founded in 1865, making it among the oldest of its kind in the western United States.

Original Governor's Mansion

Built in 1888 by a wealthy businessman, this Queen Anne-style mansion was owned by a number of important Helena residents before it was acquired by the state of Montana in 1913 as the Original Governor's Mansion (304 N. Ewing St., 406/444-4789, www.montanahistoricalsociety.org, guided tours hourly noon-3pm Tues.-Sat. summer, noon-3pm Sat. only mid-Sept.-mid-May, $4 adults, $1 children, $10 family, combination

1: Montana State Capitol building in Helena
2: St. Helena Cathedral 3: Helena at dusk

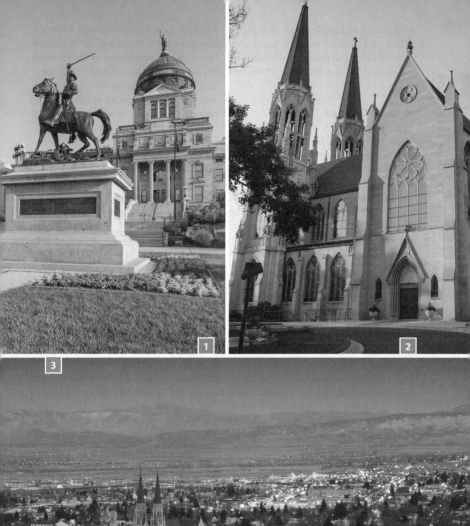

tickets for museum and tour $8 adults, $1.50 children, $19 family). Since 1959, the mansion has been owned, meticulously restored, and maintained by the Montana Historical Society.

★ Last Chance Gulch and Reeder's Alley

Rarely in the West have important gold or other mineral discovery sites gone on to become the center of big modern cities. Helena is an exception. Four prospectors (known as "the four Georgians") discovered gold in a small tributary of Ten Mile Creek. A mining camp quickly grew up around them, and the discovery site became the camp's main drag. Businesses sprouted up around the creek and never left.

Nearly 160 years after that first discovery, **Last Chance Gulch** (between W. 6th Ave. and Pioneer Park) is still at the heart of the city. But rather than a dusty collection of saloons and brothels, the area has been transformed into a marvelous pedestrian mall that includes dozens of great eateries, a few museums and galleries, wonderful shopping, and one of the most popular candy shops in the state. The area is even home to the **Last Chance Splash Waterpark and Pool** (1203 N. Last Chance Gulch, 406/447-1559, www.lastchancesplash.com, 12:15pm-7pm Mon.-Fri., 1pm-5pm Sat.-Sun., lap swim 9:30am-7pm Mon.-Fri., 1pm-5pm Sat.-Sun. mid-June-mid-Aug., $4.50 adults, $3.50 children 4-12 and seniors 65 and over, free for children 3 and under), a welcome stop on a hot day, only about 1 mile (1.6 km) from the mall. If your time in Helena is limited, Last Chance Gulch should be your first stop.

Nearby, **Reeder's Alley** (between S. Park Ave. and S. Benton Ave., across from Pioneer Park, www.reedersalley.com) is a unique little corner of downtown that reflects its more humble origins. The area has remained authentic visually, while some of the small miners' shacks, tenements, stables, and other buildings have been transformed into upscale shops and eateries. The

buildings have been designated a historic district on the National Register of Historic Places and are maintained by the Montana Heritage Commission (406/843-5247, www.montanaheritagecommission.mt.gov). Both areas are worth spending an afternoon or evening, enjoying a meal and some shopping.

Montana WILD

On the west side of Helena, near Spring Meadow Lake State Park, **Montana WILD** (2668 Broadwater Ave., 406/444-9944, http://fwp.mt.gov/education/montana-wild, 8am-5pm Mon.-Fri.) is the state's flagship education and conservation center, dedicated to all things wild. The 7,000-square-foot refurbished historic building sits on 5 acres and includes a wildlife rehabilitation center. Naturally a favorite destination with local schoolchildren, it's a great place to get an overview of the wildlife that lives in every corner of the state.

Great Northern Carousel and Exploration Works

The must-see corner of town for kids includes the **Great Northern Carousel** (989 Carousel Way, 406/457-5353, www.gncarousel.com, 12:30pm-7pm Wed.-Sun., $2), a modern, hand-built, Montana lovers' carousel with 37 animals including a grizzly bear, bobcats, bison, and trout; as well as the hands-on **Exploration Works** (995 Carousel Way, 406/457-1800, www.explorationworks.org, 10am-5pm Tues.-Sun., but call ahead or check the website for schedule changes, $7.50 general admission ages 2 and up). The museum is an interactive science center with frequently changing exhibits like space exploration, waterworks, and amazing airways. After you've exhausted your brain in the museum, head next door to the carousel for a leisurely ride and a fantastic ice-cream cone. It's kid paradise.

Tizer Botanic Gardens & Arboretum

Eighteen miles south of Helena is the tiny

town of Jefferson City and the surprisingly large and diverse **Tizer Botanic Gardens & Arboretum** (38 Tizer Lake Rd., Jefferson City, 406/933-8789, www.tizergardens.com, 10am-6pm daily Mother's Day-Oct. weather permitting, $9 adults, $7 children 5-12), a 6-acre garden and arboretum with stunning flower displays along the 0.5-mile (0.8-km) trail. It's one of only three internationally accredited privately owned arboreta in the United States, and the only full-time botanical garden in Montana. It's miraculous in this arid pine forest with Prickly Pear Creek running through to come upon such a lush and magical place. The staff is helpful in pointing out rare specimens. Attractions include a butterfly and hummingbird garden, a meditation garden, a secret garden, a shade garden, herb, vegetable, and rose gardens, test gardens, and a wildflower walk. The garden center shop is impressive, and you might be tempted to take home a rare tree. The gardens host special events throughout growing season, including high tea in the gardens on some Sundays, a fall color event, and an annual Fairy and Wizard Festival in late June that is a must for little ones. Tiny little cabins, like fairy cabins, allow you to stay overnight. It's just so surprising, this little place. And so lovely.

Broadwater Hot Springs

The only hot springs in Helena, **Broadwater Hot Springs** (4920 W. US 12, 406/443-5809, www.broadwatermt.com, 8am-10:30pm Mon.-Fri., 10am-10:30pm Sat.) is the perfect place to spend an afternoon. The natural artesian well has seasonal temperatures ranging 148-152°F (64.4-66.6°C), but the temperatures in the nicely lit outdoor pools range 81.5-99.5°F (27.5-37.5°C). The hot tubs range 103.2-106.5°F (39.5-41.4°C). The freeform pools have bench seating, which makes them ideal for soaking. There are also cold plunge pools and a rec pool for kids. A restaurant on-site, **The Springs Taproom** (11am-10pm daily, $9.50-14.50), serves standard pub fare—pizza, tacos, wings, sandwiches, and burgers—in a very cool setting. They also have beer, wine,

and cocktails. If you have your heart set on a soak, this is the place.

Marysville

Forty-five minutes northwest of Helena is the once-booming town of Marysville. The story is familiar: Gold was discovered in the 1880s, and a town grew up around it almost overnight until there were 4,000 souls eking a living out of the earth. Over the course of 20 years, the town exploded with dozens of businesses, including competing newspapers, a dozen saloons, three churches, two doctors, and two hotels. But by century's end, mining had all but ceased, and the prosperous town withered quickly as its residents fled elsewhere for opportunities.

Surprisingly, a great restaurant is to be found in the slowly decaying ghost town. **Marysville House** (153 Main St., 406/443-6677, www.marysvillehouse.com, bar opens 4pm, kitchen opens 5pm, "till closing" Wed.-Sun., $10-49) is a rustic but wonderful destination, an old train depot from Silver City, with good food in plentiful quantities. There is quite a selection of seafood and steaks, and the restaurant makes sure to point out that you won't need a salad with this meal. Dessert is roasted marshmallows over the bonfire out back. You won't find an experience like this anywhere else. To reach Marysville, take I-15 north to Highway 279 then west for 23 miles (37 km) and follow the signs for Marysville.

SPORTS AND RECREATION
Gates of the Mountains

Just outside Helena is one of the loveliest canyons in Montana. Named Gates of the Mountains by Lewis and Clark in 1805 because of the 1,200-foot (366-m) limestone cliffs that tower on either side of the Missouri River, it has become a favorite recreation area for Helena residents.

There are many ways to enjoy this scenic area on your own, but for those interested in tours, **Gates of the Mountains Boat Tours** (3131 Gates of the Mountains Rd., 20

The Fire at Mann Gulch

Not far from the Gates of the Mountains is a small but haunting little draw known as Mann Gulch. The tragedy at Mann Gulch happened on August 5, 1949, when a small fire grew with blistering hot winds into an inescapable wall of fire.

Fifteen U.S. Forest Service smokejumpers embarked on a fairly routine call that day. As they departed from their base in Missoula, temperatures in Helena hit 97°F (36°C) and the wind picked up. The cargo drop did not go as planned—heavy turbulence forced a higher than usual jump, the crew's radio was broken, and much of their equipment was scattered over a wide area—but within about an hour, by 5pm, the smokejumpers had gathered their gear, rendezvoused with a local recreation and fire prevention guard who had initially called in the fire, and headed down the slope toward the fire, which was burning up from the river. When their path to the Missouri River was blocked by fire around 5:30pm, the crew turned around and headed back uphill. At 5:53pm, with the fire rapidly gaining on them, foreman R. Wagner Dodge advised the firefighters to drop their tools in an attempt to speed their flight. The men were literally running up the mountain, a 76 percent grade in places, trying to escape 20-foot flames that were traveling an estimated 280-610 feet per minute. The fire was seconds away when, at 5:55pm, Dodge lit what has come to be known as an escape fire in an open grassy area. Despite his pleas for the men to stay with him in the burned-out area he was creating, the crew continued their mad dash uphill away from the flames. Thirteen of the men were overtaken and burned to death between 5:56 and 5:57pm. Dodge survived by lying in his burned-out area, although he was lifted off the ground three separate times by the wind created by the main fire. The only other survivors, Sallee and Rumsey, escaped by taking the shortest and steepest route through a crack in the rimrock to the summit.

The shocking tragedy—the first deaths in the relatively new field of smokejumping—was not without meaning. Copious research was done at the site to determine more about fire science and, in particular, firefighter safety. The best book on the subject is the posthumously published *Young Men and Fire* (1992) by legendary Montana writer Norman Maclean. Modern safety techniques—including safety zones, individual fire shelters, and survival training—were created in the aftermath of the disaster and are still relied on today. In August 1985, 73 firefighters were trapped while they fought a fire near Salmon, Idaho. Because of the knowledge that came out of the Mann Gulch tragedy, all 73 survived. It's worth noting that despite technology, no amount of experience can eliminate the danger from fighting unpredictable wildfires, something the nation learned again in the summer of 2013 with the tragic loss of 19 hotshots in Yarnell, Arizona.

Hikers and horseback riders can access Mann Gulch from three separate Forest Service trails leading from the north, east, and south end of the gulch. The trails range 7-18 miles (11.3-29 km) in length. For more information on the trails, contact the **U.S. Forest Service in Helena** (2880 Skyway Dr., 406/449-5201).

mi/32 km north of Helena at I-15 exit 209, 406/458-5241, www.gatesofthemountains.com, 8am-8pm daily) has 120-minute cruises ($16 adults 18-59, $14 seniors 60 and over, $10 children 4-17, free for children under 4, dinner cruise $54) from the marina; schedules change daily, so call or go online for details. Abundant wildlife inhabit the area, including bighorn sheep, mountain goats, and more than 120 bird species. You can bring a picnic lunch and get off the boat at Meriwether Picnic Area, returning later on another one.

It is also possible to hike from here to **Mann Gulch,** where 13 firefighters were killed by a fast-moving wildfire in 1949.

Canyon Ferry, Hauser, and Holter Lakes

All three lakes were created by dams on the Missouri River, and all three have become important recreational areas for people from all over southwest Montana.

South of Helena off US 287, **Canyon Ferry Lake** is the largest of the three and the newest, dating to the 1950s. Canyon Ferry covers 25 square miles and offers 80 miles (129 km) of shoreline along with endless boating and fishing opportunities. The nearby **Canyon Ferry Wildlife Management Area** provides habitat for a diversity of animals including foxes, moose, ospreys, and geese. Plentiful campgrounds and services are located around the lake, but things fill up quickly on hot summer weekends, so book in advance.

A scenic 3,200-acre reservoir 7 miles (11.3 km) north of Helena on I-15, then 4 miles (6.4 km) east on Highway 453 and 3 miles (4.8 km) north on a county road, **Hauser Lake** is home to record-breaking kokanee salmon, rainbow and brown trout, walleye, and perch. Two public campgrounds, **White Sandy Recreation Area** (6563 Hauser Dam Rd., 406/458-4744, 32 sites, $5-140) and **Black Sandy State Park** (406/495-3260, www.stateparks.mt.gov, $12-42 May-Nov., $8/vehicle nonresidents) offer terrific access to the reservoir.

Holter Lake (406/533-7600) is the most beautiful of the reservoir lakes, within view of the Gates of the Mountains north of Helena. There are three public campgrounds and recreation areas along the shoreline, designated swimming areas, two boat ramps, and plenty of fish waiting to be caught. From Helena, take I-15 north toward Great Falls to exit 226 at Wolf Creek. Turn right toward Recreation Road, then left onto Recreation Road. After crossing over the bridge, turn right on Beartooth Road and continue 2.3 miles (3.7 km) to Holter Lake Campground.

Skiing

Despite the fact that Helena is rather dry compared to many parts of Montana, it does have a pretty impressive ski hill when the weather cooperates. **Great Divide** (7385 Belmont Dr., Marysville, 406/449-3746, www.skigd.com, $56 adults, $44 students and military, $20 seniors 70 and up and children grades 1-5, free for preschoolers, $12 lighted night skiing on Fridays) has 140 trails and four terrain parks spread across three peaks and three valleys. There is terrain for everyone from toddlers testing out their ski legs to triple-black-diamond adrenaline junkies. The mountain is 23 miles (37 km) northwest of Helena.

Horseback Riding

Set in the Helena National Forest with 360-degree mountain views, **Summer Star Ranch** (7451 Owl Gulch Rd., Helena, 406/461-2659, www.summerstarranch.com, Apr.-Oct.,

Gates of the Mountains signage post

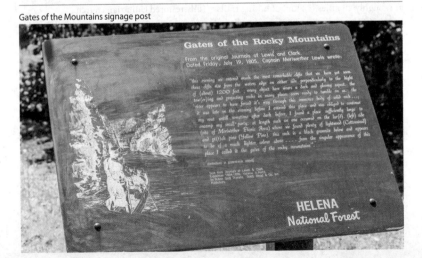

reservations required, 1-hour ride from $80 pp for 2 or more riders or $95 for single rider, 90-minute ride $110 pp for 2 or more riders or $135 for single rider, 2-hour ride $140 pp for 2 or more riders or $170 for single rider) is a great place to get out of town for a horseback ride on trails that are only open to horses. There's lots of opportunity to see wildlife, and the scenery is enough to take your breath away. They also offer sunset rides. The ranch provides housing, either cozy cabins or glamping tents, and plenty of couples decide that this is the best place in the world to tie the knot.

Hiking

Considered by many to be the best urban hiking trail in the state, the more than 7-mile (11.3-km) one-way trail along the **Mount Helena Ridge** leads gradually up and along the forested ridge overlooking the Helena Valley. It can be accessed 5 miles (8 km) south of town from the Park City trailhead or in town at the Mount Helena trailhead: Drive south on Park Avenue until you see the sign for Mount Helena City Park. Drive through the Reeders Village subdivision to get to the parking lot. Arrange a shuttle (or turn around partway) if you don't want to hike the full 14.8 miles (23.8 km) round-trip. If you depart from the Mount Helena parking area, there are roughly 20 miles (32 km) of hiking trails in the 620-acre park to explore. For more information, contact the **Helena Ranger District** (2880 Skyway Dr., 406/449-5490, www.fs.usda.gov).

ENTERTAINMENT AND EVENTS
The Arts

In a town that is becoming known for its art, the **Holter Museum of Art** (12 E. Lawrence St., 406/442-6400, www.holtermuseum.org, 10am-5:30pm Tues.-Sat., noon-4pm Sun., free) is a fascinating place to spend some time. The building was constructed in 1914 and expanded in 1999 to add 6,000 square feet of gallery space. The museum's contemporary collection includes art in a variety of media displayed in over 25 exhibitions annually, creating a unique voice in the Northwest art scene. The museum makes art education a priority and has managed to keep admission free.

Another cutting-edge artists workshop and gallery is the **Archie Bray Foundation** (2915 Country Club Ave., 406/443-3502, www.archiebray.org, 11am-5pm Mon.-Sat. year-round and noon-4pm Sun. June-Aug., free), an international hotbed of ceramic art in what was once a brick factory. Hundreds of well-known artists have come to work and exhibit here. Their annual **Brickyard Bash** in late July combines fabulous art with live music to raise money for the foundation. Classes and workshops are available for people of all ages and abilities, and some of the studio spaces are open to visitors. The grounds are open daily, year-round, during daylight hours.

There are two marvelous theaters in town that host both musical and dramatic events. The **Myrna Loy Center for the Performing Arts** (15 N. Ewing St., 406/443-0287, www.myrnaloycenter.com) presents contemporary media and performing arts from its glorious theater in the castle-like old county jail. The **Grandstreet Theatre** (325 N. Park Ave., 406/442-4270, www.grandstreettheatre.com) presents classic plays and musicals in a beautifully restored Unitarian church.

Festivals and Events

For a full listing of daily events in Helena, visit www.helenamt.com or www.helenaevents.com.

There's something going on in Helena just about every day when the summer sun is out. Mondays bring **Mondays at the Myrna** (15 N. Ewing St., 406/443-0287, www.myrnaloycenter.com), featuring a broad lineup of live music, from funk and folk to electro-pop. Every Wednesday throughout summer, a different block of Helena comes to life for **Alive at 5** (406/447-1535, www.downtownhelena.com, 5pm-9pm June-Aug.), a fun and family-oriented event that combines live music, food, and

Boulder Hot Springs and Radon Mines

In a town that is somewhat jokingly referred to by locals as "Institutionville" for its plethora of, well, institutions (the Montana Developmental Center, Intensive Behavior Center, Elkhorn Treatment Center, and Riverside Youth Correctional, to name a few), Boulder is home to some fascinating therapies indeed.

Indisputably, one of the best is the mineral-rich water at **Boulder Hot Springs** (31 Hot Springs Rd., 406/225-4339, www.boulderhotsprings.com, call ahead as hours vary daily and seasonally and the pools were open during COVID by appointment only Wed.-Sun., $8 adults 13 and over, $6 seniors 60 and over, $4 children 3-12), a historical gem about 30 miles (48 km) south of Helena off Highway 69. Backing on the Beaverhead-Deerlodge National Forest, the landmark inn was first built as a bathhouse and saloon in 1863 by a prospector who hoped to lure local miners in for a warm bath and a cold drink or two. The Victorian hotel was built in 1881 and enlarged in 1890. In 1910, under the eye of a Butte millionaire and banker, the hotel was renovated and redecorated in Spanish mission style by a snazzy New York firm. The hotel and hot springs attracted presidents and celebrities, among them Teddy Roosevelt. After countless owners and some neglect, including a temporary closure in the late 1980s, the hotel has been renovated (although not to its former glory, it must be noted) and updated, and it provides guests with simple accommodations, fantastic food, and some of the best soaking waters anywhere.

There are both indoor plunge pools and an outdoor swimming pool, varying in temperature 70-106°F (21-41°C). The indoor pools are separate for men and women and are bathing-suit-optional, giving it almost a European feel. The water is constantly moving, replenishing itself every four hours, so no chemicals are needed. Steam rooms also are available on both the men's and women's sides. Spa services, including massages, are also among the amenities.

The rooms are simple and "technology-free," and the focus here is truly on healing. Bed-and-breakfast rooms range $99-139 and include a full nutritious breakfast. Guest rooms without breakfast, and often with shared bath, range $65-70 for a single and $85-90 for a double and are more basic than the B&B rooms.

Slightly more controversial than the soothing hot springs waters are the **radon mines** in Boulder, which many people believe are the best alternative treatment for relieving chronic pain and diseases that range from gout and lupus to eczema, asthma, arthritis, and even cancer. There are a number of radon mines in town thanks to an abundance of the natural radioactive gas. One of the oldest is the **Free Enterprise Radon Health Mine** (149 Depot Hill Rd., 406/225-3383, hours vary, by appointment, $8 for 1 hour, $275 for unlimited hours over 10 days), founded in 1924 as a silver and lead mine. Visitors travel in an Otis elevator 85 feet (26 m) below the surface to sit or sleep and breathe in the radon. There is even a special area for pets to be treated. Wireless Internet is available even underground, and motel accommodations are available for those undergoing full treatment.

drink for a fantastic summer evening. And on Thursdays, crowds show up at the Great Northern Town Center amphitheater for **Out to Lunch** (40 W. 14th St., 406/447-5542, www.greatnortherntowncenter.com, 11:30am-1:30pm Thurs. June-Aug., free), with food vendors and live music. Happening the first Friday of every month is **First Friday** (406/447-1535, www.downtownhelena.com, 5pm-9pm), which invites visitors to explore downtown shops, galleries, and restaurants.

Once each summer, in mid- to late July,

the Helena Symphony joins Carroll College in presenting **Symphony Under the Stars** (406/442-1860, www.helenasymphony.org, date varies, show starts 8:30pm, free) on the hillside at Carroll College. Concerts feature classical, opera, or Broadway-oriented music, and all of them end with a spectacular fireworks display.

In late July—or sometimes early August—Helena puts on the annual **Last Chance Stampede and Fair** (98 W. Custer Ave., 406/457-8516, www.

lewisandclarkcountyfairgrounds.com) at the fairgrounds. In addition to big country-music concerts, the fair holds a rodeo, a carnival, food, and a variety of entertainment.

In mid-August, bikers and beer drinkers will revel in the combination of the **Bike Helena Shuttle Fest** (various locations, www.helenamt.com/bike-helena, see website for locations and schedule) and **Montana Brewer's Association Summer Rendezvous** (Memorial Park in Last Chance Gulch, 406/948-2739, www.montanabrewers. org, 4pm-8pm, call or visit website for locations and details, tickets $35-45). The Shuttle Fest celebrates the city's incredible mountain-biking trails and their unique free trail rider shuttle by offering free continuous shuttles for hikers and bikers to the city's best trails. And then comes the beer drinking. The Rendezvous offers live music and plenty of opportunities to taste the local brews.

SHOPPING

Eaton Turner Jewelry (1735 N. Montana Ave., 406/442-1940, www.eatonturnerjewelry. com, 10am-5:30pm Mon.-Fri.) is the oldest jeweler in the state and has been family owned and operated since 1885. History aside, this is a special store and offers a great selection of jewelry, including local stones like Montana and Yogo sapphires.

A wonderful independent bookstore, **Montana Book & Toy Co.** (25 S. Last Chance Gulch, 406/442-1594, www.mtbookco.com, 9:30am-6pm Mon.-Fri., 9:30am-5pm Sat.) offers a diverse collection of books for all readers and children's toys. Another fabulous toy store in the walking mall is **Lasso the Moon Wonderful Toys** (331 N. Last Chance Gulch, www.lassothemoontoys.com, 10am-5:30pm Mon.-Fri., 10am-4pm Sat.), which sells toys that are environmentally conscious, socially responsible, and most of all fun. As important as a bookshop or a toy store, every town worth its salt needs a good thrift shop. In Helena, it's **Funky Trunk New Liberated Consigned** (430 N. Last Chance Gulch, 406/422-4210, 10am-6pm Mon.-Sat., 11am-4pm Sun.), which

boasts a terrific selection of used, vintage, and consigned clothes, shoes, and accessories.

The **General Mercantile** (413 N. Last Chance Gulch, 406/442-6078, www. generalmerc.com, 8am-5pm Mon.-Fri., 9am-5pm Sat., 11am-4pm Sun.) is like a step back in time. The Merc serves every variety of coffee and tea, including espresso from vintage machines, and there are all sorts of cozy nooks to sip a latte while perusing a book. The store has gifts and cards galore, but it's the atmosphere in the Merc that makes it so welcoming. Also a great spot for gifts, **Eureka!** (38 S. Last Chance Gulch, 406/437-1859, www. wildflowerhelena.com, 11am-6pm daily) stocks everything from clothing to home and kitchen wares, to toiletries and candles, much of it designed in Montana.

Another unique destination in Helena is **LizE Designs Artscapes** (330 Fuller Ave., 406/459-4081, 10am-5:30pm Wed.-Fri., 10am-4pm Sat.), which sells fine and funky art as well as one-of-a-kind gifts, many crafted from found objects. In addition to her own mixed-media work, Liz showcases various guest artists who work in raku pottery, photography, painting, and jewelry, among other media.

For an experience you can't get many other places, visit **Spokane Bar Sapphire Mine & Gold Fever Rock Shop** (5360 Castles Rd., 877/344-4367 or 406/227-8989, www. sapphiremine.com, 9am-5pm daily in summer), where you can dig for your own sapphires, garnets, rubies, jasper, agates, jade, and quartz. The shop will provide you with bags of gravel and a screen to help you sift, or for $60, you can fill your own 3.5-gallon bucket and sift through it. Most of the gemstones are small, but occasionally people do find big ones. And all of them are beautiful, regardless of size. The shop also sells jewelry and gifts.

For a real taste of Montana, look no further than **The Parrot Confectionery** (42 N. Last Chance Gulch, 406/442-1470, www.parrotchocolate.com, 9am-6pm Mon.-Sat.), an absolute Montana standard when it comes to candy shops and diners. The shop makes 130 different varieties of candy, and its reputation for hand-dipped chocolates has won customers worldwide. Try a cherry phosphate from the original soda fountain, and sit up at the bar for a bowl of the secret-recipe chili. A local favorite since 1922, The Parrot should not be missed.

FOOD

For a quick bite between sights, and breakfast all day, try **Steve's Café** (1225 E. Custer, 406/444-5010, and 630 N. Montana Ave., 406/449-6666, www.stevescafe.com, 6:30am-2:30pm Wed.-Sun., $5-14) for wonderful huckleberry pancakes, breakfast burritos, steak and eggs, burgers, sandwiches, and the like. A secret menu offers specialties like pork verde chilaquiles, Irish eggs Benedict, a BLT wrap, and more. Just ask! Another good spot for a quick bite is **The Dive Bakery & Café** (1609 11th Ave., 406/442-2802, www.thedivebakery.com, 6:30am-2:30pm Mon.-Fri., $3.75-6.25), which is known for its from-scratch pastries, bread, and soup, plus delicious crepes and salads. They also serve espresso drinks.

For the best artisan bread in town (or maybe anywhere) try **Park Avenue Bakery** (44 S. Park Ave., 406/449-8424, www.parkavenuebakery.net, 7am-5pm Mon.-Sat., 8am-1pm Sun., breakfast and lunch $4-8), where you can fill up on gorgeous European-style breads, pastries, pizza, quiche, calzones, and homemade soups, salads, and dessert. Another wonderful bakery in town is **Sunflower Bakery** (1442 Euclid Ave., www.sunflowerbakerymt.com, 7:30am-5pm Wed.-Fri., 7:30am-1:30pm Sat.), which uses organic flour in their various sourdough breads and pastries. They serve coffee and tea, quiche, and soup, and are looking to add more lunch options.

No longer downtown, but still incredibly delicious and worth the drive if you are craving Southwestern food, ★ **Karmadillo's Southwestern Café** (451 Spencer Ct., 406/422-2595, 11am-8pm Tues.-Thurs., 11am-9pm Fri.-Sat., $5.75-13) serves all slow-cooked meats and beans

with salsas and crèmes prepared fresh daily. Lunch options include nachos, homemade chicken tortilla soup, tacos, enchiladas, and even a savory barbecue-beef sandwich. Dinner offers some of the same items as well as tamales, chiles rellenos, and combo plates. As good as its slow-cooked meats are, Karmadillo's also has vegetarian items and a children's menu. Check their Facebook page for the code word of the day to receive free chips and salsa. Barbecue lovers will delight in the offerings at **Bad Betty's Barbecue** (812 Front St., 406/459-2303, www.badbettysbarbecue.com, 11am-3pm Tues.-Wed. and Sat., 11am-7pm Thurs.-Fri., $7-15), which serves mouthwatering barbecue from brisket and pulled pork to chicken and ribs. They have daily specials, too, including street tacos, brisket burnt ends, and barbecue nachos.

For fine dining in Helena, **On Broadway** (106 Broadway, 406/443-1929, www.onbroadwayinhelena.com, 5pm-9:30pm Mon.-Thurs., 5pm-10pm Fri.-Sat., $20-31) is the elegant favorite, with mouthwatering pasta dishes, steaks, and seafood, and live jazz on Thursday evenings. For great Italian food, **Lucca's** (56 N. Last Chance Gulch, 406/457-8311, www.luccasitalian.com, 5pm-8:30pm Sun. and Thurs., 5pm-9pm Wed. and Fri.-Sat., $22-34) is a gustatory delight. For a really fancy Montana dinner in a beautiful setting, **Wassweiler Dinner House and Pub** (4528 US 12, 406/502-1303, www.wassweiler.com, 5pm-8:30pm Wed.-Thurs., 5pm-9pm Sat.-Sun., $22-70) is a real treat. Not far from Broadwater Hot Springs, the building was built in 1883 as an inn and bathhouse. Everything about the experience will be elegant. With such entrées as duck breast, bison sirloin, cowboy cut rib eye, and seafood pasta, the dishes are as wonderful to look at as they are to eat. Save room for dessert.

Another nice spot just off Last Chance Gulch is ★ **Benny's Bistro** (108 E. 6th St., 406/443-0105, www.bennyshelena.com, 11am-3pm Tues., 11am-3pm and 5pm-9pm Wed.-Sat., lunch $11-15, dinner $17-34). Set in a renovated historic building, Benny's does a phenomenal job of catering to the "locavore" movement by using as many fresh, locally grown ingredients as possible. Its list of Montana suppliers is vast. You can taste the best of the state in dishes like Montana-raised beef stroganoff, ginger-rubbed Montana pork loin, a local cheese board, Flathead cherry salad, and scratch-made fettuccine with chicken from the Hutterite colony. This is Montana cuisine at its best.

In the heart of the walking mall in what was Helena's last brothel, the **Windbag Saloon & Grill** (19 S. Last Chance Gulch, 406/443-3520, www.windbag406.com, 11am-midnight Mon.-Thurs., 10am-midnight Fri.-Sat., $10-17) serves burgers named after Montana politicians, sandwiches, seven different kinds of mac and cheese, plus wings, and standard bar fare. You can order funnel fries for dessert, which are funnel cakes cut into fries and drizzled with chocolate and caramel.

ACCOMMODATIONS

While Helena is long on hotels (perhaps for all the legislators who come to govern for four months every other year), most fall into the category of nice upscale chain hotels or nice upscale bed-and-breakfasts.

Still, there are plenty of nice rooms all around town. The **Best Western Premier Great Northern** (835 Great Northern Blvd., 406/457-5500 or 800/780-7234, $152-360) is shiny and new, with decor intended to conjure the Great Northern Railway days. It has all the amenities you could want in a city hotel, and small pets (under 25 pounds/11.3 kg) are welcome for $15 per night per animal for up to two animals. The hotel is ideally located in the **Great Northern Town Center** within walking distance of an eight-plex theater, shopping, a children's museum and carousel, and the walking mall at Last Chance Gulch.

Closer to the highway is the **Delta Hotels Helena Colonial** (2301 Colonial Dr., 406/443-2100, www.marriott.com, $166-364), a large, full-service, very comfortable hotel.

Additional chain hotels and motels lining the major thoroughfares include the pet-friendly **Baymont by Wyndham** (750 Fee St., 406/558-4756, www.wyndhamhotels. com, $68-130), the **Comfort Suites Helena Airport** (3180 N. Washington St., 406/513-1140, www.choicehotels.com, $127-208), **Days Inn by Wyndham** (2001 Prospect Ave., 406/442-3280, www.wyndhamhotels.com, $65-179), **Holiday Inn Express & Suites** (3170 N. Sanders St., 406/442-7500, www. ihg.com, $126-183), and **Super 8** (2200 11th Ave., 406/209-8571, www.wyndhamhotels. com, from $86). Situated right downtown in the heart of Last Chance Gulch is the pet-friendly **DoubleTree by Hilton Helena Downtown** (22 N. Last Chance Gulch, 406/443-2200, www.doubletree3.hilton.com, $132-225). One of the newest hotels in town is **Home2 Suites by Hilton** (3325 N. Sanders, 406/502-2222, www.hilton.com, $105-170). A far cry from a chain hotel, but cozy, clean, and adorable, the **Lamplighter Cabins & Suites** (1006 Madison Ave., 406/442-9200, www. lamplighterhelena.com, $115-189) have lots of character and local owners who can point you anywhere you want to go.

For a more historic option near downtown and the state capitol, **The Sanders, Helena's Bed and Breakfast** (328 N. Ewing St., 406/442-3309, www.sandersbb.com, $175-225) offers seven guest rooms in a beautifully appointed 1875 Queen Anne mansion. Many of the furnishings are original to the home, and the owners, Rock and Bobbi, are gracious and so welcoming. The breakfasts are healthy and delicious, with plenty of protein. You will be well taken care of at Sanders. Another charming and unique option for accommodations in Helena is the historic ★ **Oddfellow Inn & Farm** (2245 Head Ln., 406/578-1305, www.mt.farm, call for room options and prices, packages from $295 for 2 people including breakfast and dinner). The stately brick building was constructed in 1928 as a home for retirees, widows, and orphans. The rooms are simple, without televisions, but very inviting. There are also a variety of other accommodations including a tiny house and glamping tent. As the Oddfellow is situated on a working farm just 10 minutes from downtown, there is a wonderful farm-to-table French Bistro in the inn, **Maison** (brunch 11am-3pm Sun., $19-29, farmer's table experience 6pm Fri.-Sat., $149 pp, additional $49 pp wine pairing), which opened in 2020. The farmer's table experience happens on Friday and Saturday nights with one seating at 6pm. It's a four-course chef's tasting menu highlighting ingredients from the farm and local producers. Dessert is served outdoors, under the moonlight, in the company of the farm animals. This will be a place, an evening, and a meal to remember.

INFORMATION AND SERVICES

A good source of visitor information is the **Helena Chamber of Commerce** (225 Cruse Ave., 406/442-4120 or 800/743-5362, www.helenachamber.com, 8am-5pm Mon.-Thurs., 8am-4pm Fri.). A terrific website for planning a trip to Helena is www.helenamt. com. The site allows you to plug in your dates of travel and shows you all the available hotels and their average nightly rates.

The **main post office** (406/443-3304, 8am-6pm Mon.-Fri., 9am-noon Sat.) is at 2300 North Harris Street, and the **Lewis and Clark Library** (406/447-1690, www. lewisandclarklibrary.org, 10am-8pm Mon.-Fri., 1pm-5pm Sat.-Sun.) is at 120 South Last Chance Gulch.

St. Peter's Hospital (2475 E. Broadway, 406/457-4180, www.stpetes.org) has a 24-hour emergency room. The hospital also runs the **St. Peter's Urgent Care Clinic** (2475 Broadway, 406/447-2488, www.stpetes. org, 9am-8pm daily) and **North Clinic** (3330 Ptarmigan Ln., 406/495-7901, www.stpetes. org, 7am-6pm daily).

The **Little Dipper Laundromat** (1411 11th Ave., 6am-10pm Mon.-Sat., 7am-10pm Sun.) is attached to a bagel shop if you get hungry.

TRANSPORTATION
Getting There

The **Helena Regional Airport** (HLN, 2850 Skyway Dr., 406/442-2821, www. helenaairport.com) is just 2.5 miles (4 km) from the city center and is served by Delta/SkyWest, Alaska/Horizon, and United. The car-rental agencies at the airport are **Alamo, Avis, Budget, Hertz,** and **National. Enterprise Rental Car** has an off-airport location.

Shuttles to the airport are provided by hotels in town. The courtesy phone to contact them is located in the baggage claim area.

Greyhound (1415 N. Montana Ave., 406/447-8078) runs several bus routes to and from nearby cities, including Bozeman, Billings, and Butte.

Helena is accessible from I-15, US 12, and US 287. The city is 68 miles (109 km) north of Butte and 115 miles (185 km) southeast of Missoula.

Getting Around

Capital Transit (406/447-8080, www. ridethecapitalt.org, $0.85 single ride, $2.60 all-day pass) operates fixed route bus service (7am-6pm Mon.-Fri.), with nine loops around the city.

Helena Taxi (406/407-2738, www. helenataxi.com) offers standard taxi service. **Helena Towncar** (406/437-8585, www. helenatowncar.com) is another option. **Uber** and **Lyft** also offer service in Helena now.

Bozeman and Big Sky

The gateway to the nation's first national park, south-central Montana is a playground bursting with mountains to climb, rivers to fish, and trails to hike.

This region is home to a number of noteworthy mountain towns, including Bozeman, Big Sky, and Red Lodge. Big Timber, Livingston, and Three Forks offer more of a big plains culture despite their immediate proximity to some very impressive mountains.

The diversity of the region's geography and climate allows for a compelling range of activities. From Bozeman, you can drive 30 miles (48 km) west and hike the sacred ground at Madison Buffalo Jump State Park; head just 15 miles (24 km) south from there and you can fish along the Madison River. Just a few miles north of Bozeman is Bridger

Highlights

Look for ★ to find recommended sights, activities, dining, and lodging.

★ **Museum of the Rockies:** Renowned for its impressive dinosaur collection, this museum is also home to a planetarium and a living history farm (page 277).

★ **Emerson Center for the Arts and Culture:** A 1900s school rehabbed as an arts hub, the Emerson has more than 30 studios, a fab restaurant, and special events (page 279).

★ **Madison Buffalo Jump State Park:** A hike on this cliff is a lesson in Native American history and, if you're lucky, an exercise in solitude (page 279).

★ **Floating the Madison River:** This river's warm water is perfect for floaters, weaving through beautiful rolling terrain (page 283).

★ **Chico Hot Springs Resort:** Chico has all the trappings of a resort—hiking, riding, pool, day spa, and sumptuous cuisine—with none of the attitude (page 308).

★ **Beartooth Scenic Highway and Pass:** This highway offers room for spontaneous adventures. Bring your bike, hiking boots, binoculars, and even your skis on this summit-topping stunner (page 312).

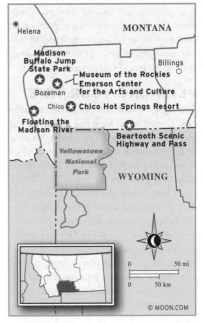

Canyon and the legendary Bridger Bowl, where you can ski deep powder on the ridge. Or head 20 miles (32 km) south of town to find yourself up Hyalite Canyon, an impressive recreation area known for its challenging ice climbs. All of these activities are possible in the same month, March; few regions in the state allow you to choose your season as easily as your activities.

While the main draw is the natural splendor and recreational opportunities, as well as the high probability of sunny weather to enjoy them, there are a multitude of ways to get to know this area: The Sweet Pea Festival of the Arts in Bozeman, the Fourth of July Rodeo in Livingston, and the "Running of the Sheep" in normally sleepy Reed Point show that south-central Montana is a distinctive blend of the Old and New West. As the hub of the region and the home of Montana State University, Bozeman is an increasingly sophisticated mountain town with a rapidly growing population of outdoor junkies, active college students, old-time cowboys, blissed-out transplants, and, more recently, COVID refugees.

PLANNING YOUR TIME

This region is vast and can require significant driving to get from one destination to the next. With its fairly central location, ease of air or highway access, and abundance of accommodations, **Bozeman** is a superb launching point for the region. You could easily spend three days here, checking out the arts scene and nightlife and enjoying the spectacular recreational opportunities in every direction. Nearby **Big Sky** is a popular destination for skiing in winter as well as for biking, hiking, and horseback riding in summer. **Three Forks** and **Manhattan** offer an excellent taste of small-town Montana and are worthwhile stops, especially if you can be there for a favorite local event: Manhattan's

Potato Festival in late August, or Three Forks' **Christmas Stroll.**

Just over the pass from Bozeman is **Livingston,** a small but vibrant community with a lot of character (and plenty of characters). You could happily spend a morning or afternoon browsing the shops and galleries downtown, and Livingston has an inordinate number of excellent restaurants to sample. The town explodes with enthusiasm and visitors over the **Fourth of July,** and if you can secure a parking spot for the parade and a ticket to the rodeo, dealing with the crowds (this is Montana, remember) will be well worth the effort.

Aptly named **Paradise Valley** links Livingston with the northernmost entrance to Yellowstone National Park at Gardiner. The mountains are spectacular and beg to be hiked. **Chico Hot Springs Resort** is the place to stay and boasts some of the best dining in the state and a long list of activities.

The plains seem to unfurl themselves, green and then golden, as you drive from Livingston through **Big Timber.** Anyone interested in Norwegian immigrant history in Montana should not miss the **Crazy Mountain Museum,** and a meal at the historic **Grand Hotel** right downtown is a treat. In **Columbus** the sheer bulk of the Beartooths dominates the horizon. There are wonderful side trips en route: a riverside hike in the **West Boulder Valley,** and if you time it right (Labor Day Sunday), the **Great Montana Sheep Drive** in Reed Point.

Red Lodge is itself a wonderful destination for skiers, bikers, hikers, and even driving enthusiasts who want to tackle the **Beartooth Highway.** It would be an easy and worthwhile place to spend a couple of days before heading back to civilization in Billings or Bozeman, or into the wilds of Yellowstone through the northeast entrance at Cooke City.

Previous: Beartooth Scenic Highway; Missouri Headwaters State Park in Three Forks; a guest ranch near Big Sky.

Bozeman and the Gateway to Yellowstone

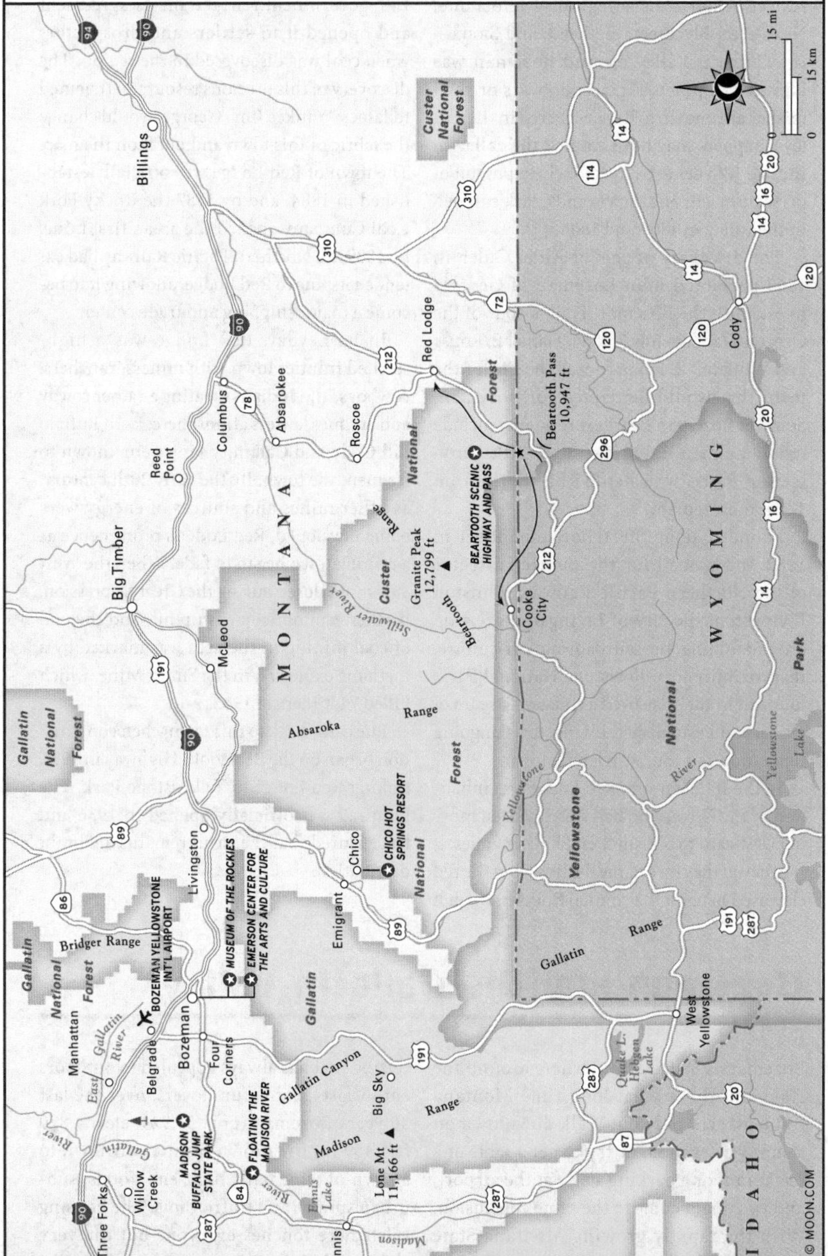

15 mi

15 km

0

Billings

Custer National Forest

Custer National Forest

Reed Point

Big Timber

Columbus

Absarokee

Roscoe

Red Lodge

Cody

Beartooth Pass 10,947 ft

BEARTOOTH SCENIC HIGHWAY AND PASS

Granite Peak 12,799 ft

Custer National Forest

Stillwater River

Cooke City

Beartooth

WYOMING

MONTANA

McLeod

Absaroka

Range

Gallatin National Forest

Gallatin National Forest

Yellowstone National Park

Yellowstone River

Yellowstone Lake

Chico

CHICO HOT SPRINGS RESORT

Livingston

MUSEUM OF THE ROCKIES

EMERSON CENTER FOR THE ARTS AND CULTURE

BOZEMAN YELLOWSTONE INT'L AIRPORT

Emigrant

Bridger Range

Gallatin

National

Forest

Manhattan

Belgrade

Bozeman

Four Corners

FLOATING THE MADISON RIVER

Gallatin Canyon

Big Sky

Range

West Yellowstone

Quake L. Hebgen Lake

East Gallatin River

Gallatin River

MADISON BUFFALO JUMP STATE PARK

Willow Creek

Three Forks

Madison River

Lone Mt 11,166 ft

Madison

Ennis Lake

Ennis

IDAHO

© MOON.COM

HISTORY

Called the "Valley of the Flowers" by the Native Americans—including Shoshone, Nez Perce, Blackfeet, Flathead, and Sioux—the Gallatin Valley around Bozeman was known as a peaceful place; no wars or skirmishes are known to have occurred in the valley. Trappers may have entered the valley in the late 18th century, most likely in pursuit of prized beaver pelts. Lewis and Clark camped in the valley in 1805 and 1806.

The discovery of gold at Alder Gulch in 1863 prompted John Bozeman of Georgia to establish the Bozeman Trail, a spur of the Oregon Trail. On July 7, 1864, Daniel E. Rouse and William J. Beall proposed the site for the town that would be named for Bozeman. Some of Bozeman's earliest residents include mountain man Jim Bridger and cattle baron Nelson Story, who herded his cattle from Texas to Bozeman.

Founded along the Yellowstone River in 1882 and named for the pioneer director of the Northern Pacific Railway, Johnston Livingston, the city of Livingston grew up around mining, the railroad, and agriculture. Its proximity to Yellowstone National Park, founded in 1872, ensured a constant stream of visitors and established Livingston's ongoing reputation as a tourist-friendly town.

In the 18th century, Red Lodge was inhabited by the Crow, who had steadily been moving westward to outrun their Sioux enemies. It is believed the city's name derives from the red clay used to paint the council tipi. Although it was part of the territory assigned to the Crow Nation by the 1851 Fort Laramie Treaty, the U.S. government reneged on its agreement and opened it to settlers and prospectors when coal was discovered in the region. The discovery of this precious resource, attributed to James "Yankee Jim" George, would change the fabric of this town and put it on the map. The town of Red Lodge was officially established in 1884, and by 1887 the Rocky Fork Coal Company opened the area's first mine. By 1889 the Northern Pacific Railway had extended its line to Red Lodge, allowing it to become a major shipping and trade center.

In its heyday, Red Lodge was a high-spirited frontier town with miners, ranchers, cowboys, and Indians creating a rather rowdy and at times lawless atmosphere. Both Buffalo Bill Cody and Calamity Jane were known to frequent the town. By the early 20th century, as other mines and sources of energy were being developed, Red Lodge's prominence as a mining town began to fade. When the West Side mine closed during the Great Depression, further economic hardship hit, and the end of coal mining in the area was marked by a methane explosion in the Smith Mine, which killed 74 miners in 1943.

Life came back to this town when construction began on the Beartooth Highway in 1931, linking Red Lodge to Yellowstone Park. The highway was officially opened in 1936 and has ensured that the town remains a vibrant destination.

Bozeman and the Gallatin Valley

Bozeman is lost. Ask anywhere around the state and that's what long-time Montana residents will tell you. Walk downtown on a sunny afternoon, or try to get a table at a restaurant or a parking space at the airport, and you might come to the same conclusion. With the rapidly growing Montana State University anchoring it and a geographical setting that has always appealed to outdoors enthusiasts and nature lovers, over the last 30 years Bozeman (pop. 53,923, elev. 4,820 ft/1,469 m) has grown from a cow town to a town of wine bars, high-end hotels, suburban sprawl, and traffic jams. The housing crisis here touches everyone but the very rich. And there are plenty of those folks here now. Whereas Bozeman used to be an ag community, a place where a 6am counter stool at the Cowboy Café was at the center of things, today it is a vacation mecca, an escape from other hotter places, a place where you can see a woman on the sidewalk in January in fuzzy mules, a fur coat but no pants, cell phone glued to her head, waiting for her toy Chihuahua to pee. "Bozangeles," some call it, both ironically and not. The character of this town has changed. And not for the better, locals would argue. But who can blame them for coming? For the wide open space and access to public land, the laid-back lifestyle, and the beauty. Oh the beauty. It's what people realized they wanted in the pandemic, and so they came. And they haven't stopped.

That said (and it's plenty, I know), the historic downtown is still the heart of this community and attracts crowd-wary locals for numerous special events. A growing number of excellent restaurants and bars appeal to everyone from broke and thirsty college students to whiskey and wine connoisseurs. A handful of galleries and some very unique shops round out downtown's offerings.

Although the city is expanding exponentially and is always on the list of Montana's fastest-growing cities, and Gallatin County (which encompasses the geography of Gallatin Valley) has been ranked the fastest-growing county in the country since 2018, the original draw—nature—is still intact, for now. Bridger Bowl and Big Sky are two excellent alpine skiing destinations nearby. The Gallatin, Madison, and Yellowstone Rivers, three blue-ribbon trout streams, are also nearby, in addition to numerous smaller streams. And there are literally hundreds of hiking and biking trails, enough to satisfy the most hard-core enthusiast.

SIGHTS
★ Museum of the Rockies

Best known for its paleontology exhibit curated by dinosaur guru Jack Horner, **Museum of the Rockies** (600 W. Kagy Blvd.,

406/994-2251, www.museumoftherockies.org, 8am-6pm daily Memorial Day-Labor Day, 9am-5pm Mon.-Sat., noon-5pm Sun. Labor Day-Memorial Day, $16.50 adults, $15.50 seniors 65 and over, $12 MSU students with ID, $10.50 children 5-17, free for children 4 and under) is a fantastic resource for the entire state. The museum tackles 500 million years of history, no small feat, with permanent exhibits that reflect Native American culture, 19th- to 20th-century regional history, an outdoor living history farm (open only in summer), a planetarium, and, of course, the dinosaurs.

The Siebel Dinosaur Complex includes hundreds of important fossils and an array of impressive life-size reproductions. The traveling exhibitions vary widely—think polar obsession, the villas of Oplontis near Pompeii, guitars, *National Geographic*'s 50 greatest photos, and even chocolate—but typically offer excellent contrast to the permanent exhibits.

The Martin Children's Discovery Center upstairs offers a great place for preschool and elementary schoolchildren to play in hands-on Yellowstone exhibits. They can camp in a tent, listen for the eruption of Old Faithful (beware—it's loud, surprising, and often scary for little ones), recline in an eagle's nest, cook up a feast in a log cabin, fish for magnetic fish, and dress up as a park ranger or firefighter. For kids with vivid imaginations, this may be the highlight of the museum. In addition, the museum offers several engaging classes for children as young as infants and excellent day camps for elementary age kids.

The gift shop is outstanding and includes a great selection of local jewelry, science-oriented toys, art, books, and even candy.

Some argue that the admission fees are too steep, particularly if you come when there is no traveling exhibit, but on a rainy day in Bozeman, the museum can provide hours of compelling exploration. Additionally, admission provides unlimited access for two consecutive days.

Bozeman

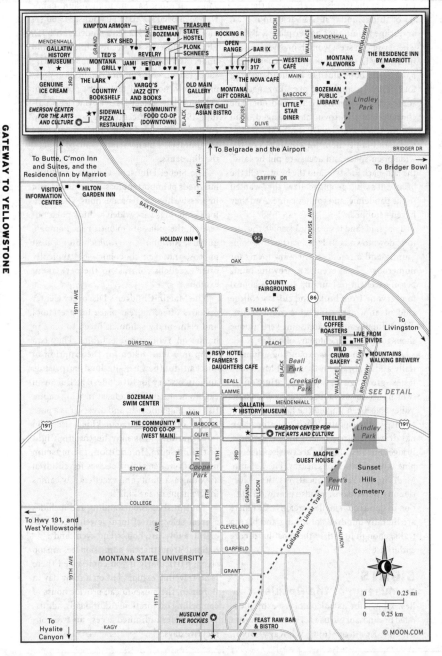

© MOON.COM

Downtown Bozeman

Historic downtown Bozeman is interesting architecturally and compelling culturally. It is without a doubt the heart and soul of the city, and more often than not it is the gathering point for the most celebrated events, including **Bite of Bozeman, Music on Main, Crazy Days,** various parades, and **Christmas Stroll.** Businesses have faced some stiff competition from big-box stores on the perimeter of town, and there is significant turnover in retail and restaurants, but local residents support downtown in meaningful ways, even starting a petition campaign to fight to keep staple businesses, like the Owenhouse Ace Hardware, on Main Street. For a list of businesses and a calendar of weekly, annual, and special events that really showcase Main Street, visit www.downtownbozeman.org.

Gallatin History Museum

Touted as the place "where history and Main Street meet," the **Gallatin History Museum** (317 W. Main St., 406/522-8122, www.gallatinhistorymuseum.org, 11am-4pm Tues.-Sat., $7.50 adults, $5 students 17 and over with ID, free for children under 17) is operated by the Gallatin Historical Society in Bozeman's 1911 county jail building. The museum shared space with the prisoners 1979-1982 before the current jail was completed. It boasts a comprehensive permanent collection of items that reflect Bozeman's early history, including an authentic 1870s homesteader's cabin, an agricultural room, substantial historical photographs, and a sheriff's room that houses plenty of artifacts and exhibits related to crime and punishment in the Old West. The Silsby Fire Engine, a top-of-the-line engine when it was manufactured in the late 1800s, is a favorite exhibit for kids. The museum offers weekly lectures, free with admission, throughout the summer.

★ Emerson Center for the Arts and Culture

Operated as an elementary school 1918-1991, the **Emerson Center for the Arts and Culture** (111 S. Grand Ave., 406/587-9797, www.theemerson.org), or The Emerson, as it is more commonly called, is the nucleus of Bozeman's robust arts scene. More than 30 studios, galleries, boutiques, and art-related businesses reside in the building in addition to Crawford Theater, one of the best in town, and an excellent restaurant, **Sidewall Pizza.** In summer, **Lunch on the Lawn** (11:30am-1:30pm Wed. July-Aug., free) is a Bozeman tradition with live music, food vendors, and lots of smiling faces.

★ Madison Buffalo Jump State Park

Farther afield but well worth the visit is **Madison Buffalo Jump State Park** (6990 Buffalo Jump Rd., 7 mi/11.3 km south of Logan off I-90, 406/285-3610, www.stateparks.mt.gov, sunrise-sunset daily, $8/vehicle nonresidents, $4/walk-in, bicycle, bus passenger). Used by Native Americans some 2,000 years ago (and as recently as 200 years ago), long before horses were brought to North America, buffalo jumps are a testament to human ingenuity. A small, covered interpretive display explains how Native Americans persuaded bison up the hill and off the cliff to their deaths, but the real lesson comes from hiking the trail (watch for rattlesnakes and cacti, both of which love the sun here) and exploring the site independently. Tipi rings can be identified, as can eagle-catching pits. Splinters of bison bone have been found at the base of the cliff. Aside from the compelling history of the area, the views from the top are magnificent and worth every step.

SPORTS AND RECREATION

Bozeman is a town of relatively young, active people, a fact that the infrastructure in town reflects.

Pools and Parks

The **Bozeman Swim Center** (1211 W. Main St., 406/582-2994, www.bozeman.net,

$5 nonresident adults 19-59, $4 nonresident children 3-18 and seniors 60 and over, $14 nonresident family Fridays, discounts for Bozeman residents) is a 50-meter Olympic-size pool inside the high school open to the public at designated times daily. The water is kept at a cool 82°F (27.8°C), ideal for lap swimming.

During summer, the outdoor pool at **Bogert Park** (303 S. Church Ave., 406/582-0806, $5 nonresident adults 19-59, $4 nonresident children 3-18 and seniors 60 and over, $14 nonresident family Fridays, discounts for Bozeman residents) is packed with families and their children. A couple of water slides keep the energy (and the crowds) at peak levels. In the park itself, an extensive playground entices children. A band shell is used for Tuesday evening concerts, and the pavilion becomes an ice rink in winter.

Farther down Church Avenue from Bogert is the **Gallagator Trail,** which follows a former railroad line abandoned in the 1930s. Entirely flat, the paved and gravel trail weaves through some lovely residential and forested areas along Bozeman Creek. Just before the Gallagator is **Peet's Hill,** the city's most popular in-town spot for a hike. A quick cruise up the hill leads you to a network of nice trails, a chance to commune with just about anyone and their dog, and ultimately to **Lindley Park,** an excellent destination year-round. In summer, there is picnicking, the fanfare of the Sweet Pea Festival in early August, and the weekly **Bozeman Farmer's Market** on Tuesday nights. Two wonderful green areas in the city's historic neighborhoods are **Beall Park** (N. Bozeman Ave. and E. Villard St.), which is popular with kids and has an arts center, a playground, and an ice rink in winter; and **Cooper Park** (S. 8th Ave. and W. Koch St.), a favorite with dogs. The city of Bozeman (www.bozeman.net) has a list of city and county parks online.

1: downtown Bozeman 2: the entrance sign to the Madison Buffalo Jump State Park 3: angler on the East Gallatin River 4: Hyalite Canyon

Hiking

Many of Montana's cities and towns have constructed an enormous letter on a mountain or hill nearby. Bozeman's B has faded away over time, but the **M** (for Montana State University) is one of the community's favorite, and often most crowded, hiking spots. Accessed from a small parking lot on the west side of Bridger Drive, just past and across the road from the Bozeman Fish Technology Center, the M is hard to miss and well worth the hike. There is a steep route up (20-30 minutes) or a longer, gentler route (45 minutes-1 hour), making mix-and-match loops a possibility. The diehards can follow the trail 21 miles (34 km) to the **Fairy Lake Campground** near the end of Bridger Canyon.

Just across Bridger Canyon Drive from the M is the **Bozeman Fish Technology Center** (4050 Bridger Canyon Rd., 406/587-9265, www.fws.gov), one of the community's best-kept secrets. In addition to classes and kid-centered festivals (the Kid Fishing Derby and the Community Watershed Festival), the site offers a great trail called **Drinking Horse Mountain.** Slightly less steep and more shaded than the M trail, and with a summit view that looks north into Bridger Canyon rather than south into the Gallatin Valley, the trail is 1.6 miles (2.6 km) to the top and offers loop options.

Hikers eager to put some serious miles on their legs and get some elevation under their belts can continue 21 miles (34 km) down Bridger Canyon to the turnoff for Fairy Lake. At the end of a bumpy 6-mile (9.7-km) road is the Fairy Lake campground and a couple of great trailheads. The 1.2-mile (1.9-km) loop around beautiful **Fairy Lake** is easy and can be loaded with huckleberries in late July and August. The water is cold but swimmable. Another trailhead at the campground takes hikers up 2,000 feet (610 m) of elevation gain over 2 miles (3.2 km) one-way to **Sacajawea Peak,** the highest point in the Bridger Range at 9,665 feet (2,946 m). The trail winds through a conifer forest and climbs several rocky switchbacks. At 8,963 feet

(2,732 m) is the **Bridger Divide,** with signed turnoffs to Hardscrabble Peak (9,575 ft/2,918 m), North Cottonwood Creek, Corbly Creek, and Sacajawea to the south. Follow the trail to the left and watch for mountain goats. From the summit, there are magnificent views in every direction. The there-and-back hike is only 4 miles (6.4 km), but with so much elevation gain, it can easily take three hours. For hikers who want to keep going (and have the ability to set up shuttle vehicles), between the Bridger Divide junction and Sacajawea Peak is a junction for the 19.9-mile (32-km) **Bridger Mountains National Recreation Trail,** running along the spine of the Bridger Range all the way to the M trailhead.

South of town is another excellent recreation area, **Hyalite Canyon** (south on S. 19th Ave. to Hyalite Canyon Rd.), one of the most popular in the state. There are excellent opportunities for boating on the reservoir, fishing in Hyalite Creek, and hiking on the various trails, including the stunning **Palisades Falls** trail, which is paved for wheelchair access. Other recreational opportunities include mountain biking, ice climbing, and backcountry skiing in winter.

Skiing

One of only two nonprofit ski areas in Montana, **Bridger Bowl** (15795 Bridger Canyon Rd., 406/587-2111, www.bridgerbowl. com, 9am-4pm daily during ski season, full day $69-84 adults, $39-54 seniors 70-79, $28-43 children 7-12, free for children 6 and under and seniors 80 and over, discounts for online tickets and multiday tickets) is only 16 miles (26 km) north of Bozeman and offers 2,000 acres of exceptional terrain and first-class facilities for about half of what you would pay at Aspen or Vail. Multiple-day tickets and ski school options are available, and there are 75 marked trails and eight lifts to get you on the mountain, including **Schlasman's,** which summits the ridge, an area long known as an "earn your turns" mecca. Though the area is hugely popular with locals and a seat in the cafeteria can be hard to find at lunchtime,

lift lines are rarely longer than 10-15 people. With so much terrain and a local tendency to ski in the trees, Bridger Bowl offers what feels like wide-open space. The mountain offers diverse terrain but is slightly more geared toward advanced skiers, with 42 percent of the trails rated "expert." The longest run is 3 miles (4.8 km), and the average annual snowfall is 350 inches (889 cm). In the summer, trails are open to hikers and mountain bikers. In early October, usually before the snow flies, the ski hill hosts the **Bridger Raptor Fest** (www. bridgerraptorfest.com), a series of films, walks, talks, and demonstrations that coincides with the largest golden eagle migration in the United States.

Just north of Bridger Bowl is the **Crosscut Mountain Sports Center** (16621 Bridger Canyon Rd., 406/586-9070, www.crosscutmt. org, 9am-4pm daily, $20 adults, $10 children 12-18, free for children under 12), a wonderful place for cross-country novices and racers alike. Crosscut boasts 16 miles (26 km) of impeccably groomed trails suitable for both classic and skate skiers, and it's also hosted numerous competitions, including the U.S. Olympic Qualifying Championship in 2002 and national NCAA events. Fat biking is becoming increasingly popular and is possible seven days a week. In summer, Crosscut transforms its trails into excellent hiking, mountain biking, and horseback riding trails. It also has a championship biathlon course and a disc golf course.

In downtown Bozeman, **Lindley Park** (E. Main St. and Buttonwood Ave.) offers extensive groomed cross-country ski trails courtesy of the Bridger Ski Foundation. The best place to park is the northwest parking lot of Bozeman Deaconess Hospital (915 Highland Blvd.). Season passes can be purchased online (www.bridgerskifoundation.org, $50 individual, $100 family), or donations can be made in the boxes at the various trailheads.

The 18-hole golf course at **Bridger Creek** (2710 McIlhattan Rd., 406/586-2333, www.bridgercreek.com) is also groomed for skiers in the winter. Buttons, which are the wear-on-your-jacket equivalent of a ski pass, can be purchased at locations in town, including **Bangtail Bike & Ski** (137 E. Main St., 406/587-4905, www.bangtailbikes.com), an excellent cycle and Nordic ski shop that also rents cross-country skis.

Fishing

Bozeman is a trout lover's paradise, with several blue-ribbon streams nearby. The **Gallatin, Jefferson,** and **Madison Rivers** flow through the valley, forming the headwaters of the Missouri River in aptly named Three Forks (31 mi/50 km west of Bozeman on I-90). Guiding since 1979, Al Gadoury of **6X Outfitters** (406/586-3806, www.6xoutfitters.com, wade or float trips $575 for 1-2 people, $700 for 3-4 people, $40-140 private water rod fee) is widely considered to be among the region's best outfitters, particularly when it comes to spring creeks and private water. As an aside, his shore lunches (think grilled moose burgers) are second to none.

Other local outfitters can offer excellent advice and guide services. **The River's Edge** (612 E. Main St., 406/586-5373, www.theriversedge.com, 8am-6pm daily summer, 9am-5:30pm Mon.-Fri. and 9am-5pm Sat. fall, winter, and spring) is one of Bozeman's oldest and most venerated. **Montana Troutfitters** (1716 W. Main St., 406/587-4707, www.troutfitters.com, 7am-7pm daily, from $535 full-day wade or float trips for 1-2 anglers) has been guiding fly-fishing excursions since 1978 and offers excellent online fishing reports. **Yellow Dog Flyfishing Adventures** (213 S. Willson Ave., 406/585-8657 or 888/777-5060, 8am-5:30pm Mon.-Fri., www.yellowdogflyfishing.com) offers first-class trips in the region and mind-blowing fishing adventures around the world.

★ Floating the Madison River

In a college town with an active and outdoorsy population, floating the rivers is a popular pastime. The calm and relatively warm **Madison River** is easily the most popular, followed by the slightly more remote **Jefferson River.** For an idyllic half-day float on the Madison, rent a 3- to 6-person raft ($45-85) or inner tubes (from $12) from **Big Boys Toys All Terrain Rentals** (8254 Huffine Ln., 406/587-4747, www.bigboystoysrentals.com, discounts for 3 or more days). Or rent tubes with coolers (from $10), kayaks (from $35), stand-up paddleboards (from $40), or canoes (from $40).

From Big Boys Toys, drive 30 minutes west on Highway 84 (also known as Norris Rd.) to the Warm Springs access. Float time down to Black's Ford is 2-3.5 hours, depending on the time of year and water flow. If you only have one vehicle, make sure to arrange a shuttle through the rental shop. Try to schedule your float on a weekday, if possible, or early in the morning on the weekend if you don't want to get caught up in the college booze-cruise flotilla.

Golf

There are three private golf courses in and around Bozeman (Valley View Golf Club, Riverside Country Club, and Black Bull Run Golf Club), and two that are open to the public. The 18-hole **Bridger Creek Golf Course** (2710 McIlhattan Rd., 406/586-2333, www.bridgercreek.com, weekdays $21 for 9 holes and $34 for 18 holes, weekends and holidays $23 for 9 holes and $36 for 18 holes) offers 6,511 yards of golf from the longest tees for a par of 71. Special family nights are ideal for little ones just picking up the game, and novice nights provide a non-stressful atmosphere for new players. Its camp offerings for kids and its group and private lessons for anyone are highly rated. **Cottonwood Hills Golf Course** (8955 River Rd., 406/587-1118, www.cottonwoodhills.com) offers a 9-hole, 1,181-yard (1,080-m), par-3 course ($10 adults, $8 children 6-12) as well as an 18-hole, 6,751-yard (6,173-m) course with a par of 70 ($24 for 9 holes, $44 for 18 holes).

Fitness and Yoga

The largest gym in the area—which has a pool, racquetball and basketball courts, and a fantastic kid's drop-off playroom—is **The Ridge** (4181 Fallon Ave., 406/586-1737, www.ridgeathletic.com, 5:15am-10pm Mon.-Thurs., 5:15am-9pm Fri., 7am-8pm Sat.-Sun., $12 day pass), an impressive facility with every class you can imagine and numerous trainers on the floor at all times. A smaller branch, known as **The Ridge Downtown** (111 E. Mendenhall St., 406/586-0077, www.ridgeathletic.com, 5:30am-9pm Mon.-Thurs., 5:30am-8pm Fri., 8am-7pm Sat., noon-7pm Sun., $12 day pass) is just off Main Street and limited to strength training and cardio equipment plus various yoga and fitness classes.

Also downtown is **Main Street Fitness** (7 W. Main St., 406/556-2200, www.mainstreetfitness.net, open 24 hours) where, for $10, visitors can have full access to the gym and its range of classes, including kickboxing, ski conditioning, and yoga.

Find your center at **Your Yoga** (20 E. Main St., 406/599-5005, www.youryoga.com). Choose from a variety of classes—from meditation and vinyasa to kundalini, hatha, and restorative. Sweat-inducing Bikram yoga can be found at **Bend Beyond Yoga** (705 E. Mendenhall St., 406/219-3837, www.bendbeyondyoga.com). Drop-ins are welcome for $25 for one class or $49 for three classes. Mats and towels can be rented. Worth noting is the meditation garden behind the studio. **Pure Barre Bozeman** (34 E. Mendenhall St., 406/577-2918, www.purebarre.com) provides an hour-long, full-body workout that uses a ballet barre and small repetitive movements with upbeat music and encouraging instructors. Drop-in classes are $23 or $105 for five classes.

ENTERTAINMENT AND EVENTS
Nightlife

In downtown Bozeman, **Plonk** (29 E. Main St., 406/587-2170, www.plonkwine.com, 3pm-1:30am daily) is an elegant wine bar as known for its tapas and desserts—start with the cheese board or ploughman's platter and finish with the chef's chocolate board

for dessert—as for its remarkably global selection of more than 600 wines. The atmosphere is a captivating integration of 100-year-old architecture, contemporary original works of art, minimalist urban design, and an eclectic collection of well-played vinyl records. In the summertime, the crowd spills outside to a handful of sidewalk tables. In a mostly family-friendly town, this is one establishment that does not welcome children or babies.

Also downtown, **Bar IX** (311 E. Main St., 406/551-2185, www.bar-ix.com, 4pm-2am Mon.-Fri., 11am-2am Sat.-Sun.) is both industrial and rustic, and it's usually hopping. Its happy hour specials and Bucket Nights are well known locally. Appealing to Bozeman's athletic crowd, **Pub 317** (321 E. Main St., 406/582-8898, www.pub317.com, 11am-2am daily) is one of the few bars that host running races. Twice each year, the Irish pub sponsors 10K or half-marathons that end back at the bar. There's usually live Irish music on Sunday, live bluegrass on Tuesday, and trivia nights on Wednesday.

An ideal spot for a gourmet Montana meal or just a mean cocktail, **Open Range** (241 E. Main St., 406/404-1940, www.openrangemt.com, drinks and dining 5pm-10pm daily summer, 5pm-9:30pm Tues.-Sat. winter) is an upscale favorite. One of the newest rooftop bars downtown—and certainly one of the hippest—is **Sky Shed** (24 W. Mendenhall St., 406/551-7703, www.skyshedbar.com, 4pm-10pm daily), on the roof of the Kimpton Armory hotel. It's not where locals hang out, but it's gorgeous and urban with loads of specialty drinks and small plates like *furikake* fries, Korean beef lettuce wraps, pork belly *bao* buns, and coconut *panna cotta*.

Popular with the college (and alumni) crowds is the **Rocking R Bar** (211 E. Main St., 406/587-9355, www.rockingrbar.com, 11am-2am daily), a favorite hangout since the 1940s. There is plenty of sidewalk seating when the weather permits, and the 20 TVs, four pool tables, and dartboards offer entertainment in this loud bar. Not exactly downtown, but not far, the **Haufbrau House** (22 S. 8th St., 406/587-4931, 11am-2am Mon.-Sat., 1pm-2am Sun.), one leg of the "Barmuda Triangle" with the Molly Brown and The Scoop, is a favorite with college students. It's looks and smells like a dive, but the open mic nights are fun and the burgers are tasty.

For an upscale brewpub experience on Bozeman's hip north side, **Mountains Walking Brewery** (422 N. Plum St., 406/219-3480, www.mountainswalking.com, 11:30am-8pm daily) has outstanding beer, brewed on-site, and lots of organic farm-to-table food, including wood-fired pizzas and small bites like crispy Brussels sprouts, plates of candied bacon, pecorino truffle fries, beer-brined wings, tacos, and more.

Theater

For a relatively small Rocky Mountain town, Bozeman has a decent number of theater offerings. Among the most popular is **Broad Comedy** (406/522-7623, www.broadcomedy.com), which produces irreverent and side-splitting satire by a female cast (geared to mature audiences only). The company has achieved global recognition and plenty of YouTube followers. If you are in town when the company is performing, be there. Broad Comedy was also the founder of (and still runs) the highly respected and always full Camp Equinox, an incredible theater experience for kids in summer.

Verge Theater (2304 N. 7th Ave., 406/551-3123, www.vergetheater.com) has been around for more than 20 years (until 2013 as Equinox Theatre Company) and produces eclectic and original shows, many of which are hilariously funny. The company took some time during the pandemic to reorganize and write a bunch of grants to secure their own future. Verge will continue to offer classes and performances at various locations around Bozeman.

There are also shows produced by students at **Montana State University** (406/994-3904) and professional theater brought to the **Brick Breeden Fieldhouse**

(1 Bobcat Cir., 406/994-7117) through **Broadway in Bozeman** (406/994-2287, www.brickbreeden.com).

One of the state's most beloved troupes, **Montana Shakespeare in the Parks** (www.shakespeareintheparks.org) is based out of Montana State University and travels all over the state bringing fantastic, outdoor (when weather permits), and free Shakespearean theater to parks and even cow pastures around the Northern Rockies in small, underserved communities. The company, which travels around to do school workshops in the off-season, has been bringing the Bard to the people since 1973. Bill Pullman is one of the company's most famous alumni. You can always catch a glimpse of them at Bozeman's Sweet Pea Festival, but going to see them anywhere is worth doing.

Music

Thanks to the eager audiences provided by the university and growing community, Bozeman also has a lively and impressive music scene. **Intermountain Opera Bozeman** (406/587-2889, www.intermountainopera.org) has been producing two professional shows annually since 1978. The shows feature world-class performers and conductors with a local chorus and orchestra and in the spring and fall. They also offer a musical each spring and special events throughout the year. The **Bozeman Symphony Orchestra and Symphonic Choir** (406/585-9774, www.bozemansymphony.org) presents a number of performances each season, starting in September, that range from late Renaissance pieces through the 20th century. It also performs annually with the Montana Ballet Company in *The Nutcracker*. **Vootie Productions** (406/586-1922, www.vootie.com) brings outstanding performers to town regularly.

Live from the Divide (627 E. Peach St., www.livefromthedivide.com, show dates vary, tickets from $30) is an independently produced hour-long public radio program celebrating the songwriters of American roots music. Tickets are sold to 50 lucky music lovers who get to sit in on the taping. Check the calendar online for the next show.

Festivals and Events

Held annually the first full weekend in August, **Sweet Pea Festival of the Arts** (406/586-4003, www.sweetpeafestival.org) is Bozeman's answer to Mardi Gras. No one is parading around half-naked—this is Montana, after all—but there is plenty of food (don't miss the tater pigs, a Sweet Pea classic), live music, theater, dance, an arts and crafts fair, both juried and open art shows, and a flower show. The weekend events are held at **Lindley Park** (east end of Main St.). Events leading up to the festival include the **Sweet Pea Ball** (Sat. before Sweet Pea weekend), **Chalk on the Walk** (Tues. before Sweet Pea), **Bite of Bozeman** (Wed. before Sweet Pea), and the **Children's Run and Sweet Pea Parade** (Sat. morning of Sweet Pea). Packed into three days, the more than 40-year-old festival is organized by some 1,500 volunteers and draws more than 16,000 visitors annually. Wristbands (from $25 adults 3-day pass in advance, $35 weekend pass at the gate, $25 day pass) are required for entry to Lindley Park, and one wristband enables you to access all the events in Lindley Park over the course of the weekend. During COVID, children 12 and under were free, but that may change post-pandemic.

Founded in 2011, in response to the increasing competition and expense for local artists to get into Sweet Pea, **SLAM Fest** (406/219-7773, info@slamfestivals.org, free), which stands for Support Local Artists and Music, runs in Bogert Park the same weekend as the other festival. Like a smaller and free version of Sweet Pea, SLAM hosts more than 50 artists and artisans from around the state, plus live music, readings, dance, food, and a beer garden.

Although Bozeman residents joke about the "nine months of winter and three months of houseguests," people take summertime recreation very seriously, and the town of Bozeman (www.downtownbozeman.org)

has created numerous ways to celebrate outside as much as possible. Residents and visitors gather on the lawn at the Emerson Center for the Arts and Culture for **Lunch on the Lawn** (11:30am-1:30pm Wed. July-Aug., free), a concert series that attracts 100-200 people and an interesting mix of food vendors. **Music on Main** (6:30pm-8:30pm Thurs. July-Aug., free) is an opportunity for folks to gather downtown on closed-off streets and enjoy live music, food vendors, and early evening activities for kids. On the second Friday of every month June-September, art lovers gather for the **Downtown Bozeman Art Walk** (406/586-4008, 6pm-8pm), an opportunity to stroll through the galleries downtown, sipping wine and tasting hors d'oeuvres along the way. Another summer event, **Crazy Days** (downtown, 406/586-4008), is a price-slashing shopping extravaganza that happens each year the third weekend in July.

Bozeman also boasts two fabulous **farmers markets.** The original is the **Bozeman Farmers' Market** (Lindley Park, www.bozemanfarmersmarket.org, 5pm-8pm Tues.). It includes everything from produce, arts, and crafts to gourmet food trucks, entertainment, and activities (like reverse bungee jumping and rock climbing for kids). The park can be packed, so plan to stay in immediate contact with little ones. For a more relaxing evening, bring a blanket and park yourself away from the masses. A larger market, the **Gallatin Valley Farmers' Market** (901 N. Black Ave., 406/388-6701, ext. 101, www.gallatinvalleyfarmersmarket.com, 9am-noon Sat. mid-June-early Sept.) runs in Haynes Pavilion at the Gallatin County Fairgrounds.

Other annual events worth checking out are the **Big Sky Country State Fair** (406/582-3270, www.406statefair.com, $10 adults, $3 children 6-12, free for children under 6), held at the county fairgrounds (901 N. Black Ave.) the third week in July, which offers carnival rides, entertainment, animals, contests (where else can your kid ride a sheep or wrestle a piglet?), and food; October's **MSU Homecoming** and **Downtown Trick** or Treat (both on Main St.); and February's **Wild West Winter Fest** (Gallatin County Fairgrounds, 901 N. Black Ave.). Bozeman's **Christmas Stroll** brings the town out the first Saturday of December to eat, shop, and enjoy the festive season.

SHOPPING

Like most regional hubs in Montana, Bozeman offers an abundance of shopping opportunities for every taste and budget level. Major stores include Target and Costco on North 19th Avenue as well as Walmart and Murdoch's Ranch & Home Supply on North 7th Avenue. **Downtown Bozeman** (www.downtownbozeman.org), however, is by far the best place to go for unique items and pure charm.

The **Country Bookshelf** (28 W. Main St., 406/587-0166, www.countrybookshelf.com, 10am-7pm daily) is Bozeman's most beloved bookstore and the state's largest independent bookstore. It is especially geared to local and regional authors, many of whom are willing to show their affection for the place with readings and book signings. On the same block is **Vargo's Jazz City & Books** (6 W. Main St., 406/587-5383, 9:30am-7pm Mon.-Fri., 10am-6pm Sat., 11am-5pm Sun.), an excellent place to get lost. The shop specializes in slightly more obscure books, CDs, and vinyl, both new and used. It's also the best place in town to get great cards.

For marvelous gifts, there are a couple of boutiques downtown. Touted as a shop "for the everyday celebration," **HeyDay** (7 W. Main St., 406/586-5589, www. heydaybozeman.com, 10am-7pm Mon.-Sat., 10am-5pm Sun.) specializes in timeless home decor and elegant gifts. From gardening to personal grooming, cooking, and entertaining, this stylish little shop is sure to make you smile. For gifts that could only come from Montana, **Montana Gift Corral** (237 E. Main St., 406/585-8625, www. giftcorral.com, 9am-8pm Mon.-Fri., 9am-6pm Sat., 10am-5pm Sun.) is the place to go.

For the hunters and outdoors enthusiasts, downtown Bozeman offers top-of-the-line shopping. Occupying two beautifully restored 1903 storefronts is an outstanding local shoe store and something of a Bozeman institution. Poised to make shoe snobs out of nearly anyone, **Schnee's** (35 E. Main St., 406/587-0981, www.schnees.com, 9am-7pm Mon.-Fri., 9am-6pm Sat., 10am-5pm Sun.) sells everything from locally made bombproof hunting boots to a selection of very hip street shoes and sandals. It also sells clothes and accessories, leather bags, and hunting and fishing gear, and takes its 100 percent satisfaction guarantee very seriously.

Bozeman has a number of notable art galleries. **Old Main Gallery & Framing** (129 E. Main St., 406/587-8860, www. oldmaingallery.com, 10am-5:30pm Mon.-Sat.) displays an outstanding collection of contemporary American, Western, and Native art. **Visions West Contemporary** (34 W. Main St., 406/522-9946, www. visionswestcontemporary.com, 10am-5:30pm Mon.-Sat.) is a dynamic space that focuses on contemporary artists in the West. For an exquisite collection of historic and contemporary Western art, **Montana Trails Gallery** (7 W. Main St., 406/586-2166, www. montanatrails.com, 10am-6pm daily) is a worthwhile stop, even if you're just looking. They curate some of the best known artists—from Thomas Moran and Charlie Russell to Clyde Aspevig and Beth Loftin.

Bozeman's most significant shopping event is **Crazy Days** (downtown Bozeman, 406/586-4008), an annual event held on the third weekend in July. Merchants reduce their inventory prices by up to 75 percent and put much of it out on the street. Early birds are the winners here; it's not uncommon to see several brand-new pairs of last year's skis being carried away by happy new owners.

FOOD

If you have recently traveled through rural Montana, Bozeman seems like a foodie mecca. With everything from sushi to tapas, the town affords diners much more than the burgers and steaks for which the state is so well known (although there is an outstanding selection of those as well).

The ★ Community Food Co-op (908 W. Main St., 406/587-4039, www.bozo.coop, 8am-9pm daily, Flying C Coffee Shop and Café closed during COVID) is a cornerstone of the community, and its downtown branch (44 E. Main St., 406/922-2667, 10am-8pm daily, deli and hot bar 11am-7pm Mon.-Fri.) is not only convenient but also offers an excellent hot bar, salad bar, and sandwich and smoothie counter. Everything the co-op does—gourmet and often locally produced groceries, mouthwatering prepared foods, and a primo coffee shop, juice bar, and bakery—is done brilliantly. The homemade soups are excellent, as is the salad bar and just about everything in the sprawling deli case. Exotic hot lunches and dinners are often available at prices that cannot be matched elsewhere.

Right downtown, the super-casual and always popular Jam! (25 W. Main St., 406/585-1761, www.jamonmain.com, 7am-3:30pm daily, $4-20) serves hearty and delicious breakfasts and lunches, ranging from crab cake Benedict and chicken and biscuit Benedict (there's even a flight of 3 favorite Benedicts!) to pulled pork omelets, sweet and savory crepes, every kind of pancake, and beet and root hash. Breakfast is served all day, but this place is always hopping so be prepared for a wait. They also serve beer and wine if it's that kind of brunch. For another upscale breakfast or lunch option downtown, The Nova Café (312 E. Main St., 406/587-3973, www.thenovacafe.com, 8am-2pm daily, $6-17) uses fresh, healthy ingredients and gets almost everything—from meats and produce to salsa—locally. The service and the food are consistently great.

Two other fantastic places for big, beautiful, and healthy meals are Feed Café (1530 W. Main St., 406/219-2630, www. feedcafebozeman.com, 7am-2pm daily, $10-16), serving gourmet breakfast sandwiches, egg dishes, soup, salads, and sandwiches in the big red barn, and The Farmer's Daughters (510 N. 7th Ave., 406/404-7999, www.farmersdaughtersbzn.com, 7:30am-2pm daily, $9.50-13), which serves healthy options like chia bowls and avocado toast, giant salads, and sandwiches in the RSVP Hotel.

As Bozeman has evolved from its ranching and agricultural heritage, many of the classic diners have been lost to trendier eateries, but one has stood the test of time. The Western Café (443 E. Main St., 406/587-0436, www. thewesterncafe.com, 6am-2pm daily, $5-15) is an old-timers classic for breakfast and lunch, including its famed chicken-fried steak and cinnamon rolls. If you want to sit in a place and feel how Bozeman used to be, this is the spot.

Also downtown and worth noting is Ted's Montana Grill (105 W. Main St., 406/587-6000, www.tedsmontanagrill.com, noon-9pm Wed.-Thurs. and Sun., noon-10pm Fri.-Sat., 4pm-9pm Mon.-Tues., $14-32), in the historic Baxter hotel. It is the flagship restaurant of local part-time resident and unequivocal philanthropist and land steward Ted Turner. Everything is made from scratch, and each meat cut is available in bison or beef. The apple cobbler is extremely good, as are the inventive burgers, which can be had either as bison or beef.

For excellent (but pricey!) Asian food, Sweet Chili Asian Bistro (101 E. Main St., 406/582-1188, www.sweetchilibistro.com, 11am-9pm Mon.-Sat., noon-8:30pm Sun., $15-42) serves up an extensive menu of fresh and flavorful Asian cuisine—mainly Thai and Cantonese specialties—along with sushi and a full bar. House favorites like Mongolian bison and saffron ginger bison are worth more than consideration. The room is dimly lit with red lights, lending some romantic ambience. This is still Bozeman though, and any restaurant is fairly casual. The fairly new Hooked Sushi (119 E. Main St., 406/577-2332, www. hookedmt.com, 4pm-9pm Sun.-Thurs., 4pm-10pm Fri.-Sat., $8-26) is a great spot for sushi and other comfort foods like ramen, fish or shrimp tacos, and more. The habanero bliss roll is a favorite. Also pretty new on the

Bozeman culinary scene, Revelry (24 N. Tracy, 406/404-1400, www.revelrymt.com, lunch 11am-3pm daily, dinner 5pm-10pm daily, weekend brunch 9am-3pm Sat.-Sun., $15-42) is a festive place for food and drinks, indoors or out, with lots of hearty pastas, sausages, burgers, sandwiches, salads, steak, and pizza.

The elegant Little Star Diner (548 E. Babcock St., 406/624-6463, www. littlestardiner.com, 5pm-10pm Wed.-Sat., 9am-2pm Sun., $18-30) boasts a frequently changing menu—including lamb kebabs, porkbelly noodle soup, Flathead Lake trout tacos, and potato and porcini pierogis—with lots of local produce and meats, plus delicious, atypical Sunday brunch fare like sour cream donuts with rhubarb jam, yellow lentil dal, grilled mushroom toast, and then the classics like huevos rancheros and breakfast burritos. With lovely ambience both on the rooftop and in the intimate dining room, this is a delightful spot for a special meal.

On the hip north side of town, the cozy Wild Crumb Bakery (600 Wallace St., 406/579-3454, www.wildcrumb.com, 7am-3pm Tues.-Sun.) is one of the favorite bakeries in town. They don't serve espresso (but you can get a great cup a few steps away at Treeline Coffee Roasters), but their artisan breads and pastries are beyond compare. Try the orange pecan sticky buns or the ham and gruyère croissant. You know what, try anything: a tart, a cake, a loaf of challah. You will be back.

On the east end of town, Montana Ale Works (611 E. Main St., 406/587-7700, www.montanaaleworks.com, 4pm-9pm daily, $14-45) combines a hip eatery with an extremely popular smoke-free bar and pool lounge. The menu offers inventive takes on Western staples like burgers and steaks, and the atmosphere, in a beautifully rehabbed 100-year-old railroad warehouse, is energetic and suitable for everyone from toddlers to grandparents; it can be loud at any time of the week, so a separate dining room is a good option for those with noise issues.

Another spot for fresh, creative cuisine is not far from the Museum of the Rockies. Feast Raw Bar & Bistro (270 W. Kagy Ave., 406/577-2377, www.feastbozeman.com, 5pm-9pm Mon.-Sat., $15-52) specializes in sustainably sourced and globally inspired cuisine. A raw bar serves everything from daily ceviche and bison carpaccio to oysters and a shellfish feast. Shared plates include Vietnamese chicken wings, crispy Brussels sprouts, and steamed mussels. And the entrées are gorgeous pieces of meat and fish.

A few steps off Main Street, tucked into the Emerson Center for the Arts and Culture, Sidewall Pizza Company (207 W. Olive St., 406/570-0730, 11am-9pm Tues.-Sun., $14-23) is a perfect spot for a bite. They have lots of shareable appetizers, salads, and pizzas with bases that range from garlic sauce to basil pesto, chicken and crushed tomato sauce. The little pepperonis on crushed tomato sauce is especially good. Another great spot for gourmet Neapolitan-style wood-fired pizza is Pizza Campania (1285 N. Rouse Ave., 406/404-1270, www.pizzacampania. net, 11am-9:30pm Mon.-Fri., 4pm-9:30pm Sat.-Sun., $11-17). Toppings include such delicacies as fennel sausage, fig preserves, goat gorgonzola, and brie. The restaurant also serves great salads and desserts, and opens up to the outside with a glass garage-style door. Patio diners can sit by the fire with a great bottle of wine.

ACCOMMODATIONS

For a long time, Bozeman's accommodations were lacking in charm, for a town with seemingly sophisticated tastes. That's changed with the addition of five terrific contemporary hotels downtown since 2015. Still, for those willing to look, there are numerous and diverse offerings, from roadside motels to upscale chains, cozy vacation rentals, and, farther afield, a historical gem.

Newer is better in Bozeman, when it comes to hotels. ★ The Lark (122 W. Main St., 866/464-1000, www.larkbozeman. com, $159-669) considers itself a base camp and works hard at getting guests out of its modern, art-filled rooms and into the wilds of Bozeman and its surrounds. A map room helps with planning, and motel employees are called guides. Still, your time inside The Lark will be a pleasure with 67 unique rooms in two buildings—the original motel and the 2018 hotel—each filled with work by local artists and craftspeople. Kids will love the bunk room, and everyone will appreciate the heart-of-downtown location, which is within walking distance to everywhere. Look out for the **Genuine Ice Cream Co.** truck (www. genuineicecream.com) just outside the hotel, dishing up handmade ice cream in flavors like fresh mint chip, matcha green tea, honey lavender, and Nutella crunch.

Another newer property in downtown Bozeman with a decidedly Scandinavian feel is ★ **Element Bozeman** (25 E. Mendenhall St., 406/582-4972, www.elementbozeman. com, from $214) a Starwood Hotel. Just a block off Main Street, this high-rise hotel (for Bozeman, anyway) has spacious rooms, a complimentary breakfast bar, evening reception, and fully stocked kitchenettes, as well as a patio grill, an indoor pool, a fitness center, and bikes to borrow.

By far the fanciest hotel in downtown Bozeman is the **Kimpton Armory** (24 W. Mendenhall St., 406/551-7700, www. armoryhotelbzn.com, $236-974), which was beautifully built in Bozeman's cool old armory and opened in 2020. It's a full-service hotel with elegant rooms (including your own Peloton in some of them!), a sophisticated restaurant (**Fielding's**, breakfast 7am-10:30am daily, dinner 5:30pm-10pm daily, breakfast $11-16, dinner $26-49) serving American regional cuisine, and a big-city chic rooftop bar. Another newer property that's long on charm and located in the growing midtown district is **RSVP Hotel** (510 N. 7th Ave., 406/404-7999, www.rsvphotel.co, from $129), a boutique hotel set in a meticulously restored roadside motel. There's a fantastic breakfast and lunch restaurant on-site (**The Farmer's Daughters**) and a new music venue immediately next door. Owned by two sisters who grew up on a wheat farm just west of Bozeman, the hotel gets every detail right and is warm, inviting, and fun.

Offering an ideal location right downtown, and the cheapest rooms anywhere, the **Treasure State Hostel** (27 E. Main St., 406/624-6244, www.treasurestatehostel.com, dorm bed from $28, private room from $42) is a find in Bozeman. Just 20 minutes from Bridger Bowl and an hour from Big Sky, the hostel is popular with skiers in winter.

The **Magpie Guest House** (323 S. Wallace Ave., 406/585-8223, www.magpiegh.com, $225-289) offers charming accommodations for up to four people in an ideal downtown location, sandwiched between the library and Peet's Hill, with all the comforts of home.

At the 19th Street exit on I-90, visitors will find the extremely comfortable all-suites **Residence Inn by Marriott** (6195 E. Valley Center Rd., 406/522-1535, www.marriott.com, from $158), with 115 suites. The hotel offers a hot breakfast each morning and social hours Monday-Thursday. Other reliable chain hotels in the area include **C'mon Inn Hotel & Suites** (6139 E. Valley Center Rd., 406/587-3555 or 866/782-2717, www.cmoninn.com, from $110), the upscale **Hilton Garden Inn** (2032 Commerce Way, 406/582-9900, http:// hiltongardeninn3.hilton.com, from $179) on the northwest side of town, and the older but well-maintained **Holiday Inn** (5 E. Baxter Ln., 406/587-4561 or 800/315-2621, www. holidayinn.com, from $158). **Travelodge** (1200 E. Main St., 406/586-8534, www. wyndhamhotels.com, from $99) is a hotel at the east end of downtown, not far from the interstate, with clean, spacious pet-friendly rooms. New in 2021, and within easy walking distance of downtown shops and restaurants, the **Residence Inn by Marriott Bozeman Downtown** (815 E. Main St., 406/586-7200, www.marriott.com, from $199) is extremely comfortable and convenient.

Bozeman Cottage Vacation Rentals (406/580-3223, www.bozemancottage.com) offers a broad array of properties to meet individual preferences for location, price, size, and style—from a lodge near Bridger Bowl to downtown cottages and riverfront cabins. There are plenty of pet-friendly offerings, and last-minute bargains can be had for those inclined to wing it. **Mountain Home** (406/586-4589 or 800/550-4589, www.mountain-home.com) has an excellent array of vacation rentals in and around Bozeman and across southwestern Montana.

INFORMATION AND SERVICES

A good place for information, travel services, and maps is the **Bozeman Chamber of Commerce** (2000 Commerce Way, southeast corner of N. 19th St. and Baxter Ln., 406/586-5421 or 800/228-4224, www.bozemancvb.com, 8am-5pm Mon.-Fri. summer, 9am-4pm Mon.-Wed. and 9am-2pm Fri. fall-spring). The chamber also staffs a **visitor center** at Bozeman Yellowstone International Airport, which offers the same assortment of information, brochures, and maps as at the chamber. Downtown shoppers can find an abundance of information, including real estate offerings from ERA Landmark, at the **Downtown Bozeman Visitor Center** (8 E. Main St., 406/586-4008 or 406/556-5001, www.downtownbozeman.org, 10am-5pm Mon.-Sat.).

The **main post office** (2201 Baxter Ln. at 19th St., 8:30am-5pm Mon.-Fri., 9am-1pm Sat.) offers a 24-hour automated postal service that accepts major credit and debit cards. The old post office still operates downtown in the federal building (32 E. Babcock St.), one block south of Main Street.

The **Bozeman Public Library** (626 E. Main St., 406/582-2400, www.bozemanlibrary.org, 10am-6pm Tues.-Fri., 10am-5pm Sat.) boasts a modern and green architectural design with lots of space to work, a nice coffee shop, and an excellent children's section. The library is one of the few places in town that offer **free Internet access.** Internet access can also be found at either of the **Community Food Co-op** locations (908

W. Main St. or 44 E. Main St., 406/587-4039, www.bozo.coop). Both restaurants turn their Wi-Fi off during the busy lunch hour so that diners can get tables.

Bozeman Health Deaconess Hospital (915 Highland Blvd., 406/585-5000, www.bozemanhealth.org) has a 24-hour emergency room. Another option is **b2 Urgent Care** (1006 W. Main St., Ste. E, 406/414-4800, www.b2cares.com, 8am-7pm daily).

Coin-operated washers and dryers can be found at **Duds-n-Suds** (502 S. 23rd Ave., 406/586-3837, 8am-8pm daily), which also boasts a car wash, a dog wash, and free Wi-Fi; and at **The Clothesline** (815 W. Main St., 406/586-3070, 7am-10pm daily), which offers drop-off laundry service as well.

TRANSPORTATION
Getting There
Bozeman Yellowstone International Airport (BZN, 406/388-8321, www.bozemanairport.com) is 8 miles (13 km) northwest of downtown Bozeman in the nearby town of Belgrade. Delta, Alaska, American, Allegiant, Frontier, Jet Blue, Southwest, Sun Country, and United all offer regular nonstop service to and from major U.S. cities, including Salt Lake City, Minneapolis, Seattle, Atlanta, Chicago, Denver, Houston, Las Vegas, Los Angeles, New York, Phoenix, Portland, Nashville, Charlotte, Boston, Newark, and San Francisco.

Greyhound travels to almost 40 towns and cities in Montana from the bus depot (1500 N. 7th Ave. 800/451-5333) at Walmart Supercenter.

Off I-90, Bozeman is easily accessible by car. It is 142 miles (229 km) west of Billings, 202 miles (320 km) southeast of Missoula, and 85 miles (137 km) east of Butte. The driving distances are slightly farther from Wyoming: Jackson is 215 miles (345 km) south, Sheridan is 270 miles (435 km) southeast, and Cody is 214 miles (345 km) southeast of Bozeman. It's worth pointing out that Bozeman can be treacherous to get to from any direction. From the east, travelers have to cross the

Bozeman Pass which is often closed for wind and snow. From the west, drivers will have to climb Homestake Pass outside of Butte, also a steep mountain pass that can be dangerous in winter. From the south, drivers will need to navigate the Gallatin Canyon, a winding single-lane road along the Gallatin River that sees lots of semi-truck traffic and a good number of accidents. Plan ahead to make it during daylight hours, and be careful. That's all.

Getting Around

From the airport, the Comfort Suites, Springhill Suites by Marriott, C'mon Inn, Homewood Suites by Hilton, Hampton Inn, Element, and several others offer shuttle service. Car-rental agencies are at the airport too; the car-rental center is next to the baggage claim. **Alamo, Avis, Budget, Enterprise, Dollar, Hertz, Thrifty, Enterprise, Go Rentals,** and **National** have on-site counters.

The only ground transportation provider within the terminal, **Karst Stage** (406/556-3540 or 800/845-2778, www.karststage.com) offers daily bus service in winter to Big Sky, West Yellowstone, and Mammoth Hot Springs. Shuttles are by reservation only in non-winter months.

Greater Valley Taxi (406/388-9999 or 406/587-6303) has a courtesy phone next to the baggage claim area. It is also a good option for getting around town while you are in Bozeman. **Shuttle to Big Sky & Taxi** (406/995-4895 or 888/454-5667, www.bigskytaxi.com) provides private van and SUV transportation to, from, and around Big Sky, as does **Big Sky Bound** (406/539-3828, www.bigskyboundshuttleandtransportation.com, $200 one-way between Big Sky and the airport 8am-8pm). **Lyft** and **Uber** also serve the Bozeman area.

VICINITY OF BOZEMAN

Belgrade

Nine miles (14.5 km) west of Bozeman on I-90, and often unfairly labeled a bedroom community of Bozeman, Belgrade (pop. 10,551, elev. 4,459 ft/1,359 m) is a great little Montana town with plenty of character. One of its best attributes is that it's not Bozeman; it feels more like a community than a tourist town. **Lewis and Clark Park** (Main St.) is the hub of the city and provides a covered picnic area, a wonderful playground, and a wildly popular splash park geared to small children. The **Belgrade Bandits** are the local American Legion baseball team, and with Little League and high school offerings, there is always a ballgame to watch.

The Fall Festival, normally held the third weekend of September, brings out the crowds for a parade, a street dance, and a host of fun family activities. The **Festival of Lights,** the first Friday of December, is another highlight with a craft show and horse-drawn wagon rides.

Belgrade has a couple of good restaurants. Long the town's most popular eatery, **The Mint Bar & Café** (27 E. Main St., 406/924-6017, www.mintcafebar.com, 4:30pm-9:30pm Sun. and Tues.-Thurs., 4:30pm-10pm Fri.-Sat., $18-42) is a good place for a martini and steak. They also have stroganoff, meatloaf, and fantastic onion rings. Another standout is **Mackenzie River Pizza** (103 Alaska Frontage Rd., 406/388-0016, www.mackenzieriverpizza.com, 11am-9pm daily, $10-22), known for their inventive pizzas, sandwiches, pasta, foodie appetizers, and salad. They have an eatery in Bozeman as well. **Bar 3 Bar-B-Q** (119 E. Main St., 406/388-9182, www.bar3bbq.com, 11am-8pm Mon.-Sat., $14-33) serves phenomenal barbecue and sides, and also brews their own beer on-site.

The **Belgrade Chamber of Commerce** (10 Main St., 406/388-1616, www.belgradechamber.org, 8am-5pm Mon.-Thurs., 8am-1pm Fri.) is a good source for local information and a friendly chat.

Manhattan

Twenty minutes west of Bozeman on I-90, Manhattan (pop. 2,074, elev. 4,245 ft/1,294 m) is a welcoming little community surrounded by potato and dairy farms, wheat fields, and mountains. The town was settled by immigrants from the Netherlands but named by New Yorkers who operated the Montana Malting Company. During the summer, the **Manhattan Farmers Market** (406/282-4350, 4pm-7pm Wed., June-Sept.) fills the small downtown with local produce, baked goods, arts and crafts, and live entertainment. The third Saturday in August is the annual **Potato Festival,** which features a Friday night street dance, pancake breakfast, a parade, 5K and 10K races, cooking competitions, an invitational car show, and music throughout the day. In December, the whole town comes together for an old-fashioned **Christmas Stroll** featuring strolling carolers, horse-drawn hayrides, the lighting of the Christmas tree, and fireworks.

Most folks in the state associate Manhattan with its most famous eatery, **Sir Scott's Oasis** (204 W. Main St., 406/284-6929, 11am-midnight Tues.-Sun., from $21), an old-school supper club with relish trays to start and sundaes for dessert. The hearty steak and potatoes you get in between will satiate even the most discerning meat lovers.

Opened in 2021 in a spectacularly refurbished 1915 auto shop, **Tailored and Tied** (114 E. Main St., 406/282-2100, www.tailoredandtied.com, hours change frequently so call ahead or check the website) is a very modern mom-and-pop shop that has a French-bistro inspired coffee shop, café, and bar in addition to their showroom—they rent furniture and more for weddings and celebrations—and loft for dining and special events. The space is lovely as can be, the food and coffee are on point, and the staff is just plain friendly. In summer they have live music on weekends and other special events.

For visitor information, contact the **Manhattan Chamber of Commerce** (406/284-4162, www.manhattanareachamber.com, 8am-noon Weds., call for additional hours).

Three Forks

Named for the three rivers that form the headwaters of the Missouri River, Three Forks (pop. 2,073, elev. 4,075 ft/1,242 m) was put on the map by Lewis and Clark in 1805. The town is rich in fur trapping and trading history and equally distinguished today by a tightly knit community and a mild climate that locals refer to as the "banana belt."

The **Three Forks Rodeo** (www.threeforksrodeo.com) is held annually in mid-July at the fairgrounds and includes a parade, two nights of rodeo, plenty of food, and entertainment. The town's **Christmas Stroll** is what every small town should aspire to: the crowning of a Christmas king and queen, fireworks, horse-drawn wagon rides, a community cookie exchange, and s'mores around the bonfire.

A couple of great outings just beyond town include **Madison Buffalo Jump State Park** (6990 Buffalo Jump Rd., 7 mi/11.3 km south of Logan, 406/285-3610, www.stateparks.mt.gov, sunrise-sunset daily, $8/vehicle nonresidents) and **Missouri Headwaters State Park** (1585 Trident Rd., Three Forks, 406/285-3610, www.stateparks.mt.gov, dawn-dusk daily, $8/vehicle nonresidents), the latter of which offers hiking, biking, interpretive trails, camping, and river access for boating and fishing.

For a historical treat in Three Forks, the ★ **Sacajawea Hotel** (5 N. Main St., 406/285-6515, www.sacajaweahotel.com) is one-of-a-kind. Lovingly restored in 2010 by the Folkvord family, local farmers who own the enormously successful Wheat Montana Bakeries, the Sac is a historic gem. There are 29 charming and comfortable rooms (starting at $116), some of which are pet-friendly, ranging from full beds to kings. And the seven new cottages (starting at $252) are elegant and private. The amenities are pretty plush and the food is sensational. Visit the Sac for a meal or just a cocktail at **Pompey's Grill** (4:30pm-9pm Mon.-Thurs., 4:30pm-10pm Fri.-Sat., 4pm-9pm Sun., $18-52).

Willow Creek

Six miles (9.7 km) south of Three Forks, the small community of Willow Creek (pop. 258, elev. 4,153 ft/1,266 m) has plenty of charm. The creek that runs through town was originally named Philosopher's River by William Clark, but the town wisely renamed it and the town for the willows that grow along the banks.

The town's half-dozen artists organize the **Willow Creek Art Walks** the third Friday of each month June-August. A local gallery not to be missed is **Aunt Dofe's Hall of Recent Memory** (102 Main St., 406/285-6996, hours vary), which supports the work of contemporary local artists. Across the street, the **Woolzie's Willow Creek Café and Saloon** (21 Main St., 406/285-3698, 4pm-9pm.Wed.-Sun., $14-39) draws diners from far and wide for its quaint ambience and savory cuisine, including the best ribs in the valley—maybe the whole state. You can't go wrong with the daily specials—everything is made from scratch. And if you can time your dinner on a night when **Montana Rose** is playing, you're in for a real treat.

Ennis

In the heart of the Madison Valley, and in the thick of some of the state's best fly-fishing, is Ennis (pop. 1,025, elev. 4,941 ft/1,506 m), 45 miles (72 km) southwest of Bozeman on US 287. The town hosts a wonderful **Fourth of July Rodeo and Parade** (for reserved-seat tickets, call 406/599-4705 after Memorial Day) each year at the fairgrounds. There is also an excellent weekly **Madison Farm to Fork Farmers Market** (First Interstate Bank, 118 W. Williams St., 406/682-3259, www.madisonfarmtofork.com, 5pm-7pm Fri. July-Sept.) and the much-touted **Fly Fishing and Outdoor Festival** (406/682-3148, www.madisonriverfoundation.org), held annually in Peter T's Park on Main Street over Labor Day weekend. A benefit for the Madison River Foundation, the three-day event offers plenty of art, food, music, fly-fishing instruction, and camaraderie.

The **fishing** is indeed the thing in these parts, and a number of good outfitters can lead you to gulpers on the Madison River and in Ennis Lake, Hebgen Lake, Quake Lake, Cliff Lake, and Wade Lake. A good place to start is **The Tackle Shop** (127 Main St., 406/682-4263, www.thetackleshop.com, 8am-6pm daily, extended hours in summer), which touts itself as the oldest fly shop in Montana, founded by Elwood Combs in 1937.

There is excellent **hiking** in every direction—the Tobacco Root Mountains and the Madison Range ring the town—and you'll find trail maps and helpful advice west

the historic Sacajawea Hotel

of town at the local **USDA Forest Service Ranger Station** (5 Forest Service Rd., 406/682-4253).

For dining, Ennis offers good choices including **Alley Bistro** (59 Hwy. 287, 406/682-5695, 11am-2pm and 4pm-8pm Tues.-Fri., 4pm-8pm Sat., $13-35), which dishes up everything from fish tacos to pot roast and veggie pizza. Another place that's a hit with locals and fishers alike is **Tavern 287** (129 Main St., 406/682-7287, www.tavern287.business.site, 11am-8pm Wed.-Mon., $17-29), which offers up such favorites as chicken pot pie, elk osso buco, bison and goat cheese ravioli, and more. A great spot for diner-style breakfast or lunch right on the main drag is **Yesterday's Soda Fountain** (124 Main St., 406/682-4246, 6am-4pm Mon.-Fri. and 6am-3pm Sat.-Sun. Sept.-May, 6am-3pm daily June-Aug., $5-10), which is part restaurant, part pharmacy, part antiques store.

After filling your belly, the creekside cabins south of town at **El Western Cabins & Lodges** (4787 US 287, 406/682-4217, www.elwestern.com, from $159) are an excellent place to hang your hat for the night. It has everything from single rooms to lodges with four bedrooms.

For more information about Ennis, contact the **Ennis Chamber of Commerce** (201 Main St., 406/682-4388, www.ennischamber.com, 9am-4pm Mon.-Fri. fall-spring, 9am-6pm Mon.-Sat. summer).

Big Sky

In the shadow of Lone Peak, tucked in the winding and rugged beauty of Gallatin Canyon, the resort town of Big Sky (pop. 3,058, elev. 7,218 ft/2,200 m) actually has four resorts: Big Sky, Moonlight Basin, Spanish Peaks, and the entirely private Yellowstone Club. Although there are not any sights per se, the town and resorts are clearly geographically blessed with mountains for skiing, hiking, climbing, and biking; rivers for fishing and floating; and trails aplenty for horses, hiking, cross-country skiing, and mountain biking. Visitors can take solace in the fact that mountains make up for museums, and the area can be used as a launching point for Yellowstone National Park (51 mi/82 km south) or Bozeman (50 mi/80 km north).

Although Big Sky has more activities than any visitor could dream of pursuing in a single trip—golf, horseback riding, fishing, skating, skiing, kayaking, wildlife-watching—it definitely feels more like a resort town than a livable community, but with a fairly new town center, their own K-12 school (so that kids don't have to be bused 50 winding mi/80 km to Bozeman), the impressive 282-seat Warren Miller Performing Arts Center, the largest hotel in the state, and their own hospital, Big Sky is growing at light speed. Still, Big Sky feels more like a collection of enclaves, resorts, and villages dotting the mountainside. The uniting factor in this area is a zeal for outdoor adventuring.

SPORTS AND RECREATION
Skiing

One thing that distinguishes Big Sky from other ski destinations in the Rockies is the plentiful elbow room—there are fewer skiers per skiable acre than in most places. **Big Sky Resort** (snow phone 406/995-5900, reservations 800/548-4486, snow sports school 406/995-5743, www.bigskyresort.com, $79-224 adults 15-69, $55-145 children 7-14, $63-183 seniors 70 and over, $1 children under 6) calls itself a ski resort without limits. It has 5,800 skiable acres and 4,350 vertical feet (1,326 m), and the area averages over 400 inches (over 1,000 cm) of the fluffy stuff annually. The ski season generally lasts from Thanksgiving to mid-April. With virtually nonexistent lift lines (except during holidays), this is an ideal place for ambitious skiers and families.

The resort's **Lone Peak Tram** takes daring skiers 16 feet (5 m) shy of the mountain's summit and offers 300 degrees of skiing from the top of Lone Peak. Manicured terrain parks with many groomed features are available for snowboarders. Even with some of the steepest terrain in the country, Big Sky offers plenty of groomers for beginning and intermediate skiers and snowboarders.

In addition to the Mountain Sports School, which offers a wide range of ski and snowboard lessons and programs in winter, Big Sky Resort has the **Basecamp** (406/995-5769), an activity center offering two zipline courses, a high ropes course, a bungee trampoline, a climbing wall, and snowshoeing.

Down the mountain is **Lone Mountain Ranch** (750 Lone Mountain Rd., 406/995-4644 or 800/514-4644, www. lonemountainranch.com, $38 adults, $25 children 13-17 and seniors 60-69, free for children 12 and under and adults 70 and over), a cross-country skier's paradise with 85 kilometers (53 mi) of beautifully groomed and forested trails on 5,000 skiable acres with 2,200 vertical feet (671 m). Snowshoeing is another option, as are guided naturalist tours, lessons, and clinics. Rental equipment (skis and snowshoes) and lessons are available, and with such magnificent terrain, this is one of the biggest bargains around. The trails are sublime, and wildlife-viewing can be excellent. For winter solitude and exploration, this is a marvelous place to be.

Fishing and Floating

The **Gallatin River** runs through the canyon beneath Big Sky and offers up a plethora of recreational opportunities. Since US 191 runs parallel to the river for 40 miles (64 km), fishing access is easy. The road is not meant for casual driving—no stopping and looking here—but there are several pullouts that can double as parking lots. Float fishing is prohibited, but the wade fishing is enticing, if somewhat tricky given the number of rapids created as the water tumbles down the canyon over beautiful car-size boulders.

Rainbows, browns, and cutthroats can all be found in these chilly waters, and the fish have to be lean and mean to battle the currents. They tend to be slightly less selective than downriver in Bozeman, where the decline slows and the water flattens out. There are caddis hatches practically all summer, and a killer salmonfly hatch in mid-June to early July. Late in the season, whopping terrestrials are the way to go.

Wild Trout Outfitters (47520 Gallatin Rd., 406/995-2975 or 800/423-4742, www. wildtroutoutftters.com, 7:30am-7:30pm daily, half-day Gallatin River wade trip $430 for 1 angler, $480 for 2 anglers, all-day Gallatin River wade trip $530 for 1 angler, $580 for 2 anglers) can offer professionally guided trips—wading or floating—including into Yellowstone National Park. **East Slope Outdoors** (44 Town Center Ave., 406/995-4369 or 888/359-3974, www. eastslopeoutdoors.com, 8am-8pm daily in summer, 10am-6pm daily fall-spring, half-day Gallatin River wade trip $325 for 1 angler, $375 for 2 anglers, all-day Gallatin River wade trip $450 for 1 angler, $525 for 2 anglers) offers equipment, rental gear, and guided fly-fishing trips.

If the tranquility of fishing appeals less than the mayhem of white water, rafting on the Gallatin River is a good option. **Montana Whitewater** (63960 Gallatin Rd., 800/799-4465, www.montanawhitewater.com, half day from $76 ages 6 and up, full day from $146 ages 6 and up) offers a range of trips to suit any adrenaline level, including half-day scenic floats, full-day white-water trips, and paddle-and-saddle overnighters. Plus, from the Gallatin Canyon base camp—which is like a small outdoors-loving city—you can

---

1: view from Lone Peak **2:** The Woolzie's Willow Creek Café and Saloon **3:** Lone Peak presides over Big Sky Resort. **4:** the Gallatin River

mix and match adventures including rafting, ziplining, fly-fishing, and horseback riding. The on-site **Blazin' Paddles Café** is a convenient food truck. **Geyser Whitewater** (46651 Gallatin Rd., next to Buck's T-4 on US 191, 406/995-4989, www.raftmontana. com, half-day lower whitewater $149 adults, minimum age restrictions vary with water conditions) is another superb local outfitter that specializes in Gallatin River trips. It also offers kayak trips, horseback riding, bike rentals, rock climbing, private boat trips, and ziplining adventures.

Hiking and Mountain Biking

In the summer, the mountain at Big Sky unfolds into a network of mountain-bike and hiking trails. The **Big Sky Scenic Lift** (406/995-5769, $31-41 adults 18-69, $23-32 children 13-17 and seniors, $5 for children 6 and under) gives riders and hikers a lift up (and down, if they choose) and a chance to tackle some thrilling terrain for every skill level. Bikes and helmets are available for rent at **Big Sky Sports** (Mountain Mall, 50 Big Sky Resort Rd., 406/995-5840, www. bigskyresort.com).

The hiking opportunities are endless around Big Sky, with three mountain ranges, the Gallatin National Forest, the Lee Metcalf Wilderness Area, and Yellowstone National Park all nearby. Some local favorites include **Ousel Falls,** an easy up-and-down 1.8-mile (2.9-km) stroll to a beautiful waterfall. (Find the parking lot and trailhead on Ousel Falls Rd., 2 mi/3.2 km beyond the intersection of Ousel Falls Rd. and Spur Road.) Picnic benches along the way make the path a good one for small children. For more ambitious hikers, **Beehive Basin** offers some excellent options. (Find the parking lot and trailhead by following the Beehive Basin turnoff—1.3 mi/2.1 km beyond Big Sky Mountain Village and 30 yards/meters before the entrance gate to Moonlight Basin—for 2.8 mi/4.5 km.) The trail is sky high at 9,200 feet (2,804 m) and offers unrivaled 360-degree views. As with all of Montana, the weather can change

quickly—snow can fall in July—and hikers need to be fully prepared for whatever Mother Nature sends their way. Farther north in the Gallatin Canyon is **Lava Lake,** a somewhat steep hike that leads you to a crystalline icy-cold mountain lake. (From Big Sky, the trailhead is 13.5 mi/21.7 km north on US 191, just north of the Gallatin River Bridge, but since left turns cannot be made from there, you will need to turn around at the first turnout and approach the gravel turnoff from the north.) The 6-mile (9.7-km) there-and-back trail is almost entirely shaded and an excellent choice on a sweltering day.

Golf

For those who choose to hoof it around the links instead of a mountain trail, the 18-hole Arnold Palmer-designed **Big Sky Golf Course** (Meadow Village, 406/995-5780, www.bigskyresort.com, $79-159, $49 twilight play after 3pm) is open to nonguests and is well worth playing. Abundant wildlife often shares the par-72 course. A driving range, bar and grill, and full pro shop are available.

ENTERTAINMENT AND EVENTS

Although it is set up as a winter resort, Big Sky does an excellent job of capitalizing on the relatively short summer with events that draw crowds from near and far. There are few better venues in the state for live music: Concerts are held in a glorious meadow surrounded by rocky peaks at the free **Music in the Mountains** series (changing venues, 406/995-2742, www.bigskyarts.org, Thursdays June-Sept. starting at 6pm). Past headliners in Big Sky have included Willie Nelson, Bonnie Raitt, and the Doobie Brothers. Other annual musical events sponsored by the Arts Council of Big Sky include **Strings under the Big Sky** (chamber music) and the **Bozeman Symphony Orchestra Pops** concert.

The weekly **Big Sky Farmers Market** (Firepit Park, Big Sky Town Center, 406/570-6579, www.bigskytowncenter.com, 5pm-8pm Wed. June-Sept.) features lots of local vendors in addition to prepared food, a great kids' area, musical entertainment, and personal enrichment that includes yoga and massage.

FOOD

Something about the high mountain air produces serious appetites, and Big Sky has a substantial selection of eateries for every taste. From the top of the mountain to the bottom, you're never more than a quick jog from your next mouthwatering meal.

The Corral (42895 Gallatin Rd., 5 mi/8 km south of Big Sky, 406/995-4249, www.corralbar.com, 8am-10pm Wed.-Sun., 4pm-midnight Mon.-Tues., bar until midnight daily, breakfast $6-16, lunch $11-18, dinner $23-38) offers up an excellent old-school take on the Montana menu. From wild game Bolognese and elk tenderloin to rib eye, chicken-fried steak, and good ol' hamburgers, The Corral's food is consistently good, with plenty of chicken, seafood, and pasta options. You can't go wrong with the smoked trout appetizer.

For great barbecue with a view, **The Riverhouse** (45130 Gallatin Rd., 406/995-7427, www.riverhousebbq.com, 3pm-10pm daily, $8-38) is known for its excellent smoked barbecue. From their fried pickles, okra, and sweet corn nuggets to beef brisket, baby back ribs, and pulled pork, owners Kyle and Greg don't let anyone leave hungry. As if the sound of the rushing Gallatin weren't enough, this wonderful riverfront venue hosts plenty of live music.

★ **Buck's T-4** (46625 Gallatin Rd., 1 mi/1.6 km south of Big Sky, 406/993-5222, www.buckst4.com, 5:30pm-9:30pm daily summer, 5pm-10pm daily winter, $18-48) is fairly unassuming but serves up some of the best cuisine in the region. Known statewide and beyond for wild game—think duck, bison, and red deer—Buck's menu reflects Montana culinary traditions with more contemporary, lighter fare. It even packages up duck bacon for diners to take home. Buck's has an extensive and impressive wine list, and its drinks make the most of the local harvest; try a wild huckleberry martini or bacon bourbon old-fashioned. Buck's keeps limited hours in the fall and spring, between ski season and summer.

For an elegant meal, **Olive B's Big Sky Bistro** (151 Center Ln., 406/995-3355, www.olivebsbigsky.com, 11am-9pm Mon.-Fri., 4pm-9pm Sat., $25-37) is a great choice. Owned by a couple from the East Coast, the restaurant offers an abundance of good seafood including lobster mac and cheese, duckling, and shrimp and grits. But the spot also serves up the best of the West: Rocky Mountain elk with huckleberry demi-glace, pork prime rib, lamb chops, and beef tenderloin. Another place for an evening meal and a stiff whiskey or two is **Copper Whiskey Bar & Grill** (in the Wilson Hotel, 145 Town Center Ave., 406/995-2233, www.coppermontana.com, 3pm-11pm daily, kitchen closes at 9pm, $15-45), which serves burgers, steak, roast chicken, and more. The service can be hit or miss, but their specialty is whiskey—they have pours from around the world and offer specialty cocktails and whiskey flights.

Blue Moon Bakery Pizzeria & Café (3090 Big Pine Dr., 406/995-2305, www.bigskybluemoonbakery.com, 7am-10pm daily, breakfast $2-8, pizza $15-28) is a good bet for everything from breakfast sandwiches and baked goods to salads and gourmet pizza pies. Another good place for an upscale meal any time of day is **Horn & Cantle** (750 Lone Mountain Rd., 406/995-4644 or 800/514-4644, www.lonemountainranch.com, 7am-10am, 11:30am-2pm, 5pm-9pm Thurs.-Tues., breakfast $25 buffet, lunch $22 buffet, dinner $21-55), which serves up gourmet local fare ranging from elk meatballs and lamb leg ragu to rib eye and more, all prepared in inventive ways and presented with flair.

For a truly unique meal during the ski season, try the sleigh-ride dinner at ★ **Lone Mountain Ranch** (750 Lone Mountain Rd., 406/995-2782, www.lonemountainranch.com, $122-162 pp), which whisks diners up a snowy trail to a candlelit cabin in the woods for a steak and potato dinner. There are two departures a day, in season, at 4:30pm and 7:30pm. Or try **dinner in a yurt** (via snowcat instead of horse-pulled sleigh) high atop Lone Mountain (406/995-3880, www.bigskyyurt.com, from $189 adults, from $149 children), which also includes time for sledding. Both experiences offer hearty meals and unparalleled ambience, and both sell out well in advance—so book ahead.

ACCOMMODATIONS

Big Sky was built as a resort, and it caters to visitors and vacationers. A wide range of accommodations, from ski-in/ski-out mountainside lodging to rustic roadside motels, inviting guest ranches, luxe resorts, and condo or cabin rentals, can address your specific needs—staying put or traveling around, skiing or golfing, walking or driving to dinner.

For the best bang for your buck, try the **Corral Motel** (42895 Gallatin Road, 5 mi/8 km south of Big Sky, 406/995-4249 or 888/995-4249, www.corralbar.com, from $140 single, $20 each additional person), which also has a terrific restaurant and bar open year-round. The guest rooms are basic but clean and comfortable, with honeyed pine paneling that evokes the best of Western hospitality. During the winter, a shuttle runs from the motel to Big Sky Resort and Meadow Village.

On top of the mountain is the **Summit at Big Sky** (Mountain Village Center, 800/548-4486, www.bigskyresort.com, studio rooms from $449), a deluxe slope-side facility with the convenience of a hotel and the amenities of a condo. It offers both residences and temporary lodging, all in a comfortable and sophisticated atmosphere. There are indoor and outdoor pools, hot tubs, a sauna and fitness facility, and fireplaces in most accommodations. The entire hotel is being remade for their 2025 vision. Lodging packages can include lift tickets. **Big Sky Resort** (800/548-4486) can arrange a variety of lodging from hotels including Summit and Huntley Lodge to slope-side rooms and condos to ski-in/ski-out cabins and homes for rent.

The two newest hotels in the Big Sky area are the **Wilson Hotel** (145 Town Center Ave., 406/995-9000, www.thewilsonhotel.com, $350-1,029), which opened in 2019 right in the heart of the town center and offers simple and nice rooms with lots of options for suites, and **Montage Big Sky** (995 Settlement Trail, 406/993-8142, www.montagehotels.com, starting at $676 night), which opened in December 2021 as the largest hotel in the state of Montana. The Montage is as glamorous as it gets in Montana, with plenty of on-site restaurants, a spa, and most of the rooms costing several thousand dollars per night.

INFORMATION AND SERVICES

The **Big Sky Chamber of Commerce** (88 Ousel Falls Rd. Unit A1, 406/995-3000 or 800/943-4111, www.bigskychamber.com, 8:30am-5:30pm daily summer, 9am-5pm Mon.-Fri. fall-spring) is an excellent resource for local information.

The **post office** (406/995-4540, 10am-5pm Mon.-Fri., 10am-1pm Sat.) is conveniently located at 55 Meadow Center Drive, Suite 2.

Your best bet for free **Internet access** is at the **Big Sky Community Library** (45465 Gallatin Rd., 406/995-4281). The library sets aside hours for community use (1pm-5pm Sun., 10am-6pm Mon., 4pm-8pm Tues.-Wed.). Call ahead or check the website for hours, which vary by season.

The **Mountain Clinic of Big Sky** is in the ski patrol building at Big Sky Resort (100 Beaverhead Trail, 406/995-2797, 9am-5pm Mon.-Fri.). For more serious medical emergencies, **Big Sky Medical Center** (334 Town Center Ave., 406/995-6995, www.bozeman-health.org) has a 24-hour emergency room about an hour's drive from Big Sky.

To wash your clothes and have a few drinks while you wait, **Sit & Spin Laundry Lounge** (115 Aspen Leaf Dr., 1F, 406/600-8416, 1pm-2am daily) is the place. They have great bloody Marys, freshly squeezed juices, and house specialty shots that look like Tide pods. They also serve specialty coffees. And they have Nintendo competitions on Thursday nights.

TRANSPORTATION
Getting There

Big Sky is about 50 miles (80 km) south of Bozeman off US 191. The closest airport is **Bozeman Yellowstone International Airport** (BZN, 406/388-8321, www. bozemanairport.com) in Belgrade, about 50 miles (80 km) north.

A variety of shuttle services run from the airport. **Karst Stage** (406/556-3540 or 800/845-2778, www.karststage.com) has a counter next to National Rent-a-Car and provides shuttles ($65 one-way with two-fare minimum) to Big Sky. **Shuttle to Big Sky & Taxi** (406/995-4895 or 888/454-5667, www. bigskytaxi.com) provides private van and SUV transportation to, from, and around Big Sky, as does **Big Sky Bound** (406/539-3828, www.bigskyboundshuttleandtransportation. com, $200 one-way between Big Sky and the airport between 8am-8pm).

Getting Around

Once in Big Sky, take advantage of the free bus service, **Skyline** (406/995-6287, www. skylinebus.com). In addition to covering the Big Sky area, buses also run between Bozeman and Big Sky. Hours vary by season.

Shuttle to Big Sky & Taxi (406/995-4895 or 888/454-5667, www.bigskytaxi.com) offers taxi service around Big Sky.

Dollar Rent-a-Car (1 mi/1.6 km from the airport, Belgrade) will deliver a vehicle to any Big Sky location.

Livingston and Paradise Valley

Rough and tumble Livingston (pop. 7,893, elev. 4,501 ft/1,372 m) has always been a crossroads of cultures. A railroad town, it was long the launching point for expeditions— both professional and leisurely—into Yellowstone National Park. Paradise Valley, the stunning agricultural and recreational corridor linking Livingston to the north entrance of Yellowstone National Park, was the stomping ground of the Crow people, a prized region for fur trappers, and the end point of the great cattle drive from Texas. The town was surrounded by mines, which drew a unique crowd, and today it probably has more literary figures and artists per capita than any other community in the state.

At one point in the early 1880s, there were 40 businesses in town, 30 of which were saloons. Such legendary characters as Calamity Jane and Madame Bulldog were residents. Evidence of those wild days is still visible in various establishments—for example, as bullet holes through the ceiling. The town still has a healthy number of bars, but in a nod to foodies, there are now an equal number of excellent restaurants.

Livingston's transformation into a haven for legendary artists, writers, and actors probably started in the 1960s. Iconic film director Sam Peckinpah took up residence in the town's Murray Hotel, and writers Tom McGuane, Doug Peacock, Tim Cahill, and Richard Brautigan all called Livingston home—and some still do. Actors including Peter Fonda, Jeff Bridges, Michael Keaton, and Dennis Quaid made their homes on ranches outside of town.

Indeed, Livingston has a rich blended culture that is evident in everything from its sophisticated galleries and gourmet restaurants to its bawdy bars, rollicking rodeo, and fly-fishing paradise.

SIGHTS

The town's **Depot Center** (200 W. Park St., 406/222-2300, www.livingstondepot. org, 10am-5pm Mon.-Sat., 1pm-5pm Sun. Memorial Day-Labor Day, donation) is a majestic building anchoring the town to its railroad heritage. In addition to being something of a community center where the town gathers for concerts and special events, the depot houses a worthwhile museum featuring history, art, and culture of the region. Electric-train buffs should ask for a tour of the basement, where the region's train fanatics have built a wonderland.

On the other side of the tracks, the **Yellowstone Gateway Museum** (118 W. Chinook St., 406/222-4184, www. yellowstonegatewaymuseum.org, 10am-5pm daily Memorial Day-Sept., 10am-5pm Thurs.-Sat. Oct.-Memorial Day, $5 adults, $4 seniors 62 and over, $4 youth 13-18, free for children 12 and under, housed in a historic schoolhouse, holds the county's archives and presents some excellent local exhibits on railroad history, pioneer life, Native American cultures, and military history.

SPORTS AND RECREATION
Fishing and Floating

If art defines Livingston, fishing feeds it. The **Yellowstone River** curves around the town and always makes its presence known. Paradise Valley lives up to its name in countless ways, fishing among them. **Nelson's, Armstrong's,** and **De Puy's Spring Creeks** are just minutes from town and offer some of the best and most consistent fishing in the state. Winter is an especially good time to fish the spring creeks because the springs flow constantly at a consistent temperature, the crowds are gone, and the rod fees go down significantly. Matson Rogers's **Angler's West Flyfishing** (206 Railroad Ln., off US 89 S., Emigrant, 406/333-4401, www.montanaflyfishers.com, 7am-7pm daily summer, 8am-6pm daily spring and fall) is a great resource, with both a fly shop and complete guiding service for the Yellowstone River and waters around the state. In Livingston, **Dan Bailey's Fly Shop** (209 W. Park St., 406/222-1673, www.dan-bailey.com, 8am-6pm Mon.-Sat., 8am-noon

Sun. summer, 9am-6pm Mon.-Sat., 9am-3pm Sun. winter) is as venerable a fly shop as ever there was, anywhere. In addition to a living history lesson—the shop was established in 1938—the staff at Dan Bailey's can offer superbly qualified advice along with renowned gear and world-famous flies. They also have outstanding maps, gear, and advice for other adventures, including hiking.

To cover a lot of water in this country, with or without a rod, floating on a raft or drift boat can be a great option. While just about any outfitter can arrange to float and fish, **The Flying Pig Adventure Company** (511 Scott St., 888/792-9193, www.flyingpigrafting.com, May-Sept., 2-hour scenic float trip from $59 adults, $49 children 12 and under, 2-hour whitewater trips from $69 adults, $59 children, full-day trips $135 adults, $115 children) is a full-service outfitter offering guided white-water rafting, horseback rides, wildlife safaris, and cowboy cookouts. **Montana Whitewater** (603 Scott St., Gardiner, 800/799-4465, www.montanawhitewater.com, half day from $66.50 adults, $56.50 children 12 and under, full day from $102.50 adults, $92.50 children 6-12) offers both scenic and white-water floats on the Yellowstone River. **Yellowstone Raft Company** (212 W. Park St., 406/848-7777 or 800/858-7781, www.yellowstoneraft.com, May-Sept., half-day raft trip from $59 ages 6 and up, full day trips from $95 ages 6 and up) was established in 1978 and has an excellent reputation for experienced guides and top-of-the-line equipment.

Hiking

With mountains towering in every direction—the Absarokas and the Gallatins south of town, the Bridgers to the west, and the Crazies to the northeast—and a stiff wind usually blowing, heading out for a hike is never a bad idea in Livingston. Six miles (9.7 km) south of town on the east side of

---

1: Livingston, a railroad town, art mecca, and angler's paradise **2:** Chico Hot Springs Resort, just north of Yellowstone **3:** the Yellowstone River

Cranky Yankee Jim's Road

James George, who earned the moniker Yankee Jim as well as a reputation for being more than a little cantankerous, came to Montana Territory as a young prospector in 1863. When gold eluded him, Jim began to hunt professionally, for meat for the Crow Indian Agency. In 1873, Jim took possession of the road from Bottler's Ranch in Paradise Valley, near present-day Emigrant, to Mammoth by squatting in the canyon along the Yellowstone when the road builders stopped construction. Jim set up a toll booth in the narrowest section of the canyon, today called Yankee Jim Canyon, and charged exorbitant fees to all travelers passing through. At the time, it was the only way for travelers to get from Livingston to Gardiner, Montana, and the brand-new Yellowstone National Park. By all accounts, Yankee Jim made a lot of money but few friends in those days.

In 1883, the Northern Pacific Railway appropriated his roadbed, much to Yankee Jim's chagrin. He negotiated the construction of another road through the canyon (parts of which are still visible along the west side of US 89 South) and reportedly used his location above the train tracks to spit on, curse at, and occasionally fire rifle shots at passing trains. His tirades were supposedly fueled by copious amounts of whiskey.

By 1893, with his road in disrepair and his penchant for alcohol steadily on the rise, Yankee Jim agreed to surrender his road for a lump sum of $1,000. Local lore inserts Teddy Roosevelt, a frequent visitor to Yellowstone National Park, as the person who convinced Yankee Jim to give up his road and his antics (or else). In 1924, Yankee Jim died penniless in Fresno, California. There are many who believe that his fortune, amassed by all those years of price-gouging in the canyon that bears his name, is buried in the hills between Emigrant and Gardiner.

River Road in Paradise Valley, **Pine Creek** is a stunning and popular spot with camping (spots fill up early) and hiking options for every ability level. A nice leisurely amble is the 2-mile (3.2-km) out-and-back trail to **Pine Creek Falls.** Hard-core hikers could hike the steep but mostly shaded 10 miles (16.1 km) round-trip to **Pine Creek Lake. Suce Creek, Deep Creek,** and **Mill Creek** all have first-rate trails and stunning scenery, but be aware of bears in the region. For gear or just good ideas, talk to Dale at **Dan Bailey's Outdoor Co.** (209 W. Park St., 406/222-1673, 8am-6pm Mon.-Sat., 8am-noon Sun. summer, 9am-6pm Mon.-Sat., 9am-3pm Sun. winter), on the main thoroughfare into downtown Livingston.

ENTERTAINMENT AND EVENTS

The Arts

One of the area's best-kept secrets is **Music Ranch Montana** (4664 Old Yellowstone Trail N., 9 mi/14.5 km south of Livingston, 406/222-2255, www.musicranchmontana.

net), a unique music venue for indoor/outdoor concerts in summer. Founded by a well-known entrepreneur and his wife in 1995, Music Ranch has a large barn with both indoor and outdoor seating, including terraces built into the hillside. Talk about an amphitheater with a view! The ticket prices for the concerts, largely country and folk musicians, are reasonable, and a dance floor right next to the stage keeps the energy up for each concert. It's family-owned and operated in the best possible way, and attending a concert at Music Ranch feels like a festive family reunion.

ART GALLERIES

Livingston is a railroad town, but to its core it is also an artists' town. There are more than a dozen galleries and many more artists, both brilliant amateurs and sophisticated professionals.

Visions West Contemporary (108 S. Main St., 406/222-0337, www. visionswestcontemporary.com, 10am-5pm Tues.-Sat.) has three galleries—in Livingston, Bozeman, and Denver—and uses the space to push the boundaries of art in the West. The stunning and often surprising work is inspired by a passion for nature, animals, the environment, and the region. Local character and talented artist Parks Reece captures the beauty of the region with a delightful and often mischievous sense of humor. The **Parks Reece Gallery** (119 S. Main St., Ste. A3, 406/222-5724, www.parksreece.com, 9am-5pm Tues.-Fri., 11am-4pm Sat.) should not be missed.

The mission of the **Livingston Center for Art & Culture** (119 S. Main, 406/222-5222, www.livingstoncenter.org, noon-5pm Tues.-Fri., 11am-4pm Sat.), is to "spark new ways of seeing and thinking through the experience of art and culture." To that end, they offer interesting exhibits—including by students at Montana State University—and classes for both kids and adults.

Festivals and Events

Since 1924, the annual **Livingston Roundup Rodeo** (406/222-3199, www. livingstonroundup.com) has enticed cowboys from across the country with its fat purse on the Fourth of July holiday. As crowds overtake the town's fairgrounds with rabid rodeo fever, regular events include barrel racing, bareback team roping, tie-down roping, saddle bronc, steer wrestling, and bull riding. The three-day event—held July 2-4—kicks off with a hometown parade and ends each evening with fireworks. This is without a doubt when Livingston most shines. General admission and reserved seating rodeo tickets are available online or by calling, but both sell out well before July.

In a town as food-savvy as Livingston, it's no surprise that there are a handful of great events to sample the local offerings. The wonderful community-centered **Livingston Farmers Market** (at the band shell in Sacajawea Park, River Dr., 406/222-0730, 4:30pm-7:30pm Wed. early June-mid-Sept.) offers up the region's fresh local bounty in a friendly and festive environment. Live music is performed until 9pm. Sponsored by the Western Sustainability Exchange (www.westernsustainabilityexchange.org), the event supports a Young Entrepreneur Leadership Program that teaches kids about the intricacies of business and the value of giving back to the community, and a Senior Farmers Market Nutrition Program provides local low-income seniors with $50 vouchers for locally grown veggies, herbs, fruit, and honey at the market.

If you want a fantastic overview of the art scene, and consequently the entire community, hit the town **art walks,** held the fourth Friday of every month late June-September; there is also a single holiday art walk each year in November-December. The town comes out in force to celebrate the arts.

SHOPPING

Downtown Livingston is a wonderful place to shop, with stores all within walking distance of one another offering a convenient escape from the town's ever-present wind along with an eclectic assortment of wares, from art and clothes to books and equipment. Most shops are closed on Sunday.

Sax & Fryer (109 W. Callender St., 406/222-1421, 9am-5pm Mon.-Fri.) is an anchor for the town and a direct link to its origins. Founded in 1883, the year after Livingston was incorporated, and still run by the Fryer family, the store offers a meaty selection of books from regional and local authors as well as magazines, cards, gifts, and office supplies. An excellent section is devoted to children's books.

B-Hive Artisan Cooperative (215 E. Lewis., 406/223-4015, www.bhivemontana. com, 10am-5pm Mon.-Tues. and Thurs.-Sat., 10am-4pm Wed.) is a hip little boutique that is artist-owned and -staffed. The collection blends various media—jewelry, yard art, ceramics, hand-blown glass, handbags, and bronze sculpture—perfect for those who don't necessarily want their gifts detailed with rusty nails or old barbed wire.

The Obsidian Collection (108 N. 2nd St., 406/222-2022, www.theobsidiancollection.

com, 10am-6pm Mon.-Sat.) offers an appealing selection of gifts, children's items, jewelry, cards, stationery, soaps, and lotions. Customers are loyal, often driving significant distances to see the latest and greatest collections. They also have a killer section of cheaters/readers for those who need a little help with menus and phones and whatnot.

For almost any kind of outdoor gear—including fly-fishing, cycling, hiking, and backpacking—visit **Dan Bailey's Outdoor Co.** (209 W. Park, 406/222-1673, www.danbaileys. com, 9am-6pm Mon.-Sat., 9am-3pm Sun.), a venerable shop indeed. Founded in 1938 by an NYC physics professor who left in order to open a fly shop in Montana, the shop has always committed to the community and worked to protect wild rivers and public land. Now owned and run by Dale Sexton, who founded Timber Trails in 1996, Dan Bailey's offers the best in all sorts of outdoor gear and athletic clothing. They rent bikes and fly-fishing gear, and are the best resource in town to guide you toward your next outdoor adventure.

FOOD

Campione (101 N. Main St., 406/333-2427, www.eatcampione.com, dinner 5pm-9pm Wed.-Sun., brunch 10am-1:45pm Sat.-Sun., $15-22) is one of the best places to enjoy a meal—if you can get a table, that is. The restaurant opened mid-pandemic but immediately gained a following since everything is made from scratch and utterly delicious. They have all sorts of traditional antipasti, both hot and cold; beautiful pastas; salads; and meat, fish, and veggie entrées. Whatever you do, save room for dessert. Reservations are strongly encouraged for this intimate eatery.

Housed in the venerable Murray Hotel, **2nd Street Bistro** (123 N. 2nd St., 406/222-9463, www.secondstreetbistro.com, 5pm-close Wed.-Sun., $16-38) serves simple but inspired cuisine—both small and large plates—with French flair and Western attitude. The Mediterranean fish stew is a local favorite, as are the upscale pizzas. All of the meat served is raised locally, and so is much of the produce. On Friday and Saturday nights, Montana prime rib is served all night. During winter months, they often have four-course prix fixe menus ($75) where diners choose from various starters, soups and salads, entrées, and dessert.

For a casual bite in a festive setting, **Neptune's Taphouse & Eatery** (232 S. Main St., 406/333-2400, 11am-9pm Thurs.-Tues., 2pm-9pm Wed., $12-35) serves a broad menu from bar food and burgers to sushi, seafood, and steak. They also serve a great selection of beers brewed down the street at Neptune's Brewery. Another favorite spot for locals and visitors alike is **Gil's Goods** (207 W. Park, 406/222-9463, www.gilsgoods.com, noon-8pm Thurs.-Mon. with extended hours in summer, $9-15), which serves up excellent burgers, wood-fired pizza, salads, and starters. The restaurant is attached to the always-busy **Murray Bar,** so diners can have a drink with their meal.

For a delicious and truly creative breakfast, try **Faye's Café** (415 E. Lewis St., 406/223-7481, www.sarahfayemontana.com, 8am-11am Mon.-Thurs., 8am-10:45am Sat.-Sun., all meals $15-18 including drink), where diners are asked to look at a colorful chalkboard and name their favorite words—from Eggs Benny and Meaty + Cheesy to huckleberry, bacon, tacos, and amazeballs—which Faye will then turn into a delicious breakfast creation.

Not gourmet by any stretch of the imagination, **Mark's In & Out Drive-In** (801 W. Park St., Livingston, 406/222-7744, www.marksbeefburgers.com, 11am-10pm daily late spring-early fall, $2-4.50) just might be the town favorite, and the most affordable. There is no seating at this seasonal walk-up or drive-up joint right out of the 1950s, but the burgers, fries, and shakes are so good that you won't mind. And there's a park across the street if you can't wait to dig in.

Every Western town worth its salt should have a **Stockman** (118 N. Main St., 406/222-8455, 11am-9pm Tues.-Sun.,

$10-29). It is an old-school bar with the essence of a supper club. The steaks, prime rib, and burgers are second to none; this is the real Montana.

If the pools bring people to ★ **Chico Hot Springs Resort** (163 Chico Rd., off US 89 S., 23 mi/37 km south of Livingston, 406/333-4933, www.chicohotsprings.com, breakfast 7:30am-10:30am daily, dinner 5pm-9pm daily, $28-50), the food is what transforms them into regulars. From the first taste of *burrata* a la Chico with a balsamic vinegar reduction, through the house-smoked rainbow trout and the gorgonzola filet mignon to the legendary flaming orange, Chico has gone a long way in defining Montana cuisine with fresh local ingredients in simple, hearty, and outstanding dishes. The Chico cookbook, available at the resort, should be in every kitchen.

Closer to town but still set in the grandeur of Paradise Valley, the ★ **Pine Creek Lodge & Café** (2496 E. River Rd., 10 mi/16.1 km south of Livingston, 406/222-3628, www.pinecreeklodgemontana.com, dinner 4pm-9pm daily, brunch 10am-3pm Sat.-Sun., brunch $10-15, dinner $12-38), is a longtime favorite and an off-the-beaten-path gem. The menu changes frequently but boasts such fare as Thai coconut curry and rainbow trout tacos you won't soon forget. Live music and outdoor barbecues take place in summer, readings by local authors in winter. The place was nearly burned down in a big 2012 forest fire, but this little enclave continues to be a wonderful part of the community. Call for reservations as opening hours can change.

ACCOMMODATIONS

It's true that Livingston has quite a collection of funky roadside motels that have seen better days, but there are some treasures around town and down the valley. Right in town, the **Murray Hotel** (201 W. Park St., 406/222-1350, www.murrayhotel.com, from $129, pets welcome for $25) is a Montana standard. It hasn't been glamorously overhauled, but the authenticity in each of the 25 unique rooms and suites works well, and the place

is rich with history, including the story of Will Rogers and Walter Hill trying to bring a saddle horse to the 3rd floor in a 1905 hand-cranked elevator. Guest rooms are well appointed, with amenities like pillow-top beds and Wi-Fi.

As for chain hotels, Livingston is growing in number. None of them have the charm of the Murray, but the newest and nicest is **Fairfield Inn & Suites by Marriott** (1629 W. Park, 406/222-4914, www.marriott.com, from $179 which can include a pass to Yellowstone National Park), which has an indoor pool, an outdoor hot tub, and a fitness room, on top of their very modern and nice hotel rooms. Pets are welcome for a $50 per stay fee. Keep in mind, rooms can soar well above the $500 mark in peak summer. There is also a pet-friendly **Super 8 by Wyndham** (105 Centennial Dr., 406/222-7711, www.wyndhamhotels.com, from $114) and a **Travelodge by Wyndham** (102 Rogers Ln., 406/222-6320, www.wyndhamhotels.com, from $72) with a restaurant on-site.

Pine Creek Lodge (2496 E. River Rd., 406/222-3628, www.pinecreeklodgemontana.com) offers unique accommodations in a beautiful setting. Cabin options (from $89) include rustic-yet-modern overhauled shipping containers, and there are also several tent sites ($39). Bathhouses are modern and clean, available to both campers and cabin guests. Pets are welcome in the cabins for $25 (free for campers). The on-site restaurant is outstanding and fun. And there are often live music events throughout the summer.

For travelers who long to stay in one place and experience life as a dude, **Mountain Sky Guest Ranch** (480 National Forest Development Rd. 132, Emigrant, 406/333-4911 or 800/548-3392, www.mountainsky.com, all rates weekly Sun.-Sun., $5,380-6,750 adults 13 and up, $4,590-5,550 children 7-12, $3,590-4,100 children 6 and under) sets the gold standard for summertime family ranch vacations. Set on 10,000 acres of mountains and forests, Mountain Sky offers impeccable service, gourmet dining, charming log cabins, and fantastic activity possibilities, including golf on a Johnny Miller course, a high-energy kids' program, endless alpine trails for horseback riding and hiking, swimming, and even a spa. With such superlative options for balancing family time and adult relaxation, it's small surprise that 87 percent of the guests return year after year, and that entire summers are often booked more than a year in advance.

★ **Chico Hot Springs Resort**

Built around a natural hot spring that was discovered in the late 1800s, the Chico Hot Springs Resort (163 Chico Rd., 23 mi/37 km south of Livingston in Pray, 406/333-4933, www.chicohotsprings.com) has become a Montana icon, as much for its sensational food and raucous saloon as for its heavenly year-round outdoor pools. The resort got its start when Bill and Percie Knowles offered weary miners a clean bed, a hot bath, and fresh strawberries with every meal. The resort has stayed true to its humble origins by offering simple, no-frills guest rooms with shared baths in the main lodge starting at $80-155. Modern accommodations are available in Warren's Wing (from $185), the Lower Lodge (from $185), and in elegant cabins (from $285) or pet-friendly rustic cabins (from $140). Cottages, houses, and chalets (call for rates and availability) can accommodate larger parties.

For travelers in search of more than a memorable meal and a luxurious soak, Chico offers a number of activities, all of which take advantage of its spectacular location just north of Yellowstone National Park in Paradise Valley. From horseback riding and dogsledding to hiking and cross-country skiing, Chico affords every visitor ample opportunity to earn their dinner.

CAMPING

There are several nice campgrounds in the Paradise Valley. The closest to town is Osen's RV Park & Campground (20 Merrill Ln.,

406/222-0591, www.montanarvpark.com, $47-59), a nice green site with plenty of shade trees, plus Wi-Fi and cable included. There's also a private bath house and laundry facilities. Another popular campground is Livingston/Paradise Valley KOA Holiday (163 Pine Creek Rd., 406/222-0992 or 800/562-2805, www.koa.com, late Apr.-Sep.), which offers plentiful tent sites (from $30) and RV sites (call for rates) in a forested area.

In the foothills of the Absarokas, Pine Creek Campground (266 Luccock Park Rd., 406/646-1012, www.recreation.gov, from $20 tents) is a gorgeous setting with fabulous hiking trails nearby. There are group sites and a group picnic area, plus tables and campfire rings, and vault toilets. Drinking water is available, as is trash collection. Campers can fish in nearby Pine Creek or hike to the falls or higher to the lake. This is bear country so don't come without bear spray and confidence about how to be in the woods without creating bear-human conflicts.

INFORMATION AND SERVICES

The Livingston Chamber of Commerce (303 E. Park St., 406/222-0850, www.livingston-chamber.com, 9am-5pm Mon.-Fri., 9am-1pm Sat.-Sun. Memorial Day-Labor Day, 10am-5pm Mon.-Fri., 10am-4pm Sat. Labor Day-Memorial Day) is housed in the former crew quarters of the Burlington Northern Railroad. It offers a wide assortment of information about summer and winter activities, including a brochure titled *What to Do in Livingston*. Stop by to meet the friendly people and pick up information on restaurants, accommodations, fishing, dude ranches, and more. A computer is available for visitors to check their email or browse the Internet.

The Livingston-Park County Public Library (228 W. Callender St., 406/222-0862, www.livingstonparkcountylibrary.blogspot.com, 10am-8pm Mon.-Thurs., 10am-6pm Fri., 10am-5pm Sat.) offers cozy spaces to work or browse through your guidebook. It has a terrific collection of fly-fishing material and even offers a genealogy service for visitors in the summer. It also has **free Internet access.** Computers are available for up to an hour at a time.

The **main post office** (406/222-0912, 8:30am-5pm Mon.-Fri., 10:30am-12:30pm Sat.) is at 105 North 2nd Street.

Livingston HealthCare (320 Alpenglow Ln., 406/222-3541) has a 24-hour emergency room. For nonemergency medical care, visit **Urgent Care** (104 Centennial Dr., 406/222-0030, 8am-7pm Mon.-Fri., noon-4pm Sat.-Sun.).

Wash clothes at **Off the Cuff** (322 E. Park St., 406/222-7428, 24 hours daily). It has coin-operated washers and dryers, laundry drop-off service, dry cleaning, and free Wi-Fi.

TRANSPORTATION
Getting There
Livingston is 116 miles (187 km) from the **Billings Logan International Airport** (BIL, 406/247-8609, www.flybillings.com) and 38 miles (61 km) from **Bozeman**

Yellowstone International Airport (BZN, 406/388-8321, www.bozemanairport.com).

From Bozeman, **Greater Valley Taxi** (406/587-6303, www.greatervalleytaxi.com) has a stand outside the baggage claim area, and rides to Livingston are around $130 for a single passenger. Livingston's lone taxi service, **Amazing Taxi** (406/223-5344, 7am-11pm daily), also offers taxi service within 125 miles (201 km) of Livingston.

From the Billings airport, **Cody Shuttle Service** (307/527-6789, www.codyshuttle.com) will transport you to Livingston (call for rates).

Getting Around
Both airports have car-rental companies on-site. At Bozeman's airport, **Alamo, Avis, Budget, Enterprise, Dollar, Hertz, Thrifty, Go Rentals,** and **National** have on-site counters. At Billings's airport, **Enterprise, Thrifty, Dollar, Hertz, National, Alamo, Avis,** and **Budget** all have a presence.

Livingston to Red Lodge

This stretch of highway is a smooth ribbon between dramatic mountains ranges—the Absarokas, the Crazies, and the behemoth Beartooths. The views stretch for miles in every direction, and although many of the scarce exits off I-90 lead to nothing more than a jumble of ranch buildings, there are some wonderful old towns that appear every now and then. **Big Timber,** still heavily populated by Norwegian immigrants, is a mining town with a railroad history and a grand old hotel. Tiny **Reed Point** is an agricultural town with big attitude. **Columbus** and **Roscoe,** barely dots on the map, offer, respectively, a well-known watering hole, the New Atlas Bar, and a great restaurant, the Grizzly Bar & Grill.

THE BOULDER VALLEY
Just east of Livingston is **Swingley Road** (from Livingston, head southeast from E. Park St. before you get to the easternmost entrance to I-90). As far as this writer is concerned, it is the portal to paradise. The road meanders through age-old farmsteads and stunning ranches, with the Boulder River carving the valley deeper into jagged peaks. The trail at **West Boulder,** which starts from the campground, offers a scenic but moderately easy 6-mile (9.7-km) round-trip hike through forest and meadow to **Boulder Meadows,** a tranquil spot with the occasional cow that is perfect for wetting a line or setting up camp. You could continue another 5 miles (8 km) to the junction of **Falls Creek Trail,**

or farther into the **Mill Creek drainage** of Paradise Valley, but the meadows are a hard place to leave. Right near the trailhead is **West Boulder Cabin** (406/222-1892 for last-minute booking, www.recreation.gov for advance reservations, $75), maintained by the U.S. Forest Service. The three-bedroom, no-bath cabin is supremely rustic (it does have electricity, a refrigerator, and cookstove, but no cell service), complete with mice-eaten mattresses, but there is no better place to wake up if early morning hiking is your thing. Reservations are required and can be made up to six months in advance.

BIG TIMBER

Not only is it perfectly situated for a roadway coffee break between Bozeman and Billings, but Big Timber (pop. 1,729, elev. 4,091 ft/1,247 m) is also an interesting little town and a worthwhile stop, with some nice galleries, a good shop or two, a great museum, and a beautiful old railroad hotel that anchors the community. An old-school agricultural community with strong mining and railroad ties, it is flat as a pancake but surrounded on either side by dramatic mountains and encircled by the Boulder and Yellowstone Rivers. Oh, and trees—thus the name.

Right off the highway is the **Crazy Mountain Museum** (2 S. Frontage Rd., southeast of I-90 exit 367, 406/932-5126, www. crazymountainmuseum.com, 10am-4:30pm Mon.-Sat., 1pm-4:30pm Sun. Memorial Day-Sept., donations appreciated), a thoughtfully laid out collection that pays tribute to the town's Norwegian heritage. Several old buildings are on-site, including the Sourdough Schoolhouse and a Norwegian *stabbur* (storehouse). There's a diorama of Big Timber in 1907, a Chinese archaeological exhibit, a gun collection, and an exhibit on the local sheep industry, among other permanent exhibits, and also plenty of rotating exhibits. The volunteer docents bring the collection to life with wonderful stories and often personal reflections.

In the heart of town is **The Grand Hotel Bed & Breakfast** (139 McLeod St., 406/932-4459, www.thegrand-hotel.com, $74-150), a stately Victorian-style railroad hotel. The guest rooms are traditional and fairly small with period antiques and private or shared bath. Downstairs, the **restaurant** (lunch 10am-3pm Mon.-Sat. $9-13, dinner 5pm-9pm Mon.-Sat. $14-42) and saloon attract visitors from around the state with butter-knife steaks, spice elk sausage, grilled herb rack of lamb, and an award-winning wine list. The food is sumptuous, and the atmosphere—with rich, dark mahogany and 1890s furnishings—leaves nothing to be desired.

Greycliff Prairie Dog Town State Park (I-90 exit 377, Greycliff, 406/247-2940, www. stateparks.mt.gov, $8/vehicle nonresidents) is just what the name suggests—a remarkable metropolis constructed and inhabited by thousands of black-tailed prairie dogs. These furry little creatures are endearing if you watch them interact for even just a few minutes. A picnic area is available, but remember to keep Fido in the car.

REED POINT

Every Labor Day weekend, the population of Reed Point swells from about 300 to more than 5,000. People come from far and wide to watch a couple of thousand sheep make their way, leaping and running, down Main Street. It's called the **Great Montana Sheep Drive** (406/322-4505, www. stillwatercountychamber.com), and it is an afternoon well spent. The annual event includes a mutton cook-off, a parade and car show, a street dance, a kids' carnival and petting zoo, local crafts sales, and a variety of entertainment. Even though it's this one-day event that puts little Reed Point on the map, it is a nice town to explore if you have time.

COLUMBUS, ABSAROKEE, AND ROSCOE

For anglers and adventurers in search of good water, high mountains, and a friendly bar with decent grub, these three hamlets fit

Running of the Sheep

It's not exactly Pamplona's Running of the Bulls, but Reed Point's **Great Montana Sheep Drive** (406/322-4505, www.stillwatercountychamber.com), also known as "Running of the Sheep," is a Montana classic. Though history might suggest this was a reaction to conflict between sheepherders and cattle ranchers, a tongue-in-cheek thumbing of the nose perhaps, the truth is that this event was started in 1980 when the town (population, according to one sign posted in town, "about 100: 99 good folks and one real jerk") gathered to auction off an 89-year-old bachelor in hopes of finding him a companion. The sheep were introduced in 1989, Montana's centennial celebration of statehood during which the relatively nearby town of Roundup was planning a cattle drive. One resident (possibly the jerk?) had the idea of a sheep drive that would actually cross in front of the cattle. The cattle confrontation was quashed, but the idea of the sheep drive took hold, and the event has been growing every year since. Roughly 2,000 sheep make their way down Main Street, sandwiched between thousands of spectators and more than 70 food vendors. The annual event also includes a mutton cook-off, a parade, a car show, a street dance, a kids' carnival and petting zoo, local crafts sales, and a variety of entertainment. The event is scheduled annually the Sunday of Labor Day.

the bill brilliantly. With the Stillwater and Yellowstone Rivers nearby, Columbus is a fishing town, and the 100-year-old **New Atlas Bar** (528 E. Pike Ave., 406/322-9818, 10am-2am daily) is one of the coolest but least-visited bars in the state. There never seem to be more than a couple of old-timers bellied up to the beautiful old bar, and with more than 60 mounts on the walls and a couple of oddities here and there (a stuffed two-headed calf, for example), this place has the feel of a cool but somewhat dingy old museum.

On the way down Highway 78 toward Red Lodge is Absarokee, a quaint little town near the Stillwater River with a handful of B&Bs and a similar number of outfitters. **Absaroka River Adventures** (113 Grove St., Absarokee, 800/334-7238, www.absarokariver.com) offers scenic floats (half day $55 adults, $35 children 12 and under, full day $130 adults, $90 children) on the lower Stillwater and on the more dramatic upper section (half day $60 adults, $40 children), which is only floatable in early summer. **Paintbrush Adventures** (86 N. Stillwater Rd., 406/328-4158, www.paintbrushadventures.com) offers guided horseback riding ($45 for 1 hour, $80 for 2 hours, $200 full day) and hiking ($150 day hike with lunch). It also offers saddle-to-paddle trips ($120 adults, $70 children),

which include a full day of rafting and horseback riding, as well as two- to seven-day pack trips, drop camps, and working ranch vacations. Cabin accommodations are available as well.

The **Grizzly Bar & Grill** (1 Main St., Roscoe, 406/328-6789, 11:30am-9pm Thurs.-Sun. with extended hours in summer, $11-51), along the East Rosebud River in Roscoe, offers a perfect setting for a delicious Montana meal. The cuisine is classic—relish trays and steaks large enough to hang off the edges of your plate—and the ambience is idyllic. Diners can enjoy a great meal on the deck overlooking the tumbling river. Ah, summer in Montana—short but so sweet.

INFORMATION

As you drive west off I-90 exit 367 to Big Timber, you can't miss the **Sweet Grass County Chamber of Commerce** (1350 Hwy. 10 W., 406/932-5131, www.bigtimber.com, 9am-4pm Mon.-Sat., noon-4pm Sun. Memorial Day-Labor Day). In a small log cabin with stunning views of the Crazy Mountains, you will find a well-informed and friendly staff ready to answer any questions you may have about the area. The center also offers a good selection of maps, brochures, and travel magazines.

Red Lodge and the Beartooth Plateau

At the edge of the massive Beartooth Plateau, Red Lodge (pop. 2,331, elev. 5,568 ft/1,697 m) is a mountain town with the Great Plains spread out at its feet. There are a couple of great places to stay and some world-class skiing just beyond town, but downtown Red Lodge is a worthwhile destination on its own. Cute shops and wonderful restaurants line Broadway, and the spectacle of nature—the rush of Rock Creek and the drama of the Beartooths—is evident from every part of the street. The town's Western hospitality combined with historic zeal for a good time make Red Lodge a fantastic getaway or a fun launching point to the wildness of the Beartooth Plateau and Yellowstone National Park.

SIGHTS
★ Beartooth Scenic Highway and Pass

Considered one of the most beautiful roadways in the country, the **Beartooth Scenic Highway** begins in Red Lodge, climbs and twists its way through 60-million-year-old mountains, and ends 65 miles (105 km) later in Cooke City at the northeast entrance to Yellowstone National Park. The scenic road has numerous switchbacks and steep grades that, once you're driving on it, clearly demonstrate why it is closed during winter. As you ascend, you come upon magnificent vistas of the Beartooth Plateau, Glacier Lake, and the canyons forged by the Clarks Fork River. After about 30 miles (48 km), you reach the mountain summit at 10,947 feet (3,337 m). Here you will encounter the aptly named **Top of the World** rest area, which provides the only services on the route. Keep an eye out for a herd of mountain goats that frequents the area.

If you plan to drive this byway, keep in mind that it is not about getting from A to B—the drive itself is the destination, and it should be undertaken with plenty of time; it lasts about three hours without stops. You will encounter an array of wildlife, including black bears, bighorn sheep, and mountain goats, as well as a broad display of vibrant wildflowers, depending on the season and moisture levels.

lake near Beartooth Scenic Highway and Pass

Take time to pull over and enjoy the vistas or explore the hiking trails and accessible lakes. With snow falling almost year-round, skiing is popular in the area June through July. Because of the extreme conditions of the mountains, the highway is only open May to October, weather permitting. Contact the **Montana Department of Transportation** (406/444-6200) or the **Red Lodge Visitors Center** (406/446-1718) for opening and closing dates.

Yellowstone Wildlife Sanctuary

This wildlife refuge is the only one of its kind in Montana. It houses indigenous animals that cannot be released back into the wild due to an injury or unfortunate dependency on humans. The **Yellowstone Wildlife Sanctuary** (615 2nd St. E., 406/446-1133, www.yellowstonewildlifesanctuary.com, 10am-4pm Tues.-Sun. May-Oct., 10am-4pm Fri.-Sun. Nov.-Dec. and Mar.-Apr., $10 adults 13 and up, $4 children 4-12, $7 seniors and military, free children under 4) cares for some 60 animals that include wolves, black bears, Canada lynx, bison, elk, bald eagles, mountain lions, coyotes, red foxes, and many more. The center says in its mission that its primary focus is to educate the public about the protection and conservation of animal residents native to the Greater Yellowstone Ecosystem by allowing visitors an up close and intimate perspective of some of the region's most beautiful species. The center's location also affords some spectacular views of the Beartooth Mountains.

SPORTS AND RECREATION

Beartooth Plateau

High atop these massive mountains is the vast and rugged grandeur of the Beartooth Plateau. It's a nature lover's paradise with spectacular scenery, unrivaled vistas, abundant wildlife, and a tangle of trails and lakes to get out and enjoy. The **Beartooth Scenic Highway** makes this remarkable place a Sunday drive destination. But if you have the time, this is a wonderland that begs to be discovered. Take a hike, wet a line—heck, throw on your skis in midsummer; just get out and enjoy this magnificent place.

The truth of the matter is, you're already pretty much on top of the world here, so you don't need to aspire much when planning a hike. The plateau is crisscrossed with trails, and as long as you are amply prepared, you can't choose a bad one. The **Clay Butte Fire Lookout Tower** is only 1 mile (1.6 km) from the highway and can be accessed by a trail that takes hikers up and above 11,000 feet (3,350 m). The views are incredible, and an interpretive display gives great perspective on the 1988 Yellowstone fires and how they impacted the entire region. **Crazy Creek Cascade** is another short hike, and the **Clarks Fork Trailhead**, just 3 miles (4.8 km) from Cooke City, offers an abundance of longer trails. Near the summit, an 8-mile (12.9-km) loop around **Beartooth Lake** offers easy terrain and lovely scenery. For trail maps, stop by the **U.S. Forest Service ranger station** (6811 US 212, Red Lodge, 406/446-2103).

Biking the Beartooth Plateau is not for the faint of heart. Never mind the insane elevation climbs and descents, the vast grizzly habitat, and the possibility of a blizzard on virtually any day of the year; the real danger is the automobiles, which are plentiful, often wide, and driven by people who can't help but ogle the mountain vistas instead of the bike traffic. You can eliminate that danger by getting off the road and onto a network of trails.

In order to fish any of the mountain lakes on the Beartooth Plateau, many of which have been stocked with trout, you'll need a Wyoming fishing license, which can be purchased at the **Top of the World Resort** (2823 US 212, 307/587-5368, www.topoftheworldresort.com) or in Red Lodge or Cooke City. Rental gear is also available seasonally at the Top of the World Resort.

Skiing

Situated in a glacial valley surrounded by the Beartooth Mountains, Red Lodge offers superb downhill and cross-country skiing. **Red Lodge Mountain** (305 Ski Run Rd., 406/446-2610 or 800/444-8977, www.redlodgemountain.com) is just 6 miles (9.7 km) from downtown Red Lodge and boasts a mountain free of crowds and with reasonable lift ticket prices (from $53 adults 19-64, from $43 seniors 65-69 and juniors 13-18, from $20 seniors 70 and over and children 6-12, free for children under 6, discounts for advance online purchase) as well as ski runs for beginners to experts. The mountain offers a higher base elevation (7,433 feet/2,266 m) than any other ski hill in the state, a spine-chilling 2,400-foot (730-m) vertical drop, 70 runs, and six chairlifts to keep you up to your elbows in the white stuff all day. The diverse terrain is groomed regularly, and the runs' features are frequently upgraded or even changed. Red Lodge offers a full-service lodge, with ski lessons, ski rentals, child care, a restaurant, two bars, and two cafeterias, all on the hill. The resort also has two cross-country trails that offer about 11 miles (18 km) of skiing. On top of the outstanding terrain and the jaw-dropping views, one of the things that makes this hill so special is the small-town friendliness of just about everyone here, from the lift operators to the people sharing a chair with you. This feels like what skiing in Montana should be.

Probably the best-known place for cross-country skiing in Red Lodge is the **Red Lodge Nordic Center** (406/446-1771, www.beartoothtrails.org, 8:30am-4:30pm daily in season, $5/day payable at the trailhead), 2 miles (3.2 km) west of downtown off Highway 78. The center is operated by the nonprofit Beartooth Recreational Trails Association (which also maintains several excellent trails for hiking when snow isn't covering the ground) and offers more than 15 kilometers (9.3 mi) of groomed classic and skate trails rated from easy to most difficult. Rentals and lessons can be arranged prior to your arrival via online booking. Other than a porta-potty, there are no services at the Nordic Center, so plan ahead.

Hiking and Fishing

Rivers, creeks, and lakes in the vicinity of Red Lodge are worth fishing or just ambling along, and with surroundings as spectacular as these, the catching may not be the point. **Rock Creek** flows through town and is a surprisingly good place to catch rainbows or browns. Public access can be found just north of town. The north-flowing **Stillwater River,** west of town toward Absarokee, is a medium-size tributary of the Yellowstone River with relatively few people fishing it and a healthy number of rainbows and browns.

Wild Bill Lake is stocked regularly and makes a fantastic family outing or introduction to fly-fishing. The area is fully accessible for wheelchairs and can be found 2 miles (3.2 km) south of Red Lodge on US 212, then 5 miles (8 km) west on Forest Road 2071.

While there are numerous gnarly trails on the Beartooth Plateau for hard-core hikers, you'll find plenty of trails just outside town that are a bit more mellow but equally beautiful. The **Nichols Creek Trail** (West Fork Rd. to Forest Rd. 2478), for example, is a 4-mile (6.4-km) round-trip out-and-back hike that follows Nichols Creek through aspen and pine forests with moderate elevation gain (1,100 feet/335 m) and a marvelous view of the West Fork Canyon.

Another popular option is the well-traveled **Basin Lakes Trail #61.** The steep, 5.1-mile (8.2-km) there-and-back trail leads to two lakes with a 1,500-foot (457-m) elevation gain. Beautiful waterfalls are along the way and, if you time it right, you can pick wild raspberries as you go. Abundant wildlife is also in the area—moose are commonly seen—so do bring bear spray and keep your eyes open. You will like run into plenty of other hikers and anglers. The upper lake is the better of the two for fishing. To get to the trailhead, drive south on US 212 from Red Lodge to West Fork Drive and head west for 2.8 miles (4.5 km). Stay left and follow the signs another 4.1 miles (6.6 km) to the Basin Lakes trailhead. Note that the West Fork Road is closed from early December to mid-April.

For a professional fishing guide—or just the right gear and good advice—contact **Rocky Fork Outfitters & Guide Service** (108 Obert Rd., 406/445-2598, www.rockyforkoutfittersguide.com, full-day float or wade for 1-2 anglers from $450, half day from $300).

Golf

To hit the links, head to the 18-hole course at **Red Lodge Resort and Golf Club** (828 Upper Continental Dr., southwest of Red Lodge, 406/446-3344, www.redlodgemountain.com, $49 adults 19 and up for 18 holes walking Mon.-Thurs., $55 for 18 holes walking Fri.-Sun., discounts for booking 48 hours in advance, juniors 18 and under, and twilight play after 4pm). Admire the jaw-dropping scenery around this challenging course, and be aware that your ball will travel farther because of the altitude.

ENTERTAINMENT AND EVENTS

Since 1950, the **Festival of Nations** has been a Red Lodge tradition celebrating the wide diversity of ethnic groups that first came to the town during the late-1800s mining boom. The cultural groups honored include both southern and northern Europeans—German, Irish, Finnish, Italian, Norwegian, Scottish, Greek—and a variety of others. The festival takes place in late July or August over two and a half days, with cultural exhibits, dancing, ethnic food, music, children's activities, and a wide assortment of daytime and nighttime entertainment. People who wear ethnic costumes get admitted free. Contact the **Red Lodge Visitors Center** (406/446-1718) for this year's dates and location. The celebration was cancelled during the pandemic so be sure to visit the website or call ahead.

The **Winter Carnival** (305 Ski Run Rd., 406/446-2610 or 800/444-8977, dates vary each year) takes place at the Red Lodge Mountain Resort and has become a favorite event among locals and visitors alike. Although the carnival selects a different theme each year (themes have included Star Wars and Teenage Mutant Ninja Turtles), many tried-and-true events make an annual appearance. The Cardboard Classic race tests the skills of its participants as they guide their original crafts—made only from cardboard, duct tape, and glue—in a competitive downhill race. Other popular activities include a scavenger hunt, a snow sculpture contest, a parade of costumes, a jalapeño-eating contest, and a dazzling fireworks show. You may even be crowned King or Queen of Red Lodge Mountain if you can telemark, alpine race, and snowboard yourself to victory.

The **Home of Champions Rodeo and Parade** (406/446-2422, www.redlodgerodeo.com, July 2-4, $17-32, $32 admits 4 on Family Day July 2) takes place each year at the fairgrounds west of Red Lodge just off Highway 78, and the parades run daily in downtown Red Lodge. Rodeo competition in the area dates back to the 1890s, when cowboys used to get together on Sunday to ride broncos at the local stockyards. Formed in 1930, the Red Lodge Rodeo Association has been hosting this annual celebration ever since. The name, Home of Champions, was coined in 1954 after a local cowboy, Bill Linderman, won his third title as World All Around Champion. A different theme is selected for the event every year, and a parade takes place at noon each day; participation is open and there are categories for all age groups. The rodeo is part of the Professional Rodeo Cowboys Association circuit, so you will see many of the nation's top champions compete in events including bareback, bull riding, calf roping, and barrel racing.

Lovers of classical music and fine art are in for a wildly unexpected treat at **Tippet Rise Art Center** (96 S. Grove Creek Rd., Fishtail, www.tippetrise.org, June-Sept.), which brings together nature, art, and music in magnificent ways. Set on an 11,500-acre working ranch, in the shadow of the Beartooths, Tippet Rise brings world-class musicians to the area for intimate performances throughout summer at a variety of indoor and outdoor venues, all of them small and visually spectacular. Tickets for concerts and films are limited to just 100 seats at most—and are available online only for as little as $10, and free for ages 21 and younger—but sell out months in advance. Tickets to the art center are available online for free, but also in very limited quantities.

SHOPPING

Shopping in Red Lodge is a leisurely stroll through the historic downtown district. Broadway has still managed to retain the charm and vibrancy of the coal-mining days with a diverse assortment of stores. **Sylvan Peak Mountain Shop** (9 N. Broadway Ave., 406/446-1770, 9am-6pm daily) is a perfect starting point for anyone in need of adventure-related gear. The store carries its own line of clothing as well as more familiar brands such as Marmot, Mountain Hardware, and Osprey. An outlet store on the main floor and a Mountain Shoppe downstairs not only sell equipment but also rent cross-country skis, telemark skis, and snowshoes. From climbing gear to boating gear, fleeces or bear spray, you will find it—plus the best insider's advice anywhere and a true commitment to protecting the great outdoors—at Sylvan Peak.

Right next door, you'll find the irresistible **Montana Candy Emporium** (7 N. Broadway Ave., 406/446-1119, 9am-9pm daily Memorial Day-Labor Day, 9am-7pm Sun.-Thurs., 9am-9pm Fri.-Sat. Labor Day-Memorial Day). The mouthwatering window displays will draw you in to this world of sweets. It is said to be the largest candy store in Montana, which is easy to believe meandering through its selection of more than 800 sugary treats. Located in the former Park Theater, decorated with nostalgic memorabilia, and selling old-fashioned candies, this store will take you back to a simpler time.

Since 1990, **Kibler and Kirch** (101 N. Broadway Ave., 406/446-2226, www. kiblerandkirch.com, 9am-5pm Mon.-Sat.) has been a pillar of the downtown shopping scene in Red Lodge. It's a home-furnishings store with a nice selection of Western artwork and accessories, and the offerings include pottery, glassware, and handcrafted leather. Since many of its products are made in Montana, you may find the perfect gift to take home.

For a unique, handmade gift, visit **Back Alley Metals** (116 Broadway Ave. N., 406/425-1533, www.backalleymetals. com, 10am-4pm Mon.-Fri.), where artists can realize any metal dream you may have, from personalized signs and art to custom metalwork like railings and gates to furniture. For art classes, workshops, lectures, demonstrations, and a marvelous gallery to peruse, try **Red Lodge Clay Center** (123 Broadway Ave. S., 406/446-3993, www. redlodgeclaycenter.com, 10am-6pm Tues.-Sat., noon-4pm Sun.). Another favorite spot for local art is **Carbon County Arts Guild & Depot Gallery** (11 8th St. W., 406/446-1370, www.carboncountydepotgallery.org, 10am-5pm Thurs.-Sat., noon-4pm Sun.-Mon.), which has new exhibitions by regional artists every month.

FOOD

Recently renovated, but still a classic, **Marli's Restaurant & Bar,** at the Pollard Hotel (2 N. Broadway Ave., 406/446-0001, www. thepollard.com, breakfast 6am-11am Mon. and Thurs.-Sat., 6am-1:30pm Sun., dinner 4:30pm-9pm Tues.-Sat., $15-36) serves up such menu items as fish and chips, cattle rancher's pie, burgers, braised short ribs, New York *au poivre,* and salmon sliders. The atmosphere is great, especially when the place hosts live music. Reservations are not accepted but you can add your party to the online waitlist.

At the heart of Red Lodge's burgeoning food scene is **Piccola Cucina at Ox Pasture** (7 Broadway N., 406/446-1212, www. oxpasture.com, 11:30am-10pm Tues.-Sun., $13-36). The small menu changes frequently to make the most of seasonal produce. From Sicilian specialties like *arancini* (rice balls) and *paccheri alla carbonara* (pasta with eggs, Italian bacon, and cheese) to grilled sea bass, rib eye, and handmade pastas, this foodie heaven puts together phenomenal flavors. They also have a great wine list. Check the website or call ahead to confirm opening days and times, and ask about the well-known chefs from around the world who show up from time to time. Even newer on the scene in Red Lodge, and equally delicious, is **PREROGATIvE Kitchen** (104 Broadway Ave. S., 406/445-3232, www.prerogativekitchen. com, 11:30am-8pm Fri.-Mon., $9-27), which serves such yummies as lamb sliders, lobster rolls, Szechuan pork belly with huckleberry jam, burgers, and lots of small artful plates made with local meat and produce.

For a casual, inexpensive, old-fashioned drive-in—or better yet, walk-up—experience, head to the **Red Box Car** (1300 S. Broadway Ave., 406/446-2152, 11am-8pm daily early Apr.-Sept., 7am-2pm Oct.-Mar., $3.60-13.50). Based in an actual 1906 boxcar from the Rocky Fork Railway, this stand serves some of the best shakes, malts, chili, burgers, and Mexican specialties you could imagine. Sit outside and enjoy your meal as you take in views of nearby Rock Creek. The Red Box Car may close at any time due to weather, so call ahead or check its Facebook page before visiting. Another excellent spot for a quick breakfast (served all day) or lunch is **The Wild Table** (113 Broadway Ave. N., 406/446-0226, www.thewildtable.com, 8am-2pm Mon.-Sat., $7-15), which serves from a new menu every week. Staples include breakfast burritos and sandwiches, *shakshuka* (poached eggs in spicy tomato sauce), English breakfasts, French toast, sandwiches, and hot lunch entrées. They serve espresso too, and their treats (huckleberry pie! meringues! triple chocolate brownies!) are beyond compare. They do have gluten-free options.

Set in a cool old Conoco gas station, **Más Taco** (304 N. Broadway Ave., 406/446-3636, 11am-4pm Tues.-Thurs., 11am-7pm Fri.-Sat., $4-12) is the place for authentic Mexican cuisine in Red Lodge. It has lots of vegetarian options and makes everything from scratch, including the corn tortillas and sour cream.

The wet burritos are legendary, and the restaurant is also known for its five versions of *al pastor*, pork roasted with pineapple and paper-thin slices of onion. Sit outside in the summer to enjoy the view, or plant yourself at the counter and watch them cook!

Attached to the Regis Grocery and known for outstanding breakfasts and organic, whole foods, ★ **Café Regis** (501 Word Ave. S., 406/446-1941, www.caferegis.com, 7am-2pm Thurs.-Mon., $5-12) is an excellent spot for a hearty, healthy, and very reasonably priced meal. The service is quick and friendly, and every delicious item on the menu—from omelets and breakfast burritos to soup, sandwiches, salads, and mouthwatering daily blue plate specials—is available to go. Grab a ready-to-go picnic lunch or find all the gourmet fixings for whatever adventure you have planned. Breakfast is served all day. The Regis Grocery has a huge selection of organic, gluten-free, and other specialty products.

ACCOMMODATIONS

In historic downtown Red Lodge, ★ **The Pollard Hotel** (2 N. Broadway Ave., 406/446-0001, www.thepollard.com, $169-300) should not be overlooked. The hotel was the first brick building constructed in Red Lodge and dates to 1893. It has played host to some of the West's most famous legends, including Calamity Jane, Buffalo Bill Cody, and famed orator William Jennings Bryan. The 39 guest rooms and suites are individually decorated, more traditional than modern, and can come with mountain views, jetted tubs, and balconies.

Rock Creek Resort (6380 US 212 S., 800/667-1119, www.rockcreekresort.com, $150-375) is about 5 miles (8 km) south of Red Lodge in a gorgeous canyon at the base of the Beartooth Mountains. The resort has 87 rooms sprawled over a 30-acre site and offers many outdoor activities. The facility has a heated indoor pool, tennis courts, a soccer field, a fully stocked fish pond, and numerous trails for hiking and biking (along with bikes for rent). Accommodations range from hotel rooms and condos to cabins and larger homes. Most have impressive views of the mountains.

If you want to stay close to downtown Red Lodge without breaking the bank, try the pet-friendly ★ Yodeler Motel (601 S. Broadway Ave., 406/446-1435, www.yodelermotel.com, $89-165). This historic, Swiss-themed chalet, owned by delightful former guides Mac and Tulsa Dean, is only three blocks from downtown. Remodeled guest rooms offer nice amenities that include cable TV, free Wi-Fi, jetted tubs, steam showers, and even a wax room to work on your skis. The rooms on the lower level are more budget-friendly and do not have balconies like the upper level, but every room is clean, comfortable, and well maintained. Plus Mac and Tulsa will give you the best advice for your Red Lodge or Yellowstone adventure.

CAMPING

Thirteen campgrounds along US 212 offer 226 sites between Red Lodge and Cooke City. Because of the elevation and volume of snow, many do not open until late June or July. Beartooth Lake Campground (21 sites, $15, July-mid-Sept.) and Island Lake Campground (21 sites, $15, July-mid-Sept.) are two excellent choices very near the summit. Campsites along the Beartooth Highway are managed by the Custer National Forest (406/446-2103, www.fs.usda.gov/custergallatin) and range in price from free to $20 per night, depending on the site.

INFORMATION AND SERVICES

The Red Lodge Chamber of Commerce (701 N. Broadway Ave., 406/446-1718 or 888/281-0625, www.redlodgechamber.org, 9am-5pm Mon.-Fri., 10am-4pm Sat.-Sun. summer, 9am-5pm Mon.-Fri., 10am-2pm Sat. winter) is at the intersection of US 212 and Highway 78. It has a 24-hour brochure room that offers local information. Inside the center you will find knowledgeable staff and plenty of state publications, visitors guides, and maps.

Access the Internet at Red Lodge Carnegie Library (3 8th St. W., 406/446-1905, 10am-5pm Mon.-Tues. and Thurs.-Fri., 10am-7pm Wed., plus noon-6pm Sat. in summer). The library has several Internet-connected computers available to the public. You can also stop by the Coffee Factory Roasters (22 S. Broadway Ave., 406/446-3200, www.coffeefactoryroasters.com, 6:30am-6pm daily), where the Wi-Fi is free.

The Beartooth Billings Clinic (2525 N. Broadway Ave., 406/446-2345, 7:30am-6pm walk-in care) offers 24-hour emergency care.

US 212 climbs another 5,000 feet (over 1,500 m) past Red Lodge. If you want to know the road conditions for the Beartooth Highway, you can stop by the chamber of commerce or check with the state of Montana Traveler Road Information (800/226-7623, TTY 800/335-7592, www.511mt.net).

TRANSPORTATION

The two major airports closest to Red Lodge are Billings Logan International Airport (BIL, 406/247-8609 or 406/657-8495, www.flybillings.com) and Bozeman Yellowstone International Airport (BZN, 406/388-8321, www.bozemanairport.com). One of the best options for getting to Red Lodge is by car; both airports have a selection of car-rental companies.

From the Billings airport, Cody Shuttle Service (307/527-6789, www.codyshuttle.com) transports visitors to Red Lodge.

Driving from Billings, take I-90 west and then US 212/310 south. Red Lodge is 60 miles (97 km) southwest of Billings, and the drive time is about an hour. From Bozeman, take I-90 east to Highway 78 and head south. Bozeman is about 150 miles (242 km) and 2.5 hours north and then west of Red Lodge.

Yellowstone National Park

Yellowstone National Park is at the heart of our country's relationship with wilderness. It's also the largest intact ecosystem in the Lower 48—all of the species that have roamed this plateau are still (or once again) in residence. For now.

Yellowstone was our nation's first national park, signed into being by President Ulysses S. Grant after a series of important and legendary scouting expeditions through the area. The region's history is lengthy and very much alive, from its prehistoric volcanic eruptions, to its occupation by the U.S. Army in the 1880s, to the controversial reintroduction of wolves in the 1990s and the more recent snowmobile usage, bison, and grizzly delisting quagmires. The stories, both far-fetched and true, and characters that have emerged from the park

Highlights

Look for ★ to find recommended sights, activities, dining, and lodging.

★ **Boiling River:** In a stretch of the Gardner River at the park's north entrance, hot water flows over waterfalls and via springs, mixing with the river water to create a perfect soaking temperature (page 335).

★ **Mammoth and the Mammoth Hot Springs Terraces:** The travertine terraces here look like an enormous cream-colored confection. Since the springs shift and change daily, a walk around the colorful terraces is never the same experience twice (page 340).

★ **Grand Canyon of the Yellowstone:** The sheer cliffs and dramatic coloring of this canyon have inspired millions of visitors. In the summer, get a rare bird's-eye view of several osprey nests (page 341).

★ **Watching the Wolves:** The wolves put on a spectacular show—with at least one reported sighting daily since 2001. The sagas of the 11 packs are dramatic, heart-wrenching, and captivating (page 348).

★ **Lamar Valley:** Known as the "Little Serengeti of North America," this scenic, glacially carved valley offers spectacular wildlife-watching year-round (page 349).

★ **Yellowstone Lake:** This beautiful lake was touted by early mountain men as perhaps the only place where you could catch a fish and cook it without ever taking it off the line (page 355).

★ **Old Faithful:** One of nearly 500 geysers in the park, and undoubtedly the most famous, this natural wonder erupts every 45-90 minutes (page 356).

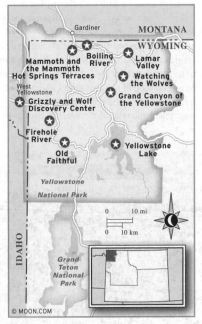

★ **Firehole River:** This river offers a stunning, heated swimming area surrounded by cliffs. The twists and turns of the cascading canyon are worth seeing even if you don't get wet (page 358).

★ **Grizzly and Wolf Discovery Center:** You're guaranteed an up-close look at two of the park's biggest and most fascinating predators at this home to grizzly bears and wolves that can't survive in the wild (page 363).

are as colorful and compelling as the landscape itself.

A vast 2.2 million acres, Yellowstone is indeed a wonderland, filled with steaming geysers and boiling mud pots, packed with diverse and healthy populations of wildlife, and crisscrossed by hundreds of miles of hiking and skiing trails. A stretch of the park called the Lamar Valley is known as the "Little Serengeti of North America," and for good reason: At certain times of the year, in a single day visitors can spot grizzly and black bears, moose, wolves, bison, elk, coyotes, bald eagles, and the occasional bighorn sheep or mountain goat. In fact, the opportunities for viewing wildlife in the park are unparalleled anywhere in the United States, and although Yellowstone may not be as picturesque as Glacier or the Tetons, it is magnificent in its wildness and uniquely American.

Seeing Yellowstone from the back of a cramped station wagon—or these days, a decked-out Winnebago—is almost a rite of passage in this country. What parent doesn't dream of hauling their children out West to see Old Faithful erupt or to catch a glimpse of a grizzly bear? And what kid doesn't want to swim in the Boiling River or lie awake in a sleeping bag, listening to the howl of coyotes? It's not exactly the last frontier it once was—there are convenience stores, beautiful old hotels, major traffic jams, and even places to get a decent latte—but Yellowstone still occupies its own corner of our national imagination; classified somewhere between American wilderness and family vacations, it conjures up foggy but perfect memories.

PLANNING YOUR TIME

One could quite literally spend a lifetime in Yellowstone without being able to cover every last corner of this magnificent wilderness, but the reality is that most visitors only have a couple of days, at best, to spend exploring the park. Something like 98 percent of visitors never get more than a mile from the road, but it's easier than you might think—and incredibly worthwhile. Three days in the park is ideal, but if you have less time, there are ways to maximize every minute.

One important consideration in planning your time in Yellowstone is to know the season you'll be traveling. Summer offers magnificent scenery, usually good weather, and the inevitable "bear jam," when drivers hit the brakes as soon as someone spots anything resembling a brown furry creature. Summer visitors to Yellowstone need to plan for traffic and often for road construction delays. Fall and spring are fantastic times to see wildlife, but the weather can change in a heartbeat—at Yellowstone's high elevation, blizzards can strike nearly any month of the year. Winter is a magical time in the park, but cars are only permitted on one road in the northeast corner. All other travel is done via snow coach, guided snowmobile tour, or on skis and snowshoes. There is no wrong time to visit the park, but knowing the advantages and disadvantages of the various seasons will help you manage your expectations.

Assuming you'll be in Yellowstone when the roads are open to car traffic, there are five entrances and exits to Yellowstone, making loop trips relatively easy. From Montana, you can enter or exit the park from the northeast at Cooke City, from the north at Gardiner, or from the west at West Yellowstone. From Wyoming, you can enter the park from the east entrance nearest Cody or from the south through Grand Teton National Park. If you're going from one state to the next, there is no more spectacular route than through the heart of Yellowstone.

A cursory glance at a Yellowstone map will reveal the main roads, which form a figure eight in the heart of the park, and the access roads leading to and from the entrances. The majority of the park's big-name highlights—**Old Faithful, West Thumb Geyser**

Previous: Grand Prismatic Spring; view of Lower Falls; a wolf in Yellowstone in winter.

Yellowstone National Park

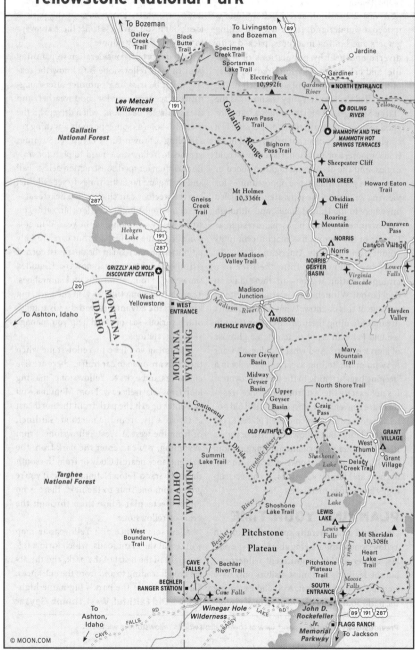

© MOON.COM

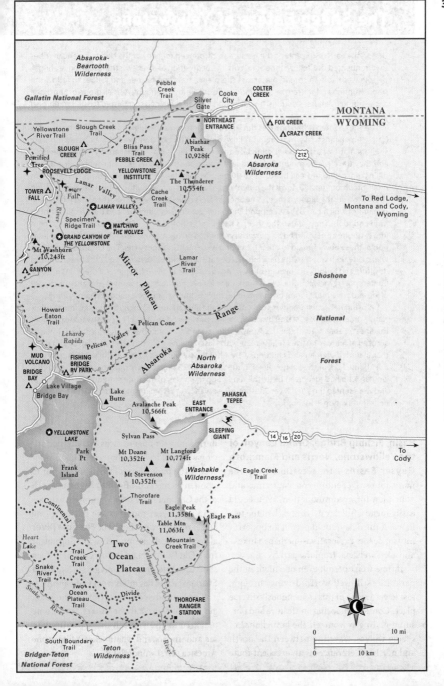

The Sheep Eaters of Yellowstone

During the early 18th century, the horse was introduced to many of the Native American tribes that frequented the Yellowstone area. With the acquisition of this new, strong, and agile animal, people were able to spread out across the plains, traveling farther and longer to follow the bison. Hunting and warfare became more efficient almost overnight. A small group of Shoshone chose not to use horses or guns, however, and instead remained committed to their traditional mountain living.

The Sheep Eaters, also known as the Tukudika, were forest dwellers considered to be the only Native Americans to have inhabited Yellowstone year-round. They lived in *wikiups*—temporary shelters made of aspen poles, pine boughs, and other brush—rather than animal-hide tipis, and they traveled the mountain ridges rather than the river paths as their counterparts on the plains did. Living in small bands of 10-20 people, they relied on their wolf dogs to help them move provisions up and down the mountains. They were named for the animal whose migration they followed: the bighorn sheep. The Sheep Eaters developed highly effective sheep traps, the remains of which can be seen around Dubois, Wyoming, and they utilized the animal for both food and tools. They heated the sheep's horns in the hot springs of Yellowstone to mold them into exquisite and strong bows, powerful enough to drive an arrow through a bison. The reputation of these bows spread to other tribes and were highly sought-after. The European outsiders who made their way into the park during the early and mid-1800s described the Sheep Eaters as destitute and forlorn, not owning or seeming to want the modern trappings of the Plains Indians. Contemporary views suggest that these people revered their environment and ancestors' way of life and were more intent on maintaining their customs than competing and conquering.

Unfortunately, their traditions did not allow the Sheep Eaters to escape the same fate as other Native Americans. Devastated by smallpox and considered an obstacle to westward expansion, the Sheep Eaters fought the U.S. Army in the last Indian war in the Pacific Northwest. Unfairly accused of murdering five Chinese miners, the last remaining Sheep Eaters, a group of 51 people that included woman and children, were relentlessly pursued in the Idaho wilderness along the Middle Fork of the Salmon River in the fall of 1879. When the army purportedly captured a woman who had just given birth, the remaining members of the tribe surrendered to save her and were sent to the Wind River Shoshone Reservation in Wyoming and Fort Hall Shoshone Bannock Reservation in Idaho.

Basin, Fishing Bridge, Grand Canyon of the Yellowstone, Norris and Mammoth Geyser Basins—are accessible from the main loops. Depending on your time and your plan for accommodations, you could easily spend a full day driving each of the two loops. A third day would permit an opportunity for deeper exploration—perhaps a hike—and a leisurely exit from the park.

If time won't permit even one night in the park, it is still well worth driving through, just to get a sense of this tremendously diverse place. Consider choosing one feature and pursuing it. To give yourself the best chance of seeing wolves, traveling between the north and northeast entrances is an excellent route

during non-summer months. Geothermal aficionados will have no shortage of choices for seeing the park's impressive features, but to swim in them, try the **Boiling River,** a stretch of the Gardner River near Mammoth, which is swimmable year-round except during spring and early summer runoff. The **Firehole River** also offers excellent summer swimming not far from Old Faithful. Landlubbers might prefer a short hike into a less-famous geyser like **Lone Star,** just a few flat miles from Old Faithful.

The best advice is this: Get off the road, get out of your car, be smart, and come prepared to give yourself the opportunity to see and understand what makes Yellowstone America's first wonderland.

INFORMATION AND SERVICES

The best resource to familiarize yourself with the park and to help plan your trip is the **National Park Service** (307/344-7381, www.nps.gov/yell). On the website, click on the link titled Plan Your Visit. The site also posts information about the different **Ranger Programs** being offered, including educational lectures and hikes.

Two official free apps can help with trip planning. **The NPS Yellowstone App** gives users live updates on the status of lodging, campgrounds, roads, and geyser predictions when in cell service. It also provides downloadable interpretive stories and self-guided audio tours that can be played when you are out of coverage areas. A more general app, the **NPS Parks App,** offers downloadable information for all the national parks in the U.S., including Yellowstone and Grand Teton. It does not provide live updates on lodging, roads, or geyser predictions.

Park Fees and Passes

Admission to the park is $35 per vehicle for seven days, $30 for motorcycles and snowmobiles, and $20 for hikers and bicyclists. An annual pass to the park costs $70. In 2021, entrance fees to the park were waived on 6 days, including Martin Luther King Jr. Day on January 18, April 17 to celebrate the start of National Park Week, August 4 to celebrate the one year anniversary of the Great American Outdoors Act, September 25 for National Public Lands Day, and Veterans Day on November 11. Check the Yellowstone website before you travel to see if any fee-free days are on the horizon. The park is open year-round, but during the winter, cars can only access the park through the north and northeast entrances.

Visitor Centers

There are 10 visitor centers in and around the park. Since days and hours vary seasonally, and all of them have been shortened due to the pandemic and staff shortages, it's a good idea to check the website (www.nps.gov/yell) before you go into the park.

The **Albright Visitor Center at Mammoth Hot Springs** (Grand Loop Rd., 307/344-2263, 9am-5pm daily) is open year-round and houses a bookstore, wildlife and history exhibits, and films on the park and its early visitors. Free Wi-Fi is also available in the visitor center. Fishers and backcountry campers can get permits in the basement backcountry office. And there are restrooms, perhaps the last for a while depending on your adventure.

The **Canyon Visitor Education Center** (Canyon Village, 307/344-2550, 9am-5pm daily summer) offers the best overview of the park's geology, including phenomenal volcano exhibits and a dynamic film. During the season, the bathrooms remain open 24 hours a day.

The **Fishing Bridge Visitor Center** (East Entrance Rd., 307/344-2450) is home to a museum, bookstore, bird and wildlife exhibits, plus information on the lake's ecology. The building was opened in 1931 and is a beautiful example of the "parkitecture"-type architecture seen in parks across the nation. The visitor center was closed throughout COVID, so check the website f or hours.

The **Grant Village Visitor Center** (west shore of Yellowstone Lake, 307/344-2650, 8am-5pm daily Memorial Day-early Oct.) offers an outstanding exhibit on the integral role of fire in the Yellowstone ecosystem.

The **Madison Information Station and Trailside Museum** (307/344-2821) at Madison Junction provides a bookstore as well as detailed information on the **Junior Ranger** program. Another prime example of "parkitecture," the Trailside Museum was opened in 1930 for early travelers to the park. It was closed in 2021, so check the website for hours.

The **Museum of the National Park Ranger** (307/344-7353) is 1 mile (1.6 km) north of Norris Geyser Basin and gives a good history of the park ranger profession.

The beautiful log building was built in 1897 after a fire destroyed the original building, and modified in 1908 to be used as soldier stations. The building was rebuilt again, log by log, after the 1959 earthquake. It was closed for 2021, so check the website for hours.

The **Norris Geyser Basin Museum & Information Station** (east of Norris Junction, 307/344-2812, 9am-5pm daily late May-early Oct.) offers visitors an excellent overview of the hydrothermal features in the park.

The **Old Faithful Visitor Education Center** (Upper Geyser Basin, 307/344-2751, 9am-5pm daily mid-Apr.-early Nov. closed winter/spring of 2022 due to staffing issues) includes exhibits, information, and films on the park's hydrothermal features, plus a bookstore and geyser eruption predictions. A Young Scientist room with hands-on exhibits is a hit with young people.

The **West Thumb Information Center** (307/242-7690, 9am-5pm daily late May-early Oct.) offers information about the West Thumb Geyser Basin on the shore of Yellowstone Lake. You can also sign up for ranger programs.

In West Yellowstone, the **West Yellowstone Visitor Information Center** (30 Yellowstone Ave., 307/344-2876, 8am-5pm daily May-Labor Day, 8am-4pm daily Labor Day-early Nov., 8am-5pm Mon.-Fri. early Nov.-mid-Apr.) hosts a National Park Service desk, plus information and publications.

Entrance Stations

Yellowstone National Park is open 365 days a year, 24 hours a day. There are five entrance stations, three in Montana and two in Wyoming.

- The **North Entrance,** at Gardiner, Montana, is the only one open year-round to wheeled vehicles.

- The **Northeast Entrance** is near the small communities of Cooke City and Silver Gate, Montana, and generally open late May to mid-October, depending upon weather and road conditions.

- The **West Entrance,** in West Yellowstone, Montana, is open to wheeled vehicles generally from the third Friday in April until the first Sunday in November.

- The **South Entrance,** 49 miles (79 km) north of Jackson, Wyoming, at the border between Grand Teton National Park and Yellowstone, is open to wheeled vehicles typically the second Friday in May through the first Sunday in November, and to snow coaches and snowmobiles mid-December to mid-March.

- The **East Entrance,** 53 miles (85 km) west of Cody, Wyoming, is generally open to wheeled vehicles from the first Friday in May to the first Sunday in November.

All entrances can be closed at any time due to weather and unscheduled changes. Visit www.nps.gov/yell before your trip for up-to-date road information, or call 307/344-2117 for recorded road and weather information.

Services

Yellowstone National Park Lodges (307/344-7311, www.yellowstonenational parklodges.com) is the official concessionaire of Yellowstone, and all reservations for lodging, dining, and special activities in the park can be made through them.

If you encounter an **emergency** when traveling through the park, dial 911, but be aware that cell coverage is spotty. Emergency medical services are attended to by rangers. There are three **urgent care facilities** inside Yellowstone. The clinic at **Mammoth** (108 Grand Loop Rd., 307/344-7965, 8:30am-5pm Mon.-Fri. June-late Sept., 8:30am-5pm Mon.-Thurs., 8:30am-1pm Fri. late Sept.-May) is open year-round, and the clinics at **Lake** (1 Lake Station, 307/242-7241, 8:30am-8:30pm daily mid-May-mid-Sept., 10am-6:30pm daily mid-Sept.-late Sept.) and **Old Faithful** (307/545-7325, 7am-7pm daily mid-May-mid-Sept., 8:30am-5pm daily mid-Sept.-early Oct.) are open in prime visiting season.

Avoid the Crowds

In September of 2021, Yellowstone National Park topped 4 million visitors in the first nine months of the year for the first time ever. In September alone, the park saw 882,078 recreational visits, up 5 percent from the year before and up 27 percent from 2019. Annual statistics echo the pattern. Visits between January and September 2021 were up 32 percent from 2020 and up 17 percent from 2019. There is nothing to suggest that the influx of visitors will slow down anytime soon, if ever. "Never in Yellowstone's history have we seen such substantial visitation increase in such a short amount of time," said Park Superintendent Cam Sholly in October 2021.

The best advice anyone can offer is to manage your expectations. Instead of hoping for solitude, expect long lines at entrance stations, extremely busy facilities and destinations, and delayed travel times due to traffic and wildlife jams. Remember that you are a visitor and act responsibly and with thoughtfulness, for your own benefit, for your fellow visitors, and for the inhabitants of the park. If you come prepared and follow a few suggestions, you can lessen your time amongst the hordes and give yourself the opportunity to enjoy the wonders of the park.

- **Buy your park pass ahead of time online** at www.recreation.gov to avoid long waits at entrance stations.

- **Avoid the park's busiest areas,** including Old Faithful, Midway Geyser Basin, Norris, and the Canyon rims. Instead stick to areas that have **fewer attractions and fewer parking lots.** It's still true that the vast majority of Yellowstone visitors never get more than half a mile from the road. If you must visit the busiest attractions, time it early or late, **before 9am or after 4pm,** when the bulk of visitors are out and about.

- As has always been true, planning a trip to Yellowstone in months other than June, July, and August is a good start. The shoulder months are busier than they've ever been, but still the **peak summer months are the busiest.** Consider a spring trip in **April or May** when the park is coming awake after a long, cold winter, and some of the animals are just starting to have their babies. Or, plan a **winter trip** when snow and ice cover everything and hide nothing. Thermal features and wildlife are more visible than ever. Plus moonlight and snow is a pretty magical combination here.

- Stay informed about **weather, road conditions, and campground availability** by checking the park website (www.nps.gov/yell). Webcams can give you an idea of the lines at North and West entrance stations. The NPS Yellowstone app will give you park alerts and road closures in real time, which can be helpful when you are figuring out where to go, or where to not go.

YELLOWSTONE NATIONAL PARK

TRANSPORTATION
Getting There
BY AIR

Yellowstone is about 90 miles (145 km) from the airports in Bozeman and Billings, 49 miles (79 km) from the airport in Jackson Hole, and 52 miles (84 km) from the airport in Cody. The **Yellowstone Airport** (WYS, 607 Airport Rd., West Yellowstone, www.yellowstoneairport.org, 406/646-7631) is served by Delta and United and is only open late May-late September.

BY CAR

The North Entrance at Gardiner, which is the only entrance open year-round to cars, is 83 miles (134 km) south of Bozeman and 170 miles (275 km) southwest of Billings. The Northeast Entrance at Cooke City is 124 miles (200 km), including the spectacular Beartooth Highway, from Billings. The West Entrance at West Yellowstone is 90 miles (145 km) south of Bozeman. The East Entrance is 53 miles (85 km) west of Cody. The South Entrance is 49 miles (79 km) north of Jackson.

BY BUS

Shuttle service with **Karst Stage** (800/287-4759 or 406/556-3540, www.karststage.com) is available from Bozeman to West Yellowstone year-round and to Gardiner during the winter and summer seasons.

Getting Around
PRIVATE VEHICLES

Your best bet to see the park on your own terms is to go by car. The nearest car-rental agencies are **Budget** and **Big Sky Car Rentals** (406/646-9564), available in West Yellowstone. Cars can also be rented from airports in Billings, Bozeman, Cody, and Jackson Hole.

When planning your drive through Yellowstone, it is best to fill up your tank outside the park. Once inside, the gas prices you'll encounter tend to be extremely high, and options are quite limited. Gas stations are located within the park at Canyon, Fishing Bridge, Grant Village, Mammoth, Upper and Lower Old Faithful, and Tower Junction. They are generally open late spring-early fall.

One of the things that makes Yellowstone so wild and enchanting is its utter unpredictability—something that relates to wildlife, weather, and, unfortunately, road conditions. A 20-year $300-million plan is currently afoot to address the structural deficiencies of Yellowstone's roads. Keep a close watch on road closures and delays that can happen at any time of year because of construction, bad weather, or even fire. For a 24-hour road report, check **Road Construction Delays and Closures** (307/344-2117, www.nps.gov/yell). Information on state roads is available from the **Montana Department of Transportation** (800/226-7623, www.mdt511.com) and **Wyoming Department of Transportation** (888/996-7623, www.wyoroad.info). **National Weather Service** (www.crh.noaa.gov) reports are available for Yellowstone and Grand Teton National Parks.

TOURS

Xanterra/Yellowstone National Park Lodges (307/344-7311 or 866/439-7375, www.yellowstonenationalparklodges.com) offers a variety of bus tours of the park during the summer, including historic Yellow Bus tours that range 1-12 hours. The **Yellowstone in a Day** tour ($130.50-138.50 adults, $65.25-69.75 kids 3-11) departs daily from Gardiner, Mammoth, and the Old Faithful Inn and covers the entire park in one day. Other options include early morning or evening wildlife tours, lake sunset tours, geyser gazers, Lamar Valley wildlife expeditions, photo safaris, boat tours, fishing trips, and custom guided tours.

Depending on your particular interests, a range of companies outside the park offer specialized tours of Yellowstone. The only one inside the park, and an outstanding option, is the **Yellowstone Forever Institute** (406/848-2400, www.yellowstone.org). Courses are broken into summer and winter semesters, and single-day field seminars fees begin around $195. Multiday tours with lodging are also available. The courses are engaging and are taught by experts in their fields. Using Yellowstone as their classroom, the instructors concentrate on "individual aspects of the ecosystem." During the summer, you can take the "Introduction to Wolf Management and Ecology" course led by a wolf biologist or "Mammal Signs: Interpreting Tracks, Scat, and Hair" with an animal tracker. There are several naturalist guide certificate programs offered in both summer and winter. Winter field seminars include "Yellowstone Block Printing," "Wilderness First Aid," "Wolves, Dogs, and Humans," and "Art of Winter Landscape Photography." The institute can provide unique (and inexpensive) lodging in its two field campuses, in Gardiner and the Lamar Valley. Or it can include standard hotel lodging at park hotels. If you take the time to browse through the course catalog, you will likely find something geared to your interests. The Yellowstone Forever Institute tours are one of the best ways to get an in-depth insider's view of Yellowstone.

The Ecology of Fire

In 1988, wildfires blazed through Yellowstone National Park. To quell the flames, the largest fire-fighting effort in U.S. history was organized, involving 25,000 people and $120 million, but it was the first snowfall of the season that would eventually rein in the fire. The fires began at the end of June and burned until November. More than 793,000 acres (roughly one-third of the park) were affected, 67 structures were destroyed, and 345 elk and 63 other large mammals died as a direct result of the fire. The entire nation watched in horror as the first national park burned. The park's fire management plan consequently came under intense scrutiny. The question on everyone's lips was, "How could this have happened?"

During the first half of the 20th century, it was widely believed that nothing good came of wildfire. In the 1940s and 1950s, all fires in Yellowstone were immediately suppressed. During the 1960s, however, the tide shifted as studies showed that fire was a natural condition helping to clean out understory and residual dead plant matter, creating less competition between tree species for important nutrients and natural elements. In addition, it was discovered that serotinous pine cones only open and release their seeds in extreme heat that can only be generated by fire. In fact, several plants and trees rely on fire for germination. It was determined that wildfires had always been a part of the ecosystem and were necessary to preserve healthy and continuous life cycles of plants and trees.

By the 1970s, the park allowed wildfires caused by lightning to burn under controlled conditions. Until 1988, 235 fires had burned; only 10 were larger than 100 acres. In June 1988, the driest year in the park's history, early summer storms produced lightning that ignited 20 fires. Eleven self-extinguished, and the rest were monitored; by mid-July only 8,500 acres had burned. Within a week, park managers agreed to extinguish all fires due to extremely dry conditions. Strong winds made that impossible, and within a week 99,000 acres had burned. By September, in order for emergency workers to battle the blaze, the park had to close to visitors for the first time in its history.

By spring, the earth was green and vibrant amid the fire-blackened swaths. With the exception of moose, which lost a significant portion of their forested habitat, the animal populations appeared as if nothing had ever happened. Elk were even reported munching on the burned bark. Yellowstone, it seemed, was different—better and healthier.

Other tour operators that offer excursions in the park include **See Yellowstone** (800/221-1151 or 406/646-9310, www.seeyellowstone.com), a full-service travel agency in West Yellowstone that can book everything from accommodations and tours to complete packages, and **Yellowstone Wild Tours** (Gardiner, 406/224-0001, www.yellowstonewildtours.com, from $650), which offers a fantastic array of private single- and multiday tours year-round. The company is owned by a wildlife biologist and staffed by naturalists, so the focus will be on finding and observing wildlife. They offer special bear and wolf tours, family wildlife tours, hiking, thermal features, and winter tracking tours. Since all tours are private, the day can be customized with pickups and meals. They also offer to document the day with a professional photographer (from $689).

PLANTS AND ANIMALS

Yellowstone is a living, breathing, evolving ecosystem that is home to a diversity of high-alpine, subalpine, and forest plants (more than 1,000 native species of flowering plants) and an extraordinary number of animals (including 67 mammal species). It is fascinating to understand how the flora and fauna relate—and react—to one another throughout the park.

Plants

What makes the plantlife in Yellowstone so interesting is neither the abundance nor the variety but rather the relationship between the plants and their environment and the way they are determined and shaped by forces of geology, climate, fire, insect infestation, drought, flood, and not least of all, wildlife. In various places throughout the park, for example, visitors will notice small fenced areas where grazing animals like elk, deer, and bison do not have access. The flora is decidedly different when it is protected from herbivores. The massive burns of 1988 and, more recently in 2016, have given rise to a plant lover's paradise where hot pink fireweed is among the first to recolonize the blackened areas. The geothermal areas have their own rare and unique plant communities. And the reintroduction of wolves caused the movements of elk to be more sporadic as they tried to avoid being eaten, which led to an increase in the number of willows and a resulting increase in various animals, including beavers, that thrive on willows. These chains of events linking plants, animals, and the natural forces that control the park are endless and fascinating.

Animals

For many, the fauna in Yellowstone is the main event. With large mammals such as elk, bison, bighorn sheep, pronghorn, bears, wolves, and mountain lions, Yellowstone is among the best areas in the country to see wildlife in its natural habitat. For those willing to get up early and be patient enough to wait, sometimes for hours, Yellowstone is like the Discovery Channel brought to life.

There are a few species of reptiles and amphibians known to inhabit the park—11 in all—thanks to Yellowstone's cool, dry climate, and some 330 species of birds have been documented since the park's 1872 founding, ranging from tiny calliope hummingbirds to majestic trumpeter swans.

But it's the big animals that draw more than 4 million people to the park annually. The omnipresent bison are the largest animal in the park, with males (bulls) weighing upward of 1,800 pounds (817 kg) and females (cows) averaging about 1,000 pounds (454 kg). Yellowstone is the only place in the Lower 48 where wild bison have existed since prehistoric times. The herd dropped to near-extinction levels at the turn of the 20th century with only 50 animals within the park boundaries. The importation of 21 bison from private herds and the subsequent 50 years of repopulation efforts led to a marked increase in numbers. By 2006 some 3,500 of these wild, woolly behemoths once again roamed the high prairies of Yellowstone, but significant population fluctuations occur,

bison along the Firehole River

primarily because of fears surrounding the disease brucellosis. In a given year, the bison population in Yellowstone ranges 2,300-5,000 animals, with the population in summer 2020 hovering around the high end at 4,680.

The most recent count in 2019 placed the number of grizzly bears in the park at around 150, with another 728 living within the Greater Yellowstone Ecosystem, and likely three to four times as many black bears. Gray wolves were reintroduced to the park (after being entirely killed off in the area) in 1995, and in January 2021 there were at least 123 wolves in nine packs living primarily within the park boundaries, and more than 500 living in the Greater Yellowstone Ecosystem. Wolverines and lynx live within the park but are rarely seen. Coyotes are plentiful and often visible from cars, and somewhere between 34-42 mountain lions inhabit the northern range. Elk populations soar in the summer months to 10,000-20,000 animals in six or seven herds, compared to the fewer than 4,000 elk that winter in the park, while moose, hard hit by the fires of 1988, number fewer than 200. In the northern Yellowstone ecosystem, there are 345 bighorn sheep, with 131 counted inside the park. There are also 200-300 nonnative mountain goats in and around Yellowstone.

Finding the animals means knowing their habitats, being willing to wait during the edges of daylight, and oftentimes just plain getting lucky. Excellent wildlife-spotting guides are available through **Yellowstone Forever** (www.yellowstone.org), but the most obvious place to start is by asking any of the rangers at the park's various visitor centers. They can tell you about recent predatory kills, bear and wolf activity, elk and bison migrations, and the most up-to-date sightings of any number of animals.

As is true with nearly every feature of the park, the importance of safety in the face of wildlife cannot be overstated. Just check out YouTube for any number of videos highlighting ill-advised visitor interactions with wildlife. Be certain to stay at least 25 yards/meters away from bison and elk and at least 100 yards/meters away from bears, wolves, and other predators. If the animals change their behavior because of your presence—if they stop eating to look at you, for example—you are too close and are creating a significant and perhaps even life-threatening hazard for both the animal and yourself. Always remember that you are the visitor here and they are the residents; show proper respect.

GEOTHERMAL FEATURES

If the animals are what bring people to Yellowstone, the geothermal features are what transfix them and lure them back year after year.

The world's largest concentration of thermal features—more than 10,000 in all—Yellowstone bursts to life with geysers, hot springs, fumaroles (steam vents), and mud pots. There are six grand geysers, of which **Old Faithful** is the most famous, and some 500 lesser geysers. Throughout the park are a number of basins where visitors can see all four types of thermal features, including **Norris Geyser Basin.**

The thermal features in Yellowstone are an indication of the region's volcanic past, present, and future, and as such they are in constant states of change. Small but daily earthquakes cause shifts in activity and temperature. The travertine **Mammoth Terraces** are literally growing and changing on a daily basis to the point that the boardwalks have had to be altered to protect visitors from different flows of searing hot water.

As miraculous as these water features are to see—with dramatic color displays and water dances that put the Bellagio fountains in Vegas to shame—and to smell (think rotten eggs), what you can't see is perhaps even more compelling: thermophiles, heat-loving microorganisms that inhabit the geothermal features throughout the park. A source of

Yellowstone's Volcano: Waiting for the Big One?

It's always interesting to watch visitors' expressions when you tell them that in Yellowstone National Park they are standing atop one of the world's largest active volcanoes . . . and that it is overdue for an apocalyptic eruption. While those two facts are true, the reality is much less threatening. Indeed there have been three super eruptions—Mike Poland, the scientist-in-charge at the Yellowstone Observatory, explains there is no such thing as a super volcano, only super eruptions—over the course of the last two million years, and the patterns do indicate that the volcano is overdue to erupt. But scientists agree that the chances of a massive eruption in the next 1,000 or even 10,000 years are very slight. For the time being, anyway, the volcano that gives rise to Yellowstone's extraordinary geothermal features is all bark and no bite—thankfully.

AN EXPLOSIVE HISTORY

The first super eruption 2.1 million years ago was 6,000 times more powerful than the 1980 eruption of Mount St. Helens, spouting rock and ash in every direction from Texas to Canada, Missouri to California. The eruption emptied the magma chamber located just underneath the park and caused a massive sinking of the earth, known as a caldera, within the confines of what is now the park. Small lava flows filled in the perimeter of the Huckleberry Ridge Caldera over the course of hundreds of thousands of years.

The second major eruption occurred 1.3 million years ago and created the Henry's Fork Caldera. The most recent massive eruption took place roughly 640,000 years ago and created the Yellowstone Caldera, which is 30 by 45 miles (48 by 72 km) in size. The perimeter of the Yellowstone Caldera is still visible in places throughout the park. Hike up Mount Washburn on Dunraven Pass between Canyon and Tower, look south, and you will see the vast caldera formed by the most recent eruption. The caldera rim is also visible at Gibbon Falls, Lewis Falls, and Lake Butte. As you drive between Mammoth and Gardiner, look at Mount Everts to the east and you will see layers of ash from the various eruptions.

TODAY'S EARTHQUAKES ARE HINTS

But volcanic activity is not a thing of the past in Yellowstone. The magma, which some scientists think is just 5 miles (8 km) beneath the surface of the park in places as opposed to the typical 40, has created two enormous bulges, known as resurgent domes, near Sour Creek and Mallard Lake. The Sour Creek Dome is growing at an impressive rate of 1.5 inches (3.8 cm) per year, causing Yellowstone Lake to tip southward, leaving docks on the north side completely out of the water and flooding the forested shore of the south side. In addition, there are roughly 1,500 earthquakes every year centered in Yellowstone, most of which cannot be felt. In 2014, however, a 4.8-magnitude quake occurred 4 miles (6.4 km) from Norris Geyser Basin. The earthquakes shift geothermal activity in the park and keep the natural plumbing system that feeds the geyser basins flowing. They also suggest volcanic activity. In early 2010, a series of more than 3,200 small earthquakes (the largest registered 3.8 on the Richter scale) rocked the park, with 16 quakes registering a magnitude greater than 3.0. A 1985 swarm recorded more than 3,000 earthquakes over three months, with the largest registering at 4.9 on the Richter scale.

DON'T WORRY!

Still, the scientists at the Yellowstone Volcano Observatory have no reason to suspect that an eruption, or even a lava flow, is imminent. For more than three decades, scientists have been monitoring the region for precursors to volcanic eruptions—earthquake swarms, rapid ground deformation, gas releases, and lava flows—and although there is activity, none of it suggests anything immediate or foreboding. Current real-time monitoring data, including earthquake activity and deformation, are available online at http://volcanoes.usgs.gov. The bottom line is that the volcano is real and active, but certainly not a threat in the immediate future, and not a reason to stay away from this awe-inspiring place.

ongoing scientific study, these thermophiles are modern examples of the earth's first life-forms and responsible for the discovery of DNA fingerprinting.

As spellbinding as they are, particularly in winter when the warm steam beckons, it is critically important to stay on boardwalks in geothermal areas and never touch the water. In addition to being boiling hot, many features are highly acidic or alkaline and could cause extreme chemical burns. The ground around the features is often thin and unstable, occasionally allowing animals to break through and be cooked. Twenty-two people have died in Yellowstone's thermal features, including one man who strayed off the boardwalk in 2016 to get a closer look and broke through the thin crust; the water was so hot that by the time help arrived, there were no remains to collect.

HISTORY
Tracing Human History

Evidence from archaeological sites, trails, and even oral histories suggests that humans inhabited the region of Yellowstone as far back as 11,000 years ago. And although the land is rich with history, not much has changed since the park was created in 1872, the invaluable blessing of having been protected as the nation's first national park. The unique geothermal features, pristine lakes and waterfalls, abundant wildlife, and the different ecosystems have endured through the years.

Yellowstone was traversed by various Native American tribes, including the Crow, Blackfeet, Nez Perce, and Shoshone, whose oral history teaches that they originated in this area. Although these nomads passed through the area, only a branch of the Shoshone, known as the "Sheep Eaters," made Yellowstone their home. The first Europeans to have visited the area were most likely fur traders and trappers who seem to have missed the unusual geothermal activity. Lewis and Clark's expedition bypassed the region completely. On their return voyage in

1806, however, John Colter separated from the group and ventured alone into the region. He is considered the first non-Native American to have seen the thermal features in the park. When Colter returned home three years later, his stories were considered suspicious. His tales of "bubbling ground," "mountains made of glass," and rivers where you could catch a fish and cook it without ever removing it from the water seemed preposterous to Easterners. Colter's descriptions of fire and brimstone quickly earned the place the nickname of "Colter's Hell." However, as more fur traders moved into the region, the stories of boiling mud, steaming land, and hot pools of water continued. Jim Bridger explored the area in 1856 and is considered by some the "first geographer" of the region. He too shared wild descriptions that were met with similar skepticism.

Expeditions into Yellowstone

The first organized expeditions into the Yellowstone area were made in 1869 and 1870. It was the 1871 government-sponsored expedition into the region led by Ferdinand Vandeveer Hayden, however, that produced a detailed account of the area. The Hayden Geological Survey was accompanied by William Henry Jackson photographs and artwork by Henry W. Elliott and Thomas Moran. Photographs and spectacular paintings and drawings were splashed across magazines and newspapers around the East so that people could see the wonders of the region for the first time. It was this report, coupled with the earnest pleas of the men who had seen the area, that prodded Congress to grant the region national park status in 1872. That year, the park had 300 visitors.

Nathaniel Langford was the park's first superintendent, but without proper funding and staff he had difficulty protecting the land. Poachers and vandals exploited the park's natural resources, creating a state of general lawlessness. By 1886 the U.S. Army had entered the park to help regain control of the region. They built park structures, strengthened and enforced regulations, encouraged visitors, and made sure the land and wildlife were protected. Transportation infrastructure improvements also helped attract more visitors to the park. The Northern Pacific Railway extended to the town of Cinnabar, north of modern-day Gardiner, near the northern entrance of the park, and in 1915 automobiles were allowed into Yellowstone, making it more accessible to the masses. Following World War II, car travel exploded, and more than a million visitors came to the park in 1948.

Shaping Park Policy

The army's leadership was not a long-term solution to managing the new national park, and in 1916 the National Park Service was created. (The birthday of the National Park Service is still celebrated every year on August 25 with a smattering of hilariously decorated Christmas trees around the park.) Since then, the park's boundaries have been redrawn to encompass 2.2 million acres (roughly equivalent in size to the state of Connecticut), and wildlife management has been continuously refined as new science emerges. One fundamental change came as a result of the 1963 Leopold Report, which suggested that "natural regulation" was superior to the long-held unnatural management in which park managers controlled animal populations and altered the course of naturally occurring events like fire. Ecological Process Management, as it has come to be called, is still the core philosophy behind park management today.

Both the grizzly bear and the gray wolf (reintroduced to the park in 1995) have seen enormous improvements to their endangered status due to Yellowstone's wildlife policies. In 1988 the park experienced the largest wildfires in its history, affecting more than a third of its land, and once again sparking furious debates about management of public resources and the value of natural ecosystems. In the spring of 2016, the U.S. Fish and Wildlife Service proposed removing grizzlies from the endangered species list in the Greater Yellowstone Ecosystem, a controversial decision that has been tied up in courts ever since.

Modern-day Yellowstone is every bit as spellbinding as it was for John Colter and Jim Bridger and the scores of Native Americans who had traveled through the park long before them. But it is increasingly complex. Issues like bioprospecting, bison management in the face of the disease brucellosis, and the delisting criteria of endangered species loom large. Despite the fact that, thankfully, the physical features of Yellowstone—its mountainscapes, geothermal features, and wildlife populations—remain largely untouched, an area of this size with more than 4.5 million visitors annually (nearly three times the populations of Montana and Wyoming combined!) cannot be immune to human influence. The challenge as we move forward is to determine a way to let Yellowstone age and evolve in its own way, on its own time, while giving people around the world access to this unique and spectacular place. It is we, the visitors, who have an opportunity to be changed forever by time spent in Yellowstone, and not the other way around.

Gardiner

Named rather inauspiciously for a mountain man who was described in the local paper in 1903 as "an outlaw and in general a worthless, dissolute character," Gardiner (pop. 879, elev. 5,314 ft/1,619 m) is actually a cute little town with plenty of places to stay, eat, and stock up and has ideal proximity to the park. The only year-round entrance to Yellowstone for automobiles, this scrubby little tourist town has a charm and an identity all its own. The Yellowstone River cuts a canyon beside the main drag, which allows for plenty of river-runner hangouts. Few other places in the world have elk congregating in the churchyard or on the front lawns of most of the motels in town. And where else do high school football players have to dodge bison dung as they're running for a touchdown? The town's architecture is a combination of glorious wood and stone "parkitecture" buildings alongside old-school Western-style buildings complete with false fronts. The towering **Roosevelt Arch,** built in 1903 and dedicated by Yellowstone champion Teddy Roosevelt himself, welcomes visitors to the park with its inspiring slogan, "For the Benefit and Enjoyment of the People." Yes, Gardiner is built around its proximity to the park, but the town has maintained its integrity by preserving its history and making the most of its surroundings.

SIGHTS
★ Boiling River

Halfway between Gardiner and Mammoth Hot Springs, straddling the Montana-Wyoming border and the 45th parallel, the halfway point between the equator and the North Pole, is the Boiling River, one of only two swimmable thermal features in Yellowstone. From the clearly marked parking area, visitors amble upstream along a 0.5-mile (0.8-km) rocky path running parallel to the Gardner River. Where the trail ends and the

steam envelops almost everything, a gushing hot spring called the Boiling River flows into the otherwise icy Gardner River. The hot and cold waters mix to a perfect temperature that can be enjoyed year-round. The area is open during daylight hours only, and all swimmers must wear a bathing suit. The Boiling River is closed each year during spring and early summer runoff, when temperature fluctuations and rushing water put swimmers at risk. Alcohol is not permitted.

Kids and adults alike marvel at the floating Day-Glo green algae. The water should not be ingested. Bison and elk frequent the area, and despite the regular crowds of people (note that 20 people constitute a crowd in this part of the West), this is one of the most unforgettable and unique ways to enjoy a few hours in Yellowstone.

SPORTS AND RECREATION
Fishing and Boating

The Yellowstone is the longest free-flowing river in the Lower 48, and as such it offers excellent boating and fishing opportunities. With the river plunging through town on its way to Yankee Jim Canyon, Gardiner is home to several outfitters that can whet your appetite for adventure, trout, or both. The **Flying Pig Adventure Company** (511 Scott St., 888/792-9193 or 406/848-7510, www.flyingpigrafting.com, 2-hour scenic floats from $59 adults, $49 children 6-12, 2-hour whitewater trips from $69 adults, $59 children 12 and under, full-day trips $135 adults, $115 children) and **Montana Whitewater** (603 Scott St., Gardiner, 406/763-4465, www.montanawhitewater.com, half day from $66.50 adults, $56.50 children 12 and under, full day from $102.50 adults, $92.50 children 6-12) both offer scenic and white-water floats on the Yellowstone River. Both companies offer add-ons like ziplining, horseback riding, and more. **Yellowstone Raft Company** (212 W. Park St., 406/848-7777 or 800/858-7781, www.yellowstoneraft.com, May-Sept., half-day raft trip from $59 ages 6 and up, full day trips from $95 ages 6 and up) was established in 1978 and has an excellent reputation for experienced guides and top-of-the-line equipment.

For anglers eager to wet a line in or out of the park in search of native cutthroats or brown trout, **Parks' Fly Shop** (202 2nd St. S., 406/848-7314, www.parksflyshop.com, 8am-6pm daily summer, 9am-5pm Mon.-Sat., 10am-4pm Sun. fall-spring) is the best place to start. This is an old-school shop with a 1920s cash register—nothing fancy here. It offers half-day trips for two people starting around $475, and full-day trips for two from $575. Anglers can pick up their licenses and any supplies in the retail shop, which stays open year-round. And since Parks' has been serving the area since 1953, its guides are keenly aware of the spots where the fish greatly outnumber the anglers. And after Thanksgiving, half of the shop becomes a **cross-country ski and snowshoe rental** shop.

Hiking

Yellowstone is a hiker's paradise, and unless you have a pet that needs to stretch its legs, hiking just outside the park is like spending the day in the Disney World parking lot. Not that there isn't stunning country in every direction, but there is something particularly alluring about hiking within the boundaries of the park.

That said, some 4.7 miles (7.6 km) south of the terraces at Mammoth Hot Springs, on the left-hand side after the Golden Gate Bridge, is the **Glen Creek Trailhead** and a small dirt parking lot. A range of wonderful hikes start from this point. Across the street on the west side of the road, a trail leads through **The Hoodoos,** massive travertine boulders that look otherworldly in this setting, and down the mountain 3.8 miles (6.1 km) back to Mammoth. If you cannot arrange either a drop-off at the trailhead or a shuttle, the return trip, another 3.8 miles (6.1 km), climbs constantly for nearly 1,000 vertical feet (305 m). Another more ambitious hike is the 9.2-mile (14.8-km) round-trip to **Osprey Falls.** The first 4 miles (6.4 km) are easy and flat, following an abandoned roadbed popular with mountain bikers. A blink-and-you'll-miss-it spur trail off the south side of the road leads hikers down into Sheepeater Canyon and the remaining 0.6 mile (1 km) to the mesmerizing 150-foot (46-m) falls. Relax, have a snack, and save your energy for the 800-vertical-foot (244-m) climb back up to the road. **Bunsen Peak** offers hikers an interesting walk through an entirely burned forest and all of its colorful rebirth, as well as a stunning view from the 8,500-foot (2,591-m) summit. The climb is steep: 1,300 vertical feet (396 m) over 2.1 miles (3.4 km). Try to ignore the hum of the radio tower near the summit—easily accomplished when the summit view fills your senses.

ENTERTAINMENT AND EVENTS

The biggest event of the year in this gateway community is the annual **Gardiner Rodeo** (406/848-7971, $12 adults), usually held in June over Father's Day weekend. The rodeo is held in the Jim Duffy arena at the northern end of town off US 89 and includes the usual competitions such as bull riding and bareback bronc riding. Women and juniors compete in barrel racing and breakaway roping. The first night of the rodeo is followed by a dance at the Gardiner Community Center, and the following day the chamber of commerce hosts a parade downtown. This is a great small-town rodeo.

But Gardiner is far from a one-event town. In late February, the **Jardine Ski Run** (406/848-7971) is a 5-mile (8-km) groomed track race where outlandish costumes are appreciated as much, if not more than, speed. With a $7 "grazing permit" you can help yourself to chili, chili dogs, baked goods, and more. Another worthwhile pursuit for the active is the **Park to Paradise Triathlon**

(406/848-7971) in late April or early May, which includes a 17.5-mile (28.2-km) bike, 4-mile (6.4-km) run, and 7-mile (11.3-km) river paddle. The much less demanding and very family-friendly **Annual Brewfest** (406/848-7971, $20 in advance or $25 at the gate) happens in mid-August and raises money for the local chamber with live entertainment, food, crafts, microbrews, and fun kids' activities like soda-tasting, face-painting, horseshoes, and kites. For more information on these events, contact the **Gardiner Chamber of Commerce** (406/848-7971, www.visitgardinermt.com).

FOOD

Known since 1960 for its "Hateful Hamburgers" and the huge personality of its owner, Helen, this fabulous burger joint was sold to the Wild West Rafting Company and is now known as ★ **Wild West Corral** (711 Scott St. W., across from the Super 8 Motel, 406/848-7627, 11am-10pm daily May-Oct., burgers $7-17). Even without Helen, this is still the kind of place you might easily drive 100 miles (161 km) to for the burgers, shakes, and old-school ambience. The limited seating is mostly outside, and there is often a line of people waiting to order. But none of that will matter when you take your first bite of a bison bacon cheeseburger or a perfectly grilled elk burger. Wild West Corral even managed to improve on Helen's by expanding the menu and cleaning the place up a bit. This is still a little slice of hamburger paradise—if you like that sort of thing.

For a good, hearty breakfast, excellent pastries, fresh Mexican food, and burgers, the **Yellowstone Grill** (404 Scott St., 406/848-9433, call ahead for hours after a temporary pandemic closure, breakfast $8-15, lunch $13-17) is sure to please. Remember though, this is small-town Montana. Sometimes the place closes when short-staffed. Or when the owners' youngest son has a Legion baseball game. Be glad for that; the important stuff still matters here. You can always have a late lunch. Another great place for a grab-and-go

meal, with fantastic book browsing while you wait, is **Tumbleweed Bookstore & Café** (501 Scott St. W., 406/848-2225, www.tumbleweedbooksandcafe.weebly.com, 7am-3pm Wed.-Mon., $3.50-9.50, sack lunches $12). They have great breakfast burritos, grilled sandwiches, wraps, soups, salads, and baked goodies. Vegetarians, vegans, and gluten-free people will be delighted with the broad offerings.

For a hearty meal almost anytime, try **Wonderland Café & Lodge** (206 Main St., 406/223-1914, www.wonderlandcafeandlodge.com, 7am-8pm Tues.-Sun., 7am-11am Mon., lunch $12-20, dinner $12-45), which serves coffee and baked goods all day, plus excellent lunch and dinner items including elk chili, trout, rib eye, pasta, and burgers. They also have free Wi-Fi and charging stations if you're in need. If pizza is what you're craving, head to **Yellowstone Pizza Company** (210 E. Park, 406/848-9991, www.yellowstonepizzaga.wixsite.com, noon-8pm daily May-Oct., $16-20), which serves 13-inch pizzas, plus pastas, salad, and appetizers.

ACCOMMODATIONS

Gardiner is built to accommodate the overflow from the park, but in reality, many of the little motels have more charm and much better value, particularly in non-summer months, than those inside the park. For the most part, it's hard to go wrong in Gardiner. There are plenty of small cabins and larger vacation rentals in the area. The folk Victorian ★ **Gardiner Guest House** (112 Main St. E., 406/848-9414, $100-165 summer, $75-115 winter) welcomes both children and pets and offers three modest but comfortable guest rooms and a cabin. Owners Richard and Nance Parks are longtime residents and an extensive source of information on the area. His fly shop and guiding company, **Parks' Fly Shop** (202 2nd St. S., 406/848-7314, www.parksflyshop.com), is one of the oldest businesses in town.

Yellowstone Park Riverfront Cabins (550 Old Yellowstone Trail S., 406/570-4500, www.cabinsontheyellowstone.com, $375/night for up to 4 people) offers comfortable cabins that can accommodate up to six people in a quiet location above the river. There is a five-night minimum. Another option for small, basic, and reasonably priced cottages right in town is **Hillcrest Cottages** (400 Scott St., 406/848-7353 or 800/970-7353, www.hillcrestcottages.com, early May-mid-Oct., $95-187). The cottages come in various sizes that can sleep 1-5 people. The **Flying Pig Adventure Company** (511 Scott St. W., 866/264-8448, www.flyingpigrafting.com) offers a host of higher-end vacation rentals ranging from cozy canvas wall tents on a nearby ranch (from $200) and cabins ($175-400) to an enormous private lodge (from $599) that can sleep up to 15. Minimum nights apply.

For more standard hotels, there is a decent selection including the riverfront **Absaroka Lodge** (310 Scott St., 406/848-7414, www.yellowstonemotel.com, $130-210), where each room has its own balcony looking into the park. And there is the barebones but clean and pet-friendly **Super 8** (702 Scott St. W., 406/848-7401, www.wyndhamhotels.com, from $62), which offers a free breakfast and Wi-Fi.

CAMPING

The difference between camping outside the park and inside Yellowstone is simply that you need to focus on reservations and availability instead of permits and regulations. There are six campgrounds in Gardiner—four national forest campgrounds and two private ones.

The private **Yellowstone RV Park & Campground** (121 US 89 S., 406/848-7496, www.rvparkyellowstone.com, May-Oct., 46 sites including pull-through and tent sites, tent sites from $48, RV sites from $91) is ideally situated on the Yellowstone River just 1.3 miles (2.1 km) north of the park entrance. They have

plenty of full-service riverfront sites, plush a wash house for campers. The other private campground is **Rocky Mountain RV Park & Cabins** (14 Jardine Rd., 406/848-7251, www.rockymountainrvpark.com, May-Sept., standard RV sites $89, deluxe RV sites $99, premium RV sites $109, discounts for seniors and military, cabins $80-215), just four blocks from the park entrance.

Those in search of a more rustic experience might enjoy checking out a national forest campground. The pack-in, pack-out **Bear Creek Campground** (Forest Rd. 493, 10.5 mi/16.9 km northeast of Gardiner, 406/848-7375, 4 sites with no services, mid-June-late Oct. depending on weather, free) and the **Timber Camp Campground** (Forest Rd. 493, 9.5 mi/15.3 km northeast of Gardiner, 406/848-7375, no services, mid-June-late Oct. depending on weather, free) are both small, isolated, and pleasantly rustic. The other Forest Service campgrounds in Gardiner are Eagle Creek Campground and Canyon Campground, both of which charge $15 per night single, $30 double (plus $5 per additional vehicle) and are about 15 minutes outside of town.

INFORMATION AND SERVICES

For information on Gardiner and the area around it, the **Gardiner Chamber of Commerce** (216 Park St., 406/848-7971, www.visitgardinermt.com, 9am-5pm Mon.-Fri., 1pm-4pm Sat.-Sun., extended summer hours) is an excellent and welcoming resource. Just a couple of doorways down, the headquarters of **Yellowstone Forever** (308 Park St., 406/848-2400, www.yellowstone.org, 8am-8pm daily) offers information about the park, as well as its own phenomenal educational tours. A great gift shop is on-site, as well as the nicest bathrooms you have likely seen in a while.

1: the Roosevelt Arch **2:** Canary Spring at Mammoth Hot Springs Terraces

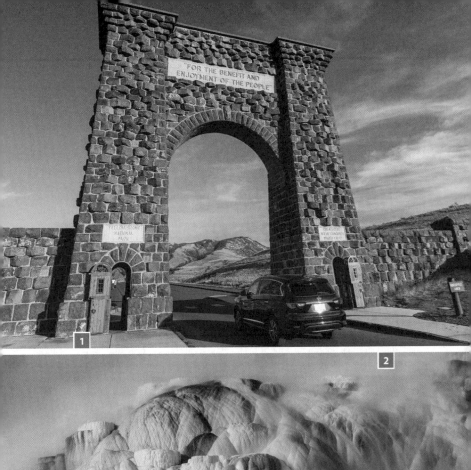

The Northern Loop

With striking panoramas, wonderful thermals, plentiful wildlife, and year-round vehicle access between the North and Northeast Entrances, this is one of the most underappreciated parts of the park. The accommodations and dining are not as fancy as elsewhere, but the crowds are more manageable, and the experience is just as good or better. Phenomenal highlights include Mammoth Hot Springs, the Lamar Valley, Tower Falls, Dunraven Pass, the Grand Canyon of the Yellowstone, and Norris Geyser Basin.

SIGHTS
★ Mammoth and the Mammoth Hot Springs Terraces

Just 5 miles (8 km) into the park and up the road from Gardiner, Mammoth is the primary northern hub of Yellowstone National Park. It is also an interesting little community in its own right, with a small medical center, the most beautiful post office in the West, and a magnificent stone church. The town of Mammoth, once known as Fort Yellowstone, was essentially built by the U.S. Army during its 1886-1918 occupation. Thinking they were on a temporary assignment, the soldiers erected canvas wall tents and lived in them through five harsh winters. In 1890, Congress set aside $50,000 for the construction of a permanent post, a stately collection of stone colonial revival-style buildings, most of which are still in use today.

The 2015 renovated **Albright Visitor Center** (Grand Loop Rd., 307/344-2263, 9am-5pm daily) is a must-see. There are films, history and wildlife exhibits, and a small but excellent selection of books and videos in the shop run by **Yellowstone Forever** (406/848-2400, www.yellowstone. org). While at the center, don't miss seeing some of the artwork produced during the

1871 Hayden Geological Survey of the park, including quality reproductions of painter Thomas Moran's famous watercolor sketches and original photographs by William Henry Jackson. Rangers on staff can usually give you up-to-date animal sightings and activity reports. The flush toilets downstairs are the last for a while.

The primary ecological attraction in Mammoth (other than the elk often seen lounging around and nibbling on the green grass) can be found on the **Mammoth Hot Springs Terraces.** Since the days of the earliest stagecoach trails into the park, they have been a visual and olfactory marvel for visitors. The Hayden Expedition named the area White Mountain Hot Spring for the cream-colored, steplike travertine terraces.

Beneath the ground, the Norris-Mammoth fault carries superheated water rich in dissolved calcium and bicarbonate. As the water emerges through cracks in the surface, carbon dioxide is released as a gas, and the carbonate combines with calcium to form travertine. The mountain is continuously growing as travertine is deposited and then shifted as the cracks are sealed and the mineral-laden water emerges somewhere else. For frequent visitors to the park, vast changes are noticeable from one visit to the next. In addition to changes in shape and water flow, the colors at Mammoth can vary dramatically from one day to the next. Not only does travertine morph from bright white when it is new to cream and then gray as it is exposed to the elements, the cyanobacteria create fabulous color shifts too—from turquoise to green and yellow to red and brown, depending on water temperature, available sunlight, and pH levels.

Liberty Cap, at the base of the terraces, is an excellent example of a dormant spring, where all but the core cone has been eroded away. **Minerva Terrace** and **Canary Spring**

are two other springs worth seeing. Their temperatures average around 160°F (71°C), and when they are flowing, they often put on marvelous color displays.

Tower Falls

Eighteen scenic miles (29 km) down the road from Mammoth Hot Springs—past **Undine Falls** and **Blacktail Plateau,** where you can see deer, elk, and bison along with some impressive lookouts—is **Tower Junction** and the breathtaking Tower Falls. The waterfall itself cascades 132 feet (40 m) from volcanic basalt. A popular spot with visitors and just steps from the parking lot, this is not a place for solitude, but it is lovely to see.

Dunraven Pass

Between Tower and the dramatic Grand Canyon of the Yellowstone is one of the most nerve-racking and perhaps most beautiful drives in the park. Climbing up the flanks of **Mount Washburn,** Dunraven Pass is the highest road elevation in the park. The spectacular summit of the road tops out at 8,859 feet (2,700 m) and offers impressive views of Yellowstone's caldera rim. Eagle eyes can also spot the nearby Grand Canyon of the Yellowstone. Hikers will have no shortage of trailheads to start from. The whitebark pines that grow along the road are a critical and dwindling food source for grizzly bears, so keep your eyes open. Because of its extreme altitude and relative exposure, Dunraven Pass is one of the last roads to open in the spring and one of the first to close when bad weather hits. For current road information, call 307/344-2117.

★ Grand Canyon of the Yellowstone

Yellowstone's most recent volcanic explosion, some 600,000 years ago, created a massive caldera and subsequent lava flows, one of which was called the Canyon Rhyolite flow, in the area that is now known as the Grand Canyon of the Yellowstone. This particular lava flow was impacted by a thermal basin, which altered the rhyolite and created the beautiful palette of colors in the rock through constant heating and cooling. Over time, lakes, rivers, and glaciers formed in the region, and the relatively soft rhyolite was easily carved away. Roughly 10,000 years ago, the last of the area's glaciers melted, causing a rush of water to carve the canyon into the form it has today. The 20-mile-long (32-km-long) canyon is still growing thanks to the forces of erosion, including water, wind, and earthquakes. A number of terrific lookouts are on both the North and South Rims of the canyon.

Before setting out for the canyon itself, visitors are advised to visit the **Canyon Visitor Education Center** (Canyon Village, 307/344-2550, 9am-5pm daily summer), which has an outstanding and vast exhibit on Yellowstone's volcanic and geothermal activity, plus other natural history. In fact, this should be a mandatory stop for every visitor who might otherwise have no appreciation for the region's fascinating geology.

On the **North Rim,** don't miss **Inspiration Point,** a natural viewing platform that gives a bird's-eye view both up and down the river. Nathaniel Langford, who would go on to be the park's first superintendent, stood in the same spot with the Washburn Expedition in 1870. He wrote:

> Standing there or rather lying there for greater safety, I thought how utterly impossible it would be to describe to another the sensations inspired by such a presence. As I took in the scene, I realized my own littleness, my helplessness, my dread exposure to destruction, my inability to cope with or even comprehend the mighty architecture of nature.

Look down, if you dare, among the nooks and crannies of rock to try to spot nesting ospreys.

Another phenomenal viewing platform can be found at **Lookout Point,** where visitors can gaze from afar at the thundering Lower Falls of the Yellowstone. Visitors who want to get closer to the spray of the falls and don't

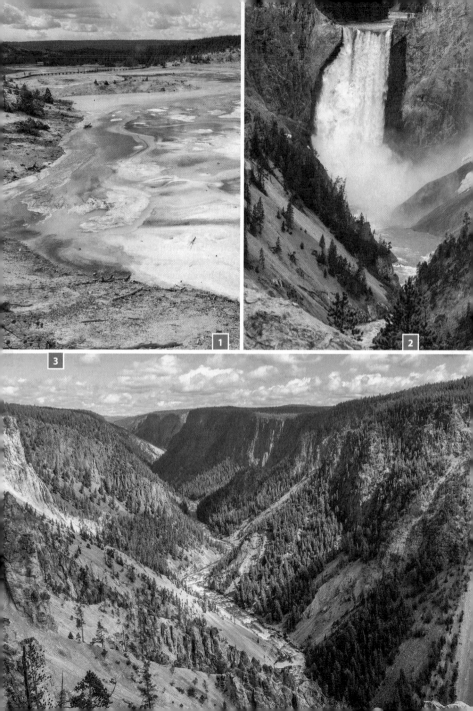

mind a long hike down, and back up again, can head toward the base of the falls at **Red Rock Point.** It's a 0.5-mile (0.8-km) trip one-way that drops more than 500 vertical feet (152 m). There is another platform at the top of the 308-foot (94-m) falls aptly named the **Brink of the Lower Falls.** This lookout also involves a 0.5-mile (0.8-km) hike and a 600-foot (183-m) elevation loss. The **Upper Falls** are just over one-third the size of the lower falls, at 109 feet (33 m), but they are worth a gander and can be easily accessed at the **Brink of the Upper Falls.** Mountain man Jim Bridger purportedly regaled friends with tales of the Upper Falls as early as 1846 and urged them to see it for themselves.

From the **South Rim,** visitors can see the Upper Falls from the **Upper Falls Viewpoint.** A trail that dates back to 1898, **Uncle Tom's Trail** still takes hardy hikers to the base of the **Lower Falls.** The trail down loses 500 vertical feet (152 m) through a series of 300 stairs and paved inclines, but what goes down must come up again. From **Artist Point,** one of the largest and most inspiring lookouts, visitors get a glorious view of the distant Lower Falls and the river as it snakes down the pinkish canyon. It was long thought that Artist Point was where painter Thomas Moran made sketches for his 7- by 12-foot (2.1- by 3.7-m) masterpiece *Grand Canyon of the Yellowstone.* More likely, say historians, he painted from a spot on the North Rim now called **Moran Point.**

Norris Geyser Basin

Both the hottest and the most unpredictable geyser basin in the park, Norris Geyser Basin is a fascinating collection of bubbling and colorful geothermal features. A 2.3-mile (3.7-km) web of boardwalks and trails leads visitors through this remarkable basin. From the **Norris Geyser Basin Museum** (east of Norris Junction, 307/344-2812, 9am-5pm daily late May-early Oct., free), which

carefully unravels the geothermal mysteries of the region, two loop trails guide visitors safely through the basin. The 1930s log and stone building that houses the museum has been designated a National Historic Landmark, and it also holds an information desk and a Yellowstone Association bookstore.

Porcelain Basin is a stark, barren setting with a palette of pink, red, orange, and yellow mineral oxides. Some of the features of note include **Africa Geyser,** which had been a hot spring in the shape of its namesake continent and started erupting in 1971. When it is active, **Whirligig Geyser,** named in 1904 by the Hague Party, erupts in a swirling pattern for a few minutes at irregular periods with a roar and hiss. The hottest steam vent in the hottest geothermal basin in the park is **Black Growler,** which has measured 280°F (138°C). The second-largest geyser in Norris, **Ledge Geyser** erupts irregularly to heights up to 125 feet (38 m).

In Norris's **Back Basin** you'll find the world's tallest geyser, **Steamboat Geyser,** which can erupt more than 300 feet (90 m) in the air. Minor eruptions of 10-40 feet (3-12 m) in height are more common. The eruptions can last 3-40 minutes and be separated by days or decades (in the past, Steamboat has gone more than 50 years without an eruption, but in 1964, it erupted 29 times). A major eruption in September 2014 happened at 11pm and was witnessed by a park ranger. Prior to that, the last major eruption occurred in 2013, and before that in 2005. In 2018, Steamboat entered an active phase with eruptions starting in March (after 3.5 years of silence), followed by two in April, four in May, three in June, and one in July. In total, there were 32 eruptions in 2018, 48 eruptions in 2019, and 48 again in 2020. As of September 2021, there had only been 14 eruptions that year. Just down the boardwalk, **Cistern Spring** is linked to Steamboat Geyser and drains in advance of a major eruption. The color is a beautiful blue, enhanced by as much as 0.5 inch (1.3 cm) of gray sinter deposited annually. By comparison, Old Faithful only

1: Norris Geyser Basin **2:** Lower Falls **3:** view from Inspiration Point

Be Safe and Smart in the Backcountry

Hiking and camping in the Yellowstone backcountry is undoubtedly the best way to understand and appreciate this magnificently wild place. But with this opportunity comes the responsibility to keep yourself safe, protect the animals from human-caused altercations, and preserve this pristine environment.

When hiking, **prevent erosion and trail degradation** by hiking single file and always staying on the trail. Don't take shortcuts or cut corners on switchbacks. If you do have to leave the trail, disperse your group so that you don't inadvertently trample the vegetation and create a new, unwanted trail.

Chances are good that you will encounter some kind of wildlife in the backcountry, so you need to be prepared to react. **Never approach an animal:** Remember to always stay at least 25 yards/meters away from all wildlife, and at least 100 yards/meters away from predators, including bears. Make noise as you hike along to give animals the opportunity to depart before an encounter. Do not hike at the edges of day—dawn or dusk—or at night, as these are the most active times for bears and other predators. Always be aware of your surroundings and pay attention to wind direction. Look for overturned rocks and logs, dug-out areas, and, of course, carcasses, all of which suggest bear activity.

If you do **encounter a bear,** know what to do. If there is some distance between you and the bear, give the bear an opportunity to leave, or take the opportunity to redirect your own party. If you run into a bear at close range, be as nonthreatening as possible. Talk calmly and back away. Never turn your back, and never run. Make sure you have your bear spray accessible. If the bear charges, stand your ground. Bears will often bluff charge to determine whether you will run and are thus prey. If the bear does attack, keep your pack on, fall to the ground on your belly, protect your head and neck with your arms, and play dead. When the bear leaves, get up and retreat. In the very uncommon circumstance that a bear provokes an attack or enters a tent, fight the bear with every resource you have.

Go to great lengths to **avoid attracting bears** by hanging all food, cooking utensils, and scented items (toothpaste, deodorant, other toiletries, menstrual supplies, and trash) in a bear bag in a tree or atop a bear pole. Designate a separate cooking and eating area away from the sleeping tents. Dispose of your trash and personal waste properly.

You need to plan your trip carefully and secure all **permits** and **backcountry campsites** through any one of nine backcountry permit offices: Bechler Ranger Station, Canyon Visitor Center, Grant Village Visitor Center, Bridge Bay Ranger Station, Mammoth Visitor Center, Old Faithful Ranger Station, South Entrance Ranger Station, Tower Ranger Station, and the West Yellowstone Visitor Information Center (307/344-2160, www.nps.gov/yell, permits available 8am-4:30pm daily June-Aug., $25 annual backcountry pass, $3 pp over 9 years old per night, $5 pp for stock parties). Some of Yellowstone's roughly 300 backcountry campsites can be reserved in advance either in person, by fax, or through the mail. Backcountry use permits are required for all overnight stays and can only be attained in person no more than 48 hours before your trip. A park booklet titled *Beyond Road's End* is available online and will help familiarize you with the backcountry regulations and restrictions.

deposits 0.5-1 inch (1.3-2.5 cm) of sinter every century. **Echinus Geyser** is the world's largest acid geyser and is almost as acidic as vinegar. Eruptions since 2007 have been rare and unpredictable, typically lasting about four minutes, but large ones have been known to reach heights of 80-125 feet (24-38 m).

SPORTS AND RECREATION

Yellowstone is indeed a hiker's paradise, with ubiquitous brown signs pointing to trailheads. Look for them anytime your legs need a stretch. In the northern loop, there are some fantastic trails in an otherwise nondescript stretch between Norris and Canyon. Drive east of Norris Junction 3.5 miles (5.6 km) or 8.5 miles (13.7 km) west of Canyon Junction to the **Ice Lake Trailhead** on the north side of the road. It is a fairly popular 4.5-mile (7.2-km) loop with minimal elevation gain. In fact, the entire trail to Ice Lake is wheelchair accessible and leads to the only wheelchair-accessible backcountry campsite in the park. Avid hikers will want to continue on to **Little Gibbon Falls,** a 25-foot (7.6-m) waterfall that is not even on the U.S. Geological Survey topographic map. Another way to see this hidden gem is to find the Little Gibbon Falls Trailhead 0.4 mile (0.6 km) east of the Ice Lake Trailhead. There is a small pullout on the south side of the road. The trail starts about 100 feet (30 m) east of the pullout on the north side of the road. From here, Little Gibbon Falls is a 1.2-mile (1.9-km) out-and-back hike.

A lengthier hike in the vicinity of Tower Junction is along the **Hellroaring Trail,** a beautiful but strenuous hike through wide open sagebrush and along fishable water. The trailhead is 3.5 miles (5.6 km) west of Tower Junction and starts with a steep descent to a suspension bridge over the Yellowstone River. Day hikers can enjoy a 6.2-mile (10-km) there-and-back hike through scenic sagebrush plateau to the confluence of Hellroaring Creek and the Yellowstone River. This is Yellowstone, so best to come prepared: Bring bear spray and a fly rod!

FOOD

By far the most unusual meal option in the park is the ★ **Old West Dinner Cookout** (307/344-7311, www.yellowstonenationalparklodges.com), which operates daily early June to mid-September from the Roosevelt Lodge and is served in Yellowstone's wilderness. The hearty steak-and-potatoes dinner with all the cowboy trimmings can be attended on horseback (1-hour rides from $98 ages 12 and over, $81 children 8-11, 2-hour rides from $110

ages 12 and over, $97 children 8-11) or via covered wagon (from $70 ages 12 and over, $55 children 3-11, free for children under 3).

Breakfast, lunch, and dinner are served daily throughout the season in the **Roosevelt Lodge Dining Room; Canyon Lodge Eatery, Canyon Lodge Falls Café,** and **Canyon Lodge M66 Grill;** and the **Mammoth Hotel Dining Room** and **Mammoth Terrace Grill** (866/439-7375, www.yellowstonenationalparklodges.com). Each restaurant has its own flair—Roosevelt Lodge tends to be heartier, with options like barbecue beef, bison chili, and Wyoming cheesesteak, while Mammoth is known for elaborate buffets and inventive small plates like goat cheese sliders, mini trout tacos, and Thai curry mussels. Canyon offers a wok station and slow food fast, with ready-made entrées like barbecued ribs, country-fried steak, and rotisserie chicken. Breakfasts include entrées ranging from pancakes and eggs to biscuits and gravy ($6-14). Lunches range $9-18, and dinners are generally $14-42. Generally, breakfast is served 6:30am-10am, lunch 11:30am-2:30pm, and dinner 5:30pm-10pm. Hours vary seasonally by restaurant and are subject to change. Call ahead for reservations, where available, or to check on hours.

ACCOMMODATIONS

There are three accommodations in the northern loop. The largest is the **Mammoth Hot Springs Hotel and Cabins** (late Apr.-early Oct. and mid-Dec.-early Mar.), which has 79 rooms, each with private bath, and another 116 cabins, four with hot tubs. The rustic cabins, two-room cabins, and deluxe hotel rooms range $124-345. Suites start at $664. Set amid historic Fort Yellowstone, Mammoth provides convenient access to restaurants, gift shops, a gas station, and the visitor center, so guests may forget they're somewhat out in the wild. Despite human and car traffic in Mammoth, wolves have been known to sneak onto the green watered

Camping in Yellowstone

As accommodations cannot meet the demand of Yellowstone's four million visitors each year, camping is an excellent option, particularly for those spontaneous souls who want to see the park without planning months in advance. More than 2,000 campsites spread over 12 campgrounds are located in the park. The five largest—Bridge Bay, Canyon, Fishing Bridge RV Park, Grant Village, and Madison—are run by Xanterra/Yellowstone National Park Lodges; all inquiries and reservations should be made by calling Xanterra (same-day reservations 307/344-7901, advance reservations 307/344-7311); these campgrounds have additional sales and utility tax fees. The other sites are assigned on a first-come, first-served basis. Try to arrive early to secure your spot; sites often fill up by 11am, especially in the busy summer months. Yellowstone also has more than 300 backcountry campsites, which require permits. Camping fees are discounted for bicyclists and hikers.

Campground	Number of Sites	Dates (Approx.)	Fees	RV Sites
Bridge Bay	432	late May-mid-Sept.	$28	call for availability and reservations
Canyon	273	late May-mid-Sept.	$33	call for availability and reservations
Fishing Bridge RV Park	310	early May-early Sept.	$52	call for availability and reservations
Grant Village	430	mid-June-mid-Sept.	$33	call for availability and reservations
Indian Creek	70	mid-June-mid-Sept.	$20	10 for 35-foot (10.7 m); 35 for 30-foot (9.1 m), walk through to assess site
Lewis Lake	85	mid-June-early Nov.	$20	25-foot (7.6-m) limit
Madison	278	late Apr.-mid-Oct.	$28	call for availability and reservations
Mammoth	85	year-round	$25	most pull-through, 30-foot (9.1-m) limit
Norris	111	late May-late Sept.	$25	2 for 50-foot (15.2 m), 5 for 30-foot (9.1 m)
Pebble Creek	27	mid-June-late Sept.	$20	some long pull-throughs
Slough Creek	16	mid-June-early Oct.	$20	14 for 30-foot (9.1 m), walk through to assess site
Tower Falls	31	late May-late Sept.	$20	all 30-foot (9.1 m) or less; hairpin turn

lawns at night to take down an unsuspecting well-grazed elk. You can imagine the surprise when early risers spotted the carcass on their way to get a breakfast burrito.

Named for Yellowstone champion Theodore Roosevelt, the ★ **Roosevelt Lodge Cabins** (early-June-early Sept.) offer a timeless rustic setting reminiscent of a great old dude ranch in a quieter corner of the park. The Roughrider Cabins (from $114) usually offer double beds and a wood-burning stove. What they lack in amenities they make up for with charming authenticity. Toilets and communal showers are available nearby. The Frontier Cabins (from $182) are slightly larger and include a private bathroom with a shower, toilet, and sink.

Set adjacent to the spectacular Grand Canyon of the Yellowstone, **Canyon Lodge & Cabins** (early June-late Sept.) is the largest single lodging property in the park. The facilities were built in the 1950s and 1960s, then added onto and renovated significantly in 2016 to bring the total to 590 rooms and cabins. Options include standard rooms, deluxe rooms, and Western cabins, which are basic motel-style units with private full bathrooms, starting at $242-500. Suites start at $940.

Reservations for all hotels inside the park should be made through **Yellowstone National Park Lodges** (307/344-7311, www.yellowstonenationalparklodges.com). Nature is the draw here: There are no televisions, radios, or air-conditioning. Internet access can be purchased in the public areas of some hotels in the park.

CAMPING

The only campground in the park's northern loop that can be reserved in advance, operated by Xanterra, the park's concessionaire, is the 270-site **Canyon** (307/344-7901 for same-day reservations, 307/344-7311 for advance reservations, late May-early Sept., from $34 nightly rate includes two showers/night), which has both tent and RV sites, 15 public restrooms with flush toilets, faucets with cold running water, and pay showers. The other six sites—at Mammoth, Tower Falls, Slough Creek, Pebble Creek, Indian Creek, and Norris—are available on a first-come, first-served basis and cost $20-25. These sites fill up quickly; your best bet is to arrive before 11am. Mammoth is the only campground open all year; all the campgrounds have some RV sites. A great feature on the Yellowstone app and website shows current availability and also what time any given site closed the day before (www.nps.gov/yell).

In addition to the campgrounds, more than 300 backcountry campsites are scattered throughout the park. Overnight permits, which are available at all ranger stations and visitor centers, are only issued in person up to 48 hours in advance; they are required for all the sites. Backcountry campsites can be reserved January-October by paying a $25 reservation fee. All requests to reserve sites must be made in person, faxed, or mailed in. Pertinent forms and information for backcountry camping in Yellowstone are available online at the National Park Service Backcountry Trip Planner (www.nps.gov/yell).

The Northeast Corner

With arguably the best wildlife-viewing in the park, especially in winter, this region is known as the "Little Serengeti of North America." The wide-open spaces of the Lamar Valley and much of the northeast corner of the park also offer some pretty dramatic mountain vistas. There is excellent fishing and hiking in the region, and just outside the park's northeast entrance is Cooke City, a cool little community with tremendous appeal to backcountry skiers, snowmobilers, and other outdoors enthusiasts.

★ WATCHING THE WOLVES

When visitors list the animals they most want to see in Yellowstone, wolves rank second, right behind grizzly bears. Since their return to Yellowstone in 1995, wolves have surprised park-goers and wildlife experts alike by being much more visible than anyone anticipated. In fact, since their reintroduction, wolves have been spotted in Yellowstone by at least one person nearly every day. Much of that is thanks to wolf researchers, including the indefatigable Rick McIntyre, who is out in the field an average of 11 hours per day seven days per week, and the ever-passionate wolf watchers (who tend to follow Rick), armed with massive scopes and camera lenses that look strong enough to spot wildlife on other planets.

The bad news is that there are roughly 123 wolves in nine packs, plus a few lone wolves, roaming throughout Yellowstone, an area that is approximately the size of Connecticut. It's always a good idea to bear those figures in mind when you have only a couple of hours and a keen desire to spot one of these majestic canines.

But there's good news too. If seeing the wolves is a high priority for you, here are five ways to improve your odds:

- **Visit in winter.** Wolves are most active and most visible (nearest to the roads and against a white backdrop) in the winter when they have significant advantages over their prey, including elk and bison. Spring and fall can offer viewing opportunities as well, but summer visitors are at a disadvantage because the wolves are often way up in the high country, far from roads. Whenever you go, don't forget your binoculars or a scope if you have one.

- **Do your homework or hire a guide.** Stop at the visitor center in Mammoth in winter (or any of the visitor centers at other times of year) and inquire about recent activity. Rangers can often tell you where packs have been spotted, if kills have recently occurred, and so forth. You could also consider hiring a guide that specializes in wolf-watching. **Yellowstone Wolf Tracker** (406/223-0173, www.wolftracker.com, $700/day for up to 3 people, $800 for up to 5 people, $900 for up to 10 people) offers 6- to 8-hour tours led by wildlife biologists. The **Yellowstone Forever Institute** (406/848-2400, www.yellowstone.org) offers multiday courses that focus on wolves.

- **Visit the Lamar Valley.** The only road open to car traffic year-round, the stretch of asphalt that winds through the Lamar Valley takes visitors through the heart of some of the park's best winter wolf terrain. There are numerous pullouts along the road for viewing, but be sure to park safely out of traffic without blocking other visitors. In the summer, along the stretch of road near the confluence of the Lamar River and Soda Butte Creek, the road is often closed to stopping thanks to a wolf-denning site not far from the pavement. Your chances to see a wolf—even pups—are good.

- **Wake up early.** Like most wildlife,

Cinderella: The Real-Life Fairy Tale of Wolf 42

In 1926 the last known wolf in Yellowstone was killed, bringing to a conclusion a decades-long campaign to rid the region of an animal widely considered a worthless pest. The murderous eviction was a tragic end to a noble creature. It took nearly 70 years for wolves to be seen not only for their intrinsic worth but their value in making the Yellowstone ecosystem whole again. This was their home, after all, and they had been unnaturally removed. Thirty-one Canadian gray wolves—*Canis lupus*—were reintroduced to the park in 1995-1996 with loud cheers and simultaneous objections.

Among the wolves brought into the park from Canada was a female who would come to be known as wolf number 42. Her sister, wolf 40, was the alpha female of the Druid Peak pack and known to rule the pack with an iron paw. She was suspected of running off her mother, number 39, and her sister, number 41. Number 42, the pack's beta female, managed to stay in the group, likely as a result of her unmatched speed and excellent hunting ability, but she could not get into her sister's good graces. The two fought constantly for four years. Both bred with wolf 21, the pack's alpha male, and wolf 40 reportedly killed her sister's first litter of pups in 1999. Wolf watchers nicknamed 42 "Cinderella" and flocked to the Lamar Valley to watch the drama unfold. Much of Cinderella's life was captured on film by Bob Landis for two *National Geographic* specials.

In a story that plays out like a fairy tale, wolf 42 got her nieces to den with her in 2000 when she had another litter of pups with 21, and after researchers saw wolf 40 approaching the den just before the pups were weaned, ostensibly to kill this second litter of pups, 42 and her nieces attacked. Wolf 40 was found dying of her wounds, and 42 not only rose to alpha status overnight and paired for life with wolf 21, but also moved into 40's den and adopted her dead sister's seven pups as her own. That year 42 and 21 raised 20 pups.

Over the course of her life—eight years, which is more than double wolf lifespan averages—she birthed 32 pups and held her alpha-female status over the Druid Pack, which climbed to 37 members in 2000, becoming one of the largest wolf packs ever recorded. She was known for her faithful and patient parenting, even coaching younger wolves in the middle of an elk hunt.

After receiving a mortality signal from 42's radio collar in February 2004, chief park wolf biologist Doug Smith hiked up Specimen Ridge on a blustery winter day. There he found Cinderella dead, killed by another pack. Wolf watchers noted wolf 21, her constant companion, atop a ridgeline howling for two days straight. The wolf watchers mourned along with him.

Cinderella was the last remaining member of the 31 wolves imported from Canada, but her legacy and story will be forever entwined with the Yellowstone wilderness and the saga of *Canis lupus* finally coming home.

wolves are most active at the edges of day. Putting yourself in the heart of the Lamar Valley before sunrise greatly improves your odds of seeing the wolves. The same is true at sunset. In this game, patience pays.

- **Watch for the wolf watchers.** They often have significant advantages, including radio telemeters that allow them to track collared wolves. These people know much about the wolves and can regale you with dramatic sagas of individual animals and entire packs. Don't be shy about pulling

over when you see them; they are often willing to let you peer through their scopes. But do be safe and courteous; turn off your engine and remain quiet.

★ LAMAR VALLEY

One of my favorite corners of the park, the **Lamar Valley** is stunningly beautiful with wide valleys carved by rivers and glaciers as well as views to the high rugged peaks around Cooke City. It's generally less crowded than other parts of the park (save for the ever-growing number of bespectacled and bescoped wolf watchers), and some of the best hiking, fishing, and camping can be had at Slough Creek. And the wolf-watching, particularly in the winter, is unrivaled anywhere else in the world. There are also grizzlies, black bears, mountain lions, coyotes, red foxes, elk, bison, bighorn sheep, and pronghorn in the area. In early summer, on occasion, there can be as many as 2,000 bison dotting the wide green expanse; it's a miraculous sight.

Lamar Buffalo Ranch

The **Lamar Buffalo Ranch Field Campus** of the **Yellowstone Forever Institute** (406/848-2400 or 307/344-8826, www. yellowstone.org/lamar-buffalo-ranch) is located away from the large crowds (of two-legged creatures, anyway) in the idyllic Lamar Valley. The institute offers field seminars at this private and unique campus year-round. If you bring your own sleeping bag and pillow, you can stay at the ranch in one of its shared or private log cabins. Propane heaters, a communal bathhouse with individual showers, and a fully equipped kitchen are housed in the common building. It's quite comfortable but not fancy. The best part is waking up each morning in the Lamar Valley, an opportunity very few

people have. You can also stay in a nearby campsite or hotel while taking a course at the ranch. Field seminars also take place at hotels throughout the park. The institute holds rooms in various lodges until 30 days before the course.

COOKE CITY

Before it was renamed for a miner and populated by hard-core modern-day prospectors in search of snow, **Cooke City** (pop. 63, elev. 7,600 ft/2,316 m) was called Shoefly. Today the town is a jumble of old buildings and some fairly salty characters, all with true Western flavor. At the end of a one-way road for most of the year (except during the height of summer when the Beartooth Highway leads visitors up and over the towering peaks), Cooke City has a remarkable sense of community, unlimited recreational opportunities, plenty of accommodations, and some excellent places to fill your belly. Nearby **Silver Gate** (pop. 29, elev. 7,608 ft/2,319 m) is equally scenic and even quieter, the Connecticut to Cooke's New York City. Pilot, Index, and Beartooth Peaks are three of the impressive summits that loom over these twin settlements, beckoning adventurers.

bison on the move in Lamar Valley

The Brucellosis Problem

Yellowstone is the only place in the continental United States where bison have existed since prehistoric times. Current policy mandates that the animals stay within the park's unfenced boundaries, and how best to enforce this is a matter of constant debate.

The park's management of the bison has changed throughout the years, just as bison numbers have fluctuated. Prior to 1967, park authorities would trap and reduce the herd to keep it manageable. After 1967, however, the guiding philosophy changed, and the bison were managed by nature alone. By 1996 the number of bison in the park had grown to 3,500. The size of the herd, coupled with winters that brought significant snowfall, led many of the bison to migrate out of the park in order to find better grazing and calving grounds. The problem of brucellosis played out on the national stage.

Brucellosis is a bacterial infection present in the bison and elk in the Greater Yellowstone area. The disease can cause spontaneous abortions, infertility, and lowered milk production in the infected animal, but the Yellowstone elk and bison populations seem relatively unscathed by the disease, despite the number of animals infected. The same tolerance of the disease is not common among cattle, however. The overwhelming fear is that bison exiting Yellowstone could infect neighboring cattle; this would be gravely detrimental to Montana, Wyoming, and Idaho beef production. Brucellosis cannot be treated in cattle and can be passed on to humans in the form of undulant fever. The government created a fairly simple inoculation program to eradicate the disease in cattle as early as 1934, but brucellosis has never been eliminated from wildlife.

Starting in the 1980s, when more than 50 percent of the park's bison tested positive for the disease, the park's approach was to control the borders with hazing to limit the number of bison that left the park. When hazing was unsuccessful, the bison were shot. The winter of 1996-1997 brought record cold and snow, and bison left the park in large numbers to forage for food; 1,079 bison were shot and another 1,300 starved to death inside the park's boundaries. This incident magnified the problem of maintaining a healthy herd while preventing the spread of brucellosis.

The National Park Service, the U.S. Department of Agriculture, and Montana, Wyoming, and Idaho are working together to see how brucellosis can be eliminated and free-roaming bison protected. A vaccination program has been implemented, with a 65 percent success rate, and the use of quarantine has proven fairly successful. Local bison rancher and wildlife advocate Ted Turner has agreed to accept some of the quarantined bison on his property. A small and highly regulated hunting season on bison is carried out each winter just outside the park boundaries.

But while there are no easy or obvious solutions, there are questions: What about elk, which also carry the disease and have been identified as the source of brucellosis outbreaks among horses in Wyoming and cattle in Idaho? No efforts to limit their natural migration in and out of the park have ever been attempted. Why are bull bison—who can carry the disease but cannot spread it through milk or birthing fluids as females do—quarantined and killed? For now, it seems, we watch, wait, and hope for a healthy, wild, and free-roaming bison population.

Sports and Recreation

The northeastern corner of the park and the area just outside it are a natural playground for fishing, hiking, cross-country and backcountry skiing, and snowmobiling.

HIKING AND FISHING

One short but worthwhile hike can be found 1.8 miles (2.9 km) west of the Pebble Creek Campground at **Trout Lake.** The hike itself is short and steep, just 1.2 miles (1.9 km) round-trip, and leaves from the Trout Lake Trailhead on the north side of the road. Anglers can bring a rod after July 15 when it opens to catch-and-release fishing for native cutthroats. In late spring and early summer, trout can be seen spawning in the inches-deep inlet, a fairly miraculous sight. There is an excellent trail around the 12-acre lake and shallow inlet and a decent chance of spotting playful otters, but hikers should take great care not to disturb the fish, especially during spawning. Bear awareness and a can of bear spray are necessary, as the bruins like fish too.

Another great place to combine fishing, hiking, and wildlife-watching—perhaps the perfect Yellowstone trifecta—is along the trail at **Slough Creek.** East of Tower Junction 5.8 miles (9.3 km) or west of the northeast entrance is an unpaved road on the north side of the road leading to Slough Creek Campground. The trailhead is 1.5 miles (2.4 km) down the road on the right side, just before the campground. The trail itself is a double-rutted wagon trail that leads to Silver Tip Ranch, a legendary private ranch just outside the park. The trail is maintained for 11 miles (17.7 km) one-way and only gains 400 feet (122 m) in elevation. All along the trail there is world-class fishing in slow-moving Slough Creek, home to a healthy population of native cutthroat trout. You may meet elk, bison, wolves, and even grizzlies along the trail, so be prepared and be safe.

MOTORIZED RECREATION

With an average of 194 inches (493 cm) of snowfall each year, mountainous terrain with elevation that ranges 7,000-10,000 feet (2,134-3,048 m), and a nearly interminable winter, Cooke City is a winter mecca with 60 miles (97 km) of groomed snowmobile trails and endless acres of ungroomed terrain for skiing and snowmobiling. Some favorite trails are **Daisy Pass, Lulu Pass,** and **Round Creek Trail.**

A number of places in town rent snowmobiles and all the necessary gear. Most important, you'll need to talk with experts about local conditions, trail closures, and avalanche dangers. **Cooke City Motorsports** (203 Eaton St., 406/838-2231, www.cookecitymotorsports.com, snowmobiles $325-385) and **Cooke City Exxon** (204 Main St., 406/838-2244, www.cookecityexxon.com, call for prices and reservations) are obvious choices in town. When the snow melts, you can rent ATVs and side-by-sides from **Bearclaw Sales and Service** (309 E. Main St., 406/838-2040, www.bearclawsalesandservice.com, for 2-6

passengers from $125/hour, $280/half day, $345-385/full day) as another way to get out and cover a lot of ground. They also rent sleds when snow is on the ground ($285-360/day). They rent all the equipment needed in any season, and you can—and should!—buy ($40) or rent ($15/day) bear spray.

Entertainment and Events

Among the biggest events of the year in Cooke City is the annual **Sweet Corn Festival,** a gathering for backcountry skiers and snowboarders usually held in late April on the weekend after the nearby ski hills have closed for the season. The weather is often sublime—think blue skies, cold nights, and warm afternoons—and the snow is like, well, sweet corn. Accommodations are not easy to come by this weekend (even floor space is pretty much spoken for), so plan ahead or bring a tent. Plenty of snowmobilers are on hand to act as taxis, enabling backcountry skiers not to have to earn their turns for once. With some of the best backcountry skiing in the West when the conditions are right, this is a welcome event.

The **Annual Hog Roast** happens in mid-March and attracts a throng of hungry snowmobilers, backcountry skiers, and, more recently, a healthy number of cross-country skiers to Cooke City. The event includes an auction, dinner, and live music.

The popular **Firemen's Picnic** is held annually on July 4, just east of town, with a good old-fashioned parade on Main Street, food, kids' games, and fireworks after dark. Another great small-town event, the **Mount Republic Chapel Bazaar**—where you can buy tools, equipment, winter and summer sports gear, clothing, books, games, and more—is held annually on a Friday and half day Saturday in mid-July.

For some culture on the periphery of Yellowstone's wilderness, check out **Montana Shakespeare in the Parks** in Silvergate Park in July or August.

For more information on any of these events, call or visit Donna—who is as knowledgeable as she is friendly—at the chamber-run **visitor center** (206 W. Main St., 406/838-2495, www.cookecitychamber. org, year-round, hours change seasonally), on the west end of town on the north side of the street; the center also has flush toilets.

Food

There are a million ways to work up an appetite in and around Cooke City. Be assured you won't go hungry (or thirsty, for that matter). ★ **Beartooth Café** (211 Main St., 406/838-2475, www.beartoothcafe.com, 9am-4pm and 5pm-9pm daily late May-late Sept., $13-27) offers excellent mountain fare—think steak and trout—with just a hint of Asian flair. The front-porch outdoor dining is a treat. Another great spot for a quick bite anytime (except April, May, October, and November when it's closed) is the **Bearclaw Bakery** (309 E. Main St., 406/838-2040, 5am-10:30am daily, rolls and coffee served from 5am, hot breakfasts from 6am), which makes from-scratch baked goods, full hearty breakfasts from chorizo toast to breakfast burritos, and light lunch. The bakery also offers a full coffee bar.

The **Prospector Restaurant** (210 US 212, 406/838-2251, www.cookecity.com, 7am-10pm daily, breakfast $6-13, lunch $13-15, dinner $13-28), inside the Soda Butte Lodge, is open year-round and particularly known for steak and prime rib—not a stretch in these parts. The Soda Butte Saloon in the lodge serves standard bar snacks.

Finally, for those wanting to pick up some supplies, the bright red ★ **Cooke City Store** (101 Main St., 406/838-2234, www. cookecitystore.com, 8am-7pm daily mid-May-Sept., hours may vary slightly based on customers and local activity) is as much a local museum and community center as it is a place to pick up some bread and a bottle of sunscreen. At the fly shop inside, **Trout Rider Fly Shop,** you can get fishing licenses for Montana, Wyoming, and Yellowstone National Park as well as pick up some flies and other supplies. It's a wonderful place and worth a visit; plus the nearest grocery store is 90 minutes away.

Accommodations

For a town with a population that hasn't made it to the triple digits yet, Cooke City has an impressive number of places to hang your hat. Lodging runs the gamut from cabins and vacation rentals to roadside motels, chain hotels, and small resorts, although not all of them are open year-round. Most of the photo galleries on the accommodations' websites are images of moose and bears or snowmobiles buried in powder rather than pictures of beds and baths. Clearly, Cooke City has morphed from a mining town into a tourist destination.

Big Moose Resort (715 US 212, 406/838-2393, www.bigmooseresort.com, from $135) is 3 miles (4.8 km) east of town and a great place to set up a base camp if you want to explore the region's trails and rivers. Open year-round, the lodge has a collection of seven old and new cabins, all of which are quite comfortable and can accommodate up to four people. There are no phones in the cabins (and no cell service in the area), but free Wi-Fi is provided, and you can schedule a Swedish massage on-site. The website gets buggy, so sometimes calling or reaching out through Facebook is the better option.

The **Cooke City Super 8** (303 E. Main St., 406/838-2070, www.wyndhamhotels.com, from $101) has rooms that are basic and clean, and the service is exceptionally friendly.

In the heart of bustling Cooke City is the **Soda Butte Lodge** (210 E. Main St., 406/838-2251, www.cookecity.com, $89-189), a full-service hotel with 32 guest rooms, a saloon, and a restaurant. The guest rooms are basic, but you didn't come to Cooke City to hang out in your hotel room.

In nearby Silver Gate, ★ **Silver Gate Lodging** (109 US 212, 406/838-2371, www. silvergatelodging.com, $150-505) offers 29 great cabins, plus motel rooms and a big lodge that can accommodate up to 10 people. Some of the accommodations are pet-friendly, but be sure to ask ahead. The setting is both quiet and communal, with barbecue grills, horseshoe pits, and a playground. And because this is Yellowstone, you can also rent scopes, which will come in plenty handy. The staff know the park backward and forward, so don't hesitate to ask about their favorite places.

Camping

Three Forest Service campgrounds are in the vicinity of Cooke City. **Soda Butte** (406/848-7375, www.fs.usda.gov, June-Labor Day depending on weather, $20/vehicle) is 1 mile (1.6 km) east of Cooke City on US 212. It has 27 sites, restrooms, food boxes, and drinking water, and fishing is available nearby. Please note that due to bear activity, this is a hard-sided campground only, and advance reservations are not accepted. Also strictly a hard-sided campground, **Colter Campground** (406/848-7375, www.fs.usda.

gov, June-Labor Day depending on weather, $20/vehicle) is just 2 miles (3.2 km) east of Cooke City and gives campers access to 18 sites, restrooms, food boxes, picnic tables, drinking water, and nearby fishing and hiking trails. Reservations are not accepted, so arrive early and have a backup plan in place.

Fox Creek Campground (307/527-6921, www.fs.usda.gov, July 15-Sept. 7 depending on weather, $20-60) is a larger, newly remodeled 33-site campground 6.7 miles (10.8 km) east of Cooke City on the Beartooth Highway with awesome views of Pilot and Index Peaks. Water is available, as are vault toilets, but cell service is not. Maximum spur length is 32 feet (9.8 m). The campground was closed due to construction on the highway through summer 2021. Reservations are not accepted.

The Southern Loop

Some of the park's biggest highlights are found in the southern loop, along with a significant number of visitors and plentiful wildlife. There are a lot of trees, many of them burned, and not as much dimension to the land as elsewhere, but the southern loop is what many people picture when they think of Yellowstone. From the sweeping Hayden Valley and the otherworldliness of West Thumb Geyser Basin to the sheer size of Yellowstone Lake and the well-deserved hubbub around Old Faithful, this section of the park has an abundance of dynamic features—some world-famous, others hidden gems—for every visitor.

SIGHTS
Hayden Valley

South of Canyon is the expansive and beautiful Hayden Valley, a sweep of grassland carved by massive glaciers named for the famed leader of the 1871 Hayden Expedition and occupied by copious wildlife that includes grizzly bears, wolves, and, in summer, thundering herds of bison. The Yellowstone River weaves quietly

through the valley, and because the soil supports grasses and wildflowers instead of trees, this is one of the most scenic drives in the park, especially during the bison rut and migration in late summer. Besides driving, hiking is an excellent way to explore the valley, either on your own (pay very close attention for signs of bear activity) or with a ranger on weekly **guided hikes** (4-5 hours, early July-late Aug., free). The hikes are limited to 15 people, and reservations must be made in advance at the **Canyon Visitor Education Center** (307/344-2550, 9am-5pm daily in summer) in Canyon Village.

Fishing Bridge

What was once the epicenter of Yellowstone fishing is today a relic of the past and a touchstone for the ongoing struggle between nature and human meddling. Fishing Bridge was built in 1937 and for years considered the best place to throw a line for native cutthroat trout. Humans were not the only ones fishing in the area, and human-grizzly encounters led to 16 grizzly bear deaths. To protect the bears and the fish, fishing in the vicinity was banned in 1973. Today, because of the sharp decline of cutthroat as a direct result of the introduction of nonnative lake trout, grizzlies are not seen as often fishing in the river.

There are some services—an RV park, a gas station, and a general store—and a 1931 log and stone structure that serves as the **Fishing Bridge Visitor Center** (East Entrance Rd., 307/344-2450, closed throughout COVID, so check the website for hours). On the National Register of Historic Places, the visitor center has a collection of stuffed bird specimens worth seeing and an exhibit on the lake's geology, including a relief map of the lake bottom.

★ Yellowstone Lake

Covering 136 square miles, Yellowstone Lake is North America's largest freshwater lake above 7,000 feet (2,134 m). In addition to being spectacularly scenic—both when it is placid and when the waves form whitecaps—the lake is a fascinating study in underwater geothermal activity. Beneath the water—or ice, much of the year—the lake bottom is littered with faults, hot springs, craters, and the miraculous life-forms that can thrive in such conditions. There is also a rather large bulge, some 2,000 feet long, that rises 100 feet above the rest of the lake bottom. The uplift is related to the ever-present geothermal activity beneath Yellowstone. Whether the bulge is gaseous or potentially volcanic in nature is the subject of ongoing research.

Aside from its geological significance, Yellowstone Lake also offers plenty of recreational opportunities, primarily in the form of boating and fishing. The water is bitter cold, though, typically 40-50°F (4-10°C), and not suitable for swimming. Eighteen-foot, 40 horsepower outboards ($62/hour) can be rented mid-June to early September at **Bridge Bay Marina** (307/344-7311 or 866/439-7375), just south of Lake Village or 21 miles (34 km) north of West Thumb. There is great fishing for native cutthroat trout as well. It's worth mentioning that early visitors to the park loved to tell stories about catching fish at the edge of the lake and then dipping their catch in the hot springs at West Thumb Geyser Basin to cook them without taking the fish off the line—a practice that would be seriously frowned upon today. Not to mention, what about the guts?

The rambling pale-yellow **Lake Yellowstone Hotel** was built in 1891 and is an elegant reminder of Yellowstone's bygone era. The lobby and deck, which overlook the

the vast Hayden Valley in summer

lake, are worth seeing, even if you are not staying here. Grab an iced tea and soak in the views; this is a stunning spot. If you can, stay for a meal and enjoy the live piano music. The crowds will fade as you gaze on the scenery.

West Thumb Geyser Basin

On the western edge of Yellowstone Lake is the eerie West Thumb Geyser Basin, a collection of hot springs, geysers, mud pots, and fumaroles that dump a collective 3,100 gallons of hot water into the lake daily. An excellent boardwalk system guides visitors through the area, but there have been injury-causing bison and bear encounters on the boardwalk, so keep your eyes open.

Abyss Pool is a sensational spring, some 53 feet deep, that transforms in color from turquoise to emerald green to brown and back, depending on a variety of factors. Similarly beautiful, **Black Pool** is no longer black because the particular thermophiles that caused the dark coloration were killed in 1991 when the water temperature rose. **Big Cone** and **Fishing Cone,** surrounded by lake water, are the features that led to the stories of fishing and cooking the catch in a single cast. Called "Mud Puffs" by the 1871 Hayden Expedition, **Thumb Paint Pots** are like miniature reddish mud volcanoes (depending on rainfall, after which they can get soupier) and are an excellent example of mud pots. Throughout the last several years, the mud pots have been particularly active, forming new mud cones and even throwing mud into the air. **Surging Spring** is fun to watch as the dome of water forms and overflows, unleashing a torrent of water on the lake.

Grant Village

On the West Thumb of Yellowstone Lake, Grant Village is a fairly controversial development dating to the 1970s and built in the heart of grizzly bear habitat and among several cutthroat spawning streams. The architecture is ugly, and the location is better suited to wildlife than visitors. In addition to the **Grant Village Visitor Center** (west shore of Yellowstone Lake, 307/344-2650, 8am-5pm

daily Memorial Day-early Oct.), which houses an exhibit dedicated to fire in the Yellowstone ecosystem, accommodations, a campground, and food services are available.

★ Old Faithful

Though often crowded, the **Old Faithful** complex brings together so many of the phenomena—both natural and human-made—that make Yellowstone so special: the landmark geyser and the incredible assortment of geothermal features surrounding it, the wildlife, the grand old park architecture of the Old Faithful Inn, and even the mass of people from around the world who come to witness the famous geyser.

An obvious stop at the Old Faithful complex is the **Old Faithful Visitor Education Center** (Upper Geyser Basin, 307/344-2751, 9am-5pm daily mid-Apr.-early Nov. closed winter/spring of 2022 due to staffing issues), which showcases Yellowstone's hydrothermal features. The $27 million facility hosts 4 million visitors annually. Efficient travelers (who are fighting an uphill battle here most of the time) can call ahead for a recorded message about daily geyser eruption predictions (307/344-2751) or check the NPS Yellowstone App.

Known as the **Upper Geyser Basin,** the area surrounding Old Faithful is the largest concentration of geysers anywhere in the world. By far the most famous is Old Faithful because of its combination of height (although it is not the tallest) and regularity (although it is not the most frequent or most regular). Intervals between eruptions are generally 60-90 minutes and can be predicted according to duration of previous eruptions. Eruptions can last anywhere from 90 seconds to five minutes. It spouts 3,700-8,400 gallons of hot water at heights of 106-184 feet. Signs inside the nearby hotel lobbies and the visitor center, a Twitter feed (@GeyserNPS), and the NPS Yellowstone App keep visitors apprised of the

1: Black Pool in West Thumb Geyser Basin **2:** crowd at Old Faithful

next expected eruptions, of which there are an average of 17 in any 24-hour period. Keep in mind that Old Faithful doesn't stop being predictable just because people go to bed or the weather turns cold—some of the most magical eruption viewings can happen without crowds. Choose a full-moon night, any time of year, and be willing to get up in the middle of the night. The vision of Old Faithful erupting in winter with snow and ice, frost, and steam in every direction is unforgettable.

If you take the time to come to Yellowstone to see Old Faithful, take the time—an hour or more is ideal—to walk through the other marvelous features of the Upper Geyser Basin. **Giantess Geyser** can erupt up to 200 feet high in several bursts. The irregular eruptions happen 2-6 times each year and can occur twice hourly, continuing 4-48 hours, and changing the behavior of many of the other geysers in the region. **Doublet Pool,** a colorful hot spring with numerous ledges, is lovely and convoluted. You can actually hear Doublet vibrating and collapsing beneath the surface. Looking something like a fire hose shooting 130-190 feet in the air, **Beehive Geyser** typically erupts twice daily, each eruption lasting 4-5 minutes. **Grand Geyser** is the world's tallest predictable geyser, erupting every 7-15 hours, lasting 9-12 minutes, and reaching heights up to 200 feet. Visible from the road into the Old Faithful complex if you look back over your shoulder, **Castle Geyser** is thought to be the park's oldest. It generally erupts every 10-12 hours, reaches 90 feet in height, and lasts roughly 20 minutes. A 30- to 40-minute noisy steam phase follows the eruptions.

★ Firehole River

Since swimming in Yellowstone Lake is not an option unless you are a trained member of the polar bear club, a dip in the heated (but far from hot!) waters of the Firehole River is one of the nicest ways to spend an afternoon. The designated and somewhat popular swimming area is surrounded by high cliffs and some fast-moving rapids both upstream and downstream, so the area is not recommended for new or young swimmers. The water temperature averages 80°F (27°C), but this avid swimmer would argue that the temperatures feel more like the 70s (about 24°C). Though quite limited, parking is accessible from Firehole Canyon Drive, which leaves the main road south of Madison Junction, less than 1,000 feet (305 m) after crossing the river. There is a toilet available but no lifeguards, so you will be swimming entirely at your own risk.

Midway and Lower Geyser Basins

Between Old Faithful and Madison Junction, along the pastoral Firehole River, are the Midway and Lower Geyser Basins, technically considered part of the same basin. In 1889, Rudyard Kipling dubbed Midway Geyser Basin "hell's half-acre" for its massive hot springs and geysers. Among the most significant features at Midway is **Grand Prismatic Spring,** a colorful and photogenic spring that was immortalized by painter Thomas Moran on the Hayden Expedition. It releases some 560 gallons of water into the Firehole River every minute. At 250 by 380 feet, and 160 feet deep, Grand Prismatic is the third-largest hot spring in the world and the largest in Yellowstone. Now dormant, **Excelsior Geyser Crater** was once the largest geyser in the world, soaring up to 300 feet high. Major eruptions in the 1880s led to a dormancy that lasted more than a century. In 1985, Excelsior erupted continuously for two days but never topped 80 feet. Today, acting as a spring, it discharges more than 4,000 gallons of heated water every minute.

Compared to the much smaller Midway Geyser Basin, the Lower Geyser Basin is enormous, spanning 12 square miles and including several clusters of thermal features. Among them are the notable **Fountain Geyser,** a placid blue pool that erupts on average every 4.5-7 hours for 25-50 minutes and sprays up to 50 feet high, the temperamental **White Dome Geyser,** the almost-constant **Clepsydra,** and the **Pocket Basin Mud Pots,** which are the largest collection of mud pots in the park. **Great Fountain Geyser** in the Firehole Lake area is the only predictable geyser in the Lower Geyser Basin and erupts every 10 hours and 45 minutes, give or take two hours, for up to an hour, reaching heights of 70-200 feet.

SPORTS AND RECREATION
Fishing and Boating

Some 50,000 anglers are lured to Yellowstone each year by the promise of elusive trout, and they are seldom disappointed by the offerings at **Yellowstone Lake.** In addition to the prized native cutthroat, the lake is home to a population of nonnative lake trout that is devastating the cutthroat trout population and threatening all the animals that eat the cutthroat trout. Introduced in 1890 into Lewis and Shoshone Lakes by the U.S. Fish Commission, the lake trout were first documented in Yellowstone Lake in the mid-1990s; scientists believe they were illegally introduced from a nearby lake in the 1980s. The average lake trout live and spawn in deep waters, feeding on as many as 40 cutthroat each year. By comparison, cutthroat trout spawn in the shallow tributaries of the lake, making them an important food source for a variety of creatures that include eagles and bears. Since the lake trout have no enemies in the deep waters of Yellowstone Lake, they are creating a serious food shortage by devouring the cutthroat. As a result, the eagles are having to eat other birds instead of fish, and Yellowstone is facing the complete elimination of some nesting bird species. All lake trout caught in Yellowstone Lake must be killed. Pick up your **fishing permit** at one of the visitor centers along with a copy of the Yellowstone fishing regulations.

You can see Yellowstone Lake by boat. Scenic or fishing boat tours as well as outboard motor rentals ($62/hour) are available from **Bridge Bay Marina,** south of Lake Village or 21 miles (34 km) northeast of West Thumb. Hour-long cruises on the *Lake Queen* ($19.50 adults, $11.50 children 3-11, free for children under 3) depart regularly from the marina mid-June to mid-September. Reservations can be made through **Xanterra** (307/344-7311 or 866/439-7375, www.yellowstonenationalparklodges.com).

Hiking

The southern loop of the park offers plentiful hiking opportunities, most of which can be combined with other interests. The **Hayden**

Grand Prismatic Spring

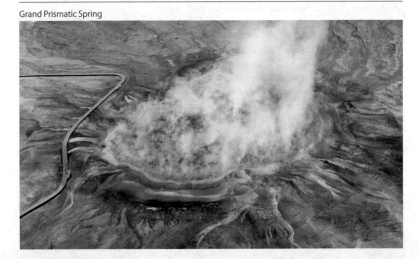

Valley has great trails for wildlife lovers, but precautions against bear encounters must be taken. The **Alum Creek Trail,** 4.4 miles (7.1 km) south of Canyon at the north end of the Hayden Valley, is a good hike. Wide open and relatively flat, the trail offers a 10-mile (16.1-km) out-and-back trip through prime bison and grizzly habitat. There are also some thermal features along Alum Creek.

Among the geysers in the Upper Geyser Basin is **Lone Star Geyser,** named for its lonely location 5 miles (8 km) from Old Faithful. An old once-paved road leads to the geyser and makes a nice level hike or bike trip. The entire out-and-back trip is 4.6 miles (7.4 km). There is parking at the trailhead on the south side of the road, 3.5 miles (5.6 km) east of the Old Faithful interchange. Lucky viewers will get to see a 30- to 50-foot eruption, which happens every 2-3 hours and tends to last 10-15 minutes.

FOOD

As the southern loop is generally the most heavily traveled section of the park, there are plenty of dining opportunities. In the park restaurants, breakfast and lunch are on a first-come, first-served basis, but reservations are strongly recommended for dinner, particularly if 5pm or 9pm is not your ideal dining hour. In almost all the venues, you will find some good vegetarian options and many items made with sustainable or organic ingredients; these are identified on each menu. If you are planning a day activity away from the center of things, the restaurants or cafeterias offer box lunches for travelers to take with them. Place your order the night before, and it will be ready in the morning. The Yellowstone General Stores at Grant Village, Lake Village, and Old Faithful also have fast-food service, groceries, and snacks.

The **Grant Village Dining Room** (866/439-7375, check website for hours but generally open daily for breakfast, lunch, and dinner, late May-Sept.) offers a pleasant view of the lake, good service, and a nice variety of American cuisine. In addition to the à la carte menu for breakfast, a buffet is available. Lunch and dinner include dishes such as prime rib sliders, smoked bison bratwurst, or spinach ravioli. Reservations are required for dinner.

The **Lake House** at Grant Village (check website for hours but generally open daily for breakfast, lunch, and dinner, late May-Sept., with shortened hours early/late seasons) sits right on the lake, with great views and a casual ambience. Breakfast is buffet only, and the dinner menu consists of regional fare like huckleberry chicken, wild game meat loaf, prime rib, and lemon pepper trout.

The ★ **Lake Yellowstone Hotel Dining Room** (307/344-7311 or 866/439-7375, check website for hours but generally open daily for breakfast buffet, lunch, and dinner, mid-May-early Oct., reservations required for dinner) is the most elegant dining room in the park, with a gorgeous view of the lake. The restaurant is committed to creating dishes with fresh, local, organic, and sustainable ingredients. Lunch is a good way to sample some of the gourmet fare without putting too large a dent in your pocketbook. Try the delicious organic lentil soup or blackened wild Alaska salmon wrap. Dinner at the hotel is sure to be a memorable experience with options like Montana elk chops, bison tenderloin, and lamb sliders.

Directly inside the hotel is the **Lake Hotel Deli** (check website for hours but generally open all day daily, mid-May-early Sept., shortened hours early/late seasons), which serves a nice selection of soups, salads, and sandwiches. The **Lake Lodge Cafeteria** (check website for hours but generally open daily for breakfast, lunch, and dinner, early June-late Sept., shortened hours early/late seasons) is a casual place for a quick bite. It serves basic breakfast standards, plenty of kids' favorites, and comfort food dishes ranging from spinach pie and fried chicken to apple-glazed pork loin.

Five eateries are located in the Old Faithful complex, but by far the most desirable is the **Old Faithful Inn Dining Room**

(307/344-7311, check website for hours but generally open daily for breakfast buffet, lunch, and dinner, early June-early Sept., shortened hours in May, Sept., early Oct.), which offers a buffet for each of the main meals daily as well as an à la carte menu. You can dine in the historic inn while enjoying its distinct rustic architecture and Western-style ambience. Lunch is a "Western buffet" with items such as farm-raised pan-fried trout, pulled pork, and wild game sausage. If you don't opt for the dinner buffet (featuring prime rib and trout), you could try pork osso buco, penne with local lamb ragout, wild Alaska sockeye salmon, and New York strip steak. Reservations are required for dinner.

The **Bear Paw Deli** (6am-9pm daily late May-early Sept., shortened hours early/late seasons), also inside the inn, is perfect for on-the-go meals. It offers a continental breakfast including bagel sandwiches, and sandwich and salad deli fare for lunch, as well as serving up several flavors of ice cream. In addition to these two eateries at the inn, there is a cafeteria and bakeshop in the lodge and a dining room and grill in the Old Faithful Snow Lodge.

ACCOMMODATIONS

★ **Lake Yellowstone Hotel** (mid-May-early Oct., rooms $285-822, suites from $1,114) is both grand and picturesque, perched on the shores of Yellowstone Lake. Originally built in 1891 and completely renovated in 2014 to celebrate its colonial revival influences, the hotel houses the nicest rooms in the park. As is true everywhere in the park, though, the appeal comes from the location and the views. If you are staying in the hotel, request a room with a view of the lake. An adjacent building, **The Sandpiper Lodge** (from $350) also offers recently renovated rooms. Individual cabins, called Lake Cottages, are behind the hotel but part of the Lake Lodge operation. These duplexes were remodeled in 2004 and are simple and modest.

There are 186 **Lake Lodge Cabins** (mid-June-early Oct., $178-276), which are clean and simple; many were renovated in 2018. Located just off the lake, the cabins are clustered around the main lodge, which is an inviting common area for guests to gather. It has a large porch that beckons guests to take a seat in one of the rocking chairs and soak in the view, as well as two fireplaces, a gift shop, and a cozy lounge. The Western cabins are a bit more spacious, with two queen beds and a shower-tub in each bathroom. The Pioneer cabins are older and more spartan, with shower-only bathrooms and 1-2 double beds. The setting is tranquil and quiet, and early risers may spot a herd of bison wandering through the property.

The ★ **Old Faithful Inn** (early May-early Oct., Old House rooms, standard West Wing rooms, deluxe West Wing rooms and deluxe East Wing rooms $193-506, suites from $942) is the most popular lodging inside the park, and for good reason. The original part of the lodge, known as the Old House, was built in 1903-1904 by acclaimed architect Robert Reamer. Situated close to the Old Faithful geyser, the lodge epitomizes rustic beauty, originality, and strength. It has a large front lobby that houses a massive stone fireplace. The larger rooms are in the wings of the inn, built in the 1910s and 1920s, while the more modest rooms are in the Old House. The inn has a wide assortment of guest rooms and rates, ranging from two-room suites with sitting rooms and fridges to simple rooms without individual baths. Since this is the most sought-after lodging in the park, make reservations well in advance.

Close to the inn are the **Old Faithful Lodge Cabins** (mid-May-late Sept., $116-192), offering much simpler and rustic lodging. If you are looking for budget-friendly accommodations that put you in the center of park activity, these are a good option. The cabins are small motel-style units that vary in condition. Many of them were renovated in 2016. The lower-priced cabins do not come with baths, but there are communal showers nearby. The cabins are scattered around a main log cabin-style lodge. Built in the 1920s, the main lodge has a large cafeteria, bakery, and fully stocked gift shop, making it popular with park visitors throughout the day.

The **Old Faithful Snow Lodge and Cabins** (late Apr.-mid-Oct. and mid-Dec.-late Feb., $146-365) are among the newest accommodations in the park. The original lodge was torn down and a new structure was built in 1999. Its architecture is intended to complement, though not duplicate, the Old Faithful Inn, and the lodge won a Cody Award for Western Design. It offers comfortable, modern rooms decorated with Western flair. It also has a few motel-style cabins, built in 1989. The Western cabins are a good value for the money; they're large rooms with two queen beds and a full bath. This is one of only two lodges (the other is Mammoth Hot Springs Hotel) open during the winter season in Yellowstone.

Grant Village is about 20 miles (32 km) southeast of Old Faithful on the West Thumb of Yellowstone Lake. Although the accommodations do not have the same rustic feel or character of the other lodges, they do offer a comfortable and modern place to stay away from the crowds. The complex is made up of six small condo-like buildings. Each building has 50 nicely furnished hotel rooms (from $306) that come with either two double beds or one queen and full baths. The rooms and exteriors were renovated in 2016.

Reservations for all hotels inside the park should be made through **Xanterra/Yellowstone National Park Lodges** (307/344-7311 or 866/439-7375, www.yellowstonenationalparklodges.com). Note that there are no televisions, radios, telephones, or air-conditioning.

CAMPING

Five of the 12 campsites in the park are in this southern region: **Bridge Bay** (between West Thumb and Lake, late May-early Sept., flush toilets, $28); **Fishing Bridge RV Park** (at Fishing Bridge north of Lake Village, early May-late Sept., flush toilets and pay showers, $50), the only campground offering water and sewer, for hard-sided vehicles only; **Grant Village** (at Grant Village south of West Thumb, late June-mid-Sept., flush toilets, $33); **Lewis Lake** (at Lewis Lake south of Grant Village, early-June-early Nov., vault toilets, $20); and **Madison** (at Madison Junction between the west entrance and Old Faithful, late Apr.-mid-Oct., flush toilets, $28). Advance reservations (307/344-7311 or 866/439-7375) or same-day reservations (307/344-7901) can be made at Bridge Bay, Fishing Bridge RV Park, Grant Village, and Madison.

West Yellowstone

West Yellowstone (pop. 1,376, elev. 6,667 ft/2,032 m) has something of a split personality—hard-core athletes training for the Olympics next to hard-core snowmobilers aiming for high-marking honors; get-too-close tourists alongside bison activists who try to put themselves in the line of fire. The winters are huge, with snow that buries everything but this town's spirit. The region shines with sensational recreational opportunities, from guided snow coach and cross-country skiing excursions to snowmobiling and dogsledding. The winters look interminable with piles of snow still scattered around town well into May and sometimes June, but with so much sun and so much to do, residents never complain about the cold.

The summers tend to be crowded as most people going to Old Faithful come through "West," as the town is known locally. With crystal-clear alpine lakes and rivers in every direction, there is no shortage of summer recreation—fishing opportunities are phenomenal, and there are plenty of places to cycle. As the hub of the region and the busiest entrance to Yellowstone National Park, West Yellowstone has plenty of good grub plus lots of comfortable beds in and around town.

SIGHTS
★ Grizzly and Wolf Discovery Center

If you have your heart set on seeing a grizzly or a wolf in Yellowstone, here's my advice: Get it out of the way before you even go into the park, like a first kiss on a first date before you order dinner. The **Grizzly and Wolf Discovery Center** (201 S. Canyon St., 406/646-7001 or 800/257-2570, www.grizzlyctr.givecloud.co, 9am-4pm daily but hours may change with the season, year-round, $15 ages 13 and over, $14 seniors 62 and over, $10 children 5-12, free for children under 5, admission valid for two consecutive days) is a nonprofit organization that acts something like an orphanage, giving homes to problem, injured, or abandoned animals that have nowhere else to go. Although there is something melancholy about watching these incredible beasts confined to any sort of enclosure, particularly on the perimeter of a chunk of wilderness as massive as Yellowstone, there is also something remarkable about seeing them close enough to count their whiskers. Watching a wolf pack interact from a comfy bench behind floor-to-ceiling windows in the warming hut is a worthwhile way to spend an afternoon. The naturalists on staff are excellent at engaging with visitors of all ages and have plenty to teach everyone.

One fantastic opportunity for curious children ages 5-12 is the **Keeper Kids** program, which is offered twice daily during the summer season. For roughly 30 minutes, the kids learn about grizzly eating habits and behavior. They get to then go into the grizzly enclosure, while the bears are locked away obviously, and hide buckets of food for the bears. When the kids exit and the bears come racing out to search for their treats—overturning massive logs and boulders in the process—the kids (and their parents!) are mesmerized. Enrollment is first-come first-served, and signup happens at the admissions counter at least 15 minutes ahead of the program.

There are also educational programs like **Raptor Rap**, about the raptors, as well as bear spray demonstrations and other programs on the wolves and bears. The center has gone to great lengths to share the personal story of each animal and why it cannot survive in the wild. They also give the bears all sorts of games and tasks—aiding in the design of bear-proof garbage cans is one example. Since these bears do not hibernate, this is a stop absolutely worth making any time of the year. Ultimately, this is a really nice place to learn a lot about bears, wolves, and raptors before heading into the park to look for them in the wild.

Yellowstone Giant Screen Theatre

Montana's first giant screen, the **Yellowstone Giant Screen Theatre** (101 S. Canyon St., 406/646-4100 or 888/854-5862, www.yellowstonegiantscreen.com, premium seating for feature films $15.75 adults, $15.25 seniors, $13 children 4-12; regular seating for feature films $11.75 adults, $11.25 seniors, $9 children) boasts a six-story-high screen with stereo surround sound that makes any subject larger than life. Nature-oriented movies rotate in and out, as do popular movies like the *Dune* and the newest Marvel Studio and other action or sci-fi flicks that benefit from the massive screen, but *Yellowstone* (premium seating $13.75 adults, $13.25 seniors, $11 children, regular seating $9.75 adults, $9.25 seniors, $7 children) is frequently on the playlist and offers an extraordinary introduction to the park's history, wildlife, geothermal activity, and mountainous beauty with giant screen grandeur. The biggest bargain in town is the 50-cent soft-serve ice cream available daily at the theater.

SPORTS AND RECREATION
Fishing

The fishing around West tends to be as plentiful as it is phenomenal. In addition to the

West Yellowstone

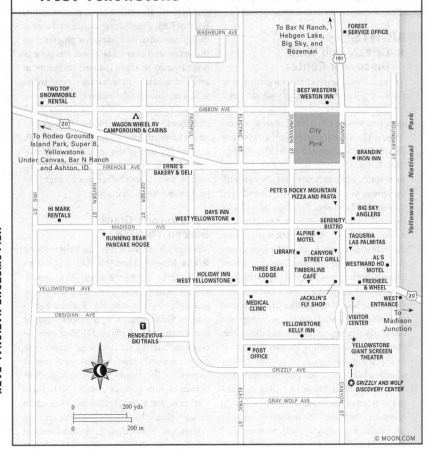

WASHBURN AVE

To Bar N Ranch,
Hebgen Lake,
Big Sky, and
Bozeman

FOREST
SERVICE OFFICE

191

TWO TOP
SNOWMOBILE
RENTAL

GIBBON AVE

BEST WESTERN
WESTON INN

20

WAGON WHEEL RV
CAMPGROUND & CABINS

City
Park

To Rodeo Grounds
Island Park, Super 8,
Yellowstone
Under Canvas, Bar N Ranch
and Ashton, ID

FIREHOLE AVE

ERNIE'S
BAKERY & DELI

BRANDIN'
IRON INN

PETE'S ROCKY MOUNTAIN
PIZZA AND PASTA

HI MARK
RENTALS

DAYS INN
WEST YELLOWSTONE

BIG SKY
ANGLERS

MADISON AVE

SERENITY
BISTRO

RUNNING BEAR
PANCAKE HOUSE

ALPINE
MOTEL

TAQUERIA
LAS PALMITAS

LIBRARY

CANYON
STREET GRILL

AL'S
WESTWARD HO
MOTEL

THREE BEAR
LODGE

TIMBERLINE
CAFÉ

FREEHEEL
& WHEEL

HOLIDAY INN
WEST YELLOWSTONE

YELLOWSTONE AVE

JACKLIN'S
FLY SHOP

WEST
ENTRANCE

OBSIDIAN AVE

MEDICAL
CLINIC

20

VISITOR
CENTER

To
Madison
Junction

RENDEZVOUS
SKI TRAILS

YELLOWSTONE
KELLY INN

YELLOWSTONE
GIANT SCREEEN
THEATER

POST
OFFICE

GRIZZLY AVE

GRIZZLY AND WOLF
DISCOVERY CENTER

GRAY WOLF AVE

IRIS ST
HAYDEN ST
GEYSER ST
FAITHFUL ST
ELECTRIC ST
DUNRAVEN ST
CANYON ST
BOUNDARY ST
ELECTRIC ST
CANYON ST

Yellowstone National Park

0   200 yds
0   200 m

© MOON.COM

YELLOWSTONE NATIONAL PARK
WEST YELLOWSTONE

big-name rivers like the **Madison, Firehole, Yellowstone,** and the nearby **Henry's Fork** across the border in Idaho, there are all sorts of small streams and beautiful lakes of all sizes. **Hebgen Lake** and **Quake Lake** are two favorites for year-round fishing.

You won't have any difficulty finding guides and gear in the town of West Yellowstone. Among the best is **Big Sky Anglers** (formerly Bud Lilly's Trout Shop, 39 Madison Ave., 406/646-7801, www.bigskyanglers.com, 7am-10pm daily during the season, 9am-5pm daily in the off-season, from $649 full-day walk/

wade or float trip for 2 anglers, $299 walk/wade clinic for 1-2 anglers), which has been outfitting and guiding anglers for 60 years. They also offer guided interpretive tours into the park. Another pretty famous name among anglers is Bob Jacklin of **Jacklin's Fly Shop** (105 Yellowstone Ave., 406/646-7336, www.jacklinsflyshop.com, 7am-10pm daily in summer, 8am-6pm daily in the off-season, $550 full-day guided float for 1-2 people; $450 half-day guided walk/wade for 1-2 people). Both outfitters are licensed to guide in and out of Yellowstone National Park, and both carry an excellent assortment of top-of-the-line gear. Bob is also happy to give private casting lessons for beginning anglers; call for rates. Anglers do not need state fishing licenses in Yellowstone, but a Yellowstone fishing permit—available at any of the visitor centers in the park—is required.

Mountain Biking and Cross-Country Skiing

Sandwiched between Yellowstone and the Gallatin National Forest on a high plateau, West Yellowstone offers excellent terrain for mountain biking. Because of its high altitude and location at the top of a reasonably flat plateau, West Yellowstone is also known for its cross-country ski trails. The town's excellent **Rendezvous Ski Trails** (look for the archway at the south end of Geyser St., 406/646-7701, www.skirunbikemt.com, passes required Dec.-Mar., $15 day pass, $30 3-day pass, children 12 and under ski free) offer roughly 22 miles (35 km) of gently rolling terrain, groomed for both skate and classic skiers, which easily converts to a single-track for mountain bikers and trail runners when the snow melts. Athletes from around the world come to train in West thanks in large part to this trail system. And it should be noted that the proximity to Yellowstone opens up a whole new world of opportunity for both mountain bikers and skiers.

The best bike and ski shop in town—which also has surprisingly stylish clothes, great gear, a Pilates studio, and killer coffee—is the **Freeheel & Wheel** (33 Yellowstone Ave., 406/646-7744, www.freeheelandwheel.com, 9am-7pm Mon.-Sat., 9am-6pm Sun. summer, 9am-5pm daily fall-spring). It rents, sells, and services bikes and skis and can offer any advice you could possibly need on the region's best rides and trails. Front suspension kid and adult mountain bikes and road bikes can be rented ($40/day) and come with a helmet and water bottle. Skate skis, classic waxable skis, and backcountry touring skis are all rentable for $35/day. Touring ski packages (for machine groomed or skier groomed trails) and snowshoes are available for $30/day. Pull sleds can be rented for $25/day. Any of this gear can be delivered to your hotel for $5/package. For those who want to rent e-bikes, **High Mark Rentals** (633 Madison Ave., 406/646-7855, www.highmarkrentals.com, $69/day) is the place. They also rent bear spray for $5/day—no money was ever better spent—and backpacks ($5/day).

Other Winter Recreation

Although snowmobiling inside the park has shifted with the four-stroke engine and guide requirements along with daily entry limits, West Yellowstone is still considered the snowmobile capital of the world for its proximity to the 200 miles (320 km) of groomed trails in the park as well as hundreds of miles of groomed terrain in the national forests surrounding West.

There are numerous places in town to rent a snowmobile, and since the park mandates that all snowmobilers within park boundaries use a guide, several outfits also offer guiding services both in and out of the park. **Two Top Snowmobile Rentals** (645 Gibbon Ave., 800/522-7802 or 406/646-7802, www.yellowstonevacations.com) has rentals for self-guided tours outside the park for $155-190 for single-riding machines and $200 for double-riding machines. Guided tours into the park start at $270 for a single-riding machine and $290 for a double-riding machine. They also have licensed guides, Yellowstone-mandated four-stroke engines, and other rental equipment, including clothing. Another outfit in town offering snowmobile, ATV, electric bike, and bike rentals is **High Mark Rentals** (633 Madison Ave., 406/646-7855, www.highmarkrentals.com, touring sleds $190-210, mountain sleds $230-260, high performance sleds for experts only $350-400). They rent Polaris, Ski-Doo, and Arctic Cat machines, and are the only place in town to rent SLP Stage 2 snowmobiles for experienced riders who want extra power for climbing and speed. Importantly, they also rent avalanche packs, beacons, and radios.

Spring Biking Through the Park

For a few magical weeks between the end of the snowmobile season and the onset of the summer car traffic, Yellowstone's roads are open exclusively to nonmotorized users. This means that bicyclists, walkers, runners, inline skaters, and roller skiers can cruise through the park in near silence with eyes focused on bison traffic as opposed to wide Winnebagos. Depending on the seasonal snow, the road between the West Entrance and Mammoth Hot Springs typically opens the last Friday in March and stays open to nonmotorized users until the third Thursday in April. Opening can be delayed in heavy snow years due to the need for plowing.

Sometime in May there is normally a brief period of bicycle-only traffic permitted from the East Entrance to the east end of Sylvan Pass, and from the South Entrance to West Thumb Junction. The roads between Madison Junction and Old Faithful, and Norris Junction to Canyon, remain closed to all traffic during this spring season for human safety and bear management.

There is something truly spellbinding about being on the open road in the park, the wind whistling through your helmet. The relative silence allows some unrivaled wildlife-viewing and necessitates great care. As nerve-racking as it can be to get engulfed by a herd of bison while driving in your car, coming across them on your bike is an entirely different scenario. Still, if you are cautious and respectful, being on your bike can allow you to feel somewhat less like an intruder and more like a resident. You can fall into sync with the flow of the rivers, the movement of the breeze, and the calls of the animals. It is an unforgettable way to experience the park.

With that said: Respect, restraint, and absolute caution are of vital importance to your safety and the well-being of the animals. Keep a good distance from all wildlife—25 yards/meters from ungulates and 100 yards/meters from predators. Remember that bison can run at speeds topping 30 mph (48 kph), and they can jump a 6-foot fence. Harbor no illusions about your immunity from an attack. The fact that you have approached silently allows for more of a startle factor for the animals and increases the likelihood of a conflict. Wear a helmet, and dress in layers: Yellowstone in spring can go from blue skies to blizzard conditions in a staggeringly short period of time. Be prepared for anything, and understand that there are no services in the park at this time. Enjoy this unique opportunity to savor the park up close. For specific information about road conditions, call 307-344-2109 (8am-4:30pm Mon.-Fri.).

For those who want to explore the backcountry outside Yellowstone National Park in a slightly quieter way, dogsledding might be the perfect choice. **Yellowstone Dog Sled Adventures** (406/223-5134, www.yellowstonedogsledadventures.com) offers half-day "Learn to Mush" tours ($235 adults, $150 children 5-12) where guests get to drive their own sled, which are appropriate for ages 5 and up. Other offerings allow guests to cuddle up in a sled while an experienced musher does the driving ($135 adult, $75 kids 12 and under).

Another amazing way to see the park is on a guided snow coach tour. Transportation between Old Faithful and Mammoth ($137 adult, $68.50 child), and an array of guided tours, can be arranged through **Yellowstone National Park Lodges** (307/344-7311, www.yellowstonenationalparklodges.com). Day tours of the Grand Canyon (from $237.50 adults, $118.75 children) include the Hoodoos, Swan Lake Flats, Obsidian Cliff and Roaring Mountain; night tours focus on steam, stars, and winter soundscapes (from $64.50). Other tours whisk visitors through a winter wonderland to destinations like West Thumb Geyser Basin (from $87 adults, $43.50 children) and the Firehole Basin (from $80 adults, $40 children).

1: a grizzly in Yellowstone **2:** West Yellowstone

ENTERTAINMENT AND EVENTS

There is plenty for visitors to do year-round in West Yellowstone. Before you arrive, you may want to visit the chamber of commerce **events calendar** (www.destinationyellowstone.com) to scope out the current happenings. The **West Yellowstone Visitor Information Center** (30 Yellowstone Ave., 406/646-7701) also has information on programs like ranger-led educational Yellowstone National Park afternoon and evening programs and snowshoe walks through the park in winter, free Music in the Park evenings, and weekly West Yellowstone rodeo shows in summer.

The **Yellowstone Rendezvous Race** (www.rendezvousskitrails.com or www.skirunbikemt.com), a one-day cross-country ski competition, is the largest event of the year. It usually takes place in early March, and 600-900 skiers come to participate. Six races are held concurrently, based on age and ability, over distances of 2-50 kilometers (1.2-31 mi). The **Kids 'N' Snow Youth Ski Festival** (www.kidsnsnow.org) is a newer event held the day after the Rendezvous Race. To encourage families to stay after the race, there are ski events (including a relay race, an obstacle course, and even musical chairs) for children 13 and younger. Throughout the ski season, look for such fun events as the monthly **Moonlight Skiing & Snowshoeing, Free Ski Day and Try It Biathlon** (Jan. 2), and **Taste of the Trails** (mid-Feb.).

The **Annual Mountain Bike Biathlon** (406/599-4464, www.skirunbike.com) takes place in June or July. There are two divisions, and first-timers are welcome to participate. The Match Class is for participants with experience and their own rifles; the Sport Class is for novices. The race covers 7.5 kilometers (4.7 mi) with two bouts of shooting. If you'd like to get some practice in before the event, you can sign up for the **Biathlon Shooting Camp** (406/599-4465) in August.

The **Wild West Yellowstone Rodeo** (175 Oldroyd Rd., 406/560-6913, www.yellowstonerodeo.com, $15 adults, $8 children) is another summertime event that runs June-August. Shows begin at 8pm and are held Tuesday-Saturday June-August; tickets are available online or at the gate.

FOOD

A great spot for a full breakfast, hot lunch, or terrific sack lunches is the long-standing **Ernie's Bakery & Deli** (406 Hwy. 20, 406/646-9467, www.erniesbakery.com, 7am-3pm daily summer, 7am-2pm daily winter, breakfast $8-13, lunch $9-14, box lunch $9-19). **Running Bear Pancake House** (538 Madison Ave., 406/646-7703, www.runningbearph.com, 6:30am-2pm daily, $8-16, box lunch $11.50) offers family-style dining for breakfast and lunch.

For the best soup, salad, and potato bar in town, try the **Timberline Café** (135 Yellowstone Ave., 406/646-9349, 6:30am-4pm and 5pm-10pm daily mid-May-early Oct., breakfast and lunch $7-16, dinner $11-38), an old-school establishment that has been feeding Yellowstone visitors and locals during the summer season since the early 1900s. Don't miss the homemade pie.

Canyon Street Grill (22 N. Canyon St., 406/646-7548, 8am-8pm daily May-Oct., reduced off-season hours, $6-17) is a 1950s-style diner with delicious burgers, fries, onion rings, sandwich baskets, and milk shakes. **Pete's Rocky Mountain Pizza and Pasta** (112 Canyon St., 406/646-7820, www.petesrockymountainpizza.com, 4:30pm-10pm summer, seasonal hours vary, delivery available after 5pm, entrées $13-18, large pizzas $20-27) serves up good pizza and hearty pasta dishes like elk sausage spaghetti and Italian buffalo ravioli. They do have gluten-free pizza offerings too.

Firehole Bar-B-Que Company (120 Firehole Ave., 406/641-0020, www.fireholebbqco.com, look online or call ahead for seasonal hours, closed November-April) smokes their meats daily, and the flavor comes out in this Central Texas style barbecue. From pulled pork and brisket to ribs and buffalo sausage, these folks serve up the real deal and they're open summer and fall, but only until they sell out the day's meat, which can often be well before sunset.

If you like Mexican street food, the best place within a day's drive from Yellowstone is, without a doubt, ★ Taqueria Las Palmitas (21 N. Canyon St., 208/760-8174, 11am-10pm daily early Apr.-mid-Oct., $5-15), known locally as "The Taco Bus." We're talking soft tacos, beans, and more, piled onto paper plates and served in an old school bus. It couldn't be less fancy or more satisfying.

For a more gourmet experience, Serenity Bistro (38 N. Canyon St., 406/646-7660, 11am-3pm and 5pm-10 daily May-Oct., $10-36) is undoubtedly the place. It serves excellent, fresh meals utilizing local ingredients whenever possible. Entrées include the bistro burger, Panang chicken, seafood pasta, trout, buffalo tortellini, elk tenderloin, and twice-cooked quail. Pasta lovers won't want to miss the butternut squash. The bistro offers gourmet salads and sandwiches for lunch and boasts the most extensive wine list in town.

Six miles (9.7 km) outside of town is the Bar N Ranch (890 Buttermilk Creek Rd., 406/333-0534, www.bar-n-ranch.com, 7am-10am and 5pm-10pm daily mid-May-mid-Oct. and mid-Dec.-early Mar., $15-45), a wonderful place for a meal. With beautiful views all around, you can indulge in terrific Western gourmet cuisine including game burgers, bison stir-fry, steaks, and pasta. One favorite is the campfire tacos with pulled pork, jalapeño slaw, and barbecue aioli. Gourmet picnic lunches are available too.

ACCOMMODATIONS

In the summer months there are more than 2,000 hotel rooms to be found in West and about 1,300 when the snow covers the ground. Guest ranches, bed-and-breakfasts, and cabin rentals are also available. See Yellowstone (800/221-1151, www.seeyellowstone.com) is a full-service travel agency in West Yellowstone that can book everything from

accommodations and private tours to complete packages. The West Yellowstone Chamber of Commerce (406/646-7701, www.destinationyellowstone.com) also has an excellent website that shows all lodging availability.

Open year-round, the Three Bear Lodge (217 Yellowstone Ave., 406/646-7353 or 800/646-7353, www.threebearlodge.com, $69-329) offers 44 guest rooms in its recently remodeled pet-friendly motel unit and 26 in the lodge, where no two rooms are alike. All guest rooms have a refrigerator, a microwave, an LCD TV, handmade furniture, and fluffy duvets.

The Alpine Motel (120 Madison Ave., 406/646-7544, www.alpinemotelwest yellowstone.com, May-Oct., $85-215) is a budget-friendly choice with a variety of units, some including kitchens, just two blocks from the park entrance. The service by owners Brian and Patty is noticeably good. Another good independent property, open mid-May to mid-October, is Al's Westward Ho Motel (16 Boundary St., 888/646-7331, www.alswestwardhomotel. net, $119-225), which has newly remodeled double queen rooms and air conditioning. It's just across the street from the park entrance and the Yellowstone Giant Screen Theatre. A couple of blocks farther from the entrance, but a long-standing and reliable choice in town, is the 79-room, pet-friendly Brandin' Iron Inn (201 Canyon, 406/646-9411 or 800/217-4613, www.brandiniron. com, $79-319).

Larger chain hotels in town include three Best Western options, the nicest of which is probably the Best Western Weston Inn (103 Gibbon Ave., 406/646-7373, www. bestwestern.com, from $290). Other options include Holiday Inn West Yellowstone (315 Yellowstone Ave., 406/646-7365 or 800/315-2621, www.ihg.com, $123-487), Days Inn West Yellowstone (301 Madison, 406/646-7656, www.daysinn.com, from $99), Yellowstone Kelly Inn (104 S. Canyon, 406/646-4544, www.yellowstonekellyinn.

com, $90-424), and, 7.5 miles (12.1 km) from town, **West Yellowstone Super 8** (1545 Targhee Pass, 406/646-9584, www.wyndhamhotels.com, $89-269).

CAMPING

With nearly two dozen private and public campgrounds in the vicinity of West, campers have plenty of choices, although most are geared to RV campers. The nearest U.S. Forest Service campground is **Baker's Hole Campground** (US 191, 3 mi/4.8 km northwest of West Yellowstone, 406/823-6961, www.hebgenbasincampgrounds.com, May 15-Sept. 30 depending on weather, $20 for 2 vehicles, $8 for each additional vehicle, $28 for electrical sites), with 73 sites (33 with electricity) set on a scenic oxbow of the Madison River. Basic services such as water and trash pickup are provided, there is firewood for sale ($6), and the fishing is excellent.

Right in town, just six blocks from the park's west entrance, is **Wagon Wheel RV Campground & Cabins** (408 Gibbon Ave., 626/848-3080, www.yellowstonerv.com, mid-May-mid-Oct., $59-79 full-hookup pull-through sites), offering a forested and quiet setting for RV camping only. Free Wi-Fi is available in some public areas.

For a truly unique experience outside of town, ★ **Under Canvas Yellowstone** (890 Buttermilk Creek Rd., 406/219-0441, www.undercanvas.com, Memorial Day-Labor Day) offers "glamping" (glamour-camping) options ($229-779) ranging from modest tipis and safari tents to luxury safari suite tents with king-size beds, private baths with freestanding tubs, and woodstoves. A variety of options are available, from shared bathrooms (the hot water showers are provided by a generator that runs from 6am to 11pm and is not quiet) to private but separate baths, influencing the price. But all of these tents and tipis are set in a mountain-ringed meadow with a creek running through. And the bedding is nothing short of luxurious. The guests are largely international, and it can be a treat to listen to campfire or next-tent pillow talk in several different languages. The only downside is that snoring is universally annoying, and with all but the most expensive tents situated so close together, light sleepers are bound to hear plenty of snorers. Still, this is comfortable camping without the work.

INFORMATION AND SERVICES

The **West Yellowstone Chamber of Commerce** (406/646-7701, www.destinationyellowstone.com), **Montana State Visitor Center,** and **Yellowstone Park Visitor Center** (307/344-2876) are all housed under the same roof at 30 Yellowstone Avenue. You can get all the information you need about the city and the state, and you can even buy your park permits. The visitor center also has a lot of information about the regular and special events held in town.

The **West Yellowstone Public Library** (23 N. Dunraven St., 406/646-9017, 10am-6pm Tues.-Fri., 10am-2pm Sat. mid-May-Sept.; 10am-5pm Tues.-Fri., 10am-1pm Sat. Oct.-mid-May) is between Yellowstone and Madison Avenues. It offers free Wi-Fi and has three computers with Internet access. Residents 18 and older with a library card can check out a hot spot for 14 days, and a telescope for up to a week.

The town's only **post office** (209 Grizzly Ave., 406/646-7704, 8:30am-5pm Mon.-Fri.) is at the corner of Electric Street and Grizzly Avenue.

Swan Cleaners (520 Madison Ave., 406/646-7892, 8am-8pm daily) is just east of the Running Bear Pancake House. It has coin-operated machines and wash-and-fold laundry services (9am-3pm Mon.-Fri.).

For nonemergency medical care, you can walk into the **Community Health Partners-West Yellowstone Clinic** (11 Electric St., 406/646-9441, www.chphealthmt.org, 9am-6pm Mon. and Thurs., 8am-5pm Tues.-Wed. and Fri. in high season, winter hours start Oct. 30). There is 24-hour paramedic emergency service available in town by calling 911.

Background

The Landscape

GEOGRAPHY

Montana is the fourth-largest state in area, with just over 147,000 square miles (380,278 sq km) of land, but ranks near the bottom in population—43rd, to be exact, with a population of 1,084,225 as of April 2020. To the north is Canada, with Montana sharing borders with Saskatchewan, Alberta, and British Columbia, while Wyoming is to the south. The western and southwestern part of the state is bordered by Idaho, and North and South Dakota flank its eastern edge. Montana is bisected by the Continental Divide, which runs

diagonally from the northwest to the south-central part of the state. The big peaks and expansive valleys dominating the landscape of western Montana, from Yellowstone to Glacier National Parks, inspired the state's name, which comes from the Spanish word for mountains. Central Montana acts as a transition to the flatter part of the state, with the Yellowstone and Missouri Rivers flowing out of the mountains and into the wide-open spaces that make up remote eastern Montana and the northern plains. Eye-catching badlands, buttes, terraces, and old grain silos dominate the horizon here, a stark contrast to the coniferous forests found farther west. Granite Peak in the Beartooth Mountains is the highest point in the state at 12,799 feet (3,901 m).

GEOLOGY

Montana and Wyoming (as well as parts of Idaho) converge around the Greater Yellowstone Ecosystem, widely regarded as the largest biologically intact temperate ecosystem in North America. Centered around Yellowstone National Park, this 31,000-square-mile (80,290-sq-km) area, or nearly 20 million acres, consists of a diverse landscape with geothermal activity and native wildlife; it is considered by scientists to be a natural laboratory for landscape ecology, geology, and wildlife preservation.

If you are worried that Yellowstone could erupt during your vacation, don't. Scientists are constantly measuring the amount of pressure in the magma chamber, which actually raises the floor of the caldera plateau—nearly 7 inches (18 cm) between 1976 and 1984, and almost 10 inches (25 cm) from 2004 to 2009. Since 2010, the rate of growth has significantly slowed down; by 2020, it was rising approximately 1 inch (2.54 cm) per year. But as if the caldera could breathe, the growth is up and down. The dome rises and falls, then rises again. Theoretically, the volcano could erupt, but scientists agree there is little evidence that a cataclysmic explosion will occur anytime soon. Due to its volcanic nature, the Yellowstone area experiences upward of 1,000-3,000 measurable earthquakes each year, but you are unlikely to feel one.

The rest of the ecosystem is mountainous and filled with large tracts of roadless land, jagged peaks, broad valleys, and flowing rivers—exactly why many people live here and even more choose to visit. Wildlife abounds, offering a rare glimpse into the lives of everything from the pine marten to the grizzly bear. Of course, people live here too, and the interaction between humans and nature is important not only historically but in contemporary matters as well.

In addition to mountains, Montana has large tracts of prairies that contain mostly dry grasses and shrubs. The iconic big sagebrush plant can be found at nearly every elevation and many land areas seem almost desertlike, right down to the tumbleweeds that roll along in the breeze.

CLIMATE

Montana weather patterns are influenced predominantly by the state's diverse topography. Generally, summers are hot and dry, often punctuated by brief but intense afternoon thunderstorms. Winters are cold and see a healthy amount of snow, particularly in the western portion of the state. Daytime highs in summer are in the 80s and 90s, with triple digits occasionally setting in. During the winter, it can get downright cold—the coldest recorded temperature in the lower 48 states was -70°F (-56.7°C) at Rogers Pass, northwest of Helena, Montana, on January 20, 1954. July and August are the warmest months, while January and February are the coldest. Snow can fall at any time of the year, but most occurs November-March. May and June are often the rainiest months of the year.

Previous: Traditional tipis remind visitors of the region's long history. 1: geyser eruption in Yellowstone 2: Glacier's Hidden Lake Overlook Trail

Humidity is generally on the low side, making the hot summer days a little more bearable. It's important to realize that when engaging in outdoor activities during the summer, you should always plan for bad weather—it can happen almost instantly at any time, even during the hottest part of the summer.

Temperatures decrease with higher altitude, so it's not uncommon in the mountains for the weather to be drastically different from lower elevations. Storms can move in without warning and can be fierce—driving hail in the summer and blizzard conditions in the winter. Rain in the valleys can often mean snow in the mountains, especially in the spring when a storm can dump several feet of heavy snow in a relatively short amount of time.

Chinook winds can blow in Montana. These unusually warm, dry winter winds blow down the east slopes of the Rockies and across the plains. They occur when moist Pacific air rises over the mountains, loses its moisture in the form of precipitation, and then warms rapidly on the leeward side. Chinooks can quickly melt snow and raise the temperature, as evidenced in January 1972, when the temperature in Loma, Montana, went from -56°F (-48.9°C) to 49°F (9.4°C) in 24 hours.

Great Falls, Montana, ranks among the windiest cities in the country. Winter winds can turn an average cold day into a bone-chilling one, while summer gusts often keep outdoor event planners working overtime.

Plants and Animals

PLANTS

The variety of habitats, ranges from grasslands and desert shrublands to forests, mountain meadows, and alpine tundra. Montana has 2,063 species in 176 plant families.

Trees

Forests cover roughly 22.3 million of the state's 93.3 million acres. Conifers—or cone-producing trees—grow most abundantly in drier areas. Montana's most prevalent conifers include ponderosa pine, Douglas fir, lodgepole pine—which combined make up some 66 percent of Montana's forests—subalpine fir, and **western larch,** which actually lose their needles every fall like deciduous trees and can live to be more than 500 years old. An infestation of mountain pine beetles has caused massive pine die-offs, increasing the threat of catastrophic forest fires. The tallest tree in Montana is a 203-foot (61.9-m) Engelmann spruce in Sanders County, and the runner-up is a 195-foot (59.4-m) ponderosa pine—incidentally, the ponderosa pine is the state's official tree—in Mineral County.

Flowers

While Montana lacks fall foliage colors, thanks to an abundance of evergreens, it more than makes up for with spring and summer displays of wildflowers. Varieties include purple **New England asters, bluebells, California poppies, camas, black-eyed Susans, fireweed, wild blue flax, sticky geraniums, fireweed, goldenrod, Indian paintbrush,** and **yellow monkeyflower.** The **bitterroot** is Montana's state flower.

Vegetation

Much of the eastern, central, and northern parts of the state consist of vast swaths of plains grassland, on which grow various species of grasses including **blue grama, bluebunch wheatgrass, needle-and-thread,** and **little bluestem.** In the shrubby grasslands, where the temperatures can be extreme and soils are generally fragile, dominant species include **blue grama, fringed sagewort, rubber rabbitbrush,**

1: bison 2: The Meadowlark is Montana's state bird. 3: grizzly bear 4: bighorn sheep

broom snakeweed, and Rocky Mountain juniper.

ANIMALS

Montana is known for their abundant wildlife. Both herbivores and predators roam the land, and with the right information a savvy traveler can seek out views of these animals. Keep in mind that it is not acceptable to approach wildlife for any reason—keep a safe distance away and never feed any animal.

Bison

Two herds of **bison**, fluctuating from 2,300 to 5,500 bison roam the area, a far cry from the millions that once lived throughout central North America from Canada to Mexico. These massive creatures graze on grasses, and males can weigh up to 2,000 pounds (907 kg), while females can weigh as much as 1,000 pounds (454 kg). Bison can commonly be seen almost any time of the year around Yellowstone, often causing traffic jams as they stand on the road. The National Bison Range wildlife refuge in Moiese, Montana, also supports a herd of 350-500 animals and has a visitor center and interpretive displays.

Elk

Elk are found throughout the mountainous region, with between 10,000 and 20,000 roaming free national park land. These regal creatures are fairly common and can be found at higher elevations in the summer and lower elevations in the winter.

Deer, Antelope, and Sheep

White-tailed deer and the large-eared **mule deer,** as well as **pronghorn antelope,** can be found throughout the region and are as often seen on the sides of highways as they are in the wild. **Bighorn sheep** are impressive, stocky animals. The rams (males) are known for their massive curled horns, which give the rugged creatures their distinctive look. Herds of bighorn sheep can be found around Big Sky, Montana, in particular.

Mountain Goats

Mountain goats inhabit many of the high peaks and can often be seen clinging to impossibly steep sides of rocky cliffs. Considered nonnative species, mountain goats were introduced to Montana in the 1940s and 1950s.

Moose

Some of the largest animals you'll encounter are **moose,** which typically inhabit river bottoms, wetlands, and willowed areas and graze on grasses, brush, and leaves. Moose can surprise you on the trail, as they are typically quiet and private creatures. Their docile nature can quickly turn deadly if they charge; give them plenty of room—at least 100 yards/meters—especially if you encounter a female with young.

Horses

The region is also home to a large herd of **wild horses,** located in the Pryor Mountains south of Billings. One of just 10 herds left in the country, many of the Pryor Mountain horses have primitive striping on their backs, withers, and legs; they are thought to be descendants of colonial Spanish horses. In 1968, interested individuals and groups convinced the government to set aside 31,000 acres in the Pryor Mountains as a public range for the wild horses, which had been living there for more than a century.

Bears

Black bears can be found in forested areas and often see much more human interaction than their larger counterpart, the **grizzly bear.** Grizzlies once roamed the entire Northern Hemisphere, and when Lewis and Clark traversed the area, there were likely more than 50,000 grizzlies across the West. Although there are still healthy populations in western Canada and Alaska, grizzly numbers in the Greater Yellowstone Ecosystem dropped to as few as 136 animals in 1975. Since the U.S. Fish and Wildlife Service listed them as a threatened species, the population has recovered to include an estimated 728 bears in the region as of 2019. The Northern Continental Divide Ecosystem in western and northwestern Montana is believed to be home to the largest number of grizzlies—approximately 1,000 as of 2020. The grizzlies along the Rocky Mountain Front have, in the last several years, started coming out of their alpine habitat to regain their status as residents of the plains, something not seen since Lewis and Clark traveled the region at the turn of the 19th century. Indeed, grizzlies today have been reported east of Great Falls, more than 100 miles (161 km) from the nearest mountain range. But despite their successes, grizzlies in the region face enormous hurdles, including habitat destruction and climate change, both of which put them in danger of human conflict. According to the United States Geological Survey (USGS), in 2020 there were at least 17 human-caused deaths for grizzlies in Montana's portion of the Greater Yellowstone Ecosystem, with reasons ranging from roadkill and self-defense to management for livestock depredations and those mistaken by hunters for black bears. The number of human-caused grizzly deaths was up over 2019 and higher than the 10-year average. Add that to the fact that grizzlies are the second-slowest reproducing land mammal in North America, and the hurdles for their survival look insurmountable. Even so, in 2017 the U.S. Fish and Wildlife Service (USFWS) delisted the Yellowstone grizzly population, but the bears will still be protected inside park boundaries. It's time for humans to protect grizzlies, and what is wild, or lose them forever.

Wolves and Coyotes

The reintroduction of the gray wolf is one of the greatest—and most controversial—wildlife success stories of the 20th century. Numbers went from zero—gray wolves were last seen in the 1930s—to more than 3,123 in some 300 packs living by the end of 2016.

You'll often see coyotes walking along the roadsides or strolling in an open meadow stalking their prey. These doglike predators have a longer and more pointed nose than wolves, a much fluffier tail, and are noticeably smaller and more delicate in appearance. Their numbers decreased substantially with the reintroduction of the wolf, thanks to food competition and conflicts between the two species.

Mountain Lions

Mountain lions, also known as cougars, are present in the region. Though their numbers dwindled to almost zero with the predator removal campaigns in the early 1900s, they managed to hang on thanks to their shy nature. These elusive cats are becoming slightly more common, and human confrontations have risen over the years. The largest cat in North America, with a length of up to 7.5 feet (2.3 m) from nose to tail, male cougars can weight 145-170 pounds (66-77 kg), and females generally weigh 85-120 pounds (39-54 kg). If you see one in the wild, chances are it will be crossing the road on a late-night hunting excursion.

Pikas and Marmots

The high country is home to the smallish pika and the larger, fuzzier yellow-bellied marmot. Both can be spotted running along rocky outcrops and scree fields at higher elevations. Listen for their high-pitched chirp.

Birds

The numerous species of birds include **bald** and **golden eagles, osprey, hawks, falcons, owls, woodpeckers, grouse, herons, pelicans,** and more. Smaller species include **jays, mountain bluebirds, warblers, western tanagers,** and **magpies.** The Red Rock Lakes National Wildlife Refuge in southwestern Montana is home to one of the largest habitats of the majestic **trumpeter swan.** For information on the excellent birding opportunities, visit www.audubon.org.

Snakes

The only venomous snake in Montana is the prairie rattlesnake, found in the eastern part of the region, typically in open arid country. Prairie rattlesnakes tend to den on south-facing slopes with rock outcrops and consume rodents as their primary prey.

Environmental Issues

As in many Western states, the environment is a controversial topic. While the state is on the conservative side politically, many of the residents—both old-timers and newcomers—have a vested interest when it comes to land, air, and water issues.

MINING

The effects of irresponsible hard-rock mining operations can be found throughout Montana, marked by a scarred landscape and contaminated water. The 1-mile-wide (1.6-km) Berkeley Pit, a former open-pit copper mine in Butte, is one of the country's largest Superfund sites. Since it closed in 1982, contaminated water has been filling the pit, which threatens contamination of the entire Clark Fork River basin. In 1998, voters in Montana approved a law that phased out the process of cyanide leaching in open-pit mines, although mining companies have tried ever since to get the decision reversed. Twelve of the 17 Superfund sites in Montana are related to mining operations.

One of the most tragic reminders of the mining industry's legacy is the situation in the northwest Montana town of Libby, where a former vermiculite mine was found to have poisoned the town's residents with a rare form of asbestos that was present in the mining dust. Health workers estimate that more than 400 people died from asbestos-related cancers, and some 3,000 residents have been sickened from exposure. There was local and national outrage when the news was made public in 2000 that the W. R. Grace Company, which owned the mine, knew all along that the asbestos was sickening workers and their families and yet said nothing. The company has since filed for bankruptcy, blaming the large number of personal-injury lawsuits, and a 20-year emergency cleanup of the town is being managed by the Environmental Protection Agency with a price tag that had reached $575 million in 2017. When the EPA wrapped up its work early, in 2018, the state of Montana took over the job of cleanup—from parks and schools to residences, a tailings mine, and 30 miles of highway—and handling future asbestos discoveries. Two documentary films have been made and several books written about the case and the tragic events surrounding the town.

AIR POLLUTION

Air quality is another concern, in particular emissions from coal-fired power plants and, in places, ongoing tire burning. Proponents of banning snowmobiles in national parks have succeeded in lowering the number of machines allowed to enter, as well as requiring all snowmobiles to be the cleaner four-stroke variety. This has divided towns where the winter economy has traditionally relied on the snowmobile tourism industry. Global warming has also affected Glacier National Park, as the number of glaciers larger than 25 acres has decreased from 150 in 1850 to 26 in 2015 and 25 by 2021—and some prediction models, based on a 2003 USGS study and 1992 temperature predictions, suggest that the park's glaciers could disappear altogether by 2030. A significant problem for air quality during most summers is smoke from massive forest fires. The Department of Environmental Quality (DEQ) (www.deq.mt.gov) monitors air quality.

Leave No Trace

Leave No Trace is an educational program that teaches outdoors enthusiasts how to protect the places they love from human-caused recreational impact. However, the Leave No Trace ethic extends far beyond backcountry and wilderness areas. As more and more people are recreating in "front country" settings, knowledge of how to apply Leave No Trace principles becomes increasingly important.

Planning ahead is the easiest way to protect outdoor places and to enjoy a safe visit. Use a map, bring a small first-aid kit, remember to bring additional clothing to keep you warm and dry, and wear suitable shoes or boots on the trails. When hiking, stay on designated trails, especially if they pass through private property. Shortcutting around corners causes erosion and damages trailside plants, especially if it's wet or muddy. Dispose of trash and biodegradable materials, such as orange peels, apple cores, and food scraps, in a bear-proof trash container. Remember, animals that become dependent on human food often have to be relocated or destroyed. Two easy slogans to remember are "Pack it in, pack it out," and "Leave it as you find it." By leaving the natural world as you find it, you will be protecting the habitat of plants and animals as well as the outdoor experience of millions of visitors.

In the backcountry, you must carry all trash out with you. Use a biodegradable soap when washing dishes, and avoid using soap within 200 feet (60 m) of a stream or spring. Allow others a sense of discovery by leaving rocks, plants, archaeological artifacts, and other objects of interest as you find them. Minimize campfire impacts by instead using portable camp stoves or fire pans. Use designated fire grates if available, and always make sure the fire is completely out before you leave camp. If you make a fire ring with rocks, disperse the rocks before you leave camp, and try hard to "leave no trace" of your being there.

Finally, always respect wildlife and be considerate of other visitors to help protect the quality of their experience. The last thing you want to do is ruin somebody else's trip of a lifetime. Keep noise to a minimum and let nature's sounds prevail; everyone will be happier for it.

WATER QUALITY

Montana is not immune to significant water quality concerns either, with mining, oil extraction, and agricultural use of pesticides, among other dangers. Various reports on impaired waters are available through the state's DEQ (www.deq.mt.gov).

FOREST MANAGEMENT

Perhaps nothing divides Westerners more than how to use and manage the forests. Whether the topic is the creatures that live in them, logging operations, forest fires, recreation, or potential wilderness, residents are passionate about their beliefs. Both sides of any issue typically have ardent followers, making legislation a painstaking process. Whether it's clear-cutting issues or motorized-vehicle access, forestry can be a touchy subject at the lunch counter. Check any newspaper in either state and you're bound to see articles and letters to the editor about these topics.

History

When examining the history of Montana, it's important to note the role geology played in creating the mountains, rivers, lakes, and valleys that are so treasured by residents and visitors alike. The Rocky Mountains were created about 100 million years ago, when giant masses of molten rock deep inside the earth began to push to the surface. The ensuing tectonic pressure stretched the land in every direction, allowing large blocks of rock to thrust upward and create the massive jumble of mountains we see today.

These new mountains were eventually buried under ice and water during several ice ages—the last one starting roughly 20,000 years ago—that carved out many of the details of today's landscape. The remnants of these glaciers can still be seen throughout the high country, particularly in Glacier National Park.

Prehistoric Residents

Dinosaurs played an important role in the region's early history. Some of the most recent and important fossil discoveries have been made here, including the largest known skull of a *Tyrannosaurus rex*. At Bozeman's Museum of the Rockies, an excellent exhibit highlights Montana's prominent role in dinosaur discovery.

The region's geologic history has made Montana a perfect laboratory for finding fossils from the Cretaceous and Jurassic periods. As the dinosaurs were dying off, the formation of the mountains caused sediment to slough off the rising peaks to form a layer over their remains. Receding glaciers then scoured the land and removed many of the layers, leaving behind fossils that can be found at or near the surface. And since much of the region remains undeveloped, most fossils have been undisturbed by humans.

The first humans most likely appeared 10,000-30,000 years ago, when Asiatic people came to North America across the Bering Strait land bridge. These people traveled south from Alaska to the Great North Trail, which ran along the eastern slopes of the Rockies. Some wandered all the way to South America. Those who stayed in the north hunted big game, including the extinct mammoth, and used tools made of chipped stone. They lived on the plains and foothills until a climatic change around 5000 BC turned the plains into a desert, and the people and animals all but disappeared.

As the climate slowly became more moderate, people returned from the south and northwest, bringing with them new techniques and cultural ideals. Bison roamed the land, providing a much-needed food source. These last prehistoric migrants are thought to be the direct ancestors of today's Native Americans. Evidence of their culture can be found in the tipi rings, pictographs (rock paintings), and petroglyphs (rock carvings) that still adorn the landscape. Buffalo jumps (also called *pishkun*) were used during this period; entire herds were stampeded off rocky cliffs and then slaughtered for their meat and hides. Two of the most remarkable buffalo jumps can be seen at First Peoples Buffalo Jump State Park near Great Falls and Madison Buffalo Jump State Park outside Three Forks.

Native Americans

Although the Flathead Indians lived west of the Continental Divide, many of the Native American tribes we associate with Montana today did not arrive until the early 1600s, moving westward after European settlement forced them from their traditional homelands. These new migrants—Plains Indians, as we refer to them today—mostly came from the Great Lakes and Mississippi Basin region, where their sedentary life was uprooted by westward expansionism. Many Native Americans abandoned their agricultural lifestyle and developed a culture of hunting as they were forced west onto the plains, where the bison were plentiful and the newly developed tipi provided a means to move around and follow the herds.

The Shoshone were among the first Plains Indians to enter Montana, displacing the resident Salish farther north. They brought with them the first horses. The Crow followed shortly after, moving throughout the valleys around the Yellowstone River. The Blackfeet brought the rifle with them when they settled in Montana during the early 1700s, and together with their allies, the Gros Ventre and Assiniboine, they quickly came to dominate the northern plains. Other groups that came to settle in Montana were the Sioux, Northern Cheyenne, Cree, and Chippewa, causing tensions with so many squeezed into a limited area as settlers moved farther west.

Lewis and Clark

It is hard to envision what monumental change would come when President Thomas Jefferson purchased the Louisiana Territory from France in 1803. This large part of the western United States was viewed as an important acquisition, and Jefferson hoped to explore this new territory to find a safe trade route from the Missouri River to the headwaters of the Columbia River and the Pacific. In other words, the West would soon be open for business.

Jefferson charged his personal secretary, Meriwether Lewis, and William Clark with the task of putting together a Corps of Discovery to explore the West. On May 14, 1804, the two set out from St. Louis with 45 men. Traveling up the Missouri River, the party spent the following winter in a Mandan village in North Dakota. Here they recruited French trader Toussaint Charbonneau, who spoke several Native languages and had traveled extensively along the Missouri. One of Charbonneau's wives was a young Shoshone named Sacagawea, who accompanied the party as an interpreter and guide.

The Corps entered Montana in April 1805 and followed the Missouri to its headwaters, near the present-day town of Three Forks. Lewis encountered the expedition's first Native American shortly thereafter, a Shoshone who led them to Sacagawea's brother and the tribe from which she had been kidnapped as a girl. The Shoshone led the party down the Bitterroot Valley and over the mountains through Lolo Pass near the Montana-Idaho border. The party then followed the Clearwater, Snake, and Columbia Rivers to the Pacific Ocean, where they built a fort and spent a long cold winter on the coast.

In the spring, the Corps backtracked across Oregon, over Lolo Pass, and into Montana in June 1806. The expedition then split into two parties, with Lewis taking the northeastern route toward Great Falls and Clark taking the more southern route to explore the Yellowstone River. The two parties met at the confluence of the Yellowstone and Missouri Rivers in August, and they were back in St. Louis by the end of September.

The Fur Trade and the Gold Rush

Although Lewis and Clark's famous expedition failed to find a manageable passage to the Pacific, it opened the door to fur trading, which would come to dominate the region in the first half of the 19th century. Trading posts sprang up along the Missouri and Yellowstone Rivers, and fashionable beaver pelts were soon finding their way to the East and Europe. By 1840, however, the mountain man era was over as beavers were trapped nearly to extinction and demand waned.

Catholic missionaries established posts near Stevensville and St. Ignatius and attempted to teach the Native Americans a different way of life. Some of these missions were successful, others were not, but their presence alone signaled that the traditional Native American way of life would soon be changed forever as settlers expanded farther into their territory.

If the beaver trade and missionary work marked the initial changes to the Native American way of life, the 1860 discovery of gold in Gold Creek near Deer Lodge signified the end of Native American autonomy. Gold was soon found near Bannack, the first territorial capital, and Virginia City, the second capital, and settlers began flocking to Montana to seek their fortunes. In 1860 there were fewer than 100 settlers in the state, but by 1870 that number had jumped to more than 20,000. Soon Montana became a postcard of the Wild West, where miners, settlers, Indians, and thieves interacted to create a dangerous, hostile atmosphere built on greed. The Bozeman Trail, established in the 1860s as an alternative to the more southern Oregon Trail, became known as the "Bloody Bozeman" for its perilous route through Indian country and several famous battles along its path.

By the 1870s, the gold rush was in full swing and the U.S. government was waging a full-on war against the Native Americans, forcing them onto reservations and land that was not traditionally their homeland. Many famous battles were fought in Montana, including George Custer's infamous "last stand" at the 1876 Battle of the Little Bighorn, where the 7th Cavalry fought several thousand Lakota and Cheyenne warriors and suffered heavy losses.

In 1877, the Nez Perce fled Oregon hoping to settle in Canada. Under the leadership of Chief Joseph, the tribe traveled across Idaho and into Montana, where they engaged with U.S. soldiers near the Big Hole River, a battle that left nearly 90 Nez Perce dead. They continued to flee, passing through Yellowstone National Park and north toward Canada, only to be captured near Chinook just 40 miles (64 km) from the Canadian border. Even though they were originally from the Pacific Northwest, the Nez Perce were sent to reservations in Oklahoma.

As gold and other minerals were being mined, the railroad came to Montana when the Union Pacific built a line from Utah to Butte in 1881. The Northern Pacific linked Chicago with Portland by 1883, opening up Montana's fortunes to the rest of the world. The Great Northern linked Minneapolis to Seattle in 1893, while the Milwaukee Road route across the center part of the state was completed in 1909.

Mining, Agriculture, and the Economy

Fueled by investors from all over the country, the large deposits of gold, copper, and other minerals quickly created vast wealth in Montana. Butte became known as the "richest hill on earth," and its three copper kings—Marcus Daly, William Clark, and Augustus Heinze—were among the richest men in the world. The competition between them to control Butte's copper mines is worth a book on its own—several have been written—and sounds like something out of a Hollywood movie. Each tried to buy courts, newspapers, politicians, banks, law enforcement, and anything and anyone that could help them or damage their opponents. In 1899, Daly teamed up with Standard Oil to create a behemoth mining company, which soon bought out Heinze's and Clark's interests and became the Anaconda Copper Mining Company. Named after the smelter town to the northwest, the company would dominate Butte for most of the 20th century.

Copper production in Butte peaked in 1917 and then started to decline, leaving the city in shambles as Anaconda began to shift jobs to places with cheaper labor, like Asia and South America. The riches of Butte, once the envy of the West, were leaving town just as fast as the mine workers. Anaconda stopped mining the massive Berkeley Pit in 1982, leaving it to become one of the largest contaminated waste sites in the country.

As the mining industry gained and then lost ground, cattle and sheep ranches continued to take advantage of Montana's abundant grasslands. By the late 1880s, there were nearly 700,000 head of cattle in the state. The passage of the Enlarged Homestead Act in 1909 brought thousands of homesteaders into the state looking for inexpensive land. Wheat farming was popular until an extended drought and a drop in market prices after World War I ruined many farmers, who were forced to abandon their farms.

Montana's post-World War I depression extended through the 1920s into the Great Depression of the 1930s. President Franklin D. Roosevelt's New Deal then brought relief to the state in the form of various projects and agencies: the building of Fort Peck Dam, the Civilian Conservation Corps (CCC), the Works Projects Administration (WPA), and the Agricultural Adjustment Administration (AAA). These "alphabet agencies" mark the first real dependence of the state on federal spending in the 20th century, a reliance that would only build.

Since World War II, Montana can be characterized by a slow shift from an economy that relied on the extraction of natural resources to one that is service-based. Such traditional industries as copper, petroleum, coal, and timber have suffered wild market fluctuations and unstable employment patterns. Agriculture has remained Montana's primary industry throughout the era. Tourism supplanted mining as the state's second-largest industry in the early 1970s. This era also saw an important shift in the state's transportation system from railroads to cars, trucks, and highways.

Montana's history contributes to its current way of life. Gone are the days of the Wild West, but each year thousands of visitors flock to see a real ghost town or Native American battlefield. The population is growing by leaps and bounds, which brings both added resources and significant challenges. Large ranching operations hark back to the days of the cowboy, and the same rivers Lewis and Clark navigated now provide a thrilling ride to white-water boaters.

Government

Montana became a territory in 1864 and was named the 41st state in 1889. Originally, the state's constitution reflected the mining and timber interests that seemed to run daily life in the early years, but in 1972 Montanans held a second Constitutional Convention, where the earlier, dated document was replaced with a more populist set of laws that placed more responsibility on the individual voter and made significant strides in protecting Montana's environment.

Montana granted women the right to vote in 1914 and two years later elected the first woman representative to the U.S. Congress. Jeannette Rankin, a lifelong pacifist and the only member of Congress to vote against entering World War II, is still the only woman Montana has elected to Congress. She served one term, worked as a lobbyist in Washington DC for 20 years, and then was elected again to Congress in 1940. Her antiwar stance fell out of favor, and she served one more term before retiring.

The Montana State Legislature is a bicameral body that meets in Helena each odd-numbered year for no longer than 90 days. It consists of a 100-member House and a 50-seat Senate. The Montana legislature has been split along party lines consistently throughout its history, especially since the new state constitution was enacted in 1972. Both parties have enjoyed similar successes over the years, and the legislature often changes hands. Montana's term-limits law survived in 2004 when 70 percent of voters shot down a measure that would have repealed term limits in the state legislature. Originally passed in 1992, the law limits representatives to four two-year terms and senators to two four-year terms. However, the term limit is for consecutive, not lifetime, terms.

Montana's postwar politics have seen some remarkable national politicians,

Changing Politics?

The political history of Montana is as colorful as the Wild West and has changed over the years to reflect the shifting population, economy, and culture that exist here.

At first glance, Montana may come across as a decidedly Republican state, but its history shows that both parties have had successes. Montanan Jeannette Rankin became the first woman elected to the U.S. Congress, in 1916 as a Republican.

Sometimes characterized as a swing state, Montana has had long-term shifts in party control throughout its history. Five of its first six governors were Democrats, and between 1952 and 1984 it elected only Democratic senators. Republicans held the governorship 1953-1969 and again 1989-2005. Democrats held the governorship 2005-2017.

If not an actual swing state, the not-always-predictable nature of Montana continues today. Montana overwhelmingly supported George W. Bush in 2000 and 2004, Mitt Romney in 2012, and Donald Trump in both 2016 and 2020. As of 2018 Montana's U.S. senators were Republican and Democrat. Montana's lone U.S. representative, Matt Rosendale, is a Republican, but starting with the 2022 midterm elections, Montana will add a second congressional seat. Montanans last supported a Democratic president in 1992 (Bill Clinton), although in 2008 the margin was just 2 percent in favor of Republican John McCain.

As university towns like Bozeman and Missoula gain population and the state's economy shifts toward tourism and the high-tech industry, Montana may become a purple state. The lines between political parties are becoming blurred but seem to be shifting slowly toward blue. But then again, as history has proved, it may only last so long.

including Mike Mansfield, Lee Metcalf, and Pat Williams. Democrat Mansfield was the longest-serving majority leader of the U.S. Senate (1961-1977) and the U.S. ambassador to Japan for more than a decade. Lee Metcalf, another Democrat, was instrumental in creating three new wilderness areas in Montana. The Lee Metcalf Wilderness Area was named for his efforts in 1983, after his death. Williams was yet another Democrat who had a hand in expanding wilderness designation and served in the U.S. House 1979-1997.

Present-day Montana politicians are also gaining notoriety on the national scene. Former governor Brian Schweitzer is a Democrat who appeals to members of both parties. In fact, his running mate in 2004 was Republican John Bohlinger. Senator Max Baucus, a Democrat, served in the U.S. Senate 1978-2014 and, as chair of the Senate Committee on Finance, played a pivotal role in the debate over health care reform. Baucus was the U.S. ambassador to China under President Obama until 2017. Montana's governor 2013-2021, Democrat Steve Bullock was quite popular and even threw his hat into the presidential race in 2020. Montana has two senators, one Republican and one Democrat, and a single Republican representative in Congress, until the new seat is filled in the 2022 midterm elections.

By some accounts, Montana is becoming a "purple" state on the national scene—once primarily red but slowly turning blue. Maybe. Montanans have voted for the Republican presidential candidate in every election since 1968, except when they chose Democrat Bill Clinton over Republican George H. W. Bush in 1992. In 2008, Montana voters gave John McCain a narrow margin—just north of 2 percent—over Barack Obama. The 2012 election results from Montana swayed much more heavily on the side of Mitt Romney over President Obama. In 2016 and again in 2020, Donald Trump won by a landslide in Montana.

An easy characterization of the shift in politics follows the state's population trends. The eastern part of the state—more rural, less industrialized—is more Republican but is losing population. The western part of Montana, from Bozeman west toward Butte and Missoula, is seeing rapid population expansion and more liberal influences taking root. Many observers argue that the younger, more intellectual western part of the state will soon "take over" Montana politics. Only time will tell.

All seven Native American Reservations in Montana function as sovereign nations with their own forms of government, and many have their own constitutions as well. Though the tribes are required to abide by federal laws, they are not responsible to the state laws of Montana.

INDIAN RESERVATIONS

The Native American population plays an important role in Montana government and politics. Tribal law prevails within reservation boundaries, and Indian reservations are federally recognized as independent political units with their own structure and legislation. As sovereign nations, tribes can have their own school systems, constitutions, police and court systems, and legislative councils. They can also regulate transport and trade within reservation boundaries. The state can't tax land or transactions that occur on reservations.

What does this mean to the visitor? Essentially, some state laws may not apply on reservations. Goods and services—mainly gasoline and tobacco—can be much cheaper on the reservations since there are no state taxes enforced. Not all land may be open to the public, and there may be additional fees for recreation, including hunting and fishing. It's best to inquire at a local store or gas station if you are traveling on reservation land.

Economy

Montana was founded on rural traditions and industries: farming, ranching, mining, and forestry. To a large extent, these industries are still dominant. Agriculture is the state's largest industry, generating some $4.82 billion in gross farm income annually from 26,900 farms and ranches. Cash crops include wheat, hay, barley, lentils, sugar beets, corn, oats, cherries, and seed potatoes. Beef cattle dominate the ranching sector, although hogs, sheep, dairy cattle, llamas, and horses are also raised. It's worth noting that there are still about 2.5 cows for every person in Montana.

Cities like Butte and Helena benefited from the mining boom of the late 19th and early 20th centuries. Butte was once one of the richest cities in the country, spurred by the large amount of copper in the area. Today, mining and resource extraction are a dwindling part of Montana's economy, even though its coal reserves are the largest in the nation, and the mountain ranges of central, southern, and western Montana hold large ore deposits of copper, gold, lead, silver, and zinc. The Stillwater Mine in Columbus is the only palladium and platinum producer in the country. Montana is the 7th-largest producer of coal in the nation and 13th in crude oil production.

Tourism is Montana's second-ranked and fastest-growing industry. More than 12.6 million visitors in 2019 spent more than $3.77 billion. Nearly every industry in the state took a significant hit in 2020, thanks to the pandemic with its lockdowns and closures across the state, and tourism was no exception. In 2020, the first quarter saw 9 percent growth in visitation and a 16 percent increase in spending over the previous year, but the story changed in March when much of the country closed down due to COVID-19. Still, Montana's tourism did not suffer as much as other states. Overall in 2020, out-of-state visitation in Montana was about 12 percent—11.1 million visitors spent $3.15

billion—compared to California, for example, which saw travel-related spending drop by 55 percent. In Montana, national parks, state parks, and campgrounds were busier than ever during the second half of 2020.

The timber industry has played a large and important part in Montana's history, but, as with mineral extraction, the boom and bust cycle is very much a part of the industry. Montana lumber production in 2009 was the lowest since the end of World War II, and the homebuilding bust from 2009 to 2012 did not help. The number of solid-wood sawmills decreased from 30 to 8 over the last three decades. Lumber prices roared back in 2017, some 22 percent higher than the previous year's prices because of a strong housing market and the reconstruction of hurricane-damaged properties in the South. Lumber prices soared again in 2020 when the demand for new home construction, repairs, and remodeling far exceeded the supply from mills in the United States and Canada. Though lumber production in the state was 428 million board feet in 2020, down more than 10 percent from 2019, sales were up some 15 percent because of the higher prices.

Other industries that contribute significantly to Montana's economic output are real estate, financial services, construction, the retail trade, health care, education, and government. Montana also has a growing high-tech sector, particularly in Bozeman, Missoula,

and Kalispell. The universities in Missoula and Bozeman are two of the state's largest employers, as are Costco, First Interstate Bank, Northwestern Energy, and Town Pump. Many of the top 20 employers are in the health care field—including hospitals and clinics in Billings, Great Falls, Kalispell, Missoula, Bozeman, and Helena.

Overall, Montana's economy has been outperforming the national economy since 2000. Unemployment rates tend to stay below national averages—3.1 percent in Montana in October 2021 versus 4.6 percent nationwide the same month. The state's GDP continues to grow at a faster rate than the majority of other states, and personal income growth has outpaced the national average—Montana was first in the country in 2020—as has wage growth, which grew 6.6 percent faster than inflation in 2021. Montana also had a relatively speedy recovery from the pandemic, compared to other parts of the country. By September 2021, payrolls across the state and employment levels were within 1 percent of their pre-pandemic peaks. The downside of such growth includes rising home prices—2021 saw a 10.3 percent increase over 2020—especially in places like Bozeman, where the average home now costs more than $500,000. Compare that to the fact that Montana still ranks 46th in the country in terms of weekly wages, 18 percent below the national average.

Local Culture

The people and culture are largely tied to the settling of the West and the Native Americans who inhabited the area. It wasn't until the 1860s that settlers started building permanent communities, as the gold rush, the railroad, and the Homestead Act lured those seeking a different and potentially lucrative way of life. Many areas were settled by immigrants and still retain their European heritage.

Montana is largely considered a conservative state, with a population that is around 90 percent Caucasian. Less than 4 percent of the population is listed as Hispanic or Latino in origin.

NATIVE AMERICANS

Although farming, ranching, and natural resource extraction certainly contributed to the growing cultural landscape, it's the

Climbing the Alphabet

One of the things you'll notice fairly quickly when driving around Montana is the seemingly endless number of large white letters on the hillsides or mountains. These hillside letters—sometimes called "geoglyphs" or "mountain monograms"—are a source of pride for many Montana localities, and in most cases they highlight the first letter of the adjacent town, school, or university. Over the years the letters have become not just visible landmarks but cultural ones as well.

Montana has the largest number of hillside letters in the country, more than 90 that represent everything from Anaconda to Winnett. The most popular hillside letter is the M in Missoula, which sits about halfway up Mount Sentinel overlooking the University of Montana campus. It's a moderate 1.5-mile (2.4-km) hike up a well-used trail and provides a panoramic view of the Clark Fork and Bitterroot Rivers and the surrounding mountains. On Saturdays in the fall, the M is often packed with students watching the football game—it offers a great aerial view of the 25,000-seat stadium.

The largest letter is the M in Bozeman, which represents Montana State University and is a popular hike for residents and visitors. The 200-foot-tall letter sits on a steep hillside on the south end of the Bridger Mountains, accessed by a trail that is also the start of the 21-mile (34-km) Bridger Mountains National Recreation Trail.

The M in Butte is actually electric, and the C near Cut Bank is one of the smallest letters in the state. The town of Anaconda actually has two letters: a C for Central High School and an A for the town's name. Even the tiny towns of Bainville and Froid—population 316 and 195, respectively—in northeastern Montana have letters. The town of Brockton has three letters—BHS—that represent the local high school. And Livingston, set amid the twists and turns of the Yellowstone, has a fish on its hillside to designate itself as the "trout capital of the world."

Montana isn't the only state with a plethora of hillside letters. It's a common sight throughout the West, with only a few erected east of the Mississippi River and nearly all of them built in a community-wide effort. Most are made of painted rocks or concrete, some are just painted on existing rock faces, and others are cut out of the vegetation.

The first letter to appear in the West was the C that overlooks the University of California, Berkeley, built in 1905. Missoula's M was built in 1908, originally of rocks, then again with wood in 1912. A blizzard destroyed that one in 1915, and it was replaced by a whitewashed granite letter that lasted until 1968, when the current concrete M was erected. Each fall the letter is lit up at the homecoming football game to welcome former students back to campus.

An interesting read on this subject is Evelyn Corning's *Hillside Letters A to Z: A Guide to Hometown Landmarks*, which explains the history of 60 letters in 14 western states.

rich Native American history that gives these states a proud and colorful representation of the past that transcends today's modern American culture. Before trappers and settlers came west, Indigenous people roamed freely across the land, following the huge bison herds that once covered the plains. Each tribe has unique customs and traditions. While Native Americans have worked to adapt to the changing world around them, they have also tried to keep the culture and traditions of their past alive. Their culture is celebrated through dance, songs, games, language,

and religious ceremonies. This rich heritage contributes to the distinct flavors of Montana.

Several museums in each state pay tribute to the American Indian, and many reservation towns host annual powwows, rodeos, and celebrations. Today, 6.2 percent of Montana's population are classified as Native American.

There are 11 different tribes represented in Montana, the majority living on seven different reservations. The following is a list of the Native American groups and the reservations that they inhabit today.

Blackfeet

The 1.5-million-acre Blackfeet Reservation is in northwestern Montana along the eastern slopes of the Rocky Mountains, bordered on the north by Canada and on the west by Glacier National Park. More than 17,320 members make up the tribe, with about 10,500 living on or near the reservation. The Blackfeet are thought to have acquired their name from the characteristic black color of their moccasins, painted or darkened with ashes, and once inhabited land near the Great Lakes before they migrated west. During this migration, the various tribes of the Blackfeet joined together to form the Blackfeet Confederacy, made up of the Piegans, the Bloods, and the Northern Blackfeet. Soon they became one of the largest tribes and remain among the 10 largest tribes in the United States today.

A worthy detour on the reservation is the Museum of the Plains Indian in Browning, where a permanent exhibit displays artifacts of the Northern Plains Indians and two special galleries feature rotating presentations.

Crow

The Crow Indian Reservation is the fifth-largest reservation in the United States, home to nearly 7,900 residents on its 2.2 million acres south of Billings. The tribe originally lived in the Great Lakes region, but it was one of the first to enter Montana in the early 1600s. The tribe was called Apsáalooke, which means "children of the large-beaked bird," and are also called Absarokee. Today, nearly 85 percent of the tribe speaks Crow as their first language. Crow Fair, held annually every August along the Little Big Horn River, was founded in 1904 and today is among the largest Native American gatherings in the northern part of the United States.

Confederated Salish and Kootenai

The Flathead Indian Reservation is home to the Confederated Salish and Kootenai Tribes, a combination of the Salish, Pend d'Oreille,

and Kootenai. There are 7,753 registered members, with about 5,000 living on or near the reservation. The 1.3-million-acre piece of land is in Montana between Missoula and Kalispell, north of I-90 among the majestic peaks of the Mission Mountains and along the shores of beautiful Flathead Lake, the largest natural freshwater lake west of the Mississippi.

These Salish-speaking people moved east from Columbia River valleys and adopted a way of life based on hunting bison while maintaining the religious and social traditions of the Northwest coast. They were generally friendly to settlers as they entered Montana.

Assiniboine

The Fort Belknap Reservation in north-central Montana is home to two tribes: the Assiniboine, or Nakoda, and the Gros Ventre. There are about 7,000 people in these two tribes and roughly half of them live on the 652,000-acre reservation.

The Assiniboine originated in the Lake of the Woods and the Lake Winnipeg area of Canada and became allied with the Cree. A division between the two tribes happened in 1744, and some bands moved west into the valleys of the Assiniboine and Saskatchewan Rivers in Canada, while others moved south into the Missouri River valley. The tribes inhabited an area from Minnesota to Montana. The Assiniboine were typically large-game hunters, dependent on bison for a considerable part of their diet and living in tipis made from the animal's hide.

The 2-million-acre Fort Peck Reservation is in northeastern Montana, 40 miles (64 km) west of the North Dakota border and 50 miles (80 km) south of the Canadian border, with the Missouri River defining its southern perimeter. About 6,800 Assiniboine and Sioux live on the reservation, with another 3,900 living off the reservation.

Gros Ventre

The Gros Ventre are closely affiliated with the Algonquin-speaking Arapaho and Cheyenne.

The Sacred Sun Dance

Very little is known about the Native American sun dance, a highly revered and often secretive traditional ceremony performed by various tribes in North America. In Montana, the Arapaho, Sioux, Assiniboine, Crow, and Blackfeet are among the nations that hold this practice sacred. The sun dance represents a spiritual rebirth and regeneration of the land. Participants acquire spiritual powers, often experiencing visions, and invoke blessings for the whole community. In 1875, Lakota chief Sitting Bull formed an alliance with the Cheyenne during a sun dance in which he had a vision of U.S. soldiers falling from the sky. Many saw his vision as foretelling the defeat of the U.S. Army at the Battle of the Little Bighorn in June 1876.

Although each tribe's sun dance has its own characteristics, there are some common elements. Sun dances involve construction of a lodge, dancing, singing, strict fasting among the dancers and subsequent feasting, the erection of a sacred pole, often body painting, and the sacrificial piercing of the chest or back. The sponsor of the dance, along with other leaders, works for months planning the event and performing certain critical rites beforehand. The sun dances themselves are known to last 3-8 days.

Before the introduction of reservation life, the sun dance ceremony provided an opportunity for the various hunting bands within a tribe to come together. Today, it serves a similar purpose in Native American communities. Often members travel from different regions of the country, and regardless of social status or religious affiliation, the sun dance provides an occasion for tribe members to reaffirm their cultural identity. Many would argue that important rituals such as the sun dance contribute to the longevity and preservation of Native American culture.

With the introduction of reservations and the determination of the U.S. government to assimilate Native Americans, many practices, including the sun dance, were banned in 1885. Some tribes did not continue with their rituals and ceremonies, and others did so in secret. When the Commission of Indian Affairs lifted the ban on ceremonies in 1934, certain tribes immediately returned to performing this sacred ceremony in public. The 50th anniversary performance of the Crow sun dance was held in Pryor, Montana, in 1991. Among the Assiniboine and Sioux, the sun dance is done annually on the Fort Peck Indian Reservation.

All three were among the last to migrate together into Montana, but they soon split up and went their separate ways. The Gros Ventre became allies of the Blackfeet, dominating the northern plains until settlers moved in and moved the tribe to Fort Belknap in 1878. About 3,500 people from two tribes live on the Fort Belknap Reservation.

Sioux

Nearly 6,800 Assiniboine and Sioux live on the 2-million-acre Fort Peck Reservation in northeastern Montana, with another 3,900 living off the reservation. Though separate, both tribes have similar languages that descended from the same language family.

The Sioux is one of the largest Indian nations in North America, and its people are divided into three linguistic groups: the Dakota, the Lakota, and the Nakota. All were originally from Canada and didn't arrive in Montana until the beginning of the 19th century, where many settled around the Fort Peck area. The reservation was created in 1888 and today is home to a large industrial park and Fort Peck Community College. The Assiniboine and Sioux Cultural Center and Museum in Poplar features fascinating displays of their history, arts, and crafts.

Northern Cheyenne

This 445,000-acre reservation is in southeastern Montana. The tribe comes from Algonquin linguistic ancestry and moved west from the Minnesota area under pressure from other tribes. Today there are roughly 12,266 members of the Northern Cheyenne, with about half that number living on the reservation. An interesting stop if you're in the area is the St. Labre Mission, established in 1884 by the Franciscan order. The building's visitor center, Cheyenne Indian Museum, and gift shop are important showplaces of Cheyenne heritage and art.

Chippewa-Cree

The 130,000-acre Rocky Boy's Reservation near the Canadian border in north-central Montana provides a home for about 6,000 members of the Chippewa-Cree tribe. It's Montana's smallest reservation, and in 1916 it was the last to be established in the state. Historically, the Chippewa lived in bands on both sides of what now divides their homelands, the Canadian border and the Great Lakes region. The Cree territory extended from eastern Canada into what are now the provinces of Saskatchewan and Alberta. The tribes began their migrations west in the 1700s, and by the early 1890s they had united in Montana to find a permanent home. The term *Rocky Boy* comes from a misinterpretation of the Chippewa leader's name, Chief Stone Man.

THE ARTS

Montana is not just filled with cowboys and ungulates; in fact boasts vibrant and varied art scenes with an interesting and colorful history. Missoula, Livingston, and Laramie have a decidedly literary bent. From books and music to landscape painting and sculpture, Montana has a remarkable range of fine art to discover.

Literature

Montana has an especially long list of literary heroes, both past and present. Andrew Garcia's *Tough Trip Through Paradise* may be the state's first famous export, a gripping firsthand account of the Nez Perce flight in the 1870s. The writing program at the University of Montana in Missoula—established in 1919 by H. G. Merriam—can largely be credited with putting Montana on the map; students and faculty have included A. B. Guthrie Jr., William Kittredge, Annick Smith, Kevin Canty, Judy Blunt, Rick DeMarinis, James Welch, Deirdre McNamer, and poet Richard Hugo. Contemporary authors that grew up in or call Montana home include Rick Bass (*For A Little While and Why I Came West*), Tom McGuane (*Ninety-Two in the Shade*), Richard Ford (*Independence Day*), Susan Henderson (The Flicker of Old Dreams), Walter Kirn (*Up in the Air*), Joanna Klink (Excerpts from a Secret Prophecy), Maile Meloy (Both Ways is the Only Way I Want It), Prageeta Sharma (Undergloom), Karen Volkman (Spar), and many more. There are thriving writing communities in Bozeman, Livingston, and Missoula, the last hosting the annual Montana Festival of the Book every October.

Fine Art

One of the best known Western artists is Charles M. Russell (1864-1926), who left Missouri for Montana in 1880 at age 16. He soon became a working artist whose colorful and detailed scenes captured the landscape, spirit, and culture of the West during the late 1880s-early 1900s. Russell was also a sculptor and writer, and the excellent C. M. Russell Museum in Great Falls houses five galleries of paintings, sculptures, drawings, and illustrations that Russell created from childhood through the end of his life. Every March, around the artist's birthday, and again in August, the city of Great Falls comes alive with art auctions, exhibitions, and events.

Bozeman features quaint streets lined with galleries and shops, offering everything from locally made stationery to the finest in Western photography, sculpture, and painting. The bustling college town of Bozeman is regionally known for its annual Sweet Pea Festival of the Arts and SLAM Fest in August, and it also boasts a well-regarded symphony as well as jazz and opera performances. The Emerson Center for the Arts and Culture houses studios, galleries, classrooms, and restaurants along with a 700-seat theater in a refurbished two-story elementary school.

The Holter Museum of Art in Helena, the Paris Gibson Square Museum of Art in Great Falls, and the Yellowstone Art Museum in Billings have some of Montana's best contemporary works on display. The Archie Bray Foundation in Helena is nationally recognized for modern pottery creations from its resident artists, and the town of Livingston boasts "14 galleries and three stoplights" and is famous for its Friday-night, wine-filled art walks.

Performing Arts

Montana is home to numerous small-town theaters as well as the large theaters associated with the universities in Bozeman and Missoula. The Missoula Children's Theatre is nationally recognized, and year-round theaters can be found in many cities, including Billings, Missoula, Bozeman, and Whitefish. Theaters in West Yellowstone, Fort Peck, and Bigfork offer excellent summer programs, and the raucous Brewery Follies in historic Virginia City plays to sold-out crowds May-September.

Montana Shakespeare in the Parks, a troupe based at the university in Bozeman, takes their show on the road each summer to rural communities. The performances are free and well regarded for their high quality, drawing actors for the cast from Chicago, Seattle, and Montana. Their plays are often summer highlights in small towns that may not see much cultural infusion the rest of the year.

For opera lovers, it doesn't get much better than Intermountain Opera Bozeman, a beloved local company that stages two remarkable productions in the spring and fall. Built under the guidance of renowned baritone Pablo Elvira, the company brings world-class talent from the Met, among others, to Montana for performances in the fall and spring.

Music

There are plenty of tunes around to keep your toes tapping, especially in the summer. Many communities have free music nights, and local bars and taverns are usually good for a fun country band and the occasional touring act. Billings and Missoula have the most offerings, including arena shows, nightclubs, and theaters.

Popular music festivals include Bozeman's Sweet Pea Festival of the Arts, Magic City Blues, and Rockin' the Rivers. Newest on the scene, and stunning if you can get one of very few tickets, are the classical concerts at Tippet Rise Art Center in Fishtail, Montana.

Essentials

Transportation

GETTING THERE

Flying into Montana is by far the best way to get here. Flights into the larger airports are becoming increasingly frequent as the region gains ground as an incredible destination for visitors. Although getting here by train or bus is possible, it's not as convenient, and stops can be far from the main travel areas—best left to hardy travelers or those on a tight budget. If you live in the West, driving is a great way to get here—major highways will carry you into the state, and well-traveled back roads will lead you to your final destination.

By Air

The cities of Billings, Bozeman, Kalispell, Helena, Butte, and Missoula are served by major carriers Delta, United, Alaska/Horizon, Southwest, and Frontier, although some flights may be seasonal. Low-cost Allegiant Air offers direct flights to Phoenix or Las Vegas from Billings, Bozeman, Great Falls, Missoula, and Kalispell. Cape Air (www.capeair.com) has some flights from Billings on 19- or 32-seat turboprops to the smaller towns of Havre, Glasgow, Wolf Point, Sidney, and Glendive. West Yellowstone's airport is open late May-September and operates daily flights on Delta to and from Salt Lake City.

If budget is your top priority, be sure to look into flights into nearby airports. With the rapid growth in Bozeman, for example, sometimes flights in and out of that airport can be hundreds of dollars cheaper than flying into Billings (140 mi/225 km) or Butte (85 mi/137 km). That's not always the case though. Smaller airports can be pricier with more limited schedules, but it's worth looking into. Keep in mind that drivers will often encounter wildlife on the roads, particularly late at night. And weather conditions can be sketchy, especially during winter. In other words, make sure the money saved on the flight is worth your time on the road. And pay attention to arrival and departure times, particularly in winter, when the nights are long and dark. Driving from Helena to Bozeman at 1am on a snowy night, for example, is an experience to avoid at all costs.

By Car

US 191 and US 93 are popular north-south routes that connect Montana with Idaho and Canada. The only major highway running north to south is I-15, which links Great Falls, Helena, and Butte to Canada and Salt Lake City. The I-94/I-90 corridor is the most direct route across the state.

I-25 heads north from Colorado up to its intersection with I-90 in Buffalo, then on to Billings, Montana. US 89 is a popular and scenic route to Jackson from Salt Lake City and heads up through Grand Teton and Yellowstone National Parks into Montana.

By Train

For a state that was quite literally built by the railroads, train service today is spotty at best. The **Empire Builder** from **Amtrak** (800/872-7245, www.amtrak.com), which travels in both directions daily through Montana between Chicago, Minneapolis, Seattle, and Portland, is the only passenger train service in the two states. Most of the stops are in the far northern part of Montana, which can be acceptable if you are going to Glacier National Park, but otherwise the train stops are long distances from the major population centers. There is bus service from Livingston to train stops in the northern part of the state.

By Bus

Greyhound (800/231-2222, www.greyhound.com) buses travel mostly along I-90 and I-94 and north-south on I-15, but service is also available on **Jefferson Lines** (800/451-5333, www.jeffersonlines.com) from Billings, Bozeman, Butte, Glendive, Livingston, Miles City, and Missoula. These routes can also be booked through Greyhound. Greyhound stations are in Arlee, Billings, Bozeman, Butte, Evaro, Glendive, Kalispell, Lakeside, Miles City, Missoula, Pablo, Polson, Ravalli, St. Ignatius, and Whitefish.

GETTING AROUND

The best way to get around is by car. Rental cars are available at the major airports, and you'll see more of the state while driving around. Consider an all-wheel-drive vehicle even if you travel only during the summer, as many of the region's most scenic roads are gravel. In addition to better traction, these vehicles typically offer

---

Previous: beargrass blooms near Logan Pass in Glacier National Park.

higher clearance. In places like Bozeman and Whitefish that are receiving record-breaking numbers of tourists, it can be wise to look at rental car rates in town (as opposed to the airports, which charge an additional tax) and in nearby towns. The same car for the same amount of time might cost half as much in Butte as it does Bozeman, for example.

By Car

The I-94/I-90 corridor follows the Yellowstone and Clark Fork Rivers and is the most direct route across the state. US 191 and US 93 are popular north-south routes; the only major highway running north to south is I-15. Some of the state's more famous back roads include US 2, which parallels the Canadian border on Montana's Hi-Line along the old Great Northern rail line, and Highway 200 and US 12, which cut east and west across the central part of the state.

CAR RENTAL

If you plan on renting a car, it's a good idea to reserve one well in advance. Unless you will be driving entirely on paved roads, which is doubtful, a high-clearance or all-wheel-drive vehicle is a good idea. Many Forest Service campgrounds are located along gravel roads, and anytime you venture off the beaten path, you're bound to encounter some type of gravel or dirt road. In the winter, all-wheel drive is a must. And be aware that rock chips on the windshield are common occurrences at any time of year. Make sure your insurance will cover it, or consider paying for added insurance from the car-rental agency.

Car-rental agencies widely include **Alamo** (800/227-7368, www.alamo.com), **Avis** (800/352-7900, www.avis.com), **Budget** (800/527-0700, www.budget.com), **Dollar** (800/800-5252, www.dollar.com), **Enterprise** (800/261-7331, www.enterprise.com), **Hertz** (800/654-3131, www.hertz.com), **National** (888/868-6204, www.nationalcar.com), and **Thrifty** (800/847-4389, www.thrifty.com).

HIGHWAY SAFETY

A few considerations apply when you are planning a road trip. In general, interstates and major highways are in good condition across the region, although short summers mean road construction can be expected at any time of the day—or night, in some cases. State highways are often narrow and winding, not compatible with drowsy or inattentive drivers. Wildlife is a concern on any road, particularly at twilight and dark, and fallen rocks can be a problem in mountainous areas. Road information can be found through the **Montana Department of Transportation** (800/226-7623, www.mdt.mt.gov/travinfo).

Distances between settlements can be great in Montana, especially in the eastern part of the state. As a rule of thumb, planning ahead is critical. Don't wait until your gas light is on to fill up your tank, and make sure your spare is inflated. Carrying emergency gear is recommended. Rest areas—even on major highways and interstates—can be hundreds of miles apart. Most major towns and cities have reliable mechanics and car dealerships, but don't expect to find parts for your old Porsche roadster in very many places.

In general, the speed limit is 80 mph on interstates and 70 mph on most two-lane highways, although it can vary quite a bit depending on location and time of day. Many two-lane roads have numerous turnouts, where slower-moving vehicles can pull over and let cars pass. Drivers are used to driving faster on these roads, so if you're getting tailgated by a local, just pull over and let them go by. Increasingly, passing lanes are being incorporated into many state highways, particularly on roads over mountain passes. Be aware that Montana has a "move over law" which requires drivers to slow down and change lanes for stopped emergency or maintenance vehicles. Courtesy would suggest you do the same for any vehicle stopped alongside the road.

WINTER TRAVEL

Winter driving takes special care, focus, and—at times—lots of caffeine. Roads can

Montana License Plates

You wouldn't know it just by driving around, but Montana's license plates have provided an interesting look at the state's population trends since the first plate was produced in 1914. In the 1930s, the state added a number to the left side of the plate that corresponded to county population—the number 1 was for the county with the highest population, and 56 was for the lowest. If you correlate these with the city that is the county seat, you get a snapshot of the state's population history—and you can tell where people are from just by looking at their plates. In lieu of road trip bingo, a fun game is to see how many plates you can identify while driving around.

When the list for the license plate was created, Silver Bow County was the largest in the state, as Butte—with a population of just under 40,000 people—was a thriving city, booming with the economic flush of mining. Great Falls was number 2, Billings was 3, and Missoula 4. Libby—in northwest Lincoln County—came in last at number 56. In 1930 the total population of the state was just 537,606; the population of Billings was a mere 16,280, and the state capital, Helena, had just under 12,000 residents.

Over the past 80-plus years, the state motor vehicle department has left the number and corresponding counties the same. That is, a car with a number 1 is still from Butte/Silver Bow County, and a truck with a number 56 is from the Libby area. However, the population snapshot paints a dramatically different picture these days. While Butte has lost more than 5,000 people since 1930, other cities have seen significant increases, leaving Butte now the sixth-largest city in Montana. Billings is the largest city, with more than 117,000 residents, and Missoula has moved up to number 2 with more than 73,000 people.

If the state did change the numbers for the license plate, Butte and Silver Bow County would now be 8, and the top five counties would be Yellowstone (Billings), Gallatin (Bozeman), Missoula, Flathead (Kalispell), and Cascade (Great Falls). Lincoln County, now with more than 20,000 residents, jumped up more dramatically than any other. It's moved from last place (56) to 10th largest since 1930. The least populated county in Montana is Petroleum County in eastern Montana, with 496 people spread across more than 1,600 square miles. It is the third least populated county in the continental United States. Generally, western Montana is growing in population and eastern Montana is shrinking, except for areas impacted by the oil boom in North Dakota. Also, transplants tend to settle in larger, more urban centers where service-related jobs are typically abundant.

Why aren't the numbers on the plates being changed? Montana drivers have a certain amount of pride regarding their heritage, and the numbers hark back to a different era. Newcomers may not pay much attention to it, but old-timers and natives certainly do. The numbers are part of the state's cultural history—something nobody wants to change anytime soon.

be rendered impassable in a matter of minutes by snow and wind, and mountain passes are especially susceptible to fast-changing conditions. Because of the area covered, it may take a while before snowplows clear the roads. And be extremely cautious when driving behind or toward a snowplow, as visibility can be diminished to nothing. Be aware that because of wildlife, salt is rarely used on roads. Instead, the roads are graveled to provide better traction in icy conditions. Loose gravel often translates into cracked or chipped windshields, so drive with caution, and never get too close to a graveling truck.

Snow tires are a must in many places, and carrying emergency supplies is strongly recommended. A good emergency kit includes a shovel, a first-aid kit, jumper cables, a flashlight, signal flares, extra clothing, some food, water, a tow strap, and a sleeping bag. Don't rely on your cell phone to save you—although service is improving, there are many dead zones.

The transportation website (www.mdt. mt.gov/travinfo) has links to current and projected weather patterns, and toll-free information numbers are updated regularly. It's a good idea to carry these numbers in your

Laws of the Wild West

Because Montana was born of the Wild West, and in many cases there still exists a hands-off, "we don't need no government" mentality. While this may work in some areas, some outdated laws and rules are being updated or eliminated. First of all, there *is* a speed limit in Montana. While the limit used to be listed as "reasonable and prudent," it was changed in 1999 after the Montana Supreme Court deemed the law too vague. Currently, the speed limit for automobiles is 80 mph on interstates, 70 mph on most two-lane highways, and 65 mph on most interstates within urban areas. In places, nighttime speed limits are lower than daytime.

Believe it or not, it used to be legal to operate a vehicle in Montana with an open container of alcohol, whether you were driving or just along for the ride. In states where distances are often measured in "six-packs," this was a big deal. After much public debate, the Montana law was finally changed in 2005, making it illegal for drivers and passengers to have any amount of open alcohol. Montana had the highest rate of alcohol-related fatalities per vehicle-mile traveled in the nation in 2002-2003, as reported by the National Highway Traffic Safety Administration, and the rates are still high. However, if you're taking a cab, bus, or limo, or riding in the back of a traveling motor home, you can still drink legally. Bottoms up!

In case you're wondering, it's also illegal in Montana to have a sheep in the cab of your truck without a proper "chaperone," and certain animals caught running at large can be castrated if not claimed within five days—at the owner's expense. Montana is still open-range country, so if you hit a black cow standing in the middle of the highway in the middle of the night, it's your responsibility to reimburse the rancher.

car. Occasionally weather information can be found on the AM band of your car radio—you'll notice signs along roads indicating where this is possible.

TRAVEL MAPS

Free road maps can be found at visitors centers and rest areas, while an excellent supplement is the **Delorme Gazetteer series** (www.delorme.com), available at bookstores and in many gas stations. These oversize companions are a must for those venturing off the beaten path, as they include topographic data, Forest Service roads and trails, camping and hiking information, fishing areas, scenic drives, and more. Sporting goods stores offer more specialized maps, from national forests and wilderness areas to Bureau of Land Management lands and mile-by-mile river guides. The free road maps you get when you enter the national parks are sufficient to use during your stay.

By Bike

Numerous back roads and accessible campgrounds make for some fun trips, but be prepared for long-distance rides and not much company. The transportation website (www.mdt.mt.gov/travinfo) offers excellent information for cyclists. You can order a **Montana Bicycle Touring Packet** online, as well as download maps and road grade information from each site.

Recreation

In the summer, rivers come alive with white-water boaters, and smaller streams entice fly-fishers seeking solitude. Wilderness areas and national forests offer miles of hiking trails, while national parks host visitors from around the world. Surprisingly, excellent golf courses are to be found here and can be relatively uncrowded, even in busy seasons. Look for unusual forms of the sport like the Cow Pasture Open in Wisdom, Montana, where golfers compete in a two-person scramble in for silver belt buckles or cellophane-wrapped cow pies. Lakes buzz with the sound of motorboats, campgrounds are full, and everyone seems to be outside doing something. Summers in the West are short, so people take advantage of them.

It's no surprise, then, that winters are particularly long, but locals take advantage of it by enjoying some of the finest and least-crowded ski slopes in the country. Great snow and majestic mountain trails make snowmobiling extremely popular, and Nordic ski centers and trails can be found in most mountain areas. Ice fishing, dog-sledding, and backcountry skiing and snow-boarding are other activities that keep folks busy when the snow flies.

NATIONAL PARKS

Glacier National Park (www.nps.gov/glac) falls entirely within Montana, and its Canadian counterpart, **Waterton Lakes National Park** (www.pc.gc.ca), is directly across the border and shares some of the same trails. Although most of **Yellowstone National Park** (www.nps.gov/yell) is in Wyoming, three of the park's entrances are found in Montana. Visitors will find a variety of accommodations in the parks, including rustic cabins, grand lodges, and tent and RV campgrounds. Popular activities include hiking, boating, fishing, and wildlife-viewing. Informational visitors centers and museums are sited in each park and offer excellent resources for history buffs.

The entrance fee in the summer for each park is $35 for automobiles, which is valid for seven days. An annual America the Beautiful national parks and federal recreation lands annual pass, which permits entrance to more than 2,000 federal recreation sites, costs $80. Campground and other lodging fees are extra. Annual passes for any of the three parks are available for $70.

Consult the National Park Service website (www.nps.gov) for more information on these areas.

STATE PARKS

Montana has **55 state parks** (www.fwp. mt.gov) that focus on both history and recreation. This diverse selection includes historic ghost towns, Native American cultural sites, and lakeside and riverside retreats. Twenty of the parks have more than 500 camping sites, which are typically open mid-May to mid-September. Camping fees for nonresidents in peak season (third Friday in May-third Friday in Sept.) range in price up to $34 per night for a site with electricity. For residents of Montana, camp fees range $6-24 during peak season. Many parks now offer yurts, tipis, and cabins ($50-72/night for nonresidents). Camping rates are reduced for both residents and nonresidents during the off-season. Cars with Montana license plates are allowed free admission to all state parks, while nonresidents are charged $8 per vehicle per park. Camping reservations can be made at www.montanastateparks.reserveamerica.com.

NATIONAL FORESTS

Much of the public land in mountainous areas is administered by the U.S. Forest Service (www.fs.fed.us), including 19.39 million acres in 10 national forests in Montana. The Forest Service is a branch of the United

Forest Service Cabins and Lookouts

Imagine waking up in your own rustic cabin, nestled in the woods next to a rambling stream. You stoke the fire, mix up a pot of cowboy coffee, and enjoy a sunny breakfast on the porch with a 10,000-foot (3,000-m) peak looming overhead. There is no one else around. Now imagine that you have to pay less than $100 per night for this. Too good to be true? Well, thanks to the U.S. Forest Service cabin rental system, it isn't.

Literally hundreds of these cabins exist, most situated in locations that people would pay millions of dollars to own a piece of. Many are old ranger stations, very few are still used by the Forest Service, and all have their own unique charms. Cabins come in all different shapes and sizes, from extremely remote backcountry sites and mountaintop fire lookouts to larger cabins with electricity and motor vehicle access. Either way, they offer an unparalleled way to enjoy the outdoors.

Each national forest has cabins for rent. You can find a list of cabins and lookouts on the Forest Service website (www.fs.fed.us). All cabins must be reserved online (www.recreation.gov), where you can enter when you want to stay and a list of available cabins will come up, or over the phone (877/444-6777 or 518/885-3639 outside the U.S.). Cabins range from $25 for small, one-room units to upward of $200 for larger rentals that sleep up to eight people. There are additional booking fees, both online and over the phone.

Cabins typically have bunk beds (bring your own bedding), wood stoves, wood, and pots and pans. Some have more, some have less. Toilet facilities are usually outside, and potable water is not always available. When you make your reservation, you'll get a list of what to bring as well as detailed directions.

Some of the more interesting rentals are historical fire lookouts, perched high atop a mountain with commanding views of the surrounding peaks. Sitting inside these lookouts, you can imagine backcountry rangers gazing out over the land trying to spot forest fires. These lookouts are especially beautiful at night, when you're out among the stars feeling like you're on top of the world. It's a must-do experience for those who want to get off the beaten path—and one you'll remember for a lifetime.

States Department of Agriculture (USDA) and manages much of the nation's forest and rangelands. All national forests contain developed hiking and biking trails, and in the winter the roads and trails can often be used for cross-country skiing. Forest Service ranger stations are good places to obtain information on camping and recreation, while most sporting goods stores sell excellent maps that pertain to specific areas. **Beartooth Publishing** (www.beartoothpublishing.com) offers a popular series of waterproof maps that highlight national forest roads, trails, campgrounds, picnic areas, and fishing access sites for specific regions in Montana. For reference, Montana is located in Region 1 (Northern Region). You'll notice signs along the highways that indicate when you enter and leave a particular national forest.

Forest Service campgrounds are widespread and offer some of the finest camping available. Fees range free-$17, depending on the type of site and the amenities offered. Free sites are often very remote and offer limited services. The Forest Service also rents some rustic cabins and lookouts starting at $25 per night. These can be a great way to enjoy the outdoors, as most are in prime locations. These cabins, as well as most campgrounds, can be reserved in advance (with additional fees) at www.recreation.gov.

WILDERNESS AREAS

As of 2021, there are 14 federally designated wilderness areas in Montana. These are roadless and closed to mechanized use, including mountain bikes. Wilderness areas generally offer solitude and amazing scenery, although some areas may be more heavily used than remote non-wilderness areas. Some wilderness areas may fall under Native American jurisdiction, so make sure you have the necessary permits before hiking, hunting, or fishing in these locations. Montana also has 44 wilderness study areas (WSAs) covering more than 1 million acres, which do not have the same protections as wilderness areas. Montana's then congressman and now governor, Greg Gianforte, introduced legislation in 2018 to remove all protections from more than 800,000 acres of WSAs. Citizens spoke out against the move and it was defeated. For more information on specific WSAs, go to www.wildmontana.org/public-lands-101/wilderness-study-areas/.

BLM PUBLIC LAND

The rest of the public land falls under purview of the Bureau of Land Management (BLM), which offers everything from camping and boating to caving and backcountry scenic byways. The BLM manages multiple resources and uses, including energy and minerals; timber; forage; recreation; wild horse and burro herds; fish and wildlife habitat; wilderness areas; and archaeological, paleontological, and historical sites. There are just over 8 million acres of BLM land in Montana. You can find out more about the BLM offerings at www.blm.gov.

HUNTING

Montana is a popular destination for those hunting elk, deer, black bears, bighorn sheep, pronghorn, pheasants, and mountain lions. In 2009 Montana implemented a wolf season, and as of 2021, the hunt continues. Montana is also trying to legalize hunting seasons for grizzly bears outside of the national parks, among other places, but passionate conservationists, including renowned primatologist Jane Goodall, have shown a willingness to fight to protect the last grizzlies rather than see them shot as trophies. Montana also has a bison hunt, for which the season, location, and quotas are determined each year.

For more information on hunting in Montana, contact the **Montana Department of Fish, Wildlife & Parks** (406/444-2535, www.fwp.mt.gov). If you would like to enlist a hunting guide, check the websites for recommendations on established outfitters or contact the **Montana Guides and Outfitters Association** (406/449-3578, www.montanaoutfitters.org).

FISHING

Legendary trout streams like the Snake, Yellowstone, Madison, Big Horn, North Platte, Big Hole, and Gallatin lure anglers looking for lunkers, especially June-September. These rivers can be crowded during the summer, but luckily there are literally hundreds of other rivers and smaller streams on which to wet a line. And for die-hard anglers, plenty of secret spots are around—think spring creeks and alpine lakes—for excellent year-round fishing.

Lake fishing is also popular, with famed walleye fishing in Canyon Ferry and Fort Peck Reservoirs. In addition, hundreds of backcountry lakes offer solitude and great fishing in a wilderness setting, and ice fishing is becoming increasingly popular during the winter.

It's important to remember that you need a separate license to fish in Yellowstone National Park. Anglers 16 years of age and older are required to purchase a $40 three-day, $55 seven-day, or $75 season permit. Children 15 and under may fish without a permit if fishing with an adult who has a valid park permit. Permits are available at park ranger stations, stores, and many businesses in the Greater Yellowstone area.

Outfitters and guide services are abundant. Although it's not necessary, using one of these outfitters is a good idea if you're new to angling or want to hone your fly-fishing skills. Guides also know the hot spots on the rivers, can tell you what is hatching on any given day, and may have access to private sites along various streams.

An excellent website for general fishing

information and a good overview of the region is **Big Sky Fishing** (www.bigskyfishing.com).

For detailed fishing information, contact the **Montana Department of Fish, Wildlife & Parks** (406/444-2535, www.fwp. mt.gov).

TOUR OPERATORS

There are many tour operators with well-researched itineraries that can cater to your specific needs and wishes. Many of these tours cater to families or a particular interest: biking, cultural and history tours, wildlife, and more. **Austin Adventures** (800/575-1540, www.austinadventures.com), for whom this writer used to guide, offers numerous multiple-sport trips (think biking, hiking, horseback riding, and rafting on one trip) in the region, including Yellowstone and Glacier National Park. The Montana-based **Adventure Cycling Association** (800/755-2453, www.adventurecycling. org) offers self-contained and supported bicycle tours in Montana and in Yellowstone. **Backroads** (800/462-2848, www.backroads. com) offers multiple-sport tours in Glacier National Park and throughout Montana. **Big Wild Adventures** (406/823-0337 www. bigwildadventures.com) offers backpacking and canoeing trips in Montana. **Yellow Dog Fly Fishing Adventures** (406/585-8667 or 888/777-5060, www.yellowdogflyfishing.com) offers custom trips around the area. In addition, operators in nearly every town offer specific adventures, such as white-water rafting, horseback riding, fly-fishing, hiking, biking, and more.

SPECTATOR SPORTS
Rodeo

Most communities have rodeos at least once during the summer, and some of the larger towns have nightly or weekly rodeos that showcase the sport's nonstop action. Some of the best rodeos are the smaller ones, often called "ranch rodeos," that feature real cowboys and cowgirls from area ranches competing against each other in real-life ranch activities. Many rodeos offer events for kids, such as greased-pig contests or wild-sheep riding. Generally speaking, rodeos are great family-oriented events, but the tenderest animal lovers may not be okay with several of the events, including roping, tying, and bronc riding.

Minor League Baseball

The **Pioneer League** (www.pioneerleague. com) has teams in Missoula (Arizona Diamondbacks), Great Falls (Chicago White Sox), and Billings (Cincinnati Reds). This rookie league plays about 70 games June-September, and most players are recent draft picks. Games often draw good crowds and are enjoyed by baseball aficionados who live in these states that have no major league sports teams.

College Football

Both the **Montana State University Bobcats** (www.msubobcats.com) and the **University of Montana Grizzlies** (www. montanagrizzlies.com) compete in the Football Championship Subdivision (formerly Division 1-AA) of college football. Both teams have won national championships, and there has been a fierce rivalry between them since the first game was played in 1897. The Grizzlies have been one of the top teams in the country for the past two decades, and games often draw crowds of more than 20,000 rowdy fans.

Travel Tips

CANADIAN CROSSINGS AND CUSTOMS

Of the many roads that cross into Canada from Montana, only two of the 13 border crossings are open 24 hours year-round—US 93 (Roosville) and I-15 (Sweetgrass/Eureka)—and both are very busy. Wait times to enter Canada midsummer can be several hours, but travelers can go online (www.cbsa-asfc.gc.ca/bwt-taf/menu-eng.html) to see the current wait times at each crossing and to sign up for border alerts. U.S. citizens are now required to carry passports (or passport cards) when crossing into Canada; Canadians entering the United States must have a passport, a NEXUS card, and an Enhanced Driver's License (EDL) or Enhanced Identification Card (EIC). Citizens of other countries must show their passports and appropriate visas and may be asked to prove that they have sufficient funds for their length of stay. U.S. citizens returning to the United States by air must present a U.S. passport.

When heading north into Canada, travelers age 21 and older can import, duty free, a maximum of 40 ounces (1.2 liters) of liquor or 24 12-ounce (0.4-liter) cans of beer or ale into the country as personal luggage. Up to 50 cigars and 200 cigarettes may be allowed entry duty free for those age 18 or over. U.S. visitors spending more than 48 hours in Canada may bring $800CAD worth of duty-free goods back with them, or $200 if staying less than 48 hours. If you're carrying more than $10,000, you'll need to declare the amount. Handguns can't be taken into Canada, although hunting rifles are allowed. Bear spray and hunting knives are also prohibited.

As of December 2021, restrictions (www.travel.gc.ca) at the Canadian border due to COVID-19 are tight and should be carefully reviewed before you attempt entry. Vaccinations are required for travel within and out of Canada. Testing, pre-registration for arrival, and proof of vaccination are required. Unvaccinated travelers will be tested on arrival and again on day 8, and are required to quarantine for a full 14 days in a designated facility. Even fully vaccinated travelers who have been anywhere but Canada or the U.S. within 14 days of entry can be selected for arrival testing, which requires quarantine in a suitable location until negative test results are confirmed. Changes can happen without warning, so be sure to study the requirements in advance.

TOURIST INFORMATION

The **Montana Office of Tourism** (800/847-4868, www.visitmt.com) is the state's official tourism organization for vacation information and to order the annual free **Montana Guidebook.** Montana has divided the state into six different tourism regions, and specific booklets are available for each one.

COMMUNICATIONS AND MEDIA

Cell Phones

Cell phone coverage is overall very good and getting better each year. That being said, rural and mountainous areas may have spotty coverage, and plenty of places have none at all. Indeed, check the storefronts in some of the smaller towns in the region (I'm looking at you, Augusta), and you'll see that cell-phone service is just being brought to the area. Verizon is the main carrier, although AT&T is increasingly available.

Internet Access

Many coffee shops and public libraries have computers available for Internet use, and most larger towns have business centers with computers and fax machines.

High-speed Internet connections are generally available, but the service is often slower and more problematic compared to larger metropolitan areas. Wireless Internet is frequently offered at coffee shops, libraries, hotels, and other public places.

Media

USA Today is the one national newspaper that can be found throughout the region, and the *Wall Street Journal* is also popular. If you want a national newspaper like *The New York Times* or the *Washington Post,* some larger towns still have smaller newspaper and magazine stores, or sections in bookstores, but you may get a copy that is a few days old at best. Large grocery stores typically have regional dailies. In Montana, the larger dailies are the *Missoulian,* the *Great Falls Tribune,* the *Montana Standard, Helena Independent Record,* and the *Billings Gazette,* although every small town seems to have at least a weekly newspaper, which can be a great source of information on local events and attractions. Other Montana publications to look out for include the *Lively Times* (www.livelytimes. com), a monthly statewide guide to entertainment. The *Montana Quarterly* and *Big Sky Journal* are excellent literary reads and feature well-written articles about the Treasure State and the Greater Yellowstone area. Many of the larger towns—Bozeman, Big Sky, Missoula, Whitefish, etc.—have interesting and often free publications about the local community, current happenings, and more. Be sure to look for them around town.

One of best sources of local and national news is **National Public Radio,** which can be heard in even the smallest of towns. **Montana Public Radio** covers western Montana (www. mtpr.org), while **Yellowstone Public Radio** (www.ypr.org) covers the rest of the state.

FOOD

One thing is certain: This is meat-and-potatoes country, which can be great for those craving a good steak, as you can find one in almost every town. Locally raised beef can be found on the menus of many restaurants, and bison is becoming increasingly popular as well. If you haven't had it, it's highly recommended, and beef lovers will generally enjoy bison. A good bison burger or tenderloin is hard to beat, but if you are asked how you like it cooked, never ask for anything more than medium. Medium rare is better, as lean wild meat can dry out more quickly. Wild-game dishes, mostly elk and venison, are also found at finer establishments, with pheasant and other regional game occasionally on the menu. If you enjoy trying new fare, this can be an exciting option.

With all the meat on the menu, you would think that vegetarians would be out of luck when dining out, but surprisingly, options abound, especially at higher-end restaurants. The "eat local" campaigns are in full swing out West, and many of the best restaurants get as much of their food as possible from local and regional growers. Despite the region being seriously landlocked, seafood is no longer necessarily a bad idea. Fresh seafood is flown in from Hawaii or Seattle daily in many places, and it is generally pretty good. Yes, there are even fresh sushi bars, and some are darn tasty. Innovative cuisine can be found in every major town, but certainly Jackson, Whitefish, Missoula, and Billings stand out.

Does Montana have a well-known meal? Well, not really. Montana is famous for its huckleberries and Flathead cherries, so a good pie or milk shake is a must. Pasties in Butte are considered indispensable regional cuisine, and Rocky Mountain oysters (calf testicles) are usually breaded and fried—not exactly gourmet, and not exactly popular or necessarily worth trying. Delicious Indian tacos load the ingredients onto fry bread, and good Mexican and Chinese restaurants can be found throughout the region. Other regional specialties include wild game, chicken-fried steak, chili, and trout.

You'll also see the standard fast-food establishments, especially near the interstates, but avoid these and try a local restaurant instead. You'll find the best food at the most random of places—and it will certainly be a more culinary and cultural experience. And remember, folks out here are friendly—if you stop and ask someone about the best place in town, they will happily point you in the right direction and will probably know the owner.

If you are traveling the back roads and small towns and get tired of ordinary bar-type food (burgers, burgers, and more burgers), consider a quest to find the best chicken-fried steak or the best piece of pie. Sometimes a personal challenge can relieve the boredom of limited options. Plus, who doesn't want an excuse to eat homemade pie for breakfast, lunch, and dinner?

ACCOMMODATIONS

It's no surprise that a wide variety of lodging options are available, from standard hotels and motels to luxury resorts and guest ranches. Generally speaking, all lodging is more expensive in the summer, and rooms fill rapidly—advance reservations are a must, especially around special events. Rooms, cabins, and even campgrounds in the national parks fill up several months—if not longer—in advance. Shoulder seasons (spring and fall) offer reduced rates and thin crowds, while rooms at the ski resort lodges fill up fast in the winter but may be wide open during the summer.

Most larger towns have numerous choices for chain motels, which are typically clustered around the interstate exits. Gateway towns to national parks also have chain hotels, as well as mom-and-pop motels sprinkled around town. Travelers used to standard hotels will be happy with these choices, but those who seek a more unique experience will want to try some of the smaller boutique hotels. It just depends on whether you would rather stay in the usual Super 8 or sleep in a room that once accommodated Ernest Hemingway or Annie Oakley. A good resource is **Historic Hotels of the Rockies** (www.historichotels.org).

Most bed-and-breakfasts in Montana are in the higher-traffic tourist areas. Many are located on the banks of a river or nestled in the pine trees and often make great escapes from the busier hotel atmosphere. A fairly comprehensive listing can be found at **BnBFinder** (www.bnbfinder.com). Very few hostels exist in Montana, but **Hostels.com** (www.hostels.com) has a list of what might be available.

Guest ranches range from traditional horse-and-cowboy dude ranches to luxury "glamping" (a portmanteau of *glamorous* and *camping*) resorts that offer spa services and high-end cuisine. An excellent resource for those seeking a real Western working vacation is the **Montana Dude Ranchers' Association** (888/284-4133, www.montanadra.com). Many of these are focused around horseback riding, fly-fishing, and family activities and often are booked in weeklong blocks. In the winter, many of these ranches offer cross-country skiing, snowshoeing, or dogsledding.

Higher-end guest ranches are becoming very popular in Montana, offering guests a chance to experience a more rustic atmosphere with upscale amenities. These are typically set in remote locations with beautiful surroundings and are private, in some cases gated from public access. Typically these are the priciest accommodations, ranging from several hundred to $1,000 or more per night.

Cabins and other vacation rentals are becoming increasingly popular, as many travelers are looking for that Western cabin experience. These can range from rustic—just beds, no plumbing—to luxurious—down comforters, a rock fireplace—and are perhaps the best way to stay. Sites like **Airbnb** (www.airbnb.com) and **VRBO** (www.vrbo.com) offer private homes and cabins for rent, while many resorts provide nightly cabin rentals. For Forest Service cabins—which can be quite primitive but in phenomenal locations—travelers can check availability and make reservations at www.recreation.gov.

Plenty of RV and tent camping sites are available for those on the road. From national forest campgrounds to large private RV resorts, there is something for everyone. RV campers will find private campgrounds in most towns, and most national forest campgrounds have room for all but the longest RVs. It's generally legal to camp on national forest land, unless you see a sign indicating that overnight camping isn't allowed. For something closer to backcountry experience without hoofing it, drive on a Forest Service road until you find a nice campsite, pull over, and set up camp. Not only is it often scenic, it's also free.

ACCESS FOR TRAVELERS WITH DISABILITIES

For the most part, Montana complies with state and federal guidelines for accessibility. Most hotels offer accessible rooms, and the national parks and even some state parks feature accessible trails. However, it's important to remember that many areas are rural, and some features may be outdated, less accessible, or nonexistent. A list of trails that are easy to navigate and/or accessible to most wheelchairs is available at www.accessiblenature.info. Another resource for travelers with disabilities is **Rocky Mountain ADA** (800/949-4232, www.rockymountainada.org). In the national parks, wheelchair accessibility information can be found on their individual websites.

TRAVELERS OF COLOR

Montana is around 90 percent white, with Native Americans, Latin American people, multiracial people, Black people, and Asian people accounting for the rest of the population, according to the 2020 U.S. census. With so few people of color, Black people and other minorities tend to be cautious when traveling in this part of the country, according to Judith Heilman, executive director of the Montana Racial Equity Project (www.themtrep.org). And for good reason: There are still a lot of sundown towns where people of color may not feel welcome or even safe. This doesn't mean you should expect to be intimidated or harassed, but it does mean you will have to be alert and aware of your surroundings.

The United States has a terrible record when it comes to land management and racial equity. People of color have been excluded from national parks—dating back to the founding of the National Park Service (NPS) in 1916 and the enforcement of segregation through Jim Crow laws—and other green settings for generations. Even though the country is becoming more diverse, parks, green spaces, and conservation spaces—which Montana has in abundance—are remaining white and somewhat elitist. An NPS poll taken in 2018 shows that even though people of color make up 42 percent of the U.S. population (and are expected to be the majority by 2044, according to the U.S. Census Bureau), only 23 percent of visitors to the national parks were people of color, and only 6 percent identified as Black. There are a multitude of social and economic reasons why this is true, and though the NPS is committed to addressing the racial disparity—by marketing to non-white communities, training staff on racial sensitivity, and working to hire rangers from more diverse backgrounds—the problem is real and poses an existential threat to our public lands. If we don't have a population that is willing to fund and fight for these natural spaces, they will cease to exist.

Which brings us back to the problems of Montana, a mostly white state with vast expanses of public land. It follows that people of color are underrepresented here and thus face real questions of both comfort and safety. The Montana Racial Equity Project based in Bozeman encourages travelers of color to be alert and aware, and to document (and film, whenever possible) any mistreatment. Generally speaking, the larger towns have more people of color and thus may feel safer and more welcoming.

It's not a bad idea to connect with communities—and there are several—that can offer insider advice for your specific destinations. A remaking of the *Green Book,* a travel guide published from 1936-1967 that identified businesses that were friendly to African American customers, the **Inclusive Guide** (www.inclusivejourneys.com) is a brand-new online community that lists safe and welcoming spaces for anyone who faces discrimination. There are also Instagram and Facebook pages targeted to people of color in the great outdoors. Outdoor Afro, Latino Outdoors, Brown People Camping, Natives Outdoors, and Black People Who Hike are but a few examples. **On She Goes** (www.onshegoes.com) is a travel website created by and for women of color. And **Travel Noire** (www.travelnoire.com), which has many articles that reference Montana, is a digital media company geared to millennials of the African Diaspora. BIPOC journalist James Edward Mills started the **Joy Trip Project** (www.joytripproject.com), which focuses on outdoor recreation. There's an excellent list of anti-racism resources on the site related to justice, equity, diversity, and inclusion of BIPOC in parks and greenspaces. One such site is **Diversify Outdoors** (www.diversifyoutdoors.com), which promotes diversity in outdoor recreation and conservation.

WOMEN TRAVELING ALONE

Overall, Montana can be exciting for a woman traveling alone. For the most part, the West is full of independent and strong women, and you won't seem out of place because of your gender in most areas. A cursory Google search turns up a wealth of stories and blogs of women chronicling their solo travels across the state. The reality is most of these women are probably white and the experience could be very different for a woman of color.

Of course, there is always the occasional weirdo, so if a place or a person makes you uncomfortable, the best thing to do is just leave. Use the same precautions and common sense that you would at home. Even in a quaint mountain town, it's probably not safe to be out, wandering alone, in the middle of the night. It's worth noting that bear spray can be just as effective on a creepy dude as it is on a curious grizzly.

LGBTQ+ TRAVELERS

It's safe to say that many people in Montana are socially conservative, and queer public displays of affection are not entirely common, although they are becoming more so. You shouldn't necessarily anticipate discrimination or hostility if you are LGBTQ+, but you'll want to be aware of your surroundings. You might not think much of expressing yourself at a back-road Montana bar, but you never know what the patrons in the corner are thinking. Sadly, this is where Matthew Shepard was brutally murdered in 1998 for no other reason than because he was gay. A lot of people in Montana still have a long way to go in terms of recognizing and celebrating alternative lifestyles. In general, "don't ask, don't tell" is the safest policy to assume when traveling here. And, as is expected, urban areas are often friendlier to LGBTQ+ travelers.

That being said, there are thriving—although often underground—gay communities in many Montana towns, particularly college towns like Missoula and Bozeman. An excellent resource for LGBTQ+ travelers is the **Western Montana LGBT Community Center** (406/543-2224, www.gaymontana.org).

HOW TO GIVE BACK

I've spent the last year and a half working on my father's memoir, the one he wrote for eight years but didn't finish before he died in 2020. My dad had a knack for remembering obscure quotes, and a gift for repeating them at often wildly inappropriate times. I mean, who toasts a new bride with "I'd rather have a bottle in front of me, than a frontal lobotomy." Dad. There was none better.

But the saying that beats in me to this day, the one he learned as a boy, and lived his whole life, is this: Of them to whom much is given, much is required. It came from a bible verse and included an "unto" and a "whomsoever." But Dad liked the simpler version. And he offered it to me whenever a thing would go right in my life: a good grade, a lucky break, a new opportunity. What it did, and what I am grateful for even now, was to remind me to slow down, to think about where I'd come from, to tally all that I'd been given, and to figure out how I was going to make myself equal to it. These days, I say it to my daughters as they go out into the world, to take it all in and to make their own marks. And now, I'm going to say it to you too.

You have a right to be here. National parks belong to all of us. So do the acres of national forest, the soaring peaks, and great expanses of plains and desert managed by the BLM. Public land is our birthright as Americans. Yours and mine. All of ours. But reaping the benefits of its beauty and solitude and rarity brings responsibilities.

So here is my ask: Slow down. Be a thoughtful traveler, a conscientious visitor. Don't just take what you want from this place, but honor it—the parts that belong to you, and the parts that don't. Find ways to give back, to make a place even better than when you found it, whether you participate in a trail cleanup or attend a gala that's raising funds for the local animal shelter, or maybe you just write a check to protect grizzly habitat and drop it in the mailbox.

There is advice in these pages: sharing proper powwow etiquette, teaching you how to be on a trail, and the ways to engage—or more often, not engage—with wildlife. But what I'm asking now is more than that. I'm asking you to do right by the wilderness here, and by the communities, by every last inhabitant and fellow visitor. I am asking you to be even better than you already are. To pay attention. To stay curious. To think bigger, feel deeper, and give more. I'm asking you to be worthy of all the gifts coming your way. Dad would have said it better, but you know what I mean.

Montana Nonprofits

This is a short list of nonprofits. For ways to give back, you can start here.

- **FAST Blackfeet:** Food Access and Sustainability Team (406/845-2404, www.fastblackfeet.org) in Browning, Montana, holds the vision that everyone has plenty of healthy food to eat, along with the inclusive,

social relationship that surrounds the sharing and eating of food in Blackfeet culture. They have provided thousands of boxes of food to families in need, and additionally offer nutrition education and outreach on the Blackfeet Reservation.

- **Indian Law Resource Center:** Working to protect the legal rights, cultures, and environments of Indian nations and other Indigenous peoples of the Americas since 1978, the Indian Law Resource Center (406/449-2006 ext. 102, www.indianlaw.org) has dozens of ongoing projects related to ending violence against Native women, environmental protection, human and land rights, law reform and Native sovereignty, and protecting sacred sites.

- **The Kids' Garden:** This Great Falls, Montana, organization (406/868-2359, www.gardensfromgarbage.org) provides hands-on education for children and adults on sustainability, gardening, harvesting, and composting methods, as well as honey and hive maintenance and cooking. The garden-grown produce and honey is donated to local elders, pantries, and kitchens in need.

- **Montana Conservation Corps:** This is a service-based organization (406/587-4475, www.mtcorps.org) committed to offering teens and young adults opportunities to learn leadership development, teamwork, civic engagement, and work-skills training with direct service to Montana lands and communities. Their programs mobilize hundreds of crews to create impactful work among themselves, as well as improving the landscape through trail work, tree planting, and invasive species control.

- **Montana Land Reliance:** Since 1978, Montana Land Reliance (406/443-7027, www.mtlandreliance.org) has partnered with the state's landowners to permanently protect agricultural lands, fish and wildlife habitat, and open space. So far, they've protected nearly 1.2 million acres in perpetuity. Anyone who comes here for solitude and the beauty of wide-open spaces owes MLR a debt of gratitude.

- **Montana Native Plant Society:** Dedicated to preserving, conserving, and studying the native plants and plant communities of Montana, and to educating the public about the values of native flora, Montana Native Plant Society (406/443-4678, www.mtnativeplants.org) encourages grassroots involvement in their six chapters and offers activities and events.

- **Montana Pool Service:** Before he was the bassist for Pearl Jam, Jeff Ament was just a kid, growing up in Big Sandy, Montana, and ripping on his skateboard wherever he could. Along with some pals, Ament founded the Montana Pool Service (www.montanapoolservice.com) to build world-class skateparks and connect youth communities in Montana through skateboarding and the arts. In 2022, the organization brought four skateparks to Indigenous communities in Montana and the Dakotas.

- **The Montana Racial Equity Project:** This grassroots organization is dedicated to education and action in civil rights and social change. They work through community organizing to offer events, forums, training, and workshops on racial equality issues. All volunteers can become advocates—to become a member and get involved, visit the MTREP website (406/624-6820, www.themtrep.org).

- **Sisters United:** The Sisters United mission (www.sistersunitedmt.org) is to empower Indigenous women, children, and communities with healing at the forefront. They are dedicated to healing through art, connecting with the land and our creator, focusing on healthy lifestyles, and educating people on the history of Indigenous people in our country. Sisters United functions as a grassroots organization that partners with numerous Montana organizations and provides healing bundles to causes including the intertwined issues of trauma healing, Indigenous education, land protection, elder welfare, cultural preservation, human trafficking task forces, domestic violence shelters, Indigenous data and research, and access to art materials.

- **Sun River Watershed Group:** Since 1994, Sun River Watershed Group (406/214-2868, www.sunriverwatershed.org) has worked on restoration of the Sun River watershed and protection of water quality resources for local communities. You can register to volunteer with the annual Bashin' Trash event, or to adopt and sponsor a river section for cleanup.

- **Vital Ground:** By conserving habitat in their work as a land trust, Vital Ground (406/549-8650, www.vitalground.org) is protecting grizzly bears and other wildlife who will not survive without wild strongholds and the land to connect them. In addition, they work in communities across the state to prevent conflicts between humans and grizzlies.

- **Western Native Voice:** Based out of Billings, Montana, Western Native Voice (406/869-1938, www.westernnativevoice.org) has been at work since 2011 to advocate on behalf of and support Native communities, offering education and leadership development, as well as engaging community members.

Health and Safety

While medical services and health care in many larger Montana towns are excellent, remember that when traveling around, you'll likely be far away from emergency medical services. Rural and mountainous highways are especially troublesome, as cell phone coverage can be spotty. Most small towns have a local clinic, and services are available in the national parks. Refer to specific areas of the text for emergency numbers, and remember that calling 911 doesn't always work in rural areas.

In general, **weather, altitude,** and **insect bites** pose the greatest risk traveling here. The summer sun can get extremely hot, and it is easy to get dehydrated, so make sure to drink plenty of water during the day. Hiking—and just walking, for some people—can be a strenuous activity as the altitude increases. It's best to carry plenty of food and water, and take your time getting to your destination. Always let someone know where you are going and when you plan to be back. The earliest and most obvious sign of altitude-related health problems is a headache, and the best remedy is drinking water and moving to a lower elevation if possible.

The common insect nuisances are mosquitoes and ticks. Mosquitoes rarely carry any diseases, but they can be annoying at certain times during the summer. While West Nile virus is becoming an increasing threat to livestock across the West, human infection is less common. Still, it's a good idea to carry bug repellent with DEET, especially when hiking or camping near water. Ticks can pose a small threat of Rocky Mountain fever or Lyme disease, and they seem to have become more pervasive in the last 10 years or so. Check every part of your skin after a day of hiking or fishing outdoors—places where you might encounter underbrush, dense trees, and grassy meadows. If you find a tick with its head stuck in your skin, pull gently with tweezers or your fingers until the tick works its way out. Don't forget to check your pets, too.

A common backcountry illness is **giardia,** sometimes called "beaver fever," from a microscopic parasite that lives in mountain streams and can wreak havoc in your intestinal tract. Avoid drinking unfiltered or untreated water directly from streams, rivers, springs, or lakes. Carry a water filter or water-purifying tablets (iodine or similar products), and you'll have nothing to worry about.

If you're camping or staying in a cabin where mice have been active, **hantavirus** can be a concern. Hantavirus is a potentially fatal disease caused by contact with rodent droppings, particularly those of deer mice. Symptoms include fever, muscle aches, coughing, and difficulty breathing. Campers should avoid sleeping on bare ground, and avoid cabins if you see signs of rodents. For more information, visit the Centers for Disease Control and Prevention (www.cdc.gov).

Winter poses different types of health concerns, namely **hypothermia** and **frostbite.** If you or someone in your party shows any signs of hypothermia—uncontrollable shivering, slurred speech, loss of coordination—get them out of the wind and inside immediately. If you're camping, a dry sleeping bag is your best bet. Dress in layers, avoid cotton clothing, always bring a hat, and—most important—make good decisions *before* you put yourself in a situation where you could be stranded in the wind and cold. If you're outside in the winter, a sign of frostbite is the whitening and hardening of the skin. The best way to warm the affected area is with other skin, but avoid warming it too quickly because thawing can be quite painful.

WEATHER

The old saying is a tad cliché but often true: If you don't like the weather, just wait five minutes. What this means is that weather in

Coronavirus in Montana

At the time of writing in 2022, Montana had emerged from periods of some of the highest Covid transmission rates in the country, but the situation is constantly evolving. With a Republican governor, Montana all but outlawed mask mandates, nor are vaccines required to enter. The majority of people you'll see do not wear masks when they are out and about, but plenty of businesses ask their employees to mask up. In general, you may feel uncomfortable in a mask, simply because you are likely to be one of only a few, but you should not expect to be harassed because of it. There are no travel restrictions in place due to COVID-19. But now more than ever, Moon encourages readers to be courteous and ethical in their travel. Be respectful to local residents and mindful of the situation in your chosen destination when planning your trip.

BEFORE YOU GO

- Check websites (listed below) for **state restrictions** and the overall health status of the destination and your point of origin. It's a good idea to check the local county health department website for the areas you intend to visit. If you're traveling to or from an area that is currently a COVID-19 hotspot, you may want to reconsider your trip. Moon encourages travelers to **get vaccinated** if their health status allows and to take a **coronavirus test** with enough time to receive the results before departure if possible. Check local requirements and factor these into your plans.

- If you plan to fly, check with your **airline** and the **local health authorities** for updated travel requirements. Some airlines may be taking more steps to help you travel safely, such as limiting occupancy; check their websites before buying your ticket. Flights may be more infrequent, with increased cancellations.

- Pack **hand sanitizer,** a **thermometer,** and plenty of **face masks.** Be prepared for possible closures and reduced services over the course of your travels.

- Assess the risk of entering **crowded spaces,** joining **tours,** and taking **public transit.**

- Expect **general disruptions.** Events may be postponed or cancelled. Some tours and venues may require **reservations,** enforce **capacity limits,** or operate during **different hours** than the ones listed. Other venues may be closed entirely.

RESOURCES

- The **Montana Department of Health and Human Services** (www.dphhs.mt.gov) can direct you to reports and demographics on COVID cases by county, connect you to local county health departments, and provide testing sites across the state.

this part of the West can change dramatically in an unbelievably short amount of time. In the summer, extreme heat can dehydrate the human body rapidly, and in the winter, extreme cold can render your body useless in a matter of minutes. Sudden changes in the weather can happen at any time of the year in mountainous areas. It can snow, sleet, hail, and rain at a moment's notice. If you're heading into the backcountry or getting ready for a three-day river float, check the forecast, but don't rely on it; plan for the worst with extra gear and plenty of food and water.

In general, Montana has a semiarid climate. There is enough moisture at certain times of the year, but summers are typically dry and warm, with July and August being the hottest months. Mountainous areas see heavy snowfall during the winter (to the delight of skiers), while the eastern areas can seem downright desertlike much of the year.

WILDLIFE

Never approach wildlife; no matter what the situation. It's just a bad idea, and each year people are hurt or killed because they ignore this basic rule. Not only are they putting themselves in harm's way, but they are often precipitating imminent doom for the animal as well. The old adage, "A fed bear is a dead bear," can be applied universally to wildlife. The problem of humans getting too close to animals, particularly in Yellowstone National Park, gets plenty of coverage these days on YouTube and the evening news. Do not become a cautionary lesson for other travelers; keep your distance from wildlife. Period.

SAFETY IN BEAR COUNTRY

Grizzly bears and black bears live here, and although encounters are rare, it is necessary to learn what to do in case it happens to you. It is also important to know how to avoid the situation in the first place. No method is absolutely foolproof, but with caution and attentiveness you can avoid most of the common mistakes that lead to bear encounters.

When out in the backcountry, it's the unexpected bear encounter you really want to avoid. The best way to do this is to let them know you are present. Make noise in areas of dense cover and blind spots on hiking or biking trails. Immediately move away from any animal carcass you come across, as there may be a bear nearby protecting it. Avoid hiking or biking in the early morning or at dusk, and travel in larger groups; the more of you there are hiking together, the more likely a bear will sense you and move away. Making noise is a great way to let bears know you are near, and in most cases they will be long gone before you have the chance to get a glimpse of them. Be aware that dogs can provoke bears and bring them right to you. And, of course, never leave food out.

If you're camping in an area frequented by bears, look for bear signs (scat, overturned rocks, decimated fallen timber, claw marks and hair on trees) around the campsite. Since bears are attracted to all kinds of odors—food, toothpaste, soap, deodorant—your cooking, eating, and food storage area should be at least 50 yards/meters from your tent. It's tempting to bring tasty items like sausage, ham, tuna, and bacon with you, but these smell good to bears too. Freeze-dried foods are your best bet. Store foods in airtight bags, and be sure to hang all food at least 12-15 feet (4-5 m) off the ground and away from tree trunks. Some designated campsites have bear storage containers or food storage poles.

Carrying **pepper spray** (sold in most sporting goods stores, but it's worth noting that the Grizzly and Wolf Discovery Center in West Yellowstone is the only place you can buy bear spray at cost) is a must in bear country, and it has been proven useful in fending off bear attacks. These sprays only work at close range (10-30 feet/3-9 m) and can quickly dissipate in the wind or sometimes blow back in your face. Carry the spray in a holster or on a belt across your chest for easy access. It's important to note that these spray canisters are not allowed on commercial airplanes, they expire after a certain date, and they should not be left in a very hot place like a closed car. Also, test your container every now and then in light or no wind to make sure it works.

If you happen to encounter a bear, and it notices you, try not to panic or make any sudden moves. Do not run—bears can run more than 40 mph in short bursts—or try to climb a tree. Make yourself visible by moving out into the open so the bear can identify you. Avoid direct eye contact with the bear, but talking in a low voice may convince the animal that you are human. If the bear is sniffing the air or standing on its hind legs, it's most likely trying to identify you. If it's woofing and posturing, this could be a challenge. Stand your ground if the bear charges; most charges are bluffs, where the bear will stop short and wander away.

If a grizzly does charge and knocks you to the ground, curl up in the fetal position with your hands wrapped behind your neck and your elbows tucked over your face. Keeping your backpack on may offer some protection. Remain as still as possible, as bears will often only sniff or nip you and leave. This is considered playing "active dead." If the bear rolls you over, as it will likely try to do, roll yourself back over on your stomach and keep your neck as protected as possible. Remain on the ground until you know the bear has vacated the area.

In general, black bears are more common and seem to have more interaction with people. In many places they can be a nuisance—getting into garbage, breaking into homes—but don't think that they are not dangerous. Black bears will generally try to avoid you and are easily scared away, but if you encounter an attacking or aggressive bear, this usually means it views you as food. In this case, most experts recommend fighting back with whatever means possible: large rocks or sticks, yelling, and shouting.

It's a rare event when a bear attacks sleeping campers in tents at night—as tragically happened to a California biker camping behind the post office in Ovando, Montana, in 2021—but if you find yourself in that situation, defend yourself as aggressively as you can. In these circumstances, bears are viewing you as prey and may give up if you fight back. Never play dead in this case, and to thwart off an attack, always keep pepper spray and a flashlight handy.

Before you go into the backcountry, brush up on your **bear identification.** You can't tell what kind of bear you see by its color alone. Grizzlies are often larger and have a trademark hump at the top of their neck. Grizzlies also have more of a dish-shaped face profile, compared to a straighter profile of black bears.

OTHER WILDLIFE

Although bears get more press, there are other animals you need to be aware of when traveling. **Moose** are huge animals that are prone to sudden charges when surprised, especially females traveling with young. If you travel through Yellowstone National Park, you'll encounter numerous **bison,** large animals with sharp horns. Although it may be tempting to walk up to them, avoid doing so. While they are not vicious, bison can charge if provoked and have maimed and even killed visitors in the past. Be aware that these lumbering beasts can sprint the length of a football field in six seconds and can leap a 6-foot fence. Likewise, **elk** in the park can seem downright docile, but it's important to remember not to approach them. They too have attacked, stomped, and gored visitors who got too close.

Mountain lions generally keep a low profile, but as humans encroach on their habitat, encounters are becoming more frequent in the West. Most attacks have been on unattended children, and they rarely target adults. If you happen to find yourself in a situation with a mountain lion, be aggressive and fight back if necessary, or throw rocks and sticks to try to make it go away.

Rattlesnakes can be found in the central and eastern parts of Montana, especially in the drier prairies. Rattlesnake bites are rarely fatal (less than 4 percent when antivenin is used in time), and the snakes generally avoid humans. Be careful where you step when hiking around these areas, and pay attention if children are with you. If you surprise or step on a rattlesnake—chances are you'll hear its trademark rattle before you do—it may coil and strike. Any bite from a rattlesnake should be regarded as a life-threatening medical emergency that requires immediate hospital treatment by trained professionals. Bear in mind that dogs can get two doses of a rattlesnake vaccine in order to give them a better chance to get to the vet before the toxin kills them.

With all of the incredible wildlife-viewing opportunities, it can be easy to get complacent when taking pictures or hiking around. Treat all wildlife with respect and care, and never feed or approach any type of wild animal. If you are lucky enough to see many of these critters, observe them in their natural habitat and then carry on. The last thing you want is to become a statistic.

Resources

Suggested Reading

INFORMATION AND TRAVEL

Fifer, Barbara, and Vicky Soderberg. *Along the Trail with Lewis and Clark,* 2nd edition. Helena, MT: Farcountry Press and *Montana Magazine,* 2001. Full of colorful maps, this is the most in-depth guide to the Lewis and Clark Trail.

Graham, Keith, and Neil Chaput de Saintonge. *Chasing Time.* Helena, MT: Riverbend Publishing, 2017. This wonderful and engaging photo book tells the story of Montana through its 68 active one-room schoolhouses.

McCoy, Michael. *Montana Off the Beaten Path,* 10th edition. Guilford, CT: Globe Pequot Press, 2020. This book guides travelers to the unexpected, and at times outlandish, places in Montana.

Merrill-Maker, Andrea. *Montana Almanac,* 2nd edition. Guilford, CT: Globe Pequot Press, 2005. Written by a former legislative researcher, this tome compiles thousands of interesting facts about Big Sky Country.

Montanans Inc. *Montana: A Profile in Pictures.* New York: Fleming Publishing, 1941. What I love about this tiny little picture book is that so little has changed in more than 70 years. Swap out newer cars, modern fashions, and perhaps some racier skis, and nearly every one of these photographs could have been taken in the last decade.

Rowland, Russell. *Fifty-Six Counties.* Bozeman, MT: Bangtail Press, 2016. This artful travelogue, told by a fourth-generation Montanan and novelist, visits the strangest and most beautiful corners of the state.

Snyder, S. A. *Scenic Driving Montana,* 4th edition. Guilford, CT: Globe Pequot Press, 2021. This book covers 24 jaw-droppingly beautiful drives around the state.

Spencer, Janet. *Montana Trivia.* Helena, MT: Riverbend Publishing, 2005. A quirky and fascinating compendium of factoids about Montana, this book covers geography, history, entertainment, sports, arts, science, and nature.

Therriault, Ednor. *Montana Curiosities: Quirky Characters, Roadside Oddities & Other Offbeat Stuff.* Curiosities Series. Guilford, CT: Globe Pequot Press, 2016. A perfect book to carry along in the car, or in the backpack, this offbeat book highlights so many of the quirky, wonderful, and don't-blink-or-you'll-miss-it places and faces of the state.

Vasapoli, Salvatore. *Montana: Portrait of a State.* Portland, OR: Graphic Arts Books, 2008. If you need nudging on why to choose Montana or want a way to reflect on your trip the rest of the year, this coffee-table picture book of Montana nature porn, and more, is just the ticket.

HISTORY AND CULTURE

Ambrose, Stephen E. *Undaunted Courage.* New York: Simon & Schuster, 1996. This has long been considered the definitive account of Lewis and Clark's extraordinary expedition.

Baumler, Ellen. Girl from the Gulches: The Story of Mary Ronan. Helena, MT: Montana Historical Society Press, 2003. This important and highly readable history through memoir is the best record of what it was like to grow up on the Montana mining frontier.

Baumler, Ellen. The Life of the Afterlife in the Big Sky State. Lincoln, NE: Bison Books, 2021. Written by a historian from the Montana Historical Society, this book is a groundbreaking history of death in Montana, with sensitive perspective on the evolution of customs and burial grounds.

Cheney, Roberta Carkeek. *Names on the Face of Montana.* Missoula, MT: Mountain Press Publishing, 1983. In its eighth printing, this is a classic for anyone who wants to know the stories behind names like Freezeout Lake, Ekalaka, Deadman's Basin, and more than 1,000 others.

Colton, Larry. *Counting Coup: A True Story of Basketball and Honor on the Little Bighorn.* New York and Boston: Grand Central Publishing, 2000. This powerful work of nonfiction tells the story of Sharon LaForge, a 17-year-old Native American basketball player fighting to grow up on the reservation.

Egan Jr., Ken. *Montana 1889.* Helena, MT: Riverbend Publishing, 2017. Historian Ken Egan Jr. brings characters to life in this exquisitely crafted history of the year Montana became a state.

Fritz, Harry, Mary Murphy, and Robert Swartout. *Montana Legacy: Essays on History, People and Place.* Helena, MT: Montana Historical Society Press, 2002. This wonderful collection of essays reflects the state's surprising diversity.

Horner, John R. (Jack), and James Gorman. *Digging Dinosaurs.* New York: Harper Collins, 1990. A popular science book for good reason, it redefined the way we think of dinosaurs as parents.

Howard, Joseph Kinsey. *Montana: High, Wide and Handsome.* Lincoln, NE: University of Nebraska Press, 1943. Before "Big Sky," this compelling text was the source of one of Montana's earliest taglines.

Hungry Wolf, Adolf, and Beverly Hungry Wolf, compilers. *Indian Tribes of the Northern Rockies.* Skookumchuck, Canada: Good Medicine Books, 1993. With historical photos and copies of treaties, this volume offers a well-rounded cultural and historical overview of numerous tribes.

History of Montana in 101 Objects. Helena, MT: Montana Historical Society Press, 2021. This beautiful and fascinating book brings together objects, interpretive essays, and photographs by Tom Ferris to draw attention to the diversity of experiences that made Montana.

MacDonald, Douglas H. *Montana Before History.* Missoula, MT: Mountain Press Publishing, 2012. An excellent look at archaeological sites across the state, this book dives into the oldest known evidence of humans in Montana and how they lived.

MacGregor, Carol Lynn, editor. *The Journals of Patrick Gass.* Missoula, MT: Mountain Press Publishing, 1997. A well-edited and annotated version of the journals of Patrick Gass, a member of the Lewis and Clark expedition, this work focuses on the day-to-day activities of the Corps of Discovery.

Malone, Michael P., editor. *Montana Century: 100 Years in Pictures and Words.* Helena, MT: Falcon Publishing, 1999. This gorgeous coffee-table book looks at the faces, places, and events that shaped Montana in the 20th century.

Malone, Michael P., Richard B. Roeder, and William L. Lang. *Montana: A History of Two Centuries.* Seattle and London: University of Washington Press, 1991. First written in 1976, this authoritative history of Montana deals with prehistory, Native American studies, ethnic history, women's studies, oral history, and contemporary political history.

Montana Place Names from Alzada to Zortman. Helena, MT: Montana Historical Society Press, 2009. Written over the course of two years by five staff members from the Montana Historical Society Research Center, this book is backed by extensive research and access to the best historians in the state.

Munn, Debra D. *Montana Ghost Stories.* Helena, MT: Riverbend Publishing, 2007. A fun read for ghost lovers, this short volume spins tales of 11 favorite Montana ghosts.

Robinson, Ken. *Historic Tales of Whoop-Up Country.* Charleston, NC: Arcadia Publishing, 2020. This book offers a fascinating historical look at the lawlessness on the Whoop-Up trail from Fort Benton to Lethbridge in the 1870s.

Spritzer, Don. *Roadside History of Montana.* Missoula, MT: Mountain Press Publishing, 1999. Organized insightfully by natural travel routes, this book is filled with nice overviews of towns and regions as well as interesting little anecdotes.

Ulrich, Paul G. Montana Stories. Butte, MT: Paul G. Ulrich, 2021. Divided into two parts—Butte and everything else—this book of stories creates a historical tapestry for the state.

LITERATURE

Bass, Rick. *For a Little While.* New York: Little, Brown and Company, 2016. Though he is most often celebrated for lyrical nonfiction driven by his passion for Montana's Yaak Valley and all things wild, Bass's fiction is second to none. This collection reflects 30 years of his most brilliant short stories, many of them set in Montana.

Bass, Rick. *Winter: Notes from Montana.* Boston: Houghton Mifflin, 1991. Written by one of the state's most well-known contemporary writers, this lovely book celebrates the quietude of Montana's longest season.

Blew, Mary Clearman. *All But the Waltz.* Norman, OK: University of Oklahoma Press, 2001. Blew is a strong voice for central Montana in this hauntingly beautiful collection of essays spanning five generations of her family in the state.

Blunt, Judy. *Breaking Clean.* New York: Vintage Books, 2002. This unflinching memoir tells the story of Blunt's ranch upbringing and the life she ultimately had to flee.

Doig, Ivan. *This House of Sky: Landscapes of a Western Mind.* New York: Harcourt, 1978. A moving memoir that launched his long career, this work by Ivan Doig captures small-town Montana as it once was.

Fromm, Pete. *Indian Creek Chronicles: A Winter in the Bitterroot.* New York: Picador, 2003. Hired to tend salmon eggs during winter in Montana 40 miles (64 km) from the nearest road, this memoir is the author's exquisite introduction to the icy solitude of a Montana winter.

Grady, James, and Keir Graff. *Montana Noir.* New York: Akashic Books, 2017. This dark short story anthology gives readers a fascinating look into the seedier sides of Big Sky Country from some of its most talented writers.

Guthrie Jr., A. B., *The Big Sky*. Boston: Houghton Mifflin, 1947. This timeless novel about three frontiersmen gave the state its well-known moniker.

Harpole, Tom. *Regarding Willingness: Chronicles of a Fraught Life*. Bozeman, MT: Riverfeet Press, 2020. Sometimes called the thinking man's Evel Knievel, Harpole has lived a thousand lives, each of them fascinating. This collection of essays gives hilarious and heartbreaking looks into 16 of them.

Harrison, Jim. *Legends of the Fall*. New York: Bantam Doubleday Dell Publishing Group, 1978. Perhaps the most well-known of Harrison's works—thanks to the Hollywood adaptation starring Brad Pitt—this novella is a masterpiece, 100 years in 100 pages.

Henderson, Susan. *The Flicker of Old Dreams*. New York: Harper Perennial, 2013. Set against the dying town of Petroleum in eastern Montana, this beautiful novel tells the story of resilience and redemption.

Hugo, Richard. *Making Certain It Goes On*. New York: W. W. Norton, 1984. A collection of Hugo's poems, this is an absolute classic.

Kittredge, William, and Annick Smith. *The Last Best Place: A Montana Anthology*. Helena, MT: Montana Historical Society Press, 1988. This is the ultimate reader's guide to Montana literature, with nearly 1,200 pages of literary selections spanning Native American stories and myths to contemporary fiction and poetry with everything in between.

Maclean, John N. *Home Waters: A Chronicle of Family and a River*. New York, NY: Custom House, 2021. In this memoir the son of Norman Maclean offers a lyrical companion to his father's classic, a must read for lovers of *A River Runs Through It.*

Maclean, Norman. *A River Runs Through It*. Chicago: University of Chicago Press, 1976. The book that launched a thousand drift boats.

Maclean, Norman. *Young Men and Fire*. Chicago and London: University of Chicago Press, 1992. The posthumously published work by the author of *A River Runs Through It,* this nonfiction work about the fire that claimed 12 airborne firefighters is considered a modern tragedy and a magnificent piece of literature.

McGuane, Thomas. *Crow Fair*. New York: Alfred A. Knopf, 2015. Tom McGuane is a poet, a philosopher, a wild man, a master. His latest collection of short stories, set in the state he loves, should not be missed.

McMurtry, Larry. *Lonesome Dove*. New York: Pocket Books, 1985. Another can't-miss classic about the legendary Texas cattle drives.

Meloy, Maile. *Both Ways Is the Only Way I Want It*. New York: Riverhead Books, 2009. A fresh voice in short fiction, Meloy has a sly and bittersweet understanding of Montana and is a marvelous storyteller.

Stegner, Wallace. *Collected Stories of Wallace Stegner*. New York: Random House, 1990. A wonderful collection of Stegner's masterful fiction.

Stegner, Wallace. *Where the Bluebird Sings to the Lemonade Springs*. New York: Penguin Books, 1992. A classic and luminous Western writer, Wallace Stegner writes about the land and the human condition in these 16 brilliant essays.

Watson, Larry. *Montana 1948.* Minneapolis, MN: Milkweed Editions, 2007. This is a novel about love and courage, of power abused, and the terrible choice between family loyalty and justice.

Welch, James. *Riding the Earthboy 40.* New York: Penguin Books, 1971. The only book of poetry by one of the West's most remarkable poets, this collection is magnificent and timeless. Sherman Alexie called it the most important book of poetry in all of Native American literature.

Welch, James. *Winter in the Blood.* New York: Penguin Books, 1974. Welch's first novel, about a young Native American man living on the Fort Belknap Indian Reservation, is a heartbreaking and beautiful classic.

Zupan, Kim. *The Ploughmen.* New York: Henry Holt & Company, 2014. Zupan's searing novel about an aging killer and a troubled young deputy in Montana has earned him comparisons to Cormac McCarthy.

RECREATION

Birkby, Jeff. *Touring Hot Springs Montana & Wyoming: The State's Best Resorts and Rustic Soaks.* Helena, MT: Falcon Guides, 2019. Pack this one along to find all the best soaking spots.

Fischer, Kit. *Paddling Montana.* Guilford, CT: Globe Pequot Press, 2015. Detailed paddling info for more than 30 river trips.

Harrison, Melynda, and Mariann Van Den Elzen. *Ski Trails of Southwest Montana: 30 of the Best Cross Country and Snowshoe Trails Around Big Sky, Bozeman, and Paradise Valley.* Butte, MT: First Ascent Press, 2007. This book offers great suggestions for everyone from newbie skiers and families to pros.

Lomax, Becky. *Moon Montana, Wyoming & Idaho Camping.* Berkeley, CA: Avalon Travel, 2014. Hands down, the best and most comprehensive guide for camping in the region.

Robbins, Chuck. *Flyfisher's Guide to Montana.* Tucson, AZ: No Nonsense Fly Fishing Guidebooks, 2007. Belgrade, MT: Wilderness Adventure Press, 2018, second edition. Both a fisherman and a writer, Chuck Robbins gets onto the back roads and into the fish all across the state.

Schneider, Bill, and Russ Schneider. *Hiking Montana.* Guilford, CT: Globe Pequot Press, 2014. The 35th anniversary edition, this hiking guide offers excellent advice, clear directions, and descriptive details, plus great maps for hiking trails across the state.

Straub, Patrick (Paddy). *Montana on the Fly: An Angler's Guide.* Woodstock, VT: Countryman Press, 2008. A comprehensive guide to Montana waters and outfitters.

MAGAZINES

A longtime literary publication for Montana and the Northern Rockies, including Wyoming and Idaho, *Big Sky Journal* (subscriptions 800/731-1227, www.bigskyjournal.com) is published five times annually and includes special issues devoted to fly-fishing and the arts. Regular features by well-known writers focus on ranching and rodeo, hunting, fishing, art, and architecture.

Montana Outdoors (subscriptions 800/678-6668, www.fwp.mt.gov/mtoutdoors) is an excellent publication produced by Montana Fish, Wildlife & Parks, focusing on the state's natural resources, including fishing and hunting. The magazine has won countless awards and is a fantastic resource for natural historians. You can read the current issue online.

Montana Quarterly (subscriptions 406/333-2154, www.themontanaquarterly.com) is a beautiful magazine that tackles the issues of the state—politics, science, arts, and culture—head on. Their editorial policy is simple: "Montana, warts and all."

For history buffs, there is no better

publication than *Montana: The Magazine of Western History* (subscriptions 800/243-9900, www.mhs.mt.gov/pub), produced quarterly by the Montana Historical Society.

Mountain Outlaw (www.mtoutlaw.com) is a free publication out of the Bozeman and Big Sky area that examines the lifestyle, culture, and issues relevant to the region.

A remarkable literary magazine that captures the beauty and grit of the state, *Whitefish Review* (www.whitefishreview.org) comes out twice annually and includes important interviews with Montana figures and work by the best and brightest across the country.

MAPS

Montana Atlas & Gazetteer. Yarmouth, ME: Delorme Publishing, 2017. The most indispensable map book you'll find, these topographic maps cover roads and trails all over the state.

Montana Benchmark Road & Recreation Atlas. Washington DC: National Geographic Maps, 2014. From an outfit that knows how to make a map, this 128-page atlas shows the backroads and the recreational opportunities you'll find there.

YELLOWSTONE AND GLACIER
History

Black, George. *Empire of Shadows: The Epic Story of Yellowstone.* New York: St. Martin's Press, 2012. Black offers a fascinating look at the gripping and unexpected history of our first national park.

Clayton, John. *Wonderlandscape: Yellowstone National Park and the Evolution of an American Cultural Icon.* New York: Pegasus Books, 2017. Using iconic figures—including painters, naturalists, and entrepreneurs—as the storytelling mechanisms, John Clayton paints a fascinating cultural picture of the park.

Everts, Truman, and Lee H. Whittlesey. Lost in Yellowstone: Thirty-Seven Days of Peril. Salt Lake City, UT: University of Utah Press, 2015. This book captures one of the most remarkable stories of survival in Yellowstone's history.

Gourley, Bruce T. Historic Yellowstone National Park. Guilford, CT: Globe Pequot/Lyons Press, 2021. Bruce Gourley captures the most interesting moments in the park's history.

Guthrie, C. W. *Glacier National Park, The First 100 Years.* Helena, MT: Farcountry Press, 2008. A marvelous volume compiled to celebrate the park's centennial in 2010, this book features exquisite photos and artwork in addition to compelling history.

Haines, Aubrey. *The Yellowstone Story: A History of Our First National Park.* Yellowstone National Park, WY, and Niwot, CO: The Yellowstone Association for Natural Science, History, and Education and The University Press of Colorado, 1996. This comprehensive volume tackles the park's early years, from primitive exploration to early development.

Minetor, Randi. Historic Glacier National Park. Guilford, CT: Globe Pequot/Lyons Press, 2016. This history reveals the human stories of Glacier and what it was like for early explorers.

Righter, Robert W. *Wind Energy in America: A History.* Norman, OK: University of Oklahoma Press, 2003. Righter gives readers an excellent, in-depth look at the saga of wind energy across the West.

Saunders, Richard L., editor. *A Yellowstone Reader: The National Park in Folklore, Popular Fiction, and Verse.* Salt Lake City: University of Utah Press, 2003. This volume offers a core sample of historical literature that spans the late 19th century through the 1980s.

Whittlesey, Lee H. *Death in Yellowstone: Accidents and Foolhardiness in the First National Park*. Lanham, MD: Roberts Rinehart Publishers, 1995. Who doesn't love reading about a little gore and some good old-fashioned stupidity when traveling through Yellowstone?

Natural History

Blakeslee, Nate. *American Wolf: A True Story of Survival and Obsession in the West*. New York: Crown Publishing, 2017. There's nothing like a good wolf story, and Blakeslee portrays Yellowstone alpha female O-Six against the backdrop of conservation politics.

Grinell, George Bird. The Father of Glacier National Park: Discoveries and Explorations in His Own Words. The History Press, 2020. George Bird Grinnell kept meticulous journals and records, which are compiled here, along with his written stories and personal correspondence, to tell the early story of Glacier.

Johnsgard, Paul A., and Thomas D. Mangelsen. *Yellowstone Wildlife: Ecology and Natural History of the Greater Yellowstone Ecosystem*. Boulder, CO: University Press of Colorado, 2013. With stunning images by Mangelsen and detailed natural histories of the animals that call the park home, this is an outstanding book for wildlife lovers.

Mangelsen, Thomas, and Todd Wilkinson. *Grizzlies of Pilgrim Creek*. New York: Rizzoli, 2015. The project of famed photographer Tom Mangelsen and environmental writer Todd Wilkinson, this gorgeous, oversized book tells the story of grizzly bear #399, one of the most beloved and oft-seen bruins in Grand Teton National Park.

Murie, Margaret, and Olaus Johan Murie. *Wapiti Wilderness*. Boulder, CO: University Press of Colorado, 1985. A magnificent read by two of the region's now deceased but beloved conservationists, the chapters alternate between his work studying elk and her descriptions of their fascinating life together.

Olsen, Jack. *Night of the Grizzlies*. Moose, WY: Homestead Publishing, 1996. Perhaps better read *after* your camping trip in Glacier, this is the account of a 1967 night in which two campers were killed in Glacier in two different locations by two different bears.

Peacock, Doug. *Grizzly Years: In Search of American Wilderness*. New York: Holt Paperbacks, 1996. A classic by one of Montana's favorite authors, who was the model for George Hayduke in Ed Abbey's novels, this narrative tells of one man's 20-year quest to understand and appreciate this magnificent creature.

Phillips, Michael K., and Douglas W. Smith. *The Wolves of Yellowstone*. Stillwater, MN: Voyageur Press, 1996. Told with fabulous color photos and intimate details by the two men who oversaw the project, this book tells the story of the wolves' reintroduction to Yellowstone in 1995.

Riis, Joe, with contributions from Arthur Middleton, Emilene Ostlind, Gretel Ehrlich, and Thomas Lovejoy. *Yellowstone Migrations*. Seattle: Mountaineers Books, 2017. This marvelous photographic exploration of the last great migrations of elk, pronghorn, antelope, and mule deer features rich, meaty essays by some wonderful writers.

Schreier, Carl. *A Field Guide to Yellowstone's Geysers, Hot Springs and Fumaroles*. Moose, WY: Homestead Publishing, 1999. This slightly larger-than-your-pocket book is the authoritative guide to Yellowstone's best-known thermal features, with information about the origin of their names, regular and irregular activity, statistics, and anecdotal histories.

Schullery, Paul. *Searching for Yellowstone: Ecology and Wonder in the Last Wilderness.* Helena, MT: Montana Historical Society Press, 2004. A fascinating and compelling environmental history of the world's first national park.

Schullery, Paul. *Yellowstone Bear Tales.* Boulder, CO: Roberts Rinehart Publishers, 1991. Read this for hair-raising accounts of bear encounters by one of the park's most respected natural historians.

Wilkinson, Todd. *Yellowstone Wildlife: A Watcher's Guide.* Minocqua, WI: NorthWord Press, 1992. This is an excellent guide for where to see wildlife, with fascinating must-know information about each creature.

Recreation

Henry, Jeff. *Yellowstone Winter Guide.* Boulder, CO: Roberts Rinehart Publishers, 1998. This full-color guide is a must for travelers seeing Yellowstone in its quietest and arguably most magical season.

Lilly, Bud, and Paul Schullery. *Bud Lilly's Guide to Fly Fishing the New West.* Portland, OR: Frank Amato Publications, 2000. Written by the father of Western trout fishing and one of the West's most respected natural historians, this book weaves Lilly's personal history as an angler, guide, and conservationist with the history of fly-fishing in the region along with sage advice.

Lomax, Becky. *Moon Glacier National Park.* Berkeley, CA: Avalon Travel, 2021. Lomax wrote the definitive resource for visitors to this phenomenal park.

Marschall, Mark C. *Yellowstone Trails: A Hiking Guide.* Yellowstone National Park, WY: Yellowstone National Park Association, 2008. Another great hiking guide, this one includes descriptions of more than 100 trails ranging from day hikes to backpack trips.

Schneider, Bill. *Hiking Yellowstone National Park,* 3rd edition. Guilford, CT: Globe Pequot Press, 2012. This excellent hiking guide offers short, moderate, and long hikes throughout Yellowstone.

Internet Resources

Montana Office of Tourism
www.visitmt.com
Searchable by region and town, places to go, things to do, and a variety of other user-friendly options, the website is superbly organized and easy to navigate.

Montana Kids
www.montanakids.com
The kids' version of the Montana Tourism site is loaded with fun facts, games, and information on the state.

Montana Travel and Tourism Information
www.travelmt.com
Searchable by region, this website provides hotel, restaurant, shopping, recreation, and business information for each city and town in the state.

Winter Montana
www.wintermt.com
Another product of the state of Montana, this site is invaluable for visitors during Montana's longest season.

National Park Service
www.nps.gov
The NPS website is helpful for making plans to visit any of the national parks.

Montana Fish, Wildlife & Parks
www.fwp.mt.gov
This official state site is useful for finding state parks, fishing and hunting information, and other recreational opportunities.

U.S. Forest Service
www.fs.usda.gov
The Forest Service's website is helpful for pursuing recreational opportunities—including multiuse trails, campgrounds, and cabin rentals—throughout Montana.

Recreation.gov
www.recreation.gov
This government-run site allows visitors to make reservations at public campgrounds.

Montana Outfitters & Guides Association
www.montanaoutfitters.org
An ideal source for visitors looking for professionally guided hunting and fishing trips or other types of outdoors experiences.

Museums Association of Montana
www.montanamuseums.org
A great database of museums across the state.

Montana Bed-and-Breakfast Association
www.mtbba.com
A useful resource for visitors looking for a B&B experience.

Traveler Updates
www.mdt.mt.gov/travinfo
The best resource for up-to-date road information comes courtesy of the Montana Department of Transportation.

Index

XYZ

List of Maps

Photo Credits

Title page photo: © illvorasate | Dreamstime.com; page 2 © Montana Office of Tourism and Business Development (MOTBD); page 3 © MOTBD/Chuck Haney; page 8 © (top left) MOTBD; (top right) MOTBD; (bottom) Brizardh | Dreamstime.com; page 9 (top) courtesy Linda Mohammad; (bottom left) MOTBD; (bottom right) MOTBD; page 10 © MOTBD/Noah Couser; page 12 © (top) MOTBD/Donnie Sexton; (bottom) MOTBD/Tim Kemple; page 13 © (top) Coltonstiffler | Dreamstime.com; (bottom) MOTBD; page 14 © (top) Katinka2014 | Dreamstime.com; (bottom) Alexey Kamenskiy | Dreamstime.com; page 15 © MOTBD/Donnie Sexton; page 16 (bottom) courtesy Linda Mohammad; page 18 © (bottom) Kayleigh Bishop Källberg | Unsplash.com; page 19 © (bottom) Acareylau | Dreamstime.com; page 22 © (bottom) Isu83boo | Dreamstime.com; page 25 © (top) Kwiktor | Dreamstime.com; (bottom) Bertl123 | Dreamstime.com; page 27 © Margiew | Dreamstime.com; page 28 © (top left) MOTBD/Donnie Sexton; (top right) MOTBD/Donnie Sexton; page 33 © MOTBD/Chuck Haney; page 37 © (top left) MOTBD; (top right) MOTBD; (bottom) Jacob Boomsma | Dreamstime.com; page 41 © (top left) MOTBD; (top right) MOTBD; (bottom) MOTBD; page 48 © (top) MOTBD; (left middle) MOTBD; (right middle) MOTBD; (bottom) MOTBD/Bob Webster; page 60 © (top left) MOTBD; (top right) MOTBD; (bottom) MOTBD; page 63 © MOTBD; page 65 © Carter G. Walker; page 66 © (top) MOTBD/Chuck Haney; (bottom) MOTBD/Chuck Haney; page 71 © (top) Carter G. Walker; (bottom) MOTBD; page 74 © (top) Rick Graetz; (bottom) Pictureguy66 | Dreamstime.com; page 76 © Carter G. Walker; page 80 © MOTBD; page 81 © (top left) MOTBD/Donnie Sexton; (top right) Gerald Voss | Dreamstime.com; page 87 © (top) MOTBD/Jacob Moon; (bottom) MOTBD; page 102 © (top) mtnmichelle | istockphoto.com; (bottom) Carter G. Walker; page 109 © (top) MOTBD; (left middle) MOTBD; (right middle). MOTBD; (bottom) Robert Philip | Dreamstime.com; page 113 © MOTBD; page 119 © MOTBD; page 121 © NPS/Tim Rains; page 122 © (top left) NPS/Jacob W. Frank; (top right) Carter G. Walker; page 126 © MOTBD/Noah Couser; page 134 © (top) NPS/Jacob W. Frank; (left middle) Carter G. Walker; (right middle) NPS; (bottom) NPS/Jacob W. Frank; page 138 © Carter G. Walker; page 144 © (top) NPS/Jacob W. Frank; (bottom) NPS/Jacob W. Frank; page 150 © (top left) MOTBD; (top right) MOTBD/Donnie Sexton; (bottom left) Carter G. Walker; (bottom right) NPS/Tim Rains; page 154 © NPS/Jacob W. Frank; page 156 © Tim Kemple/MOTBD; page 157 © (top left) Karin Hildebrand Lau | Dreamstime.com; page 164 © MOTBD; page 167 © (top left) Dspataro | Dreamstime.com; (top right) Carter G. Walker; (bottom) MOTBD/Mike Schirf; page 180 © (top) Carter G. Walker; (bottom) MOTBD; page 190 © Steve Boice | Dreamstime.com; page 192 © (top left) MOTBD; (top right) MOTBD/Donnie Sexton; (bottom) Victoria Ditkovsky | Dreamstime.com; page 194 © (top) Adeliepenguin | Dreamstime.com; (bottom) Carter G. Walker; page 200 © MOTBD/Donnie Sexton; page 207 © Ronniechua | Dreamstime.com; page 209 © (top) MOTBD/Donnie Sexton; (bottom) MOTBD; page 216 © MOTBD/Donnie Sexton; page 217 © (top left) MOTBD/Donnie Sexton; (top right) Daniel Larson | Dreamstime.com; page 223 © (top) MOTBD/Donnie Sexton; (left middle) MOTBD; (right middle) Radkol | Dreamstime.com; (bottom) Jesse Kraft | Dreamstime.com; page 240 © (top) MOTBD/Donnie Sexton; (bottom) MOTBD; page 246 © MOTBD/Donnie Sexton; page 251 © Mtsue | Dreamstime.com; page 254 © (top left) Carter G. Walker; (top right) Carter G. Walker; (bottom) Joe Sohm | Dreamstime.com; page 261 © (top left) Glenn Nagel | Dreamstime.com; (top right) MOTBD/Donnie Sexton; (bottom) MOTBD/Bob Webster; page 265 © CheriAlguire | Dreamstime.com; page 272 © Bobby J Norris | Dreamstime.com; page 273 © (top left) Leigh Anne Meeks | Dreamstime.com; (top right) MOTBD/Donnie Sexton; page 280 © (top) Coffe72 | Dreamstime.com; (left middle) CheriAlguire | Dreamstime.com; (right middle) Taseret | Dreamstime.com; (bottom) Flashon Studio | Dreamstime.com; page 294 © MOTBD/Donnie Sexton; page 297 © (top) MOTBD; (left middle) Carter G. Walker; (right middle) MOTBD; (bottom) MOTBD; page 303 © (top left) Miroslav Liska | Dreamstime.com; (bottom) Philip Bird | Dreamstime.com; page 312 © Robert Crum | Dreamstime.com; page 319 © Wyoming Office of Tourism/Martin Ruegner; page 320 © (top left) NPS/Neal Herbert; (top right) MOTBD; page 330 © Linda Bair | Dreamstime.com; page 339 © (top) NPS/Neal Herbert; (bottom) NPS/Jacob W. Frank; page 342 © (top left) NPS/Neal Herbert; (top right) NPS/Jacob W. Frank; (bottom) NPS/Neal Herbert; page 350 © NPS/Jacob W. Frank; page 355 © NPS/Jacob W. Frank; page 357 © (top) NPS/Jacob W. Frank; (bottom) Wyoming Office of Tourism; page 359 © NPS/Jim Peaco; page 367 © (top) MOTBD; (bottom) MOTBD; page 371 © MOTBD/Bob Webster; page 373 © (top) Bennymarty | Dreamstime.com; (bottom) MOTBD/Noah Couser; page 375 © (left middle) MOTBD; (right middle) MOTBD/Donnie Sexton; (bottom) MOTBD/Donnie Sexton; page 392 © MOTBD/Donnie Sexton

ACADIA
NATIONAL PARK
SEASIDE TOWNS · FALL FOLIAGE
CYCLING & PADDLING

HILARY NANGLE

ARCHES &
CANYONLANDS
NATIONAL PARKS
HIKING · BIKING
SCENIC DRIVES

JUDY JEWELL & W. C. McRAE

MOON

BANFF
NATIONAL PARK

HIKE · CAMP
SEE WILDLIFE

ANDREW HEMPSTEAD

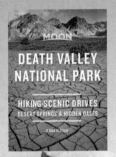

MOON

DEATH VALLEY
NATIONAL PARK

HIKING · SCENIC DRIVES
DESERT SPRINGS & HIDDEN OASES

JENNA BLOUGH

MOON

GLACIER
NATIONAL PARK

HIKING · CAMPING
LAKES & PEAKS

BECKY LOMAX

MOON

GRAND
CANYON

HIKE · CAMP
RAFT THE
COLORADO RIVER

TIM HULL

MOON

GREAT SMOKY
MOUNTAINS
NATIONAL PARK

HIKING · CAMPING
SCENIC DRIVES

JASON FRYE

MOON

JOSHUA TREE
& PALM SPRINGS

HIKING · SCENIC DRIVES
DESERT GETAWAYS

JENNA BLOUGH

MOON

ROCKY
MOUNTAIN
NATIONAL PARK

HIKE · CAMP
SEE WILDLIFE

ERIN ENGLISH

MOON

SEQUOIA &
KINGS CANYON

HIKING · CAMPING
WATERFALLS & BIG TREES

LEIGH BERNACCHI

MOON

YELLOWSTONE
& GRAND TETON

HIKE · CAMP
SEE WILDLIFE

BECKY LOMAX

MOON

YOSEMITE
SEQUOIA &
KINGS CANYON

HIKING · CAMPING
REDWOODS & WATERFALLS

ANN MARIE BROWN

MOON

ZION &
BRYCE
WITH ARCHES, CANYONLANDS, CAPITOL REEF,
GRAND STAIRCASE-ESCALANTE & MORE

HIKING · BIKING
SCENIC DRIVES

JUDY JEWELL & W. C. McRAE

Spending only
a few days in
a park? Try
Moon's Best of
Parks guides.

MOON

- BEST OF -

GLACIER, BANFF,
& JASPER

MAKE THE MOST OF
ONE TO THREE DAYS
IN THE PARKS

TOP SIGHTS, TOP HIKES,
TOP SCENIC DRIVES

BECKY LOMAX & ANDREW HEMPSTEAD

Plan an epic adventure with
Moon USA State by State and
Moon USA National Parks!

ROAD TRIP GUIDES

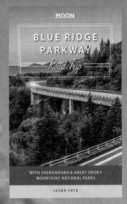

MOON

BLUE RIDGE PARKWAY
Road Trip

WITH SHENANDOAH & GREAT SMOKY
MOUNTAINS NATIONAL PARKS

JASON FRYE

MOON

CALIFORNIA
Road Trip

SAN FRANCISCO, YOSEMITE, LAS VEGAS,
GRAND CANYON, LOS ANGELES,
& THE PACIFIC COAST HIGHWAY

STUART THORNTON

MOON

NASHVILLE TO
NEW ORLEANS
Road Trip

NATCHEZ TRACE PARKWAY • MEMPHIS •
TUPELO • MISSISSIPPI BLUES TRAIL

MARGARET LITTMAN

MOON

NEW
ENGLAND
Road Trip

SEASIDE SPOTS, MAJESTIC MOUNTAINS &
FALL FOLIAGE, COZY GETAWAYS

MILES HOWARD

MOON

NORTHERN
CALIFORNIA
Road Trips

DRIVES ALONG THE COAST, REDWOODS, AND MOUNTAINS
WITH THE BEST STOPS ALONG THE WAY

STUART THORNTON & KAYLA ANDERSON

MOON

OREGON
TRAIL
Road Trip

HISTORIC SITES, SMALL TOWNS, AND
SCENIC LANDSCAPES ALONG THE LEGENDARY
WESTWARD ROUTE

KATRINA EMERY

MOON

PACIFIC COAST
HIGHWAY
Road Trip

CALIFORNIA,
OREGON & WASHINGTON

IAN ANDERSON

MOON

PACIFIC
NORTHWEST
Road Trip

OUTDOOR ADVENTURES AND CREATIVE CITIES
FROM THE COAST TO THE MOUNTAINS

ALLISON WILLIAMS

MOON

ROUTE 66
Road Trip

JESSICA DUNHAM

MOON.COM | ROADTRIPUSA.COM

MAP SYMBOLS

▰▰▰ Expressway	○ City/Town	✈ Airport	⚒ Golf Course
══ Primary Road	◉ State Capital	✈ Airfield	🅿 Parking Area
── Secondary Road	✹ National Capital	▲ Mountain	▰ Archaeological Site
═══ Unpaved Road	✪ Highlight	✦ Unique Natural Feature	⬧ Church
----- Trail	★ Point of Interest		⬧ Gas Station
·········· Ferry	• Accommodation	⬧ Waterfall	⬭ Glacier
▬▬▬ Railroad	▼ Restaurant/Bar	⬧ Park	▨ Mangrove
▰▰▰ Pedestrian Walkway	■ Other Location	⬧ Trailhead	▨ Reef
▥▥▥ Stairs	△ Campground	⬧ Skiing Area	▨ Swamp

CONVERSION TABLES

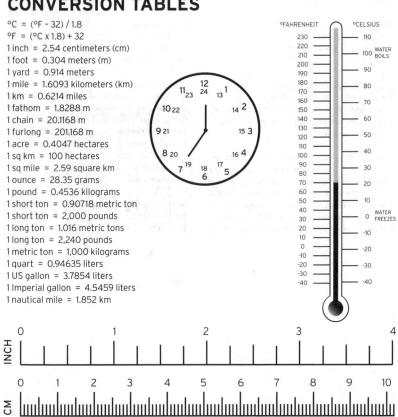

°C = (°F - 32) / 1.8
°F = (°C x 1.8) + 32
1 inch = 2.54 centimeters (cm)
1 foot = 0.304 meters (m)
1 yard = 0.914 meters
1 mile = 1.6093 kilometers (km)
1 km = 0.6214 miles
1 fathom = 1.8288 m
1 chain = 20.1168 m
1 furlong = 201.168 m
1 acre = 0.4047 hectares
1 sq km = 100 hectares
1 sq mile = 2.59 square km
1 ounce = 28.35 grams
1 pound = 0.4536 kilograms
1 short ton = 0.90718 metric ton
1 short ton = 2,000 pounds
1 long ton = 1.016 metric tons
1 long ton = 2,240 pounds
1 metric ton = 1,000 kilograms
1 quart = 0.94635 liters
1 US gallon = 3.7854 liters
1 Imperial gallon = 4.5459 liters
1 nautical mile = 1.852 km

MOON MONTANA

Avalon Travel
Hachette Book Group
1700 Fourth Street
Berkeley, CA 94710, USA
www.moon.com

Editor: Kimberly Ehart
Acquiring Editor: Nikki Ioakimedes
Series Manager: Kathryn Ettinger
Copy Editor: Deana Shields
Graphics and Production Coordinator: Ravina
  Schneider
Cover Design: Toni Tajima
Map Editor: Albert Angulo
Cartographers: Erin Greb and Karin Dahl
Indexer: Greg Jewett

ISBN-13: 978-1-64049-717-7

Printing History
1st Edition — 2019
2nd Edition — February 2023
5 4 3 2 1

Front cover photo: St. Mary River, Glacier National
  Park © Robert Bohrer | Dreamstime.com
Back cover photo: Old Faithful geyser, Yellowstone
  National Park © Shriram Patki | Dreamstime.com

Printed in Malaysia for Imago

Get inspired for
your next adventure

Follow **@moonguides** on Instagram or
subscribe to our newsletter at **moon.com**